Oman
in History

Oman
in History

Oman in History is published by Immel Publishing Ltd.

Production Director:	Dr Peter Vine
Editor:	Paula Casey-Vine
Main Translators:	Jean O'Hanlon
	Yassin H. Yassin
Other Translators:	Fouad Alaaraji
	Abdassamad Clarke
	Mohamed Alhourani
Translation Revision:	Abdullah Al-Harrasi

Cataloguing in Publication Data
A CIP catalogue record for this book is available from the British Library.

ISBN 1 898 162 115

Immel Publishing Ltd.,
20 Berkeley Street, Berkeley Square, London W1X5AE
Tel:- 0171 491 1799. Fax:- 0171 493 5524

Contents

Foreword

In the name of God, the Beneficent, the Merciful.

Lo! We have revealed it in a Lecture in Arabic, that ye may understand. We narrate unto thee the best of narratives in that we have inspired in thee this Qur'an, though aforetime thou wast of the heedless.

Oman in History is the end result of a major effort to summarize the historical events that occurred in Oman. On behalf of the Omani people and as recognition of His Majesty's leadership, we dedicate this effort to Sultan Qaboos bin Said bin Taimur, Sultan of Oman, since he is the instigator of Oman's modern development. The great stride forward which he has orchestrated has brought Oman from the dark ages of backwardness and ignorance to the brink of the twenty-first century.

His Majesty has fulfilled his promise to establish a contemporary and modern state in Oman. This great historical achievement is only one block in a huge and magnificent construction which has as its foundations:

- The protection of Oman's Arab identity; the Omani people have always had a heartfelt belief in the generous mission of Islam.
- Deepening and strengthening of national unity among the people of Oman, as well as maintenance of rights, obligations, equality and equal opportunity for all Omani people, within the framework of Allah, the homeland, and the Sultan.
- The removal of the walls of isolation which Oman has lived behind for a long time. With open arms, with heart and soul, with the great heritage of our ancestors, with will and determination, with our solid belief in Allah, we will move forward.

Under the leadership of His Majesty, Sultan Qaboos, Oman has raised the banner of friendship, peace and stability in international relations based on:

- Non-interference in the affairs of others, and at the same time refusing to accept interference by others in our internal issues.
- Pursuance of the policy of peace and good neighbourliness.
- Mutual respect for state security.
- Exchange and co-operation between states.

Oman in History is a product of the experiences and genuine efforts of many people who are aware that Oman values and respects its history and at the same time looks forward to building a bright future. This book does not attempt to create a history. Such was written by the actions of the Omani people: through the centuries, the sacrifice of generation upon generation has endowed Oman with a great historical heritage. As a tribute to these martyrs scientific methodology and Arab thinking was scrupulously followed in recording historical events in this great undertaking.

This book is more than a record of important historical events, it is also a detailed account of Oman's history as assiduously researched and thoroughly investigated by the many Arab experts, from the Union of Arab Historians and elsewhere, who have collaborated in this honourable work. These respected contributors have valued the heroic history of the sons of Al-Muhallab bin Abi Safra and Malik bin Fahm, recognizing at all times the fundamental legacy of these upright individuals who supported what is right and forbade what is wrong. The Omani people are very grateful for their sincere and diligent work.

I would like to convey my gratitude to all governmental and civil organizations for their hard work, tremendous efforts and good co-operation. My thanks also to Sultan Qaboos University for hosting the important conference on 'Oman in History'. It was a happy occasion to see so many specialists in Omani history from all over the Arab and Islamic world, even from some countries that were directly connected to the history of Oman.

Finally, I would like to register my special thanks to the committee responsible for the supervision and preparation of the materials for this book. Because of their monumental work and continuous efforts we were able to avoid duplication within the text and to overcome many difficulties. On this occasion, I would especially like to thank His Highness, Faisal bin Ali bin Faisal Al-Said, the Minister for National Heritage and Culture, for opening the conference and for his support. The conference organized under his auspices was welcomed by all participants.

And God is behind the intention. And it is He who guides to the even path.

Abdul Aziz bin Mohammed Al-Rowas,
The Minister of Information, Chairman of the Chief Supervisory Committee for the preparation of the book *Oman in History*.

Introduction

The need became apparent in recent times for a book which would present the history of Oman in some detail; which would address this history across the ages in a chronological fashion; and which would encompass culture alongside history. We do not, so far, have available to us a book which tackles all of these matters. Or if it does, or partly does, this is done in such a cursory way as to fail to satisfy the ungratified need for a knowledge of the history and civilization of Oman; or the history is rendered after the traditional manner which was not noted for its attention to the modern investigative method. At all events the civilization of Oman has not up until now benefited from adequate study and investigation.

The Ministry of Information has been most fortunate in this context in being furnished with a considerable body of research work which came to it from a number of Arab scholars and historians for the purposes of this book. A committee of nominees in the field of historical study was set up to discuss this research work and review it thoroughly. The final abridgement of this book took place after the studies had been presented and discussed at a scientific symposium convened for this purpose at the Sultan Qaboos University in the month of Rabia Al-Akher 1415 AH/ September 1994. The symposium ran for four days and was attended by an elite of Arab historians from institutes in every quarter of the Arab world, along with the University's teachers and students.

The studies presented spanned a diverse pattern of interest. Some covered ground already dealt with in others as one might indeed expect. It was essential that these studies be culled to avoid repetition, and then a mechanism devised to link either whole studies or sections of them or in some instances the information extracted from them to give continuity and sequence to the subject matter and ensure that the book assembled disconnected fragments of fact or historical judgment into a comprehensive whole. This was the most difficult of the tasks involved in the abstraction, abridgement and revision.

It needs to be said that the nature of the work of extracting and summarizing this book from many very different studies, indeed the summarizing of single chapters or single points from various study sources, was bound to leave a residue of repetition which if not evident in a recurrence of passages may occur in a recurrence of historical meaning or fact, where for instance one study offers us an example to illustrate a particular point and another study offers it again to illustrate something else. So notwithstanding the strenuous efforts we made to strip out as much of the overlapping material as possible the reader will encounter a certain amount of repetition of this type, though rarely and to an insignificant extent. While we feel it is not sufficient to harm the book, it will no doubt catch the attention of the discerning reader.

Again it is in the nature of the task of summarizing a book from many research sources, while preserving the text in the interests of serving the original goals of the work, that disparities of style and material would stand out in the end result. There were chapters which revealed an ease of style and exuberance of idiom and others in which this was not apparent to the same degree. This obstacle was handled with the intention of giving the book the overall guise of its having been written by one author so that the reader would not be discomfited by the disparity of style. We cannot claim to have been a hundred per cent successful in this treatment in view of the nature of the work and what has grown out of it.

The style and phraseology of the various scholars was thus preserved virtually intact except where some slight amendment was necessary or the addition of a sentence or short passage to connect sections or maintain the sequence of chapters, to clarify meaning or maintain a uniform style. These additions are present only in the most restricted sense and only where absolutely necessary.

At any rate those who undertook this work applied their most painstaking endeavours to overcome the obstacles and challenges which arose during the abridgement of the source material. This involved going over the material word by word, the rechannelling of certain information and annotation of some material to give the work a deserved overall profile. This then is how the book came to attain its final level of distinction. If it has been successfully achieved then the success is due to the grace of God, praise be to Him on high, for He is our sole support, He is the Lord and the Source.

Supervisory Committee
History of Oman

PART I

The Geography of Oman

Studies Presented and Summarized in this Part

Oman in the Writings of the Arab Geographers, by Dr Youssef Ghawanima, Dean of Faculty of Arts, Yarmuk University, Jordan.

The Nature of the Relationship between Oman and the Central Authority of the Islamic State in the First Century AH, by Dr Khalil Baghdad.

Oman as Presented in the Writings of Travellers in the Middle Ages, by Dr Zubeida Atta, Minia University, A.R.E.

The Omanis and their Role in the Indian Border Events in the First and Second Centuries AH, by Dr Saad bin Said Al-Hamidi, Associate Professor Faculty of Languages and Social Sciences, Imam Mohammed bin Saud Islamic University, Southern Branch, Abha, K.S.A.

Oman and its Trade with the Far East and East Africa in the Islamic Era, by Dr Sohar El Sayed Abdul Aziz Salem, Alexandria University.

A Study of the Geopolitical Components of the Sultanate of Oman, by Dr Mohammed Ramzi, Damascus University.

Historical and Archaeological Research in the Province of Dhofar, Sultanate of Oman, prepared by Professor Juris Zarens, South West Missouri State University, U.S.A.

Oman — Situation

Oman's Situation and Significance Throughout History

Oman occupies the far south-eastern corner of the Arabian peninsula, its geographical boundaries clearly defined by nature from earliest times. To the north it extends as far as Musandam on the Strait of Hormuz, while its interior merges with the Rub'al-Khali or Empty Quarter to the west and south-west. From Bahrain and Qatar it is separated by the Rimal Baynouna and from the Hadramaut by the Rimal Al-Ahqaf, which run into the Rub'al-Khali[1]. These geographical attributes have contributed to Oman's unique character, its long association with the sea being an outstanding feature. Oman's coastline is cut by numerous long deep bays from which rise steep vertical cliffs. The interior of the country is, for the most part, composed of a massif averaging 1500 metres in height. The 'backbone' of this massif, Jebel Al-Akhdar south-west of Muscat, rises to around 3000 metres. Gorges or steep wadis criss-cross the plateau. Some of the wadis run down towards the Gulf of Oman and the Arabian Sea, the most important of them being the Wadi Sama'il, the most fertile of all the wadis, which discharges west of the city of Muscat. Others decant into the Rub'al-Khali.

Oman has a coastal plain overlooking the Gulf of Oman known as the Batinah Plain into which waters from the high massif pour down to feed a rich growth of grains, cereals and fruits as well as date palms. Another coastal plain skirts the Arabian Sea. Known as Jarbib, it is watered by wells and *falajes* (water channels) and supports a variety of fruits and vegetables, as well as plantations of banana and coconut palm. To the west of this plateau lie many oases, the most famous of which is Buraimi.

When we come to classify Oman's interior regions, topography can play a useful part. Between coastal plain and mountain range are rocky lowlands inhabited from ancient times. From time immemorial too, Omanis have settled the valleys which slope down from these mountains. And the open desert has long been home to free-ranging desert tribes. These diverse geographical regions combine to form a vast area of land totalling 312,000 sq kms, although today's Oman does not compare in size with the Oman of earlier times, when it encompassed a number of adjacent districts from neighbouring Arab territories[2]. In the first century after the Hegira it stretched southwards as far as Shihr and west to the Rub'al-Khali, down to the coast on the south, south-west and north-east, and up as far as Bahrain in the north[3].

If the natural geography of Oman sets it off as distinct from the rest of the Arabian peninsula, then its place on the regional map also has a crucial significance and Oman has played an influential role in establishing the powers of autonomous states[4]. The geographical location of Oman is more than merely a factor to be considered - it is a vital national resource with a central part to play in the complex web of internal and regional relationships and interests, more particularly because of its strategic coastal setting. For, as we know, its coastline extends for more than 1700 kms[5] along the Gulf of Oman to the Arabian Sea and on to where this sea merges with the Indian Ocean. Oman commands the Strait of Hormuz on its southern side, this Strait constituting the sole means of access by sea to the Arabian Gulf from the Arabian Sea and the Indian Ocean.

This magnificent setting was to contribute to the growth of one of Oman's outstanding claims to distinction - its supremacy on the high seas. It is easy to see the connection if we look at the hazards with which passage by land to the neighbouring regions was fraught. Between Bahrain and Oman, for instance, lies intractable desert[6] as well as many desolate and sparsely populated regions. The Omanis were thus obliged to seek out a passage by sea and in time applied themselves to achieving mastery over the sea and extracting the maximum benefit from their nautical skills. In due course this seafaring nation began to play a principal role in the trade of the Arabian Gulf and the Indian Ocean. First it was to become the principal marine base of the Gulf, commanding its southern access gates, and then the major centre of interaction between two worlds - the Far East, represented by India, China and South-east Asia on the one hand, and East Africa and Egypt, and thence the European West on the other.

The Gulf, controlled by Oman at its entrance point on the southern side, is not as might be thought an arm of the Indian Ocean, but rather a separate sea in itself. In fact it combines no less than three seas: the Sea of Persia, the Sea of Bahrain and the Sea of Oman, which together form a single body of water enclosed by the Persian coastline on the eastern rim and the Arab littoral on the west. The waters of this Gulf discharge into the Indian Ocean, which extends to the Far East in one direction and in the other to the Arabian Sea and the Berberine Gulf (a reference to Berberine Somalia) which runs down to Safala in Mozambique and of which the Red Sea (Suez branch) is an offshoot[7].

It is reasonable to expect that such an important location will have a bearing on the course of historical events in Oman, and on its political stance with respect to its neighbours, as indeed its position in the far south-eastern corner of the Arabian peninsula defines Oman as a part of the Arab World[8]. In this context, events occurring at the centre of the Arab Islamic State would be reflected in Oman and in the other Arab territories. The stability and interests of Oman interacted with the stability and interests of the Arab Islamic State and the welfare of each was a matter of mutual concern and benefit. Oman's position was a focal point of its attachment and dialogue with the Islamic State and it was in this context that many of the travellers and geographers wrote about it, particularly during the Islamic Age.

Oman in the Writings of the Arab Geographers

Arab geographers described Oman in their various narratives, emphasizing its pre-eminence as a maritime and trading nation as well as its relations with

China, India and the East African coast and some of the islands of the Indian Ocean. They also described its flora and they have given us their own personal observations or descriptions recounted to them by others or transcribed by them from the writings of others. This material gives us a valuable account of the territories of Oman.

At'Tajir Suleiman (d. 237 AH/851 AD)[9] tells us in his account *Silsila Al-Tawarikh* (The Annals), concerning the traffic of ships and trading schooners going out from Siraf [10] and the district of Oman to India and China: 'Most of the Chinese merchant ships take on their cargo at Siraf, the merchandise having been brought down to Siraf from Basra, Oman and other ports and there loaded onto the Chinese ships. They then sail for Muscat, being the last port of call of Oman. From Siraf to Muscat was a distance of 200 *parasang*. In this sea were the Mountains of Oman and the place known as Al-Dardour (or whirlpool), a narrow pass between two underwater rock formations plied only by smaller ships. The Chinese ships do not pass by this place. Here also are the two mountains known as Kaseer and Aweer (the Destroyer and the Wrecker). Only a tiny portion of these is visible above water. If it passes these mountains safely, a ship will soon arrive at Sohar. On the return journey ships anchor at Muscat to take on sweet water, then make sail for India, calling en route to Kolom Melli[11] With a moderately good wind behind them they can cover this distance in a month. The Chinese ships bring silk to the Arab countries'.

Abu Zayed Al-Hassan Al-Sirafi, in *Akhbar Al-Sin Wal Hind* (Chronicles of China and India), notes that Oman was famed for its sea captains and pilots and it maintained a supply of these to Chinese, Indian and Arab boats[12]. Of Oman's relationship with the islands of the Far East it was said that on the island of Killeh[13] were wondrous wares: aloes and camphor, sandalwood, ivory, lead, ebony and brazilwood[14], as well as aromatics[15] of every variety. These goods were transported from this island to Oman, and on the same journey the boats carried Arab goods to India[16].

In *Al-Masalek Wal-Mamalek* (Roads and Kingdoms) about Oman and its territories, Ibn Khordathuba (d 272 AH/885 AD) notes that Oman's annual income from *kharaj* or land tax was 300,000 dinars, giving an indication of the importance of its position in world trade at that time. Merchants would call in there on their way from Al-Abila[17] in the south of Iraq to India, Sind and China. The goods which they brought back from the Far East were musk and aloes, camphor, cinnamon and the like. On the return voyage they would sail on to Europe, travelling up the Red Sea and Gulf of Suez and across Egypt, bearing with them servants and odalisques, silk, skins, silk fabric, furs, sable and swords[18].

Al-Hamdani (d 334 AH/945 AD) in *Siffat Jeziret Al-Arab* (Features of the Arabian Peninsula), describes Yemen as being in the south of the peninsula with El-Sham (Syria) lying to its north: 'To the west is the Sharm Eilat Bay and the unbroken coastline of the Red Sea as far as the pavilions of Egypt. On the Eastern side are the lands of Oman and Bahrain, Kazima and Basra. The central area is divided between the Hijaz, the Nejd and Al-Oroudh'[19]. Of the ocean at Oman where it meets the Hijaz, Al-Hamdani says that it 'joins the lands of the Yemen to the lands of the Negroes and Abyssinia[20]. The main town in Oman is Sohar and the villages are in greater part gathered into the valleys[21]. The Azdi

This map was taken from
by the Arab sai
This book is a
Soviet Orient

...*book "Thalat R'amanjat Al-Jahoula"*
...*avigator Ahmed bin Majed.*
...*gst the publications of the*
...*stitute in Leningrad, 1957.*

Thalath
Rahmanjat Al-
Majhoula *by the
mariner Ahmed
bin Majed.*

Sila

**CHINA
(Bilad Al-Sin)**

Ghour Is.

Siniya

Sitwa

*OCEAN SEA
(Al-Bahr Al-Mohayt)*

Nalbari Is.

Felu Sinbilin

Af.

Serjil

Firk. *Fini*

James Filleh *Tinburk*

Ghobat Qafasi

SIAM

Solar *Sina*

Falalu

SUMATRA

Sinda **Kaban**

JAVA

tribes who settled Oman are for the most part: the Yahmad, Wahdan, Malik, Al-Hareth, Oteik and Jadid'[22].

According to Al-Istakhri (d 340 AH/951 AD) in *Masalek Al-Mamalek* (The Roads of the Kingdoms), the Arabs did not have to share their lands with other non-Arab inhabitants. These lands were enclosed by the Persian Sea (Arabian Gulf) which extended from Abadan, into which fed the waters of the Tigris and Euphrates, to Bahrain and onwards from there to Oman, there to be released onto the shores of Mahra, Hadramaut and Aden, thence to the Yemeni coast, on to Jeddah and along the coastal border of the Hijaz and finally to Eilat (latterday Aqaba)[23].

Al-Istakhri gives us a good description of Oman: '(It) is distinguished by its suitability to the many date palms and fruits which grow there, such as banana, pomegranate, lotus fruit and others. The capital of the Omani territories is Sohar on the sea coast. It has an active sea trade and is visited by (trading) boats. It is Oman's most populated and prosperous city and you will not find in all of the lands of Islam a city of more people or greater affluence than Sohar[24]. There are many other cities in the land of Oman. Its area is 300 *parasang* [25]. The distance between Oman and Bahrain is a journey of one month and from Oman to Mahra is around one month's journey also'[26].

Birzek bin Shahrayar (died around the middle of the fourth century AH/10th century AD) recounts in his book *Aja'ib Al-Hind Birru Wa Bahru Wa Jaza'iru* (The Wonders of India, Land, Sea and Islands), how the inhabitants of Oman were renowned for seafaring: 'Among its legendary sea captains was Yazid Al-Omani, the captain of *Al-Zinj*. This mariner relates how he had once seen in the land of the Negroes two great mountains enclosing a valley which bore tracks of fire. When he asked about them, he was told that there was a time of year when this valley ran with a fire which annihilated everything in its path - animals, plants and men'. There is no doubt but this fire was what we call volcanic lava[27].

In *Kitab Al-Buldan* (The Book of the Countries), Ibn Al-Faqih Al-Hamdani (365 AH/975 AD) describes Oman as 'the finest of the two lands and foremost amongst them'[28]. He continues: 'The world had three hashoush or date gardens - Oman, El-Abila and Siraf[29]. It is noted for its fish, its spears and dates. Amongst the renowned varieties of date are the *fardh ballaq* and *khabout*'[30].

Ibn Hawqal (d 380 AH/990 AD) again outlines the Arab territories in *Surat Al-Ardh* (Image of the Earth): 'Bounded by the Persian Sea (Arabian Gulf) from Abadan, where the Tigris enters the sea, to Bahrain and on to Oman, then curving along the coast of Mahra, Hadramaut and Aden, thence to the Yemen and on to Jeddah, from where it extends past Al-Jar and Medin as far as Eilat.[31] Among the places he mentions on the coast of Oman are Ras Al-Jamjama[32]and the city of Sohar.

The districts of the Arabian peninsula as described by the Arabs in the Middle Ages.

Describing Oman, he writes of a country of districts distinguished by their wide open spaces in which grow date palms and fruits - among them banana, pomegranate and the like. 'These are hot lands, and yet a light snow falls on some of its mountains. Its capital is Sohar on the coast. Sohar has innumerable merchants and a busy trade. It is the most populated city in Oman and also the most prosperous. You will not find in the lands of Islam on all the coast of the Persian Sea a more populous or wealthier city than Sohar. Oman has many cities'[33].

Al-Maqdisi (d after 390 AH/999 AD) in *Ahsan Al-Taqasim* (The Best Classification), divides the Arabian peninsula into 'four vast and glorious districts' and 'four superb cantons.' The districts are: the Hijaz, the Yemen, Oman and Hajar. The cantons are Al-Ahqaf, Shihr, Yamama and Qurah[34]. He describes the district of Oman as a splendid one measuring 80 *parasang* square[35] with a profusion of date palms and gardens. The inhabitants are supplied with water drawn from nearby wells by cattle, the wells being mostly in the mountain regions[36]. The capital of Oman is Sohar. Its other cities include Nizwa Al-Sirr, Dhank, Hafit, Daba, Salut, Julfar, Samad, Bisia and Manah[37]. Of Sohar he says that it is the capital of Oman, and that 'no city on the Sea of

Contemporary view of Nizwa.

China today (fourth century of the Hegira) compares with it in splendour or in the nobility of its inhabitants. It is a city of abundance and merchants and fruits and finery, wealthier than Zubayd and Sana'a in Yemen, with wondrous souqs. It is a graceful town built along the sea's edge, its houses made from baked brick and mud[38]. The buildings there are tall and handsome and the inhabitants prosperous in bearing. Sohar is the vestibule of the sea route to China, the treasury of the Orient and of Iraq and the deliverance of Yemen. It is watered by sweet wells and pleasant canals. Beyond the souqs by the sea is a fine mosque with a handsome tall minaret and a *mihrab* (prayer niche) with a spiral which when it turns appears first yellow and then green and then again red'[39].

Al-Maqdisi also furnishes a description of Oman's other cities. Of Nizwa he says that 'it is in the mountains, a sizeable town with homes built from clay. The mosque is situated in the heart of the souq. The town's inhabitants drink from streams and wells. If the valley becomes flooded in the rains, the waters enter the mosque[40]... Al-Sirr[41] is smaller than Nizwa and encircled by date palms. Its mosque is also located in the centre of the souq and it is watered by streams and wells. The town of Dhank has only a small number of date palms. Hafit on the other hand has many and its mosque is in the centre of the market-place. Salut is to the left of Nizwa, while Daba and Julfar are on the side of the Hajar lands[42]. There are towns named Samad and Bisia and Manah and Al-Qal'ah[43] and Dhank'[44]. Where he writes of Muscat he says of it that it is the first habitation to greet boats arriving from Yemen. He found it to be a handsome place rich in fruits. Tu'am he notes was peopled largely by a tribe of the Qureish noted for their courage and strength[45].

Al-Maqdisi's account of the commerce of the Arabian peninsula observes that trading there is profitable, 'for it has the two seaports of Dunia and Souq Menna and a sea linking it to China. Jeddah and Al-Jar are the treasuries of Egypt and Wadi Al-Qara the repository of El-Sham (Syria) and Iraq. Yemen is the storehouse of headcloths and carnelian stones, of skins and of slaves. To Oman are exported the tools of the apothecary's trade and every kind of fragrance as well as musk and saffron, brazilwood and teak and sasem (a kind of tree from which arrows are made), ivory, pearls and silk brocade, onyx, sapphires, ebony, coconut palm and cane sugar crystals, Alexandrite, aloes, iron, lead, bamboo, green plants, sandalwood, quartz, pepper and the like. Aden is supplied by it with ambergris, drinks and cordials, leather shields, Abyssinian slaves and servants as well as tiger and leopard skins. By means of the merchandise of China is wisdom spread abroad'[46].

The system of weights and measures operating in Oman at the time of Al-Maqdisi were the *saa* {a cubic measure of varying magnitude}, the *mudd* {a variable dry measure} and the *makuk* {a variable liquid measure equivalent to the contents of a drinking cup}. On board the seagoing ships were two *saa* in one of which the sailor was given his daily rations, while the larger one was used to carry on business. Their dry weight was a *rotl,* this being the *munn* known throughout the Islamic countries[47]. The currency employed by the inhabitants of Oman was the *dinar,* this being the equivalent of 30 *dirhams*. The dirham used in Oman was known as the *tesswah* [48]. It was customary for the citizens to pay the Sultan one *dirham* in respect of each date palm owned by them[49]. Oman's total *kharaj* (land tax), in the view of Qadama bin Jaafar, was 300,000 dinars annually. It was also customary to take from merchants arriving in Oman a tenth (of the value of their merchandise) and on occasion the Sultan took a third of the merchant's income. From time to time the merchants were subjected to a thorough inspection[50].

Nasir Khusru (d 481AH/ 1088 AD) describes Oman in his book *Safar Naama* (Peaceful Journeys) as a *wilaya* or province: "If the traveller travels south of Al-Hassa he will come upon it. It is an Arab land, three sides of which are impenetrable desert, the weather is hot and the coconuts known as *narjileh* flourish here. South of Oman is Aden, and eastwards across the water lie the two islands of Kish and Makran'[51].

Abu Eid Al-Bakri (d 487 AH/1094 AD) in his book *Jeziret Al-Arab* (The Arab Peninsula), transcribed from *Al-Masalek Wa Al-Mamalek* (Roads and Kingdoms), says of Dhofar that it is a stopping place for the Aaraba Arabs and the home of exalted and mighty kings and chieftains and princes. 'To be found there are sabres and garments - the robes and gowns of Aden and Sana'a -

Two views of contemporary Sohar.

embroidered and ornamented. As well as these are ambergris, onyx, carnelian, slaves, Khurasannee and Mahra, camels , Arabian horses, pure gold and other goods and wares'[52]. He remarks that in the land of Oman are pearl fisheries where the divers earn from one *kerat* to one half dirham per day. 'It is customary for them to dive from first light until midday and then to break open the shells up to the end of that day. The pearls of Oman are of a good quality and greatly prized. It is known that seed pearls from Oman have been sold for as much as 10 - 15,000 dinars'[53].

In the account of Al-Bakri on Oman he describes coastal plains, which give way to hard ground as one leaves the coast towards the mountains inland. Among the cities he makes note of Muscat on the sea coast, observing that it is a fortified town encircled by a mountain with running water flowing down into the city. It is a city of many date palms and gardens and a variety of fruits. The staples of the inhabitants are wheat, barley, rice and millet'[54]. Sohar is a substantial city on the sea coast and it is watered by wells. The town of Nizwa is bigger than Sohar and Saham, another city, is fed by springs. It has a multitude of date palms and sugar cane grows there'[55].

Al-Bakri notes that the land tax or *kharaj* of Oman is 80,000 dinars annually: 'From here one may travel by sea to the shores of the Arabian peninsula, Africa, China and India. It conducts a vast and far-reaching trade and inns and caravanserai have been built there to accommodate foreign merchants arriving from

overseas or residing there. There is a proverb which says: 'Who has lost his livelihood let him go to Oman' (where his fortunes will be restored). In gratitude for their good fortune one of the lords of Oman some time after the year 420 AH made a gift to the Kaaba of *mihrabs* (prayer niches) wrought from silver, the weight of each *mihrab* being more than one *qantar*, as well as silver candleabra, exquisitely worked. The *mihrabs* were encased within the Kaaba at a position facing the door'[56].

Al-Idrisi (d 565 AH/1169 AD) says of Oman in his book *Nozha Al-Mishtaq fi Akhtaraq Al-Ifaq* (The Recreation of Him who Yearns to Traverse the Lands): 'Adjacent to the land of Mahra and its neighbour on the northern side is Oman. This is an independent land inhabited by its own people. It has many dates and fleshy fruit, such as banana, pomegranate, figs, grapes and the like... Among its most famous cities are Sur and Qalhat on the sea coast. Both of these are small and yet flourishing towns. The inhabitants drink from wells and small quantities of pearls are fished here. The distance between Sur and Qalhat is a day's journey, though not by sea[57]. On the coast of Oman is Ras Jamjama[58], a high mountain on the sea's edge eastwards of Ghab Al-Hashish. Navigation along the Oman coastline is hazardous because of massive rock formations just beneath the surface of the water on which boats are wrecked if they approach too close. The vicinity of Ras Jamjama is famed for its pearl diving[59]. Just off the coast of Oman are two islands, Ibn Kawan, which is 52 miles long and 9 miles across, and Kishe Island. Close to Ibn Kawan is Al-Dardour (or the whirlpool), a place where the waters swirl in an unceasing vortex. If a boat approaches too close, the waters will spin and turn until they have trapped it in their embrace. Close by the two (submerged) mountains Kaseer and Aweer is a strait, through which pass smaller ships, though never the Chinese boats. These two mountains are submerged beneath the surface of the water, with no part of them visible. The sea captains know their whereabouts and take care to avoid them. Between Siraf and Muscat on the coast is a spur which juts out into the sea and facing this is a small island'[60].

Al-Idrisi writes of the building of ships on the Oman coast, in particular at Sohar and Marbat. 'The type of boat built here is made from coconut wood and the leaves of the date palm. After the wooden planks have been sawn they are stitched together using a rope made from coconut fibre (coir) in the manner in which ropes are woven from palm fronds[61]. Oman is famed for a type of grease used for sealing breaches in the boats[62]. There are also larger boats which they build from local or imported woods. Omani sailors travel the Indian Ocean and the Arabian Sea in these boats, carrying goods and precious wares as far as the coasts of Africa, India and China. And they bring back with them the merchandise of these countries[63].

'Among Oman's coastal towns is Dama [Al-Seeb], no more than a village in winter with a depleted population. In summer, however, all is teeming life, when the divers arrive to search for pearls along the coast. Here is splendid pearl fishing and the area is noted for the quality of its pearl'[64].

The city of Sohar, according to Al-Idrisi, is one of the oldest cities of Oman, and one of the wealthiest in ancient as well as recent times. 'Merchants flock here every year in countless numbers from all over the world. All the wares of the Yemen are assembled here and every manner of trade and traffic is conducted. The citizens are prosperous and commerce is profitable. It is famed for the profusion of date palms in its environs as well as fruits, including bananas, pomegranates and quince. It has many varieties of delicious and wondrous dates. Ships setting out from Sohar plied the sea routes as far as China until this traffic was severed as a consequence of pirates preying on the merchant ships. They would pounce on the boats in sudden forays out of the islands off the coast of Oman, and the merchant boats moved their trade to Aden'[65]. Muscat he describes as a fabled city on the Oman coast at a distance from Sohar of around 450 miles[66]. 'Towards the northern shore of Oman is the island of Kishe, a square land mass measuring 12 miles in each direction. This island has a fine fort as well as plantations, goats, cows and vines'. He goes on to describe its reputation for pearl diving[67]. 'Among Oman's coastal towns, as well as Sohar, Dama and Muscat, are Al-Hail and Julfar. Pearl fishing is conducted off the coasts of these last two settlements and alongshore as far as Sohar. Facing them out to sea is one side of a large underwater rock mass or mountain showing only small portions here and there and otherwise out of sight. This rock mass is

The Earth after Al-Sherif Al-Idrisi.

Niyazeeh Mahak Lasgart Al-Herab Majuj Bulgaria Turkey Izkesh Yajuj Kharaz Sea Gaziah Khalkhiyah Qiaq zerbaijan Alshash Nagargar Iraq Persia Khurasan Tibet Makharkhir Kernan Magaza China Makran India Shahr Oman Sind Ramy mah z Comores Yemen Sarandeeb INDIAN SEA Waqwaq Safala Barbarah Zinj a menace to boats and those which approach too close are liable to be smashed to pieces"[68].

Al-Idrisi in his account of Oman continues, saying that its area measures 900 miles[69]: 'It is hot in summer but a light snow falls on the peak of Jebel Shams in winter. Between Oman and the Nejd is unbroken open road. The road from here to Mecca is extremely arduous overland because of the many desolate regions and the scarcity of inhabitants. On the northern and western sides, Oman borders the land of Yamama'[70].

Ya'qut Al-Hamawi (d 626 AH/ 1228 AD) says in his book *Mu'jam Al-Buldan* (The Lexicon of Countries): 'Oman is the name of an Arab district on the coast of the Sea of Yemen and India. It is in the first province, and is situated at 74 degrees and 30 minutes longitude, and 19 degrees and 45 minutes latitude[71]. It is east of Hajar and consists of many adjacent lands. There are numerous date plantations and cultivations. .. The capital of Oman is Sohar of which the Prophet said: "I know one of the Arab lands that is called Oman which is by the sea coast. The one pilgrimage [to Mecca] from Oman is better than two from other places"[72]'. Describing Sohar he says it is the capital of that part of Oman which lies beyond the mountain[73], he goes on to cite Al-Maqdisi's observations about this town and its pre-eminence as a city of Oman and centre for trade with the East[74].

Nizwa he describes as an inland mountain[75] encircled by a number of large villages which, grouped together, share this name. 'The district of Nizwa is noted for its robes of silk brocade. These exquisitely worked robes are finer than any to be found in the Arab countries. Coverlets made from this type of work are costly and greatly prized'. Al-Hamawi saw some of these and commended them and it is evident that these exquisite vestments were exported beyond the borders of Oman to other countries[76].

Muscat, according to Ya'qut, was a name given to several diverse places among which were: 'Muscat Al-Raml on the desert road to Basra, Muscat the city on the Oman sea coast as well as Muscat on the Caspian Sea before reaching *Bab Al-Abwab* or the Gate of Gates[77]. Qalhat is another of Oman's seaport cities having facilities for boats from India. It has no old buildings and Ya'qut believed it to have been built after the year 500 AH. It was one of the most renowned and finest cities of Oman, densely populated and the chief port of Oman on the Indian Ocean and Arabian Sea'[78].

'Julfar is a prosperous town known for its goats and cheeses and cooking fat, which it exported to the neighbouring countries[79]. One of its villages is Kelba, set on the coast[80] and Khor Fakkan, another coastal township separated from the Great Sea by a mountain. It has dates and sweet water springs[81]. Ibn Said Al-Maghrabi (d 673 AH/1274 AD) says of Dhofar in his work *Kitab Al-Jughrafia* (The Book of Geography), that it had been 'a mighty city now laid waste'. It lies at 73 degrees longitude and 15 degrees latitude, after which one encounters the coastal cities of Shihr. This is the land of ambergris and frankincense (olibanum). One of its towns is Marbat, on a small north-facing inlet at 74 degrees longitude and 14.5 degrees latitude. Eastwards of this town on the same bay is the modern Dhofar. In the time of Ibn Said Al-Maghrabi (the seventh century AH) Dhofar was a seat of (government) of Shihr and its celebrated port to which were dispatched Arab horses for transport onwards to India. It was said that in this town were to be found the many and diverse medicaments of India such as coconut, tanbal (a plant), betel nut and jujube. North of the inlet are the Al-Ahqaf sands, and north of Al-Ahqaf the Frankincense Mountains run from west to east'[82].

Al-Qazzouini (d 682 AH/1283 AD) notes that Dhofar is celebrated for the good quality of Dhofari onyx and for its olibanum bushes, 'which are unique to these mountains in all the world. The frankincense trade yields a good return for the Sultan. When the stem of the bush is cut with a knife the frankincense resin runs out, whereupon it is collected and brought to Dhofar. The Sultan takes a portion of this and returns the rest to them'[83].

Omani making an incision in a frankincense tree.

Ibn Al-Majawir (d 690 AH/ 1291 AD) in his book *Siffat Balad Al-Yemen Wa Mekkah Wa Baadh Al-Hijaz* (Description of Yemen, Mecca and Part of the Hijaz) describes Oman as 'universally blessed, its mercantile interests vast. Qalhat and Muscat and Sohar are among its prominent cities. The distance between Qalhat and Taiwi is three *parasang* and to Muscat is six[84]. Oman is noted for its fishing, and its inhabitants live off fish and dates'. Ibn Al-Majawir remarks that Muscat was the anchorage of Sohar[85]. Boats arriving from foreign lands were accustomed to anchor (there), and to take on a variety of goods before proceeding to Karman and Sigistan. The merchandise would be distributed in Khorasan and beyond the river as well as Zaulistan and Al-Ghour (in the Jordan Valley) and Carmel'[86]. A measure of the extent and range of Oman's trade is the fact that Sohar had 192 weigh-bridges for weighing merchandise for vendors and purchasers[87], a pointer to the prominence of Oman's trading status in the Middle Ages.

Al-Dimeshqi (d. 727 AH/1326 AD) gives an account in his narrative *Nakhbet Al-Dahar fi Aja'ib Al-Birr wal-Bahar* (The Passage of Time in the Marvels of Land and Sea) about pearls and pearl fishing. 'Diving is found in four places - the island of Kharg in the jurisdiction of Persia, Oman, Qatar and the island of Serendib (Sri Lanka). There are two types of pearl: the larger goes by the name of *dorr* and the small *lu'lu'*. The best quality *dorr* is perfectly round, pure and translucent, of a respectable size, and weighs between a half and one and a half miskal. The finest *lu'lu'* is clear and spherical. Pearls come in several colours, among them round yellow, red, green and blue'[88]. Al-Dimeshqi notes that Oman was famed for its aloes, this being a resin produced 'by a tree with a leaf resembling the leaf of the liquorice plant. The leaf edges have small thorns and these are longer and coarser than the leaves of the lily and exude a sticky gum. The Omani gum is black and glossy. Oman exports also blue *muqal*, this being a fragrant gum resembling olibanum which comes from a large tree which grows in the region between Shihr and Oman[89]. The bush (*Boswellia carteri*) which produces olibanum or oriental frankincense grows in Oman, particularly around the region of Dhofar and these bushes also grow in Yemen'[90].

View of Dhofar.

Al-Dimeshqi describes Oman as being on the coast of the Indian Ocean. 'The coastal terrain is made up of level plain and sands and beyond this is *hozoun* (rough intractable ground) and mountains. Oman is renowned for its date palms, bananas and pomegranates. Its first capital was Sohar, until it was destroyed. The city of Qalhat was built at a later date and this became the chief port of Oman. Sur and Muscat were other cities of note, both set on the sea coast. Inland were Adam, a walled city, and Meeh[91], another walled town into which flow waters from the high neighbouring ground.

'Nizwa lies in a valley between two mountains and the Bahla Fort, strategically placed on a high/forbidding promontory. Then there is the city of Julfar. One of the features of Oman are its *falajs* which resemble streams and which bring water to the coastal cities and villages and which irrigate the areas of cultivation. Some decant directly into the ocean'[92].

Aboul Feda (d 732AH/1331 AD), writing of the Arabian peninsula in *Taqwim Al-Buldan* (Tales of Countries), notes that 'the sea which encloses the peninsula from the western side and then skirts the coast from Yemen as far as Eilat, is the *Bahr Al-Qalzam* or Red Sea. On the eastern side is the Sea of Persia (Arabian Gulf), extending from Basra to Bahrain and then on to Oman'. He describes Oman as being situated 'at the mouth of the Persian Gulf (Arabian Gulf), situated at 74 degrees longitude and 19 degrees and 45 minutes latitude[93]. The peninsula is bound on the south by the Indian Ocean which stretches from Oman to the coast of Mahra, then follows the shores of Yemen as far as Aden'. Describing the town of Marbat, he says: 'This is on the coast of the Gulf of Dhofar and in the hills above it grow the bush which produces frankincense which is exported to many countries'[94].

Al-Homeiri, who died in the eighth century of the Hegira/fourteenth century AD, describes Sohar in his narrative *Al-Rawdh Al-Mi'tar Fi Khabar Al-Aqtar* (Scented Gardens in the Annals of the Regions): 'A large city on the sea coast,

View of Dhofar.

the capital of Oman, with an area of one *parasang* square. Its inhabitants drink from wells. It is said to be the oldest and wealthiest city of Oman in both ancient and recent times. Merchants flock here every year from every part of the world. All the wares of the Yemen are assembled here and every manner of trade and traffic is conducted. It was the anchorage for ships from China and India and these ships would load up with diverse goods and set sail from here. This remained the situation until the

The fort of Bahla.

island of Kishe built up a fleet, mounting expeditions into the coastal regions of Yemen. This had an adverse influence on both travellers and merchants and benefited no-one for trade declined and ships no longer called into Oman. Prior to this Sohar was the port of call for the mercantile trade, exporting to all countries and enriching its inhabitants in the process. Sohar has cultivations of date palm, bananas, pomegranate and quince and many delicious varieties of dates'[95].

In Al-Homeiri's account, Oman was an independent state inhabited by its own citizens, known for its dates and fruits, including bananas, pomegranates, figs and grapes. It measured 80 *parasang* square[96], with plains and sandy areas along the sea coast and rough ground and mountains to the interior. 'One of its many cities is Oman[97], a fortified city on the coast, with streams flowing down into the town from the mountains surrounding its interior. It has many date palms and gardens and a variety of fruits. In the town are inns and baths which were built to serve visiting merchants. The staple food of the inhabitants is wheat, barley, rice and millet. The walls of the city have iron gates and there are many souqs within. It is the port city for the China sea trade, and the merchandise of Siraf is brought here in small skiffs and loaded onto the great oceangoing ships which set sail in a good wind for India and China.

Muscat is on the road to Oman on the coast and voyagers to India and China call in there, travelling southwards until they reach Muscat. This city is between two mountains and ships anchor at it port to take on fresh water from the wells. These ships also take on board stones and rocks from Muscat to cast at enemies should they encounter them on the high seas. Shihr in the Hadramaut is at a distance of 90 *parasang*'[98].

Finally Al-Qalqashandi (d 821 AH/1418 AD), in his travelogue *Subh Al-'Aasha* (The Morning of the Night-blind: On the Art of Writing), describes Oman as follows: 'Its capital is Oman[99] on the coast below Basra. It is a splendid city with an anchorage for boats from Sind and India and Zinj (Africa).

View of Muscat.

No city on the Persian Sea compares with it. It is a country of the Azd and measures around 300 *parasang* with many fruits and palms. It is extremely hot however. In olden times the capital of Oman was Sohar'. This city in the time of Al-Qalqashandi (ninth century AH/fifteenth century AD) was in ruins[100].

To sum up, Arab geographers wrote frequently of Oman throughout the period from the third to the ninth century of the Hegira and these accounts gave us

an abundance of information about the position of Oman and its importance, its influence, its crops and resources, its major cities as well as its merchant traffic with the diverse foreign lands at that time.

This splendid picture of the Orient as handed down to us by these geographers was completed and illuminated further by the accounts of the travellers who traversed the seas and wandered among the inhabited lands of east and west. Oman was one of the stopping places where they rested up and in their accounts of it they gave us a detailed picture of what they saw. So what did they say?

Oman in the Writings of Travellers in the Middle Ages

Oman was one of the important confluence points of Islamic culture, and its own history had roots deep in the past, going back many thousands of years. This coastal nation was the dominant power of the Gulf and merchant ships from India, China, Egypt and the Arabian peninsula called at its ports[101]. In this way it became a link between the Arabian peninsula and the old world. Parts of it were very fertile and travellers were unrestrained in their descriptions of its marvels and its dates. It bore the vestiges of many past civilizations - the great cultures of Mesopotamia, China, India and Egypt left their mark here, as well as Greece and Rome - and historians from the latter states wrote about its ports.

Many travellers and geographers visited the area and wrote down their impressions. Their descriptions differed in accordance with the times in which they lived. The centres of civilization and renaissance as well as the trading pre-eminence of its ports changed over the centuries. Furthermore the travellers of the first period were mostly geographers such as Ibn Hawqal and Al-Istakhri and their information was influenced by the special position played by geography and history[102].

The travellers of the thirteenth and fourteenth centuries, among them the Italian, Marco Polo, and Ibn Battuta, have handed down to us a detailed account of the country and its affairs and ports as well as the habits and customs of its people.

These geographers noted that the Omanis were pre-eminent in seafaring commerce, trading in goods from faraway lands. Abu Abida Abdullah bin Al-Qassem was the first to travel to China in the Islamic Era, in the year 133AH/750 AD. He confirmed the strategic location of Oman and its trading importance at that time. Its position at the junction of the sea routes between China and India to the east and Iraq to the north and east and the Red Sea to the west[103] was one of the factors that assisted the Omanis in mounting voyages to China and India. They purchased silk, camphor, musk, spices and porcelain from China, and from India teak, rice and foodstuffs. In exchange they brought the goods of the east - linen and cotton and wool, metal implements, crude iron and gold ingots. The most important exports of Oman itself were horses and frankincense.

If we return to the writings of our travellers we find the geographer and historian[104], Al-Mas'udi, who made many voyages starting from the year 309 AH across Persia and Karman and India, Malabar, Mansoura and Serendib. He

Dolphins.

travelled to China and crossed the Indian Ocean from Madagascar, returning to Oman before setting off for Azerbaijan and El-Sham and finally settling in Egypt[105]. In the course of his visit to Oman he was dazzled by its bustling trade, especially at Sohar which had a far-reaching reputation as a trading centre. He described his journey across the Indian Ocean and observed that the Ocean extended from the coast of Abyssinia to the far reaches of India and China, covering 8000 miles, and that most of the mariners on the high seas were from Oman. They were the best sailors of their time and many were sea captains. They had extensive knowledge of the sea and of pearl fishing in the Sea of Oman and the Gulf. He said that as well as pearls this region was noted for carnelians, sapphires and gold and that Oman in particular was famed for its copper as well as perfume and ambergris, teak and wood[106].

Fishing was also one of Oman's principal livelihoods and he mentioned a type of fish which was probably the whale. The centres with the most active trade were the coastal cities of Qalhat and Sohar, known to the Persian as Mazoun. Muscat had not yet gained fame. He described it as a port town where sea captains would take on sweet water from the wells.

The Shihri people, descendents of the Arab tribe of Qutha'ah, were also skilled in commerce, and he noted that they spoke a corrupted dialect. The city had

the best camels and they had also the best ambergris. The merchants of Oman prepared various types of ambergris. He wrote that the region known as Al-Hallad had wooden signs erected in the sea to guide the boats heading for Oman.

Tail of Humpback Whale.

Omani horses.   If we continue our journey in time until we arrive at the seventh century Hegira - the thirteenth century AD - we encounter the famous traveller Marco Polo, Italian born and bred, who lived for 17 years at the court of the Moghul kings. He visited Oman on his return journey and here we see how the situation had changed since the time of Al-Mas'udi in the fourth century. Oman still retained her sea supremacy and trading enterprise, but the hierarchy of cities had altered. Sohar had begun its decline while Dhofar and Qalhat had risen to take its place[107].

The first city he passed through on his journey was Iskabir (Shihr)[108], and he remarks on its fame as a trading centre, exporting the finest produce and wares of Oman, of which the most prized was olibanum or frankincense. White frankincense was counted the best variety and it was obtained from a small bush, the stem of which was cut until a liquid seeped from the cut after the bark had been removed. The frankincense resin oozes from this wound and is left to harden. He observed that the governor of this town had a monopoly of the trade in frankincense and bought it for a price of ten byzantiums (gold ducats) a qantar and sold it to the merchants for forty.

Horses were an important side to the exports of this town and they were sold for a high price for export to India. Oman's most significant crop was dates. Dates of the highest quality were grown and a drink composed of rice, sugar and dates was known there. There was not a great variety of cultivation, for they confined themselves to rice and millet and were importers of foodstuffs.

While trade was the principal livelihood, fishing was also important, fish representing a prime source of nutrition which they dried and prepared as food for their livestock and cattle, who were accustomed to eating this. Dhofar was an important port and it was from here that horses embarked for India and frankincense also. In this district are many cities and forts.

Here Marco Polo describes the city of Qalhat, referring to it as Qalaiati and its significance as a trading centre, and he notes that it is not far from Muscat. It was a possession of Hormuz which he believed to be subject to the governorship of Kerman. He mentions that the ruler was accustomed to retire there when exposed to danger from any of the other cities because of its unassailable aspect. Like Dhofar it did not produce grain, but imported it. Of the town port, and it is likely that he means Muscat, he says that the ships bring to this port cloth and spices which the merchants sell in exchange for horses.

Marco Polo remarks that the port had a fort occupying a lofty and impervious position at the entrance to the Gulf such that no boat could enter or leave without permission. A levy was imposed on the merchants. Its commanding position made it truly the door not only to the Gulf but to the sea itself, for a resident of the fort had a view of every ship that passed by. This place was a

Ruins at Qalhat.

sanctuary for ships passing through on great voyages and its defence was facilitated by the fact that all ships approaching the coast were visible from the fort. The prince who controlled this stronghold had mastery of the surrounding seas. The local inhabitants lived on dates and fresh or salted fish. It was said that dates were the staple food and that the inhabitants chopped them into every kind of dish and ate them without bread[109].

In the century after Marco Polo, the fourteenth AD, lived the Maghrabi traveller Ibn Battuta. He provides us with a marvellous description of Oman and the customs of its inhabitants. Ibn Battuta visited India and from there travelled by sea to Dhofar with the help of a steady wind in the space of one month. He mentions that on another occasion he had covered the distance from Calicut to Dhofar in 28 days and he describes this city as being hemmed in by desert. He paints a portrait of the city as he saw it, with the Sultan's palace at the entrance to the town. It was the custom to beat drums outside the palace of the Sultan just after the afternoon prayer every day and he would convene a council every Friday to consult with the townspeople. On Mondays and Thursdays he met with his soldiers. Whenever he went out of the city he was armed and accompanied by his slaves, mounted on a camel-borne litter which hid him from view. The affairs of state he entrusted to a vizier or minister. The inhabitants were dependent for their survival on fish, which they also fed to their animals[110].

Ibn Battuta cast his inquiring eye over local society, noting that the townspeople resembled the Maghrabis and that they were a god-fearing people. Every house had a rug made from palm fronds hanging on the wall of the house which the master of the house would use when performing his prayers, just as was the custom in the *Maghreb*. Even the names they gave to the surrounding districts were similar to those used by the people of the *Maghreb*. It was one of their agreeable practices to shake hands in the mosque at the morning and afternoon prayer. The first row would face the *qiblah* (prayer niche) and the row behind would extend their hands to them and so on. This practice was also observed after the Friday prayer.

The inhabitants were also characterized by their modest bearing, pleasant disposition and hospitality to strangers. Their garments were made from cotton which they purchased from India and they wore a robe fastened at the waist instead of trousers. Most of them wore this robe gathered in at the waist and draped another across their backs to keep out the heat. They bathed several times a day.

It was, Ibn Battuta says, the habit in this town when a boat came in from India or some other faraway place for the slaves of the Sultan to go down to the shore and row out to the ship in *sambuqs* (a type of ship) bearing a full set of apparel for the ship's master or his deputy and for the owner of the ship and the captain, as well as the *karani* (or the ship's scribe) who kept the ship's log. They were furnished with mares which they mounted and drums were beaten before them from the seashore up to the house of the Sultan, where they paid their respects to the vizier and the chief sentry. The welcome party visited the ship's crew with hospitality three times a day and after three days the crew were entertained at the palace of the Sultan.

Ibn Battuta describes the noteworthy places in the town and enumerates the mosques, mentioning a small mosque of some repute which had been endowed by a pious man from Dhofar named Abi Mohammed bin Bakr bin Issa. This mosque was a sanctuary for persons who had incurred the Sultan's disfavour, and at the time of his own visit to Oman the Sultan's scribe was ensconsed inside and remained there until a reconciliation had been arranged.

On his way to Oman Ibn Battuta called in to Hasek, where he found the inhabitants to be fishermen. The olibanum bush from which was extracted frankincense grew in the town. A species of fish was known there which resembled a seal. Their homes were made from fishbones and the ceilings were of camelskin. He speaks of a big pole which guided boats to Oman. He noted that most of the seamen and a great number of the merchants whom he encountered during his travels were Omanis. They were accustomed to bring with them a type of food cooked from corn and honey and dates which was eaten by most of the Omani merchants. He noted that the master of the ship on which he travelled was from the island of Masira[111]. He also made reference to the importance of the coastal town of Qalhat, mentioning that it was a stronghold town. No person was permitted entry without the prior approval of the town governor. If a person was allowed in he was taken on his arrival before the governor of the town he was visiting. He pointed out that the town governor was answerable to Qotb Al-Din Timhattan, the King of Hormuz. The city had well-stocked souqs and a mosque with walls inlaid with faience which was built by a pious lady named Mariam.

The inhabitants lived on rice, which they imported from India, as well as fish. They spoke a local dialect. Ibn Battuta visited a nearby town called Tibi, and found there gardens and streams and trees. This town was at a distance from Oman[112] of six days' journey across the desert.

Of the other towns in Oman, Ibn Battuta remarks on the fertility of the soil 'which supports many gardens. Their capital is Nizwa, a town at the foot of a mountain, around which are gardens and streams. The inhabitants are renowned for their courage and fearlessness. They belong to the Ibadhi sect and they pray four *ruqqah* on Friday. When the Imam has completed his reading, they gather to eat a communal meal. Members of the congregation give according to their means and then they all sit down to eat together from trays supplied by the mosque'.

He observed that the governor of the town was an Arab from the Azd tribe who went by the name of Abi Mohammed bin Nabhan. The name Abi Mohammed was a characteristic of all of the Sultans of Oman. He was accustomed to sit outside the door of his house holding council. He had neither friend nor minister and no-one was prevented from meeting him, not even strangers from beyond the town. Al-Qariat[113], Killia[114] and Sohar he mentions as among the towns affiliated to Oman, all of them built on fertile land.

It is clear from the accounts of these travellers that Oman's trading supremacy was maintained over a lengthy historical period. This importance grew at the end of the period and the number of cities proliferated. After Sohar's decline, Dhofar flourished, then Qalhat and Muscat. Oman's navigators and mariners were the best in the Gulf and its ships plied the high seas carrying merchandise and spreading civilization, goodwill and welfare wherever their feet touched dry land.

An Omani boy in traditional costume.

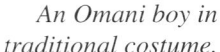

Traditions are respected among Omani society.

The People and Economy of Oman

The Inhabitants of Oman at the Dawn of Islam

Al-Bilathuri is of the view that most of those who settled Oman came from the Azd tribe[115]. These were Arabs from Qahtan in Yemen. Living close by them were a not inconsiderable number of others of a different origin, though these were dispersed throughout the *bawadi* or open spaces[116]. One of the tribes of Oman was the Bani Baraq from an offshoot of the Bani Amr who had split off from the Azd. Hodheifa bin Mohsen Al-Barqi was one of these. He became a Muslim and was sent by the Prophet to the people of Oman on a mission to collect the *zakat* or alms tax[117].

The Atki were another group of settlers who traced their ancestry to Al-Azd bin Umran bin Amr, a faction of the Azd[118]. The Bani Najiah Al-Azdioun were descended from Najiah bin Al-Jamaher or Al-Jamaheer bin Al-Ashaar of Qadai'a[119]. The Bani Najiah were yet another of the settled tribes, not related to the above but descended from Sama bin Lu'ai. They were Nazarene Adnanis and shared no more than a name with the Azdi Bani Najiah[120].

According to reliable references, the Bani Hudaid were the branch of the Azdi tribe who colonized Oman. They joined forces with Luqait Dhu'l Taj but later abandoned him when the armies of Abu Bakr arrived to subdue the rebellious tribes there[121]. And we must not forget the Bani 'Ulaf and the name 'Ulaf Rubban bin Thaalaba bin Helwan bin 'Umran bin Al-Haf [122] . Mu'awiyya and Mohammed, sons of Al-Hareth Al-'Ulafian, belonged to this tribe [123]. Men from these tribes played prominent roles in the Islamic Opening or spread of the Islamic Empire.

There were Arabian tribes in Oman whose origin was other than the Yemenites listed by Al-Bilathuri. These were referred to by him as the 'citizens of bawadi', the Bani Mazin bin Shaiban[124]. Ibn Durayed said: 'There is not one amongst them with a reputation (worth preserving). However Abi 'Uthman Al-Nahawi is related to them because his mother was one of them'[125].

Of the Bani Malik bin Fahm bin Daws bin Zahran, another Omani tribe, it was said by Ibn Durayed that they were kinsmen of the Daws Al-Azima tribe[126]. The Salimi[127] were from this tribe. They were Bani Zakia and Thaalaba bin Malik and they were descended from the Bani Amru bin Malik bin Fahm of whom was Sabia bin Ghazal who was given precedence over Abu Bakr by the citizens of Oman[128] . The Al-Hat of Kandu were another tribe associated with a place of the same name[129]. Likewise the Al-Tana'im were connected to Tan'am[130]. These are just some of the many tribes who colonized Oman in the distant past and who went on to develop thriving human settlements there.

Centres of Human Civilization in Oman

It would be impossible to overestimate the role played by Oman and its coastal cities in linking the Oman sea coast with the interior and the inhabitants of the Arabian peninsula. Oman was settled by migrations from the Arab hinterland and was a point of contact with the outside world through its ports and the islands scattered about its coastline which were active centres in the evolution of human culture and civilization.

Oman had amongst its cities and ports many which were prominent centres of habitation - Julfar (Ras Al-Khaimah), Daba, Sohar, Muscat, Tana'am, Hatta, Salut and others.

Julfar (Ras Al-Khaimah)

Julfar[131], of which Al-Maqdisi (d circa 375 AH) said that it was a city of Oman[132], was described as being close to the sea and resembling at that time Hajar[133] (Bahrain) in scale and importance. No doubt it was, like its sister cities in Oman, a market for the exotic merchandise of China, India and Yemen such as 'apothecary's tools, essences and aromatics including musk, saffron, brazilwood and teak, sasem, ivory, pearls and silk brocade, onyx and sapphires, ebony and coconut, crystal sugar, Alexandrite and aloes, iron and lead, bamboo, sandalwood, quartz crystal and pepper[134]. These wares were then borne to Iraq and the East (probably Iran)'.

It seems that the combined ports of the Omani sea coast, of which Julfar was one, constituted a trading entrepôt into which were gathered the exotic wares of the Far East for re-distribution throughout the Middle East. Ya'qut Al-Rumi says of Julfar that it had 'goats and cheese and butter in abundance' and that these were 'exported to the neighbouring countries'[135].

Sohar

This, the pre-eminent city of Oman, was the metropolis of the territory adjacent to the mountain. The metropolis of Tu'am, on the other hand, was on the coast. The geographers rivalled one another in their portrayals of Sohar. Al-Idrisi claimed it to be the oldest and richest city of Oman both past and present. He noted its foremost status as a trading centre saying: 'Countless foreign merchants come to this place every year and all of the wares of Yemen are displayed here and every manner of trade and traffic is conducted. The inhabitants are men of substance and their commerce is profitable'[136].

Al-Maqdisi also made reference to this supremacy and gives an account of its attractions and its revenues, its souqs and its mosques, as has been outlined above in some detail[137]. Ya'qut transcribed the narrative of Al-Maqdisi on the importance of Oman and its affairs in his *Kitab Mu'jam Al- Buldan* [138]. Some of the sources interpret the name Sohar as being taken from that of Sohar bin Aram bin Sam bin Nuh. It was thought that Sohar derived from Sahraa (or desert)[139]. Al-Mas'udi calls it Sinjar in his account: 'Oman's capital city is Sinjar, known to the Persians as Mazoun[140]. A distance of 50 *parasang* separates it from Muscat, which is a small village where sea captains take on sweet water from the wells there' [141].

Muscat

This was the second city after Sohar, the two cities being 230 kms apart[142]. The various sources agree on the existence of freshwater wells in Muscat which were adequate to meet the needs of the town and its trade when Muscat's status as a trading centre grew[143]. Ibn Battuta noted that Muscat was famous for a type of fish which was known as the *qaib al-mas* or the diamond heart[144].

Muscat.

Nizwa

Al-Istakhri and Ibn Hawqal both report that this was the place where the Shurats had gone on an occasion when a difference arose between them and the Bani Sama bin Lu'ai faction who were elders of the town and district. One of the Bani Sama, a man known as Mohammed bin Al-Qassem of the Bani Sama, went to the Caliph's assistant who dispatched a reinforcement under the command of a man called Ibn Thor. The troops entered Oman, the Bani Sama were saved and the Shurats withdrew to Nizwa[145].

Daba

Daba lies between Oman and Bahrain[146] on the Hajar side and is close by the sea, according to Al-Maqdisi[147]. It was a market town along the lines of the traditional Arab souq[148]. When Bahrain and Yemen and Yamama became centres of the Riddah or Secession after the Prophet's death we have no reports of apostacy in Oman, with the exception of a single incident which took place in Daba. A difference had arisen over the

Daba.

payment of *zakat* by one of the mistresses of the town. Hodheifa bin Mohsen Al-Ghulfani or Al-Barqi was anxious that this protest might prove to be a manifestation of secession, so he laid on an attack and routed the people of Daba. The matter ended with a delegation being despatched from Oman to seek an audience with the Caliph Abu Bakr. There they made clear their allegiance to Islam and resolved not to depart from this allegiance. Hodheifa Al-Ghulfani had misunderstood the townspeople of Daba and the Caliph ordered the return of captives after he had severely berated Hodheifa[149] . These were the most notable cities and ports in Oman, and they remained outstanding centres of civilization in ancient and Islamic times. Oman's offshore island possessions were also notable repositories of culture and learning.

Oman's Most Important Island Possessions

There were islands in the Arabian Gulf which were held to be possessions of Oman and they were governed frequently over the centuries by rulers of Omani Arab stock. The islands engaged in the ocean trade with China, India and South-east Asia and the East African coast. The foremost of these islands were:

Zirbad Island

Ya'qut Al-Hamawi says of this island that it is a Persian province. He quotes from Ibn Sirian's history: 'In the year 309 AH Abdullah bin 'Amara, the Lord of Zirbad Island, died after a reign of 25 years. He was succeeded by his brother Jaafar bin Hamza, who governed for six months until he was assassinated by one of his servants, whereupon Batal bin Abdullah bin 'Amara took over the reins of power'[150].

Omani Arabs of the 'Amara family governed the island successively, up to the beginning of the fourth century AH[151]. They were descendants of the Bani Julanda, who were Azdi Omanis'. On this subject Al-Istakhri says of the Arabs who colonized Persia and the coastal rim of the Arabian Gulf that 'the 'Amara family who were known as the Julanda, were of this tribe. They control a vast kingdom and have many estates and a line of strongholds on the sea coast of Persia as far as Kerman. They claim that they have governed this place since before the time of Moses'[152].

Qais Island (Kishe)

Ya'qut Al-Hamawi had this to say of the island: 'Qais is an island in the Sea of Oman having a circumference of four *parasang*. It is a handsome town of gardens and fine buildings. The overlord of this sea, being the ruler of Oman, has a residence there. It commands a third of the revenue of Bahrain. There is a facility for boats from India and from this island you can see the land and mountains of Persia. It has souqs and treasures and pearl divers'[153]. Qais was to alternate between Arab and Persian suzerainty. Its name was ascribed to Qais bin 'Amara of the 'Amara family who were a well known offshoot of the Julanda clan[154] . Qais Island inherited dominance of the sea trade from Siraf, after the masters of Qais had attacked that city and brought it under their control. Siraf declined in importance as a trading port[155], and as it declined so Qais gained in stature until it was to become one of the outstanding regional ports[156].

Ibn Battuta notes that Qais' influence on the sea trade began to decline in the fourteenth century AD and trading supremacy passed from it to Hormuz[157].

Jask Island

Ya'qut says of Jask: 'It is a large island between Qais (the island better known as Kishe) and Oman, facing the city of Hormuz at a distance of three days' journey. It has buildings and houses occupied by the troops of Qais Island's king. These are splendid able men, unequalled in fortitude and in their experience of war at sea as well as their handling of ships and boats...'[158].

There is no doubt that the Omanis' knowledge of the seasonal winds assisted them in achieving dominion over the seas and over merchant traffic in the Arabian Gulf and the Indian Ocean. Their practice of making the outward voyage in summer and returning in winter is clear enough evidence of their deep understanding of seasonal wind patterns and of the intelligence which Omani navigators and merchants applied in exploiting the prevailing winds to best effect in their conduct of the sea trade[159].

Oman's Economic Riches

Oman became known[160] for pearl fishing, a livelihood shared by most of the towns along the Arabian Gulf and its islands. Al-Mas'udi, in *Murooj Al-Thahab* (Meadows of Gold) details the process of pearl diving in the Persian Sea off the coasts of Kharg, Qatar, Oman and Serendib (Sri Lanka) and he notes the attributes of pearls obtained there[161].

Sahib Aja'ib Al-Hind relates how an Omani diver called Muslim bin Bishr extracted a pearl of matchless beauty and sold it to the Caliph Haroun Al-Rashid for 70,000 dirhams. He sold him another for 30,000 and returned to Oman with 100,000 and became the master of a mansion and estates[162].

Al-Istikhri and Ibn Hawqal both made reference to this unique pearl and Al-Homeiri in *Al-Rawdh Al-Mi'tar* (Rain-fed Gardens) recounts how a man from Oman betook himself to Mecca with two magnificent pearls, the like of which had not been seen. He sold them for 2000 gold dinars to a man from Samarkand and left Mecca on the same day. When he was a few days' journey out he was overtaken by a messenger sent by the Lord of Oman enquiring who had sold the two pearls and accusing the man of having stolen them from his palace. Enquiries were made as to the whereabouts of the purchaser who was not to be found, having left with the two pearls for Damascus. One of them was traced to the ruler of Damascus who was persuaded to return it for 10,000 dinars. The messenger then went on to Samarkand and managed to trace the second to its owner, who handed it over for the sum of 15,000 dinars. Al-Homeiri says that these two pearls were from Oman[163].

Ibn Faqih remarks that Oman was also known for its spears and celebrated throughout the Islamic Era[164] for its delicious dates[165]. Ibn Battuta confirms this, noting that Oman was known to export dates to India and its neighbours[166].

An additional resource was Oman's well respected reputation for the breeding of pure Arabian horses. This reputation had travelled as far as India and India bought horses from Oman as well as from some other countries. Of the Indians Ibn Battuta has this to say: 'The horse they sought for racing they found in Yemen and Oman and Persia. The price of one was between one and four thousand dinars'[167].

Oman was also renowned from earliest historical times for the making of copper implements and this status was maintained throughout the Islamic

Era[168]. It was also known far and wide for the abundance of its offshore fishing. Of this Ibn Faqih says: 'A world of fish lies offshore from Mahirdian to Oman'[169]. He confirms this in a later passage of his book[170], as does Ibn Battuta, writing of Muscat's renowned fishing grounds[171].

It is worth mentioning here that some of the Hadith attributed to the Prophet in which he remarks on the virtues of Oman makes reference to the Omanis' engagement with the sea and with fishing. In a Hadith of Mazin bin Ghadhuba he reports: 'I said: "O Messenger of Allah, Invoke Allah's blessings on the people of Oman". And he replied: "May Allah guide and reward them". So I said: "Please say more, O Messenger of Allah". And he said: "May God give them virtue and contentment as well as their daily means". I said to him: "O messenger of God, the sea sprinkles around us: pray to God for our provisions and cheerfulness", and the Prophet prayed, "O Lord, expand for them their provisions and increase the bounteousness of their sea". I said, "more", and the Prophet said, "O Lord: inflict not over them an enemy from those not among them. Say Amen, O Mazin"[172].

Mahra, of which the capital is Shihr, and which Al-Istakhri and Ibn Hawqal considered to be part of Oman[173], was a producer of frankincense, which spread its fame to the far corners of the known world. Its inhabitants were by trade fishermen, camel breeders and date planters[174]. These products, along with ambergris, were sold in Shihr. *Silsilat Al-Tawarikh* (The Annals) describes it thus: 'Its territory included the *Bahr Al-Zinj* and the African territories on this sea coast. There are few (sperm) whales in this sea for most of them are found near African shores and the coast of Shihr in the Arab lands. The Shihris are a race descended from Qadai'ya bin Malik from Homeir and other Arabs'[175]. Ibn Khordadhuba and Al-Maqdisi both refer to kandar or frankincense which was one of the cultivated treasures of Mahra[176]. Arab sources include the names of numerous valuable crops in Oman, such as dates and fleshy fruits, including banana, pomegranate and lotus fruit[177]. The island of Qais, which frequently came under the rule of Omani overlords, was famed for extracting pearls[178].

Oman was distinguished by these and many other rich resources from earliest history through the Islamic Era and into modern times. Many crafts and artisan skills developed over time which are still actively pursued today. In turn this indigenous productivity stimulated the trading activities with other countries in which Oman excelled.

The Geopolitics of Oman and its Impact in the Modern Era

Having presented something of the people and heritage of Oman in the Islamic era, we will now attempt to set out the more prominent features of the geopolitics of Oman and examine their effects on the modern age. These geopolitcal components are many and diverse. First to be considered must be Oman's geographical setting and the way in which this is reflected in any assessment of its strategic importance; next the affects of the natural and climatic features of Oman on patterns of commercial and other activity, along with their political and economic overtones; then the Omani people themselves, who, in their diversity and with their cultural and educational skills, are a critical factor in casting either a positive or negative light on the circumstances of the Sultanate at any time and on the influence it is likely to wield in the international arena. Finally, we will address the impact the geological make-up of the Sultanate has had in creating natural resources, such as cultivable ground and mineral deposits, reflecting the economic and political value of the Sultanate[179].

To address these geopolitical elements and outline the effects they have had on the political structure is to throw more light on the paths to economic, social and political development in the Sultanate. This is even more true if we examine the root principles of this development process and the analyses and conclusions they support. Success will be with the one who plans for the future of this country and who acts with its progress and advancement and interests in mind.

The Geopolitics of Place

A glance at any map of the world is enough to convey Oman's formidable strategic location. Lying at the fulcrum of the Islamic world, its long sea coast marks off the far eastern boundary of the Arab world from the Indian Ocean whose shores link the African continent with the shores of the Pacific Ocean.

An understanding of Oman's place at the heart of the Middle East and its relationship with the civilizations and political entities around it is central to any explanation of the political interactions which impact on this region, both as far as internal dynamics are concerned and externally in the context of the pressure exercised by international powers. From the Sultanate's central location between east and west at the entrance to the Arab Gulf, which would come to be known as the 'Petroleum Gulf', Oman shares with Iran control of the access point to the richest oil producing region in the world, the Strait of Hormuz, through which more than 60 per cent of the world's petroleum

*The location
of Oman.*

supplies[180] pass. This figure includes 90 per cent of Japan's and 70 per cent of the European Union's petroleum supplies, as well as 50 per cent of the requirements of the United States.

Even before the discovery of oil, when it became one of the regions at the production face of the world's fuel supply, Oman's geographical bearings were significant in the context of the struggles between the great sea-trading powers which wracked the region. Oman overlooked an important sea route for the trade in spices, incense and silk and other rare and exotic commodities, commodities which were in their time more precious than oil is today. So it is hardly surprising to learn that at every stage of its history it had to contend with intense and protracted struggles between rival powers attempting to take possession of the country and its ports[181]. All of this points to the Sultanate's strategic bearings, making this location one of the critical regions of confrontation in the modern contest for world dominance. This was true even before the end of the Cold War and the collapse of the Soviet Union and the abrupt changes which came about in what was known as the Eastern bloc.

If it was Oman's position on the map that drew upon it the attention of the world powers then this interest increased with the passage of a major part of the world's oil trade through the Strait of Hormuz, the navigable portion of which lies within the territory of Oman. In view of the importance which has attached to oil as a strategic commodity and lifeline for Western countries, the industrial powers have pursued every means to ensure the protection of the oil supply line. This they have achieved by maintaining an international equilibrium sustained by the continued tension between the superpowers. This was of course prior to the collapse of the Soviet Union and its spheres of influence

It is possible to view the political and other aspects of the geographical location of Oman in the context of three historical periods during which the effects on the Sultanate were reflected in different ways. The first period begins with the rise of the prominent ancient civilizations on the eastern and south-eastern seaboard of the Arabian peninsula. The second stage spans the sixteenth, seventeenth and eighteenth centuries and the third covers the modern period, beginning with the nineteenth century and continuing on up to today.

Phase One

From the beginning of the early historical period the regions adjacent to the eastern and south-eastern portions of the Arabian peninsula were the activity centres of a number of powerful political powers, since they were at the junction of and had exclusive control over land, sea and trade routes from the known parts of the ancient world, from Africa, Asia and Europe. Because of this, these regions were to become centres of the world's trade movements.

Babylon and Assyria were among the first empires to control the Asian land trade from the Arabian Gulf to the eastern shores of the Mediterranean. Later the Persian empire would emerge and expand to gain influence over a vast area and to control the region's trade.

When the Islamic Empire rose to world pre-eminence in the early and Middle Ages, the countries of the Arabian peninsula on the Arabian Gulf and the Gulf of Oman regained their influence over the world's ancient trade routes. Baghdad adopted the mantle in this part of the Islamic world which was to pass after a number of centuries to Spain, Portugal, England and Holland respectively. The merchandise of the sea trade with China, Indonesia, India and East Africa was directed to Baghdad through the Arabian Gulf and its trading centres on the Gulf of Oman and the Strait of Hormuz. From there goods were passed to the markets of Europe, carried by the fleets of Venice and Genoa sailing out from European ports.

Phase Two

The period from 1498 to 1507, after Portugal had occupied the trading ports of East Africa along with Aden and Muscat, was one of commercial stagnation. Oman's ports in the Arabian Gulf and East Africa suffered massive destruction from a series of naval onslaughts by Portugal and from the tyranny and ruin which were characteristic of its rule and which were to become hallmarks of the war against Islam and to give rise to the installation of Crusader stations in East Africa, the Gulf of Aden and Muscat.

Nonetheless the Portuguese stranglehold, which lasted for more than a century and a half, was to fail in its objectives for a number of reasons, the most important of which were:

• Oman's spirited resistance.
• New rivalries between the European powers (Portugal, Britain, Holland and France).
• Reverses suffered by the Portuguese and in particular their rout at Wadi Al-Makhazen in the *Maghreb* (Morocco) which weakened their power in Africa and Asia.

Phase Three

The torpor that hung over the population centres on the Arabian Gulf was not to lift until the end of the eighteenth century when the winds of post-Revolutionary France came knocking on the doors of the Gulf sheikhdoms. Napoleon hastened to seize control of the world's sea trading routes and to cut off Britain's access to India. Gradually the region began to recover from its long paralysis once again to throw itself into the arena of world struggle.

During this historical period several powers wrestled and collided in their attempts to obtain a base from which to rule the Gulf and its coastal states, for this area was the principal link in the chain of protection for the colonial powers' various possessions and interests on the Indian Ocean and Far Eastern littoral. These interactions took on a labyrinthine complexity which had few parallels in the world's other geopolitically significant areas. The region was bound up repeatedly by alliances entered into by different foreign powers in different periods of history. Frequently the allies of one era became enemies at another time. This extreme rivalry to gain control of the region played on the diverse political events occurring inside the Sultanate and the adjacent territories. Sometimes the Sultanate would be adversely affected by these pressures. Most often it was able to bring its influence to bear by setting a deliberate course to serve the strategic interests of one or other of the conflicting parties.

Much has been written on the Sultanate's political history during this period. However the intricacy of the political situation and the various external and internal cross-currents make any fair assessment of these circumstances somewhat difficult to achieve. Some analyses abandoned objectivity altogether in their approach and conclusions, notwithstanding the essentially simple outline of the events. It is therefore worth summarizing these events again in a spirit of objectivity and in such a way as to take into consideration the issues of power and internal politics in the region, the impact made by the European powers wrestling with it, along with the political stress lines and flashpoints, and the role of each of the two power groups in putting together the geopolitical map of the Sultanate and the way in which this map evolved during the nineteenth century.

The basis of English strategy was to erect or support barrier states in order to protect its possessions, interests and routes of empire from other powers which posed a threat to these interests. These barrier states were then involved in its defence, at the same time imposing on them a portion of the cost of defence by making the barrier states dependent for their existence on British support. The British fleet was ever an agile tool in executing this strategy and was therefore in constant need of forward bases to lend it logistical support. Britain began to take possession of such bases in 1214 AH/1799 AD when it occupied the island of Perim at the Bab al Mandab Strait in a move to contain the French menace as exemplified by Napoleon's Egyptian Expedition in 1213 AH/1798 AD. Subsequently it occupied the island of Socotra in the year 1834 and Aden was occupied forcibly in 1255 AH/1839 AD. As a result of treaties entered into by Britain with the Arab Gulf Sheikhs it had by the advent of the second half of the nineteenth century achieved clear control of the sea routes in the Gulf.

When Germany emerged after 1287 AH/1870 AD as a victorious military power, having overcome its rivals in Europe, it began to recognize the strategic significance of the coastal regions of the Arabian Gulf which overlooked the sea routes linking the European states with their regions of influence (in Africa and Asia). Oman, which controlled the Strait of Hormuz, stood out among these regions. Germany set about joining forces with the Ottoman State in pursuit of its strategy, which was exemplified by its securing of Turkey as a bridgehead to the Indian Ocean. In this way it sought to drive a wedge between Russia on the one hand and its two allies, France and Britain on the other. In 1319AH/1901 AD the Ottoman State granted Germany a concession to lay a railway line from Berlin to Baghdad, passing through Mosul, Baghdad and Basra and terminating at the Arabian Gulf. Britain put up a vigorous resistance to this project, then arrived at a draft treaty with the Ottoman State in 1913 in which England would participate in the above project. However, World War One broke out before the draft had been signed and ratified by the two countries.

As the Ottoman State was approaching final collapse at the turn of the twentieth century, opportunities abounded for the European states to achieve their goals in the various territorial possessions of the 'Sick Man of Europe'. As a consequence of all of this various struggles and alliances were to alternate in which the common denominator was the winding up of the Ottoman State and division of its possessions.

The end came after World War One (1332-1337/1914-1918), arising out of which came the collapse of the Ottoman State (and the establishment of the Turkish Republic on its present territory) and the loss of its possessions in the Arab region[182]. This was to assist Britain in copperfastening its influence over the route to India to protect its Indian empire, a goal the pursuit of which had debilitated the Arab region, for Britain in its greed had openly extended its protection such that the Arab region had become both fortress and base for the protection of routes to diverse parts of the British empire while Britain maintained its control over the peripheral states of the Arabian Gulf - where the odour of petrol had begun to waft outwards.

The Arab independence struggle between the two World Wars, however, added to the events which had overtaken the world situation - profound political shifts and transformations, as well as the emergence of major new contenders in the arenas of power conspired to warn Britain that it was in danger of losing total control of the Arab regions if it were to seek to retain exclusive influence there. It was obliged to accept the partnership of a number of European states in the control and exploitation of the region, along with that of the United States, which had come to have economic and political interests there in the form of oil on the one hand and a need to maintain the balance of power on the other. The protection of these interests required the enforcement of its own specific strategy implemented through the aegis of the broad Western alliance in the region and as well as special local alliances. Thus did the United States come to be the latest Western capitalist power to enter the arena[183]. After the United States had stepped into the role of leader of the Western world in the aftermath of World War Two, its interests began to expand across the globe and were particularly strong in the Arabian Gulf region with its gigantic American petroleum companies, as well as in the fringe areas of the Gulf. Oman, with its oil and its strategic location, was to become one of the prime regions of interest to the United States and a focus of its efforts to achieve a world balance of

H.M. Sultan Qaboos.

power with what was at that time the Soviet Union.

The Sultanate of Oman was not slow to grasp the importance of its own position and the significance of a region which was at the centre of a cross-current of elaborate international relationships, overlapping in turn the interests of the great regional powers. And so Oman hastened after 1970 to ensure that the Gulf would become a zone of peace and it strove to promote bonds of conciliation and harmony throughout the region. This exercise was not confined to the Arab side of the Gulf but extended also to Iran. In this Oman was executing not a passive response to its geographical circumstances but rather a positive response to the demands of maintaining the process of development and modernization. If we examine the positions taken by Oman we find that it gave serious priority to enhancing its international standing by developing balanced relations with the world's nations, irrespective of the nature of their political and economic ideologies. With its own renaissance Oman set out on a journey to comprehensive development, assisted in this by its special advantages over the rest of the Gulf states, viz. its area and its population density. Among the outstanding features of Oman's foreign policy is that it is bound in to Oman's status as an elder state with a history of influence as a regional power, this being particularly true of the first half of the last century. In addition, it revolves on factors firmly linked to the implications of its location on the one hand and the various goals it has set for itself in its progress to development on the other. In this context we should make brief reference to the following:

Firstly, Oman's early grasp of the importance of its position at the approaches to the Arabian Gulf, with its long coastline along the Gulf of Oman and Indian Ocean; as well as its understanding of the nature of international rivalry, particularly that which engaged Britain and France throughout the nineteenth century, gave it cause to consider exploiting its external relations in the role of a neutral intermediary, or on occasion to limit the impact brought to bear on it by some international power. This it achieved by establishing relations with the contending power on the one hand while at the same time expanding the scope of its relations with the other international power whose influence had been brought to bear. Thus it is not surprising that Oman should have not only diplomatic relations but indeed exchange treaties with Britain and France as well as the United States, dating to the second half of the nineteenth century.

Secondly, among the most important influences attaching to Oman's geographical position are those which derive from its status as a coastal nation and from the length of the Omani coastline. The effect of these has been to cause Oman to be permanently concerned with the reinforcement and development of its naval power. This naval power was an effective tool in the protection and safeguarding of the Omani state as well as the reinforcement of its economic and political ideology. An examination of the period when the State of Oman extended to East Africa and, on occasion, the other shore of the Gulf will illustrate this clearly.

Thirdly, always conscious of the importance of maintaining a balance in its external relations, the Sultanate has been careful from the start of its modern renaissance period, as directed by His Majesty Sultan Qaboos bin Said, to extend the scope of its diplomatic relations as far afield as possible, always insisting that the basis of these relations would be mutual respect including respect for sovereignty, non-interference in internal affairs, and diplomatic exchange on the basis of good intent in the service of shared interests. This policy is conducted irrespective of the political or social structure governing the other country. Oman had amicable relations with West and East before the collapse of the Soviet Union and now good relations govern the bonds between Oman on the one hand and the Russian Federation and the East European countries, Central Asia and China on the other. Oman has, moreover, carved out for itself a policy of positive neutrality and non-alignment at international level and the achievement of security and stability at regional level, building on the mutually respectful relations enjoyed by the Sultanate and Sultan with many and diverse countries.

Fourthly, perhaps the most important practical example of the interaction between place and politics is that embodied in Oman's stance during the Iraq-Iran war (1400-1408 AH/1980-1988 AD). Oman's position had a considerable impact not only on containing the level of tension in the Arabian Gulf and keeping a lid on the conflagration, but also through its practical intervention on more than one occasion in alleviating or indeed resolving some of the difficulties associated with continuation of the war. Meanwhile Oman was able through its practical and farsighted politics not only to maintain open communications on an ongoing basis with both parties, Iraq and Iran, but also to endeavour to bring the parties closer. And at a time when the Sultanate was calling repeatedly for a peaceful end to the struggle on the basis of international legitimacy and protection of the rights of both parties, including such as would permit the deep and permanent bonds between the peoples of the region, bonds rooted in neighbourliness, religion, progress and partnership, to be preserved, the Sultanate stood guard also over the security and continuity of shipping in the Gulf and the Strait of Hormuz in service to international trade, while exercising every conceivable strategy to prevent the area from falling victim to the consequences of world polarization with all of its negative implications.

Oman took such a balanced stand when Iraq invaded Kuwait in August 1990. This wise and practical stance was based on Arab as well as international legitimacy. Through this stance it took into consideration Oman's national interests and Arab interests, as well as the interests of both Iraq and Kuwait, who are basically two brotherly countries, irrespective of any temporary circumstance.

The most recent of Oman's political stances, consciously embodying the interaction between place and politics, arose out of the bloody events in the Yemen which broke out in May 1994 when its actions were guided by a commitment to stopping the war and fostering the process of dialogue, while preserving internal coherence. Furthermore in all its communications and consultations, both before and after the conflict, Oman confirmed its full commitment to the peace and stability of Yemen and the consolidation of its national unity.

Fifthly, even as the Sultanate tried to maintain secure and uninterrupted shipping in the Strait of Hormuz, especially during the 'Tanker Wars' in 1406-1408 AH/1986-1988 AD, the long Omani coastline on the Gulf of Oman and Indian Ocean enabled it to furnish an important alternative for the transport of oil from the other oil producing member states of the Arab Gulf Cooperation Council to outside the Strait of Hormuz without passing through the waterway. This came in the form of a proposal to extend a pipeline for the transport of oil from the producing regions in the Gulf to Omani ports in the Gulf of Oman. This project obtained the good favour of the Gulf Cooperation Council, but the project has been temporarily deferred.

Physical topography of Oman.

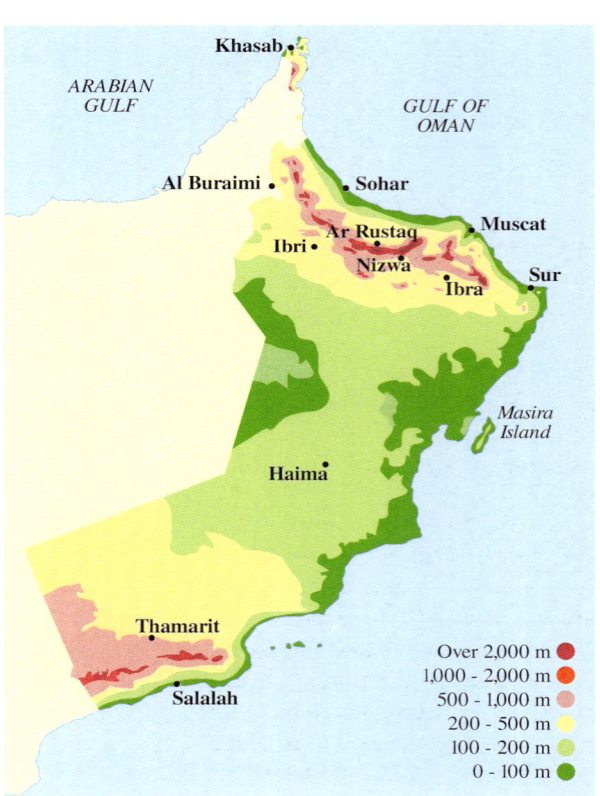

Sixthly, at the heart of the politics of the renaissance led by H.M. Sultan Qaboos is a commitment to achieving Arab cooperation and unity, to supporting this work by means of positive conflict resolution through dialogue, and to fostering a departure from the use or threat of force in favour of the principles enshrined in relevant Arab and international treaties.

These are incontrovertible principles, accepted internationally. It is worth noting here that the Sultanate has generally taken a vigorous role in peace-making and in the restoration of good neighbourly relations between various Arab countries. It is important to be aware of the developments to which this region has been exposed, particularly in the last decade, and which culminated in the establishment of peace. And if we look at the positions and policies taken by Oman in more than one situation and on more than one occasion, it will be seen that these have had a positive impact on the Sultanate's relations and on the influence it wields in the region, an impact which will help to propel it along the road to development and recon-struction.

For the most part, the challenges to the maintenance of influential relations caused by profound changes in the technology of transport, communications and economic practices have confirmed and reinforced the significance of geographical location in the case of the Sultanate.

The Geopolitics of Natural and Climatic Components[184]

No picture of geopolitical phenomena in the Sultanate would be complete without a description of the physical lines of Oman, sketching a natural theatre above and around which circulate political events and power struggles. Oman's inhabitants apply themselves on this stage to their various economic and political activities, influenced by their natural and climatic environment, at the same time bringing their own influence to bear in a variety of ways in accordance with their level of technological expertise. The shape taken by the terrain and its surface features are many and varied. Oman has many habitats, and this feature has had a useful and effective impact on history, culture and politics. The first of the constituent habitats which we encounter is the coastal one.

The mountains around Nakhal.

The coastal environment has claimed a substantial share of the attention of Oman's settled peoples throughout history. It is on the shores of Oman that the land mass of the Arabian peninsula, a terrain sometimes known as the 'Arab coat of mail', ends abruptly. One of the salient features of this seaboard, and one which has had a crucial influence on the activities of coastal dwellers over a long history, is the shallowness of the waters along much of the coastal reef, making these stretches unsuitable for the construction of large sea ports. Also characteristic of this coastline are the many tongues of shallow water which penetrate for up to several kilometres into the land mass. These are known as *akhouar* or inlets, and they have been central to the lives of the coastal dwellers in helping to shape the events of their history as well as their economic and political activities. The extremities of these inlets were deemed appropriate sites for locating human settlements which were also the departure points for fishermen in their struggle with the sea. In the shallow waters Omani man found the protection which would strengthen him against his enemies on land and sea. From here doughty bands of resistance fighters launched lightning raids on the foreign merchant ships of the imperialist powers, which had imposed their stranglehold and forced protection on the region and its neighbours on the Arabian Gulf and South Arabia. In addition, coastal shallows and sheltered inlets suited to the pearl oysters have long had a part in easing the economic difficulties of Oman. Among the features of this coast were extensive and unfolding salt marshes, vast portions of which would be covered by the tide waters, and on this waterlogged and briny ground no form of cultivation was reasonably possible.

The desert.

If we now move from the coastal marine environment and its role in moulding the economic and political outlook of its inhabitants to the arid interior, we find a habitat which is utterly different in its economic and political impact. This habitat represents another aspect to the struggle of Omani man with his environment and his attempts to carve out a living for himself.

This habitat encompasses the narrow coastal plains and overlooking these the flat rocky outcrops of mountains cut by flood gorges. Beyond this hilly ground and inclining towards the interior of the Arabian peninsula stretches arid desert, enclosing a number of diverse desert terrains broken by many small areas of cultivation scattered here and there where water is located.

The interior of the Sultanate, which for the most part rises well above the coastal areas, consists of an ancient plateau ascending to more than 1300 metres. At the centre of this range is the Jebel Al-Akhdar, some of whose peaks reach 3000 metres above sea level. The gorges running from the south-west due north-east define the rocky outline of these elevated regions sloping towards the coastal plain.

These coastal plains and the mountains beyond with their wadis and terraced slopes, because of their elevation and aspect in the path of the summer monsoons, draw considerable rain, a minimum of 250 cms, enabling the practice of agricultural and pastoral activities, including the cultivation of a variety of fruits, grapes, pomegranates, peaches, walnuts, olives and almonds, as well as mulberry trees[185]. In addition to the seasonal rains, these agricultural areas benefit from water distributed by *falajes* (irrigation channels) and gushing streams.

Jebel Akhdar is one of the principal sites for the cultivation of fruit and it is noted in particular for its singular varieties, such as those which require a relatively moderate climate. In the low mountain foothills and the coastal plain known as Batinah, date cultivation is very important, in fact accounting for the main income of this region. As well as dates, the coastal plain produces tobacco, cane sugar and cotton in plantations which depend for irrigation on water distributed from mountain springs by means of canals.

Some of the inhabitants of the oases in the interior and in the foothills raise goats and sheep, and some of the coastal dwellers engage in fishing and trade, along with the textile, copper, leather, and ceramic crafts for which some of the cities are famous, Nizwa in particular.

From out of this geographical diversity we can observe a number of features which could be said to have a direct or indirect connection with the geopolitical features of the Sultanate. The geographical environments of the marine, mountain and desert regions combine together to draw a geographical groundmap on which the inhabitants act out their economic and political lives. Interacting with these natural and climatic elements were the products of a cultural legacy and economic livelihood which preceded the discovery of petroleum and the transformation which attended it.

Insofar as the Sultanate is for the most part arid, the problem of maintaining a supply of water is a demanding one if cultivated areas are to be extended and agriculture intensified. Besides an organic connection that binds the people, generation after generation and century after century, to their land is the belief that communities having an attachment to the land never die out irrespective of the challenges and reversals thrown at them by the changes of their rulers and sovereign authority.

The climate, which could be described as generally dry over most of the Sultanate with the clear impact this has on agricultural development, constitutes along with rivers and their associated ground water one of the fundamental geographical components of the strategic make-up of the Sultanate. This would be in keeping with a normal understanding of geopolitics, where climate plays a key part in sketching in the areas which can be settled and cultivated. In Oman, this means dense and settled habitation in the oases and districts where ground water comes to the surface; in the many valleys and the narrow coastal plains; and finally in the elevated regions and plateaus which encounter considerable rainfall. Against this it imposes a haphazard and nomadic lifestyle in the arid regions.

These climatic circumstances and the attendant water picture were among the geographical elements that had a strong impact in determining the basic features of the economic, political and social structure in the Sultanate. The heat and drought gave water resources a vital importance equivalent in impact to the importance of geographical place.

It is the capacity of its water resources that determines the size of a habitation, as well as the species and scope of the agricultural and animal resources that can be supported. In addition, the size of habitation must remain in a permanently adjusted equilibrium with ground water capacity. The Sultanate is ever preoccupied with maintaining the natural balance in its water sources by diversifying its means of supply, such as in attempts to control the wadis and seasonal floodwaters and the use of scientific methods to obtain ground water which has collected from insubstantial current rains or from the rains of past geological periods, and finally by means of sea water distillation.

As a result of this never ceasing dynamic between geography and man, it is hardly surprising that human activity should gravitate towards the oases where well water is in supply and where pastoral activities materialize when summer rains allow the growth of herbage. Here also a limited agriculture will be possible, practised by the wadi dwellers as a marginal activity though not as a basic livelihood.

If obstacles created by natural geography have had a part in making communications between the plains and the small wadis and oases nigh impossible in the past, thus ensuring that the pattern of habitation in these places would be intermittent, they could not have been the primary causes of this fragmentation and isolation and no doubt there are other contemporary obstacles which have a part and which are linked into the political circumstances experienced by the Sultanate.

Even though natural geography inhibited the establishment of contact between parts of Oman, there were other factors which strengthened this communication. Thus history establishes that the pattern of Arab culture and consciousness, embodying factors which value unity and solidarity, gave the Arabs the strength when it was needed to triumph over every natural hazard and to link areas of habitation and population centres through firm bonds of nation and faith; and it confirms that mankind, with his body of ideological values and heritage is not incapable of uniting diverse natural districts into a cohesive whole irrespective of their distance from one another and of the difficulties posed by geographical and climatic circumstances. How then might he fare if he were to arm himself further with advanced technology in the pursuit of his activities and enterprises'.

The Geopolitics of Habitation[186]

If we now take a look at the human component of Oman's political geography, represented by the size, growth and distribution of the population, their diverse buildings and dwelling places, as well as economic, social and settlement patterns; and arising from these cultural and educational standards, productivity and economic relations, we can see that there is no doubt but that these components are important and fundamental insofar as they are the factors which by

their interactions with nature constitute the principal aspects of the economic and political value system of the Sultanate. By their development and advance will Omani society attain its high economic, social and political aspirations and increase its political stock in a region rightly counted as one of the most ancient, vigorous and enterprising regions of the world. The profound changes now underway in the Sultanate, and the accelerated transformation of the political infrastructure and economic, social and political support structures, demands the injection of a new kind of manpower capable of responding to the special requirements of these new circumstances. Any failure to achieve a balance between these transformations and their manpower requirements will reflect in a negative way on the political and economic development of the country, and drive it to greater dependence on foreign employees, with all the risks and drawbacks attendant on such a path.

Conscious of the importance of the population component in any consideration of current realities or in sketching an outline of the future as envisaged in the various development plans and programmes, the Sultanate has taken care to bring population data up to date in its awareness of the importance of being able

to furnish relevant population data for use in the development plan or in examining and evaluating the various results of this plan. This recognition resulted in the census carried out at the end of 1993. Its results showed the population of the Sultanate to be 2,018,074 persons[187], of whom 74 per cent were nationals, and 26 non-national residents. There were 755,071 male Omanis, a ratio of 51 per cent, and 725,460 females, or 49 per cent, these being normal ratios in line with recognized international measurements[188].

In the light of the figures presented by the census we can refer to the improved health care which the Omani citizen now enjoys and how this is reflected in a reduction in average mortality. The World Health Organization has emphasized in its latest report the success achieved by the Sultanate in this regard.

It is likely in the light of the established average population growth patterns that the Omani population will increase to not less than 1.6 million by the end of 1995 and to 2 million by the end of the century. If we assume that the non-Omani population will remain at its present level, then the total population of the Sultanate will be around 2.5 million.

The discovery of petroleum and its steadily increasing production in the years since 1388 AH/1968 AD have stimulated the level of immigration into Oman as well as the return of a large number of Omanis who had left the country to look for work.

A demographic map of the population distribution in the Sultanate shows that the majority of the inhabitants are concentrated in the environs of the province of Muscat and the Batinah district. The population of the province of

Muscat is thus 549,150 and of Batinah 564,677. Dhofar has a population of 189,094, Musandam 28,727, Dhahira 181,224, Dakhalia 229,791, Sharqia 258,344 and Al-Wasta 17,067[189].

The actual population distribution between rural, desert and urban districts in Oman today is very different from the picture in the past. When H.M. Sultan Qaboos bin Said launched the Oman renaissance oil wealth was to play a signit- icant role in the acceleration of development. It was also as a result of this new affluence that certain places - due to the implementation of infrastructural projects - drew more benefit from the effects of the development plans. And so there was a migration from rural and desert areas into the cities and in particular to Muscat, its population rising to more than a quarter of the entire population of the Sultanate[190].

As a consequence a large metropolitan community came to occupy the major cities[191]. Sohar and Salalah and Nizwa and Sur, all of them cities which grew at the expense of the neighbouring rural and desert areas, underwent a similar phenomenon.

The government is acutely aware of the implications of a desertion of the rural and desert areas in favour of the nearby cities, which are not in themselves the end destination for migrants, but rather stopping places on the way to Muscat. And while Muscat is close to collapse from the pressure of their numbers, country and desert are being abandoned *en masse* by their inhabitants. It has put in place local social development programmes with the goal of distributing investment along geographical lines so as to benefit different regions and population centres throughout the country and its inhabitants[192].

In order to close the standard of living gap, current focus is on the least developed regions. The implentation of this programme will serve to support the development of present population centres and to preserve them from the dangers of migration to the densely populated urban centres. All of which leads to the final matter to be considered, that is protection of the environment from pollution and destruction.

The Sultanate is one of the Arab Gulf countries where the inhabitants of rural and desert areas have not severed their ties with their districts. And so at the start of the 1980s the population of the rural areas was 75 per cent of the total population. It looks as though this ratio decreased in the '80s as a result of internal migrations. However a study of future projections (in the light of the Omani's bond with the 'land' and internal social development projects) shows that this percentage is likely to go no lower than 50 per cent at the onset of the new century.

The Sultanate of Oman is a peninsula surrounded by water on three sides and land on the fourth, the Rub'al-Khali or Empty Quarter, a practically impassable desert. And so Oman has always been protected on the land side, destined to become a stronghold refuge for those in need of sanctuary . Meanwhile the Omanis directed their attention towards the sea and beyond the ocean and in this way Oman came to have an arm extended along many routes to Iran, India, China and East Africa. This situation prevailed up to the start of the 1970s. During this time Oman was to give up a part of its population to emigration and the most important destination for migrants at the midpoint of this century were the Arab Gulf states where the oil bonanza had manifested itself before Oman.

Omani farmers cultivated the Batinah and Jerbib Plain and they watered their small farms in the scattered oases in the interior and eastern part of the country. The most important other occupations were fishing and the grazing of herds. And as the trade convoys once asserted Oman's supremacy on the sea, so today it has retained its seafaring reputation.

The situation changes at the dawn of the Omani renaissance which began in 1390 AH/1970 AD when the Sultanate, like it neighbours, found itself unexpectedly in a situation in which the indigenous workforce in the Sultanate was inadequate to meet the need for burgeoning growth. This was in spite of the return of a great number of Omanis to their country in answer to the call put to them by the leader of the triumphant march (the accession has concerned itself with bringing Oman foursquare into the twentieth century). The country was in danger of severe reversal and therefore proceeded to engage a large and diverse number of foreign workers, enabling it in a brief period of time and in a manner little short of miraculous to alter the circumstances of the inhabitants, in particular their economic circumstances. The average income of the citizen of the Sultanate was still lower than the income of his brother in neighbouring Gulf states. Nevertheless, income continues to increase, giving rise to the emergence of a consumer society hungry for the latest offerings of the developed industrial countries. In both private and public sectors demand grew for the appliances and commodities of the modern age. Oman began to be transformed from a traditional into a fast developing modern society.

Fishing is a traditional Omani occupation.

The density of cultivation does not play a crucial part in the economy of the Sultanate and the role of agricultural activity in the GNP is restricted. It is an activity which has been affected by the dominance of one resource - oil - over all others, including the agricultural, pastoral and fishing sectors. A better view of the population distribution pattern throughout the Sultanate will be that which shows the relationship between the size of the population and its urban habitat, along with the level of economic base furnished for the population. The demographic map of the populated areas in the Sultanate shows the old traditional pattern of spread as imposed by environmental circumstances and the older lifestyle transforming into a new pattern in which strong emphasis is on the larger metropolitan districts and modern urban centres at the expense of a defection from the desert and rural areas and small traditional communities. The population of the Sultanate is now distributed within a restricted area marked by local geographical and economic features and showing an emphasis on larger population concentrations. And though the Sultanate still differs from the rest of the Arab oil producing countries of the Gulf, the urban gathering in the province of Muscat stands at almost a quarter of the total population and is still rising, and the petroleum wealth which arrived later in the Sultanate than the other Gulf states is sharing in the acceleration of this increase.

Age distribution analysis demonstrates that Omani society is one of mixed youth in which the very young predominate, so that those aged 15 years of age and under constitute 51.81per cent of the population, with 43.53 per cent of the population between the ages of 15 and 59 and 4.66 per cent over 60. The rise in

Oman still has substantial inshore fishery resources caught by traditional methods.

the proportion of young people is evidence of an increased level of fertility on the one hand and of a drop in the death rate on the other[193].

Oman remained traditional in its lifestyle, economy and social mores up to the start of the renaissance, when the central features and values of society changed. The new citizen of Oman with his new economic lifestyle came to be part of a society in which the people were no longer perceived as oppressed by the harsh circumstances of geography. Instead a powerful new social framework emerged which interacted with this environment using a new understanding and new weapons, and from a standpoint of power derived from science and technology. This comprehensive and continuing development was able to rely for its forward movement on a solid economy. Thus today's picture of the constituents of the economic and political situation as drawn up by the new Omani man, differs utterly from the old picture. The area is in the throes of change, and this change is a tireless and swift progression across the geographical stage, while its reflection on the political geographical components are also swift and significant.

The emergence of Islamic civilization was to have a dramatic effect on the Sultanate as its characteristically rich and multi-faceted civilization, encompassing religion, language and social structure, was to have a clear impact on the social and political customs and practices of individuals and communities. And just as the influences brought about by man and by Arab culture go back in history to the origin of the Arabs, so also do these still share in a large way in moulding the strong bonds which hold people together today and which bring geographically distant communities close and so offer a picture of the social structure of modern Oman. This picture confirms that man, with his values, heritage and ideology and his preoccupation with progress, can conquer isolation, apathy, backwardness and weakness in order to liberate himself to unite and build a strong and developed society and invite into place new economic and political values which will enhance his country's strategic importance.

Geopolitics of Natural Resources[194]

View from the coastal village of Mahoot

The geological profile and general rock composition are factors with a bearing on the strength or weakness of the economy and politics of the Sultanate. The most important effects of the geological landscape on the geopolitics of Oman are concentrated in two areas: the first being the pattern of surface and ground water drainage and the structure of the alluvial plains, these being the fundamental ground support of settled life; the second, mineral resources, one of the most crucial bases of economic activity in modern times.

In relation to the pattern of water drainage, the scope of the older quartz rock composition which characterizes a substantial part of the Sultanate is distinguished by rocks of low porosity and solid composition. Flood waters and seasonal flash floods run quickly along the surface of these formations and it is not possible to deepen their beds. Insofar as most of this older composition is located in the dry region, this terrain therefore lacks any form of permanent surface flow. In the sedimentary basins of the quartz areas, however, water which falls in the form of torrents is allowed to collect and so these areas can be sources of oasis life, as is the case in the Buraimi region and its environs. Oases proliferate in the regions where quartz and sedimentary compositions meet. Here also floods permit the growth of coarse vegetation along their pathways and this in turn allows the appearance of a nomadic pastoral life along the extent of these flood valleys. This pattern of living

takes on a guise of permanence in the nearby oases such that these flood valleys become a living domain in which pastoral life is conducted.

So if water and the problems of agricultural settlement are challenges against which the Omani people must pit themselves, the oil boom when it came brought welcome relief from the pressure of these problems by contributing to

Land harvest.

Drying dates.

increased investment in land reclamation and water management. Statistics show that the percentage return from oil in the gross domestic product is still as high as 75 per cent, despite the efforts made to diversify the domestic national product. What is more, the Sultanate's oil exports are on the point of becoming its only exports, the receipts from these exports representing around 94 per cent of the government's income.

Insofar as oil has come to constitute the principal mineral resource of the Sultanate, our discussion of natural resources can be confined to the geopolitics of petrol in order to demonstrate the extensive impact the petroleum industry has had on the current destiny and politics of the Sultanate.

The discovery of petrol, its production and exportation, coming on the heels of a revolution which radically altered the lifestyle and economic bearing of the Sultanate, was to carry it swiftly from the status of a traditional economy of meagre yields and returns to one of great wealth and expansion. This economic quantum leap had a profound effect on the population, in both qualitative and quantitative terms. While the population itself increased, the demographic patterns altered also in terms of age and type. At the same time inward migration increased and economic activity took on new shapes and patterns.

Camel races.

Prior to the oil boom the economy of Oman was heavily dependent on pearl diving and sea fishing as well as trade, agriculture and pastoral activities, and, since the inland environment of the mountain and desert areas is poor in resources, the sea was the focus of much of the activity of indigenous Omanis throughout history, as well as the pillar of economic life.

By the end of the 1960s and the onset of the oil investment boom, petroleum revenue had set in motion an economic and social transformation and created a new set of geographical, cultural and demographic circumstances in Oman. The labour force moved away from traditional activities towards a more modern economic ethos and the Sultanate entered a phase of extensive development encompassing the features of a well rounded economic life.

In pursuit of Muscat's deliberate policy of diversifying its economy and gradually reducing dependence on petrol as a sole source of income, three new spheres of activity have come to light which would be significant in realizing this objective. These are agriculture, industry and tourism. The agricultural sector constitutes one of the vital axes of the development effort in the Sultanate. The country's present cultivable area is in the region of 198,000 hectares, with an irrigated area of around 55,000 hectares. The potential inherent in this sector points to room for expansion in agricultural productivity based on better water management, improved farming methods and moderniziation of this sector's institutional framework, including developments in finance, advice, training and marketing. This is aside from plans to implement new investment projects which would have a well-structured and institutional nature. The average population growth targeted for this sector is around 6.6 per cent during the fourth Five Year Plan (1991-95). This must be set against an average annual growth rate of around 5.3 per cent during the third Five Year Plan (1986-1990)[195].

In the 1970s the Oman government intensified its efforts to increase production and to stimulate more effective investment in agriculture. A comprehensive agricultural census was carried out with a view to providing information on agriculture and livestock in the population centres and desert areas, thereby facilitating the formation of more effective agricultural development programmes. This went hand in hand with the intensification of a national plan of instruction in methods of raising production. A major programme of development was undergone in the Jebel Al-Akhdar region, as well as a programme to improve, develop and diversify the cultivation of vegetables and fruits, grain crops and fodder.

Industry has in the past achieved relatively high growth rates and the industrial sector has been deemed a suitable field of endeavour where the private sector might exercise its development skills. The government offers its support to industry in the form of grants and incentives, easy loans and exemptions. The relative importance of the industrial sector has increased in the gross domestic product from 0.8 per cent in 1980 to 3.4 per cent in 1985[196].

In the first four years of the fourth Five Year Plan (1991- 1995) the average growth achieved by the industrial sector was 15 per cent annually, exceeding the plan's annual targeted average of 12 per cent. The industrial policy and legislation put in place in the two industrial years 1991 and 1992 were extraordinarily successful in achieving the required growth averages. From out of this legislation came the extension of subsidies to all establishments and companies, a privilege previously restricted to public stock companies. New programmes are geared to stimulating young graduates of universities and technical institutes to undertake industrial projects having capital requirements not exceeding 100,000 Omani riyals through the aegis of non-repayable grants up to a ceiling of 40 per cent of the investment costs of the project, as well as interest free loans to a ceiling of 40 per cent of the costs of projects located in the province of Muscat. Projects located outside this jurisdiction carry grants of up to 60 per cent of the costs. In addition to these schemes, the government has set about constructing industrial zones designed to scientific standards as an encouragement to potential investors in industry, following on the success attained by the Al-Raseel Industrial Zone in the capital Muscat.

The Sultanate has taken its first cautious steps into the domain of tourism, an area with potentially high yields in view of the country's many archaeological sites and its stimulating climatic diversity on the coast and in the interior, both north and south. The Government has entered a dialogue with the International Tourism Organisation affiliated to the United Nations with a view to putting in place a tourist strategy to develop and modernize this sector up to the year 2005.

The Sultanate's tourist strategy is based on the need to define a set of discerning and intelligent policies which will have regard for the protection of local customs and traditions as well as of the natural environment. Liasons have taken place with Arab and international organizations in order to benefit from their technical and scientific expertise in this regard; and representatives of these organizations have visited the Sultanate to examine at first hand its own ideas and views in the context of the Omani environment, and to benefit in turn from its experience, so that a rational and appropriate tourist policy can be worked out.

It is clear from this that the future of the Omani economy will be in diversifying income in the agriculture, industry and tourism areas. Noteworthy in this respect is the foresight with which the Sultanate has begun to move forward to an age beyond oil, for oil is a depletable non-renewable resource, and only by diversifying its economy and sources of revenue through increased investment allocations for industry and by stimulating efforts in these areas, in particular those arising out of the recommendations of serious studies and involving the transfer and harnessing of technology.

Nevertheless it must be acknowledged and accepted that it is no simple matter to transform Omani society, particularly in such a brief period of time, from a life of involvement with sea and desert and a traditionally-based economy into a modern industrial economy and lifestyle based on scientific and technological principles. In order not to be unrealistic in our expectations we should not neglect to mention or be surprised if there are certain negative aspects to this process. The route to industrialization is not free of hazards and risks. Challenges must be faced and the industrialization process is going to require additional national human resources with upgraded skills and expertise. The creation of these resources demands new competencies, as well as more time, additional training and patience if the process of industrialization is not to lead to unforeseen problems.

Finally, it is clear that a group of realities exist which have had a direct or indirect bearing on the political and economic events which the native Omani has etched through his various economic activities, giving them a political and economical meaning and value.

This district was until recent times one of the poorer regions of the world. Its environment is harsh, with an extreme climate, poor soil and scarcity of fresh surface water. It is an environment which does not offer its inhabitants much choice in determining their lifestyle and economic activities. On the contrary, they were obliged from early times to find their opportunities on and in the sea, and so they travelled the sea and plied their trades with distant coasts and dived to its depths for pearls and cast their nets on its waters to catch the fish which were their staple diet - until oil was discovered in the Sultanate.

The introduction of this valuable new resource and the progressive increase in production gave the Sultanate a precious addition to its traditional importance, in the form of capital funding for the expansion of agricultural and industrial and commercial investment. The Sultanate's average daily oil output rose in 1970 to 332,000 barrels per day. By 1975 this figure had risen to 341,000 bpd, at the end of the second Five Year Plan in 1985 it was 498,000 bpd, and by 1989 it had reached 641 bpd. In 1970 the value of local production was 71.6 million Omani Rials. After the rise in petrol prices in 1973 this revenue from this resource rose in 1975 to 486.8 million Omani Rials. Oil revenue continued to rise throughout this period to peak at 1639.1million Omani Rials in 1985. Since then the slide in oil prices has meant a drop in oil revenue - to 1417.2 in 1989 - despite increased production[197]. In 1993 Oman increased its oil production from 750,000 to 800,000 bpd to compensate for the price drop. And yet its oil export returns, constituting 75 per cent of its income sources, decreased by an average 8 per cent in 1992 to reach 1590 million Rials ie $4130 million against 1740 million Rials ie $4520 million in 1992.

All of this points to the occurrence of widesweeping changes in the economic and political affairs of the Sultanate while giving its geographical bearings additional weight as represented in its being able to supply the capital resources required to expand investment in agriculture, industry and commercial activity.

From another viewpoint, it could be said that the discovery of petrol added another geographical component for consideration in assessing the Sultanate's strategic dimension in the international geopolitical arena, as represented in the international jostling for power in the region. It is a power struggle which has not diminished since the collapse of the Soviet Union and its satellites. But the Sultanate, with its strategic and vital position and in its capacity as a producer state influential among the other producers, has become an effective player in the geostrategy of oil.

Notes for Part One

[1]   Abdullah Youssef Ghoneim, *Districts of the Arabian Peninsula in the Early Arab Writings and in Modern Studies,* Kuwait, 1981, p42.

[2]   Adel Ridha, *Oman and the Arabian Gulf,* Cairo, 1969, p91.

[3]   Abdul Rahman Al-Aani, *Oman in the First Islamic Periods*, Baghdad, 1977, p27.

[4]   Ahmed Al-Jamili, *The Sultanate of Oman - A Study in Political Geography,* Master thesis, Institute for Arab Research and Studies, Baghdad, 1988, p7.

[5]   Mohammed Rashid Abbas, *Political Developments in Oman and its External Relations*, Master thesis, Institute for Arab Research and Studies, Baghdad, 1988, p10.

[6]   Al-Istakhri, *Al-Masalek Wa Al-Mamalek* (Roads and Kingdoms) Study by Mohammed Jaber Abdul Aal, 1961 edition, pp 27-8, Ibn Hawqal, *Surat Al-Ardh*, Beirut printing, pp 45, 47.

[7]   Al-Sayed Abdelaziz Salem, *Merchant Shipping in the Gulf in Early Islam,* Paper presented to the Congress of Studies in the History of the Eastern Arabian Peninsula - Qatar, vol.1, 1976, p400.

[8]   Al-Idrisi, *Jeziret Al-Arab*, from Nozhat Al-Mishtaq Fi Ihtiraq Al-Ifaq, Baghdad, 1971, p43.

[9]   At-Tajir (The Merchant) Suleiman, *Silsilat Al-Tawarikh,* Paris printing, Sultan's Printing Press, 1811, pp 15, 16, 27, 28.

[10]   Siraf, a great city on the coast of the Sea of Persia, in ancient times the sea gate to India (Ya'qut, vol. 3, p294).

[11]   Kolom Melli, a port on the southern side of the Malabar Coast, this being the west coast of India. cf. Dr Rajab Mohammed Abdul Halim, *The Omanis, Navigation, Trade and the Spread*

      of Islam, Muscat 1989, pp67, 72.

[12]   At-Tajir Suleiman, *Silsilat Al-Tawarikh,* Al-Sirafi's second book written in 565 AH at the end of the book of Al-Tajer Suleiman, p67.

[13]   Killeh, an island having a port of the same name. Also known as Killeh Bar, it is on the western coast of what was the Malayan Archipelago in the present province of Kedah. cf. Dr Rajab Mohammed Abdul Halim, *The Omanis, Navigation, Trade and the Spread of Islam,* Muscat 1989, p106.

[14]   Brazilwood or *baqam,* a gum used for dyeing (deep red colour) or the tree which produces this. This is an arabization. cf. Ibn Mandhour's *Lissan Al-Arab* (The Arab Tongue), Dar Sader, Beirut, undated, vol.12, p52.

[15]   *Al-Afawiya* or aromatics, which are added to perfumes in the way that spices are used to enhance food. cf. Ibn Mandhour's *Lissan Al-Arab* vol.13, p53.

[16]   At-Tajir (The Merchant) Suleiman, *Silsilat Al-Tawarikh,* the second book by Al-Sirafi written in 565 AH at the end of the book of At-Tajir Suleiman, p67.

[17]   Ibn Khordathaba, *Al-Masalek wa Al-Mamalek,* Lyons, Brill, 1889, p149. Al-Abila, a town on the banks of the Tigris at Basra on an arm of the Gulf which runs up to Basra. It is older than Basra (Ya'qut, vol.1, p77).

[18]   *Ibid.,* pp 154-5.

[19]   Al-Hamdani, *Siffat Jeziret Al-Arab,* A Study by Mohammed Ali Al-Akoua', Dar Al-Yamama Publications, Riyadh, KSA, 1934, p3. Eilat is a city on the Red Sea Coast at the juncture of the Hijaz and El-Sham (Ya'qut, vol.1, p292. Kazima, an opening on the sea coast on the route to Bahrain from Basra at a distance of two days' journey from Basra. Ya'qut, vol.4, p431.)

[20]   *Ibid.,* p10.

[21]   *Ibid.,* p265.

[22]   *Ibid.,* p374.

[23]   Al-Istakhri, Al-*Masalek wa Al-Mamalek,* Lyons ed., 1927, pp12-13. Abadan, a place below Basra near the ocean (Gulf). Abadan was a domain of Hamran bin Abban Mawalli Othman bin 'Affan granted to him by the Caliph Abdul Malik bin Marwan (Ya'qut, vol.4, p74).

[24]   *Ibid.,* p25.

[25]   *Ibid.,* p25. Al-Istakhri again notes that the area of Oman is 300 *parasang* and Al-Maqdisi, in *Ahsan Al-Taqasim fi Ma'arfat Al-Aqalim,* p93, on the area of Oman, says it is 80 *parasang* square. In fact there is no dispute between the two. Al-Istakhri was describing the total area of Oman, while Al-Maqdisi was describing a single province, the province of Oman. It was common in the past as well as the present to name a province after the state itself, and the province, governorate or district is naturally smaller than the state. Additionally Al-Istakhri and other Arab geographers did not intend the figures they presented in their writings to represent the precise dimensions of the countries they visited or wrote about. Rather they were referring to the inhabited portion which they had seen or visited. The interior territories, the deserts, and uninhabited sands they did not see and so these areas did not for the most part enter into their calculations. Thus the 300 *parasang* or 80 *parasang* are the dimensions of the populated areas of Oman or the size of the portions which were traversed by whoever Al-Istakhri or Al-Maqdisi respectively took their accounts of Oman from. Oman was much larger than this, particularly during the Islamic Era when its borders extended from Bahrain to the Hadramaut.

[26]   *Ibid.,* p27.

[27]   *Ibid.,* p27.

[28]   Ibn Al-Faqih Al-Hamdani, *Kitab Al-Buldan,* Lyons ed., Brill, 1302 AH, p197.

[29]   *Ibid.,* p205. Hashoush, a dense date plantations (Al-Muhait Dictionary).

[30]   *Ibid.,* pp16, 30, 92, 114, 135, 253.

[31]   *Ibid.,* p294.

[32]   Situated on the coast between Sur and Dhofar south of Ghibbet Al-Hashish.

[33]   Ibn Hawqal, *Kitab Surat Al-Ardh,* Al-Hayat Publications, Beirut, p27-30.

[34]   Al-Maqdisi, *Ahsan Al-Taqasim,* 2nd ed., Leiden, Brill, 1967, p68.

[35]   The correct figure is 80,000 *pararsang.*

[36]   *Ibid.,* p93.

[37]   *Ibid.,* p70.

[38]   *Saj,* a species of large-leafed tree which grows to an enormous height and breadth (Al-Muhait Dictionary).

[39]   *Ibid.,* p93.

[40]   *Ibid.,* p93.

[41]   Al-Sirr, a town in the district of Al-Dhahira.

[42]   He probably means that Daba and Julfar are on the road to Hajar.

[43]   There is more than one township named Al-Qalaa, one of them being a town in the Hoddan Mountains and the other Qalaa Al-Awamer near Izki.

[44]   Al-Maqdisi, *Ahsan Al-Taqasim,* 2nd ed., Leiden, Brill, 1967, p93.

[45] *Ibid.,* p93.

[46] *Ibid.*, p97

[47] *Ibid.,* pp98-9. Al-Bikri says of them that they also used the *keelja* and the *mann,* the *keelja* constituting 9 *mann.* Al-Bikri, *Jeziret Al-Arab min Kitab Al-Mamalek wa Al -Masalek,* A Study by Abdullah Youssef Al-Ghoneim, Dar Al-Salasel, Kuwait, 1977, p37.

[48] Al-Maqdisi, *Ahsan Al-Taqasim,* 2nd ed., Leiden, Brill, 1967, p99.

[49] *Ibid.*, p105.

[50] *Ibid.*, p105.

[51] Nasir Khusru, *Safar Naama,* translated by Yahya Al-Khashab, Dar Al-Kitab Al-Jadid, Beirut, 1970, p144.

[52] Al-Bikri, *Jeziret Al-Arab min Kitab Al-Mamalek Wal Masalek,* A Study by Abdullah Youssef Al-Ghoneim, Dar Al-Salasel, Kuwait, 1977, p35.

[53] *Ibid.,* p36.

[54] *Ibid..,* p37.

[55] *Ibid.,* p37.

[56] *Ibid.,* p38.

[57] Al-Idrisi, *Nizwat Al-Ishtaq fi Akhtaraq Al-Ifaq,* vol 2, Rome ed. 1971, p155.

[58] See note 32 *supra.*

[59] Al-Idrisi, *Nizwat Al-Ishtaq fi Akhtaraq Al-Ifaq,* vol 2, Rome ed. 1971, p156.

[60] *Ibid.,* p164.

[61] Al-Idrisi, *Wasf Al-Hind Wama Yijawarha min Al-Bilad,* Fifth Volume, *A Study by Maqbul Ahmed,* Islamic University, Alikarah, India 1954, p12.

[62] Al-Idrisi, *Wasf Al-Hind,* Fifth Volume, p22.

[63] Al-Idrisi, *Wasf Al-Hind,* Fifth Volume, p37, and Volume Two, p167.

[64] Al-Idrisi, *Wasf Al-Hind,* Fifth Volume, p156.

[65] *Ibid.,* pp156-7.

[66] The correct distance between Muscat and Sohar is 230 kms.

[67] Al-Idrisi, *Wasf Al-Hind,* Fifth Volume, p157.

[68] Al-Idrisi, *Wasf Al-Hind,* Fifth Volume, p162.

[69] The correct area of Oman is now 312,000 sq kms. See note 25 *supra.*

[70] Al-Idrisi, p158.

[71] Oman lies between 53°30 and 59°45 longitude and between 16°30 and 25° latitude.

[72] Ya'qut, *Mu'jam Al-Buldan, Dar Ahya'Al-Tirath*, Beirut, 1979, vol4, p150.

[73] Sohar is a city on the coast of the Sea of Oman (Gulf of Oman).

[74] Ya'qut, *Mu'jam Al-Buldan, Dar Ahya'Al-Tirath*, Beirut, 1979, vol.3, p393-394.

[75] Nizwa is an inland city of Oman.

[76] Ya'qut, *Mu'jam Al-Buldan, Dar Ahya'Al-Tirath*, Beirut, 1979, vol5, p281.

[77] *Ibid.,* vol 5, p127.

[78] *Ibid.,* vol 4, p393.

[79] *Ibid.,* vol 2, p154.

[80] *Ibid.,* vol 4, p476.

[81] *Ibid.,* vol 2, p400. To the Arabs a *khor* is a coastline such as that of the Gulf. Originally *hor* it was arabized to *khor.* (Ya'qut, vol.2, p400).

[82] Ibn Said Al-Maghrabi, *Kitab Al-Jughrafia,* a Study by Ismail Al-Arabi, Al-Maktab Al-Tajari Liltaba'a Wal Nashr, Beirut, 1970, p102.

[83] Al-Qazzouini, *Athar Al-Bilad Wa Akhbar Al-Ab'ad* (Monuments of Countries and Reports of Faraway Places), p56.

[84] Ibn Al-Majawar, *Siffat Al-Yemen Wa Mekkah Wa Baadh Al-Hijaz,* amended by Oscar Lufgren, Medina Publications, 2nd ed., 1986, p284. He says, The origin of the name Muscat is *maskat* {from the verb 'to become silent or still'}. When the Companions of the Prophet arrived there the population were pacified and the place became Maskat or the 'silent/reticent' place. In time this became corrupted to Muscat.

[85] By 'Oman' is meant here the city of Sohar.

[86] Ibn Al-Majawar, *Siffat Al-Yemen Wa Mekkah Wa Baadh Al-Hijaz* amended by Oscar Lufgren, Medina Publications, 2nd ed., 1986, p284

[87] Ibn Al-Majawar, *Siffat Al-Yemen Wa Mekkah Wa Baadh Al-Hijaz* amended by Oscar Lufgren, Medina Publications, 2nd ed., 1986, p285

[88] Al-Dimeshqi, *Nakhbet Al-Dahar fi Aja'ib Al-Birr wal-Bahar,* Maktabat Al-Metheni, Baghdad, after the Petersburg ed., 1866, pp77-8.

[89] *Ibid.,* pp81-2.

[90] *Ibid.,* p82.

[91] Probably refers to the present day city of Manah.

[92] Al-Dimeshqi, *Nakhbet Al-Dahar fi Aja'ib Al-Birr wal-Bahar,* Maktabat Al-Metheni, Baghdad, after the Petersburg ed., 1866, p218.

93 Aboul Feda, *Taqwim Al-Buldan,* Dar Al-Taba'a Al-Sultaniya, Paris, 1840, p22.

94 *Ibid.,* pp78, 99.

95 Al-Homeiri, *Ar Rawdh Al Mi'tar fi khabar Al-Aqtar*, Study by Ahsan Abbas, Library of Lebanon, 1st ed., Beirut, 1984, p354-355.

96 See note 25 *supra*.

97 Possibly means Qalhat.

98 Al-Homeiri, *ibid.*

99 Possibly means Muscat.

100 Al-Qalqashandi, *Subh Al-'Aasha fi Sana'at Al-Inshaa,* photocopied, Ministry of Culture and National Guidance, Cairo, (b.t.), vol.5, p55.

101 Ya'qut Shehab Al-Din Ibn Abdullah Al-Hamawi, *Mu'jam Al- Buldan,* Beirut, 1984, p150.

102 Ibn Khordadhuba (Aboul-Qassem Abeed Allah), *Al-Masalek Wal Mamalek,* Baghdad; Al-Hamdani (Abu Bakr bin Mohammed), *Kitab Al-Buldan,* abridged version; and Al-Hamdani (Abu Mohammed Al-Hassan bin Yaaqoub), *Kitab Siffat Jeziret Al-Arab*, all wrote about Oman's importance as a trading nation and the routes which led there.

103 Al-Hamdani, *Kitab Siffat Jeziret Al-Arab*, p48. Ibn Khordadhiba, *Al-Masalek Wal Mamalek*, p60.

104 Al-Hassan bin Ali bin Hussein bin Ali Al-Mas'udi, a citizen of Baghdad of Maghrabi ancestry. Al-Mas'udi (Abu Al-Hussein Ali bin Mas'udi) *Murooj Al-Thahab Wa Ma'aden Al-Jawhar*, Beirut, p65.

105 *Ibid.,* p65.

106 *Ibid.,* p60. Hassan Saleh, in his book *Adhou' 'Ala Tarikh Al-Yemen* (Light on the History of Yemen), p153, on pearls and their production in the Gulf area and Oman's exports. Amer Ali 'Umair Al-Marhubi, *Oman Qabal Wa B'ad Al-Islam* (Oman before and after Islam), Oman, 1980, pp14-15.

107 Marco Polo was born in Venice in 1204 AD. His father, an Italian merchant, took him to the court of Kublai Khan, the Tatar ruler, where he lived for 17 years. Marco Polo, *Travels of Marco Polo*, Cairo, 1977.

108 Marco Polo, p339.

109 Marco Polo, p34.

110 Ibn Battuta, *Travels of Ibn Battuta,* p265.

111 Ibn Battuta, *Travels of Ibn Battuta,* p270.

112 Possibly means Oman's interior regions.

113 Al-Qariat, the town of Qariat (without the definite article).

114 Killia, may mean the present day town of Kelba on the coast of the United Arab Emirates.

115 *Futuh Al-Buldan* - Critically edited and published by M.G.De Goya, 2nd ed., Brill, Leiden, 1968, p76.

116 Al-Qalqashandi, *Nahaiya Al-Orab fi Ma'arafat Insan Al-Arab* - Study by Ibrahim Al-Abiari, 2nd ed., Dar Al-Kitab Al-Lubnani, Beirut, 1400 AH/1980 AD, p169. Qaren ibn Hazm, *Jamharat Insan Al-Arab* - Study by Levi Provencal, Dar Al-Maaraf, Cairo, 1948, p347; and Ibn Al-Atheer, *Al-Libbab fi Tahdhib Al-Insab (*Reason in the Revision of Kinship), vol. 1, Dar Sader ed., Beirut, 1400 AH/1980 AD, pp107, 157.

117 Al-Bilathuri, *Futuh al-Buldan*, p76; and Ya'qut Al-Hamawi, *Mu'jam Al-Buldan*, vol. 2, Dar Sader ed., Beirut, p435; Qaren Al-Tabari, *Tarikh Al-Rasal Wal Muluk* (History of Messengers and Kings) Volume 3 - Study by Mohammed Aboul Fadl Ibrahim, 2nd ed., Dar Al-Maaraf, Cairo, 1976, p314, and Ibn Hajar, *Al-Adaba fi Tamayyez Al-Sohaba (*Afflictions in Characterizng the Companions*)*, Volume 2 - Study by Mohammed Al- Bajawi, Dar Nahdhat Masr, Cairo, pp44-6.

118 Ya'qut Al-Hamawi, *ibid.*, vol. 2, p436; and Ibn Hazm *Jamharat Ansanb Al-Arab* - Study by Levi Provencal, Dar Al-Maaraf, Cairo, 1948, pp348-50.

119 Ya'qut, *ibid.,* vol. 2, p434; Ibn Kathir, *Al-Bedaiya Wal Nahaiya* (Beginning and End), 2nd ed., Maktabat Al-Maaraf, Beirut, 1974, p329. Ibn Kathir confused the Luqait Dhu'l Taj and the Bani Julanda, kings of Oman and in this differs from the other sources. See also same reference, p33. Al-Tabari, vol. 3, p314.

120 cf. Al-Qalqashandi, *Nahaiya Al-Orab fi Ma'arafat Insan Al- Arab* - Study by Ibrahim Al-Abiari, 2nd ed., Dar Al-Kitab Al-Lubnani, Beirut, 1400 AH/1980 AD, pp168, 429 and Omar Ridha Kahala, *Mu'jam Qaba'il Al-Arab* (Lexicon of Arab Tribes), vol. 3, 3rd ed., Al-Risala Est., Beirut, 1402 AH/1982 AD, p1116.

121 *Tarikh Al-Yaaqoubi* (or Jacobite history), vol. 2, Dar Beirut, Beirut, 1400 AH/1980 AD, pp194-5.

122 Khalifa bin Hodeid bin Assad bin 'A'idh bin Malik bin 'Amr bin Malik bin Fahm bin Ghonam bin Daws bin 'Adnan bin Abdullah bin Zahran bin Malik bin Nasir bin Al-Azd bin Al-Ghouth, of whom Rashed bin 'Amr Al-Hodeidi was a relative. See *Kitab Al-Tabaqat* - Study by Dr Akram Dhia' Al-'Amari, 2nd ed., Dar Tayeba, Riyadh, 1402 AH/1982 AD, p202.

66

[123] *Ibid.*, p201.

[124] See also Al-Bilathuri, *ibid.*, p435; and Khalifa bin Khayat, *Tarikh Khalifa bin Khayat* - Study by Dr Akram Dhia' Al-'Amari, 2nd ed., Dar Tayeba, Riyadh, 1405 AH/1985 AD, p296; and Al-Qadhi Atthar, Abu Al- M'aali, *Al-Aqd Al-Themin*, p121.

[125] *Al-Ishtiqaq* (Schism) - Study by Abdul Salaam Mohammed Haroun, Maktab Al-Khanji, Cairo, p351.

[126] *Ibid.*, p497.

[127] Ibn Durayed said they were called Salimi because of their invincibility, *ibid.*, p501.

[128] *Ibid.*, p501.

[129] *Ibid.*, p242; and Ya'qut, *ibid.*, vol 2, p217.

[130] Ibn Durayed, *ibid.*, p137.

[131] There is another village called Julfar which Ya'qut described as one of the villages of 'Maru'. See *Mu'jam Ai-Buldan*, vol. 2, p154. It is not mentioned anywhere else.

[132] See *Ahsan Al-Taqasim fi Ma'arafa Al-Aqalim* - Study by M.G. De Goya, 2nd ed., Brill, Leiden, 1967, p 93.

[133] *Ibid.*, p93.

[134] *Ibid.*, p97.

[135] Ya'qut, *ibid.*, vol 2, p154.

[136] Al-Idrisi, *Nozhat Al-Mishtaq fi Ihtiraq Al-Ifaq*, pp156-7. Naqoula Ziada, *The Eastern Coastline of the Arabian Peninsula*, paper submitted to the Qatar Symposium, 1976, from p257f.

[137] Al-Maqdisi, *Ahsan Al-Taqasim*, pp92-3.

[138] Ya'qut Al-Hamawi, *Mu'jam Al-Buldan*, Beirut ed., 1957, vol 3, p494.

[139] *Ibid.*, pp392-3.

[140] Al-Maqdisi, *Ahsan Al-Taqasim*, p30. Sayeda Kashef, *Oman fi Fajr Al-Islam*, pp12-13.

[141] Aboul Hassan Ali bin Al-Hussein Al-Mas'udi, *Murooj Al-Thahab Wa Ma'aden Al-Jawhar - Study by Mohammed Mohieddin Abdul Hamid*, vol 1, p149.

[142] Al-Idrisi.

[143] Ibn Al-Faqih, *Mukhtasar Kitab Al-Buldan* - Abridged Version, p11. Al- Mas'udi, *Murooj Al-Thahab*, vol. 1, p14p.

[144] Rihlat Ibn Battuta *(Travels of Ibn Battuta)*, Beirut ed., 1960, p648.

[145] Al-Istakhri, *Al-Masalek Wal Mamalek*, p27. Ibn Hawqal, *Surat Al-Ardh*, p44. Ibn Battuta, *Al-Rihla*, p 271. The Banu Sama bin Lu'ai were an Omani Nazarene clan descended from Sama bin Lu'ai bin Ghaleb. One of the most noteworthy men of this tribe in the political arena was Al-Fadhal bin Al-Hawari who went to war against the Imam Azzan bin Tamim, a Yamani Azdi. Credit is due to a number of the Bani Sama for establishing an Arab presence as well as Arab trading supremacy on the eastern shore of the Arabian Gulf. Jaafar bin Abi Zuheir of the Bani Sama bin Lu'ai was one of a delegation of the Persian kings to the court of Haroun Al-Rashid. This serves to confirm the growth of Arab Omani influence on the eastern shore of the Arabian Gulf and its economic dominance. They retained a presence in Persia up to the start of the fourth century of the Hegira (Farouq Omar Fawzi, *The Arab Expansion in the Eastern Provinces of the Arabian Gulf*, p64- 8, Mohammed Aboul Faraj Al-'Ash, 'Arab Islamic Currency Minted in the Eastern cities of the Arabian Peninsula', paper presented to the Congress of Studies of the History of the East of the Arabian Peninsula, Qatar, 1976, from p304.

[146] Al-Homeiri, *Al-Rawadh Al-M'itar*, p232.

[147] Al-Maqdisi, *Ahsan Al-Taqasim*, p93.

[148] Ya'qut Al-Hamawi, *Mu'jam Al-Buldan*, vol 2, p435. Sayeda Kashef, *Oman fi Fajr Al-Islam*, p32.

[149] *Op. cit.*, p33. For further information on the Riddah (Secession) movement and the views of other Arab Omani sources on this see Farouq Omar Fawzi, *The Arab Gulf in the Islamic Era*, 1st ed., 1983, p42.

[150] Ya'qut Al-Hamawi, *Mu'jam Al-Buldan*, vol. 3, p163.

[151] Farouq Omar Fawzi, *The Arab Expansion in the Eastern Provinces of the Arabian Gulf*, p66.

[152] Al-Istakhri, *Al-Masalek Wal Mamalek*, p85.

[153] Ya'qut Al-Hamawi, *Mu'jam Al-Buldan*, vol. 4, p422.

[154] Farouq Omar Fawzi, *The Arab Expansion*, p66.

[155] Naqoula Ziada, *Arab Geography and Travels*, Dar Al-Kitab Al-Lubnani ed., 1962, p235. Ahmed Al-Shami. *Trade Links between the Gulf States and the Countries of the Far East*, p333.

[156] Ya'qut Al-Hamawi, *Mu'jam Al-Buldan*, vol. 3, p295.

[157] Ibn Battuta, *The Travels* (Al-Rihla) p273.

[158] Ya'qut Al-Hamawi, *Mu'jam Al-Buldan*, vol. 2, p95. For information on Jask's subordination to the Arab ruler of Qais Island, see Farouq Omar Fawzi, *The Arab Expansion*, p66.

[159] Obada Kahila, *The Arabs and the Sea*, p47. Salaheddin Al- Shami, 'Arab Voyages in the Indian

Ocean and their Role in Serving Geographical Scholarship'. Article in *Alam Al-Fikr* magazine, no.4, 1983, p23.

[160] Al-Istakhri, *Al-Masalek Wal Mamalek,* p30. Ibn Hawqal, *Surat Al-Ardh,* p 52.

[161] Al-Mas'udi, *Murooj Al-Thahab,* vol 1, p148.

[162] Ibn Shahryar Birzek Al-Nakhedha Al-Ram Hormuzi, *Kitab Aja'ib Al-Hind BarruhWa Bahru hWa Jaza'iruh* Cairo, Al-Saada Press, 1908 after Leiden ed., 1883, pp101-3.

[163] Al-Homeiri, *Al-Rawadh Al-M'atar,* p413.

[164] Ibn Faqih, *Mukhtasar Kitab Al-Buldan* - Abridged Version, p16.

[165] *Ibid.,* p30.

[166] Ibn Battuta, *Al-Rihla,* p271.

[167] *Ibid.,* p328.

[168] Al-Mas'udi, *Murooj Al-Thahab,* vol. 1, p112.

[169] Ibn Faqih, *Mukhtasar Kitab Al-Buldan* - Abridged Version, p114.

[170] *Ibid.,* p135.

[171] Ibn Battuta, *Al-Rihla,* p648.

[172] Sayeda Kashef, *Oman at the Dawn of Islam,* p27.

[173] Al-Istakhri, *Al-Masalek Wal Mamalek,* p27. Ibn Hawqal, *Surat Al-Ardh,* p44.

[174] Ibn Hawqal, *ibid.,* p44.

[175] *Silsilat Al-Tawarikh,* Paris, 1811, pp182-3.

[176] Ibn Khordadhuba, *Al-Masalek Wal Mamalek,* p147. Al-Maqdisi, *Ahsan Al-Taqasim,* p98.

[177] Ibn Hawqal, *Surat Al-Ardh,* p44. Ya'qut Al-Hamawi, *Mu'jam Al- Buldan,* vol. 3, p393.

[178] Ibn Khordadhuba, *Al-Masalek Wal Mamalek,* p62. Ibn Battuta, *Al-Rihla,* p594.

[179] This study, which is first and foremost a geographical one, set out to show the important role played by its most prominent geographical features on the Sultanate's political make-up and what these critical components contribute to this structure in terms of its strategic significance. This is not in any sense to suggest that these geographical components should be considered in isolation in establishing Oman's strategic influence, for other geographical elements which did not come within the scope of this study play a role also.

[180] A giant oil tanker passes through this Strait every 11 minutes, on its way into the Gulf or on the outward journey.

[181] A brief perusal of the history of the Arab East will confirm this for us. From the fourteenth century the imperialist powers of the time began to entrench in various parts of the Arab world. In 1569 AD France signed a treaty with the Sublime Porte which granted it protection rights over parts of the Ottoman Empire and this was succeeded particularly in the nineteenth century by a series of other treaties concluded with France, Imperial Russia and Britain which granted them rights of intervention to secure their interests.

[182] See page 16 of Daniel Doran's book *World Oil and Political Monopolies* as follows: '*World War One provoked the anxiety and hunger of the United States of America for petrol and so began an aggressive and relentless struggle which was to continue for ten years between American and British companies and in which each party sought to secure new petroleum reserves. The Arabian Gulf region was one of the most crucial arenas of this contest'.*

[183] The giant American oil companies were not concerned with the production of petrol outside the North American mainland prior to World War One. By 1920 however five of the larger American oil companies had begun to jostle the British and Dutch oil companies in the Arabian Gulf region.

[184] Dr Amin Mahmoud Abdullah notes (pp 68, 75) of his book *Studies in the Geopolitics of the Contemporary World*: 'The study of the natural features of the various political districts will be of assistance to us in deciding the significance of these regions in relation to others. Any degree of undulation can leave its mark on the political map. The most powerful states in the world were greatly benefited in their advance to progress by having a climate harmonious to human endeavour'.

[185] Dr Mohammed Saudi, *The Arab World* p227.

[186] Its settled inhabitants are a state's precious human resource, for they fashion its political circumstances. Without settled inhabitants there is neither production, construction, culture nor political influence. The value of a settled population can be assessed by their level of vigorous activity and effectiveness, the ratio of young people in the population and of its working men and women as well as their average age. One of the factors contributing to increasing the effectiveness of a population is solidarity and interrelationship, and the presence of leadership and its qualifying traits, as well as the levels of education and technical training.

[187] *Annual Statistical Report,* published by the Ministry of Development, Sultanate of Oman, 22nd ed, October 1994, p46.

[188] *Ibid.*

[189] *Ibid.*

[190] *Ibid.*

[191] Muscat took in a number of other cities to constitute the Province of Muscat.

[192] *The Good March*, Ministry of Information.

[193] *Annual Statistical Report*, published by the Ministry of Development, Sultanate of Oman, 22nd ed, October 1994, p55.

[194] It is agreed in economic and political circles that it is vital for every state to rely absolutely on its natural resources and its economic potential in erecting a political structure. And so mineral resources such as petrol, coal, iron ore and uranium have a vital importance in providing a geographical basis for assessing a state's strategic value.

[195] *The Fourth Five Year Plan* (1991-95), issued by the Development Council, July 1991, p203.

[196] *The Third Five Year Plan* (1986-90), issued by the Development Council, p119.

[197] See: *The Sultanate of Oman - Statistical Yearbook,* 10th ed, June 1990, pp316, 465, 466.

PART II

Oman in Early History

Chapter One: Oman at the Dawn of History

Chapter Two: Omani Society in the Early Historical Periods

Chapter Three: Images from Omani Civilization in the Early Historical Period

Studies Presented and Summarized in this Part

Oman in the Middle Islamic Period, by Dr Ali Mansour Nasir, University of Bahrain.

Aspects of Oman's Early History and its Cultural Relations, by Dr Ridha Jawad Al-Hashemi, Baghdad University.

The Rise of the Omani State and its Development in a Geographical and Historical Context, by Dr Mohammed Harb Farzat, Damascus University.

Oman in the Cuneiform Texts, by Dr Fawzi Rashid, Arab Federation of Historians, Baghdad.

Oman at the Dawn of History

The Origin of the Name 'Oman'

'Oman' describes an Arab district on the coast of the Arabian Sea and the Indian Ocean at 34° 30' longitude and 19° 45' latitude, east of Hajar. Opinions differ as to the origin of the name, some sources linking it to the Qahtani tribe of Oman and others linking it linguistically to a word having the meaning of 'settling' or 'staying'. Ibn Al-Qabi says: 'Oman means those who occupy a place, as in the adjective *aamen*, or *amoun* i.e. a settled man. From this was derived Oman'. He continues: 'If a man *a'amana,* he made his permanent residence in Oman'[1]. Al-Zujjaji says: 'Oman was named after Oman bin Ibrahim Al- Khalil', while Ibn Al-Kelbi says: 'It was named after Oman bin Siba' bin Yaghthan bin Ibrahim, God's Khalil (or close friend), because he was the person who built the city of Oman'[2]. Sheikh Al-Rabwa, on the other hand, ascribes the name to Oman bin Loot, the Prophet, (Lot)[3], And it is said that the Azdis called Oman *Omana* because they came from a valley at Ma'rib which went by the name of Oman and they likened it to this place[4].

One of the earliest Roman historians to mention Oman was Yalainous who lived in the first century of the Christian Era (23-79 AD). He presents in his writings a city which he names *Omana*. This name recurs in Ptolemy (who lived in the second century AD). In the view of Grohimmann, the Omana which these two historians describe was in fact Sohar, the pre-eminent regional economic centre of the Classical Age[5].

Oman was known by other names: the Sumerians and Mesopotamians called it *Magan*, perhaps alluding to the ship-building craft for which Oman was famous, for according to cuneiform scripts, a *magan* was a type of ship's chassis. The Persians knew it as *Mazoun*.The name Oman occurs in Arab references as an independent district. Al-Istakhri and Ibn Hawqal both refer to Oman as a district, sovereign in itself with a sovereign people[6]. Ibn Khaldun had the clearest definition of Oman, noting that it was one of a group of Arab districts which emerged as independent states in the Arabian peninsula, these being Yemen, the Hijaz, Shihr, the Hadramaut and Oman. He described their manner of government, calling them 'individual sovereign districts'[7].

Whatever is the case, the name *Oman* evidently goes back to early history and if it appears most likely that Oman got its name from a valley in Yemen called Oman or from a Yemeni tribe of the same name, then we have evidence pointing to very early migrations from Yemen into Oman, showing Oman to have been crossed by Arab strains from earliest times. But how are we to find out more about this Arab district in early historical times?

Study of Oman's Early History

Any exploration of the early history of Oman will involve two parallel lines of inquiry, the first requires reference to written texts, in particular to the writings of explorers and geographers. These sources, however, do not serve the scholar who wishes to delve deep into the country's past. If we consult Classical references (Greek and Roman) or Chinese sources, we will find our information limited for the most part to the time of the Christian Era and a short period before this[8].

Historical events and the activities of Omanis during the time of the early or later migrations or during the historical periods commencing from the start of the third millenium BC are, as is the case with the other districts in the Arabian peninsula and the Arab Gulf, completely unknown to us. Scraps of information from cuneiform writings give scholars the only hope of access to past events in this important region of early human civilization.

The decades since World War Two have spurred studies of the early history of the Gulf and the Arabian peninsula, based for the most part on early cuneiform sources from Iraq, and these have had an important role, in common with other archaeological and historical studies, in generating a proliferation of archaeological excavation works throughout the Arabian peninsula, in particular those areas of early settlement around its periphery, as well as the oases and the coastal areas. Where textual references are not scarce is where they refer to the preoccupation of the coastal dwellers with navigation and trade with distant lands[9]. Cuneiform sources were also helpful insofar as they set in train a new era of studies of early Arab history, or of specific chapters of it, a significant part of which was occupied by the history of Oman.

Archaeological excavation and discoveries provide the second strand of our investigation of Oman's early history, particularly in view of the results which have spurred concentrated effort in recent decades, and which establish conclusively the tremendous age and historical significance of early Arab history generally and the splendid role the Arabs played in the development of human civilization and in ensuring its succession and endurance.

Scholars from Arab countries, including Oman, have been notable in this field of study. *The Journal of Oman Studies,* published by the Ministry of National Heritage and Culture in the Sultanate of Oman, is a good example of this. Published without interruption since the first issue came out in 1395 AH/1975 AD, its studies and reports of various archaeological expeditions in Oman are amongst the most comprehensive and reliable references for students of the early history and civilization of this important corner of the Arab world[10].

Points of Departure in the Study of Early Omani History

Oman is set in the south-eastern portion of the Arabian peninsula, where it follows the edge of the Arabian Sea, enclosing a gulf which bears its name. It is counted as the central point of contact between the extremities of the Arab world and the Indian sub-continent. And though Oman is mostly celebrated for its oceangoing skills and for its sea crossings, relations with its near neighbours on the Arabian peninsula are etched deep into the earliest periods of its history. These ancient bonds are attested to by the numberous archaeological remains of ancient active land routes[11].

Cuneiform texts assert the importance of Magan (Oman) in the export of copper to Iraq, a claim which has led in recent years to a flurry of archaeological field studies being conducted in Oman in search of proof[12]. Thus early Omani history and civilization constituted a part of a broad spectrum of historical and cultural activities of the Arab Gulf region, in the shaping of which the old routes with their centres of civilization played a conspicuous part. We believe that this methodological approach will provide the most satisfying point of departure for a study of Oman's early history.

The second point of departure concerns the role played by the Omanis in early ocean navigation. It is a well known fact of early navigation that it flourished in the Arabian Gulf but was interrupted over a long period in the Red Sea and parts of the Arabian Sea, this being apparently for reasons connected with the technicalities of ship-building and the skills of mariners[13]. Oman's reputation on the high seas was distinguished from that of the other seagoing communities on the Arabian Gulf by the size and grandeur of its ships and perhaps also by the fame of its trade in copper which found a brisk market in the cities of Mesopotamia. Cuneiform scripts identify Magan with a particular type of ship. referred to as the 'Magan ship'. The textual reference to these ships is part of a Sumerian poem which recounts a voyage by Gilgamesh to Ard Al-Hayat (land of life), from which we may infer that the Magan ships were the greatest and strongest ships of the time[14]. Confirmation of this understanding of the Magan ships is found in the introduction to the Canon of Ur-Nammu in which he boasts that he can cause these ships to re-anchor at the quays of Ur, that he can increase the frequency of their visits and cause them to be famous[15]. This would seem to suggest a type of merchandise which the cuneiform sources identify with Magan, the most prominent goods being copper, stone and timber[16]. From this we may deduce that the fame of Omani sea skills in past centuries was based on a long history of navigation going back deep into Oman's past, and this long time span saw many changes from one era to another in the direction of voyages and goods traded.

Most importantly, trade and seafaring were not considered to be merely two economic activities. At heart they were activities around which revolved the various interactions between civilizations; and they were the means by which bridges of friendship and understanding were put in place and the common interests of nations and cultures were shared, in addition its role in cementing the bonds of early Arab civilization.

References in cuneiform texts describe a political and administrative system of government led by a ruler named Manu Danu who reigned in approximately the twenty-third century BC at a time contemporary with King Naram-Sin, a king of Akkad in Iraq. Another text from the time of the Akkadian king, Sargon, grandfather of Naram-Sin, speaks of the many Magan (Omani) ships that have arrived in Akkad[17], implying the presence of a powerful and thriving state, active in commerce and with a vast seagoing trade.

The third point of departure for the study of Oman's early history is aimed at discovering the extent of the strategic influence enjoyed by Oman as a direct result of its relations with the Arabs, on the one hand, and with the external world on the other. These relationships were for the most part rooted in commerce and buttressed by regular voyages by Omani ships and Arabian camel caravans which journeyed out from the various quarters of the Arabian peninsula, including Oman, to markets abroad, in particular those which bordered the peninsula.

When shipping ceased in the Red Sea as a result of difficulties caused by the growth of coral and the absence of favourable winds, this had the effect of spurring into life the Arabian caravan trade which transported the merchandise of the Arabian peninsula as well as India to the markets of El-Sham (Syria) and the port cities of the Mediterranean and Egypt[18].

The Arabian caravan trade would never have come to command this influence and significance in the early economic history of the Arabs but for the taming of the camel - the ship of the desert -which was to become at the onset of the first millennium BC a domesticated Arab animal serving on a grand scale the transport of goods as well as communications between the territorial domains of the Arabs and the centres of civilization on their periphery in Iraq and El-Sham (Syria) and Egypt[19].

Because of the location of Oman, separated by scorching desert (the Rub'al-Khali) from the rest of the Arabian peninsula up to the domestication of the camel (around the start of the first millennium BC), and also because of the nature of its merchandise and its marketplaces, most of the trading and mercantile activity of the Omanis was aimed at servicing the Arabian Gulf and Mesopotamia. This is confirmed by the cuneiform texts, together with information yielded by archaeological excavations at the ancient centres of civilization in the Arabian Gulf area and Oman. Archaeological excavation work found circular tombs on a small island facing the city of Abu Dhabi, which goes by the name of Umm Nar[20], and this was followed by the discovery of similar tombs in the Hilli area near the township of Al-Ain, as well as the tombs of Badi'a bint Saud and Jebel Hafit[21]. From this one may deduce that the districts of the southern quarter of the Arabian Gulf shared a single cultural ambience.

Thus the first strand of our investigation, the historical writings, open up for us an important aspect of early Omani history, insofar as it concerns the seafaring and trading activities of its inhabitants, as well as its relations with its immediate neighbours. The second strand, from which we may also glean some aspects of the history of Oman, looks at the results of archaeological excavations and exploration.

Archaeological Excavations

The oldest remains found on the eastern and western coasts of Oman go back to the fifth millennium BC[22]. There are also clear pointers to the presence of small settlements on Omani soil even earlier than this, as far back as the sixth millennium BC, uncovered at Al-Qurm near Muscat, where tombs and remains and personal items were stumbled upon. Most of the inhabitants of this place lived by extracting their nutritional requirements from fish and oysters taken from nearby shores, while others were hunters who lived by hunting game in the form of gazelle in the wadis and the depths of the interior. Burial remains point to the existence of a form of institutionalized religious life complete with recognized rites. The discovery of both male and female jewellery suggests that a degree of skill in craftsmanship had been achieved[23].

Archaeological remains at Bat.

Between 1972 and 1973 successive excavations were undertaken in Oman. Scientific expeditions were conducted to various locations in search of burial sites from the third millennium BC: these discoveries add a new link to the chain of excavations which have followed one another in the Gulf regions over the past four decades. One of the most rewarding archaeological excavations to have taken place in the Arabian Gulf was that on the island of Umm Nar near Abu Dhabi in 1959, when a settlement was uncovered dating possibly to the early part of the third millennium BC. Found there were the remains of dwelling places as well as burial sites and kilns used in the firing of earthenware[24]. It would appear that a common way of life and culture was shared over a large area, as is evidenced by the discovery of a number of stone tombs following the same pattern close to Jebel Hafit near Al-Ain. These contained pottery remains dating to around 3400-3000 BC. Pottery similar to this was unearthed at Bat[25] near Ibra and samples of the same pottery again at the Ibra site[26]. The most striking feature in relation to the construction of these tombs is the craftsmanship employed in the overlaying of the dome-shaped roof with a limestone casing and the sub-sectioning of the interior into two or three chambers. This would tend to give material expression to religious beliefs as reflected in the social customs and daily life of these early settlers, and which would richly reward further study into their origins and the factors influencing them.

If we add to the archaeological discoveries of the Arabian Gulf countries the findings in this area of interest at Tibba Yahia in Karman and Bajour in Baluchistan, it becomes possible to draw up a map of the routes of contact and exchange between the two great civilizations which grew up on the land of Mesopotamia and the peninsula (Sumer and Akkad) and in the Sind Valley[27]. Dilmun in the northern part of the Gulf and Magan in the south were vigorously active over a period of 2000 years in maintaining these contacts. A German expedition led by Konrad Schliephake (of Wurzburg) observes that the diligent activity of the Mesopotamian fleet in the Gulf, propelled by the need to obtain raw materials, was matched by the activity of the Egyptian fleet in the opposite gulf or Red Sea in its pursuit of the merchandise of Punt (Yemen and the part of the African coast facing it). In this exchange of activity in the first millennium BC was the basis laid of a new civilization in the Arabian peninsula which would be founded on trade in frankincense, myrrh and perfumes, and which would carry these exotic wares between the Indian Ocean and the Mediterranean Basin[28].

Scientific reports published recently (1987) on the yields from archaeological excavations carried out at a number of sites in Oman (in the central district of Batinah) over the space of a decade, with the object of confirming the existence of an early historical background on which to structure a politically and economically effective society having the political substance to direct its dealings with other states and societies, show a number of fruitful conclusions. One study published by B. Costa and T.G. Wilkinson[29] on the hinterland of Sohar paints a clear picture of mining, agricultural and commercial activities in the district going back to earliest times and continuing up to the Islamic Era.

Early Iraqi sources (Sumerian and Akkadian) also mentioned a land 'between Dilmun (Bahrain) and Meluhha (probably Sind)', and this we assume to be Magan, which was known to be a source of copper. Though opinions differ it is likely that the country alluded to is Oman, which had large copper deposits in the north of the country. Analysis of the green rocks and the appearance in them of magnesium hydrosilicate support this thesis. Copper was extracted easily from the rock and from excavated mines, and a form of sulphur ore was also mined[30]. Costa and Wilkinson set forth in the above study[31]a comprehensive and detailed scientific report confirming the existence of active mining skills at a very early period of antiquity in this district, especially in the mining of copper. The mining territory lies beyond the cultivated areas at a distance of 25 kilometres inland from the coast, set into the western rockface surface of Al-Hajar Al-Gharbi (the Western Stone) mountains. The discovery of stone remains in this district points to its having been colonized by small communities at the start of the third millennium BC, communities which apparently worked the mines. Raw ore was extracted from the mine and smelted in primitive furnaces and primitive dwellings were constructed to house the workers.

The exploitation of these mines continued up to the Middle Islamic Era. Their principal site of activity from the end of the Sassanid period up to the twelfth century of the Christian Era was Arja and the remains of human settlements are to be found there which may have had some connection with mining. Earthenware and pottery found here may also date to this time. Worthy of note was the discovery of copper seams at a depth of 90 metres beneath the ground surface along with pieces of wood and rope. These remains were investigated by means of carbon-dating (C14) and found to date to the ninth century of the

Christian Era. Al-Mas'udi (four century AH/tenth century AD) referred to the copper mines of Oman. More important than this, however, is the presence of a systematic mining code of Omani origin referred to by the two authors. This also dates to the tenth century AD. Other mines at Wadi Al-Jizzi near Sohar were exploited from the twelfth century. Apart from these brief references we are not offered any further details. But there is no doubt that - and this is confirmed by the two authors - the code revolved around the subject of mining and incorporated a form of contract between the owners of the site and those exploiting the mine. These were long lease contracts valid for in the region of 100 years. However, the documents are silent in relation to information about the mine labourers or the mining methods they employed[32].

The extraction, mining and use of copper were not confined to Oman during the remote historical periods before the Christian Era or indeed later. The fourth and third millennia BC were distinguished by the use of copper at early centres of civilization on a wide scale, particularly Egypt and Iraq. From it they fashioned bronze ingots - after first smelting it with tin- until this era of early civilization came to be known as the Bronze Age. Egypt had in the copper mines of Sinai a rich and nearby source to meet its needs for this mineral. Thus Pharaonic memorial texts are likely to contain reports on trading expeditions to these mines and the securing of the communicating roads there, as well as the provision of the support services necessary to facilitate the task of the labourers working the copper mines or transporting the copper to Egyptian cities. The textual references return again and again to the importance the Egyptians gave to the copper mines in Sinai during the era before and leading up to the Twentieth Dynasty i.e. for a period of almost 2000 years from around the middle of the fourth millennium BC and up to the start of the first millennium BC[33].

Arising out of the efforts of the Egyptians to provide copper, added to their accelerated and persistent efforts to monopolize the supply of Lebanese cedarwood, the main focus of early Egyptian trade and the direction of state policy was turned towards Sinai and the shores of Lebanon. Iraq meanwhile got its meagre supply of this important metal from two sources, Oman, via the sea route in the Arabian Gulf, and also Anatolia. Information gleaned from texts dating to the third millennium BC[34], together with archaeological evidence of human settlements spread about a wide area along the coasts and islands of the Arabian Gulf[35], show that the copper supplied to the Iraqis from the start of the fourth millennium BC came from the copper mines of Oman by means of sea crossings of the Arabian Gulf. This supply line served to enhance trading relations between Iraq and Oman. The shipping lanes in the Arabian Gulf provided clear and open routes for the transport of goods in ancient times and served in the absence of any other route or means of communication between the two countries.

Also assisting the growth of trading relations during the fourth and third millennia BC, relations which were founded on and built around the trade in copper, were the other primary materials offered by Oman and other centres on the Arabian Gulf, or procured by means of voyages in the Arabian Gulf. These included stone of various types, including precious stones, and various species of timber. And so copper, timber and stone were foremost among the commodities which Iraq endeavoured to supply by means of the merchant trade in the Arabian Gulf.

With the middle of the second millennium BC came the increasing use of iron as a metal, particularly in the crafting of weapons. This followed the rise to repute of the Indo-European races in the countries of the Ancient Near East, particularly following the Hyksos invasion of Egypt in or around the seventeenth century BC. The Kassites invaded Iraq in approximately the fifteenth century BC and the Hittites and Mitani came to fame in the north of Syria and Mesopotamia. Although the demand for copper continued, the emergence of iron with its superiority over copper and bronze in the manufacture of weapons saw a falling off of the extensive trade in copper in favour of iron. Perhaps this explains why the Assyrians turned their attention away from the commerce of the Arabian Gulf[36].

As mentioned already, the domestication of the camel and its extensive use by the inhabitants of the Arabian peninsula as a vehicle of both transport and communication, had the effect of reducing the importance of the Gulf sea trade. New horizons and new trading opportunities were opened up for the Arabs of South Arabia as a whole, among them the Omanis. This was in keeping with the demands of these new markets and the political, human and intellectual transformations occurring in the Near Eastern region during the first millennium BC. New commodities were brought to market and the demand for incense, perfumes and aromatics grew until they became foremost amongst the goods traded.

And so Oman's trade and merchandise came to be to a great extent directed towards markets in the west and north and to be linked into the vast trade of the South Arabian caravans along what was known as the Incense Route. This view is supported in Musnad writings from many locations in Oman and the Gulf countries. Livestock, camels, perfumes and gold came to be among the commodities offered by the Arab trade of the first millennium BC, commodities which the Assyrians and other nations strove to obtain[37].

The Arab trade began to broaden its scope in the supply of foreign goods to the markets, often to an extent which surpassed the supply of local Arab goods. An example was cinnamon in respect of which the Omanis played a prominent role in maintaining a supply from its source in India. With their advanced oceangoing skills and spurred by favourable conditions they could make the sea crossing from the Gulf of Oman to the western shores of India to arrive at the hidden source of cinnamon and a variety of other wares and important merchandise.

By means of the changes referred to previously, the word *Magan* began to take on a wide geographical meaning in the first millennium BC such as to encompass all of the South Arabian districts from the Bab El Mandab Strait to the Strait of Hormuz. The region was similar in many of its natural features, climate, rains, plant and animal life. It was also the land of perfumes, incense, copper, gold and precious stones. And so the Assyrians were astonished to find the merchandise which they had intended to come by by means of voyages in the Arabian Gulf arriving from the south of El-Sham (Syria) and Egypt. Here we should take note of the route taken by voyages on the Nile and which were completed by means of the Red Sea in the direction of the Land of Perfume

(*Punt* to the Egyptians) and which is said to have been in the south of the Arabian peninsula. It is worth noting here that many of the cities of Palestine and the Lebanese coast, especially Gaza, were considered to be Egyptian as far as the Assyrians were concerned. So perhaps the Assyrians did not limit the meaning of Egypt to the land of the Nile Valley alone, but counted among the lands of Egypt parts of southern Syria and Palestine. And Magan was south of these. All of these routes were tributaries of the Incense Trade Route which ran from the south of the Arabian peninsula, once called Magan, and later Oman and Yemen respectively[38].

This thesis is opposed by an argument the substance of which is the absence of a mention of Magan in the Greek sources describing the Arabian peninsula and its various districts. Our response is that Greece dealt with the Arabian territories from a foreign perspective. The Greeks did not enter this territory, and consequently they employed their own names and terminology when they wished to make reference to them. Typical of these were the descriptions *Arabia Petraea, Arabia Deserta* and *Arabia Felix*, and there were many other such names. It is worth noting here that Herodotus named the Red Sea the *Arabian Sea* and the Arabian Gulf the *Red Sea*[39].

At all events the centres of civilization, with their various political and military structures and interrelationships, along with the principal commodities traded, the routes of communication and means of transport employed, all did (and still do) play a role in establishing the principal axes of world trade and creating the basis of diverse relations including cultural relations.

Oman, in particular, and the south of the Arabian peninsula generally benefited from the fact that when demand for copper declined a substitute commodity was found in perfumes and aromatics; and when the sea routes in the Arabian Gulf were discovered, the caravan routes became active in order to open up a new horizon of communications including communication with the Mesopotamia. Then when the importance of the caravan routes faded with the emergence of sea routes in the Red Sea and Arabian Sea, the southern region of the Arabian peninsula rose again, and its cities and ports returned to prominence, and thus it remains to this day.

The activities of the indigenous Omani in antiquity were not confined to mining, trade and seafaring. Agriculture was also one of his busy livelihoods. For strong nations throughout history always grounded their strength in a thriving and diverse economy, of which agriculture, and this is especially true of the economies of the past, occupied a prominent position.

Despite the fact that we do not yet have complete information about the early activities of settled Oman, nevertheless the picture of an advanced agricultural economy together with what we have demonstrated of a flourishing trade, combine to give a broad but clear sketch of the country in early times.The advanced nature of agriculture in early Oman is confirmed in the light of two important pieces of evidence: the first, and this we understand from some of the cuneiform texts, was that agricultural goods were imported from Magan (Oman). Onions, as well as *ghadhab* (or whale hides) and timbers, were counted among the agricultural products for which Oman's external trade with Iraq was famous[40].

The second piece of evidence is embodied in the remains of scores of miles of ancient irrigation canals scattered throughout the districts of Oman, known locally as *aflaj*. In consideration of the importance of the *aflaj* from the historical point of view as well as in the technical mastery which they display and the information they convey to us of relationships with other Arab centres of culture, they deserve some detailed attention.

View of a falaj *at Barkat Al-Mawz.*

Aflaj and Water Springs

Although water is fundamental to the life of the human race, it is not sufficient in itself as a factor for the civilization of mankind until man has applied his intelligence and best endeavours to harness it. Water can make for a full storehouse or a famine; it can transform the progress of man and it can be a vehicle in the advance of a civilization. This holds true in the territories where water is plentiful such as the Valley of the Tigris and Euphrates (Mesopotamia), and the Nile Valley and again in lands where water is a scarce resource, such as Oman. We note the diverse methods and means on which the people of these different countries rely to manage and utilize water.

In the Yemen, Hadramaut and Oman mountain barriers collect the rainwaters of the monsoon winds which blow in upon them from the direction of the Indian Ocean. These rains water a vast area or are carried in the form of floodwaters along flood gorges between the mountains to various places beyond. Or they may soak down into the ground where a rocky layer will store the water, raising the level of the ground water, or emerging in the form of springs and waterspouts which gush forth here and there until life and civilization grow up and revolve around them. Because of the flourishing agriculture and the density of plant life in the southern parts of the Arabian peninsula, the Classical writers named it *Arabia Felix*.

In any event, textual sources give us many references to the progressive role of Arabs in the science of irrigation. The results of archaeological expeditions and excavations in various parts of the Arabian peninsula and the Arabian Gulf all concur insofar as they speak of advanced scientific levels of competence, of skills beyond imagination and unrivalled expertise in the handling of water from a variety of sources and in placing it at the service of the Arab civilization of the past[41]. *Falaj* is an Arabic word meaning a stream, or it is said a small stream or running water from a spring or rivulet. The *falaj* is the rivulet of cultivation, its plural is *aflaj*[42].

A basic principle of this novel system of irrigation is the seepage of ground water by means of underground canals constructed at an incline which differs from the incline of the ground water surface rock layer. The canals surface at ground level close by the agricultural settlements and cities which they serve for distribution. The *aflaj* system is not inconsistent with what linguists would call a canal and is essentially a pipeline of clear water running underground, a definition which equally fits the description of a *kadhama* or a *nafaq* or an *ardab*[43]. *Aflaj* are constructed in different ways. The canal is concealed beneath the ground surface right up to its egress point where it is required for human consumption. It appears and then disappears again. Sometimes the *aflaj* owners will carve out races at certain

points along the canal in order to use them in working stone mills[44].

Oman's *aflaj* networks are most common in the vicinity of the mountain range known as the Jebel Al-Akhdar, in the eastern area and the interior and on the Batinah Plains which slope towards the Gulf of Oman and the Arabian Sea; and again on the Dhahira Plains which run along the edge of the Rub'al-Khali; and in the environs of Sohar on the Gulf of Oman; as well as Buraimi, Ibri and other districts of Dhahira[45].

The traditional system of irrigation by means of aflaj *in the Jebel Al-Akhdar.*

Early Arab engineers were celebrated for their skills in irrigation and were known as *qanaqin*[46]. In more recent times Omani tribes have gained a superior reputation in the excavation and maintenance of *aflaj*[47]. While the technical skills employed in constructing these *aflaj*, and the fact that Oman was dependent on them for its sole source of supply of irrigation water to large and vital areas of cultivation, point to their great age, the *aflaj* which have been uncovered nevertheless offer inadequate archaeological information to surmise how long these projects took to construct. Equally we lack certain vital historical information necessary to establish the age of these *aflaj*.

Falaj Darus

Herodotus relates that the land of Arabia had a great river called Kours which flowed into the Red Sea, adding that the Arab kings were accustomed to lay pipelines made from bull's hide or other animal skins to deliver water from the river to parts of the desert where they would feed wells. And he said that these wells were at a distance of 12 days' journey[48]. In an Arabic narrative about Al-Qazzouini, a reliable source in the district of Ahqaf in the south-western part of Oman is quoted as saying that the king delivered there an underground stream to a distance of 40 *parasang*. It emerged at the town and from this stream rivulets ran along the pathways and streets and he ordered that the path of the stream and its rivulets be painted and they were painted with gold[49].

Ibn Al-Mujawar speaks of the existence of many wells in Aden, among which was the Well of Saffron, the waters of which, he says, were delivered to the farthest reaches of Yemen[50]. These historical narratives clearly intimate that the *aflaj* system originated with the Arabs and that its origins go back into the recesses of time, at the very least to the fifth century BC, this being the century in which Herodotus lived and wrote. To this we can add that Danish archaeologists discovered, south of the town of Awali in Bahrain, a chain of circular stone edifices resembling chimney vents showing slightly above the ground. On closer examination the Danish scholars confirmed that the vents led to a stretch of canal excavated in stone at a depth of 20 feet below ground level to carry water from spring sources in the central hills of Bahrain on a course below ground level towards the cultivations of the low coastal area to the west of the island[51]. This was an early prototype of the *falaj*, a means of transferring abundant waters from one site to another which had need of them. And though no archaeological evidence has been found to date these canals, the fame throughout history of Bahrain and the coastal regions facing it at Al-Ihsaa and Al-Quteif in matters of agriculture and irrigation, lead us to infer a great age in speaking of these irrigation projects. The only historical pointer offered to date on the subject of underground canals - or *aflaj* - has come to us from a canal built by the Assyrian King Senharib (Sennacherib) (704-681 BC) at Erbil in the north of Iraq[52].

Erbil, home of Senharib's irrigation project, resembles in some of its natural features the district of Dhahira or Batinah in Oman, in particular the chain of mountains and broad valleys which encircle it, and insofar as the mountains on both places receive abundant rainfall. Erbil was one of the most prominent centres of early Iraq, famed far and wide for its system of irrigation canals, known locally as *kahariz*. One of the authorities working in this district on the development of agriculture and irrigation counted around 365 canals or *kahariz* in a survey. In most of these water had stopped flowing as a consequence of neglect and the accumulation of soil and dirt in the canal basin, but 60 of them were still in satisfactory operation at the time that the survey was carried out[53].

Senharib's canal was the early prototype for these canals in Erbil, carrying water from the mountains to the city of Erbil. We can say today that the system of irrigation by means of underground canals, *kahariz* or *aflaj* gives us a picture of cultural interaction and exchange of expertise and practice between Iraq and the Arab Gulf.

Perhaps the continuing work of excavation in Oman and its neighbours on the Arabian Gulf will find evidence to gauge the antiquity of this highly evolved irrigation system. Insofar as Oman and the districts of the Arabian peninsula and the Arabian Gulf are so dependent on sophisticated irrigation methods because of their hot dry climate and absence of rivers, such information is of crucial interest to them. It is no coincidence that the Omanis refer to their *aflaj* as *Daoudiat* when they trace their ancestry to Suleiman bin Daoud (Solomon son of David)[54]. In this is a clear inference of the great age of the *aflaj* which must be linked to the oldest signs of cultivation in Oman.

Omani Society in Antiquity

The Omanis and their Trade with Mesopotamia in Antiquity

We still have much to learn about the circumstances in which early human settlements in Oman came to be formed, however, we do know that the progress made by archaeological inquiry into the ancient history and civilization of the Arabian Gulf region in recent decades has led to the discovery of the roots of an ancient Arab civilization in Oman and parts of the Gulf which had strong ties with Mesopotamia and the Arab East as well as with the Indian seaboard. It is only rational to suggest that it would not have been possible for Oman to maintain the economic exchange at agricultural, artisan and commercial levels that it did, as well as its broad interaction over land and sea with sophisticated urban societies contemporary with it without itself being possessed of a socio-political framework and having some form of state structure. There are many pointers from which we can infer that Oman enjoyed a significant relationship with Sumer, Akkad, Babylon and Assyria, and that its ports and its merchant trade were the subject of interest of the great powers who took control of the facilities of the Arab Orient from the Persian Era (the Achmaenids) up to the Islamic Age.

If we pass to the dawn of antiquity when the earliest states were founded in the Tigris Valley, in Egypt and in Syria (the third millennium) Magan was one of the more powerful mercantile economies contemporary with these. Sargon and later his grandson Naram-Sin[55] were careful to protect the well-established and regulated trading relations that existed with Magan to ensure a continuity of supply of the necessities of life. The most important of these was copper from which weapons were wrought as well as domestic implements, vessels and ornaments. There were anchorages for ships at Magan, as there were at Akkad, which could receive ships bearing heavy loads bound for long voyages.

This society, which conducted a far-reaching sea trade providing the known world with a crucial primary resource, exercised its best efforts in the activities of mining and ship-building and the systematic promotion of trading relations with other countries.

It was inevitable that the economic interests of the various states would collide from time to time, leading to confrontation and war. Naram-Sin drew attention to this in a text in which he describes a war he precipitated against Manu (Manium) Danu, the Lord of Magan. Trade relations between the Mesopotamian states and Magan were not long in resuming after this interruption, however, and merchandise was once again carried from Magan on boats loaded with copper, gold ingots and precious stones, as well as varieties

Oman and its trading contacts in past ages.

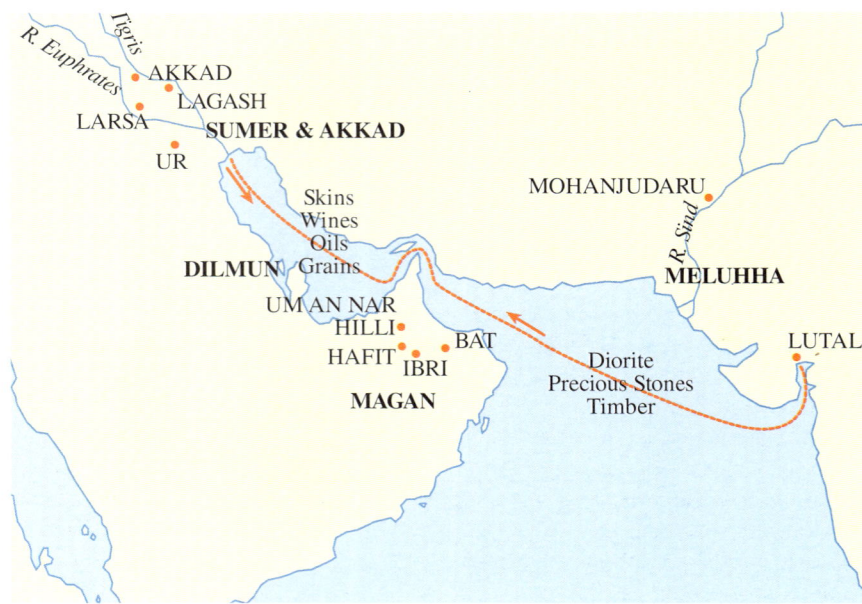

of cane, wooden divans and various panelwoods, dates and perfumed oils bound for the cities of Ur, Lagash and Larsa.

The Lagash ruler, Gudea, procured from Magan and Meluhha, i.e. the Sind Valley, gold and copper, diorite, coral, perfumed essences and ebony wood with which to build the Temple of Nanjersu[56]. Lagash was unable to maintain its dominion of the Gulf sea trade after the rise of the Third Dynasty of Ur and it is most probable that a bloody war broke out between the Mesopotamian states with the purpose of wresting control of the sea trade with Magan from the princes of Lagash[57].

Archival texts from Larsa which date to the Third Dynasty give us some more detail on the position of Magan in world trade in the context of its relations with the Mesopotamian states and in particular with Ur[58]. One of a group of dispatches addressed to Aya Naser, a prominent merchant mariner from Ur and procurement agent for copper from Dilmun (Dispatches UET 22, 29, 71, 81) recounts how copper was imported from Magan by way of Dilmun. These documents infer that large quantities were involved. Text UET v 796, for instance, describes a quantity of 13,000 mina of copper using the measurements current at Dilmun. The *thiql* or *mithqal* was generally speaking 8 gms and the mina 6 x 8. Copper was transported in the form of ingots of gutareum, each weighing 4 *waznat* or *talents* (UET 678).

Another text relates how an individual named Luan Lila in the second year of the reign of Abi Sin, last of the Third Dynasty kings of Ur (UET 1511), obtained quantities of wool, precious garments, oils and leather goods by means of which to purchase a quantity of copper arriving by boat from Magan. Luan Lila was a merchant of note in his time who traded directly with Magan.

A third text from the fourth year of the reign of Abi Sin records that the same merchant obtained quantities of clothes and wool from stores in the temple of Nana for the price of a quantity of copper imported from Magan.

Dr Oppenheim observes that copper was not the only material imported from Magan: other commodities were precious stones, ivory and onions, these latter much celebrated at the time as the 'onions of Magan' as were the 'onions of Dilmun' in the time of Sargon. Oppenheim describes the growth of new trading practices in which the state organized military style trading expeditions which characterized for instance the time of Sargon. These were replaced by great trading houses which oversaw the trade in raw materials. Merchants would accompany their merchant ships - and this practice was common to both the Third Dynasty of Ur and the Larsa Dynasty - to Dilmun, and thence to Magan, where they would attend in person the delivery of the goods they brought with them from Ur, and take delivery of the goods which were being purchased for the return voyage.

Since there are no known written records about Magan it is difficult to state much about the structure of the merchant trade or its manner of dealing with its trading partners. Records from Mesopotamia however show us clearly the importance wielded by Greater Magan in the economic system of the ancient East and the Arabian peninsula throughout the Third Dynasty of Ur[59].This no more than confirms the previous testimony of others - it was a geographical-economic-political unit known from the third millennium (UET 1193) which continued to exist in one shape or another as the circumstances of state dictated.

The fall of the Third Dynasty of Ur brought a change of fortune to direct trading relations with Magan. Dilmun moved closer to the Mesopotamian states in the role of intermediary between these states and the Orient. Evidence of the existence of direct trade is lacking after this point, for the internal affairs of Sumer and Akkad and Babylon were inclined to be reflected in their external trading practices. After the fate of Larsa and when Babylon had risen to dominion over Mesopotamia, there was a major shift of focus towards the Westland (the Amurru) and North and trade with Magan went into a long period of stagnation.

Active trading relations, after this long suspension, were resumed under the Assyrians according to a text[60] dating to the time of King Senharib (Sennacherib) (704 - 681 BC). Once again the merchandise in which Magan specialized was loaded and dispatched to the ports of Mesopotamia, passing through Dilmun. This merchandise included bronze implements - spades and trowels and spear tips and the like - as well as spices, essences and timber procured from the Orient by way of Magan and Dilmun.

It would appear that the impediments to contact with the Orient did not begin to fade for a thousand years. We have very little exact information concerning what transpired during this long interval in the way of human migrations in the region, of changing affairs of state and the repercussions of these on Magan (Oman).

We do find further testimony to the continuation of relations between Assyria and the Gulf countries up to the end of the Assyrian Age (seventh century BC). An inscription dating to the time of Assyria and Babylon at the Temple of Ishtar in Nineveh speaks of Khondaru King of Dilmun and next to it Ramit Bat King of the Land of Kubi (Jubi). This was most likely Jubin, which was renowned in the time of Gudea as being close by Dilmun and Magan and Meluhha, the source of stone and timber[61]. In the sixth century BC after they had conquered and added all of the Near Eastern countries to their Empire, the Achmaenids inherited the ancient trading routes in the Gulf and opened up the area to a revival of exchange between India and the Mediterranean Basin, and this exchange was to continue without hindrance right up to the Macedonian conquest. If in this discussion of the emergence of Omani society and its progress through ancient history we have so far alluded to Assyrian and Babylonian texts, there are other texts even older than these which have mentioned Oman, describing the enterprise of its citizens and their longstanding relations with Mesopotamia. We refer of course to the cuneiform inscriptions.

Oman in the Light of Cuneiform and Other Ancient Texts

One historical reality which cannot be contradicted concerns the merchant trade which existed between Oman and the cities of the Arabian Gulf before the southern provinces of Iraq had been constituted (in around 5000 BC) into an organized state. The information available to us states incontrovertibly that the ships arriving at Iraq's ancient ports were not of Iraqi origin but belonged to Meluhha, Magan and Dilmun. This historical fact alone confirms that these cities engaged in merchant commerce and that they owned sailing ships with which to obtain the commodities and raw materials necessary to their existence. And when the Iraqi provinces were brought under a single administration and farming villages began gradually to transform into towns, the demand for stone, timber, copper and precious stones rose, and once again the ships resumed their voyages to Meluhha, Magan, Jubin and Dilmun and arrived bearing merchandise to market in the cities of Iraq. Iraq's southern provinces had no timber of any kind and so lacked the principal raw material required for ship-building. Thus when southern Iraq first began to emerge as a state it did not have the fundamentals required to build a merchant fleet except by first importing timber in foreign-owned ships.

All of the Iraqi kings who speak of Iraq's trade with the cities of the Arabian Gulf observe that they had ships from Meluhha and Magan and Dilmun anchored in their city ports[62]. This is clear recognition by the kings that dominion over the trade routes in the Arabian Gulf was not theirs but belonged to the three abovementioned cities. The other point which confirms that Iraq's trading ships were not involved in the Arabian Gulf trade for a relatively long time after the cities had begun to trade is the Sumerian word for trade, *dam jar*. Sumerian scholars assert that this is a derivation from the word *tamkarum* (from the peninsula), a further indication that the inhabitants of Meluhha, Magan and Dilmun were trading before the Sumerians. Before placing material evidence in support of the above points, it might be helpful to present some information about the Omani cities which enjoyed this long stretch of trading relations with the cities of Iraq and of the Arabian Gulf.

Meluhha
The name Meluhha in the cuneiform inscriptions is a compound of the syllable *mie* meaning 'many' or 'abundance', this being the device used to indicate the plural, followed by *luh*, meaning 'pure' or 'clear' and finally *ha*, a conjunction.

Thus the meaning of the word *meluhha* would be 'materials of great purity,' a theme in harmony to a great degree with the type of merchandise which the citizens of Mesopotamia obtained from the city of Meluhha. Sargon, the Akkadian king, tells us that teak and marble were imported from Meluhha[63]. Again Prince Gudea, (2144-2124 BC) the second ruler of Lagash, who ruled from 2164-2109 BC, recorded that he imported precious stones from the above city, including carnelian and lapis lazuli, as well as copper, zinc and gold[64]. If we contemplate these materials we find that they are all characterized by their clarity and purity because they are constituted from precious material. In this way did the city come to be entitled Meluhha. The cuneiform method of writing did not proceed by the same principles that we use in writing today. Rather it selected an image appropriate to the characteristics of the city in question. The ancient Iraqis used this procedure in arriving at the inscription for Meluhha which had the meaning of 'materials of great purity'. This constitutes the direct reason why the citizens of Mesopotamia came to name the faraway places from which they imported exotic commodities, in particular gold and precious stones, 'Meluhha'. Evidence in support of this is the first appearance of this name around the middle of the second millennium BC in relation to Ethiopia, for the Iraqis of this time were accustomed to import gold and precious stones from this place.

Furthermore, if we look to the cuneiform texts and to the succession of trading cities alluded to in the inscriptions, we find that the furthest trading station with which early Iraq maintained a commercial exchange was Meluhha. Through the commodities and materials which the citizens of Mesopotamia imported from Meluhha by way of a chain of other trading posts we can infer that its location was represented by the south-eastern sector of Oman, i.e. Ras Al-Hadd. There are of course many scholars who hold the view that Meluhha was on the other side of the Arabian Gulf, that is to say to the west of India where the Indus civilization came into being. And though we are certain that the site of this city was Ras Al-Hadd, these other scholars are right insofar as the early Iraqis were accustomed to lend the name Meluhha to any distant place from which they imported gold[65].

In support of this notion we have cuneiform texts, which commence from around the middle of the second millennium BC or earlier, applying the name Meluhha to the district of Ethiopia on the African continent, and it was around this time that the inhabitants of Mesopotamia and in particular the Assyrians began to trade with Ethiopia and this country is as we know a very great distance from Mesopotamia.

An example during the Arab Islamic Era comparable to the flowering of Meluhha was the rise to prominence of the islands which the Arabs knew as Waq Waq. Information available to us identifies these islands with Japan. Nevertheless we find the same name applied liberally in other Arabic sources to various far distant places. Nevertheless, irrespective of how many other places come to light bearing the name Meluhha this will not influence one way or the other the categorical fact that the early name for Ras Al-Hadd was Meluhha.

Because it was the pattern of early Iraq to import lapis lazuli from Meluhha and because we know for a certainty that the lapis lazuli used by the Mesopotamians was from mines which were and still are in Afghanistan, we

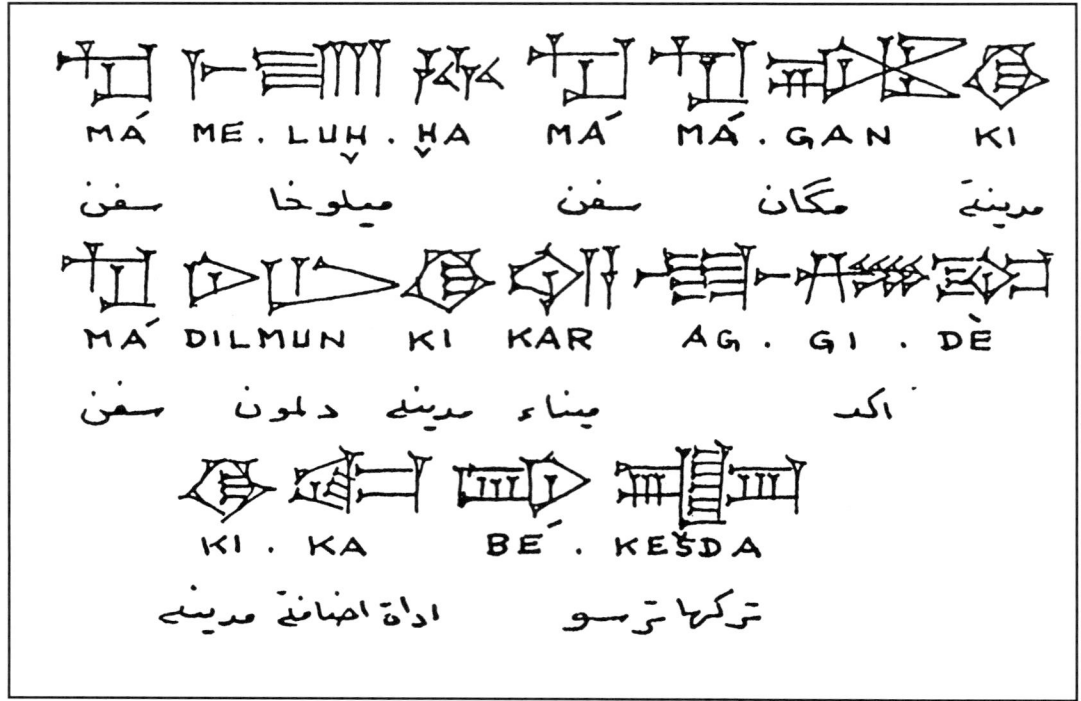

The text is by the Akkadian king Sargon. It translates: He allowed ships from Meluhha, the city of Magan and the city of Dilmun to anchor at the city of Akkad.

can infer that the merchants of Meluhha were the sole intermediaries in supplying the merchants of Iraq with this precious Afghan stone, because the cuneiform inscriptions all insist that the Iraqis of the time imported lapis lazuli only from the city of Meluhha.

Proof that lapis did come from Afghanistan is found in the stone's Sumerian name, pronounced *zard jin*[66]. This Sumerian name means, in the language of ancient Afghanistan, 'like gold', and this makes sense if we know that some of the forms of this stone have a yellow streak which looks remarkably like gold. The Afghan name is both a reference to the rarity of the stone and also to the gold-like streaks.

Before closing this tale of Meluhha it might befit us briefly to refer to the cuneiform text which was called 'the Elegy of the City of Akkad'. The people of this city were known as owners of the black lands and it is probable that this description is a reference to the fertility of the soil or to the abundance of trees in its environs, for the southern part of Iraq was known as the black land in consequence of its profusion of date palms.

Magan

Historians of early Iraq and specialists in the study of cuneiform texts are all in agreement that the modern name for the ancient city of Magan is Oman and indeed the city of Magan (Oman) closely resembles the Ru'us al-Jebel peninsula[67].

The Mesopotamians were particularly partial to the diorite which they procured from Magan. Monuments carved from this stone and still extant are material proof to add to the evidence of the cuneiform texts that Omani ships supplied diorite at the behest of Iraqi merchants from the time of Sargon of Akkad (2340-2284 BC). The early Iraqis' fondness for the stone was shared by the Lagash Prince Gudea (2144-2124 BC) who mentions it in inscriptions as being 'superior to any other known mineral, even to gold itself'[68].

This stone was used in ancient Iraq in the manufacture of cylindrical seals and weights specifically because of its extreme hardness and durability as well as its rarity in Iraq and the difficulty ordinary people had of coming by it, thereby frustrating would-be swindlers of weights and counterfeiters of cylindrical seals.

As well as diorite the early Iraqis imported a variety of timbers which were acquired by the merchants of the said city from India. The inscriptions which speak of Magan show us that this city was famed for building merchant ships, for its name was expressed by the two signs *ma* meaning ship and *gan* meaning skeleton or chassis, giving us 'ship's chassis', and confirming the city's shipbuilding reputation. Indeed the fame of Oman's shipwrights continued into modern times and their skills were celebrated throughout the Abbassid period - witness the embarkation of Sindbad on his voyages from this place - and up to the start of the nineteenth century.

We can now build on these facts to assert that it was Magan which supplied Dilmun (Bahrain) and other trading posts along the Arabian Gulf seaboard with ships throughout antiquity.

Jubin

The Lagash ruler Gudea left inscriptions in which reference to Jubin followed immediately the mention of Meluhha and Magan. He observed that it was the

Jebel Al-Akhdar.

home of the *khaloub* or oak tree, and oak was one of the timbers imported from Magan. Scholars of the cuneiform inscriptions place Jubin in the region of the Jebel Al-Akhdar, for this was the only region in the south of the Arabian peninsula possessed of trees which Iraq required in constructing its civilization[69]. In the knowledge that this name did not appear in the cuneiform sources prior to the reign of Prince Gudea (2144-2124 BC), it is probably safe to surmise that this trading city was constituted and began to engage in trade in the last quarter of the third millennium BC. Prior to this historical record Magan was exporting timber.

Dilmun

There is no difference of opinion as to Dilmun being the present-day island of Bahrain. Dilmun was a trading post linking the cities previously mentioned with the cities of Iraq. Proof of this is found in the fact that King Ur-Nanshi, (c. 2520-2490 BC), founder of the First Dynasty of Lagash Kings (c. 2520-2355 BC), noted that Dilmun ships would bring merchandise from foreign lands to disembark at the ports of Lagash[70]. This reference, along with the other references to Dilmun, confirm that it was strictly a trading port and not a source country for the goods in which it traded. This fact about Dilmun confirms for us that the mercantile trade in times of antiquity was confined to Iraq and Oman. Iraq exported grain, oils, fermented drinks and skins to the cities of the Gulf and imported the merchandise mentioned above from the ports of Oman.

References to Magan and Meluhha in the Cuneiform Texts

From the study of Sumerian cuneiform texts from the first half of the third millennium BC it becomes clear to us that Iraq was importing Omani goods, not directly from Magan, but rather indirectly on board ships from Dilmun.

This we know from two inscriptions bequeathed to us by the previously mentioned King Ur-Nanshi of Lagash[71] and it shows us that the petty Sumerian states were commissioning Dilmun ships with a view to gaining access to its merchandise. Dilmun was after all much closer to Iraq than Magan or Meluhha. This situation was to change when Sargon came to power and ships from Magan and Meluhha once again docked at Iraqi ports.

Proof of this reference is contained in a later passage of the king's text: 'The ships of Meluhha and the ships of Magan and the ships of Dilmun cast anchor in the port of the city of Akkad'. This is a clear indication that King Sargon of Akkad (3340-2284 BC) broadened the scope of Iraq's commercial exchange with the Arabian Gulf cities as well as embarking on a policy of direct trade with Meluhha and Magan.

It looks as though the Akkadians by one means or another were enabled to put in place firm relations with Magan such that it was to become in the nature of a province of Akkad. This we learn from an inscription given to us by King Naram-Sin, grandson of Sargon, when he says that all the provinces of the Akkadian Empire rose against him at the time of his accession to the throne and this included the revolt of Magan[72]. Naram-Sin (2260-2223 BC), his inscriptions tell us, was obliged to gather together a military expedition force and set out for Magan to put down the insurrection. When he had achieved his purpose he took captive its ruler Manu Danu, whose name in Akkadian means 'he who is powerful like him'. On his return to his capital (Akkad) he took with him a quantity of diorite from which he had carved a statue of himself and this statue was unearthed in the city of Susa, the Elamite capital.

As well as the diorite stone from which Naram-Sin had carved the statue of himself, a calcite vessel was found and the inscription on this vessel states how the vessel had come from the spoils captured by King Naram-Sin in the city of Magan (Oman).

The means by which these relics which had been seized by Naram-Sin in Magan came to be found in the city of Susa, the Elamite capital, arose out of the conquest by the Elamite King Shtrok-Nakhuntu in the year 1171 BC of a number of Iraq's pre-eminent cities. In a series of lightening strikes these cities were sacked and the precious objects found in Susa were amongst the king's spoils[73].

Information left to us by King Naram-Sin tells us that in his lifetime this king restricted his trading partnership to Magan alone, and none of his texts make mention of any other Gulf city. In all probability this was because of his having occupied the Magan city-state and a treaty having being concluded as a consequence between Magan and the Akkadian State, sealed on the basis that Iraq would import from no other source than Magan.

It would appear that this commercial relationship persisted up to the collapse of the Akkadian Empire. The writings of the Second Lagash Dynasty (2164-2109 BC), whose kings ruled Iraq during the period of the Kuti occupation of parts of Iraq, confirm that the kings of this dynasty traded with Meluhha, Magan, Jubin and Dilmun. The collapse of this dynasty however and the accession of the Third Dynasty of Ur to power in a united Iraq caused the trading relationship to be resumed to its past level with Magan. King Ur-Nammu (2111-2094) BC, founding king of the Third Dynasty of Ur (2111-2003 BC) and law-maker, whose canon is the earliest we have on record, remarks in his introduction to this canon that he has brought back the ships of Magan to anchor at the port of Ur[74].

During this long stretch of history in Mesopotamia, trade peaked between the Mesopotamian and the Arab Gulf region, i.e. the districts of Dilmun and Magan, to the extent that many merchants from these districts took up their abode in Sumeria itself while in turn many Sumerian merchants set up residence in Dilmun and Magan[75].

Another Sumerian text going back to King Ibi Sin (2082-2004 BC), last king of the Third Dynasty of Ur, remarks that cargo has arrived at Ur, and specifically for the Temple of Nina, from a number of trading ports around the Arabian Gulf. The text also relates how the city of Ur had sent by way of a sea transit of the Gulf to Oman (Magan) sesame oil and wool in exchange for the copper of Magan[76].

First Dynasty Babylonian texts make no reference to trade between Oman (Magan) and this dynasty held power from the start of the nineteenth century up to the sixteenth century BC.

In the age which followed the First Babylonian Dynasty i.e. the Kassite Era, it looks as though trade was restored to its previous level if we are to go by the

Annals of some of the Kassite kings of the districts neighbouring Dilmun. This would not be unnatural since relations had been resumed with Magan/Oman.

During the Middle Assyrian Age, in particular the reign of King Tawakalti Naturta the First (1244-1208 BC), we have a text attributed to this king who is mentioned in the capacity of King of Dilmun and Miloukha[77].

It is likely that the district of Dilmun at the time of the Assyrian Empire took in all of the territory on the western coast of the Arabian Gulf including Oman, so that many of the remains and artefacts discovered in Oman, such as pottery, metal objects and stone vessels as noted above show a direct connection with those found in the Assyrian capitals.

The Chaldean Dynasty which lasted from 632-539 BC had trading relations with the districts situated to the north of Babylon and extending as far as the Mediterranean coast. In consequence, trade between Babylon and Oman in particular and the other trading posts in the Arabian Gulf generally, was restricted and no further reference is made to Oman for the rest of this era[78].

Following the Macedonian conquest of Mesopotamia Alexander sought to found an empire vast in extent whose capital would be Babylon. His dream was not to be realized however, for he died in Babylon in the year 323 BC and his dream of empire died with him.

Mesopotamia and its neighbouring areas, after the death of Alexander, were ruled by the Seleucids who founded their dynastic rule by taking Babylon for their capital, only to build another capital which they called Seleucia and sited on both banks of the Tigris about 30 kms south-west of Baghdad.

Once again under the Seleucids trade was revived with Magan and many settlements dating to this time have been found in Oman. At this time also several Greek voyagers and geographers travelled to Oman and wrote about what they had experienced[79].

Some archaeologists and scholars of ancient texts have sought to establish that Oman is unrelated to the Magan of the Sumerian, Akkadian and Babylonian inscriptions insofar as they believe the location of Magan to be either in the far south-west of the Iranian Plateau[80] or on the Indian sub-continent[81]. These endeavours are destined to failure however, for if we look at the continuity of trade between Mesopotamia and Oman from earliest recorded history (that is the Early Sumerian Era) and up to the Islamic Era, in particular when Baghdad was at the peak of its greatness, we note that the trading practices and trade routes used by these merchants did not alter. As this situation flourished so did Oman become the centre of contact between the Mediterranean Sea on the one hand and the Arabian Gulf, Arabian Sea and the Indian Ocean on the other; and in timewitness to the flowering and passing of many civilizations. Its influence in linking the coastal states of the Indian Ocean and the *Bahr Al-Zinj* (off the East African coast) and the China Sea gained new significance when with the rise of Islam and Oman's conversion to the new faith, it set about binding these disparate regions, through its far-flung trade and mercantile explorations, with ties of the emerging civilization of Islam. For its seafaring trade never once abated throughout the ages. Certainly this will provide us with a useful defence in our discourse about Oman and its activities in these domains during the Islamic period. Let us then direct our attention to Oman in the Age of Islam.

Images from Omani Society in Antiquity[82]

Before we take a look at the external characteristics of Omani civilization in the Islamic Age and later periods, it would befit us to take a brief look at the shape of this society at the time of earliest recorded history and pre-history insofar as we have information, artefacts and intelligence accumulated from various excavation works undertaken by archaeologists in Oman. Certainly we can in the future expect more knowledge to come to light of Omani civilization in this bygone age as the excavations so assiduously pursued by Oman progress and as the area of exploration is gradually extended.

It would be useful here to refer to the fact that excavations have found the remains of human settlements in Oman going back to pre-historic times, and even to the Stone Age. So we had better briefly examine these remains and through them perhaps glimpse something of this ancient civilization in historic and pre-historic times.

Oman in the Stone Age

Wattia in the district of Muscat is the oldest human settlement and dates to the Stone Age in the east of the Arabian peninsula, making it thus in the region of 10,000 years old. Archaeological remains of different dates were discovered here, the earliest representing the Stone Age and then the Heliocene Age, interrupted by the transition period of decline, and finally the Bronze Age. Findings consisted of stone implements, animal bones and potsherds, shells and fire hearths. These latter were dated to 7615 BC and are the oldest signs of human settlement in the area.

An early tomb in Samad.

Among other discoveries were sherds of hand-moulded pottery, which bore the distinguishing marks of the Sultanate's pre-Bronze Age pottery. Also found were a number of heavy flint implements made from slivers of quartz as well as sharp and pointed tools and scrapers.

On a mountain rockface in the Wattia district animal drawings were discovered in which animals were represented along with humans in the guise of hunters. Similar drawings were found in the Wadi Sahtan and Wadi Bani Khorous in Rustaq. These drawings consist of human figures carrying spears, lances and arrows and confronted by wild animals. Other drawings show tame animals such as camels and bulls mounted by humans.

Siwan in Haima is another Stone Age location in Oman and flint implements found there include arrowheads, knives, chisels and circular stones which were used for throwing at wild animals. This site was given an age of 200,000 years.

Oman in the Fourth Millennium BC

The hunting culture of early Oman, as represented at separate sites in Ras Al-Hamra in the north west of Muscat, is a good indication that this region had already been settled by man in the fourth millennium BC. Eleven sites were enclosed altogether, all of them sharing common features. The most important site was at Ras Hamra (No. 5).

This site consists of settlements heaped one above the other. The layer representing the dwellings is composed of sand, shells and fishbones, ash and coal. An interesting feature of this settlement is that it was found to be entirely devoid of pottery remains.

Other archaeological testimony found at this site came in the form of a symmetrically shaped pit such as might be used for the disposal of waste matter, as well as fire hearths, flint tools, including hammers, knives, chisels, snare weights made from rock crystal and hunting hooks fashioned from copper and seashells. The organic remains pointed to the principal activity of this colony having been the hunting of fish and turtle, for these composed the staple diet of the settlers of this period.

Of the plant life represented at this site there was evidence that the lotus tree was widespread; swamps of mangrove were indicated also and sorghum and mulberry seeds found. The inhabitants of this time built their homes from branches and reeds. The dwellings were circular in plan with a central excavation.

A burial ground was unearthed at this site which contained 220 burials in which the skeletons were lying on one side in a foetal position facing the sea (the source of their subsistence), their arms folded upwards and back. In some cases the hand was folded firmly and carefully over an oyster and in one case this was replaced by a pearl.

This pearl would be one of the oldest examples of a pearl found in the Gulf, dating as it does to the fourth millennium BC. In many cases the skeleton was adorned with jewellery made from shells, including rings and bracelets, along with necklets made from stone beads with shell pendants shaped like leaves.

Oman in the Third Millennium BC

The third millennium BC is represented in many locations throughout the Sultanate, including Bat, Ras Al-Hadd and Samad Al-Shan.

Bat is east of the province of Ibri and revealed a burial site located at a distance of 1-2 kms north of the village. The site contained 100 burials and the constructions were of stone.

A circular edifice constructed from blocks of a local stone and incorporating two walled enclosures, one inside the other, constituted the burial structure. Stone joists supported the roof and a small narrow entrance passage gave access to the interior. The smooth black stone used here and for which the tombs of Dhank are renowned place the origins of this site in the third millennium BC.

There were parallels between the tombs in the southern portion of the burial ground and those at Umm Nar in the United Arab Emirates, in the fine quality of the terracotta earthenware found there and in the existence of the interior walled enclosure in the delineation of the burial site, which had the effect of sectioning it into several chambers.

Other archaeological testimony included the vestiges of six square-based stone towers marking out and enclosing rectangular shaped dwellings. It was calculated that the height of one of the six towers was more than ten metres. Carbon dating has placed the origins of this structure in 2750 BC.

Water channels were uncovered at the site which were probably used to deliver water from a remote spot and which would make them thus the earliest

Oman's archaeological sites from different periods.

Clay pot making is still a traditional skill in Oman.

examples of the system of irrigation by means of *aflaj* for which Oman has long been celebrated. The World Heritage Series has assessed Bat as the secondmost site of archaeological importance in Oman, after Bahla.

The second site dating to the third millennium BC is Samad Al-Shan. This site is in the eastern part of Oman in the *Wilaya* of Al-Mudhaibi at a distance of 120 km south of Muscat. Here we have a number of ring-shaped graves huddled together. They are built from large stone blocks and three different types were identified:

- The men's graves contained iron and copper weapons, such as daggers, knives and arrowheads as well as large earthenware jars and shells used as drinking vessels.
- The women's graves had deep stone vessels and earthenware flasks for storing viscous liquids such as essences, and shells containing a green substance used as a cosmetic, together with a variety of shells.
- Dual graves, containing the skeletons of men and women together.

Archaeological study of the earthenware artefacts established the principal distinguishing features of the pottery of Samad Al-Shan and placed its origins in or around 500 BC. The pottery was hand-built from a coarse clay and fired to a moderate temperature. It was coated inside and out and there decorated after one of three principal patterns:

- A fishbone design
- A grid of crossed lines
- Inscriptions from South Arabia.

These date to the period 200-50 BC and were impressed onto the clay vessel before firing. The size and function of these vessels were as follows:

- Large jars for storing water
- Vessels of a whitish colour used for storing grain
- Earthenware flasks for the storage of viscous liquids
- Small dark-coloured bottles which were probably used for burial purposes only

As well as the abovementioned discoveries, recently unearthed was the skeleton of a she-camel. It was well-situated and not isolated from the rest of the burial. A necklet of stone beads around the camel's neck dated the burial to the Iron Age.

In the eastern district of Sur is Ras Al-Hadd on the east coast of Jebel Saffran at a distance of 200 metres from the line of direction to the Indian Ocean, making this site a prime subject for the study of historical communications between Oman and the Indian sub-continent.

Discoveries at this site include an edifice constructed from brick and sub-divided into several elongated chambers. It is thought that these were used for storage. A workshop for carving flintheads was also identified in which were found fragments of red shert, this being a type of flint specifically associated with the pre-historic period. The workshop was used as a production unit for making jewellery from shells, such as rings, beads and pendants.

Site-workers found a variety of pottery, the most important being the pieces dating to the third millennium BC. This is of the Harappan type and so probably belongs to the civilization period of the last of the Mohanjudaru Dynasty in India. Red terracotta earthenware was also present, with dark stripes and illustrations. This is the finest of the pottery which was used in this district facing the Arabian Sea. Other archaeological discoveries here were pieces of burnished pottery of the Sassanid Islamic period and also African ware and Chinese porcelain.

The buildings were distinguished by their unique use of brick. This is the only district where brick was used during the Bronze Age in Oman and its environs, including the south of Iran and Baluchistan and the Sind Valley. From this perhaps we can surmise that the inhabitants of Ras Al-Hadd were - in the third millennium BC - pioneers in the introduction of brick as a construction material, a practice which was to persist for more than 1500 years in the Gulf of Oman.

If we look at the construction of the burial sites at Ras Al-Hadd across time we note that the direction of the entrance passage inclined slightly from the southeasterly direction towards the south and we find that there are more burial chambers. This suggests the repeated use of the site. The most common artefacts found were flint implements - chisels used for boring small beads, hammers, stone snare weights and shell ornaments such as rings, necklets and oyster shells containing antimony (kohl). A variety of beads was also unearthed, made from red carnelian and lapis lazuli, as well as green porcelain vessels, dating to around 1800 BC. There were also enormous quantities of bones, of fish, turtles and sharks.

Oman in the Second Millennium BC

Classified under this period are sites scattered throughout Oman such as the Mikhailif site in Batinah and Al-Waset in the Wadi Al-Jizzi in the district of Batinah in which many vessels made from smooth soapstone have come to light. There were also ornaments characteristic of this period, as well as bronze spearheads and arrowheads and knives.

Oman in the First Millennium BC

The Sohar site is the most important site in Oman representing the first millennium BC. A settlement was unearthed there in which were found constructions above the buildings of the first century AD, showing how the settlement continued to grow and flourish. The artefacts found here show Sohar to have been a significant trading centre at this time. Merchant seals were found and a type of fine terracotta earthenware, probably imported from India. Other forms of pottery were porcelain from China of a type found in abundance in the first century of the Islamic Age, confirming that trade with China was flourishing then. This trade continued to grow up to the fourteenth century AD.

The succession of strata at the site shows the gradual decline of trade and subsequent stagnation of the city after this period as a result of the overlordship of Hormuz passing to Qalhat near the city of Sur, so that trade and its attendant enterprise and tax revenue were relocated there.

The fortification of Sohar was raised by order of one of the princes of Hormuz with the purpose of imposing a trade blockade on the town, until the town was severely reduced and the inhabitants were forced to flee. Information about this period came to us in the form of the scant remains and the poverty of the dwellings. After the Portuguese had been expelled from the region Sohar saw a revival of trade and an increase in its mercantile exchanges with the Far East.

Among other archaeological pointers in Sohar are its square fort supported by four towers at the four corners. The fifth tower is in the centre of the north-west face. The fortress is surrounded by an external wall, and this is the last remnant of the original fort, the central structure having been much altered.

In addition to the prominence that attached to Sohar historically, it had a significant economic asset in its mining industry which was served by, amongst others, two vital natural advantages:

- The Wadi Suq and Wadi Al-Jizzi were both passes through the Oman Mountains.
- Copper sediment is present in abundance along the length of the Wadi Al-Jizzi, where the sedimentary rocks are for the most part both large and heavy. Thirty two copper-smelting sites were identified in this district, the main sites along the Wadi Al-Jizzi being Arja, Al-Bida, Al-Aseel, Al-Seeb, Towi, Abila and Al-Waset.

A view of artefacts discovered at Ubar.

At Arja was evidence of the production of copper at the Zahra settlement dating to the third millennium BC. Copper was smelted at this site on a continuous basis up to the first millennium BC. If we compare the operation at this time with the activity of the Middle Ages, we find that it was confined to the use of one single furnace and production was not high.

In respect of the period before Islam, we have carbon dated evidence from coal found in Arja giving it a pre-Islamic date and it looks as though the heavy ore residue was probably used during the late Sassanid period. The copper was also used during the period of Sassanid control in the Yemen. The early

Islamic Era was the principal copper producing period in this region and this is mirrored by the evidence of development at the site. The settlement and its copper-smelting livelihood however continued to be productive up to the sixth century AH/twelfth century AD and the whole operation was thriving in 800-900 AD. There were several copper production units at Arja, although there is nothing to suggest that they were in use at the same time or continually in the period lasting 150 years. The specific function of each unit was identifiable from the scanty copper remains. These also showed that the smaller units were used for a shorter time.

Among the sites going back to the first millennium BC are those artefacts of Khor Rory (Samharam) dating to the first century BC and the first century AD. This city is marked by fine limestone architecture and is set on the coast at the end of a small rift bay and a few kilometres to the east of the Salalah Plain.

Khor Rory is protected by walled fortifications built with closely and precisely packed stone. Five of these blocks were found bearing inscriptions in the alphabet of South Arabia describing the founding of the town. It had been built with the precise objective of taking control of the incense and olibanum trade and was the centre where these precious commodities were assembled for export to foreign countries. The remains of an ancient temple were unearthed towards the centre of the northern face of the town. Its walls were uncovered,

Ruins of an ancient temple at Samharam.

The ancient city of Samharam is located at Khor Rory.

along with three sacrificial altars. There was a relief carving of a bull on one of the altars, suggesting the deity worshipped at this temple was a lunar one, for the Himyarites worshipped a lunar god represented by a bull. Around the altars were the ashes of sacrifice offered to the deity and these consisted of bones of fish, chickens, larger animals and birds. Also present was a small residue of frankincense.

Other archaeological findings at this site included a small bronze statuette of an Indian girl playing a *nai*, a type of flute. She was incomplete and parts of the statuette were missing. It was dated to the second century AD.

The importance of this statue lies in its presence at the site insofar as it constitutes material evidence of a relationship between India and the Arabian peninsula. A total of 14 bronze coins were found, along with a bronze bell inscribed with the name of the moon deity who was the patron god of the city.

Early Islamic sites included Al-Bleyd (Balid) in south Oman which in olden times was known as Dhofar. It was founded in the tenth century AD (fourth century AH) but was destroyed and rebuilt in 1221 AD, before succumbing to gradual decline during the sixteenth century as the Portuguese expropriated its export trade to India.

The layout of this town was that of a long strip along the sea's edge. It was encircled by a wall which had three gates used for entering the town. The traces of a large mosque were uncovered, and this also was of an elongated rectangular design, pitched on elevated ground and surrounded on every side by galleries. This special gallery is a feature of all the mosques of Dhofar. An open courtyard was noticeably small in comparison with the roofed area. The walls of the *qiblah*, *mihrab* and *minbar* were also identified. The column used to support the ceiling had eight sides as is the case in most of the mosques in Oman today.

From the archaeological evidence we may visualize a prosperous and gracious city enjoying the benefits of a busy centre of trade and industry in the southern region. It was moreover the port from which horses, fish oil and frankincense were dispatched to India in return for cotton and rice. The city was also noted for the weaving of fine cloths from silk and linen and various cottons. It had a trading history with East Africa and Egypt as a result of the revival of the old historical crossings of the Red Sea. Other findings pointing to the existence of trade with Asia were the bronze coins, some dating to the Islamic Era, still others to the Chinese civilization.

Frankincense was above all else the commodity which brought the name of Dhofar in the south of Oman to prominence historically. Dhofar occupied a conspicuous place in the early civilizations as the prime source of this exotic commodity and also of gum. Frankincense was in the forefront of the commodities traded in the dim past, particularly once it had caught the attention of the early historians around 400 BC. First Herodotus, and later Pliny, Ptolemy and finally Strabo and Diodorus gave us in their accounts a sense of the importance of the trades in frankincense and gum in olden times. And indeed the nature of the demand for frankincense at the time had no parallel in any other commodity.

Field studies carried out in Dhofar show that frankincense was transported by land and sea to the far corners fo the world. The port of Ras Fartak (or Jebel

Al-Qamr) was the port where the crop was collected for outward transport to Yemen and other arts of Asia by way of the port of Aden. The land route commenced to the west of Dhofar and passed through the Nejd to the south of the Arabian peninsula, then swung north again to Najran and on to Gaza.

The most significant route mentioned by the early historians and geographers was the one which linked Dhofar with the east of the Arabian peninsula and continued to the land of the Sumerians in Iraq.

The renowned geographer Ptolemy I was the first geographer to draw up a map of the district of Dhofar in which he identified the region where frankincense was cultivated as the Salalah Plain (Khor Rory). Ptolemy also singled out a place in Dhofar[83] which he named *Suq Al-Omaniyeen* (the Omani Marketplace). Other investigative studies show that the Omanis controlled the principal districts on the south coast of the Arabian Sea. Muslim historians moreover made reference to Ubar or Wabar, placing it in the northern part of Dhofar. Nashwan bin Said Al-Homeiri also referred to this place, but believed it to be in the territory occupied by the Aad tribe (that is the eastern part of Yemen). The historian Al-Tabari speaks of Wabar without adequately specifying its whereabouts in a reference to its having been stricken with drought. At all events there are innumerable references to the fact that the Aad clan were settled at Ubar or Wabar. The Qur'an also records a tale of the Aad who were destroyed and buried without their domicile being known.

From the above we may deduct that Ubar or Wabar was not the name of a city but rather of a substantial territory the precise location of which shall remain for now a matter of debate between historians and archaeologists.

From the earliest times Dhofar was a habitat uniquely suited to the cultivation of the frankincense bush, although it would appear that the use of frankincense as a traded commodity did not occur before the Neolithic Period, that is some 8000 years ago. During the Islamic Era, the routes used for the trade in this commodity were those very routes of the Neolithic Period which were constructed by the Arabs and Romans over the old routes. The Frankincense Route from Oman to Egypt travelled by way of the Negev and Sinai down through the ages from its distant origins. And so the question which should now be asked is this: Are there any signs of trade between Dhofar and the east of the Arabian peninsula during the Neolithic Period?

It is certain that South Arabia was once endowed with many rivers and lakes and in consequence was well populated and traversed by many roads, in particular across the Rub'al-Khali. This latter we know from the evidence of vessels and implements associated with the age of the Neolithic Period and which were found all along the length of the route and at various sites throughout the Arabian peninsula, all sharing common features of technique and decoration. Also found were wall paintings on rockfaces in the west of the peninsula and in Yemen. Further finds along the route to Sumer in Iraq were all characterized by the same feats of decoration.

Oman did not confine its exports to raw frankincense or olibanum. By blending this with a form of tallow they were able to process it into incense for they were well aware of the demand for incense for use in the religious rites of past societies. Ivory and perfumes were also among the exports of Oman at this time, i.e. the Neolithic Period.

Investigative surveys stumbled on a quantity of Sumerian tablets bearing the word *bokhur* (incense) and in records we find a more precise descriptive meaning in '*bokhur* which is extracted from the frankincense bush'.

To summarize, from approximately 5000 BC and up to around 1800 BC, Iraq's need for incense as supplied by Dhofar grew apace. Some time around 2000 BC the region probably witnessed a change of climate and the environment began to experience drought and gradual desertification. This approximated the time the inhabitants began to domesticate the camel for use in the overland caravan trade. Archaeological findings in the peninsula and in Egypt prove that the land trade became an established reality *circa* 1500 BC.

At all events the locality known as Shasir was a principal trade centre of the Nejd/Dhofar district for the land route to the north which began at the start of the Neolithic Period and which appears to have been associated with trade between Dhofar and the north of the Arabian peninsula to Sumer in the south of Iraq.

Who knows, perhaps the trade links between Dhofar and Sumer ascertain that this commerce extended also from earliest times to the trade with Gaza and Ancient Egypt?

The Bronze and Iron Ages came to an end and still Shasir continued to thrive. Recent excavations unearthed the traces of fine buildings, suggesting a place well-populated on the trading activities of its citizens. During the Middle Ages many sources refer to their uncommon enterprise in the export of incense and horses and gum. It is likely that Shasir retained its trading prominence up to the start of the sixteenth century when its inhabitants uprooted and re-settled in the surrounding regions.

Field surveys carried out in 1993 on the Salalah Plain found a great similarity in the buildings excavated, particularly at the Ain Hamran site, with those of the Shasir district which shared many identical architectural features.

These same field studies led to the discovery of a large group of buildings at

Old building in Salalah.

Balid in Salalah. These studies ascribe considerable significance to this locality as a busy trading post engaged in the export and import of goods, as evidenced by the presence of a variety of coins and ceramic vessels dating to the fourteenth century AD. Archaeologists also found parallel samples in Shasir, establishing that a link existed between the region to the interior of Dhofar and the coast right up to the fifteenth century.

From this brief outline we can see that Oman was home to a civilization which went back in time continuously to the pre-Islamic Age. Throughout the Islamic Age itself Oman enjoyed a cultural expansion which was no less than the equal of the other Islamic lands with which it communicated through trade and navigation. In this Oman and the Omanis enjoyed an advantage over the other Muslim peoples and countries for the reasons we have explained in earlier chapters.

We have demonstrated how Oman stood out among its peers as a merchant and seafaring state. Perhaps we should take a look at how it achieved justifiable prominence as a centre of learning, wisdom, culture and civilization.

Notes for Part Two

[1] Ya'qut Al-Hamawi, *Mu'jam Al-Buldan*, vol 4, p150.

[2] *Ibid*.

[3] Sheikh Al-Rabwa, *Nakhbet Al-Dahar* (Passages from Time), p218.

[4] Sarhan bin Said Al-Azkawi, *Kashef Al-Ghumah Al-Jami' Li Akhbar Al-Umma*, p32, handwritten copy, Taimouriya Collection, Egyptian National Library, under ref 2582.

[5] See Grohimann's article in the Islamic Encyclopaedia. A. Grohimann, *Encycliobidis de l'Islam*, Leiden, Brill, 1936, p104-2- 1044. Ci. Huart, *Histoire des Arabes* II, Paris, 1913, pp257-82.

[6] Al-Istakhri, *Al-Masalek Wa Al-Mamalek*, p27; Ibn Hawqal, *Surat Al-Ardh*, p44.

[7] Ibn Khaldun, *Al-'Abr* (The Lessons). vol. 4, p198.

[8] S.A. Huzayyin, *Arabian Far East -Their Commercial and Cultural Relations In Graeco-Roman and Iran-Arabian Times*, Cairo, 1942, p6f.

[9] G. Bibby, *Looking for Dilmun*, Proof Ed, 1973. See also, *An Introduction to the Monuments of Saudi Arabia*, Monuments and Antiquities Administration, Ministry of Information, Kingdom of Saudi Arabia, 1395 AH/1975 AD.

[10] See our communication to this magazine in, Ridha Jawad Al- Hashemi, 'A New Magazine Specialising in the Monuments of the Gulf and the Arabian Peninsula', *Sumer Magazine*, Baghdad, 1980, pp359- 62.

[11] Ridha Jawad Al-Hashemi, 'Burial Grounds in the Gulf Area and their Cultural Meaning', *Sumer*, 1980, p33.

[12] A. Hastings, G.H. Humphries and R. H. Meadow, 'Oman in the Third Millennium BC', *Journal of Oman Studies (JOS)*, vol.1, p69f. M. Tosi, 'Distribution and Exploitation of Natural Resources in Oman', *JOS*, vol 1, p187ff.

[13] Ridha Jawad Al-Hashemi, *Monuments of the Arabian Gulf and the Arabian Peninsula*, Baghdad, 1984, p35ff.

[14] J. Pritchard, *Ancient Near Eastern Texts Relating to the Old Testament*, 3rd ed, with supplement, Princeton, 1969, p49 (ANET).

[15] *Ibid*, p523.

[16] Ridha Al-Hashemi, *Monuments of the Arabian Gulf and the Arabian Peninsula*, Baghdad, 1984, p523.

[17] ANET, pp266, 268.

[18] Ridha Jawad Al-Hashemi, *The Caravan Trade in Ancient Arab History*, p24, Institute of Arab Research and Studies, Baghdad, 1984.

[19] Ridha Jawad Al-Hashemi, 'The History of the Camel in the Light of Archaeological Remains and Ancient Writings', *Faculty of Arts* magazine, Baghdad, no. 32. Appendix 1978, pp185-232.

[20] *Kuml*, 1962, p190f.

[21] *The Monuments of the United Arab Emirates*, Survey of the Tourism and Monuments Administration, Ministry of Information and Culture, 1975.

22 *The Monuments of the United Arab Emirates,* Survey of the Tourism and Monuments Administration, Ministry of Information and Culture, 1975.

23 M. Tosi, S. Durante, *JOS,* 3, pt2, 1977.*

24 G. Rachet, 'Oun Annas' in *Dictionnaire de l'Archaeologie,* Paris, 1983, avee Bibliographie.

25 K. Frifelt, *JOS,* 2, 1976.

26 B. De Gardi, *JOS,* pt3, 1977.

27 L. Oppenheim, *Mesopotamian Civilization,* trans, France, 1970; M. Wheeler, *Indus Civilization* 1953/1972.

28 Konrad Schliephake, *Die Arabsche Halbim*l, Wurzburg, 1982.

29 B. Costa, T.G. Wilkinson, *From Excavations and History - A Study in the History and Civilization of Early Oman.* B. Costa and T.G. Wilkinson are the two historians who studied the history and civilization of early Oman working with others on a field study at Arja and Tiwi in search of evidence relevant to early methods of water supply. Costa led a survey of Omani Monuments, while the English Orientalist Wilkinson assisted him with this expedition which set out in January 1978 to work on Phase One of the excavation of the district of Arja. A year before this these two scholars participated in an encounter with a number of other scholars entitled 'An Unofficial Encounter/ on the exploitation of natural resources in early Oman'. Costa was responsible for another study published by the Ministry of National Heritage and Culture under the title, *The Arja Copper Mining Settlement.* Wilkinson has published many historical studies about Oman including a study on the *aflaj* and one on the scholars of Oman and a third on the Bani Julanda in Oman, along with other studies published by the Ministry of National Heritage and Culture as part of the book series *Turathna* published by this Ministry. See, B. Costa, *The Arja Copper Mining Settlement,* Ministry of National Heritage and Culture, No. 46, pp27, 32; Awad Mohammed Khalifat, *The Emergence of the Ibadhi Movement,* Muscat, 1978. p33.

30 G. Weisgerber, *JOS,* 4, 1978, Malullah bin Ali bin Habib Allawati, *Outline of the History of Oman,* 1989, p9.

31 Paolo Costa and Tony F. Wilkinson, 'The Hinterland of Sohar, Archaeological Surveys and Excavations within the Region of an Omani Seafaring City', *JOS,* vol. 9, Mascte - Londres 1987, p238, fig 110.

32 Monique Kervran, Paolo Costa et T.F. Wilkinson 'The Hinterland of Sohar', *Bull. Cret. des Ann. Islam,* no. 6, 1989, pp228-9.

33 ANET, p229.

34 Robert England, 'Dilmun in the Archaic Corpus', pp35-3 in, Daniel (Ed), *Dilmun - New Studies in the Archaeology and Early History of Bahrain.* Berliner Biet Zum vordren Orient Band -2 (BBVO-2), Berlin - 19.

35 Joan Oates, 'Seafaring Merchants of Ur' in *Antiquity,* vol. 1, 11, no. 203 (1977), p221f.

36 M. Kervran, P. Mortensen and F. Hiebert, 'The Occupational Enigma of Bahrain between the 13th and 8th Century BC', p13f. *Dilmun,* 14, 1987/8 (Dilmun - Magazine of the History and Archaeological Society of Bahrain).

37 Ridha Jawad Al-Hashemi, 'The Arabs in the Light of the Cuneiform Sources', *magazine of the Faculty of Arts, Baghdad,* issue 22/1978, pp639-83

38 *Ibid.*

39 Herodotus, 89.

40 Ridha Al-Hashemi, *Monuments of the Arabian Gulf and the Arabian Peninsula,* Baghdad, 1984, p59ff.

41 Ridha Al-Hashemi, *The Aflaj - an Ancient Arab Irrigation System,* p19ff.

42 Ibn Mandhour, Mada *Falaj (The Aflaj).*

43 Ibn Sayedu, *Al-Mukhassas,* vol. 10, p34; G.B. Gressey, 'Qanat, Karez and Foggaras', in, *The Geographical Review,* vol. 1, 1958, New York, p27f.

44 T.G. Wilkinson, Sohar Ancient Fields Project, *JOS,* vol. p165.

45 Donald Hawley, *Oman and its Modern Renaissance,* London, p130.

46 Ibn Sayedu, *Al-Mukhassas,* book 10, p131.

47 Donald Hawley, *Oman and its Modern Renaissance,* London, p131.

48 Herodotus, 7-9.

49 Al-Qazzouini, *Athar Al-Bilad Wa Akhbar Al-Abad* (Monuments of Countries and News of People), Dar Al-Sayyad, Beirut, p16.

50 Ibn Al-Majawar, *Siffat Bilad Al-Yemen Wa Mekkah Wa Baadh Al-Hijaz,* amended by Oscar Lufgren, Leiden, 1951, p131.

51 G. Bibby, *Looking for Dilmun,* proof edition, 1973. p66f.

52 Fouad Safar, 'Irrigation Works undertaken by Senharib', *Sumer,* Baghdad, vol. 1, 1947, pp77-86.

53 R. M. Parson Co, 'Ground Water Resources of Iraq', Baghdad, 1955-1956. Taken from, Cressy, *op. cit.,* p41.

[54] Hawley, *op. cit.*, p128.

[55] Sargon and Naram-Sin, Two kings of ancient Iraq.

[56] W.F. Lee, ans, *Foreign Trade in the Old Babylonian Period*, Leyden, 1960, pp11-12

[57] D.O. Edzard, *Das Reich der III Dynastie von ur*, Fisherweltgeschichte 2, p133

[58] A.L. Oppenheim, *The Seafaring Merchants of Ur*, ibid.

[59] *Ibid.*, p15.

[60] *Idem Keilschrift Texte aus Assue Historesahen Inhalts* = KAH122.

[61] A.L. Oppenheim, *idem*, p17.

[62] Archiv Fur Orientforschung, Band, Graz, 1963, H. Hirsch, *Die Inschriften der Konige von Agade*, p87.

[63] A. Falkenstein, *Die Inschriften Gudeas von Lagash*, I, Einleitung, 1966, pp48-9; Sumerische und Akkadische Hymnen und Gebete, p416.

[64] H. Hirsch, *Die Inschriften der Konige von Agade*, p49.

[65] Adam Falkerstein, *op. cit.*, No. 2, pp48-9.

[66] R. Labat, *Manuel Depigraphie Akkadienne*, Paris, 1959, No. 586, p247.

[67] Adam Falkenstein, *op. cit.*, No. 2, p48.

[68] Dr Fawzi Rashid, *Principles of the Sumerian Language*, 1972, p48.

[69] Dr Fawzi Rashid, *Translations of Sumerian Royal Texts*, 1985, p142.

[70] H. Steible, *Die Altsumerischen Bau und Weihinschriften*, Teul I, p103.

[71] Dr Fawzi Rashid, *Translations of Sumerian Royal Texts*, 1985, pp61, 65.

[72] H. Hirsch, *Die Inschriften der Konige von Agade* (= AFO, BAND XX, 1963), p17.

[73] H. Hirsch, *ibid.*, p17.

[74] Dr Fawzi Rashid, *Canons of Ancient Iraq*, Baghdad, 3rd ed., 1987, p26.

[75] This is in spite of the fact that the cuneiform texts do not specifically mention the merchants of Magan and that they only mention the merchants of Dilmun which the Sumerians called *Alik Dilmun*. It is not unlikely that the name means the merchants of the two, Dilmun and Magan or indeed the three city-states, Dilmun, Magan and Meluhha which may well be located in the south-west of Oman (Hadramaut).

[76] G. Bibby, *Looking for Dilmun* (1971).

[77] I. Gelb, *Magan and Meluhha in Early Mesopotamian Sources*, RAAO, No. 64, 1970. This confirms our supposition that the site of Meluhha during the Sumerian and Akkadian Ages was not beyond the coastal territories of the Arabian Gulf or the Arabian Sea.

[78] One text dating to the eleventh year of the reign of Nabonidus, last of the Third Dynasty Babylonian kings (567 BC) contains a reference to the province of Dilmun.

[79] Oman is mentioned in Pliny, XII, 2 under the name *Omana*.

[80] I. Gersheuitch, 'Sisso at Susa', *Bulletin of the School of Oriental and African Studies*, vol.19, 1957.

[81] R. Thapar, 'A Possible Identification of Meluhha, Dilmun and Magan', *Journal of the Economic and Social History of the Orient*, No. 18, 1975.

[82] The material in this chapter was prepared by the Monuments Department at the Ministry of National Heritage and Culture, Sultanate of Oman.

[83] There is no original of this map. However, copies of it appeared in the twelfth century AD and it was mentioned in both Arabic and European sources in the eleventh century AD.

PART III

Oman in the Age of Islam

Studies Presented and Summarized in this Part

Omani Mariners Lords of the South in the Islamic Age, by Dr El-Sayed Abdul Aziz Salem, University of Alexandria.

Relations between Oman and Yemen in the Early and Middle Ages, by Dr Mohammed Said Shukri, University of Aden.

Features of Oman's History during the Time of Al-Risala (The Message of Islam), by Dr Ramzia Mohammed Al-Taraqji, University of Baghdad.

The Companion Mazin bin Ghadhuba and the Conversion of Oman to Islam, by Dr Shaker Mamhoud Abdul Moneim, Al-Mustansiriya University, Iraq.

The Nature of the Relationship between Oman and the Central Authority of the Islamic State in the First Century of the Hegira, by Dr Khalil Shaker Hussein, Al-Mustansiriya University, Iraq.

Oman in the Middle Islamic Period, by Dr Ali Mansour Nasir, University of Bahrain.

Oman's Relations with North Africa, by Dr Farhat bin Ali Al-Jaabeiri, University of Qairouan.

*The Mahlab Family and their Role in Politics and War up to the end of the Ummayyad Perio*d, by Dr Abdul Moneim Abdul Hamid Sultan, Sultan Qaboos University.

The Arabs of Oman and their Role in the Events of Thighr Al-Ḥind in the First and Second Centuries of the Hegira, by Dr Saad bin Said Al-Hamidi, Faculty of Arabic Language and Social Sciences, University of Imam Mohammed bin Saud Al-Islami - Southern Branch, Abha, Kingdom of Saudi Arabia.

The Omanis and their Role in Preserving the Arab Islamic Identity of Oman, by Dr Mustafa El-Shakaa, University of Ayn Shams.

The Rule of the Bani Nabhan in Oman, compiled by Abdullah bin Nasir Al-Harithi, Sultan Qaboos University.

Trade Contacts between Oman and East Africa in the Middle Ages, by Dr Sabah Ibrahim Al-Sheikhli, University of Baghdad.

Oman from the Dawn of Islam to the End of the Ummayad State

The Conversion to Islam

The Omanis' Arab roots are deep. It is said that a major migration took place during the earliest part of recorded history from the north of the Arabian peninsula south to Oman and its coastal periphery, as a result of drought affecting the heart of the peninsula. The exact date of the migration is not known, nor whether it occurred as a single great human movement or a succession of these. The migrants were from the tribe of Nazar (Nazarenes) and these were Adnani Arabs from the north. Arab sources relate how Oman was the focus of an intense influx from Yemen when, in the time of Sharhabil Yaafar Al-Himyari in the mid-fifth century AD[1], the Ma'rib dam was breached and destroyed. As a result of his inability to repair the structure adequately to guarantee its stability the inhabitants fled the city, the Lakhm and the Azd to various parts of the Arabian peninsula. Some of the Azd travelled into the eastern part of Oman, while the Awas and the Khazraj settled in Yathrib. The Bani Amru bin Amer, who were descended from Mazin bin Al-Azd, headed north towards the hills of El-Sham. Al-Bilathuri describes how the Azd, after they had left their home country, went first to Mecca and there they separated, one party setting out for Oman, another to As'Sirah, a party to Al-Anbar and Al Hirah and another to El-Sham[2].

In fact, there is little precise information available with which to date the migration of the Azd to Oman and no fixed evidence of the course this migration took, whether from the Hadramaut out of Ma'rib or by way of Yamama and Bahrain out of As'Sirah (Aseer). Phillips refers to the Azd tribe which inhabited Ma'rib at the end of the first century AD. He remarks that they fled from Ma'rib across the Hadramaut Valley, arriving down to Saihout (in Shihr) under the command of Malik bin Fahm who went on by sea to Qalhat (15 miles north west of Sur), whence he embarked on a series of ferocious battles with the Persians to liberate Oman and become its first independent overlord[3].

It is said that this great hero, Malik bin Fahm bin Ghanam bin Daws Al-Azdi, was the first of the Azd to enter Oman. He was father to Guthaima Al-Abrash, King of Al-Hirah. Al-Awatbi says that Malik crossed into Oman with an armed force of more than 6000 men and horses. On finding the Persians there he retired to close by Qalhat and took up a position on the coast with a view to protecting his flank[4]. He then set about the task of ousting the Persians from Oman and engaged in a protracted and bloody war with them to this end. The Persians sought to terrorize the Arabs by bringing a number of their

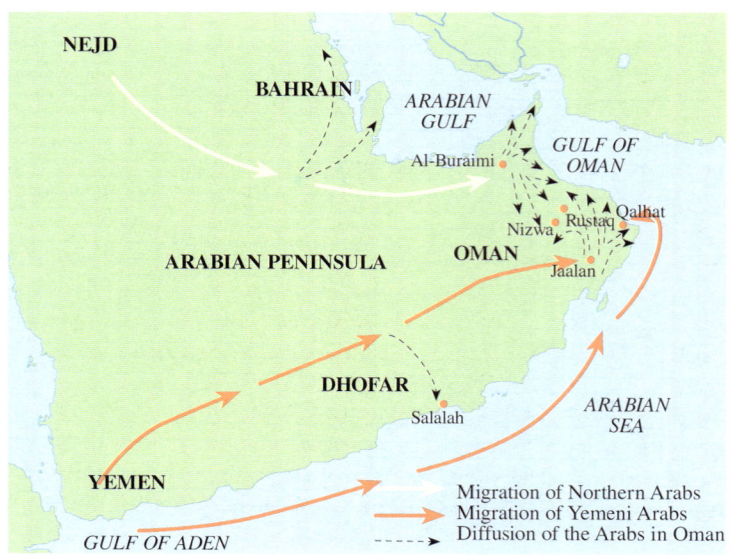

Arab migratory movements and settlement patterns of the tribes in Oman.

elephants to the front of their battle lines. But the Persian elephants did not intimidate Malik and his fighting men. They fell upon the beasts with spears, swords and arrows and the elephants turned on the satrap's troops, crushing many of them.

Though the Persians put up a spirited resistance, the courage of Malik and his Azdi tribesmen surpassed imagination and the Persians were forced to sue for peace. Under the settlement agreed, Malik was to hold his peace for a year in which the Persians would complete their departure from Oman. They made him a pledge to this effect and backed it up with tribute and so Malik assented.

The Persian king was enraged at the implications of this arrangement and he summoned a commander from amongst his great satraps and *asawirah* (horsemen)[5] and gathering an escort of 3000 men he dispatched them as a reinforcement to Oman by way of Bahrain. Malik set upon them energetically with his inferior force and attacked them repeatedly until he had routed them utterly, whence Malik bin Fahm attained mastery of Oman and he seized all of the wealth and possessions of the Persians.

This showdown with the Persians made the Arabs of Oman fiercely conscious of their independence and as fiercely proud of their Arab identity and lineage. The Omanis wrapped up their defeat of the Persians by descending on Persia itself when Selima bin Malik bin Fahm succeeded in wresting control of Karman from the Persians. Karman remained in the hands of the Omanis until after the death of Selima bin Malik when a disagreement ensued between the sons. The Persians inflicted defeat on them and regained control of their father's possessions in Karman. As their influence faded, they left Karman and a portion of them made their way to Oman.

After their defeat by Malik bin Fahm the Persians failed to recover their influence in Oman, until in due course Malik's possessions and those of his sons came to an end. When the sovereignty of Oman fell to the family of Julanda bin Mustakbir, a relative of Maawiya bin Shams, and Persia came to be ruled by the Bani Sassan (the Sassanids), they were reconciled with the Julanda in Oman.

For some time before the Julanda came to power the Azd tribe had been pouring steadily into Oman. Among the first to settle after Maawiya bin Shams Al-Azdi was Omar bin Amru bin Amer and his sons Al-Hajar and Al-Aswad. From these two are descended many of the tribes of Oman[6].

The Bani Al-Aswad took part in the Muslim Conquests after the emergence of Islam, and a branch of them was to travel as far as Andalucia whence they went down to Bajana seaport, and they partook in a *jihad* by sea. Of the Bani Maawiya bin Shams Al-Azdi were Gaifar and Abd, sons of Al-Julanda bin Karkar bin Al-Mustakbir bin Mas'ud bin Al-Jarar Abdul Azi bin Ma'wila bin Shams, King of Oman at the time of the Prophet. Ibn Hazm recounts how the Prophet sent them a dispatch inviting them to adopt Islam. This they did with full and complete conviction and along with them the people of Oman[7]. This was in the eighth year of the Hegira, soon after Amr bin Al-A'as had adopted the faith[8].

Of the Azdi conquest of Oman Al-Bilathuri says: 'It is said that the Azd conquered Oman and there were there as well as the Azd many from the *bawadi* (desert)'[9].The Azd of Oman at the time of the emergence of Islam were composed of several branches and clans, the most important of whom as we have mentioned were the Bani Ma'wila bin Shams bin Umar bin Ghanam bin Ghalib bin Uthman bin Zahran bin Ka'b bin Al-Hareth bin Ka'b bin Nasir bin Abdullah bin Malik bin Nasir bin Al-Azd[10].

Another branch of the Omani Azd came from Al-Hodan bin Shams, brother of Ma'wila bin Shams[11]. A delegation of these approached the Prophet after Mecca had fallen to the Muslims under Maslia bin Mazin Al-Hadani. Another detachment of them migrated after the coming of Islam to Basra and others stayed in Oman[12]. It is not known in which year the Azd came to Basra nor with any precision how many of them arrived[13]. The Omani Azd also included the Bani Malik bin Fahm bin Daws bin Adnan bin Abdullah bin Zahran bin Ka'b bin Al-Hareth bin Ka'b bin Abdullah bin Malik bin Nasir bin Al-Azd[14]. Others of those who settled Oman were Nawa and Al-Ashaqer, to whom was related the poet Ka'b Al-Ashqari[15]. Some of them after the arrival of Islam migrated to Basra while most of them stayed in Oman[16].

Another offshoot of the Azd of Oman were the Ateik[17] bin Al-Assad bin Omran bin Amru bin Amer bin Haretha bin Imri Al-Qais bin Thalaba bin Mazin bin Al-Azd. Also of the Ateik was Mahlab bin Abi Safra[18]. The citizens

A re-enactment of the battle against the Marzupan which was led on the Omani side by Malik bin Fahm.

of Daba were Bani Hareth bin Malik bin Fahm.

The Yahmad were yet another branch of the Azd who settled Oman and they were the Yahmad bin Hami bin Othman bin Nasir bin Zahran[19] and some of these also went to Basra after Islam[20].

The Azd were not the only inhabitants of Oman. At the dawn of Islam several well-known Oman tribes were settled there and these included Sama bin Lu'ai[21], whose ancestry was traced by genealogists to the Qureish. The Bani Sama preserved their tribal bloodline and did not intermarry with the Azd, though they were allies[22]. Al-Bakri says of the Bani Sama that they carved out a life for themselves in Oman that was 'fierce and they were fearless and wealthy and invincible'[23]. Some of these also went to Basra after the arrival of Islam[24].

Among the Azd who were settled in Oman at the time of the Muslim Conquests were a number of branches of the Abdul Qais. These were settled in Oman since the earliest times, as noted by Ibn Durayeed: 'The Itlad are a central strand of the Abdul Qais. They are the Omani Itlad because they have been there for a long time'[25]. *Mu'jam Ma Ista'jam*[26] has a passage on the migration of the tribes: 'Tribes of the Abdul Qais entered the heart of Oman and became partners of the Azd and these are the Itlad of Oman'.

Branches of the Qutha'a also were settled in Oman at the dawn of Islam[27]. If, as we have seen, most of the Omani tribes were of Yemeni origin, the migration was essentially from Yemen directly or by way of other areas. Indeed the landscape and the special features of the natural and human environment shared by Yemen and Oman prepared the ground for a closeness which recognizes no boundaries in the matter of human and historical continuity and mutually beneficial exchange. Both land and sea routes facilitated the exchange of influences and gave economic synergy to the products of land and sea, such as fish, pearls, incense, olibanum, *wars* (a plant used to dye clothes red) and coffee, as well as the exchange of animals. All of this was responsible for strengthening the contact between Yemen and Oman as a result of which many of the migrations, when they occurred, set out for Oman and in consequence a great many of the Omani tribes were of Yemeni origin. These and many other tribes also of Yemeni or Adnani origin were the residents of Oman at the arrival of Islam. They were quick to respond to the call to the new faith and sent delegations and men to the Hijaz to know more about the new faith. Mazin bin Ghadhuba Al-Tay Al-Sama'ili was one of the first to set out for Medina and one of the first Muslims of Oman. Who then was this splendid Omani Companion (of the Prophet)?

The Companion Mazin bin Ghadhuba Al-Tay

He was Mazin bin Ghadhuba bin Sabi'a bin Shamasa bin Hayyan bin Murr bin Hayyan bin Abi Bishr bin Khatama bin Saad bin Nabhan bin Amru bin Al-Ghouth bin Tay[28]. Tay came from Al-Ta'a meaning to go deeply into. These people are Bani Adad bin Zayed bin Yashgab bin Areeb bin Zayed bin Kahlan. Taya was father of Fatra and Al-Ghouth and Al-Hareth and each of these was responsible for a proliferation of tribal branches and offshoots, so many indeed that they would be near impossible to trace to the various places where they eventually settled. They were constantly on the move as their needs and livelihood demanded and in line with the tribal alliances they formed[29].

Some of the commentators say that Taya was the father of this tribe and that he went out from Yemen with his kin and his tribe to Hijaz and roamed the hills of Aga and Salmi with them[30], and that Taya after his travels in the north settled in the vicinity of the Bani Assad whom they conquered and dislodged from the two mountains, so that these came to be known as the Two Mountains of Taya. These two mountains wielded a powerful influence in directing the lives of the Tayes and earning them their reputation for high-mindedness, wisdom and valour[31], in view of the outstanding features of the territory they occupied from the standpoint of trade and cultivation, military advantage and strength of fortification.

Notwithstanding the difficulty of the terrain in and around the Taya Mountains, Wadi Rek close by had dates and sweetwater wells. The town of Fayed was four miles away to the right of the road to Mecca and became a market town during the season of the *Hajj*[32].

Mazin bin Ghadhuba's Clan

The sources do not offer much in the way of information about the family of Mazin Al-Tay and biographies are few. Perhaps this is because his social status was limited and his role in the early conversions to Islam was an extremely fortunate one. The sources of his biography say that his mother was Zeinab bint Abdullah bin Rabi'a bin Howeis, and she was one of the Bani Nimran[33]. This would suggest the abovementioned 'Ghadhuba' in his name could have been either a surname or a true name for his father, for the Arabs sometimes gave feminine names to men, such as 'Rabi'a.' At all events we have no information to tell us which is the correct view.

Brought up in the city of Sama'il in the interior of Oman, he had a brother by the same mother and from these came the Bani Samit and the Bani Khatama and Fahra[34]. Mazin mentions that he had a son named Hayyan in his own account of his encounter with the Prophet Mazin said, 'I was blessed with a son and I named him Hayyan bin Mazin'[35]. Among his near descendants were Ahmed bin Harb and Ali bin Harb Al-Tay[36] of whom Ibn Al-Atheer said that he was the grandfather of Ali bin Harb bin Mohammed bin Ali bin Hayyan bin Mazen bin Ghadhuba Al-Tay[37]. These were distinguished Imams[38] and communicators of the Prophet's Hadith. Born in 175 AH/791 AD in Azerbaijan, Ali had a great knowledge of Arab affairs and was a poet and a man of culture; he saw Al-Maani bin Omar Al-Mosuli who quoted some Hadiths from his father and he in turn from Ibn Uyayna and Al-Qassem Ibn Yazid Al-Jarami and a number of renowned *huffadh* (who had memorized the entire Qur'an) and he quoted from others and Al-Nissai quoted some Hadiths from him.

Abu Zakaria Al-Azdi said of him in *Tarikh Mosul*, Ibn Hayyan in *Al-Thiqaat* and Al-Khoteib Al-Baghdadi in *Tarikh Baghdad* that he was a communicator of Hadith and was learned in the affairs of the Arabs, a man of culture and a poet. He travelled to the court of Al-Moattaz in the year 204 AH/819 AD and there his Hadith were written down. For this he was given an honorarium; and so it was up to the time of Al-Motadhid. He died in Mosul in the year 265 AH/878 AD [39] at the age of 92.

Ahmed[40] bin Harb bin Mohammed bin Hayyan bin Mazin bin Ghadhuba was born in 174 AH/790 AD. This was recounted by Ibn Uyayna and Abi Mu'awiyah. Ahmed shared his brother's high esteem and Nisa'i gave a full account of him and his brothers Ali and Abdul Rahman. However, differences have arisen as to the authenticity of this account. Muslim found the account to be a reasonable one and Ibn Abi Hatem said: 'I have come across him but I have not quoted from him'. Ibn Hayyan also verified his authenticity. Mazin died in Idhna[41] on the El-Sham coast in 263 AH/876 AD. This is what was recalled by sources in his family.

The Companion Mazin bin Ghadhuba Al-Tay Converted to Islam

Mazin bin Ghadhuba Al-Tay's story is told in the Arabic book: *Prominent Prophecy of the Clerics*[42]. Ibn Hayyan[43] stated that Mazin had many close colleagues. Ibn Hajar[44] refers to Ibn Al-Sakan and to Al-Tabrani and Al-Fakihi's book *Mecca* as well as Al-Baihaqi's *The Indications*. According to these sources Ibn Al-Sakan and Ibn Qaana'e heard from Husham bin Al-Kalbi that his father had told him that Abdullah Al-Omani had said that Mazin had declared in a lengthy speech that he had destroyed the idols and 'come before the Messenger and converted to Islam'.

Ibn Abdul Birr[45] also pointed out that Mazin had close colleagues. The story goes that one day he visited the Messenger and asked him for help. 'Oh, Allah's Messenger, I am a man who cherishes excitement, women and alcohol. I lose my money and then regret my mistakes. Pray to Allah to save me from these adversities. I have no son, pray to Allah to let me have one'. Mazin then said that: 'He prayed for me, Allah helped me, and my prayers were answered. I married four female slaves, and I had a son. I learnt sections of the Holy Qur'an by heart and I went on the pilgrimage many times.'

The *Taj Al-Arous*[46], states that Mazin bin Ghadhuba Al-Tay was a chosen person. Ibn Al-Atheer[47] also corroborated the same story which was summarized by Ibn Abdul Birr. The story was explained in more detail by the author of *Kashef Al-Ghumah*[48].

But Abu-Na'eem described Mazin Al-Tay as one who was a guardian of an idol at Sama'il, and that they killed a sacrifice before the idol - the precise name of which seems to be in dispute by different authors. However, the majority, as pointed out by Ibn Durayed in his book *Al-Jamhara*, concur that it was Bajir[49] - the name of an idol worshipped by Al-Azd and the neighbouring tribes of Tay and Qutha'a during Al-Jahilya.

The story-teller relates that when Mazin killed the sacrifice, he heard a voice saying: 'Listen Mazin: you will be happy if you listen to me, while on the surface it may seem alright, deep down it is evil. A prophet from Mudhar has been sent to spread the word; to bring news of Allah's religion. Abandon your stone statue and you will be freed from damnation and the fires of Hell'[50].

A few days later another sacrifice was slaughtered, and again a voice was heard saying: 'Come to me...come, you will hear something you may know. This is a prophet, sent to teach the true way. Believe in him, to save yourself from the coal-fires of Hell'[51].

Historical narratives indicate that Mazin was alarmed and frightened by what he heard, hoping that everything would be alright. While he was contemplating, a man from Hijaz arrived and asked for some water to drink. Mazin enquired from the man whether he had any problems or brought any news. The visitor told Mazin that if he met a man named Mohammed bin Abdullah bin Abdul Muttalib bin Hashim bin Abd Munaaf[52] that this person would tell them to accept Allah's call. Mazin immediately linked the message he had been given when he slaughtered the sacrifice with that which the Hijazi man had told him (historical narratives do not mention the name of this man).

Mazin is then reputed to have broken the idol into pieces and to have recited a poem whose approximate translation is:

I broke Baajir to pieces when he was a god
and I rested in his shade.
Al-Hashimi (ie the Prophet) *showed us the falsehood of our ways.*
His religion was not known before.

Traveller - tell Amr and her brothers
that I, who once claimed Baajir as my god,
says that the true God has talked.

Mazin Bin Ghadhuba's mosque in Sama'il.

Mazin was referring to Amr and her brothers in the tribe of Bani Khutama led by Khutama bin Sa'ad bin Al-Ghawth bin Tay. As we have already mentioned, this was the famous branch of the tribe to which Mazin himself belonged[53]. Following this experience Mazin made the journey to visit Mohammed, and dedicated himself before Him, to Islam, declaring his faith in poetic verse, approximately translated as follows [54]:

To you[55], Allah's Messenger, my horse carried me,
across the vast deserts of Oman to Al-A'arj[56].
In all the world, you are the only one who can help me;

Who can forgive my sins and help me to succeed[57],

Of those who do not obey Allah's religion[58]:
their thoughts are not mine
and their aims are not mine.

My life was debauched by adultery and alcohol,
My youth gone and my physique[59] worn-down.
Renew my soul,
help me to fear alcohol,
help me to desist from adultery.

My hope and objective is Al Jihad,
for Allah is my pilgrimage and fast[60].

The original verse has been greatly distorted by numerous word of mouth translations with the almost inevitable distortions that result, as well as the final imperfections of translation. However, it is clear that Mazin bin Ghadhuba Al-Tay lived and was one of the first Omani people to be converted to Islam.

Additional evidence of Mazin's existence as one of Allah's Messenger's close compatriots, is provided by some Hadiths of the Prophet. Ibn Al-Sakan refers to Mohammed bin Khalaf, who was known as Wakee' in the *Nawadir Al-Akhbar*, and so through Ibn Manda; Abu Naa'eem; Al-Hassan bin Kutheir and to Yahya bin Abi Kutheir who reported that his father said: 'I heard Mazin bin Ghadhuba say: "I heard Allah's Messenger saying that you must be honest to be guided to Heaven".' It is a correct Hadith, in meaning at least. According to Ibn Manda[61] this Hadith is *gharib* (strange) because it is only known through this source.

However, it was not the only Hadith that referred to Mazin within the books of Hadiths. On one occasion it was reported that Mazin had asked the Messenger to pray for the people of Oman. Mazin said: 'Thou, Allah's Messenger, may Allah bless You - pray to Allah - may He be exalted - for the Omani people'. He prayed to Allah asking Him to guide the Omani people to follow the true path. Mazin is reported to have asked the Prophet to extend His prayer: 'Thou, I beg you to speak more to Allah!' he said and Allah's Messenger once more prayed, beseeching Allah to make the Omani people chaste; to protect their livelihoods and let them be satisfied with their lives.

Mazin continued in his request for the people of Oman: 'Thou Allah's Messenger . . . around us is a great ocean . . . pray to Allah to protect our livelihoods and our camels and sheep'[62]. Once more Allah's Messenger prayed, asking Allah to protect their livelihoods, and to enrich them from their sea!

Once more Mazin requested help for Oman and Allah's Messenger prayed that no enemy should rule over the Omani people. Finally He instructed Mazin to say 'Amen' for Allah would help those who say 'Amen'. And Mazin said: 'Amen'[63].

The following year, Mazin bin Ghadhuba returned to visit Allah's Messenger and told him: 'Thou the Son of the blessed and kind people. Allah has blessed some people and their relations from Oman with your religion . . . profits, catches and well-being have all improved'.

The Prophet replied that Islam was His faith and that Allah would increase the fish catches and well-being of the people of Oman. He promised that Allah would bless each person who followed Him, even those who believed in Him without coming to see Him, or who had not personally met with those who had seen the Prophet. He said that Allah would bless the people of Oman by expanding Islam throughout Oman[64].

It was true that the Omanis had converted to Islam. The Prophet sent them his letters and his messengers. What were the contents of these letters?

Letters of the Prophet Sent to Oman

The historical narratives are not in complete agreement on the exact time at which Islam entered Oman during the life of the Prophet Mohammed. Available historical documents claim that the Messenger took the initiative to call upon Gaifar and Abd, sons of Al-Julanda, the rulers of Oman[65] to submit to Islam. They do not agree upon the exact date when this approach was made but they concur that this communication did in fact take place. One such document mentioned that the Prophet Mohammed contacted Oman's leaders following Al-Hudaibia's reconciliation in the year sixth Hegira[66]. Another document ties the date of this communication to the period following the conquest of the holy city of Mecca in eighth Hegira[67]. A third historian claimed the event took place when the rulers of Oman had followed *Hajat Al-Wada* or the Farewell pilgrimage[68].

Historical documents state that the Messenger Mohammed sent Amr bin Al-A'as Al-Sahmi as his delegate to Gaifar and Abd, sons of Al-Julanda[69]. So far as the communication itself is concerned, the learned and distinguished historian, Ibn Khaldoon, states that the contact was made at some point between Al-Hudaibia's reconciliation and the death of the Prophet Mohammed [70]. The most likely time was following the signing of Al-Hudaibia's reconciliation agreement, when the Messenger Mohammed took diplomatic steps to spread Islam beyond the Hijaz. It was a time at which He wrote many letters to the kings and leaders of the neighbouring countries, including Oman's leaders.

It is a well established fact that, following the conquest of Mecca, the Prophet (Peace be upon Him) concentrated on the expansion of the Islamic State. The ending of Qureishi resistance marked a crucial landmark in the history of Islam and Muslims. Islam was now the greatest power in the Arab countries. Whilst the Arab tribal leaders had been sitting on the fence for some time, waiting to see what would happen in the conflict between Islam on one hand, and Qureish and her allied tribes the other, the Muslim conquest of Mecca, thanks to Allah, transformed Islam into a most powerful force. The Qureish were thus convinced of the path to take and they provided their own support to serve the growing Islamic cause.

At that time, the Messenger Mohammed preferred to follow peaceful diplomatic means. He contacted the kings and leaders of the neighbouring countries, and among them were the two kings of Oman: Gaifar and Abd, the sons of Al-Julanda. Historical books indicate that the Messenger Mohammed wrote

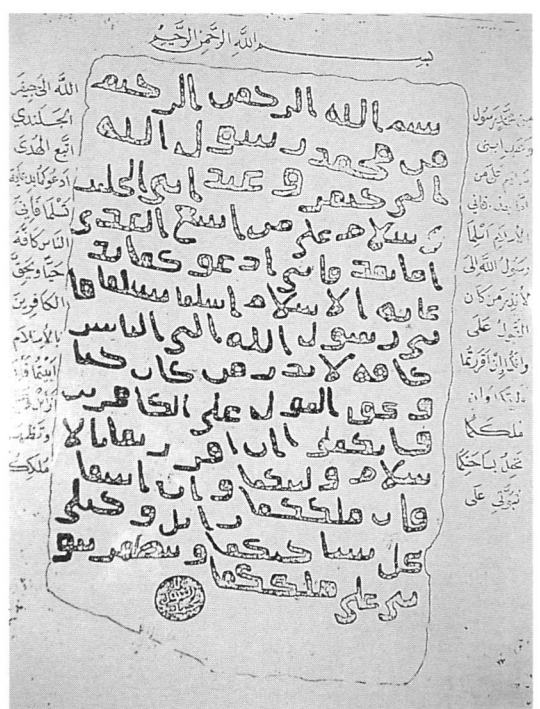

letters[71] to the people of Oman and that Amr bin Al-A'as was dispatched with one such letter which he carried to Gaifar and Abd the sons of Al-Julanda. An approximate translation into English of this letter from the Messenger is given below:

In the name of Allah, the Beneficent, the Merciful . . . from Mohammed bin Abdullah to Gaifar and Abd, sons of Al-Julanda, peace is upon him who follows the guidance, now and after . . . I am calling both of you, in the name of Islam. You will be safe if you submit to Islam. I am the Messenger of Allah to all of the people. I bring news of Islam to all the people, and will fight the infidels. I hope you will accept Islam, but if you do not, then you will lose your country, and my horsemen will invade your territory, and my prophecy will dominate your country.

The full text of this letter was mentioned in the book *Mode of Life* of Zain Dahlan, who referred to a Muslim, Abi Birza - Allah be pleased with him - who stated: 'Allah's Messenger had sent a man to one tribe but

Copy of a letter from the Prophet Mohammed to the King of Oman.

they insulted and beat him. He returned to the Messenger and told him: " If you go to the Omani people, they will never insult or beat you".' Imam Ahmed conveyed to us that Omar - Allah be pleased with him - told him that he heard Allah's Messenger Mohammed (Peace be upon Him) saying: 'I know the land called Oman, on the borders of the sea, and if my delegate visits those people, they would never shoot an arrow or throw a stone on him'.

In the *Lion of the Forest* Ibn Al-Atheer mentioned that Amr bin Al-A'as visited the monarch of the Al-Julanda, and told him: 'Thou Julanda, despite the fact that you are far away from us, you are not far from Allah, you must pray only to the one who created you. You should not attribute an equal to Allah, you have to understand that he created you and will end your life and bring you back again. Study this illiterate prophet who has told us about the world and Doomsday. If he asks for any reward, don't give it to him. If he leans on himself then don't bother about him. But look into what he is promulgating. Is his message the same as what the people say? If it is the same then ask him for evidence and choose the right way. If what he says is different, then you have to accept his promise and heed his warnings'. Al-Julanda is reported to have responded: 'In the name of God, he who has introduced me to this illiterate prophet does not demand anything that he does not first do himself, and he does not order one to refrain from evil before he himself denies temptation. He is very modest and is not haughty. He convinces people without aggravating

The Arab-Islamic state at the time of the Prophet Mohammed.

them. He is faithful to promises and accomplishes his duty. You will know his people when you know his secret. I witness that he is a Prophet'.

Ibn Hajar correctly reported that Al-Julanda recited poems, as the following translation of one section indicates:

> *Amr told me never to turn back to the old ways,*
> *it is the best of advice.*
> *I told him that his words were full of wisdom,*
> *Omani Julanda will take the right path for Oman.*
> *O! Amr, I converted to Islam as soon as I knew of it,*
> *an orator in the two valleys is reaching out to the people.*

It has been claimed that such an eloquent conversation occurred between Amr and Gaifar. but other sources state that Al-Julanda recited only one poem. There was another story that the conversation described above did indeed take place between him and Amr. What are the facts behind these accounts? Considering that every monarch in Oman at that time was called Al-Julanda could it be that Al-Julanda himself was in fact Gaifar? Or was this Al-Julanda the father of Gaifar and Abd? Another book recorded a different set of events, suggesting that the Prophet Mohammed sent Zaid Thabit bin Zaid or Amr bin Akhtab in the sixth year of Hegira with a letter to Al-Julanda, and sent Amr in the eighth year of Hegira to Gaifar and Abd, delivering the letter to them.

In one book, we read that Amr bin Al-A'as said:

I travelled to Oman, and visited Abd who was better than his brother and behaved himself. I told him that: "I am the messenger of Allah's Messenger to you and your brother". He replied: "My brother is older than I and his rank is higher than my own. I will introduce my brother to you and he will read your letter". Then he asked me: "What are you going to say to him?" I replied that I would ask him to submit to Allah alone and nothing other than Allah, and to believe that Mohammed is his servant and messenger. He said: "O! Amr, you are the son of your people's Master....How did your father Al-A'as Bin Waa'el, who we respect very much, decide?" I said: "He died and did not believe in Mohammed. I wished that he was the Messenger's follower. I was like him before, until Allah - may He be exalted - led me to the right way and I converted to Islam". He asked me: "When did you follow Mohammed?" I said: "Recently". He then asked: "Where did you convert?" I told him that I converted before Al-Najashi, and I told him that Al-Najashi had already converted to Islam. He asked: "What was the attitude of your people?" I told him that they approved and that they followed suit. He then asked: "What about the Christian priests and bishops?" I replied that they also had converted. He replied to me in disbelief saying: "Look Amr, what you say is not more than a lie." I said that I told the truth and that lies were prohibited in our religion. He then said: "Did Hercules know about Al-Najashi's submission to Islam?" I told him that he did. He asked: "What was the outcome?" I told him that Al-Najashi used to pay tax to Hercules, but when Al-Najashi placed his faith in Mohammed (Peace be upon Him), and submitted to Islam, he decided, and swore by Allah, that he would never pay Hercules, even if Hercules asked him to pay a single drachma. Hercules was told about what Al-Najashi had said and Hercules' brother asked him: "How come your slave has decided not to pay you tax and to believe in a new religion?" Hercules replied: "What can I do for a man who chooses his religion. In the name of God, if I was not the country's leader, I would do what he did".

He then said to me: "Think Amr about what you are saying". I replied: "In the name of Allah, I have told you the truth". Then Abd asked me: "What is his advice and from what does he want the people to desist?" I said: "He wants everyone to be obedient to Allah - may He be exalted. He forbids disobedience and has ordered us to do everything that is good and to be good to relatives. He forbids oppression and injustice. He also forbids adultery, alcoholic drinks and the worshipping of stones, as well as the prohibition of praying to idols and the cross". He said: "What a great thing he is leading the people to. If my brother agrees with me, we will travel to, and will believe in, Mohammed. But my brother is selfish with his property and would not wish to become a follower". I said: "If you submit to Islam, then Allah's Messenger will assign you to be the leader of your people, and will take the alms from the rich and give it to the poor". He said: "It is really a wonderful story, but what are the alms?" I told him that Allah's Messenger had imposed a certain amount of tax on the wealthy people. When I mentioned the cattle, he asked me: "Do you mean that some of the pasturing cattle will be taken?" I replied that they would. He said: "My God, I don't think that all my people will accept such a rule".

Amr bin Al-A'as continued his account, stating:

remained a few days at Gaifar's city who conveyed my mission to his brother who in turn invited me to visit him where he lived. His soldiers took my arm, and he told them to enter. When I went in they refused to allow me to sit. I looked into his eyes and he asked me: "Tell me what you want". I gave him the closed letter. He took it and finished reading the letter and passed it over to his brother to read it. Then he said: "Would you tell me what Qureish did?" I said: "They trusted and followed Him, whether through sincere belief in the religion or whether forced by the sword to accept it". He then asked: "Who supports him?" I replied: "The people who accepted and chose Islam as their religion, they understood Islam with the help of Allah. They were in darkness. I do not know any one left in this area who is not believing in Islam - except you. If you do not submit to Islam and follow it, the horses will crush you and destroy your followers. If you submit to Islam, then you will be assigned to be the leader of your people, and the horses and soldiers will not enter your place". He said: "Give me one day to think and come back tomorrow". On the next day I returned to him, but he did not allow me to enter his room. I went to his brother and told him that they did not allow me to see him. He came with me and entered the room and Gaifar said to me: "I have reflected upon what you demanded, but I should be the greatest weakling of all the Arabs if I were to give another man rule over all that I possess". I then told him: "I am leaving tomorrow". When he was certain that I was really returning, he went to have a private talk with his brother. On the next morning, he called me and dedicated himself to Islam, together with his brother and his people. They paid their alms, and ruled their people. They helped me and stood side by side with me against any opposition. Both submitted to Islam and many people followed them too.

Allah's Messenger (Peace be upon Him) died while Amr was still in Oman.

These narratives show us that the Prophet sent a letter with Abi Zaid Al-Ansary to Al-Julanda in the sixth year Hegira; or to Gaifar and Abd as we have mentioned above. He also sent a letter with Amr bin Al-A'as in the eighth year of Hegira, and a third letter to the people of Oman with Abu Shada Al-Damai of Dama. He said: 'We received the letter of the Prophet written on an animal skin, and the letter said - "From Mohammed, Messenger of Allah to the people of Oman, now and for all time, you must convert to Islam and witness that there is no God but Allah, and I am Allah's Messenger, pay the poor-rates, build the mosques, or I shall invade you".' Abu Shada said: 'We did not find somebody who could read the letter, until we found a boy who read it to us'.

The fourth letter from Allah (peace upon Him) to the people of Oman was carried by Abdullah bin Ali Altamali and Masslia bin Hazzan Al-Hadani, both of whom lived in Oman and jointly led a delegation which visited Allah's Messenger. Submitting themselves to Islam before Him, and promising their loyalty, He wrote a detailed letter concerning the alms that should be paid to the poor.

As a result of these letters, and the direct contact between many of the Omani people and the Messenger, Islam spread widely throughout Oman. One of the keys to its early establishment in Oman was that the Messenger promised the sons of Al-Julanda that they could stay in power if they would submit to Islam, and they followed His advice. Ibn Al-A'as was given the task of collecting the alms-tax from the wealthy people and distributing it among the poor people all over the country instead of sending it to the Islamic capital Al-Medina Al-Munawara. It was these kinds of socially just policies that impressed the Omani people who embraced Islam without any hesitation[72].

As we have seen, the two sons of Al-Julanda submitted to Islam. Ibn Sa'd included a detailed account of Amr bin Al-A'as description concerning how honest they were in their submission and how they responded to him. He became the alms collector[73]. Aba Zaid Al-Ansary undertook the task of teaching the people of Oman how to pray, to read the Qur'an, and to understand all the principles of the Islamic faith[74]. At the same time, numerous Omani delegations visited Al-Medina Al-Munawara, the Islamic capital. One important source mentions two Omani delegation to Al-Medina, one led by Asad bin Yabroh Al-Tahi and the other led by Salma bin Iyath Al-Azadi. They submitted to Islam and declared their loyalty to Islamic power in Al-Medina[75].

Another source describes a further delegation of Al-Azd who visited the Messenger. Abu Na'eem, through Soweid Ibn Al-Harth Al-Azadi said:

I was with the seventh delegation of my people visiting the Messenger. We entered his place and talked to him. He was happy to listen to us and in the meantime was impressed by our appearance. He asked: "Who are you and what are you doing?". We replied: "Believers". He smiled and said: "there must be certain tenets to support every belief. What tenets will you speak of with regard to your own faith?". We replied: "fifteen tenets and attributes, five of them are principles of belief which came through your messengers, five you ordered us to follow, and the other five were inherited from Al-Jahiliya who is still respected. But if you advise us to abandon some of them, we shall obey".

The Messenger said: "What are the five that my messengers ordered you to believe in?" We said: "you ordered us to believe in Allah, His angels, His books, His messengers and the resurrection after death". He then asked us: "What are the five that my messengers ordered you to follow?" We replied: "You ordered us to say that there is no god but Allah; Mohammed is Messenger of Allah; pray when the time of prayer has come; give alms to the poor; fast during Ramadhan; and make the Pilgrimage to Mecca" when possible.

He then asked: "What are the five from Al-Jahilya which you have inherited and still observe?" We said: "When prosperous we say thanks; when misfortunate we are patient; when death is unavoidable we accept it; when asked a question we never lie; and when our enemy is injured we do not rejoice". He then told us: "You are wise and learned men, your knowledge and skills in jurisprudence make you very close to being prophets". He then added: "I shall give you another five good tenets and then you will have twenty of them[76].

" In addition to the fifteen that you have mentioned, you should also not take more than you need to eat; not build more houses than you need to live in;

not compete for inheritance; fear Allah to whom you will return; and refrain from evil". They then departed and observed his advice (Peace be upon Him)[77].

The Messenger (Peace be upon Him) called the people of Oman to convert to Islam, and He prayed for them, especially when He came to know that the two kings of Oman were sincere and dedicated in their following of Islam. It is not surprising, therefore, that the Messenger prayed for the people of Oman, saying: 'Allah bless the people of Oman, those who believe in me without seeing me'[78].

Historical documents all concur that the two Omani kings responded positively to the Messenger's call. Both of them dedicated themselves to Islam without fear or wavering. Both advised the Omani people to follow suit, and they also converted to Islam with the exception of the Persians, who were in Oman at the time, and who rejected the initial call to Islam. In the meantime Gaifar and Abd realized that Islam had become a powerful spiritual influence for them, and one which provided important moral support to their citizens. Thus strengthened, they were able to expel the Persians and foreign aggressors from the country.

The Al-Azd tribal leaders visited Gaifar bin Al-Julanda and told him that the Persians would no longer be their neighbours and they decided to stand together in order to expel the Persians from their country. Gaifar contacted the Persian leaders, telling them that an Arab Prophet has been raised, and that they could choose between submission to Islam as they had done, or leave Oman. Their response was however negative, refusing on both counts.

Following this rebuttal, the Al-Azd clans united together, and engaged in a bloody fight against the Persians, defeating them. A large number of Persians were entrenched at the city of Dastajord. Besieged from all sides by the Islamic Arab forces, the Persians eventually sought a treaty. The peace terms demanded by the Arabian forces called for a full retreat of the Persians to their own country, together with their families and belongings. They departed Oman by sea to Persia[79].

The Persian expulsion was the culmination of a long held Omani dream. As we have already seen, the two sons of Al-Julanda, Gaifar and Abd continued to rule Oman, while Amr Ibn Al-A'as remained, as the representative of the Messenger, in order to collect the alms[80]. When Amr received news that the Prophet had died, he returned to Al-Medina. The Islamic state thus entered into a new phase of its development: the era of *Al-Khulafae Ar-Rashideen* (literally translated as 'The Just Caliphs') or the Orthodox Caliphate.

Let us look now at the kind of relations that developed between Oman and *Al-Khulafae Ar-Rashideen*?

Oman in the Era of Al-Khulafae Ar-Rashideen

Abu Bakr Al-Siddiq extols Oman's conversion to Islam commenting that when Amr Ibn Al-A'as departed from Oman for Al-Medina, he was very confident concerning the country's dedication to Islam. Following the death of the Master of Mankind (ie the Prophet), a delegation of Omani people headed by Abd bin

Al-Julanda, one of the two Kings of Oman, accompanied Amr Ibn Al-A'as back to Medina. Other Omani leaders were also among the delegation, like Ja'afar bin Jashm Al-A'atki and Abu Safra Sariq bin Dhalim. The delegation met the loyal follower, our master, Abu Bakr Al-Siddiq, the successor of Allah's Messenger.

Sariq bin Dhalim rose and declared: 'Thou, the successor of Allah's Messenger, we are the people of Qureish and here is a token of our respect, it is for Allah's Messenger, we are handing it over to you' [81].

Abu Bakr Al-Siddiq appreciated their efforts and many speakers followed suit and said: 'You, the Azd people, are honoured by the fact that Allah's Messenger appreciated your dedicated efforts'. Amr bin Al-A'as missed out nothing in appraising the Azd people of Oman.

The leaders of *Al-Ansaar* (defenders) of Al-Azd in Al-Medina Al-Munawara, paid homage to Abd bin Al-Julanda and his delegation. In the afternoon, Abu Bakr asked the people from Al-Ansaar and *Al-Muhagireen* (i.e. immigrants who followed the Prophet Mohammed when he left Mecca to Al-Medina) to attend a meeting. Abu Bakr gave a speech and began with thanks to Allah, mentioning the Prophet and praying for him; and then, directing his speech towards his Omani guests, he said:

O people of Oman, you voluntarily converted to Islam. Allah's Messenger did not invade your country with his horses and camel riders[82]. You did not disobey him, while some other Arabs did. You were not involved in dividing people, but you united your people. May Allah unite all your people. The Prophet Mohammed (Peace be upon Him) sent Amr Ibn Al-A'as to you without an army or weapons. You accepted his call even though he came from so far away from you. You fed him, even when he gave orders to you, when you were very strong and had a large population. No one did so many favours as you did, and no one did such honourable and respectable work like you. You must be very proud of yourselves because Allah's Messenger has so sincerely praised you. You will be honoured until the end of time! Amr lived happily among you as a Muslim, and he was grateful for your hospitality right up to the time of his departure. Allah has blessed you through Abd and Gaifar, the sons of Al-Julanda, for their submission to Islam. Allah has blessed them because of you, and blessed you because of them.

You were prosperous, and when Allah's Messenger (Peace be upon Him) died, you showed your generosity, your benevolence. We highly appreciated it. You accepted responsibility for, and you participated in, the great mission; and you sacrificed your men and your wealth. Allah will bless your hearts and tongues. There will be more work to be done, and I am sure you will be my trusted people! I am not afraid at all, that you will change your religion or you will harm your country. Allah will bless you all [83].

It is important to note here, that the speech of Abu Bakr Al-Siddiq, directed to the Omani delegation led by Al-Julanda, in the presence of a large gathering of *Al-Muhagireen* and *Al-Ansaar*, was one of considerable historical importance. It has unique social and political implications since it confirms the truly moral behaviour and thinking of the people of Oman; and underlines their high standards and legendary hospitality. The speech also helped to solidify the Omani peoples' faith, which remained very strong.

Abu Bakr's attitude towards the Omani delegation was so positive that he sent a letter to the people of Oman, applauding and thanking them for all their efforts. The successor of Allah's Messenger recognized Gaifar and his brother Abd as the leaders of their people, and granted them the right to collect tithes from their people.

The Omani records mention that Gaifar and his brother carried on their mission until their death. Abbad bin Abd bin Al-Julanda succeeded them during the time of Ottoman and Ali[84].

The Omanis and the Arab *Riddah* (Apostacy)

Omani commentators relate that Abd bin Al-Julanda, when he was introduced to Abu Bakr Al-Siddiq as part of the Omani delegation, was urged by the Caliph to take up the struggle against the *Murtad'deen* or the recanters (who had returned to their old gods after the death of the Prophet). The Caliph assembled a fighting party and issued them with their orders and Abd bin Al-Julanda set out in command of this company until he reached and redeemed the territory of the Jafna clan[85]. Amongst this fighting party was a man named Hassan bin Thabet Al-Ansar. Abd bin Al-Julanda fought valiantly and on their return from the Jafna country Hassan bin Thabet reported: 'The stature of Abd has been witnessed in the lands of the heathens and of Islam. There is not a man more resolute or more admirable or clear-thinking than Abd. He descended on (the enemy) in the morning and he darkened their day for them'[86]. This delighted Abu Bakr Al-Siddiq who said: 'Oh, Abu Al-Walid, it is just as you say. And your words are not yet adequate, for the nobility of his character is even greater than this'[87].

We do not hear anything of Ar'Riddah or apostates in Oman, with the exception of the incident transmitted by Al-Bilathuri (d 279 AH/892 AD) in *Futuh Al-Buldan*, Al-Tabari (d 310AH/922 AD) in his history and Ibn A'atham Al-Kufi (d 314 AH/926 AD) in *Kitab Al-Futuh* , as well as the writings of those scholars who transcribed from the abovementioned, such as Ibn Al-Atheer (d 630 AH/1232 AD) in his book *Al-Kamel fi Al-Tarikh*. They note that the Azd recanted and Luqait bin Malik Dhu'l Taj Al-Azdi withdrew to Daba. Abu Bakr Al-Siddiq dispatched Hodheifa bin Mohsen Al-Ghulfani (or Hodheifa bin Mohsen Al-Barqi) of the Azd and Akrama bin Abi Jahl bin Hisham Al-Makhzumi or Arifja Al-Barqi to meet them. Encountering Luqait and his escort they killed him and sent captives from Daba to Abu Bakr. It was said of Luqait bin Malik that he was known to the heathens as Al-Julanda. Gaifar and Abd fell back and took refuge in the mountains and the sea. Gaifar wrote to Abu Bakr informing him of what had happened and requesting assistance. Abu Bakr instructed his commanders to proceed with his troops to Oman and if they were close by to take direction from Gaifar and Abd.

Whatever the outcome, this movement died out and the Oman delegation were received in Medina to present the view of the Omanis on the origins of this movement. By the time the Omani delegation had arrived in Medina, the

Caliph Abu Bakr Al-Siddiq had died and Omar bin Al-Khattab had assumed the Caliphate. Omar ordered the return of the captives to Daba but not before he had severely chastised Hodheifa[88].

Here let us defer to the opinion of the Omani religious savant Nur Al-Din Abi Mohammed Abdullah bin Hamoud bin Salem Al-Salimi, one of the recognized *ulamas* (learned men) of the fourteenth century of the Hegira (twentieth century AD), who insists that Omani sources must always be relied on in matters concerning the history of Oman. Speaking of the Daba incident and the *Riddah* movement, he says: 'This is a summary of the incident of Daba from Omani writings. These are more dependable as sources and the most knowledgeable in content. Ibn Al-Atheer in his *Al-Kamil (fi Al-Tarikh)* (The Complete Book of Chronicles) did not correct what they said'[89].

Certainly the earliest Omani commentators repudiate suggestions that there was a *Riddah* movement in Oman convincingly saying: Sheikh Khalaf bin Ziad, who died in 134 AH/751 AD said in his *Sirah* (biography): He informed us that Abu Bakr sent an alms collector to the Omanis to collect the *sadaqa* or wealth tax and as law abiding citizens they handed over the tax, with the exception of one woman who quarrelled with some of the alms collectors in the course of which the woman was struck. She called to her people to come to her aid, crying out: '*Ya Al Malik* (Oh Malik Clan)'. This was a heathen rallying cry punishable by death, in the belief of Muslims. And so combat was joined and the tax collectors were victorious. When Hodheifa Al-Ghulfani appeared he seized as many captives as he could handle from among the citizens of Daba and set out with them for Medina. The Omani delegation arrived in Oman, but Abu Bakr had passed away. Omar bin Al-Khattab returned the captives and spoils and a total of 300 of them became Muslims[90]. We note that this historian is citing in his account Al-Bilathuri, Al-Tabari, Ibn Al-Atheer and others, making him an acceptable and credible source.

Matters Settle Down After the Daba Incident

At all events matters settled down in Oman and the government remained in the hands of the Julanda family throughout the time of the Orthodox Caliphate, despite definite historical information that the two successive Caliphs Abu Bakr and Omar bin Al-Khattab had appointed a *Wali* (governor) to Oman. Notwithstanding the *Wali*, it would appear that the sovereignty of the sons of Julanda was not contravened and they managed to preserve both their interests and their status without diminution. It would appear that the appointment of these prefects was by way of establishing as a hard fact in Oman the existence of a central authority of the Arab Islamic State. Meanwhile the actual role of the *Wali* was confined to the collection of alms tax and the teaching of the *Sunnan* (sanctioned procedures) and of the fundamental concepts of Islam, while liaising between the Julanda family and the Islamic authorities in Medina as well as offering opinions and advice[91].

It was enough for the central Islamic authority to maintain the political situation in Oman to an extent that reassured it that its concerted efforts to reunify the Arab Islamic State would not be interrupted and that its forces would be free to open up new fronts in the north and east. The Omanis had a pivotal role in this strategy.

It is worth noting here that the Caliph Abu Bakr Al-Siddiq had appointed Hodheifa bin Mohsen to Oman and this appointment was renewed when Omar bin Al-Khattaɔ became Caliph with Bilal Al-Ansari for an assistant[92]. A radical development now took place in the relations between Oman and the central Islamic Authority when Othman bin Affan assumed the Caliphate. The administration of Oman became attached to that of Basra such that Oman became militarily and politically an affiliate of the Basra administration[93].

This proceɔure can be explained by the fact that the central Islamic authority needed to reinforce the eastern front with combatants in support of the Arab Islamic military effort. The authority of the Julandas was not undermined by this procedure for once again they were able to pursue their administrative and commercial policies in Oman, a status which was to be maintained throughout the period of the Orthodox Caliphates.

In order thɩs to ensure that the Azd and Qutha'a and other tribes of Oman would continue to have an active role in the conquests of the *Mashriq* (Orient)[94], when the Muslims had won a victory at the battle of Jalula, a fighting party led by Othman bin Abi Al-A'as sailed for the eastern shore of the Gulf. With them weɾe combatants from the Azd, Raseb and Abdul Qais tribes. The fighting party embarked from Julfar and made for the island of Ibn Kawan, which they liberated from Persian control. The Muslims managed once again to rout the Persians from the island of Qeshm and so expanded the territory of the Islamic State[95].

The primary sources are silent on the matter of naming any of the *walis* of the Arab Islamic Caliphate during the reign of Othman bin Affan and it looks as though the Islamic authority was satisfied enough with the administration of Basra and the presence of the Julanda family in Oman.

Oman saw the appointment of a new *Wali* Al-Hellu bin Awf Al-Azdi under the Caliph Ali bin Abi Taleb[96]. This appointment demonstrates the special esteem in which Oman was held throughout the time that it was a *wilaya* of the Islamic State. Political relations between this state and Oman were not adversely affected during the civil war which followed the assassination of the Caliph Othman bin Affan and the Caliphate of Ali bin Abi Taleb, for Omani tribes had neither act nor part in this civil strife nor in the bloody assassinations of the Caliphs. Indeed the administration in Oman was at this time more independent than it had been before the advent of the authority of the Arab Islamic State[97].

Oman's Participation in the Islamic Conquest

The great period of Arab Islamic Conquest continued from the time of the death of the Prophet in the eleventh year of the Hegira (632 AD) up to the end of the Ummayyad Era, that is for something over a century. The territory now controlled by the Arabs stretched as far as India and China in the east and to the Atlantic Ocean or *Bahr Al-Dhulmat* (Sea of Darkness) in the west; and in a line from the Black Sea and the Mediterranean to the Pyrenees in the north; and to the Arabian Sea and the Sudanese desert in the south.

Islam spread far and wide throughout the inhabited world and to territories far beyond those conquered by the Arabs through the influence of pious Muslim savants and theologians as well as preachers and merchants. The Omanis were particularly active in this latter respect, helping in the spread of Islam to lands conquered and unconquered.

Scientifically researched historical studies of the first wave of conquests are eloquent about the role of the Omani Azdi tribes in these conquests; and about the deployment and subsequent settlement by some of the tribes and their principal offshoots in various countries; and on the principal arenas of the Omani *jihad* on land and sea during these great conquests. The Omanis were particularly noted for their superior contribution, in person and possessions, to this struggle.

Among the few historical narratives which have come down to us, we know that the Caliph Omar bin Khattab requested the *Wali* of Oman Othman bin Abi Al-A'as Al-Thaqafi after the battle of Jalula (16 AH/637 AD) to make the sea crossing of the Gulf in order to engage the Persian king. He duly set out with 3000 or 2600 fighting men, most of them Azd from Julfar[98], to the island of Kawan where the Persian commander was based. The Persian commander sued for a peace with Othman bin Abi Al-A'as and no battle ensued. When Yazdegird the Persian king heard of this, however, he wrote to his viceroy in Karman instructing him to sail for Kawan and provoke trouble amongst the Arabs there. So he rerouted three or four thousand men from Hormuz to Ras Al-Qasm (an arabization of the original 'Gash'). They were met by Ibn Abi Al-A'as on the island of Qasm and a ferocious battle ensued in which (the Persian) Shahruk was killed and the heathens defeated. It was said that Yazdegird sent Shahruk (or Ibn Al-Hamra) to meet the Arabs with 40,000 horsemen[99]. This Arab victory was won by the Omanis and Shahruk was slain by the hand of an Omani.

Certainly the decisive victory of the Omanis over Shahruk was one of the most significant factors in allowing the Arabs to break out of their encirclement from the south and east. This Omani victory settled once and for all Persian hopes of restoring their kingdom or conquering the Arabs.

The Omani effort did not stop at diverting Persian attacks on the southern front. They took part in the conquests on other fronts also, including the Iraqi front. One of the consequences of the extensive participation of the Omani Azdis in the Islamic Conquests was that many of them carved out a life for themselves in Basra after this city was built in the lifetime of Omar bin Al-Khattab. The Omanis persisted in their endeavours for the faith over the passage of time[100].

Othman now became Caliph and the migration of Omani Azd to Iraq in this period grew apace. Most of them headed for Basra which had become a gathering place and capital of the Eastern Provinces in the time of the Ummayyads. It goes without question that Oman would maintain a relationship of some nature with this State, whether good or bad. So what was in fact the nature of the relationship?

Oman and the Ummayyad State

When internecine squabbles broke out between the Muslims at the time of Othman bin Affan and when Ali bin Abi Taleb became mediator between him and Maawiya bin Abi Sufian, Oman's attitude to the Ummayyad Caliphate began to change. Around 37 AH/657 AD, following a meeting of the two rulers

Amr bin Al-A'as and Abdullah bin Qais Abi Moussa Al-Ashaari whereby they deposed Ali bin Abi Taleb as Caliph of the Muslims, Oman withdrew altogether from the Ummayyad sphere of influence .

Omani historical sources and narratives agree that after the internecine strife and sundering of the *Umma* of Islam and the accession to sovereignty and power of Maawiya bin Abi Sufian, the Ummayyads had neither standing nor interests in Oman[101], for the centre of power of the Arab Islamic State moved from Kufa to Damascus after Al-Hassan bin Ali had abdicated from the Caliphate in the year 41 AH in favour of Maawiya bin Abi Sufian. The overriding preoccupations of the Ummayyad Caliphs were the restoration of stablility and security in the principal quarters of the Arab Islamic State and Iraq in general. And so they entrusted the administration of Kufa to Al-Mughayera bin Shaaba Al-Thaqafi and Abdullah bin Amer became *Wali* of Basra until he was replaced by Ziad bin Abia Al-Thaqafi in the year 45 AH/665 AD[102].

Despite these political developments which took place in the power structures of the Arab Islamic State, the administration of Oman remained under the control of the Julanda family who were forceful in guarding their administrative independence, particularly after the Ummayyads came to power. For all we know, perhaps the transfer of power from Kufa to Damascus gave Oman even greater independence, given the geographical distance which now separated it from the seat of central power. One pointer to this interpretation is in the fact that the Ummayyad government did not appoint a *wali* to Oman[103].

Assuming that the Julanda family refused to submit to the Ummayyad Caliphate, the Caliph Maawiya bin Abi Sufian was more than capable of restoring matters to their previous situation should he have wished, as would Al-Hajjaj bin Youssef at a future date. This was particularly so in view of the fact that his *walis* in Basra and Kufa had succeeded in imposing order and stability and subduing the opposition to Ummayyad rule[104]. But Maawiya did not send a *wali* and he did not harm Oman.

In any case, the political situation began to deteriorate during the reign of Yazid bin Maawiya (60-64 AH/679-683 AD) and resistance started to raise its head in the Hijaz and Iraq after the surrendering of the Caliphate by Maawiya bin Yazid in 64 AH, leaving the seat of power vacant. The political vacuum which ensued in the Arab Islamic State precipitated a power struggle[105] in which the central authority in Damascus began to lose control over the provinces at the extremities of the Islamic State. Onto this stage stepped Najda bin Amer Al-Hanafi, leader of the *Khawarij* (or Separatists, a dissident Islamic sect), who had managed to seize control of Bahrain and to spread his influence as far as Oman. With the purpose of attaining this objective, he had sent an armed expedition to Oman under Attia bin Al-Aswad Al-Hanafi. Oman at that time was under the governorship of Abbad bin Abd bin Al-Julanda, assisted by his sons Suleiman and Said in regulating the political and commercial affairs of Oman. Attia Al-Hanafi surprised the Julanda and having killed Abbad Al-Julanda went on to take Oman by force, and in doing so removed it from the field of Arab Islamic central authority[106].

It would not have been the choice of the Muhakkimah in Damascus that Basra, Bahrain and Oman and other places in Maghreb should slip from Arab grasp without a thorough investigation. While they knew from experience that they did not have the power to pose a direct threat to the Ummayyad authority, yet they were able to harrass the Ummayyad forces using tactics of direct confrontation and sudden strikes. They chose regions geographically distant from the centre of the state from which to stage these activities which they intensified in such areas as enjoyed natural advantages to facilitate their military manoeuvres and sudden ambushes.

In this latter aspect the *Khawarij* were able to hold Oman within their sphere of influence insofar as its landscape was distinguished by many strategic and well fortified vantage points. This and the preoccupation of the Arabian State at the time of Marwan bin Al-Hakam and his son Abdul Mulik bin Marwan (64-73AH/683-692AD) with the matter of an endless succession of rebellions and, set in this context, its attempts to achieve the unification of the Arab Islamic State, helped to generate the circumstances which spurred the *Khawarij* in the Gulf to pursue their activities with vigour[107].

The sons of Julanda had managed to put together a strong following in Oman and were biding their time for an opportunity to rid the country of the *Khawarij*. The opportunity came when the *Khawarij* commander Attia Al-Hanafi returned to Bahrain, leaving behind his deputy Abi Al-Qassem as governor of Oman. In these favourable circumstances the Omanis, led by the Julanda, mutinied against Abi Al-Qassem and routed him and his forces, thus ridding the country of the *Khawarij* once and for all. The commander tried in vain to subdue Oman a second time, but the Omanis again held their ground and once again the *Khawarij* failed to regain their foothold in this important part of the Arab world[108].

Al-Hajjaj bin Youssef Al-Thaqafi, however, did succeed in this and in truth the appointment of Al-Hajjaj bin Youssef Al-Thaqafi as Amir of Iraq and the Islamic *Mashriq* (Orient) in the year 75 AH/694 AD by the Caliph Abdul Mulik bin Marwan is deemed a turning point in affairs between the central authority of the Islamic State and Oman. Al-Hajjaj's political leanings were towards the centralization of government and the administration of all of the associated provinces and districts was linked directly to the central government. We do not find it strange then to come upon Al-Hajjaj drawing Oman into his plans for centralization and this is how it came to be under direct administration from Damascus[109].

A modern historian observes that the Azd tribes in Oman under Said and Suleiman, sons of Abbad bin Abd bin Al-Julanda bin Al-Mustakbir, publicly declared their resistance to the policy of Al-Hajjaj bin Youssef Al-Thaqafi[110]. And since we have no precise evidence of the stand taken by the sons of Al-Julanda, we cannot be certain if their resistance was founded in their opposition to the policies of Al-Hajjaj bin Youssef which threatened the very basis of their authority in Oman or to the policies of the Ummayyad State and the Caliph Abdul Mulik bin Marwan.

If we look to the views of Omani historians, we find that the opposition of the Omanis to Ummayyad rule was specifically attributable to the policies of Al-Hajjaj bin Youssef, and it was he whom they deemed responsible for precipitating the military confrontations between Omani and Ummayyad forces[111]. The Julanda family found in the policy of Al-Hajjaj bin Youssef a real threat to their interests and a clear indication that their own role in the administration of Oman was being extinguished after 80 years of surviving in the shadow of the Arab Islamic State.

One modern historian remarks that the Omanis had refused to pay the *zakat* (obligatory alms tax) to the central powers of the Ummayyad State after Maawiya bin Abi Sufian had assumed power. This remained the case until the Caliphate of Abdul Mulik bin Marwan[112]. The same author in another context notes that the Azd tribes mounted a revolt under the command of Said and Suleiman, sons of Abbad bin Abd bin Al-Julanda bin al-Mustakbir. And he alludes to the independent stand pursued by the Julanda family by which they exploited at every turn the political turmoil in which the Arab Islamic State was embroiled from the accession of Maawiya bin Abi Sufian to the seat of power insofar as they did not recognize the Caliphate of Maawiya bin Abi Sufian[113].

It goes without question that an inference such as this is supported by both Omani and non-Omani sources[114], though there are Omani historians who reject out of hand any notion that Oman infringed its allegiance to the central government under the Ummayyads. Whatever the case, any response to Al-Hajjaj's decision ending the administrative independence of the Julanda family in Oman must fall within the scope of larger political developments which were taking place at the heart of the Arab Islamic State during the Caliphate of Abdul Mulik bin Marwan and which accelerated after its success in quelling the various rebellions and restoring the unity of the State. At any rate the central government was no longer content to maintain the previous pattern of relations between Oman and the Arab Islamic State. This may help us to understand better the nature of the events that unfolded in the context of political developments at this time in the Ummayyad State.

Primary sources do not assist us much with information as to the cause of the shift in relations which was to culminate in military confrontation. Information is scant and such information as does exist does not acquaint us much with the circumstances which led to the sudden termination of the old mode of relations between the Caliphate and Oman. The preoccupation of the early historians with events happening at the centre of the Islamic State and its principal districts left them little opportunity to record events which they did not perceive as being of crucial interest to the central government[115].

At all events the date that the military expeditions to Oman commenced is not recorded. It is probable that the first military expedition set out shortly before the Abdul Rahman bin Mohammed bin Ash'ath movement (81-83 AH/700-702 AD). The result was a devastating failure[116]. The first expeditionary force, under the command of Al-Qassem bin Shaawa Al-Mezni, came by sea and dropped anchor off the coast of Hatat. They encountered tough resistance from the Omanis, who scattered the attacking force and killed their commander Al-Qassem[117]. When the fugitives arrived back home, Al-Hajjaj sensed the seriousness of the situation and he put together a set of measures which he hoped would bring him success in a future military endeavour.

The first of these moves was the containment of the Azd tribes in Basra so that they could not extend assistance to the Azd of Oman. The second move was the dispatch of two separate expeditionary forces to Oman. The leader of the first of these was Majaa bin Shaawa Al-Mezni who was the brother of Al-

Qassem who had been killed in the first expedition. The total fighting force was 40,000 men and they were divided into two separate detachments of 20,000 men each, one of which took the land route while the other went by sea[118]. Al-Hajjaj bin Youssef put together the entire troop from Nazarene tribesmen who had no connection with the Azd and Atta surrendered command to Majaa who was spurred by the fact that the Omanis were responsible for the death of his brother.

The land force set out for Oman and Al-Hajjaj bin Youssef sent dispatches to the Caliph to keep him thoroughly acquainted with the progress of this military expedition. The land contingent was first to arrive, only to find Suleiman bin Abbad Al-Julanda ready with most of the fighting army of Oman to take on the Ummayyad forces. The two armies met at the water's edge below the wasteland which is now east of Falaj and north of Wadi Bawshir near Muscat. Calamity overtook the Ummayyad army and they were put to flight[119].

It would appear that the Julanda had made their preparations to encounter the land contingent sent by Al-Hajjaj and had not counted on the naval contingent which had now arrived and disembarked at Julfar (present-day Ras Al-Khaimah). It was this force that was led by Maja'a Al-Mezni - we do not know who led the land force. In due course Majaa reached the coast of Barka where Said bin Abbad Al-Julanda found himself compelled to take on this superior battleforce despite his own depleted numbers. Combat was engaged and went on throughout the day until nightfall when Said took advantage of darkness to withdraw to the Jebel Al-Akhdar with his immediate family and those of his brother Suleiman[120].

When Suleiman heard that the Ummayyads had landed a naval force he went out to the Ummayyad fleet and set fire to more than 50 ships. The remainder put to sea with the combatants aboard and retired to Julfar after Suleiman had managed to defeat Maja'a and his men near Sama'il[121].

Al-Hajjaj was informed of the difficulties his forces were encountering and he promptly dispatched a reinforcement party of 5000 fresh troops, made up of men from El-Sham who had previously been used by Al-Hajjaj to put down the rebellion of Abdul Rahman bin Mohammed bin Al-Asha'ath Al-Kindi[122]. Historical accounts confirm that the Julanda sons, Said and Suleiman, were corralled in the Jebel Al-Akhdar and they were without adequate means to continue the fight for their strength and numbers were diminished, and this against an Ummayyad army which was constantly being replenished. Added to this was the fact that the Ummayyad forces had managed to take possession of the coastal cities. Against this background the Omani resistance effort began to flag and Said and Suleiman Al-Julanda opted to take refuge in *Bilad Al-Zinj* (the land of the Negroes) on the East African coast, abandoning Oman to the forces of Al-Hajjaj bin Youssef. Here they came to play an honourable part in the spread of Islam in East Africa[123].

And so Oman lost its independence and became a province of the central State, attached to the *Wilaya* of Al-Hajjaj bin Youssef in Iraq. Al-Hajjaj appointed Al-Khiar bin Sabra Al-Majashai *Wali* of Oman.

Matters were to remain thus until the death of Abdul Mulik bin Marwan when the seat of power passed to his son Al-Walid bin Abdul Mulik (86-96 AH/705-715 AD). When Al-Hajjaj bin Youssef Al-Thaqafi died in the year 95

AH/714 AD Al-Walid bin Abdul Mulik appointed Yazid bin Abi Muslim as *Wali* of Iraq and Yazid in turn dispatched a new *Wali* to Oman, Saif bin Al-Hani Al-Hamdani[124].

When Suleiman bin Abdul Mulik took over as ruler of the Ummayyad State (96-99 AH/715-717 AD), the Ummayyad grip began to relax in Oman and the Omanis began by degrees to recover their internal independence. Under Suleiman the local viceregents were discharged and Saleh bin Abdul Rahman bin Qais Al-Leithi took charge. Subsequently he felt that Omani administrators could be reinstated and Saleh bin Abdul Rahman would oversee them.

Subsequently, Suleiman bin Abdul Mulik appointed Yazid bin Al-Mahlab Al-Azdi *Wali* over Iraq and Khorasan. Yazid assigned his brother Ziad to Oman. It was said of this man in the Omani narratives that 'he remained a viceregent beneficent to its citizens up to the death of Suleiman bin Abdul Mulik'[125].

The narratives observe that Suleiman's successor, Omar bin Abdul Aziz (99-101 AH/717-720 AD), appointed Adi bin Artaa Al-Fazari *Wali* of Iraq. Adi in turn appointed viceregents to Oman who did such harm to the country that the Omanis wrote to Omar bin Abdul Aziz to complain and he sent Omar bin Abdullah Al-Ansari to them as *Wali* and their lot improved. He remained a much venerated *Wali* among the Omanis who paid their *sadaqat* (alms tax) to him happily and voluntarily, and this was the situation up to the death of Omar bin Abdul Aziz[126].

It would appear that Oman gradually acquired a large measure of internal independence during the rule of Suleiman bin Abdul Mulik. When Omar bin Abdul Aziz died, his *Wali* Omar bin Abdullah Al-Ansari left Oman and said to Ziad bin Al-Mahlab: 'This country is as your nation and your affairs are there', and Ziad bin Al-Mahlab did indeed apply himself to the affairs of Oman up to the appearance of Abu Al-Abbas Al-Saffah, into whose hands was delivered the affairs of the Ummayyads and who was to lay the foundations of the Abbassid Caliphate.

In the same year that the Abbassid Caliphate came into existence the first Ibadhi Imamate came into being in Oman in the person of Al-Julanda bin Massaoud bin Gaifar bin Al-Julanda. Full independence from the newly instituted Abbassid State was now attained by Oman. The spirit which achieved this has to be due in great part to the emergence of the Ibadhi rite in Oman in which the Omanis found a powerful motivation to confront any state which might seek to impose its influence on their country. We should then take a look at how this doctrine first made its appearance in Basra, found its way to Oman and Yemen and what impact it had on the events which took place in these two countries and on their relations with the Ummayyads and subsequently the Abbassids. We should also examine how the Ibadhi sect reached North Africa and founded there a powerful state which had a substantial role in the spread of Islam among the Berbers of the Great Sahara and the countries beyond the Sahara which are commonly known as West and Middle Sudan. This will be the subject of the following chapter.

The Al-Mahlab Clan of Oman
and their political and military role up to the end of the Ummayyad Era

The Origins of the Al-Mahlabs and the Part they Played in the Time of the Orthodox Caliphate

Throughout their long history the Al-Mahlab clan retained a bond with their mother country, Oman, and indeed Oman's name was linked with most of the outstanding achievements and momentous events which involved the Al-Mahlabs in the course of their political and military campaigns. When Abu Safra, father of Al-Mahlab, went out with the Islamic armies to take part in the Conquests in the time of Omar bin Al-Khattab, Omanis served in the armies led by him. They had their own *quartier* in Basra which had grown into a metropolis, and the city in time came to be known as 'Al-Mahlab's Basra' and its citizens as *Mawali Al-Mahallab* or Al-Mahlab's servants in recognition of the strength of their ties with the Al-Mahlabs and the Omanis. So who were these Al-Mahlabs? And who was Abu Safra?

The Al-Mahlab family trace their ancestry to Al-Mahlab bin Abi Safra. Abu Safra's name was Qati bin Sariq bin Dhalim[127] who in turn traced his origins to the Yemeni Azd[128] who migrated to Oman when the annihilation of the Ma'rib Dam, and other calamities cited in the ancient narratives, drove out the tribes from Yemen to disperse to new homes in the far quarters of the Arabian peninsula. The Azd were accustomed to identify the various clans by a distintuishing characteristic so we had the Surat Azd and the Shinu'a Azd and the Omani Azd, all of them descendents of the aforementioned Azd[129]. Omani genealogists believe that Abu Safra was from the city of Adam in the Omani interior and that the Al-Busaid in Oman are descended from Abu Said Al-Mahlab bin Abi Safra[130].

Ibn Hajar in *Al-Isaba* reviews evidence that implies that Abu Safra was a Companion and that he had met the Prophet to whom he declared his allegiance to Islam. He says that it was the Prophet who had given Abu Safra this name: 'Abu Safra was presented to the Prophet in order to pledge his allegiance. He was at the time wearing a yellow (*safra* in Arabic) robe and when the Prophet noticed him he remarked "And who might you be?", to which he replied: "I am Qati bin Sariq bin Dhalim". The Prophet said to him: "You are Abu Safra. May you repudiate theft and transgression". Abu Safra declared his submission and he said: "I have eighteen sons and I have been blessed with a girl and I have called her Safra". And the Prophet said: "And you are then Abu Safra"[131].'

Ibn Hajar acknowledges that this version of events is a controversial one. Some of the commentators reject outright Abu Safra's status as Companion and deny a meeting with the Prophet. The author of *Al-Isti'ab* declares that Abu Safra was a Muslim at the time of the Prophet and did not go to see him but did join a delegation to the Caliph Omar bin Al-Khattab[132].

The accounts of the two abovementioned authors demand a moment's pause to tie in the information they afford us with what is available to us from Omani sources. It is quite likely that Abu Safra did go to meet the Prophet in Medina to make his declaration of submission. The Omani sources believe that Islam was quick to take hold in Oman when the call to the faith went out from the Hijaz. The first to declare his faith was Mazin bin Ghadhuba, a citizen of Sama'il who travelled to Medina and had a meeting with the Prophet before whom he declared his faith; and he was soon followed in his conversion by others[133]. Ibn Saad in *Al-Tabaqat* recalls that a delegation went from Oman to Medina to present themselves to the Prophet and announce their conversion. They asked the Prophet if he would send back with them someone who could teach them the ways of the faith[134]. This was before the start of the Conquests and before the Prophet had sent his message to the rulers of Oman, Abd and Gaifar, sons of Julanda, calling on them to adopt Islam[135]. If we keep in mind that Abu Safra was a prominent citizen and one of the lords and masters of Oman, and that his standing among his people became even more exalted when he adopted Islam[136], then we do not find it unlikely that he should have gone to Medina and had a meeting with the Prophet as Ibn Hajar claims.

Concerning the insistence by the author of *Al-Isti'ab* that Abu Safra did not meet the Prophet but did meet Omar bin Al-Khattab, we suggest that this account lacks precision, for it is accepted that Abu Safra met Abu Bakr Al-Siddiq after he became Caliph. The narratives that we have at our disposal are in agreement that shortly after the death of the Prophet Amr bin Al-A'as returned from Oman, where he had been *Wali* since the year 8 AH, to Medina accompanied by an Omani delegation of some 70 horsemen under the command of one of the country's leaders. This commander was Abd bin Julanda and Abu Safra was a member of the delegation[137]. The purpose of this delegation was to pledge allegiance to Abu Bakr Al-Siddiq on his assuming the Caliphate. Amr bin Al-A'as in the course of his journey 'found the population to have recanted. He reached the Muslims in Medina and they gathered around him to hear his news and he told them that there were soldiers encamped all the way from Daba to Medina'[138].

As the Omani delegation arrived at the approaches to Medina they met the Caliph Abu Bakr and Abu Safra was received on behalf of the Omanis. Amr bin Al-A'as came forward sound and in good health and Abu Safra presenting him said:'This (man) was entrusted to us under a mandate of the Prophet to which we committed ourselves and we now pass him back to you'. And Abu Bakr Said: 'May God reward you'[139].

The author of *Al-Aghani* (The Songs) confirms this account saying: 'The delegation of the son of Julanda was of the Azd, the Omani Azd, and there was a delegation which included Abu Safra and he went in to Omar with Ibn Julanda'[140]. So perhaps the Omani delegation met first with Omar bin Al-Khattab and subsequently there was an encounter with Abu Bakr; for the narrative speaks of only one visit by Ibn Julanda and that is the one we have described and which included Abu Safra.

Following this we come to the account of Abu Safra in his capacity as one of the commanding officers who had led Muslim expeditions into Persia at the time of the Caliph Omar bin Al-Khattab. Omar had instructed the *Wali* of Oman, who was at that time Othman bin Abi Al-A'as Al-Thaqafi, to monitor the movements of the Persian army in the Gulf and to engage them where appropriate. Abu Safra, being both knowledgeable and experienced in matters of navigation and seamanship, had the confidence of the Omanis and when Omar bin Al-Khattab asked the *Wali* to dispatch a naval party across the Gulf to Persia and Othman bin Abi Al-A'as in turn asked the Omanis to recommend an able counsel to him in the matter of the expedition, they recommended Abu Safra[141].

The *Wali* commissioned the fighting force and assembled a party of around 3000 troops, most of them Omani Azd. Abu Safra was amongst these, leading the Bani Umran who were his own kinsmen[142]. With him also were three of his sons: Najaf, Mughayera and Habib[143]. Othman bin Abi Al-A'as succeeded with the help of this fighting force in harrassing the Persians up and down the Gulf. He seized control of the island of Kawan and banished the Persians to the east bank of the Gulf and routed them again in Karman, where Abu Safra and his sons and his men fought with fortitude and valour[144].

Abu Safra went on to fight many encounters with the Muslims along the Persian front during the time of Othman bin Affan. Ibn Khaldun describes how Othman bin Abi Al-A'as sent his brother Al-Hakam from Bahrain to Persia with 2000 men. He marched to Tawj with Jaroud Al-Abdi and Abu Safra the father of Al-Mahlab at his side. The Persian king dispatched his noted commander Shahruk with a party to meet the invader. They met at Tawj where the Persians were defeated and Shahruk killed. The Muslims now pursued the defeated army to Sabour, where they laid siege to the city until the inhabitants sued for peace[145].

In the wake of this victory Abu Safra went down to Tawj and seized it as a base for himself and his family, clansmen and troops. Later, during the Caliphate of Othman bin Affan, he transferred to Basra where he was received graciously by the *Wali* of the day Abdullah bin Amer[146] and the Azd fighting party led by Abu Safra attached itself to the *Wali's* forces in Basra[147].

After the death of Othman bin Affan, when the Caliphate passed to Ali bin Abi Taleb and the great struggle broke out between him and Maawiya bin Abi Sufian, Abu Safra had a meeting with the Caliph Ali in the aftermath of the Battle of the Camel in Basra. From the dialogue that ensued we can impute that Abu Safra was a leader of the Azd tribes in Iraq at this time, for when Ali revealed the grievances he had endured at the hands of his people Abu Safra said to him: 'Wallah, O Prince of the Faithful, if I had been among them no two of them would have raised their sword'. Ali now asked Abu Safra if he would lend him one of his sons to carry the standard of faith to those who had fled after the Battle of the Camel, in the hope of convincing them to return. Al-Najaf bin Abi Safra refused this undertaking in fear of the consequences of the Battle of the Camel. Al-Mahlab, however, took on the task and the banner of the Muslims was given to him. As a result of his efforts most of the fugitives were persuaded to return to Basra, where the inhabitants now saw 'good fortune in the banner of Al-Mahlab'[148].

We do not know the year of Abu Safra's death, except that he died in Basra during the *Wilaya* of Abdullah bin Al-Abbas in the Caliphate of Ali bin Abi Taleb. It was said that he died on the march to Saffin[149] from which we can gather that it was in or around 37 AH.

The Al-Mahlabs and Their Role in the (Maawiya Bin Abi) Sufian Period (40-65 AH)

There is no clear reference in the sources at our disposal to the individual who headed the Abu Safra clan after the latter's death. All pointers however would indicate that the most prominent personality in the clan at that time was his son Al-Mahlab. Although Al-Mahlab was one of the younger brothers[150], word of his battle skills, horsemanship and high standing had gone before him, and he was first choice to lead the family on the death of Abu Safra. The sources think it most likely that his reputation was gained as a result of his participation in the invasion of Sind in the year 44 AH/ 664 AD. This savage battle had involved a confrontation with Turkish horsemen who were nonetheless annihilated by the superior skills of the Muslims[151]. Al-Mahlab at this time commanded a fighting force which was drawn from his own tribesmen, the Omani Azd[152]. This is a further pointer that he succeeded his father in taking over command of his troops.

An account by Ya'qubi describes how Maawiya bin Abi Sufian wrote to Ziad bin Abih his *Wali* in Kufa: 'There is a man, a Companion of the Prophet, named Al-Hakam bin Amru Al-Ghafari. Appoint him *Wali* of Khorasan'. Ziad did as instructed and (Al-Hakam) invaded Herat and conquered Jarjan with the help of Al-Mahlab bin Abi Safra[153] who had proved himself courageous and able in fighting the enemy. Al-Mahlab now advanced into wild and rugged terrain and against the most intransigent populations in pursuit of his military endeavour, displaying a formidable strength and lust for combat.

When Al-Hakam bin Amru Al-Ghafari invaded the Turk-held mountains in 47 AH/ 667 AD Al-Mahlab was one of the commanders of this expedition. During one phase of the campaign Al-Hakam's army found itself locked into a Turkish ambush with all access to roads and mountain passes cut off by the Turks. From this tight corner Al-Hakam surrendered command to Al-Mahlab who managed by ruse and manoeuvre to capture one of the enemy guard and threaten him with his life to show them a way out of the impasse. His efforts were successful and the army managed to escape with their lives and the spoils of war[154].

Al-Mahlab's battle acuity and cool head in critical situations enabled him to become one of the most formidable commanders on the Eastern Front and the *Walis* of Khorasan were eager to share the company of Al-Mahlab bin Abi Safra. When Said bin Othman bin Affan in the year 56 AH/ 675 AD set out as the new *Wali* of Khorasan district Al-Mahlab was among his commanders[155]. Al-Mahlab took part in many campaigns at this time, in particular the invasion of Samarkand. It was said that Said bin Othman and Al-Mahlab had their eyes gouged during this campaign[156].

In the Caliphate of Yazid bin Maawiya, Salama bin Ziad (61 AH/ 680 AD) was appointed *Wali* of Khorasan and Sijistan and left Damascus with a rallying call to the people of Basra to send forth their men with him, the new *Wali* of Khorasan, if they wished to be part of a *jihad*. Al-Mahlab took up the call and with him a number of the leading notables of Basra, accompanied by their horsemen[157]. Salama's armies marched on Bukhara where Queen Khatoun ruled. Sensing the gravity of the approaching threat the queen announced her desire to marry King Saghad in a pact under which he would come to rule Bukhara and make a stand against the Muslims. King Saghad went out with an army of 120,000 men and against this vast horde Salama pitted his smaller army, placing Al-Mahlab's fighting force in the vanguard. After protracted and savage combat Al-Mahlab's men prevailed; the Turks were defeated and King Saghad slain[158].

Salama bin Ziad remained *Wali* of Khorasan up to the death of Yazid bin Maawiya in the month of Safar 64 AH/ 683 AD[159]. Salama hoped to conceal the fact of the Caliph's death to prevent an outbreak of tribal unrest, but the news spread soon after the installation of Maawiya II as Caliph. Salama called on the masses to declare their allegiance to the successor and thus ensure the continuity of the Caliphate. This they did, and then revoked it again two months later[160].

When the situation became critical for Salama he departed Khorasan, appointing as his successor Al-Mahlab. Al-Mahlab however was more than aware of the tribal warfare that was engulfing Khorasan and El-Sham and he was reluctant to involve himself in such bloody feuding. This was especially so since most of the tribes and in particular the Qaissiya were not prepared to accept Al-Mahlab as *Wali* of Khorasan. Salama bin Ziad was thus prompted to offer the *Wilaya* to Abdullah bin Hazm Al-Salami, whom he encountered at Nisapur; and Al-Mahlab withdrew peacefully from Khorasan even before the new *Wali* had arrived[161].

The Al-Mahlab Clan and Their Clashes with the Azariqite During the Period of Zubeiri Control in Iraq

Al-Mahlab returned from Khorasan in 64 AH/ 683 AD and rested amongst his men in Basra. From the accounts available to us it is apparent that Abdullah bin Al-Zubeir was aware of the standing of Al-Mahlab and of the necessity of grafting men of his calibre into his ranks. Abdullah bin Al-Zubeir induced Al-Mahlab to meet him in Mecca where the two men held an exchange of views. Ibn Khalakan gives us an account of an incident that occurred during this exchange. While the two men were alone in consultation Abdullah bin Safwan bin Amiya bin Khalaf broke in on them and said: 'Who is this who occupies your time, O Prince of the Faithful?' Abdullah bin Al-Zubeir said: 'You don't know him?' and when Abdullah replied that he didn't Al-Zubeir said: 'This is the lord and master of the Iraqis'. And Abdullah said: 'Then he is Al-Mahlab bin Abi Safra'[162].

It would appear that this consultation convinced Al-Zubeir that Al-Mahlab should govern Khorasan as his deputy, that place being still in a state of upheaval. Al-Mahlab called in to Basra on his way to Khorasan in the year 65 AH/ 684 AD where he found that under the leadership of Naf'a bin Al-Azraq the Azariqite thorn had further penetrated the city. There were barbarous encounters between the two sides that did not relent even with the death in combat of Al-Azraq himself in 65 AH/ 684 AD. The war continued unabated until victory went finally to the Azariqites who now managed to come within reach of Basra. Then the inhabitants turned to Al-Ahnaf bin Qais and begged him to take command and he in turn referred them to Al-Mahlab bin Abi Safra'[163].

Al-Mahlab was at this time on the return journey from his meeting with Abdullah bin Al-Zubeir bearing the evidence of his investiture as *Wali* of Khorasan. He was met by a reception party of the notables of Basra who briefed him on the progress of the Azariqite war[164].

Al-Mahlab, however, dictated terms without which he would not agree to dedicate his efforts to this crucial war against the Azariqites. To the Basrans he said: 'By God I won't go out unless they concede to me what I have won and give me from their Treasury what I need to strengthen my forces for the task'. And they agreed[165]. They committed their pledge to writing and dispatched it to Abdullah bin Al-Zubeir and he signed it[166]. Al-Mahlab now set about making preparations for his campaign against the Azariqites. He managed to marshall an expeditionary force of around 12,000 men[167], most of them from his own Omani Azd. When he inspected the Treasury of Basra, however, he found there insufficient resources to meet the requirements of his army so he negotiated with the merchants of Basra, pointing out to them that their trade was destined to cease altogether as long as the goods supply from Ahwaz and Persian was cut, for the Azariqites had taken control over these districts. He asked them for money and promised that they would be compensated with the revival of their commerce. The merchants of Basra complied with his request 'and Al-Mahlab got what he needed for his troops'[168].

From the outset the Al-Mahlab family were prominently represented in Al-Mahlab's army, which left Basra in 65 AH. To his right were his sons Yazid and Habib; to the left his sons Mughayera and Qabissa. Another son, Abdul Mulik, led a wing of the right flank and yet another, Al-Mufaddal, a wing of the left flank. In his own company were his sons Ziad and Marwan, and before him his son Mohammed and his brother Al-Ma'arek bin Abi Safra[169].

One of the first tasks of the campaign was to repel the Azariqites who had affixed themselves to the eastern bank of the River Euphrates and to recapture the bridge spanning the river so that the army might cross over. Al-Mahlab sent his son Mughayera across by boat and the latter landed on the eastern bank where he engaged the Azariqites and dislodged them from their ground base until Al-Mahlab was able to take the bridge and cross over with his full army. The Azariqites were forced to withdraw and Al-Mahlab let them go and forbade a pursuit[170].

In his strategy throughout this campaign Al-Mahlab made good use of the tactics of close pursuit while studying the enemy's flank and holding back from engaging them in combat which he believed would not be to his advantage. Now he rested at his camp for 40 days, collecting the *kharaj* and building up his forces. One outcome of this strategy was a stronger army and a deepening of the confidence vested in him by the citizens of Basra, in particular the merchants. Al-Mahlab settled with the merchants and enriched his friends and men hastened to join him in his campaign against the Azariqites, drawn by the promise of spoil and reward[171] until the army had grown to 20,000 men[172].

Al-Mahlab then set out in wary pursuit of the Azariqites who had retreated to Ahwaz. A pitched and bloody series of battles was fought in the vicinity of Ahwaz in which the Al-Mahlab group, which included Al-Ma'arek, distinguished itself, though Al-Ma'arek bin Abi Safra himself was killed close by the River Tiri[173]. Here the Azariqite, in an endeavour to wind up events in their favour, rallied their forces to engage Al-Mahlab in a separate battle and they assembled at Li and at Salbari in Ahwaz[174].

The two armies met in a desperate encounter, the Azariqites intensifying their pressure on Al-Mahlab until they had managed to scatter his forces in disarray. Sorely beset Al-Mahlab's army was on the point of defeat when Al-Mahlab 'sustained a massive blow to the head and fell from his horse, whereupon his men gathered round him in fierce protection'[175]. The Azariqites exploited this turn of events and instilled terror into Al-Mahlab's army by dispatching their herald to cry out: 'Al-Mahlab has been slain!'[176]. This did further damage to the morale of the troops until Al-Mahlab, grasping the seriousness of the situation, climbed onto a low hill close by the battlefield and laid hold of the Azd and Yahmad youth who were crying out[177] and harangued them: 'Give me your attention for the space of an hour'[178]. And the men from his tribe of Oman came back to him[179]. 'Al-Tabari says that around 3000 returned to his ranks and he calls these the Omani squadrons'[180].

Seeking to compensate for his dearth of men in face of the Azariqites' superior army, Al-Mahlab instructed his escort to prepare to attack, making use of the fact that a part of the Azariqite cavalry had departed in pursuit of his own defeated men in the direction of Basra. He directed them to collect ten rocks apiece and to assemble them in bags with a view to surprising the Azariqites with a sudden hail of rocks. 'This would both drive back the cavalry and fell the men'[181]. Al-Mahlab now advanced against the Azariqites with his men. The first thing the enemy knew was that Al-Mahlab had descended on them and they were being pelted with stones from every side. The Omanis then closed in to finish them off and before long a great many of them had been slaughtered along with their leader Ubaidillah bin Al-Mahuz, and Al-Mahlab overran their camp and seized its contents[182].

He quickly sent a dispatch to the *Wali* of Basra to spread the news of the victory and inform him of his safety and on receipt of his letter the people of Basra rose and sent back the fugitives who had fled in terror of the Azariqites[183]. While this was going on Al-Mahlab was also arranging parties of men and cavalry in ambushes along the return route of the Azariqites who had pursued the remnants of his defeated army in the direction of Basra. These now fell upon the returning Azraqites and finished them off. Only a few managed to escape. The year was 66 AH/685 AD[184].

The Azariqites retired to Karman and Isfahan and Al-Mahlab took the district of Ahwaz and spent the rest of the year 66 AH/ 685 AD collecting *kharaj* and distributing rations and spoils to his troops. The wealth and generosity dispensed by Al-Mahlab drew to his ranks a great influx of the citizens of Basra and he enlisted them and was generous with them until his army had grown to 30,000[185]. Al-Mahlab remained at his base in Ahwaz and kept up the pressure on the Azariqites until Al-Hareth bin Abdullah was discharged from office as *Wali* of Basra and the post was granted to Mus'ab bin Al-Zubeir by his brother in 67 AH/ 686 AD[186].

When Mus'ab took over he sent a dispatch to Al-Mahlab while the latter was pursuing hostilities with the Azariqites and from the tone of the message we can infer the high esteem in which the Al-Mahlab family were held for their efforts to contain the Azariqite menace: '...If the people were to give every man his due you would be without doubt the first among Arabs. In your compliance and gallantry you represent to us every quality that we love and respect. We wish you the rewards of Allah in better and greater abundance. You are to us the last word and you are dignity and excellence to us'[187].

Mus'ab bin Al-Zubeir was anxious to confront the movement led by Al-Mokhtar bin Abi Ubaid Al-Thaqafi in Iraq because of the gravity of its threat to the Zubeiri revolution. He understood the urgency of rooting out Al-Mokhtar so that he could turn his attention to Iraq and to this end sought to assemble his foremost commanders. He wanted Al-Mahlab, who was acutely aware of and familiar with the Azariqite threat to Iraq, at his side and he wrote to him entrusting him with command of the march to Kufa where Al-Mokhtar was ensconced; and requested him to delegate the continuing war on the Azraqites to his sons and to meet him in Basra[188].

Al-Mahlab set out for Basra 'in a great host of men and chattels and a massed army and the people of Basra were delighted'[189]. Mus'ab received him graciously on his arrival and Al-Mahlab made ready for the war on Al-Mokhtar. Every Arab tribe was represented by one of its chiefs and Al-Mahlab was at the head of the Azd[190] and commander of the force[191]. Al-Mahlab and his men fought valiantly in their encounters with Al-Mokhtar[192] and the forces of Mus'ab bin Al-Zubeir, after a protracted campaign, succeeded in finishing off the threat of Al-Mokhtar who was himself slain in the fighting, allowing Al-Mus'ab to seize his possessions[193].

Now that Mus'ab was free of the menace of Al-Mokhtar, he wrote to Ibrahim bin Al-Ashtar, calling on him to submit. He did so and Mus'ab entrusted the territories which had been in the possession of Al-Ashtar - Moghul, Al-Jezira, Armenia and Azerbaijan - to Al-Mahlab and he discharged him from the war against the Azariqites[194]. Omar bin Ubaidillah bin Moammar Al-Tamimi he dispatched to Persia with the task of (containing the Azariqites) and directed Al-Mahlab to make his way to Mosul and Al-Jezira and Armenia[195].

Omar bin Ubaidillah it seems was taken in by accusations that Al-Mahlab dragged out the war in order to amass wealth. He believed that his own strategy would enable him to wind up the Azariqite campaign; and so he marched to Khorasan where he met the Azariqites near Sabour. The latter defeated him, however, and he was escorted to Ahwaz. Infuriated, Mus'ab was obliged to go himself to protect Basra from falling into their hands. The enemy force now turned towards Kufa but Mus'ab's deputy there managed to head them off and they returned to al-Ra'i and seized it after killing its *Wali* Yazid bin Al-Hareth. Meanwhile the leader of the Azariqitees, Al-Zubeir bin Al-Mahouz, was killed and they elected as his successor Qatari bin Al-Fuja'a who withdrew to Karman to raise funds and regroup before marching on Ahwaz. There he gained a series of victories until Basra was again threatened. Mus'ab's administrator in Basra in 68 AH/ 687 AD was Al-Hareth bin Abi Rabi'a and he wrote to Mus'ab of the threat of the Azariqites to his city and exorted him: We have no-one for this (task) but Al-Mahlab'[196].

Mus'ab realized the error he had made in sending Al-Mahlab to Mosul and discharging him from the Azariqite war, and he recalled Al-Mahlab and gave him command of the war against the Kharijites, of whom the Azraqites were an offshoot, with orders to prepare for a march. Matters now resumed their old pattern when Ibrahim bin Al-Ashtar was dispatched to administer the territories and Al-Mahlab came down to Basra where he selected men and marched with such men as enlisted making his way to the Azraqite encampments. He drew them into a series of bloody battles in the districts of Solaf 'and for eight months they were engaged in intense fighting, the likes of which had not been seen'[197].

Al-Mahlab continued to press the Azariqites until the year 71 AH/690 AD during which time the Ummayyad Caliph Abdul Mulik bin Marwan travelled to Iraq to bring it back under the influence of Damascus and his army managed to defeat and kill Mus'ab and subdue Iraq. Al-Mahlab pledged allegiance to the new ruler of Iraq and Abdul Mulik bin Marwan (the Ummayyad Caliph) granted him Ahwaz[198].

Al-Mahlab's *Wila'a* or viceregency was thus transferred from the Zubeiris to the Ummayyads shortly after the slaying of Mus'ab bin Al-Zubeir and Abdul Mulik took control of Iraq in 71 AH/690 AD. Al-Mahlab had in all probability sensed the winds of change and foresaw that ultimate victory would go to the Ummayyads. At all events his expectations were fulfilled when the Ummayyads succeeded in putting an end to the Zubeiri revolution of Abdullah bin Al-Zubeir and he was killed in Mecca in 73 AH/692 AD[199].

Al-Mahab's Defeat of the Azariqites in the Period of Ummayyad Control over Iraq and the Mashriq

We have already mentioned that Al-Mahlab, after pledging his allegiance to Abdullah bin Marwan, was appointed to the province of Ahwaz. Abdullah, moreover, thanked him for the stand he had taken and praised him appreciatively. In 72 AH/691 AD Abdul Mulik entrusted the *Wilaya* of Basra to Khaled bin Abdullah bin Usaid who promptly dismissed Al-Mahlab from the war against the Azraqites and charged him with the collection of *kharaj* in the district of Ahwaz. Disdaining the counsel of his advisors the citizens of Basra put it directly to him that he should re-entrust the conduct of the war against the Azariqites to Al-Mahlab because of his knowledge and experience in the matter. But Khaled had taken a malevolent dislike to Al-Mahlab because of his legendary fame and the high esteem in which he was held by the Caliph and he said to his entourage: 'O ye Qureish, by God Al-Mahlab has carried off the good fortune of this city and the Prince of the Faithful thinks no-one can stand before Al-Mahlab'[200]. Khaled then sent his brother Abdul Aziz bin Abdullah to take Al-Mahlab's command of the Azariqite war[201] in the hope of appropriating some of the exalted standing enjoyed by the Al-Mahlabs in the eyes of the

Caliph, but Abdul Aziz's force was quickly dispatched by Qatari bin Al-Fuja'a, the new leader of the Azariqites.

The Caliph was enraged when news reached him of the conduct of his *Wali* in Basra in discharging Al-Mahlab from the Azariqite war. In a furious letter which confirmed Al-Mahlab's high influence and the Caliph's personal regard for his heroic endeavours he railed against the *Wali*: 'May God revile you for thinking to send your brother, a bedouin from Mecca, into battle while committing Al-Mahlab to the collection of *kharaj*, he who is most auspicious (in war), unrivalled in tactics, proficient and able in war, a warrior of warriors. Go and stir up the people for an encounter at Ahwaz. I have written to Bashir in Kufa[202] to supply you with an army. Go march with them and do not take so much as a look at the enemy without the presence of Al-Mahlab, peace be with you'[203]. On seeing the amassed armies of Kufa and Basra advancing on them the Azariqites retired to the depths of Persia. Khaled sent the commander of his left flank to pursue them and himself returned to Basra while Al-Mahlab stayed in Ahwaz[204].

In 74 AH/ 693 AD Abdul Mulik ordered his brother, to whom he had attached the *Wilayas* of Basra and Kufa, to give Al-Mahlab command of the war against the Azraqites and to grant him unrestricted licence to enlist such services as he needed from the citizens of Basra. The war was to be left in Al-Mahlab's hands and his view respected. And Abdul Mulik cautioned him against succumbing to the tactics of Khaled bin Abdullah before him, threatening him with dismissal if this were to occur[205].

Bashir summoned Al-Mahlab and read out to him Abdul Mulik's letter entrusting him with the war against the Azariqites and he was given full freedom to select what men he needed. Al-Mahlab gave the task of enlisting the men to one of his relatives, Judi'a bin Said Al-Azdi, brother of his son Yazid's mother, and directed him to take over the administration and choose his people[206].

Al-Mahlab set out from Basra with 10,000 men from his own tribe, the Azd of Oman and 8000 men from various other tribes. With these armies he entered Ahwaz, which the Azariqites had left for Sabour in Persia in order to regroup for a fresh round of fighting with Al-Mahlab. Al-Mahlab himself spent no more than a few days in Ahwaz before going out again to the city of Ramharmaz with his troops[207].

On his arrival at Ramharmaz and encountering an Azariqite force there, Al-Mahlab had a trench dug around his encampment and thus fortified himself against the surprise assaults of the Azariqites, known to him through his protracted campaign against them. The Kufite army under the command of Abdul Rahman bin Makhannaf now approached and encamped close by. Ten days had not passed when news reached them of the death of Bashir bin Marwan in Basra. It was 74 AH/693 AD[208].

When the troops of Kufa and Basra heard of Bashir bin Marwan's death they promptly abandoned the objective for which they had come to Ramharmaz and a great number of them absconded. It was this factor above others which led the Caliph Abdul Mulik bin Marwan to seek out a strong man to take on the affairs of Iraq; one who would wield power with an iron fist and restore the dignity of the Caliphate among the insubordinates and Azariqites who had between them wrought havoc on the eastern provinces of the Islamic State. When Al-Hajjaj bin Youssef Al-Thaqafi was ordered to Iraq in 75 AH/ 694 AD one of his first tasks was to send deputations to Al-Mahlab and to dismiss those who had deserted their command and abandoned the war without justification. In the celebrated speech which he delivered to the citizens from the *minbar* in Kufa, Al-Hajjaj harangued them: 'We have heard that you rejected Al-Mahlab and that you accepted the mutiny of rebels in your city. I swear to you by God that there will not be one left among you after three days but I will have wrung his neck and rent his home'[209].

Al-Hajjaj followed this assault in Kufa with a similar one in Basra. The able-bodied men of the town were given three days to enlist and the troops hastened to join their regiments[210].

Al-Hajjaj now wrote to Al-Mahlab instructing him to proceed against the Azariqites and he made known the confidence he had vested in him and in his ability to take on this crucial duty as well as the need he had for his continued support, saying: 'Bashir sent you on this mission against the Azraqites, but he misappropriated your services for (his own purpose); but I truly have need of you, so have hope for the outcome and continue the fight'[211]. Al-Hajjaj also recognized the terms of the agreement Al-Mahlab had made with the citizens of Baghdad at the outset of the Azariqite war in 65 AH, that he should have the proceeds of the *kharaj* in the territories he conquered 'and the money was brought to him from the lands of Persia in bags sealed with the imprint: "This is what it has pleased Allah to grant to Al-Mahlab bin Abi Safra from the countries he has redeemed and which he shall deliver to his Azd kinsmen and none shall impede him in this"[212].'

We note from this period of combat against the Azariqites that the leadership of the armies in Ramharmaz was not united, despite Al-Hajjaj's orders and his assignment to Al-Mahlab of command of the war against the Azraqites. The Basrans were led by the Al-Mahlab and the Kufites by Abdul Rahman bin Makhannaf. Al-Hajjaj's armies were successful at first and expelled the Azariqites from Ramharmaz 'with few casualties'[213] according to the account of Al-Tabari and it looks as though this was typical of Azariqite tactics when they sensed a concentration of the Caliph's armies and the danger of a confrontation. They retreated to Sabour and then down to the city of Karzon[214] to reorganize their ranks and Al-Mahlab and Abdul Rahman bin Makhannaf followed them. These events took place in the month of Ramadan in 75 AH/ 694 AD and pitched battles were fought by the two adversaries with heavy losses on both sides. Amongst those killed was Abdul Rahman bin Makhannaf, but Al-Mahlab and his men stood their ground bravely[215].

Al-Hajjaj sent Aatab bin Warqa to succeed Ibn Makhannaf in command of the Kufites. Seeking to benefit from the experience of Ibn Makhannaf when the latter disdained Al-Mahlab's advice to entrench and to be alert to the outra-geous ways of the Azariqites, Al-Hajjaj's orders were clear: if hostilities were engaged he was to heed the counsel of Al-Mahlab and submit to his authority. Aatab chafed at these instructions but had no choice but to obey them[216]. Unfortunately, tribal loyalties began to play on the minds of the commanders. Aatab resented Al-Mahlab and strained under his leadership. Furthermore differences arose between the two men and they were near to coming to blows on one occasion during a meeting of Al-Mahlab's council. Al-Mahlab raised his staff to strike 'Aatab and would have done so had not Al-Mughayera bin Al-Mahlab intervened to separate the two men[217]. Al-Hajjaj realized too late the injudiciousness of having sent two rival commanders against the Kharijites and used the opportunity of 'Aatab's complaint against Al-Mahlab to recall him to Kufa. Al-Mahlab at once transferred 'Aatab's command to his son Habib[218].

So command of the Azariqite campaign was reunited under the Al-Mahlabs and Al-Mahlab was able during this phase of the campaign to inflict severe blows on the Azariqites in Persia and Karman. He harried them for 18 months without let-up[219] and in this time succeeded in constraining their supply lines by seizing most of the territories of Persia and sealing off the supplies from this rich terrain[220]. Throughout this period Al-Hajjaj followed closely the campaign of Al-Mahlab and his sons against the Azariqites and he urged him to bring the war to a speedy conclusion, suspecting that the longer the war went on the greater would be the demand for funds. He wrote to Al-Mahlab in these terms and Al-Mahlab replied that he was awaiting the correct opportunity to inflict final victory on this enemy. There were but three instances when this could occur: the death of the Azariqite leader Qatari bin Al-Fuja'a; a fracturing of the movement from within; or a blockading of them from without until they died of hunger[221]. Al-Hajjaj was not convinced of these explanations however and continued to bedevil Al-Mahlab with letters and dispatches telling him to end

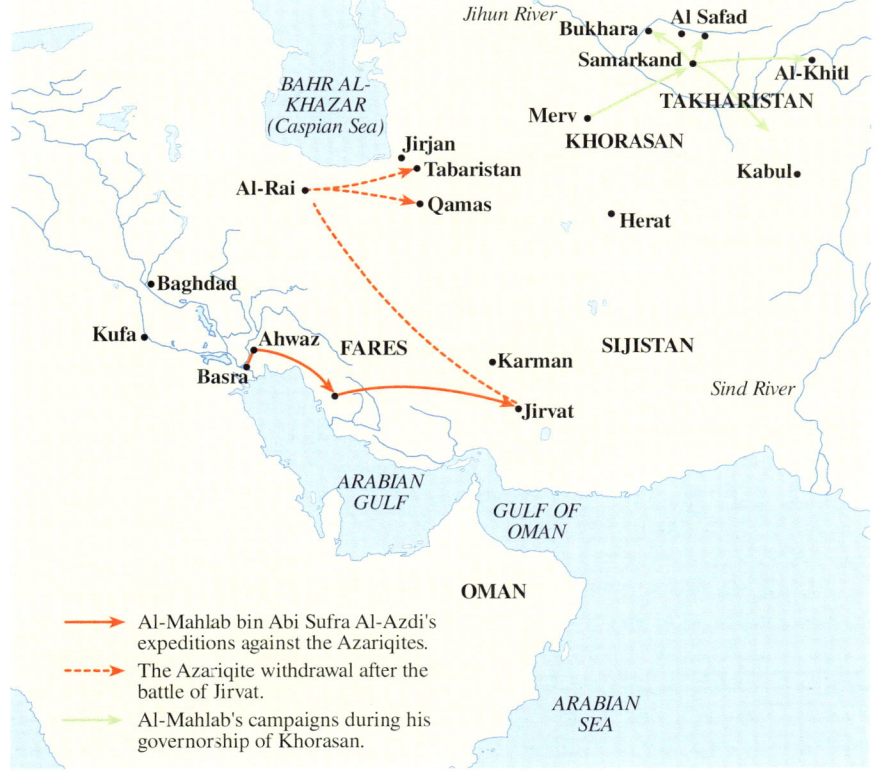

The Al-Mahlab family and their role in combating the Azariqites.

the war with the Azraqites.

This phase of the campaign saw the most furious of the battles between the Al-Mahlab clan and the Azariqites. Any student of history who follows the course of this campaign, which has come down to us in some detail from various sources, will be conscious of the military genius and rare fortitude which distinguished Al-Mahlab and his kinsmen and the clansmen who led his troops and who mounted assaults and battles under his command. Within his troop forces were a great many Omanis[222], who constituted the aforementioned 'Omani squadrons'[223] within his army.

Al-Mahlab continued to push back the Azariqites from one city to another and from one place to another, sometimes employing the tactic of the sudden attack and sometimes strike and defend and sometimes a refusal to engage[224]. He would counsel his sons: 'Do not be the first to engage (your adversary), unless he has first oppressed you; in this way will your victory be assured'[225]. He would forbid them from pursuing an enemy unless his rearguard was in flight and he counselled his son Mughayera against pursuit if the enemy was wounded 'for a wounded dog is a vicious one'[226].

The Al-Mahlab family were proud of their Omani Azd connections and in a perilous situation, one that required that they stand shoulder to shoulder and be ready for sacrifice, they sought refuge with these clansmen of whose fealty and courage they were assured. When Attia bin Al-Aswad of the Azariqite horsemen turned his attention to one of the campaigns against Al-Mahlab, Al-Mahlab entrusted the task of tackling him to his son Yazid, saying to him: 'Son, this Attia bin Al-Azwad is approaching with the Azraqite horsemen. Go with your trusted brothers and meet the loathesome ones with courage'. Yazid 'had only to call out "Azd cavalry!" and they came to him from every side'[227].

The campaign continued from 75 AH/ 694 AD to 77 AH/ 696 AD, a period of almost 18 months without a break; and then a split occurred within the ranks of the Azariqites[228]. An internal schism rent the movement in 77 AH/ 696 AD and when Al-Mahlab was told of this he said to his companions: 'Rejoice!, for this is what I have wanted from these *Khawarij* (Kharijites), may God bring them ruin and perdition'[229].

Al-Mahlab now sought by ruse to aggravate the internal dissent within the Azariqite movement. He monitored closely the progress of the widening gap between the factions and made no haste to take them on[230] for he was alert to the danger that an assault at this stage would have the effect of reuniting them. He bided his time until the squabbles had ceased and a faction of around 10,000 men[231] had departed under Qatari bin Al-Fuja'a in the direction of Jervat in Karman. Another faction under Abd Rabbu Al-Kebir consisted of 7000 men and a third under Abd Rabbu Al-Saghir had 4000 men. All of them were eager to take on Al-Mahlab with a view to presenting a picture before their people of steadfastness and endeavour, as well as precedence over the other factions[232].

Al-Mahlab now threw a blockade around the town of Jervat with Qatari and his men inside. The situation inside the besieged city deteriorated rapidly until Qatari was forced to emerge and face his destiny in a clash with Al-Mahlab's army. It would appear that Abd Rabbu Al-Saghir, vexed at the predicament of Qatari, attempted to come to his aid with his 4000 Azariqites. Al-Mahlab assigned his son Yazid the task of obstructing Abd Rabbu and preventing him from joining battle with Qatari. Yazid dispatched the supporters and Abd Rabbu and most of his escort were slain and their camp overrun and seized by Yazid's men[233]. Al-Mahlab meantime had captured Jervat[234] after Qatari had evacuated the town without a battle, anxious to avoid a clash with Al-Mahlab. He fled with his army to Al-Rai, accompanied by Ubaidah bin Hilal and his attachment of Azariqites. At Al-Rai they separated, Qatari making for Tabarastan[235] while Ubaidah bin Hilal with a company of his men repaired to the city of Qumas[236].

The definitive battle of this campaign took place around the city of Jervat. Abd Rabbu Al-Kebir had marshalled for this battle as many men as he could muster and spurred them to vengeance against Al-Mahlab, who had captured Jervat and seized the possessions of their companions and cousins. As was customary for Al-Mahlab throughout his long struggle with the Azariqites he now handled his enemy with the shrewd intelligence of a commander who had studied his adversary well and grasped his intent. Scarcely had he heard the news that the Azariqites were marching on Jervat than he ordered his escort to exit the town in the manner of a broken force. Coming upon Abd Rabbu with the Azariqites at the approach to Jervat they informed them of Al-Mahlab's departure and he, thinking he had victory within his grasp, entered the town with his men and walked straight into the ambush that had been laid for them by Al-Mahlab. No sooner had Abd Rabbu entered the town than Al-Mahlab returned with all his troops and laid siege to him within; and so Abd Rabbu found himself in the identical situation of Qatari a short time before. Al-Mahlab ordered his escort to refrain from engaging the Azariqites and tightened the siege until the trapped army was forced to emerge[237]. Al-Mahlab now mobilized his men into flying columns, each headed by one of his sons, and he rallied them: 'Go into combat for Allah, for you are the warriors of Allah and for your father, and defenders of the faith of Allah. None is superior to you in war. So fight and endure and know that you do not own the necks of men but you own your own submission'[238].

A ferocious battle took place in the environs of Jervat in which fighting intensified until the horses were wounded and weapons broken and horsemen slain. Seeing the end was near Abd Rabbu descended from his horse and broke the hilt of his sword, his companions following suit. Al-Mahlab assembled his sons and the heroes amongst his men and rounded on them and brought the battle to a close, crying out: 'Never has there been such a day as this'[239]. This battle yielded a ruinous defeat on the Azariqites. Abd Rabbu Al-Kebir was slain and with him almost 4000 of his companions; and their blood flowed down to the Wadi Jervat and turned the waters red'[240]. Few were spared and some fled and some sought the protection of Al-Mahlab and this he granted.

In the wake of his victory Al-Mahlab entered the city of Jervat and seized what he found in the way of goods, valuables, women and children. These were captured as earlier they had captured the Muslims[241]. After this conclusive battle the pursuit of Qatari bin Al-Fuja'a was undertaken and the Azariqite leader was killed in the same year, 77 AH/ 696 AD, by a faction in Tabarastan. So also was Ubaidah bin Hilal, at a fort where he had ensconced himself in Qumas[242]. Thus ended the menace of the Azariqites against the Ummayyad State, after a long and bitter campaign led in most of its many phases by Al-Mahlab and his clan.

Al-Mahlab wrote to Al-Hajjaj immediately after his victory and dispatched a messenger. When the messenger entered the council of Al-Hajjaj the *Wali* asked if they had reached a resolution in their war against the Azariqites and he asked for a news of the Al-Mahlabs. The messenger replied: 'Al-Mughayera is their horseman and master; and Yazid is a valiant horseman; the most generous and open-handed is Qabissa; and let him not be ashamed who flees the strength of Mudarrak; Abdul Mulik is a poison infusion {ie very resourceful and intelligent}; Habib is instant death; and Mohammed a jungle lion; and Mufaddal will not forbear to assist'. And Al-Hajjaj said: 'Which of them was the most intrepid?' And the messenger replied: 'They were linked as a hollow chain, you could not tell from whence it came'[243].

Al-Hajjaj was pleased with the man's words about the Al-Mahlabs. He wrote to Al-Mahlab to thank him for his efforts and he apologized to him for his criticism during the campaign about delays in the war against the Azariqites[244]. He urged him to delegate as governor of Karman whichever of his sons he saw suited to the office and to hasten to him, bringing his family and his horses and he was to leave none behind. When Al-Mahlab arrived at Al-Hajjaj's court and the latter saw evidence of his deference and piety he called out: 'O, people of Iraq, you are the servants of Al-Mahlab'[245], and he requested that Al-Mahlab bring forward the horsemen who had gone fearlessly into such desperate battles and stood their ground so bravely in the war against the Azraqites, so that he might describe to him their heroic deeds.

When the truth of these deeds was confirmed, Al-Hajjaj gave generously to the men, saying: 'Of these it can be said that they are truly great in action and deserving of reward; for they are men of war and conquerers of the enemy'[246]. Al-Hajjaj wished to reward Al-Mahlab generously so he appointed him *Wali* of Khorasan. Khorasan, then, was the prize which Al-Mahlab bin Abi Safra won as a reward for his efforts and his heroism in the war on the Azariqites. In the year 78 AH/697 AD Abdul Mulik bin Marwan discharged Umayya bin Abdullah bin Khaled from Khorasan and Sijistan. This governorship had been independent of Al-Hajjaj in its administration[247] and the *Wali* of Basra now drew these districts within his jurisdiction and entrusted them to Al-Mahlab. But first Al-Mahlab needed to rest awhile in Basra after the long strain of the war against the Azariqites and he deputed his son Habib to go ahead of him to Khorasan. Al-Hajjaj agreed to this and he bade Habib farewell in person and dispatched him with 10,000 dirhams. Habib remained ensconsed in Khorasan for ten months until Al-Mahlab arrived in 79 AH/698 AD[248].

We note that Al-Mahlab during his viceregency of Khorasan (78-82 AH/ 697-701 AD) did not rest on his laurels but actively pursued his military expeditions, fighting an unbroken war on this front against the enemies of Islam who were endeavouring through the subjugation of these territories to undermine the Ummayyad State, and 'he dreamt of Samarkand and Bukhara and the cities of Takharistan. And every time a conquest was made a fifth (of the tribute) went to Al-Hajjaj and a portion as spoil to his companions and the citizens of Khorasan were greatly delighted with the *Wilaya* of Al-Mahlab'[249], for his honourable stand in the Holy War and for what he brought back in the spoils of war.

In 80 AH/699 AD Al-Mahlab struck out eastwards in a campaign of conquest and invasion and crossed the River Baluch with his men and marched on Kush, a village in Jerjan[250]. Here he received a deputation in the shape of the nephew of the king of Khotal[251] who was at the time embroiled in a wrangle with the king. Bent on the conquest of this territory, Al-Mahlab took with him his son Yazid, dug a ditch around Al-Khotal and captured the city. Yazid, having reached agreement with the inhabitants on a ransom payable to him[252], then left the town. Al-Mahlab meanwhile sent his son Habib to Bukhara with an army of 40,000 men and the Bukharans were routed. When he had brought the district under his subjection Habib returned to his father in Kush[253] which Al-Mahlab had picked as a base of operations from which to launch the various conquests. Al-Mahlab remained in Kush arranging matters and collecting *kharaj* and disdained the rash provocations of those who in their craving for the spoils of war besought him to invade this or that place. When it was put to him that he should advance to Saghad and beyond he replied: 'I have not the good fortune on such an expedition to ensure the protection of my troops and their safe return to Merv'[254].

During this period the rebellion of Ibn Al-Ash'ath Al-Kindi erupted against Al-Hajjaj and the Ummayyads. Ibn Al-Ash'ath attempted to win over the *Wali* of Khorasan but Al-Mahlab would have nothing of this invitation to civil strife. He wrote to Ibn Al-Ash'ath making clear his views and his loyalty to the legitimate authority saying: 'You have placed your foot, oh Ibn Mohammed, in a long stirrup of transgression against the nation of the Prophet Mohammed. Allah Allah look to yourself that you do not bring perdition on the (nation of Islam) or shed the blood of Muslims. Do not spread division among the people nor violate the oath (of allegiance)'[255].

Al-Mahlab stayed in his *Wilaya* and remained fast in his loyalty to the Ummayyads; until news of the death of his son Mughayera in 82 AH/ 701 AD dealt him a devastating blow. Mughayera was his father's deputy in Merv and Al-Mahlab, distracted with grief, instructed his son Yazid from his base in Kush to go to Merv and oversee the burial rites of his brother; counselling him what to do as the tears rolled down his beard[256]. As soon as he could arrange his affairs in Kush he left the town and made for Merv, but was on the way struck down by an mortal illness. Sensing his approaching death he summoned his sons to his side, assigning Yazid as his successor and beseeching the others not to contravene him. Mufaddal said: 'Even had you not put him forward we should have done so'[257]. Al-Mahlab then showed them a bundle of arrows and asked his sons: 'Can you break them if they are together?' And they replied: 'No'. He then asked them: 'Can you break them if they are separate?' And they replied: 'Yes'. And Al-Mahlab said: 'So also it is with men'.

As we have learned from most historical references, Al-Mahlab counselled his sons shortly before his death and he died at Merv and was buried there. His son Habib prayed for him; and the month was Dhul Hijja and the year 82 AH/701 AD[258].

Yazid Bin Mahlab's Relationship with the Ummayads up to the Death of Omar Bin Abdul Aziz

Following the death of Al-Mahlab, his son Yazid wrote to Al-Hajjaj to inform him and Al-Hajjaj appointed Yazid to succeed his father in Khorasan[259]. Yazid installed himself and stayed in Khorasan to organize his affairs.

In 83 AH/702 AD Al-Hajjaj bin Youssef Al-Thaqafi was still at war with Ibn Al-Ash'ath. The most crucial confrontation of this year was the notorious battle of Deir Al-Jamajam near Kufa in which the army of Ibn Al-Ash'ath was broken and his escort scattered[260]. What interests us about this battle is that a faction of Ibn Al-Ash'ath's army wound up after the defeat in Sijistan and on being asked to leave made with their armies for Khorasan where Yazid bin Al-Mahlab was *Wali*. Their purpose was to seize the district and build up their armies and they pressed Ibn Al-Ash'ath in this objective, earnestly soliciting him with arguments. Ibn Al-Ash'ath responded favourably and so they marched on Khorasan. On reaching Herat, however, strife broke out as a result of fractious elements within the ranks and a portion of the army under Abdullah bin Abdul Rahman withdrew in Al-Fin. Furious, Ibn Al-Ash'ath abandoned his command and retired with his personal escort from the campaign[261].

The remainder of Ibn Al-Ash'ath's army rallied at Herat under Abdul Rahman bin Al-Abbas bin Rabi'a, a total of around 20,000 men. News of this marshalling of forces reached Yazid bin Al-Mahlab in Khorasan and along with it an account of what had happened to his deputy at Herat, Al-Ruqad bin Ubaid, when the latter had attempted to obstruct the progress of the invading army. The deputy had been slain and Yazid now sent a grim warning to Abdul Rahman[262].

Abdul Rahman bin Al-Abbas explained to Yazid that he had not come to wage war or to colonize the district but rather to rest his men for an onward march. Yazid watched closely as events unfolded in Herat with the customary military caution of the Al-Mahlabs. On being briefed that Abdul Rahman was receiving tribute from the territories he occupied, Yazid understood at once that a commander resting his army did not collect *kharaj*[263]. So Yazid went out with his men in the direction of Herat, appointing his brother Al-Mufaddal as deputy. Behind in Merv, the capital of Khorasan, he left affairs in the hands of his uncle Jadia bin Yazid. On reaching Herat he sent a second warning to Abdul Rahman bin Abbas saying: 'You have rested and grown fat and you have collected *kharaj* and now you have what you collected and more. So be off with you for I am loath to fight you'[264]. But Abdul Rahman bin Al-Abbas did not respond to this attempt at conciliation and tried instead to win over Yazid's troops to his side. Informed of this, Yazid understood that there was nothing to be gained from further admonitions and instructed his brother Al-Mufaddal to advance. In the bloody battle that ensued Abdul Rahman's army was defeated and most of his escort fled the battleground. Yazid ordered his men to refrain from a pursuit. A great many of the enemy were captured, among them Mohammed bin Saad bin Abi Waqqas who said to Yazid when he was taken to him: 'I beg of you in my father's prayer to your father'. And Yazid gave him his freedom[265].

We have it on record that Habib bin Al-Mahlab pressed his brother Yazid to withhold the Yemeni captives when dispatching the prisoners to Al-Hajjaj since he knew that Al-Hajjaj would break their necks. Habib argued: 'How would it look to the Yemenis if you did such a thing?' And although Yazid knew the risk he was taking in thwarting Al-Hajjaj, he nevertheless deferred to Habib and withheld the Yemeni prisoners. As to the rest, they were placed in fetters and sent to the *Wali* who had them all killed[266].

When Al-Hajjaj had rid himself of the rebellion of Abdul Rahman bin

Mohammed bin Al-Ash'ath in the year 83 AH he set his mind to curbing Yazid bin Al-Mahlab and he dismissed him from Khorasan, leaving him shorn of status or means. 'Al-Hajjaj had broken the spirit of Iraq's inhabitants with the sole exception of Yazid and his family and their resolute followers in Khorasan. With the defeat of Abdul Rahman bin Mohammed, there was no one left to threaten him save Yazid Al-Mahlab'[267]. Al-Hajjaj was wont to speak of Yazid as his greatest rival for the office of Caliph in Damascus and he feared that Yazid might undermine his power and take control of the *Wali's* subject provinces. In Ibn Khalakan's account we see that 'He (Hajjaj) detested Yazid and the nobility of his descent and fearing that he might one day take his place lost no opportunity to malign him'[268]. Yazid Al-Mahlab became Al-Hajjaj's overriding preoccupation at this time and he consulted astrologers again and again asking them who would take his place and they were saying 'a man named Yazid.' Al-Hajjaj knew of no other besides Yazid Al-Mahlab who could fit the description[269].

Historians describe how Al-Hajjaj searched for a means to convince Abdul Mulik bin Marwan to dismiss Yazid from Khorasan and in several letters to Abdul Mulik he disparaged Yazid and the Al-Mahlab clan, charging them with being Zubeiris[270]. Abdul Mulik was well aware of the worthless nature of these allegations given the victories the Al-Mahlabs had won over the enemies of the Ummayyad State. Nevertheless Al-Hajjaj continued to press him until the Caliph wrote back to him: 'You have said much of Yazid and the Al-Mahlab family. So name me a man appropriate for Khorasan'. He named Maja'a bin Sa'ad Al-Sa'adi and Abdul Mulik wrote again saying: 'What caused you to vilify the Al-Mahlabs is what caused you to choose Maja'a. Show me a man who is resolute and effective in your service'. So he named Qutaiba bin Muslim and he became *Wali*[271].

We understand from the above that Abdul Mulik was wise to Al-Hajjaj's true sentiments and the malice he nursed against Yazid and the Al-Mahlab family; that he was intent on tearing down their reputation. So we may assume that the Caliph's accession to Al-Hajjaj's demand and his dismissal of Yazid bin Al-Mahlab from Khorasan in favour of Qutaiba bin Muslim in the month of Rabia Al-Akher 85 AH was probably a move to prevent civil upheaval and a collision between Yazid and Al-Hajjaj which could only have adverse results. Al-Hajjaj now wished to discharge Yazid from Khorasan and to bring him to Iraq in such a way as not to antagonize him or cause a mutiny. So he wrote to him not of his dismissal but of the succession of his brother Al-Mufaddal and he asked if Yazid would meet him in Iraq[272].

Yazid was aware of Al-Hajjaj's motives but despite sound advice to delay his departure for Iraq in the hope that perhaps Abdul Mulik would relent and revoke the dismissal, Yazid nevertheless, faithful to the principles instilled in him by his father, refused the advice of his entourage saying: 'I come from a family who take joy in submission and I scorn sedition and dissent'[273].

Here one of the narratives tells us that Yazid's disposition in his last days at Khorasan changed, when he became odious to his people and abandoned the advice of his father; until the people of Khorasan despised him and wrote to Al-Hajjaj[274]. We are not disposed to give much credence to this account as justification for the dismissal of Yazid for we know that Al-Hajjaj was not as

A handwritten copy of the Holy Qur'an.

occupied with Yazid's treatment of his subjects or their opinion of him as he was with other matters, as we have outlined. Where this narrative falls down, and most of the accounts testify to this, is in the fact that when Yazid went out of Khorasan to Iraq he was received in every quarter with hospitality and 'in every town he passed through (the citizens) spread aromatic plants before him'[275].

Al-Hajjaj detained Yazid and most of his family, subjecting them to the worst forms of torture, and they were fined 6,000,000 dirhams[276]. Yazid remained in Al-Hajjaj's prison until 90 AH/708 AD when he managed to escape with those of his brothers who were with him from the clutches of Al-Hajjaj. He sought sanctuary with Suleiman bin Abdul Mulik and took refuge with him[277]. Suleiman bin Abdul Mulik (brother of the Caliph) had not forgotten the heroism and fame of the Al-Mahlab family and their efforts and services to the Ummayyad State. He sent in the company of Yazid and his brothers his son Ayoub whom he told to enter the presence of Al-Walid in accord with Yazid bin Al-Mahlab. Suleiman sent with them a letter to his brother justifying his protection of Yazid saying: 'I have sheltered Yazid bin Al-Mahlab for he and his father and his brothers are of our calling from past and recent times, and I shelter only those whom I have learned to be compliant and heroic and effective in the (service of) Islam, such as he and his father and his family'. Suleiman had undertaken to restore to Yazid all of the money he needed[278]. Al-Walid bin Abdul Mulik now guaranteed Yazid and the Al-Mahlabs their safety and wrote to Al-Hajjaj telling him to let them be and Al-Hajjaj assented. Abu Uyaynah bin Al-Mahlab, who had had a fine enforced against him and was at this time in the presence of Al-Hajjaj, was relieved of the fine; and Habib bin Al-Mahlab, who was undergoing torture in Basra[279], was released. Yazid proceeded to Suleiman bin Abdul Mulik. Suleiman gave Yazid a splendid reception and lavished valuable gifts on him and these Yazid returned in kind. The friendship between the two men grew with time and no slander managed to come

Manuscript from Oman's past.

between them[280]. Things remained thus up to the death of Al-Walid bin Abdul Mulik, when Suleiman succeeded to the Caliphate in 96 AH/ 714 AD.

It would be reasonable to assume that the Al-Mahlab family with Yazid at the helm would fare well under the Caliphate of Suleiman (96-99 AH/ 714-717 AD). And indeed the new Caliph had barely taken office when he summoned Yazid bin Al-Mahlab and bestowed on him honours and awards[281]. Yazid became *Wali* of Iraq and Suleiman charged him with chastising the family of Abi Aqil who were clansmen of Al-Hajjaj[282]. Yazid disdained the task and entrusted it to his brother Abdul Mulik[283]. And though Suleiman had granted Yazid a free hand with Al-Hajjaj's kinsmen and adherents, Yazid's character and disposition did not bear the stamp of Al-Hajjaj's and he was of more of a mind to show pardon than take revenge on his adversary. An example of this is apparent in his treatment of Yazid bin Abi Muslim, Al-Hajjaj's scribe and special aide. Suleiman had had him arrested and now instructed Yazid bin Al-Mahlab: 'Take him and show him the colour of torture until you get his money out of him'. But he replied: 'O Prince of the Faithful, I know of this one - he has no money. He was not the kind to hold on to it'. Yazid knew of a favour which had been granted him (by Abi Muslim) and he delegated the task to Suleiman Al-Sai'gha[284].

In 97 AH/ 715 AD Suleiman bin Abdul Mulik granted Yazid bin Al-Mahlab power over Khorasan as well as Iraq, and Yazid in turn appointed his brother Ziad *Wali* of Oman[285]. In entrusting Yazid with the government of Iraq Suleiman had in mind that he would assume responsibility for the war, *kharaj* and public worship - a sovereignty of broad and sweeping powers. From this position Yazid looked at the ruined finances of Iraq and its provinces in the wake of Al-Hajjaj's drastic reign and its strangulation of population and resources, and he felt that if he were to torment further the population and press them for more taxes he would be in their eyes no better than Al-Hajjaj. So Yazid pressed the Caliph to be granted the government of Khorasan and the order appointing him came unexpectedly[286].

It is evident from Ibn Al-Atheer's narrative that Yazid was enticed away from the collection of *kharaj* and that he passed on this task to Saleh bin Abdul Rahman. Saleh pressed Yazid for money until the latter became uneasy about remaining in Iraq. Yazid was famed for his liberality which he exercised to the point of extravagance; and when (he set out) a thousand tables to feed the population Saleh prohibited this. And when Yazid wrote a deed of contract to Saleh for the value of items purchased, Saleh refused to accept it and said that *kharaj* could not be collected as Yazid wished[287].

We can assume that the high aspirations of Yazid and the Al-Mahlab family found Iraq's ill fortune constraining, since Iraq held few opportunities in the domain of conquest and invasion for Yazid. Perhaps this is what spurred him to hasten to the governorship of Khorasan, that province with which the Al-Mahlab clan were so thoroughly familiar in their struggle against the Azraqites and their confrontations in pursuit of *jihad* and the spread of Islam. Conquest was the route by which the Al-Mahlabs had enabled themselves to acquire fame and the spoils of war. Through conquest perhaps he might achieve high standing and the immense wealth that subordinates men and marshalls victory. Yazid bin Al-Mahlab set out for Khorasan in 97 AH/715 AD preceded by his son Mukhallad and he left behind him the government of the cities of Iraq. His brother Marwan took over his possessions and affairs in Basra[288], for Basra was a district of special interest to the Al-Mahlabs.

Yazid bin Al-Mahlab, having assumed his duties in Khorasan, was not long about preparing to embark on a new course to achieve the objectives that were dear to him. His authority once established in his *Wilaya*, he put down revolts in Jarjan and Tabaristan and took on the Turks and the Deilemis. From within the Al-Mahlab family he chose men to administer and command, appointing his son Mukhallad to Samarkand and Mudarrak bin Al-Mahlab to Baluch and Mohammed bin Al-Mahlab to Merv, while Yazid's own rule was mighty in Khorasan[289]. This enabled him to undertake a succession of successful conquests and invasions. He wrote to Suleiman bin Abdul Mulik of these, citing the surplus in spoil at 'twenty million' after he had paid his soldiers and distributed their rations of spoil[290]. When Suleiman died and Omar bin Abdul Aziz took on the Caliphate as his successor, he asked Yazid to produce this money saying there was no evidence that it had been handed over to the Treasury. Yazid was asked to present himself in Damascus and on claiming ignorance of the money, was cast in prison until he could come forward with the sums due to the Muslims[291]. On being informed in captivity that Omar bin Abdul Aziz was on the point of death, and knowing that his relations with the heir apparent Yazid bin Abdul Mulik were strained in the extreme, and that he should fear for his life if the latter assumed the Caliphate, Yazid hatched a plot which had the happy outcome of his escaping from captivity[292].

The Al-Mahlab Revolt Against Yazid Bin Abdul Mulik

Omar bin Abdul Aziz died and Yazid bin Abdul Mulik took over the Caliphate in 101 AH/ 719 AD. One of his first priorities was to be the arrest of Yazid bin Al-Mahlab. Yazid however managed to get himself to Basra and to take possession of this city[293]. Seizing the Treasury he liberally distributed the contents to his followers. The administrators he dispatched to Ahwaz, Persia and Karman and he announced a revolt against the Ummayyads[294]. Al-Hassan Al-Basri called on the Basrans to abandon him[295] and when Yazid bin Abdul Mulik amassed a great army led by his brother Muslima bin Abdul Mulik, one of the outstanding heroes of the Conquests, there was terror in the ranks of Ibn Mahlab's army. He spurred them on however[296] and the two armies met at a spot close to Kufa called Al-Aqar. Here Ibn Mahlab was defeated and slain and the rest of his family and army fled in the direction of Basra. The year was 102 AH/ 720 AD[297].

Those still alive of the Al-Mahlabs assembled in Basra and sailed for Qandabil which had been abandoned by its ruler. The Ummayyad armies followed them there and they were slaughtered almost to a man[298].

The defeat of Yazid and the affliction that befell the Al-Mahlabs were a consequence of a split having arisen within the ranks of Yazid's army; as well as Al-Hassan Al-Basri's exhortation to the people to desert him[299]; and the recklessness which caused him to ignore the risks before him as well as delusions about the strength of his adversary[300]. This disaster was to bring and end to the Al-Mahlabs' role in events for many years to come. One of their descent, Suleiman bin Habib bin Al-Mahlab, was mentioned in noteworthy events in the districts of Basra and Ahwaz (129 AH 746 AD), possibly for services to the emerging Abbassids[301]. Generally speaking the Al-Mahlabs inclined to the call of Abbas, probably in vengeance against the Ummayyads. The Abbassids rewarded Sufian bin Maawiya bin Yazid bin Al-Mahlab; for he was the person who declared the revolt in Basra and wore the signal black of the Abbassids. When they had taken power and finally defeated the Ummayyads, he was charged with the government of Basra and they returned to him the possessions of the Al-Mahlab family which had been seized by the Ummayyad authorities[302].

This then summarizes our view as to how Al-Mahlab and the Al-Mahlabs of Oman came to play their part in the defeat of the Azariqites and rid the Islamic State of the peril posed by this fanatic sect which had plagued it for so long; how they ruled Khorasan and wielded vast influence in Basra and Iraq until they lost everything in a revolt against the Ummayyad State in the Caliphate of Yazid bin Abdul Mulik - with the outcome we have seen.

We now move to examine the role of the Omanis in another arena, that is conquest and *jihad* and the spread of Islam as revealed in the splendid activities of the Omanis during the conquest of Thighr Al-Hind and the propagation of the faith in this region. So how did this come about and what actually happened?

The Omanis and Their Role in the Events of Thighr Al-Hind

The connection between Oman and the Indian sub-continent was not such as would warrant the establishment of the type of military relations that existed between the Byzantine and Islamic States and which persisted for many years. Perhaps the existence of such an arrangement had more to do with Oman's gradual absorption into the larger Islamic State and the absence of a temporal power in some parts of India which at the time entertained many diverse powers.

These relations (if we can use that term) go back to the early Islamic Period. The sources at our disposal observe how Omar bin Al-Khattab, the Second Caliph, assigned in the year 13 AH/634 AD Othman bin Abi Al-A'as Al-Thaqafi to the viceregency of Bahrain and Oman.

Al-Bilathuri's account tells us that Othman deputed his brother Al-Hakam bin Abi Al-A'as to represent him in Bahrain and went himself to Oman where he put its affairs in order and brought stability and the authority of the Caliphate to bear on this province[303].

From Oman Othman bin Abi Al-A'as set out to invade India; in Ali bin Mohammed bin Abi Seif's account, assigning one of his armies to undertake a sea expedition to Tana on the west coast of India. When the army returned with victory and spoils, Othman wrote to inform Omar of this and the Caliph Omar rebuked him roundly saying: 'O Thaqifi (Taifi) brother, you took with you worms in the timber {weak men} and I swear if any of then had been injured I would have taken their equal from amongst your people'[304].

It would appear that Othman had sent two other naval expeditions one of which was under the command of his brother Al-Hakam[305], and these had been dispatched to Barous or Barouj[306]. The second expedition under Mughayera arrived at the seaport of Deibul where they were set upon by the Sindis. The Muslims were victorious[307] and it looks as though the greater portion of the participants in this expedition were Arabs from Oman and Bahrain, for we know that these were the Arabs of the peninsula most noted for their seamanship. Another fact worth noting is that Arab tribes have been mentioned on more than one occasion as having invaded Persia from Bahrain across the Arabian Gulf in the company of Othman bin Abi Al-A'as[308] and perhaps after him Al-Ala' bin Al-Hadramf; amongst these were the Bani Najiah, the Omani Azd, the Bani Abdul Qais and the Bani Tamim. Perhaps Othman bin Abi Al-A'as, a Taifi whom we must presume knew nothing whatsoever about the sea or how to cross it, was persuaded into his venture by the Omanis[309].

It would appear that the Islamic Caliphate, particularly at the time of the Orthodox Caliphs and the Ummayyads, were greatly dependent on the Arabs of

Oman and Bahrain in the conquest of India, and we find the names of many Omani Arabs in the list of commanders of overland military expeditions in Makran and Sind (the central regions of the western part of India).

Over and above what we have already mentioned about the role of the Bani Najiah and the Azd there were Omanis or persons of Omani origin who distinguished themselves in planning and effecting the events of Thigr Al-Hind and who later played an effective role in the administration of districts there. Khalifa bin Khayyat and some of the other sources say that in 42 AH/662 AD Abdullah bin Amer bin Keriz, *Wali* of Iraq as it was then, appointed Rashed bin Amru Al-Judaidi[310] *Wali* of Thighr Al-Hind (that is Makran and the Sind provinces) and Rashed led a number of expeditions in India and into Sind[311].

The role of the Omanis in the events of Thighr Al-Hind in the first and second centuries of the Hegira.

Some two years into the viceregency of Rashed Al-Judaidi, that is in 44 AH/664 AD, we come upon Al-Mahlab bin Abi Safra, the legendary Ummayyad commander and an Omani Azdi by descent, taking on the issue of Thighr Al-Hind for a brief period before he became caught up in the successful invasions of Qaiqan[312] and Qandabil[313]. He then turned north to subdue Betta or Benna and Lahore[314]. So the enemy's armies were defeated and when Abdullah bin War Al-Abdi became *Wali* of Thighr Al-Hind in 45 AH/665 AD we find mention of Hatem bin Qabissa bin Al-Mahlab amongst the commanders on whom Abdullah bin Sawar depended[315].

We see from the account of Khalifa bin Khayyat that on another occasion in 48 AH/668 AD, that is at the close of the first viceregency of Sinan bin Salma bin Al-Mohabbaq Al-Hadabi he entrusted the affairs of Thighr Al-Hind to Rashed bin Amru Al-Hodeidi[316]. On this viceregency of Rashed, Ali bin Hamed Al-Kufi casts some light. He recalls that Maawiya bin Abi Sufian sent for Rashed bin Amr, a man of honour and exalted status, and (when Rashed came) sat him down beside him and advised him on the affairs of India, then directed the *Sherifs* and high officers to submit to him and heed his orders saying: 'Rashed is an honourable man. Therefore heed him and heed his instructions and support him in war and do not disobey him'. Rashed then departed to take up his duties and on reaching Thighr Al-Hind encountered Sinan bin Salma, an Arab of the nobility. Rashed was greatly taken by Sinan's character and disposition and extolled his virtues.

After consulting on the affairs of Thighr Al-Hind until he had attained a full grasp of the situation, Rashed embarked on a series of successful military expeditions and subjected the inhabitants of Balia Mountain to payment of the *jizzia*. He then led an expedition into the interior of Qaiqan which yielded substantial spoils and booty and he suppressed the Kharijites and seized control of the roads[317].

In the second year he led another expedition against the Kharijites and transgressors of Islam. This expedition took a course across Fahraj in Karman and through the province of Sijistan. It was when he was on this campaign and after he had arrived at the Jebel Al-Mandhar that he found his path blocked by a great crowd of some 50,000 of the inhabitants of these districts. Rashed was forced to yield to a vicious engagement with them which began at dawn and continued till noon. Rashed was slain in this battle and Sinan became *Wali* for the second time[318].

Some of the narratives hold that Rashed bin Amr had also attacked Qaiqan, as well as Toghul in Sind, and that he had conquered the district of Al-Meed or Al-Mind[319]. This should clear up any allegation that Omanis did not only play a distinguished leadership role, but their advice was also sought on the overriding issues of Thighr Al-Hind at this time.

In line with some of the historical sources, in the period 65-78 AH/ 684-697 AD, that is the period in which the Ummayyad State witnessed its most severe trials, an Arab force emerged in Thighr Al-Hind which disdained allegiance to the Ummayyads. This group was known as the forces of Maawiya and Mohammed, sons of Al-Hareth Al-Allafiyeen[320] 'of the Bani Allaf, described by Al-Bilathuri as 'Rubban bin Tha'laba bin Helwan of the Azd of Oman'[321].

This force succeeded in gaining control of Thighr Al-Hind (Makran and Sind) for a period of between 10 and 13 years. So what was the situation in Thighr Al-Hind at the time of the activities of the Al-Allafiyeen? What were their goals? How did they govern? Were they of the Ibadhi rite as some believe? To these and other questions we have not yet found an answer.

The explanation that some historians come back to again and again is that the reason for the departure of the Al-Allafiyeen goes back to the killing of one of their allies or relatives named Safhawi bin Lam Al-Omani[322] at the hands of Said ibn Aslam Al-Kalabi, Al-Hajjaj's administrator, whom he sent in or around 78 AH to Sind. However we find this a rather unconvincing argument because the latter went to Al-Thighr at the end of the period of the Allafiyeen, which leads some of the sources to argue that the Allafiyeen had control of Al-Thighr from the year 65 AH/684 AD[323].

On the contrary it may be said with more justification that the Allafiyeen's revenge on Said bin Aslam was the reason that the Ummayyad Caliphate and its Prince in Iraq at that time, Al-Hajjaj bin Youssef, took on the *wilayat* of the *Mashriq* (Orient) in revenge and to defeat the Allafiyeen.

Al-Kufi tells us that on his approach to Makran, Said bin Aslam betook himself to kill Safhawi bin Lam - and perhaps the latter was one of the Omanis of the Bani Allaf (or Rubban) here at Thighr. A group of the Allafiyeen, amongst them Mohammed bin Maawiya Al-Allafi, sought vindication by killing Said and they attacked him and some of his men at a place called Marj. He was slain along with a number of his men. The rest of them who had recourse to flight returned to Iraq and told Al-Hajjaj what had transpired. So he sent Maja'a bin Sa'r Al-Tamimi and directed him to pursue the Allafiyeen, but he was not there more than a year when he died in 79 AH/698 AD[324].

The Allafiyeen fled from Makran and took refuge with the King of Sind. Al-Hajjaj however dispatched Mohammed bin Haroun Al-Nimeiri promptly on Maja'a's death and he succeeded in pursuing the Allafiyeen and exterminating them for good[325]. And so, just as the power of the Allafiyeen emerged in mysterious circumstances, we are left with scant information on a situation replete with questions and possible answers[326].

The Omani role in Thighr Al-Hind does not stand out just for its performance in thwarting the power of the Allafiyeen. Al-Bilathuri[327] recounts that Al-Hajjaj, before he sent Mohammed bin Al-Qassem Al-Thaqafi in 92 AH/911 AD, had ordered Badil bin Tohfa Al-Bajli who was in Oman to march to the Deibel Thigr, a seaport to the south-east of present day Karachi at a distance of around 40 kms. It would seem that Badil's expedition was not very well formed and he was killed in the effort[328]. Most probably there were Omani elements amongst the soldiers of Badil, although the historians do not say, but it is a fact that it set out from Oman.

About four years after this in 96 AH/715 AD, Habib bin Al-Mahlab bin Abi Safra was sent to Thighr Al-Hind immediately after the murder of its *Wali* Yazid bin Abi Kabsha Al-Suksuki[329]. It appears that Habib did not persevere in this post, remaining for around two years, for at the start of the Caliphate of Omar bin Abdul Aziz in 98AH/ 717 AD the *Wali* of Thighr Al-Hind was discharged and another individual replaced him[330].

Thighr Al-Hind witnessed the tragedy of the sons of Al-Mahlab bin Abi Safra Al-Ateiki and his family. The sources relate that a clash took place between Yazid bin Al-Mahlab bin Abi Safra who was *Wali* of Iraq under Suleiman bin Abdul Mulik in 96AH/715 AD and the armies of Yazid II bin Abdul Mulik bin Marwan in 102 AH/720 AD. Those of the sons of Al-Mahlab who had not been butchered fled -these were Mudarrak, Al-Mufaddal, Abdul Mulik, Ziad and Maawiya - with what was left of the Al-Mahlab family and embarked by ship for Qandabil (present day Gandav in Pakistan). This followed a plan devised by Yazid before he was killed with Wada'a bin Hamid Al-Azdi. Yazid had appointed Wada'a *Wali* of Qandabil on an understanding that if the Ummayyad armies were defeated Yazid would reward him further; and if the outcome were the reverse Wada'a would grant refuge to (Yazid's) people[331].

However Wada'a did not fulfil his promise. On the contrary he prevented the Al-Mahlab family from entering Qandabil on the pretext of his loyalty to the Ummayyads, then faced them with the Caliph's army which had been sent by Yazid II in pursuit of the Al-Mahlabs under the command of Halal bin Ahwaz Al-Mazini Al-Tamimi[332]. It might be asked how events would have transpired in Thighr Al-Hind if Wada'a bin Hamid had enabled the Bani Al-Mahlab and their followers to enter Qandabil, particularly if we recall the long and illustrious descent of this family in leadership and influence. Despite this the substance of the information we get from the sources is that a great many of the men of the Al-Mahlab family were slaughtered in a dreadful and bloody massacre which probably finished off the children. All that remained were around 50 high-ranking women of the Al-Mahlabs who were taken captive and treated as infidels[333]. Al-Bilathuri says that Mudarrak bin Al-Mahlab was killed in Qandabil along with Mufaddal, Abdul Mulik, Ziad, Marwan and Maawiya bin Al-Mahlab. Maawiya bin Yazid was killed with others[334] named by Ibn Khaldun as Minhal bin Abu Uyaynah bin Al-Mahlab and Omar bin Yazid bin Al-Mahlab as well as 13 others, most of them were children who were killed by Yazid II himself[335]. Abu Uyaynah bin Al-Mahlab and Othman bin Al-Mufaddal escaped to Ratbil and Khaghan, kings of the east[336].

Did this massacre herald the demise of the Al-Mahlab family? The truth is, in spite of the exaggerations of some of the narratives, that this was not so, and we find at the end of the era of Hisham bin Abdul Mulik in around 124 AH/ 741 AD, a member of the Al-Mahlab family named Marwan bin Yazid bin Al-Mahlab was amongst the commanders on whom depended the *Wali* of Sind or Thighr Al-Hind of that time, Amru bin Mohammed bin Al-Qassem[337]. Then, in 142 AH/ 759 AD in the Caliphate of Abi Ja'afar Al-Mansour and by his order we find Omar bin Hafas bin Abi Safra Al-Ataki, also known by the surname Hazarmarad, appointed to Sind and India[338].

Also mentioned as one of the *Walis* of Thighr Al-Hind and certainly of Sind was Suleiman bin Qabissa bin Yazid bin Al-Mahlab bin Abi Safra, who was connected with Al-Khalil bin Ahmed Al-Farahidi (d 175 AH/ 791 AD)[339]. Al-Mahdi (158-169 AH/ 774-785 AD) in the year 159 AH/ 775 AD employed Ruh bin Hatem bin Qabissa bin Al-Mahlab bin Abi Safra over the province of Sind[340]. Abi Hazm recalls that Yazid bin Hatem Al-Mahlabi, brother of Ruh, also served as *Wali* of Sind[341].

Al-Rashid engaged Dawud bin Yazid bin Hatem Al-Mahlab as Viceroy of Sind (or Thighr Al-Hind) in 184 AH/ 800 AD and Al-Ya'aqubi gives us a reasonably good picture of the events which hampered the progress of the conquests as a consequence of the tribalism which had overtaken the country. The efforts of the emirs resulted in the restoration of internal stability and separation (of the factions) without the Arab tribes coming to blows there. After the appointment by Al-Rashid of Dawud bin Yazid the latter sent his brother Mughayera at the head a force to be joined by him at a later stage. Al-Ya'aqubi says: 'When Mughayera approached, the inhabitants of Mansoura closed the gates and forbade him to enter unless he could give them an undertaking that he would not use the zealots on them or that they could leave the city *en masse* before he entered. So those who still had a breath of life in them came out and Mughayera entered; whereupon he rounded on the Nazarenes and they fought and defeated him. When Dawud bin Yazid was told this news as he reached the town he unleashed his sword and in the attack that followed an immense number of the Nazarenes were killed. Dawud now proceeded to Al-Mansoura where battle was joined and raged for 20 days and the war between the two sides did not subside for several months when the city fell. He then marched on to the cities of Sind and did not cease to conquer and destroy until he had subdued the country'[342]. Khalifa bin Khayyat records that Dawud remained in the viceregency of Al-Hind up to the end of the Al-Rashid reign 192 AH/807 AD[343].

It looks as though Dawud stayed longer than this. He was succeeded as *Wali* by his son Bashir in the time of Ma'moun 196-218 AH/ 811-833 AD and it was said that he clashed with Ma'moun and was dismissed[344]. It is most probable that Mohammed and Ghassan, sons of Abbad, were also of the Bani Al-Mahlab. These it was who gave Ma'moun their assurance of the falseness of the allegations made concerning Bashir bin Dawud Al-Mahlabi's differences with him. Ghassan bin Abbad was the Mahlabi who ruled Thighr Al-Hind (Sind) for Ma'moun in the year 213 AH/828 AD in line with Al-Tabari's account[345]. Thus the Al-Mahlabs maintained their bonds with a land which they and their people knew thoroughly and well.

From what we have seen, it is clear the extent to which the Arabs of Oman were present and active in the events of Thighr Al-Hind and the extent to which the Caliphate was dependent on the efforts and experience of these Arabs, probably on account of their naval activities as well their proximity to India. It could be said that this experience and contact went back to a time deep in history and through them they learned to relate to the land and its people.

It is evident that the Arabs of Oman played a substantial role in Thighr Al-Hind. This role which began at the time of the Orthodox Caliphs continued through the Ummayyad Era and into the Abbassid Era; we also need to examine the relationship the Omanis had with this Caliphate, so that we may judge what impact this relationship had on the course of events and on the history of Oman itself. This is the subject of the next chapter.

Oman and the Abbassid State

Oman in the First Abbassid Age (132-232 AH/749-847 AD)

With the emergence of the Abbassid State (132 AH/749 AD) Abu Al-Abbas Al-Safah appointed his brother Abu Ja'afar Al-Mansour over the districts of Oman, Yamama and Bahrain. Abu Ja'afar chose Jinnah bin Abada bin Qais Al-Hina'i to administer Oman. This man only held the post for a short time however before he was dismissed and his son Mohammed bin Jinnah took his place[346]. The sources do not say why he was removed but they do infer that Mohammed was an Omani, a fair administrator who improved their lot and so was loved[347].

Mohammed bin Jinnah was much taken with the philosophy of the Ibadhis so that they called him to recognize their authority. The Omanis were quick to accept and they granted the Imamate to Julanda bin Mas'ud[348], who became the first Ibadhi Imam of Oman. In this way Oman departed the sphere of influence of the Abbassids in the time of Abu Al-Abbas Al-Saffah[349].

No doubt the Abbassids, preoccupied with the possible affects of external threat and internal discord - specifically the remnants of Ummayyad power and the internal Alawite revolts - on their fledgling state, were temporarily disinclined to give their attention to what was happening in other states, including Oman[350].

Matters settled down in the time of Julanda bin Mas'ud who showed himself to be a judicious arbitrator and the people delighted in his rule. Ibadhi influence spread far and wide from Oman to other parts of the Islamic world in his time. Al-Julanda was amongst those who attended the induction of Imam Taleb Al-Haq Abdullah bin Yahya bin Yahya Al-Kindi in Yemen in 129 AH/746 AD. Many of the practices of the Ibadhis came to Oman from Yemen, the Hadramaut and Basra after the Ibadhi Imamate had been declared[351], serving to underpin its influence and reinforce Oman's independence from the Abbassid State.

Oman was granted full independence under Al-Julanda bin Mas'ud from the Abbassid State; however, this independence earned the ill-will of those Abbassids who, since they had seized exclusive control of the Caliphate, had come to be concerned with the allegiance of the eastern districts of the State, including those on the Arabian Gulf, for reasons of political, economic and religious significance to their central power. The Abbassids had begun to contemplate new conquests in India and Central Asia and these new objectives required them to be reassured of their control over the military access routes across the Arabian Gulf. The sole means to this objective was seizure of the major sea access points[352].

The Imamate resisted Abbassid pressure until the inevitable clash occurred between the two sides. Abu Al-Abbas Al-Saffah in 134 AH/ 751-2 AD dispatched a force by sea to Oman under the command of Khazem bin Khuzima[353] with the purpose of drawing into battle Shaiban Al-Yashkari and his *Safari* (Soffaride) followers who had fled to the islands of the Gulf. On hearing however that Khazem was headed their way they withdrew to Oman only to be faced down by the Imam Al-Julanda. In the ensuing engagement the Ibadhis triumphed and Shaiban Al-Yashkari was slain with many of his Soffaride followers[354].

By his action in dispatching the threat of Shaiban Al-Yashkari, Al-Julanda bin Mas'ud managed to smooth the way for the Abbassid army who were now advancing to subject Oman to the authority of the Abbassid State. Khazem Al-Tamimi, who had originally set out in pursuit of the Soffarides, now demanded of the Ibadhis that they declare their fealty to the Abbassid State and summoned Al-Julanda to meet him.

The meeting was held and Khazem took the opportunity to thank Al-Julanda for his campaign against Shaiban Al-Yashkari and then asked him to bring his followers back within the fold of the Abbassid authority. Al-Julanda took counsel with his companions but they were adamant and Al-Julanda communicated their refusal to Khazem[355]. Battle was engaged between the two parties at Julfar (Ras Al-Khaimah). Both factions were well matched but the Abbassids resorted to ruse and set fire to the Omani camps. Occupied with the quenching of the fires to save their children, Khazem's followers now set upon them with sword and blade and a great slaughter was inflicted on the Omani army[356]. Al-Julanda himself was killed. He had been Imam for two years and one month. Also killed was Hilal bin Attia Al-Khorasani and many of the Ibadhis and the First Ibadhi Imamate in Oman was brought to an end[357].

All of the sources report that as many as 10,000 Omanis were killed in this battle. Khazem took the heads of some of the more illustrious among them and dispatched them to the Abbassid Caliph. He then took control of the affairs of Oman for a time until he was recalled by Abu Al-Abbas to Baghdad[358].

A story is told that a man from Oman set out on the *Hajj* in the company of a man from Basra who would not be still at night and did not sleep. The Omani inquired about his condition and the man, who did not know that his companion was from Oman, said: 'I went with Khazem bin Khuzima to Oman and we fought there people the like of whom I have not seen; and from that day to this I have not known sleep'. And the Omani said to himself: 'And you deserve no better for you were amongst those who fought'[359].

The death of Al-Julanda created a political vacuum and led to clashes amongst his followers and the Abbassids found themselves unable to subdue Oman. The Omani Ibadhis would not submit to the Abbassid *Wali* and they continued to resent the Abbassids and to resist their administration in Oman. Meanwhile differences arose between the sons of Al-Julanda with all that this implied in tribal unrest[360].

The Abbassid authority established itself in Oman over the course of the 44 months that followed the killing of Al-Julanda. This entrenchment is ascribed to the tyranny and corruption that characterized the sequence of governors who ruled Oman during this period and whom the Omanis called the

Jababera (the Tyrants). In the words of one Omani historian: 'The Tyrants seized control of Oman and succumbed to corruption. They were oppressors and despots'[361].

Among these *Jababera* were Mohammed bin Za'ida and Rashed bin Al-Nadhar, both Julanda. Once again however, in 177 AH/ 793 AD unity and harmony were restored in Oman when the Ibadhi *ulema* and jurists came together under Moussa bin Jaber Al-Azkawi, took the reigns of tyrannical power from the Julanda family and advertized a Second Imamate, appointing Mohammed bin Abi Affan. This latter proving to be insufficiently flexible however, he was removed and his place taken by the Imam Warith bin Ka'b Al-Azdi who ruled with justice and impartiality[362].

Oman maintained this independence for a period of 11 years until in the term of Imam Al-Warith bin Ka'b, the Abbassid Caliph Haroun Al-Rashid, in an attempt to clamp down on this independence and enforce more stringently the authority of the Islamic State on Oman, dispatched Issa bin Ja'afar bin Suleiman with 1000 cavalry and 5000 men. Dawud bin Yazid Al-Mahlabi wrote to Imam Warith telling him of the landing of Issa and his troops, whereupon the Imam sent out Fares bin Mohammed to face the invading army. The two armies met at Hitta and the Abbassid commander was defeated and took to his fleet. Abu Humaid bin Falaj Al-Hadani Al-Saluti pursued him, accompanied by Amr bin Omar, in three boats. Issa was captured and brought captive to Sohar where a crowd attacked the prison at night and killed Issa before the *Wali* and Imam could be informed. On hearing of Issa's killing Haroun Al-Rashid resolved to send an army to Oman but died before he could carry out his plan[363].

The Omanis were united in their allegiance to Ghassan bin Abdullah Al-Yahmadi as Imam after the death of Al-Warith bin Ka'b in 192 AH/807 AD. He held the post for 15 years and seven months and some say 25 years and seven months and seven days[364].

Ghassan was one of the foremost of the Imams. He was alert to the many perils facing Oman, in particular the persistent raids of Indian corsairs, and he was the first to build up a naval force with the purpose of pre-empting any attempts to violate the stability of Oman or its trade and economy. While the Imam Ghassan was building the Omani fleet, he did not neglect his efforts to stabilize the interior. Against the outlaws offshore he dispatched such heroic men as Abi Rashid bin Mohammed and Saqr bin Mohammed bin Za'ida, both Julandas. He killed them and their groups and Nizwa was regarded as the centre of Islam[365]. Ghassan served for 15 years distinguished by welfare, prosperity, stability and respect for human dignity. With the death of Ghassan passed this stable interval in Oman's history while the Imamate now devolved on Abdul Mulik bin Humaid.

Imam Abdul Mulik bin Humaid

Abdul Mulik bin Humaid was one of the Bani Ali bin Sawda bin Ali bin Amru bin Amer bin Ma'Al-Sama Al-Azdi. He was acknowledged as Imam on Monday of the last week of the month of Shawwal in 208 AH/ 823 AD, although it was said elsewhere of him that he was installed on the day after the death of the Imam Ghassan, and that would have been before the end of the month of Dhul Qaada in 207 AH/822 AD.

On the basis of the first assertion his term of office would have begun approximately 11 months after the death of Ghassan; if the second is true then he was really installed on the day after the death of Ghassan who passed away after the dawn prayer on Sunday of the last week of Dhul Qaada 207 AH/822 AD. The historian, Nur Al-Din Al-Salimi, does not think this to be the case, but having regard to the tensions prevalent at this time in the Imamate, the predominant view is that this version is the correct one. He pledged his allegiance, after the manner of his two predecessors, Al-Warith bin Ka'b and Ghassan bin Abdullah that is to say to: 'the accepted and absolute prohibition of all abominable acts, forbearance in the way of Allah, the exposure of truth and suppression of falsehood, *jihad* in the way of Allah and struggle against the oppressor; and all are barred from the truth until they have sworn fealty to Allah. Forbidden to them are the spoils (of war) and children as captives; and they shall not impute a Hegira after that of the Prophet nor denigrate as polytheists those (the Muslims) of the two creeds. (That there is no God but Allah and that Mohammed is His Messenger)'[366].

During the Imamate of Abdul Mulik the *Qadria* and *Murji'a* faction was active in Sohar and these Islamic separatists called on the people to embrace their doctrines. Their call won a positive response and their influence soon spread outwards to Tu'am and other towns of Oman. Hashem bin Ghilan, the Muslim savant, feared for the Muslims and for Islam in face of this new threat and wrote to the Imam Abdul Mulik. Insofar as it illustrates the manner of communication between the *ulema* and the Imamate and the manner in which an affair such as this is broached and concluded; how the subject of the letter is introduced - that is to say the Imam is informed about the activities of the faction and this information is followed by a recommendation as to how they might be handled - it is worth reprinting in full. In its specific recommendations it constituted a set of directives from this scholar to the Imam on how he might best confront this faction.

To Imam Abdul Mulik bin Humaid from Hashem bin Ghilan...
In the Name of Allah, the Beneficent, the Merciful. Peace be upon you. I thank Allah of Whom there is none other and I ask by the power of Allah that you and I may find a means to resolve this dissent among the ulema with the distress it has caused; and I call on the assistance of Allah.

And so: What we seek in this life and in the hereafter is safety and the mercy of Allah. I write to you in good health and I thank Allah who gives you good health and sustains your faith and your fear; for it is He who provides for you and guides and supports you in His knowledge and beneficence, He who is the Most Gracious One. I tell you, may Allah have mercy upon you, that there were Muslim Imams before you who were known to some who are known to us and these told us that the first thing they did for their congregation was to teach them their faith and the roots of Islam; and they made clear to them what was allowed and what was prohibited by Allah. Those who were not Muslims among them, such as the Khawarij and others who were in doubt and others like them were not left thus; and (in time) the people adopted Islam. Among them were those who embraced Islam wholeheartedly out of conviction and a need for the faith; and some did so out of fear and they did not come to know Allah, but avoided all heresy and all religions other than Islam. When, may Allah have mercy upon them, they were told of someone who had not become a Muslim they would send him a disposition about their religion and if he accepted the faith they would treat him like any other; but if he refused and sought to alter the doctrine of the Muslims they ordered him out of the country. If he went then they let him be but if he did not conform and did not leave they coerced him until he adopted Islam.

And so Allah strengthened their faith and heresy abated and the truth prevailed among them and iniquity was quenched until they passed away, may the mercy of God be upon them.

We are told that the adherents of the Qadriya and Murji'a are in Sohar. Their doctrine has spread and they have called on the masses to join them and have increased their following until they have since appeared in Tu'am and other (cities). And you would be right to deny them this, for we fear they will increase their influence amongst the Muslims. So instruct Yazid or write to him and tell him not to abandon the heretics to the propagation of their doctrines so that all falsehood and heresy are denied. Write to him, may Allah have mercy upon you, that he show them the error of their ways; and he should write to all those who have come under their sway and show them the way of Islam and the evidence of divine decree and the atonement of the persevering. Say that if they do not submit to this they shall be imprisoned and punished; that any who has received the message and persists in his ways his punishment shall continue and his captivity be extended. We have desired to inform you of these matters and we have written to you what we were told and which has caused us anguish. Have regard to it, may God grant you and us His mercy, peace and the mercy of God be upon you[367].

Imam Abdul Mulik bin Humaid ruled with satisfactory propriety and authority until he was advanced in age and his sight and hearing failed. Perhaps it was this that led to restiveness amongst his troops and to the *ulema* criticizing some of his rulings and decisions, and which prompted these *ulema* to write to the Imam and admonish him,[368] whence, fearing a descent into chaos, the scholar Moussa bin Ali took over the affairs of state.

Imam Abdul Mulik died on the night of Friday the third of Rajab in 226 AH/ 840 AD after a term of 18 years. His successor, installed on the following morning, was Imam Muhanna bin Gaifar Al-Yahmadi Al-Azdi.

Imam Muhanna bin Gaifar

The rule of Imam Muhanna was enlightened from the first day. He declared his oath to abhor abomination and was mindful of the dangers confronted by Oman. The greatest of these came from the direction of the sea, for Oman's coastline stretched for more than a thousand miles, and he knew the importance of building a strong land army with which to protect both land and sea.

So the Imam Muhanna strengthened the Omani naval force to a level which made it a significant adjunct to the Islamic navy at the height of its power. The Omani fleet built by this Imam totalled 300 fully armed ships and these were in a constant state of military preparedness, ready to embark at a moment's notice[369].

The land army relied as circumstances warranted on combat fighters and horsemen and incorporated garrison troops distributed throughout the various districts. The Nizwa garrison alone consisted of 10,000 men, 700 camels and 600 horses.

Imam Muhanna, and in this he showed himself to be a perspicacious leader of men, was cognizant that internal stability was the basis for stable government, and he did not falter in face of the dissidents among the Bani Julanda led by Mughayera bin Rawshen Al-Julandani who had entered Tu'am and killed Abu Al-Wadah and the Imam's *Wali*. Imam Muhanna prepared a strong army and sent it against them. Fighting broke out in Buraimi and the Julanda clan were defeated; some were killed and the rest fled.

There was another great and accomplished Imam of the Bani Kharous. This was Al-Salt bin Malik bin Bal'arab Al-Kharousi Al-Azdi who was inducted on the day that Imam Muhanna died, that is the twenty-sixth of Rabia Al-Akher 237 AH/ 851 AD[370]. Al-Salt vowed allegiance as did his just predecessors to internal conciliation and external *jihad*. At that time Oman encompassed a vast territory which included Socotra, Makla, Hadramaut and Mahra; until the strength of the Omani authority and fleet were tested when a fleet of Abyssinian Christians attacked Socotra without the knowledge of the Imam, annihilating it and violating property and honour. They tolled the bells and declared them Christian. A poem reached the Imam which had been written by a pious Muslim woman of Socotra in which she called for help and incited him to rise to the defence of the Muslim island as follows:

Tell the Imam whose favour we seek
Son of the noble, the high-born, and prolific

Son of horsemen valiant and sublime
Masters among the Arabs

Tell him that Socotra has gone far from Islam
From the law and the Qur'an and other books[371].

This verse had the effect on the Imam Al-Salt of the battle cry 'O Mo'tatham' of the Muslim woman in Amouriya, when Al-Mo'tatham had led an army of horsemen (to the rescue) and was victorious. Imam Al-Salt dispatched a fleet of 100 warships bearing cavalry and soldiers who emboldened in the spirit of Allah reclaimed the island from the usurpers.

Imam Al-Salt remained in government for 35 years, from 237 to 272 AH/851 to 885 AD. It was not his death that brought his rule to an end - and this is an established historical fact - but rather his dismissal as a result of a withdrawal of popular favour. Moussa bin Moussa went down with a crowd to the village of Farq near Nizwa with the intention of besieging the Imam and to obtain their demand for his removal. The Imam's death came three years after this incident, to be precise in Dhul Hijjah 275 AH/ 888 AD.

The reader of history will see that the Imam Al-Salt's term marked the consecutive office of six Abbassid Caliphs: Al-Mutawakkil, Al-Muntassir, Al-Musta'een, Al-Mu'tazz, Al-Mahtadi and Al-Mo'atammad. The Abbassids had no contact with Oman during the office of Al-Salt. In fact they held no dominion over the country from the time of the Orthodox Caliphs up to the time of Al-Motadhid. Thus it can be said that the Abbassids in terms of sovereignty and influence had no impact on Oman through the terms of ten Caliphs.

The Disturbances During the Period of the Bani Kharous Imams

Oman was peaceful and strong throughout the rule of the aforementioned Imams. When Imam Al-Salt stepped down, however, unrest took over and a power struggle ensued between many factions. This is one of the unfortunate consequences of the enfeeblement of a state; and from the time of the departure of Imam Al-Salt Moussa bin Moussa bin Ali inducted Rashed bin Al-Nadhr Al-Hamidi the *ulema* (or scholars of religion) and the secular notables bickered amongst themselves. Of one faction it was thought that their procedures were false and a departure from the way of the just Imam - these were known as the *Rustaqiya* from Rustaq: the other faction, known as the *Nizwaniya* from Nizwa, held an opposite view.

More than one Imam ruled Oman after the Imam Azzan bin Tamim in whose reign occurred a lengthy civil war. Of the Imams who succeeded Imam Azzan not one of them remained in office except by the stratagem of others. Azzan bin Tamim ruled as Imam and in his reign the civil war raged and wrought havoc in the country.

It was in the term of Azzan that the Abbassids under the Caliph Al-Motadhid began to turn their minds again to an invasion of Oman. This was not in small part due to the fact that the Imams who ruled Oman at this time were unequal to the task, leaving the field open to the feuding of restless tribes; steadily the country descended into chaos until a civil war had engulfed it in which the Nazari and Yemeni tribes occupied centre stage. When the Nazaris had lost many men and were facing severe pressure Mohammed bin Al-Qassem and Bashir bin Al-Mundhar of the Bani Sama bin Lu'ai sought help of Mohammed bin Nour, the Abbassid *Wali* of Bahrain who had been appointed by Al-Motadhid in 280 AH/ 893 AD. On hearing their complaints of what had befallen them at the hands of the Yamanis and their appeal to him to go with them to Oman, his ambitions of splendid rewards were fuelled and he responded to their supplications, directing them to go and see the Caliph in Baghdad[372]. Having come to an agreement with them, Mohammed bin Al-Qassem went to Baghdad and met the Caliph Al-Motadhid. The Caliph gave his approval and Mohammed bin Al-Qassem returned immediately to Bahrain[373].

News reached the Omanis that a delegation had gone to Bahrain to seek the assistance of the *Wali* and it was hoped that this would unite the Omanis against an invasion. But it would seem that the Omanis were in no position to defend their country as a result of the differences that had splintered the country and fragmented the people, some supporting the Nazaris and some the Yamanis. Many Omanis fled the country at this time and the rest succumbed to fate. These were the circumstances in which Mohammed bin Nour the *Wali* of Bahrain turned towards Oman with an army of 28,000 fighting men, most of them Nazaris[374].

Mohammed bin Nour captured Julfar (Ras Al-Khaimah) and Nizwa, defeated the Omanis and killed their Imam Azzan bin Tamim and sent his head to the Caliph in Baghdad. He then set about inflicting the most terrible crimes on the people of Oman. A great many of the Omanis were killed and only those who had been delayed were saved. He settled in Nizwa and then took possession of all of Oman. The country was ravaged until the remaining people and land lay in ruins, the population reduced to abject penury. He cut off hands and feet and ears and gouged out eyes. The people were subjected to punishment and shame, their rivers buried and books burned and Oman slipped from the grasp of its people[375]. One of the side-effects of Mohammed bin Nour's rampage was the attempt made by Ahyaf bin Hammam Al-Hina'i to rally the Omanis against him and the Omanis did actually succeed in banishing him to Dama (Al-Seeb) and were at one stage at the point of victory over his forces. But as the struggle progressed, events turned to his favour, Ahyaf was defeated and Ibn Nour returned to rule Oman once more[376].

Mohammed bin Nour did not remain long in the position of *Wali* of Oman. He abandoned the task and returned to Bahrain after Ahmed bin Hilal had been installed to succeed him by the Abbassid State. Ahmed had been a scribe of the Caliph Al-Muqtaddar in Baghdad before becoming *Wali* of Oman[377] and Ahmed became administrator over all of Oman. His residence was in Bahla and Nizwa was administered by a man named Baihera[378].

Ahmed sought to earn the goodwill of the Caliph by means of the costly gifts he sent him. Al-Mas'udi recalls that on his passing through Oman in 305 AH/ 917 AD he saw gifts from Ahmed bin Hilal being loaded destined for the Caliph Al-Muqtaddar, amongst them monkeys in large baskets[379], along with perfumes, spears, black birds that spoke Persian and Indian, and a collection of colossal snakes, turtles and other curiosities and marvels from the ocean depths[380].

The Banu Sama bin Lu'ai continued to govern Oman under Abbassid suzerainty, with Mohammed bin Al-Qassem Al-Sami at their head. He it was who had sought the assistance of the Caliph Al-Motadhid to restore stability to Oman. This government lasted 40 years until power passed from this family as a consequence of internal differences.

Though the Ibadhi Imamate which had been in place for more than a century faded out as a political entity in the provinces, the authority of the Abbassid Caliphate did not extend to all of Oman. Instead it was confined to the coastal areas and northern region while the Omani tribes continued to give their allegiance to the Ibadhi rite and disdained to cooperate with the succession of *Walis* sent to rule them by the Abbassids[381]. During this time Oman was paying an annual tribute to the Abbassid State which was collected by an appointee of the Abbassid authority assigned specifically to this purpose[382].

Cracks appeared in Oman's fragile peace after the death of the Imam Al-Hawari bin Matraf and the Ibadhi Imamate collapsed leaving Oman without an Imam for some time. Finally, Mohammed bin Yazid Al-Kindi was sworn in, pledging allegiance to their defence and protection. But he did not pledge his oath to the *shiraa* for he owed them money; and so he was unable to face down the armies of the Abbassid *Wali* who surrounded him. He fled from Oman and the Omanis installed Al-Hakam bin Al-Milaa in Nizwa. This Imam was weak and without experience in administration, enabling the Abbassid *Wali* to take control of Nizwa[383] and to strengthen his grip on Oman.

The Imam Rashed bin Al-Walid tried to curb the Abbassid influence in Oman but he was not suited to this task and the Abbassid *Wali* after a succession of confrontations was able, assisted as he was by the continuing internecine bloodletting, to oust the Imam and appropriate his power[384]. This bloodletting cost Oman dearly and not least of its losses was the loss of its political identity.

The economic circumstances of the country plumbed new depths of adversity with the flight of much of the population of Oman with their wealth and belongings and dependents to more stable population centres nearby. Some of the *aflaj* became silted up, trees were cut down in acts of vengeance by one tribe against another or by the Abbassid governors to weaken the resistance of the masses[385].

In these circumstances the *Wali* was able to close the stranglehold on the country. In the words of one Omani historian: 'The despotic Sultan (that is the Abbasid *Wali*) took possession of every district and quarter'[386].

Oman in the Second Abbassid Age (232-656 AH/847-1258 AD)

The Carmathians and Oman

The Abbassid grip on Oman did not last long. The Omanis managed to banish the Abbassid *Wali* to Nizwa and they elected a new Imam. He was followed by others, none of whom managed to unite the country nor to muster the allegiance of the tribes in face of the Carmathian assaults. It would appear that Oman sustained its first Carmathian attack in 294 AH/ 905-6 AD under the command of Abi Said Al-Jinabi the Carmathian commander in Bahrain. The historical accounts differ on the extent of the success of this first attempt but it is probable that the Abbassid *Wali* with the aid of the Nazaris was equal to the attack[387].

The second Carmathian attempt came in 305 AH/ 917 AD and the third in 318 AH/ 930-1 AD, taking advantage of the opportunity presented by Al-Muqtaddir Billah's withdrawal of the Abbassid army from Oman. This was as a result of an agreement having been reached in which the Omanis would pledge allegiance to the Caliphate and pay an annual tribute to the central treasury. The Carmathians were successful on this occasion and brought Oman under their control without any recorded opposition and the tribute was now transferred to the Carmathians instead of the Abbassids. Carmathian rule was not severe and the population retained a considerable degree of internal freedom and autonomy. And so they elected a new Ibadhi Imam, Mohammed bin Yazid Al-Kindi[388].

The Carmathian Period coincided with the consecutive terms of seven Imams spanning 30 years. These were Azzan bin Al-Hazbar, Mohammed bin Al-Hassan, Azzan bin Khadar, Abdullah bin Mohammed, Al-Salt bin Al-Qassem, Mohammed bin Al-Hassan for the second time, Al-Hassan bin Said who died in 287 AH/900 AD. Other Imams succeeded these but in a haphazard manner and a great many of them were dismissed from office; of some we have only an obscure record; others were not elected but assigned to office by consensus and opposing factions were wont to polarize the electorate to prevent them from rallying to the Imam after his election[389]. All of this helped to augment the power of the Carmathians in Oman.

By the end of 318 AH/930 AD the Carmathians had extended their influence over much of Oman - in the time of Abi Taher Al-Qarmati - and this occupation was to continue in an intermittent fashion up to the year 375 AH/985 AD[390]. The power wielded by the Carmathians oscillated from strong to weak in line with the prevailing situation in Oman and the influence of the Abbassid power in Baghdad.

The period of Oman's history extending from the end of the third to the tenth century of the Hegira or the tenth to the sixteenth century AD goes by the description the Dark Ages,[391] when events collided and rulers multiplied, some of them monarchs, some Imams, and Oman would not submit to one regime. These were dark and difficult times and chaos reigned in Oman.

Added to the internal strife in Oman were the events taking place in the Gulf region: the *zinj* revolt (of African slaves) in Basra and the Carmathians in Bahrain challenged even the central Abbassid authority. Over and above this were the attempts by the Abbassids to subject Oman, represented in a succession of invasions. These events were to culminate in the independence of the Abbassid *Walis* and the institution of monarchies[392].

Oman in the Time of the Bani Buwaih (the Buwayhids)

Youssef bin Wajih wrested control of Oman, and the sources give us no information as to how this came about, except to say that his people were the Bani Sama bin Lu'ai who had attained dominion over the Imams with the help of the Abbassids[393].

Relations between Oman and the Abbassid State at this time were becoming more turbulent. The Omani princes did not consider themselves bound by the directives coming from the Abbassid State. The Emir Youssef bin Wajih blithely ignored the instructions of the Abbassid *Wazir* Al-Abbassi Abi Ali bin Muqlah to deal harshly with Abi Al-Abbas Al-Khoseibi the former Abbassid minister and Abi Suleiman bin Yahia in prison in Oman; in fact he ordered their release. Ibn Muqlah had been the cause of their exile to Oman and imprisonment there[394].

Youssef bin Wajih did not stop there. He began to think of seizing Basra and became bent on occupying it, in particular after the *Baridiyeen* who were in control of the city at this time imposed high tariffs on Omani goods. The first attempt to conquer Basra was in 331 AH/942 AD[395]. With this purpose in mind he readied a powerful fleet, sailed for Basra; and was on the point of capturing it[396] when he was betrayed by a Basran sailor who crossed over to join the *Baridiyeen*. Ibn Wajih failed in his mission and most of his ships were destroyed; and the *Baridiyeen* richly rewarded the Basran sailor whose action had saved the city[397].

The second attempt came ten years after the first debacle and this time Ibn Wajih exploited the tensions between Muizz Al-Dawla the Buwayhid ruler in Baghdad and the Carmathians in Bahrain. The year was 341 AH/ 952 AD and the Carmathians had rejected what they saw as the interference of Muizz Al-Dawla in their alliance with the rulers of Basra and his advance to conquer the city. So Ibn Wajih mustered his forces with the support of the Carmathians.

A silver dirham minted in Oman in 319 AH at the time of Youssef bin Wajih.

On the other side was Muizz Al-Dawla's vizier, Al Abu Mohammed Al-Mahlabi. The two met in a sea battle in which Ibn Wajih and his Carmathian allies were defeated. A huge number of his men were killed and the rest captured and Al-Mahlabi seized his boats[398].

The Omanis had installed Imam Said bin Abdullah bin Mohammed bin Mahboub bin Al-Rahil in the year 320 AH/ 930 AD and this Imam managed to take control from Ibn Wajih and repossess many of the cities of the interior; restricting Youssef bin Wajih's influence to the coastal districts. After the death of Imam Said bin Abdullah in the village of Manaqi in one of the municipalities of Rustaq in 328 AH/939 AD Rashed bin Al-Walid was sworn in (328-342 AH/939-53 AD) and this Imam retained the interior districts which had been under the rule of his predecessor Imam Said[399]. Ibn Wajih had been murdered by his servant Naf'a in 342 AH/953 AD who took his place, and Naf'a was endeavouring to cement his relations with the Abbassids. Naf'a sent an elephant as a gift which was transported by sea to Basra thence to Baghdad.

Naf'a occupied himself with the war on the Ibadhi Imams in 342 AH/ 953 AD and instability returned, worsening steadily up to 351 AH/ 962 AD when Muizz Al-Dawla decided to occupy Oman. An expedition was sent under Abu Mohammed Al-Mahlabi but as a result of the death of the commander the expedition did not arrive in Oman[400].

Muizz Al-Dawla, returning to his plan to invade Oman in 354 AH/ 965 AD, prepared an expeditionary force led by Kardak Al-Naqib. On reaching his destination, he asked Naf'a to submit to Muizz Al-Dawla and to have the Friday sermon delivered in his name. Naf'a declared his allegiance to the Buwayhids after some hesitation and acceded to all of Kardak's demands and the latter having settled affairs in Oman departed for Baghdad. At around this time a revolt was mounted against Naf'a in which he was ousted and replaced by Al-Nawkani, who was a wealthy Omani, as monarch[401].

This new turn of events in Oman drew a fearful response from Muizz Al-Dawla, who threatened Al-Nawkani in a letter delivered by hand by Kardak demanding that he step down from power. Al-Nawkani assented but the Omanis now rose against him and he fled into exile with a vast treasure which he had accumulated. He went by sea to Basra but on the way encountered Kardak who relieved him of his money and jewels, bound Al-Nawkani in fetters and threw him overboard. The treasure he had seized he handed over to Muizz Al-Dawla on his return to Baghdad[402].

The overthrow of their king had the effect of exacerbating the situation in Oman and unleashing a new struggle for power amongst the tribal leaders. The civil strife worsened to the point where in 355 AH/ 965 AD a faction sought the aid of the Carmathians in Bahrain to help restore stability. The Carmathians then sent a force to Oman under Ali bin Ahmed Al-Kateb who was commander of their armed forces[403].

Ali bin Ahmed made use of the prevailing turbulence in Oman and watched for an opportunity to oust the elected Emir Abdul Wahab bin Ahmed bin Marwan who had assumed power after the assassination of his predecessor Ibn Taghan. Ali bin Ahmed managed to win over an African detachment of the army amounting to some 6000 men and they proclaimed him Emir after first driving out the Emir Abdul Wahab. These machinations by the Carmathian general occurred without the approval and against the wishes of the Omanis.

The Carmathian occupation was not to last. Naf'a, the former Emir, sought the assistance of Muizz Al-Dawla in Iraq who prepared to take on the Carmathians in Oman. He made ready a fleet of about 100 troop-carrying ships and gave command to Abu Al-Faraj Mohammed bin Abbas Fassanjs. This force landed at Siraf where it was joined by reinforcements sent by Addad Al-Dawla Al-Buwaiyhi to the assistance of his uncle Muizz Al-Dawla. The combined armies inflicted a crushing defeat and heavy battlefield losses on the Omanis and took possession of the country in 355-6 AH/965-6 AD[404].

Abu Al-Faraj Mohammed bin Abbas who had taken over the affairs of Oman now succeeded in stamping the authority of the Buwaiyhids under the protection of the Abbassid Caliphate on Oman, after it had been cleansed of the last vestiges of Carmathian influence. Abu Al-Faraj abandoned Oman after the death of Muizz Al-Dawla and passed the reins to Omar bin Nabhan Al-Tay who bowed to the authority of Addad Al-Dawla in Oman[405].

The death of Muizz Al-Dawla had aggravated events in Oman, troubled now by a bloody insurrection of the *zinj* against Omar bin Nabhan Al-Tay, the Abbassid minion in Oman. This uprising gained force and violence until it had overtaken all of Oman and Omar bin Nabhan had been killed. Ibn Hallaj was selected as Emir in his place[406].

In response Addad Al-Dawla sent another expedition, this time from Karman and led by Abu Harb Taghan, to put down the *zinj* uprising. The force came ashore at Sohar and Taghan managed to defeat the *zinj* and end their pretensions. The scattered remnants of their army were pursued to Buraimi where they were cut down by Taghan's men, while the Omanis used the opportunity given them by Taghan's killing spree to regroup with a view to ridding themselves once and for all of the Buwaiyhid yoke; and they elected as their Imam Hafas bin Rashed[407].

In the light of these circumstances Addad Al-Dawla, sensing danger, conspired to kill the Imam and a new expedition was sent to Oman under Al-Mutahhar bin Abdullah. Al-Mutahhar subdued Oman in 364 AH/974 AD[408]. After a short interval he departed on the orders of Addad Al-Dawla - and the Omanis lost no time in returning to the attack and swore in their Imam Hafas bin Rashed for the second time. Power was passed to the Imam and the country came under his rule. Oman fell again into the grasp of the Buwaiyhids after the death of Hafas, but the grip was weak as a consequence of trouble within the house of Buwaiyhi when Addad's death provoked a struggle for succession. His successor Sharaf Al-Dawla, on acceding to power in Baghdad and noticing the effect that Buwaiyhid neglect had had on weakening their authority in Oman, resolved to revive their previous influence and so yet another army made its way to Oman under Abu Al-Nasir Khouashadhaa. Abu Al-Nasir defeated the opposing force but he wasted no time in selecting a deputy to whom he entrusted the affairs of the Buwaiyhid Sultan and himself departed from Oman[409].

Sherif Al-Dawla's deputy was not of the calibre required to administer the affairs of Oman and in due course resistance had mobilized against him.

Seizing their opportunity the Omanis declared an insurrection against their weak *Wali*, overthrowing him, and along with him the last shreds of Carmathian influence in Oman. It was 375 AH/985 AD and the Omani Ibadhis were back in power in their country, pursuing Abbassid loyalists until they had established their authority.

The Rise of the Bani Makram State in Oman

This political state of affairs was not to last however. There was no let-up in the internecine squabbling, driven by the lust for power; and in due course the Abbassids regained their grip on the country. A deputation of the Bani Makram who were among the prominent clans of Oman appealed to the Buwaiyhid rulers of Baghdad for support in a war against the Imams who were the effective power in Oman. This came at a propitious time for the Buwaiyhids who were anxious to restore their authority and the Bani Makram were enabled to capture control of most of the major cities in Oman in the name of the Buwaiyhids.

The Bani Makram remained in government as suzerains of the Buwaiyhids even dedicating the Friday sermon in the name of the Abbassids. Relations between the Bani Makram and the Buwaiyhids remained sound even despite a troubled patch when Abu Mohammed bin Makram was dismissed and replaced by Al-Farakhan bin Shairan[410] who came from outside the Bani Makram clan. This occurred in 392 AH/ 1001 AD, but Abu Mohammed was returned to office years after his dismissal and earned a noteworthy record in guiding the affairs of Oman and the approval of the Buwaiyhids; and in due course power was passed to the magistrate Abi Bakr[411].

When Abu Mohammed bin Makram became ill he appointed his son Aba Al-Qassem Ali bin Makram who evinced from the outset of his rule an intense abhorrence of the Imams. One of these rebelled against him but he managed to put down the uprising and stayed on to rule Oman until his death in 429 AH/ 1037 AD, to be succeeded by his son Abu Al-Hassan bin Al-Qassem bin Makram[412].

The failing power of the Buwaiyhids in Baghdad created a suitable climate for the entrenchment of the Bani Makram as rulers of Oman. They assumed independence in their affairs and installed a dynastic monarchy from the time of Abi Al-Qassem Ali bin Makram[413], but their power was enfeebled by internal jockeying for position. A struggle developed between two brothers, Abi Al-Jeish and Al-Mahdhab, which had the outcome of Abi Al-Jeish assassinating his brother Al-Mahdhab and he ruled alone until he died and Ali bin Hattal took over as king[414].

Ali bin Hattal's rule was oppressive in the extreme: he plundered the wealth of the merchants of Oman and impoverished the inhabitants until a groundswell of hatred built up against him. When news of this reached Baghdad Kaligar gave it due significance and gave orders that he was to be curbed. He delegated this task to his general Abu Mansour bin Maafina who made contact with one Mortada, a representative of the Bani Makram, and requested his assistance in mounting an expedition against Ali bin Hattal. Mortada succeeded in defeating

Ibn Hattal and Abu Mansour bin Maafina decreed Abu Mohammed bin Makram Emir of Oman in 431 AH/ 1039 AD[415].

Disturbances soon convulsed the country once again and the people rose against the rule of the Bani Makram. In 433 AH/1041 AD Kaligar sent a new military force against Oman which succeeded in restoring tranquillity and order. But the power of the Bani Makram rulers was almost exhausted and before long dominion was in the hands of women and slaves. This was an opportunity for the Ibadhi Imams to make another upward thrust. They regrouped for a new attempt to wrest control from the Buwaiyhids and succeeded in overthrowing them. Abi Al-Mudhaffar Bani Kaligar who had installed himself as Emir of Oman was seized and incarcerated and the period of Buwaiyhid rule came to an end in 442 AH/1050 AD[416].

The Decline of Buwaiyhid Influence

The Ibadhi Imams returned to power shortly before the collapse of Buwaiyhid rule in Oman and the people elected as Imam Khalil bin Shadhan in the first decade of the fifth century AH. He ruled for much of the first half of that century and carried out sweeping reforms throughout the country. He reduced taxation and governed with justice and discretion. Oman remained under the rule of the Ibadhi Imams who succeeded Imam Khalil without any obvious indication of interference from the Abbassid State.

Oman had now removed itself fully from the domain of Abbassid influence and was to retain its independence despite persistent Abbassid attempts to woo it back into its embrace. The Abbassid State, however, was nearing its end, its power almost spent, until it was finally overthrown by the Moghuls in 656 AH/1258 AD. Oman meanwhile pursued a course along a route far removed from the influence of this feeble Caliphate and before long, that is around the first half of the sixth century AH, it had entered a new era, that of the Bani Nabhan, who were to rule Oman for around five centuries. Which brings us now to a discussion of the Bani Nabhan Era.

Oman at the Time of the Bani Nabhan
(549-1034 AH/1154-1624 AD)

Omani historians are agreed that the rule of the Bani Nabhan in Oman lasted five centuries, spread over two periods. The first of these was known as the First Nabhan Period and lasted 400 years beginning with the death of the Imam Abi Jaber Moussa bin Abi Al-Maali Moussa bin Najad in 549 AH/1154 AD and ending with the defeat of Suleiman bin Suleiman bin Mudhaffar Al-Nabhani, the celebrated poet king, and the induction of Mohammed bin Ismail as Imam of Oman in 906 AH/1500 AD. This period was flawed by invasions and wars waged by the Bani Nabhan from within and without, interspersed with government by the Imamate from time to time.

The second reign, which was known as the Later Nabhan Period, extended from 906 AH to 1034 AH (1500 AD to 1624 AD) and was characterized by a variety of events which included the troubled succession of the Imams, and power struggles amongst the Bani Nabhan clan on the one hand and between the Bani Nabhan and some of the other Omani tribes with ambitions for power on the other. However by far the most important incident of this period was the occupation by the Portuguese of the coastal regions of Oman.

It could be said that the influence of the Nabhan was restricted to the interior of the country for some of their rule while at other times it extended to the coast. At yet other times some of the dissident tribes managed to isolate the coastal districts from the authority of the Nabhan government.

In view of the extended rule of the Nabhan for over five centuries, their era came to be known as the Nabhan Era. And though most historians are of the view that the rule of the Nabhan was one of tyranny and outrage because of their oppression of citizen's rights, an unbiased scientific assessment would not wish to concede to such uncontested views which forfeit in their general approach genuine scientific investigation.

The Nabhan Era offers us a fertile domain of new study, in respect of which, perhaps, the future will bring us news of other sources to clear up some of the mystery surrounding this important period of Oman's history.

In the struggle which went on between Suleiman bin Suleiman bin Muddhaffar and the Imams, the Nabhan managed to turn things to their favour and by means of a series of battles generally characterized by surprise raids, the Nabhan succeeded in restoring their authority[417]. And so the question which now presents itself is this: What were the origins of the Bani Nabhan and what was their ancestry?

The Origins and Ancestry of the Bani Nabhan

The Bani Nabhan trace their origins to the Al-Ateik tribe, these being an ancient Arab Azdi tribe of Oman. The Ateik had played a pivotal role in the history of Islam through one of their renowned offshoots, the family of Al-Mahlab bin Abi Safra[418], whom we know as the outstanding Omani commander who succeeded with the help of his own tribe and the Omani Azd in defeating the evil of the Azariqites. It is known that the Ateik originated with the Arab Azd tribe the Qahtani, who can be traced back to Ya'rub bin Qahtan bin Hood - the messenger of God[419].

A good indication of their descent comes to us via the words of the celebrated Nabhan poet and contemporary of the First Nabhan Period, Abu Bakr Al-Sitali[420], who eulogized the Nabhan kings in his poems; to be succeeded in this vainglorious activity by the Nabhan poet King Suleiman bin Suleiman bin Muddhaffar[421] - who lived through the end of the ninth century and the beginning of the tenth AH (fifteenth/sixteenth century AD) - and again by Al-Kidhawi, court poet of the Nabhan kings during the Second or Later Nabahan Period[422].

The Emergence of the Bani Nabhan

An examination of the rise of the Bani Nabhan demands that we enquire how the Bani Nabhan first came to govern Oman and whence they became the Nabhan kings in the period covered by the study. A tribal schism and a subsequent struggle waged against the incumbent power in Oman gave rise to internal fragmentation and drew the interest of external forces who were eager to assert their influence and control over Oman. It was this that brought the Bani Nabhan to power[423].

One of the problems which looms large before us in studying the history of Oman in the period 549-809 AH/1104-1406 AD is an interlocking of events and inconsistency of dates which collide and contradict one another. Thus the dates of the accession and deaths of the Imams to which Omani historians give great prominence are completely entangled and confused so that there is not one date of accession about which there is undisputed agreement.

Al-Sitali was poet to the Nabhan kings and he provides us in his *diwan* (poetry collection) with three dates relating to different events in the Nabhan Era. The first was the year 474 AH/1081 AD[424]; the second was 501 AH/1107 AD[425] and the third 559 AH/1164 AD[426]. If we suppose that the first date was the start of his poetical career and the start of the reign of the Nabhan and that the last was the last of his versifying for the kings, the interval is 85 years; and assuming he had started to compose poetry of this elevated standard at an age of not less than 20 years then he would have lived to be more than a hundred years[427].

Al-Azkawi points out that the period between the death of the Imam Mohammed bin Khanbash in 557 AH/1161 AD and the induction of the Imam Malik bin Al-Hawari in 809 AH/1406 AD[428] comes to 252 years and that there does not seem to be any mention of Imams in this period. However he says elsewhere: 'Perchance these years between Mohammed bin Khanbash and Malik bin Al-Hawari were the years when the Nabhan kings ruled, and perhaps their reign was longer than 500 years for between these years there were Imams and perhaps the Nabhan were kings of one kind of territory and the Imams of another'[429].

Ibn Ruzaiq described the Nabhan kings as mighty kings, noble and heroic in character. It was extremely difficult to describe their individual reigns in any detail because there were so many of them and because each one was identical to the next in rank and power, 'although Al-Fallah bin Al-Mohsen was the most famous, liberal and shrewd'[430]. However Badger, who translated the work of Ibn Ruzaiq, assumed Al-Fallah bin Al-Mohsen to be the first king of the Nabhan and every Orientalist and Arab historian who followed him copied him *verbatim* with the exception of the Omanis[431].

When we read closely into what Ibn Ruzaiq said we find that he did not say that Fallah bin Mohsen was the first of the Nabhan rulers. What he said was that he was the most celebrated of them. In fact Fallah bin Mohsen was the third Sultan in the succession of the Later Nabhan Period and ruled in the second era of Nabhan power. Again it seems to us that these historians have placed the names of more than one of the Nabhan kings from the Later Period into the First Nabhan Period, while failing to mention the names of the kings of the First Period.

These kings set up residence in Nizwa and Bahla[432]. Their rule was dynastic in that the son inherited the crown from his father or brother from brother. Where there was neither brother nor son the nearest relative of the dead king inherited the throne. Their rule was autocratic and while there is no room for the comparison of these rulers, who were known to the Omani jurists as the 'mighty oppressors'[433] with the lawfully elected Imams who were characterized by asceticism and fortitude and piety, yet we are not inclined to take a one-dimensional view of this period of government; or accept the generally uncontested views of others without some debate. For while there is no doubt but there was perniciousness and corruption, there were some who were reformist and suited to their task as governors. They cannot be dismissed as tyrants as some of the historians would have us do.

We can give as an instance Al-Sitali's comments on some of the rulers. He spoke glowingly of the modesty and excellent character of the Nabhan King Abi Al-Arab Ya'rub bin Omar who was known for his love of wisdom and of the *ulema*. Again he extols the Sultan Abi Al-Hassan Dhahal bin Omar and salutes him on his return home after performing the religious duty of the *Hajj*[434]. A good description of the disposition of the Nabhan kings and their generosity and modest ways comes from the record of Ibn Battuta's visit to Oman and encounter with the Nabhan King Abi Mohammed where he says: 'He was wont to sit outside the door of his house in council, and he had neither keeper nor minister and none were prohibited from entering, neither stranger nor other. He was generous to guests after the custom of the Arabs and he would entertain them hospitably and give them (gifts) commensurate with their rank. His was an excellent disposition'[435].

It seems to us that it would be extreme to place the full burden of the ruinous situation of this period on the shoulders of the Nabhan kings, for the responsibility was not theirs alone but also that of their contemporary *ulema,* as well as the territorial administrators and the general populace, in particular given that wars and clashes were rife throughout the country for much of the rule of the Bani Nabhan.

Wars of the Nabhan Kings with their Rivals

The rule of the Bani Nabhan was, perhaps more than any other period in the history of Oman, blighted by tribal strife and power struggles. When the Imamate for one reason or another lacked an Imam who could sustain control of the affairs of state, the situation reverted to anarchy and chaos as the tribes resumed their squabbling for precedence. This disorderly situation was to continue in Oman for more than 250 years and it would seem that in this period the country was deprived of an Imamate; and fighting was at its most intense between the Nabhan and other Omani tribes, and between individuals within the Nabhan family itself. This internecine squabbling did not stop between cousins; the slaughter and contention for power went on between brothers also.

We are unable to follow the events of this ongoing conflict from the time of the foundation of the Nabhan state because our only source for this period is Al-Sitali, the poet whose poetry was intended as a panegyric to the First Nabhan kings, and he refuses to address their negative traits as represented in their bloody power struggles. The Nabhan king, poet Suleiman bin Suleiman, made reference to this struggle in a verse in which he implored his brother Husam bin Suleiman to cast aside the war and settle for peace and conciliation[436]. However it would seem that Husam was not responsive to this type of solicitation and resolved to wrest power from the grip of his brother Suleiman and indeed met his death in the pursuit of this fraternal strife.

Add to this the fact that the Nabhan king became embroiled in a dreadful clash with the leaders of the other Omani tribes, including the Bani Amr and the Al-Awamer, the Bani Umair and Bani Rabi'a, the Bani Ka'b and the Al-Taya family and the Bani Man'a and the Al-Shiriheen, the Sawalem and the Nawafel, all of which merely led to the tribes uniting against him. It was said that in one encounter over 7000 men were cut down[437].

The one piece of solid information that Omani historians give us about this tribal strife concerns the uprising of the Al-Rayyes family against the Nabhan kings at the time of King Kahalan bin Omar bin Nabhan at the end of the month of Shawwal in 675 AH (the beginning of April 1277 AD). A large expedition force from the Al-Rayyes clan set out, supported by the Al-Hodan tribe[438] and prompted by a malevolence they harboured for the Nabhan kings, and proceeded towards the district of Aqar in Nizwa, residence of the Nabhan kings at the time. When King Kahalan bin Omar heard of the approach of this fighting party he went out with his escort from the encampment and a company drawn from the inhabitants of Aqar to impede their access to Nizwa[439].

On hearing that Kahalan along with the resident population had evacuated Aqar, the attackers found a way to avert a clash and enter the unprotected city. They achieved their purpose and they claimed the war by dupery and entered the city unopposed, whereupon they stormed the souq and plundered its contents, then set it ablaze until the fires reached the stores of the Nizwa main mosque. These were gutted along with everything in them including their library of books. They then turned upon the dwellings of the inhabitants which they sacked before taking the women captive.

On the following day Kahalan returned with his supporters from the town and camp and they assembled at *Siraa* at the approaches to the town of Nizwa. They were in total 7000 fighting men and they were not long about storming the enemy encampment, that is of the two tribes, the Al-Rayyes and the Al-Hodan. In the ensuing battle 300 men were killed from both sides and the enemy were defeated and returned to whence they had come[440].

Some of the later sources say that the attacking force of the two tribes numbered 7000 fighting men. Some of the same sources contain a distortion of the Arabic word *sirat* making it into *shiraa*[441], by which they mean the escort who had gone out with King Kahalan. However as is known the word *shirat*[442] is an Ibadhi term meaning those fighting men or *fedayeen* whose office is to escort the Imam and protect the Imamate and not a system antagonistic to the Imams as is the system of the Nabhan kings. A pointer to the accuracy of this view is given in the *Sirat* of Ibn Mudad where he says: 'On the second day, the first of the month of Dhul Qaada, Kahalan arrived at the encampment and they assembled at Al-Sirat. The army set upon them and they were about 7000 men in all'[443].

If this was the nature of the Nabhans' relations with their rival tribal chiefs, what can have been the state of their relations with the Ibadhi Imams?

The Nabhan Kings and the Ibadhi Imamate

In this respect we must first take a look at the Imams about whom the sources have afforded us some information and examine their relations with the Nabhan kings. From the outset the sources describe the situation in Oman as disturbed when the Nabhan kings took power, for with the death of the Imam Mohammed bin Khanbash in 557 AH/1161 AD Oman underwent a regime of disorder and anarchy and the writing of this part of its history is clouded by darkness and obscurity. Says Al-Azkawi[444] of this time: 'The citizens of Oman were sorely stricken at his (the Imam's) death and mourned him in a way that they had never mourned any before him'. He then paints for us a picture of the oppressed circumstances and the relentless conflict under which the Omani subjects chafed. And the desire of the masses to elect an Imam to unite them was not to be fulfilled through all of this extended period from 557 to 809 AH/ 1161 to 1406 AD. Miles[445] commented that for all of 40 years no conflict or power struggle was waged by the Nabhan and the Ibadhi *ulema*, until the election of election of Imam Malik bin Al-Hawari in 809 AH/ 1406 AD. He is evidently referring to the power struggles between the Nabhan kings and the Imams. In fact they were all Ibadhis. Moreover the interval was longer than he describes; for a period of 252 years no Imam held office until finally the *ulema* and secular notables met and agreed to install Malik bin Al-Hawari as their Imam.

Malik bin Al-Hawari 809-832 AH/ 1406-1428 AD was thus considered to be the first Imam of the Nabhan Era. Here we have an early example of the contra-dictions which have frustrated efforts to record the history of the events of this time in the attempt of Al-Salimi, who began his account of the period of the Nabhan Era Imams as starting with Al-Hawari bin Malik and then: 'shortly afterwards Malik bin Al-Hawari and it is not known if these are two successive Imams or that the names were inadvertently reversed. As there is a difference as to the dates when they died, perhaps one was the father of the other'.[446]

Al-Salimi gives preponderance to neither but Al-Siyabi persists with one account in which he says that the Imam inducted was Al-Hawari bin Malik[447]. Against this contradiction in the information supplied we believe in taking the proponent's view that the successor was Malik bin Al-Hawari and that Al-Hawari bin Malik is not the reversal of the name as was the belief of Al-Salimi. An observation by Al-Azkawi confirms this, where he says that seven years after the death of Malik bin Hawari, Abi Al-Hassan bin Khamis bin Amer became Imam in the month of Ramadan 839 AH/1436 AD[448].

Malik bin Al-Hawari was inducted in the city of Nizwa when an expeditionary force was sent out under Abdullah Al-Malqab who was known as *Alhoul* to invade the city of Rustaq and bring it under subjection. So the commander set ablaze the walls of the Rustaq fort to pressurize the inhabitants within the fortification to hand it over; until eventually they surrendered.

The Imamate of Abi Al-Hassan bin Khamis[449]

The Imam Abi Al-Hassan bin Khamis bin Amer was the third Imam of the Nabhan Era after Mohammed bin Khanbash, who died in 557 AH/ 1162 AD, and Imam Malik bin Al-Hawari. Zambaru and those after him who took his view considered this Imam to be the first of the Bani Nabhan Era, closing their eyes to an examination of any circumstances they found difficult to decipher[450]. Al-Azkawi and Ibn Ruzaiq both mention the two Imams Mohammed bin Khanbash and Malik bin Al-Hawari. At all events Abi Al-Hassan became Imam in Ramadan in 839 AH/April 1435 AD and Al-Salimi is the only one to mention that the Bani Salt went out against him and waged war on him with the backing of the Bani Rabi'a. The Imam ordered that the Rabi's date palms be cut down to punish them for this support. He died on Saturday the eleventh of Dhul Qaada in 846 AH/23 March 1443 AD. His Imamate thus lasted for seven years[451].

The period when the Imamate was vacant between the Imam Malik bin Al-Hawari and Imam Abi Al-Hassan bin Khamis bin Amer was scrutinized by Al-Siyabi, citing Ibn Ruzaiq. He says: 'Abu Al-Hassan succeeded Ahmed bin Mohammed Al-Rabakhi. Perhaps then (this latter) held office during this interval of six years which we have noted between Malik bin Al-Hawari and Abi Al-Hassan?'

It is obvious that the time period between the Imam Malik bin Al-Hawari and Imam Ahmed bin Omar bin Mohammed Al-Rabakhi was seven years as we have noted above. Indeed the Imam Abu Al-Hassan who was mentioned in the previous (paragraph) was another Imam and not the Abu Al-Hassan bin Khamis bin Amer who concerns us. We will discuss him later.

The Imamate of Omar bin Al-Khattab bin Mohammed Al-Kharousi[452]

As the violence and arbitrariness of the Nabhan kings intensified in their effects on country and population, the distinguished notables and *ulema* assembled and assigned Omar bin Al-Khattab Al-Kharousi as their Imam in 885 AH/1480 AD.

He had not held the post for more than a year when the Nabhan King Suleiman bin Suleiman and his adherents rose against him[453] and a vicious battle ensued in the village of Hamamet[454] in the *wadi* of the Bani Rawaha. Al-Siyabi is alone in mentioning the helpers of the Nabhan king, saying: 'The most assiduous in assisting the Sultan in this onslaught were the Bani Rawaha who were at his behest'[455].

The Imam and his army lost the battle and so lost his Imamate. He was re-inducted for a second time, but we are not afforded a date for this happening. He had yet to face other battles and encounters with this Nabhan king and his supporters, although ultimately he would prevail against them[456].

Ibn Ruzaiq[457] in his narrative puts the first accession of Imam Omar bin Al-Khattab at 835 AH/ 1431 AD, while Zambaru[458] places it in 855 AH/ 1451 AD without saying whether he is referring to the first or second term.

This opinion is not shared by the united view of the historians we have cited previously, nor again by the report of Ibn Ruzaiq himself regarding the Imamate of Abi Hassan bin Khamis when he agreed with other historians that this commenced in 839 AH/1435 AD and that the Imam died in 846 AH/1442 AD. If we accept this then the first term of Imam Omar bin Al-Khattab would have been in 885 AH, as we suggested above, and probably the second term began in 887 AH/1482 AD as will come clear to us below.

Ibn Ruzaiq likened the Omani Imam Omar bin Al-Khattab Al-Kharousi to the Second Orthodox Caliph Omar bin Al-Khattab in his judiciousness and fairness, discretion and forcefulness, in his promotion of truth and his fight against the iniquitous and corrupt[459].

The Death of Imam Omar bin Al-Khattab Al-Kharousi

None of the historians have mentioned the date of the Imam's death, though they do have a date for the accession of Imam Mohammed bin Suleiman, his immediate successor. This was 894 AH/1448 AD[460]. Ibn Majed[461] however, who was a contemporary of these happenings, but whose information we feel is somewhat weak, has an account of the ambitions of the King of Hormuz, and his expansionism and aggression on his neighbours: 'His son Saif bin Zamel took Oman (from)[462] Nabhan bin Shehab by sword from Suleiman bin Suleiman bin Nabhan in the year 893 AH. It was ruled by an Imam of the Ibadhi to whom they granted the revenue. Its inhabitants came out in his support and its strongholds were levelled and Omar bin Al-Khattab the Ibadhi (became) their leader'. If we are to analyze this historical text we will have to clear up certain points in it:

• The Nabhan bin Shehab mentioned in the text has never been mentioned by Omani historians.
• The correct name for Suleiman bin Suleiman bin Nabhan as described by Ibn Majed is Suleiman bin Suleiman bin Mudhaffar bin Suleiman bin Mudhaffar bin Nabhan Al-Nabhani.

What we can manage to glean[463] from Ibn Majed's comments is that the person referred to, whether he be Saif bin Zamel or Nabhan bin Shehab, took possession of Oman 'by the sword' that is to say by force from Suleiman bin Suleiman, and it was ruled by an Ibadhi Imam to whom was paid the 'revenue' that is the *zakat* . The Omanis went to the aid of this Imam who ruled them and that Imam was Omar bin Al-Khattab. We believe that the matter was confused by Ibn Majed and the Imam he describes was Omar bin Al-Khattab himself. Perhaps in this he wished to refer to the exalted and learned Imam Mohammed bin Suleiman ibn Ahmed bin Mafrah who installed as Imam Omar bin Al-Khattab for the second time as we have described.

Imam Mohammed bin Suleiman

Mohammed bin Suleiman bin Ahmed bin Mafraj, the Bahlawi judge, was a leader of the *ulema* of Oman when he was installed as ruler and magistrate before the succession of Imam Omar bin Al-Khattab. For this reason he was known by the title *Al-Qadhi* (judge). Subsequently, it was he who installed Omar bin Al-Khattab as Imam for the second time and the Imam Omar delegated to him the task of constituting a council of magistrates to rule over the possessions of the Bani Nabhan as we have previously mentioned. He himself became Imam on the death of Imam Omar in 894 AH/ 1488 AD, but did not remain long in the post. It is probable that he was dismissed or resigned for the magistrates were no match for the agitators stirred up by Suleiman bin Suleiman after his return from Qasm island. Suleiman nursed a malevolent hatred for this Imam, for it was he - and not his father as Al-Siyabi says -who had drawn up the council of magistrates to govern the possessions of the Nabhan kings.

Imam Omar Al-Sherif

The sources do not give the rest of this Imam's name or his family origins. He assumed the Imamate after the resignation of Imam Mohammed bin Suleiman bin Ahmed bin Mafraj. We do not have the date of his accession from the historians but we know that he held office for one year, then departed the Imam's quarters in Nizwa for Bahla, thus ending this brief term of office[464]. Now the aforementioned Mohammed bin Suleiman took office as Imam for a second term. However he also was to hold office only briefly and resigned again to be succeeded by the just and irreproachable Ahmed bin Omar bin Mohammed Al-Rabakhi who ruled commendably and died in office. He was buried in Nizwa.

Imam Abu Al-Hasan bin Abdul Salaam

Abu Al-Hasan bin Abdul Salaam succeeded to the Imamate in Nizwa on the death of Imam Al-Rabakhi and retained the post for a year or slightly less until Suleiman bin Suleiman rose against him and put an end to the Imamate or, in Ibn Ruzaiq's version of events, until he died in office.

In Al-Azkawi's account Mohammed bin Suleiman, who was known as *Al Qadhi*, was now reinstalled for the third time, but Al-Salimi disagrees: 'Suleiman bin Suleiman retained sovereignty by the exercise of force and tyranny, subjecting all beneath him with might and force', until the accession of Imam Mohammed bin Ismail. We can infer the truth of this from the unstable state of affairs and endless rebellions and wars of this period and from the brevity of the terms of successive Imams as a consequence of the constant struggle between the Imamate and the secular Nabhan regime as represented by the revolts and assaults of Suleiman bin Suleiman.

Imam Mohammed bin Ismail Ismaili Al-Hadari[465]

One fixed historical fact is that Suleiman bin Suleiman Al-Nabhani had certain characteristics which the notables found alarming and which caused them in time to want a leader who would be properly equipped to run the affairs of state. They chose Mohammed bin Ismail Al-Hadari and installed him as Imam in 906 AH/1500 AD, seeing in him a character stamped with the qualities of competence and probity. These were the internal events which prevailed in Oman throughout the time of the Nabhan. But what was the nature of their relations with external forces and foreign powers?

The Relationship of the Bani Nabhan with External Powers

The Nabhans' relations with outside powers had two aspects, one negative and the other positive. The negative aspect was represented in the invasion of Oman from abroad. This was a direct result of the internecine strife and fragmentation which left Oman at the mercy of its enemies. A succession of raids was mounted, mostly by the Persians. Al-Sitali makes note of Persian assaults in the reign of the Nabhan King Muammar bin Omar bin Nabhan, but says that the Omanis fought them off[466]. However the Persians were successful on three occasions in occupying Oman and its possessions for a period of time.

The First Persian Invasion

The history books tell us that in the year 660 AH/1261 AD and in the reign of the Nabhan King Abu Al-Maali Kahalan bin Nabhan, Mahmoud bin Ahmed Al-Koushi, King of Hormuz[467], attacked Oman and took possession of the port of Qalhat, whereupon he demanded of Abu Al-Maali that he hand over the proceeds of Oman's *kharaj*. Abu Al-Maali declined to do so giving as a pretext that Oman was not fully under his control. Al-Koushi gave notice that he would go out himself in the company of armed brigade to collect from whoever would not pay the *kharaj* and Abu Al-Maali, seeing that he was serious and hoping to win him over by artifice, apologized on behalf of the people of Oman for their inability to pay the sums demanded. The king of Hormuz became enraged at this and when a delegation of Omani Bedouin approached at his invitation he lavished on them gifts of garments and money and asked for their assistance in executing the demand for money and they gave him their support[468].

When the king of Hormuz arrived at Dhofar, the inhabitants came out against him and a large number of them were killed in the attempt. The king now concentrated his forces on the coast where they quickly set about sacking the souqs and then the dwellings of the inhabitants, stripping them of valuables and seizing their slaves. Twelve thousand captives were taken in all and, rounding up these spoils and valuables along with the captives, they made for their ships. The king of Hormuz assigned a third of his army to accompany the ships and bade them to hasten to Qalhat where they should rejoin the rest of his army. Meanwhile he gathered the company he had with him and headed in from the coast, marching towards the interior[469].

One narrative of Omani source[470] describes these events saying that soon the Persians 'began to suffer from a lack of provisions on the road inland, the weather bore down on them, and a *mann*[471] of meat cost one dinar. They were wracked with thirst because of the shortage of water along this road and it is said that 5000 or more soldiers died from this hardship'. However this piece of information will not gratify the seeker of truth for it is vague and does not explain how the men came to be in this severe situation.

It would surely not make sense for a great commander and sovereign of a substantial realm to embark on an adventure of this nature without a comprehensive logistical plan. It is more likely that what Ibn Ruzaiq tells us is closer to the truth, that when the king of Hormuz arrived at the territory of the Al-Qari tribe, who were nomads inhabiting a very high mountain in Dhofar, they sought the help of ten men of the tribe to guide them along the route to the interior.

But when they were well inland the guides escaped at night and they found themselves helplessly abandoned amidst high sands and empty desert.

Lost in this vast wasteland, individually and in groups they straggled hither and tither until they came upon food and water. Without enough water for their animals these died of hunger and thirst. Thus perished the king of Hormuz and most of his army[472]. Those who did not die of hunger and thirst were set upon by the desert dwellers[473], and only a very few survived, marching until they reached Julfar (present-day Ras Al-Khaimah) and from there they crossed to the island of Hormuz. We will not take seriously Ibn Ruzaiq's allegation that not one of them survived, for this is certainly an exaggeration.

As to those who returned from Dhofar by sea, they anchored at Qalhat[474] and assigned a garrison, whence most of them proceeded onwards to Tiwi. There they were blocked by the Bani Jaber and other Omani tribes accompanying them. The enemy were slain to a man and buried there in common graves known today as the Turkish tombs. Ibn Ruzaiq in his book *Al-Fet'h Al-Mubeen* observed that men from the Bani Jaber and their clansmen attacked the enemy garrison protecting the ships in Qalhat port and defeated them utterly; then captured their ships and burnt the fleet[475].

The Second Persian Invasion

This was an invasion by the rulers of Shiraz. It occurred in 674 AH/ 1276 AD during the reign of the Nabhan king Omar bin Nabhan. Fakhr Al-Din Ahmed bin Al-Daiya and his brother Shehab Al-Din, the two sons of the ruler of Shiraz in Persia, both invaded Oman at the head of an expeditionary force of 4500 cavalry.

When the aggressors landed at Sohar they were met by King Omar bin Nabhan who was encamped with his army at a well-protected site in Haiy Asem. He was defeated with the loss of 300 men and the Persians marched on to Nizwa. There the inhabitants put up an inadequate defence and were overcome and the invaders took possession of the town on the 15 Dhul Qaada (2 May) of that year. They looted the souq and dwellings and, not satisfied with this, proceeded to demolish the souq and burn any books they found there. They evicted the citizens of Nizwa and ensconsed themselves in their homes. This done they marched on to surround Bahla[476] the second capital of the Bani Nabhan, but despite a long siege they failed to open the town.

During the course of this siege the enemy commander Fakhr Al-Din Ahmed bin Al-Daiya fell fatal victim to an arrow wound and his death broke the resolve of his army who were defeated and driven from Oman[477] after a sojourn of four months during which they had wrought death and depravity, plunder and pillage on the country. The inhabitants suffered terribly under this occupation, for over and above the corruption and tyrannous deeds they had endured prices had soared to the point where the people were without food. All of the historical accounts agree that 674 AH 1275 AD was the year that this invasion occurred with the exception of Ibn Ruzaiq who in his two books *Al-Sh'aa Al-Sha'a and Al-Fet'h Al-Mubeen* add that it was in 664 AH/ 1265 AD[478]; which suggests that Ibn Ruzaiq is not precise in his recording of the dates of historical events and details.

The Third Persian Invasion

We now come to the third invasion. Ibn Mudad and Al-Mawali each afford us a description, so we know that in 866 AH/1461-2 AD Nur Shah bin Luqma, king of Hormuz, invaded Oman at the head of a great army of some 20,000 troops including a thousand cavalry[479].

After a triumphant march in which the king took possession of Oman, he seized Bahla - seat of the Nabhan King Suleiman bin Mudhaffar who had fled to Al-Ihsaa - as a garrison base for his troops and placed them under the command of Ghassan bin Kulaib who had been a special advisor to Suleiman bin Mudhaffar at the level of vizier and was considered his closest confidant. The same historical accounts assert that Suleiman bin Mudhaffar returned at a later stage to Oman and power was restored to him; but they do not explain how it was that he returned to power nor whether this was achieved by force or by conciliation. Or whether the Omanis rose against the occupier and banished him from their country.

Whatever the situation - and we do not have a clear view - this Suleiman bin Mudhaffar betook himself to East Africa as we will describe later and there founded the Nabhan Kingdom of Patta (Bat). It was said that he returned to Oman, though it is likely that this was on a visit and not as ruler, for we hear of no subsequent role for this man.

His two young sons Suleiman and Husam became embroiled in a contest for the succession which culminated in Suleiman's victory over his brother. He however proceeded to take on the Imams and the tribal leaders until the Imam Mohammed bin Ismail succeeded in wresting control from him as previously noted.

Al-Mawali dates this invasion to 806 AH/ 1403 AD, although at the end of his discourse on this matter he says that this happened after *Siniy Al-Fatra* (or the years of the period which extended from 557 AH/1162 AD to 809 AH/ 1406 AD) during which the Imamate was vacant in Oman and the country in the hands of the Bani Nabhan kings. So it seems that the date mentioned by Al-Mawali for this invasion does not tie in with the date he has given at the end of his discourse on this subject and we believe that the date given by Ibn Mudad, that is 866 AH/ 1461 AD, is the correct one[480].

The Bani Nabhans' Relations with External Powers

Some Omani historical accounts speak of the Nabhan rulers as having many and diverse relations with foreign powers, in particular political ties which were cemented by the exchange of visits. These ties were largely with Oman's immediate neighbours, especially those in the Gulf region, along with East Africa and some of the Asian kingdoms.

If we accept the narrative of Al-Sitali, poet to the Bani Nabhan kings, which makes reference to the Nabhans' relations with East Africa from an account of his own visit there, it is evident that the Nabhani bonds with the East African kingdoms were deep, for Al-Sitali extols three of their kings, Sabkhat bin Ali[481], Bakhtan[482] and Ishaq bin Omar[483].

Notwithstanding this, much obscurity surrounds the reign of the Nabhan kings. Only scraps of information have survived but these give us an adequate enough profile of the nature of the relations between the Nabhans and the East Africans.

Oman's relations with East Africa in the Nabhan Era

The Omani bond with East Africa goes back deep in time, in particular the trading history shared by the two regions. It was in East Africa that Omanis would seek sanctuary when oppression weighed heavily on their country, forcing them to abandon it. Sometimes the oppression was economic in nature when drought or economic crisis overtook them, sometimes political when tribal leaders and princes were forced into exile. This latter was the case when Said and Suleiman, sons of Abbad bin Abd bin Al-Julanda, fled the persecution of Al-Hajjaj bin Youssef Al-Thaqafi. Sometimes the cause was social, a consequence of tribal warfare and blood revenge which drove some of them to flee for their lives to East Africa. Thus the Omanis' colonization of East Africa was of long and continued standing.

The specific relations of the Nabhan kings with East Africa however, their exile there and establishment of a Nabhan kingdom at Patta are probably linked to the return of the Imams to the government of Oman with the swearing in of Malik bin Al-Hawari as Imam of Oman in 809 AH/1406-7 AD[484]. It is probable that this happened at the time of the Nabhan King Mudhaffar bin Suleiman bin Mudhaffar bin Nabhan or the time of his son Suleiman bin Mudhaffar - father of the poet Suleiman bin Suleiman who left Oman after he was ousted from power by the king of Hormuz Nur Shah bin Luqma, as we have recounted. Having taken refuge in the kingdom of Patta he married one of the daughters of King Al-Muda'u Is'haq and then inherited power on the king's death or as a result of the latter's stepping down in deference to his daughter and her husband[485].

If this then summarizes the internal and external politics of the Bani Nabhan and the events that unrolled during the First Period of their reign, what were the events that marked the briefer Second Nabhan Period?

The Second Period of Nabhan Rule (906-1034 AH/1500-1624 AD)

We have noted that the Imamate was suspended during this period with the exception of the three Imams who ruled at its outset. These were Barakat bin

Mohammed Al-Ismaili Al-Haderi, Omar bin Qassem Al-Fadhili and Abdullah bin Mohammed Al-Qaran. We have also noted the failure of the jealous *ulema* to reform society's ills. Thus was clouded the Imam's pledge to confront abomination; and anarchy overwhelmed the country and slaughter and butchery marked the unceasing and relentless struggle for power.

One of the most significant incidents of this period was the accession to the throne of the Nabhan King Sultan bin Mohsen bin Suleiman Al-Nabhani which he accomplished by seizing Nizwa in 964 AH/1556 AD[486]. Again King Suleiman bin Mudhaffar bin Sultan bin Mohsen seized power in the interior and took Bahla as his centre of government. Among the better points of his rule were his success in reunifying the country and the assistance he contributed to Muhanna bin Mohammed Al-Hodheifi the leader of Sohar, enabling the latter to threaten Persia.

Nevertheless he took to persecuting the Jahadhem tribe and banished them - albeit unrepentant - from their tribal homeland for a period of 30 years. It was not long before his supporters had split into two factions, the Bani Maan and Bani Shukail remaining in alliance with him while the Bani Al-Nir and the Bani Hanaa under Khalaf bin Abi Said and Saif bin Mohammed bin Abi Said declared him to be their enemy and allied themselves with the Emir of Sama'il Umair bin Hamyar Al-Nabhani; and so a tribal oath was taken by these against the Nabhan King Suleiman bin Mudhaffar along with the Emir of Rustaq Malik bin Abi Al-Arab and Abi Al-Hassan Ali bin Qotn Al-Jiberri, leader of the Jobour. These allies enabled the Jahadhem to gain back their tribal lands from Suleiman bin Mudhaffar and return to them, while the contest between the two sides continued at full intensity; until Suleiman died and was succeeded by his nephew Arar bin Fallah bin Mohsen, who was in turn succeeded by his brother Nabhan bin Fallah bin Mohsen[487].

When Bahla was the sovereign power base for the Nabhan kings in this period every leader coveted the sovereign office in order to secure possession of this city, cement his power base and guarantee his standing amongst the tribes. The Emir Umair bin Hamyar Al-Nabhani did just this and seized Bahla and thus gained power. His efforts were assisted by an alliance with the Bani Hanaa joined by the citizens of Nizwa and Manah, who went out and expelled his rivals in the districts which fell within his domain. These were Sultan bin Hamyar and his associates and they travelled to Sohar and remained there with its leader Mohammed bin Muhanna Al-Hodheifi. If during the First Nabhan Era the Nabhans' closest supporters were the Bani Ruwaha, particularly at the time of the poet King Suleiman bin Suleiman bin Mudhaffar, in the Second Nabhan Era the closest supporters of the kings were the Bani Hanaa.

Struggle in Dhofar

No sooner had these incidents drawn to a close than the struggle moved to the district of Dhahira which was under the control of the sons of the Nabhan King Fallah bin Mohsen. With the death of Makhzoum bin Fallah bin Mohsen, who had seized the city of Yanqul, the two cities of Yanqul and Maqniat fell into the hands of his brother Nabhan who was loathed by the citizens of Maqniat for his outrages against them and his arbitrary rule. They appealed to King Umair bin Hamyar who had a vast army led by Saif bin Mohammed bin Abi Said Al-

Hina'i. With this help they seized Maqniat, then made for Yanqul . On hearing that they were headed his way Nabhan left the city to seek the aid of his uncles of the Al-Rayyes clan. The date was 2 Safar 1026 AH/ 20 March 1617 AD. At Yanqul King Umair bin Hamyar appointed a deputy to run the affairs of the city and returned to its citizens the wealth and belongings which had been appropriated from them. He stayed awhile in the city then returned to Maqniat and saw why the citizens had sought his help against the persecutions of Nabhan. He reduced the crop levies on them to a tenth of the date harvest and field crops whereas Nabhan had exacted half of the date crop and a quarter of the field crop. Moreover he pledged the proceeds of the state levy to whoever would take on the fortification of the city and the running of its affairs. Omar bin Abi Said Al-Hina'i took on these functions and then returned with Saif bin Mohammed to Bahla[488].

Omani historical sources record that the latter portion of the Second Nabhan Period existed in a climate of anarchy which led to the utter fragmentation of the social order until the country was given a glimmer of hope in the form of one discerning ruler. He was Nasir bin Murshid Al-Ya'rubi who was put forward by the notables to the Imamate in 1034 AH/ 1624 AD and Oman entered a new era of cohesion and solidarity, a golden age in which stability and peace governed the country's affairs and reforms were instituted.

In the middle of the month of Rabi'a Al-Akher (the end of April) of the same year Nabhan with his aid of his uncles the Al-Rayyes clan regained all of Yanqul with the exception of its fortification which was in the hands of the Bani Ali tribe. These sought the support of the Jobour who inhabited the northern desert region. They came to the support of their allies and together the Bani Nabhan were beaten and the Al-Ya'ruba Period began. Before we close the curtain on the Bani Nabhan in this matter we should briefly note some of the characteristics of their long reign.

Features of the Nabhan Era

The Bani Nabhan ruled by means of an absolutist political regime. Their autocratic methods stood in sharp contrast with the simple asceticism of the elected Imams. The Nabhans led lives of decadent luxury and built citadels and fortifications to ward off the threats of their rivals.

Add to this the arbitrariness of many of the Nabhan kings and the seizure by others of property by unlawful means, their exaction of oppressive taxes on the whole country which defied the rules of Islam and the principles on which were based the collection of *zakat*. For the Prophet said: 'It is not written to give a fifth of an oke in *sadaqa*. And it is not written to give 20 *mithqal* in *sadaqa*. And it is not written to give a fifth (for) defence *sadaqa*. And it is not written to give 40 sheep as *sadaqa* and it is not written to give five loads as *sadaqa* {ie whoever has less than these goods is not obligated by *sadaqa* or charity}'[489].

It could not be said either that strong government was a characteristic of the period of Nabhan rule, for this era was distinguished from start to end by its many power contests and unceasing civil strife and disorder. They fought amongst themselves, with the other tribal leaders and with the elected. The least disparaging thing that could be said about their reign was to call it a period of ruling clans or of petty city states. There was no strong central government to enforce its administration on the whole country. This was the background to the discontent and exasperation experienced by the Omanis in the period of Nabhan rule. Their power was absolute and their government arbitrary. Omani historians recoiled from recording their history so that much of this period of Oman's past is veiled in blackness. Their history has escaped us; and so it has come to be called the 'Dark Age' of Omani history.

If the Nabhan Period was grim in many of its aspects, this was not the case in another district over which the Nabhan had control. This was the Kingdom of Patta on the Lamu Archipelago on the coast of East Africa. One of the Nabhan kings went from Oman to found a kingdom there, a place of civilization, science, culture and the flowering of Islam; and there he enjoyed an amicable relationship with the peoples of the coast and the interior.

The Nabhans of Patta may have put in place this relationship and sealed the ties between Oman and East Africa. But it was not the first time that this happened. The history of Oman's contacts with East Africa go back deep in time and it was trade more than anything else which instituted and cemented the bonds of an old and meaningful relationship. It is imperative therefore that we take a look at the history of these contacts to have a better understanding - and that shall be the subject of the next chapter.

Trade Contacts Between Oman and East Africa in the Middle Ages

Just as the Arabian Gulf area in general and Oman in particular enjoyed longstanding contacts with East Africa going back to well before Islam, the Omanis were the first explorers of the East African coast and more influential than any other external party in the mark they left on the region. Their purpose was trade with the Africans through this region of the African continent.

It is said that the history of the Omanis in East Africa is tied in with the history of its trade. Unfortunately, however, this history is not on record, at least not in any full or detailed form. Published Omani sources are not knowledgeable about the circumstances surrounding trade relations between East Africa and Oman, even though this trade was a source of enrichment for the Omanis. Moreover concerning the records discovered in East Africa, besides the fact that they are historically recent and based on oral sources, their principal concern lies in the area of the political history of the clans that ruled East Africa[490]. So we will have to rely on the Arab geographical and navigational sources of the Middle Ages which include valuable information about the trade between Oman and East Africa. It is acknowledged that the merchant activities of Arab Muslims were one of the factors which spurred the Arab geographers to travel to the districts of East Africa and to inform outsiders of their customs and ways as well as describing the inhabitants of these countries, their temperament and the goods they furnished to the market.

Beginning with the fourth century AH/ tenth century AD we find an Arab traveller giving a condensed description of his voyage from Oman to East Africa in his book *Murooj Al-Thahab Wa Maaden Al-Jawhar*. This was Abu Al-Hassan Ali bin Al-Hussain bin Ali Al-Mas'udi who was born at the end of the third century AH/ninth century AD in Baghdad of a Hijaz family. It looks as though the report of his trip to East Africa is the only source of knowledge of Oman's trade with East Africa[491].

Al-Mas'udi made several voyages with Omani merchants in pursuit of their trade. He encountered frights and horrors in the waters of East Africa and he travelled with Omani Arab Azd sailors as far as the far south-eastern shores of Africa. For three years he lived with them in East Africa, writing down his observations, then returned with them to Oman. He did not settle in Oman for long but took to sea once more and returned to East Africa.

Al-Mas'udi brought us knowledge of East Africa and he wrote at a time when the Gulf trade became active in this region. Moreover he was not transcribing the writings or hearsay of others, but rather writing down what he himself saw and heard. Thus was laid a fixed and firm foundation for the history of Arab-African trading relations with particular reference to Oman[492].

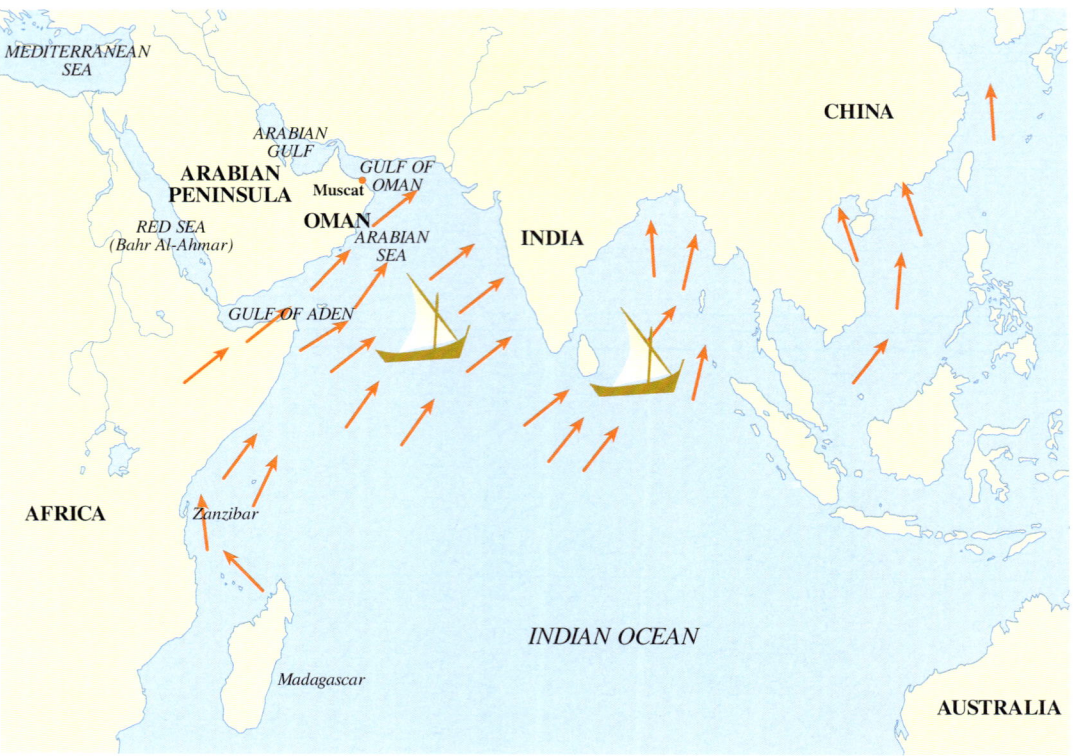

The role of the south-westerly summer monsoons in Omani trade.

For all that he wrote about Oman's trade contacts with East Africa with special reference to the coast to coast trade route, we are confident that Al-Mas'udi's knowledge of these affairs is far greater than is evident in the account he gives us in his book *Murooj Al-Thahab*.

In the fourth century AH/tenth century AD we received other descriptions of Omani trading voyages in East Africa. Birzek bin Shahrayar wrote through the eyes of Omani sea captains who specialized in the crossing to East Africa, showing us the regions reached by Oman's sea merchants.

The Arab geographers continued between the fifth and seventh centuries AH/ eleventh and thirteenth centuries AD to confirm the existence of Arab trading activities in East Africa[493], activities which reached a peak in the eighth century AH/ fourteenth century AD. In this context we have the great Arab traveller Ibn Battuta who explored the countries of the Islamic world alone and arrived on the shores of East Africa from Aden in 732 AH/1331 AD and returned from there to Oman on the merchant sea route; and on his return wrote down what he had seen of Arab commerce in the cities of East Africa along with the trading practices followed there.

The books of navigation constitute a record of Oman's trade, mercantile and political relations with districts of the known world of that time, among them the districts of East Africa. Some Omanis sought to study the laws and first principles of navigation in the Indian Ocean, among the most famous of these being Ahmed bin Majed and Suleiman Al-Mahri who composed greater and lesser groups of treatises which greatly assist the scholar in his quest for a

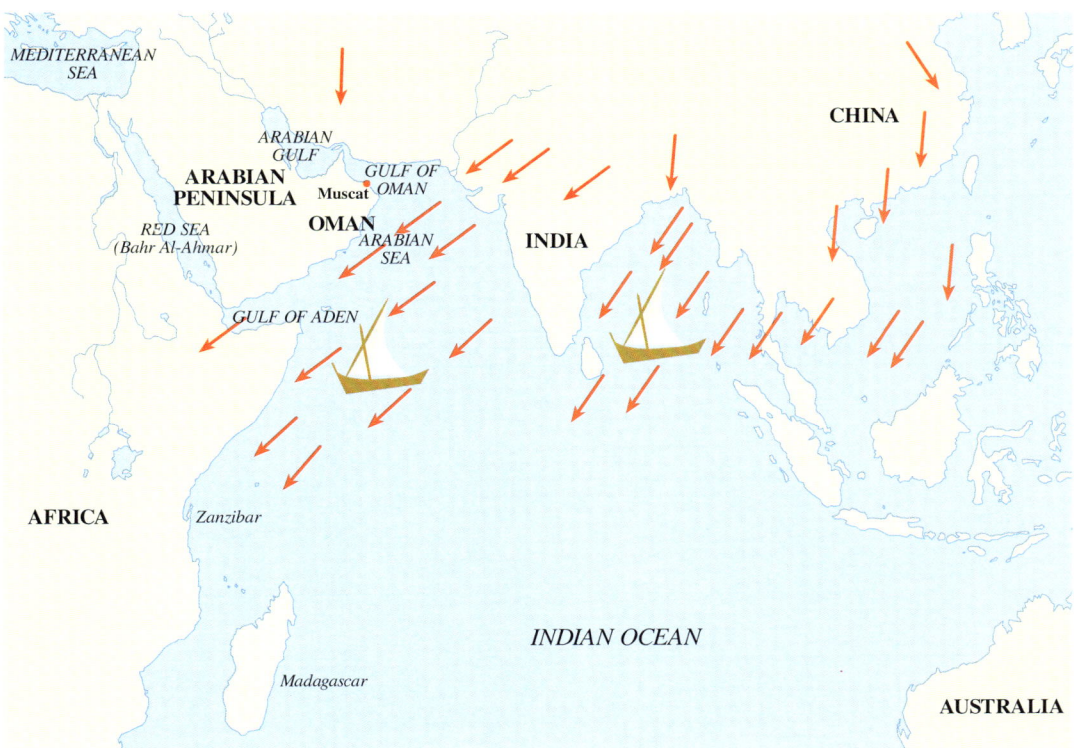

knowledge of trade and navigation activity. To these navigational compositions we can ascribe our knowledge that the merchant sea voyage to East Africa demanded a thorough familiarity with the first principles of the science of navigation. To these also we owe our knowledge of the seasonal patterns of Oman's trade with East Africa and the goods which they travelled to bring home. We will come back to this in the second part of this chapter.

The role of the north-easterly winter monsoons in Omani trade.

Factors Governing Oman's Mercantile Contacts with East Africa

One of the incontrovertible facts furnished to us is that the first and foremost element of the contact between Oman and East Africa was trade. It was this that spurred the Omanis to make the sea crossing to East Africa, carrying with them the goods needed by the people of this region to barter for their traded goods. The question that comes to mind is this: Why did the Omanis direct their trading activities towards East Africa? The answer is deeply intertwined with a number of factors, amongst them:

- Oman's age-old role in navigation and the merchant trade: The bonds of Oman's coastal dwellers with the sea are as old as they themselves, and these coastal dwellers came to acquire navigational skills that would equip them to master the Indian Ocean between Oman and East Africa on their sea journeys, unmindful of the huge waves[494] they encountered; all of which suggests that the Omanis acquired their navigational skills and knowledge of the sea routes and the principles of seamanship in the service of their trading objectives with East Africa.

- The geographical bearings of Oman's seaports: These Omani city ports became important transit centres for the import and export trade between the markets of the known world in the Middle Ages. This and its involvement with the known trading routes was what earned Oman its special position as a centre of the entrepôt trade. It was said: 'Who seeks to trade let him go to Aden and Oman'[495]. Oman's ports were celebrated for their profusion of merchandise and merchants and air of wealth and prosperity[496]. The country had become the gateway from the Arabian Gulf to East Africa, distinguished by its abundant resources. The Omanis transferred most of the East African trade across to Oman, from whence the goods whould be distributed to other centres of demand[497].

- The relationship of place between Oman and East Africa: geographical conditions spurred the Omanis to direct their trade towards East Africa.

- Part of the allure of East Africa was its combination of exotic and essential goods which brought high profits. And so Omani merchants risked life and limb on hazardous voyages to secure them.

- The natural climate of East Africa: this climate facilitated Omani trade with East Africa, in that the seasonal monsoons which prevailed in the Indian Ocean region allowed the Omanis to make two planned voyages each year. In November of each year the winds veered south-westwardly and the ships went out from the Gulf of Oman to the Indian Ocean, then followed a course parallel to the East African coast. In April the operation was reversed when the winds began to blow from the south and south- west, enabling the ships to return home to Oman laden down with a great diversity of African goods. In addition to this Oman's position allowed it to make use of the monsoon winds to arrive at the East African coast[498].

- The increase in Oman's trade after the emergence of Islam: a new dimension was added to relations between Oman and East Africa after the arrival of Islam as a result of fresh incentives stemming from religious and political factors. Contact between the two areas strengthened with the growth of trade. The Omanis had experienced a reinvigoration as a result of their conversion to Islam and they brought the message of the new faith with them to East Africa while pursuing their trade[499].

Throughout this time, the political and intellectual struggles which Oman witnessed in the Middle Ages caused many Omanis to leave their homeland and set up residence in East Africa. There many of them abandoned their livelihoods, among which of course was trade. One of the first Omani groups to take sanctuary in East Africa and to record this history for us was the Al-Julanda family[500].

During the reign of Said and Suleiman of the Julanda family, Oman became a refuge for those who opposed the rule of the Ummayyad Caliphs. As a result the Caliphate resolved to bring Oman back to compliance with the Central State, and the *Wali* of Iraq Al-Hajjaj bin Youssef Al-Thaqafi dispatched an army to Oman, which was an administrative district under its influence; and this expedition was successful in its objective[501].

The brothers Said and Suleiman were forced to gather their families and belongings and, with a number of their followers and tribal kin, sail for East Africa. Of this incident Sarhan bin Said Al-Azkawi says[502]: 'When Suleiman and Said sensed their inadequacy in the face of Al-Hajjaj's army, taking their offspring and chattels and whichever of their kin went out with them, they attached themselves to one of the countries of *zinj* (black Africa) where they lived and died'. Al-Azkawi did not specify the place that the Julanda family disembarked and settled in East Africa. Kirkman[503] attributes this to the fact that the names of the places in East Africa had no meaning in the context of Oman's political affairs. They belonged in the domain of the merchants and seamen. However the Julanda family were compelled to sojourn in Patta (Bat), one of the islands of the Lamu Archipelago[504]. We have however one singular text on the foundation of the city of Lamu in the manuscript (Report of Lamu)[505] in which was said: 'The first citizens of Lamu are Arabs who came from the city of Damascus in Syria and the person who sent them was Abdul Mulik bin Marwan. After these other Arabs came when news reached them of the Arab emigrants to the Swahili coast. The leader of these Arabs was Haj Said'.

This text referred to the residence of Said Al-Julanda on the Lamu Archipelago. His reason for choosing this place to settle was because other Arabs had come here before him and settled. Moreover the events which caused this influx had occurred during the time of the Ummayyad Caliph Abdul Mulik bin Marwan and this coincided with the time of the flight of the Julanda family to East Africa. What makes this text even more important is the fact that it is the only one which concerns itself with the first Omani migration to East Africa.

For the second time we find an important pointer to the arrival of the Omanis on the East African coast. At the start of the seventh century AH/ thirteenth century AD there was a another great influx of Omanis, driven again by political factors. This was the Nabhani ruling family of Oman, a family who had seized control of Oman at the end of the sixth century AH/ twelfth century AD, following a protracted struggle with the other forces prevailing at the time. The manuscript *History of Patta* says: 'The Sultan Suleiman bin Mudhaffar Al-Nabhani when he was exiled by the Ya'ruba made his way to Patta in 601 AH/ 1204 AD and stayed there. He had with him a great treasure and he married the daughter of the Patawi ruler[506] and became ruler of the area as a wedding gift from the father of the bride'[507].

Thus Patta became at this time a centre of Nabhani power which soon extended its influence as far as the East African coast; until the Nabhani had their ambitions curbed by the Ya'ruba authority in Zanzibar[508]. Kirkman[509] is suspicious of this narrative which tells of the arrival of the Nabhani to Patta and their accession to government of this city at the start of the seventh century AH/ thirteenth century AD. Nevertheless, he still insists that the arrival of the Nabhani to Patta was inextricably bound up with events in Oman and the overthrow of the Nabhani government there, though he does not think it likely that the Nabhani arrived in East Africa as early as this. At any rate what interests us in this context is that the Nabhani along with all of the other Omani migrants had a positive effect on resuscitating Arab trading activities in East Africa and this revival was instrumental in creating an ingathering of Omani merchants to the ports and cities of East Africa[510].

It would be useful here to remind ourselves that the Omani presence in East Africa after Islam altered the pattern of relations between Oman and this region. At the outset it led to a transformation of the temporary Arab trading posts which had arisen along the East African coastline prior to Islam to serve Arab trading contacts with the peoples of these districts into permanent centres promoting the exchange of trade and the political interests of the Arabs along this coastline. This would suggest that the Omani families who came to East Africa successfully rose to high position in the organization of the East African merchant trade to the benefit of the Arabs and the Omanis[511].

The Trade Route Between Oman and East Africa and the Trading Posts Along this Route

Anyone who wishes to learn about the trade crossing from Oman to East Africa must first and foremost go back to the writings of the Arab geographers, for in their writings and literary compositions these men took special care to describe this route in terms of the various stages of the voyage and the stations along the way where the ships put down anchor. If the writings of the earliest geographers do not go into much detail about these stages, it is enough that they mention a sea route between Oman and the *Bilad Al-Zinj*[512]. The bustling trade between Oman and East Africa from the fourth century AH/ tenth century AD onwards as a result of the resurgence of Arab trading activity with this region, after trade with the Far East had begun to face a variety of problems[513], led the Arab geographers to write in detail about the Oman-East Africa trade route.

Before we begin to describe the historic voyages of the Omanis to East Africa we should note that the Omanis knew the East African coast as four geographical regions. These were Berbera, Zinj, Safala (Mozambique), and Waq Waq[514]. They also knew the cities of every district, in particular those which were sources of the commodities which they had come to purchase[515].

The first stage of the trade route began with the departure from Oman towards Mahra and Shihr (Hadramaut) thence to Aden[516]. From Aden the ships set a course due south- west past the island of Socotra to arrive at the first landing in East Africa, i.e. Berbera and its bay, the Berbery Bay[517]. The Omanis knew the borders of this district and the length and breadth of the bay, for it was the waterway which they had to pass to gain access to the territories they were destined for in East Africa. Al-Mas'udi says of this[518]: 'There is a bay off the coast of Abyssynia which extends to the Berbery region of the *Bilad Al-Zinj* and Abyssinia and which goes by the name of Berbery Bay. It is 500 miles long and the width is 100 miles. Omani sailors cross this bay to the island of Qanbaloo in the *Bahr Al-Zinj* (Zinj Sea)'.

The most prominent port visited by Omani ships was Berbera or Hafuni (Hafun) and Bandar Moussa[519]. It should be pointed out here that the Omani ships were not - if we are to go by his description - carrying goods on the first stage of the voyage, suggesting that Berbera was no more than a transit stage for the merchant ships.

The ships now went out from Hafuni to the second East African district on their itinerary, that is *Bilad Al-Zinj*, to begin the second stage of the voyage. The Omanis knew this district thoroughly as an abundant source of the commodities they required. It extended from the city of Mogadishu (in Somalia) to Safala (Mozambique)[520]. Al-Mas'udi[521] calculated the area of this district at around 700 *parasang*. The first city where the Omani ships anchored here was Mogadishu which was described by Ibn Said Al-Maghrabi[522] as 'the celebrated Islamic city of the *Bilad Al-Zinj* region mentioned frequently by travellers'.

Mogadishu was an important reception centre for merchants arriving at this place. Probably the best testimony to its trading influence in this coastal area comes from the Arab traveller Ibn Fatima who says: 'Its inhabitants are gathered into quarters. It is a transit port'[523]. Mogadishu continued to maintain this trading prominence and it was described again in the eighth century AH/fourteenth century AD by Ibn Battuta the famous voyager, saying that it was an extremely large city, that its citizens were powerful merchants and ships were constantly coming in to anchor at its quayside from every place. Its citizens he said were always ready to welcome merchant ships arriving at port and to take what goods and wares they were carrying[524].

Among the coastal stations of the *Bilad Al-Zinj* called on by the Omani ships after Mogadishu were Marka and Birawa which were not more than a day's travel from Mogadishu[525]. Then they would make their way to Patta and Lamu, both cities on the Lamu Archipelago so similar to one another as to be hard to distinguish. The former was the political capital and the latter the commercial capital of this archipelago and so we find both geographers and sailors referring to them both as one. Both cities were situated on a long inlet, Patta on the right hand side of the bay and Lamu on the left[526]. After stopping here the Omani ships would head south to Malindi and Mombasa, both of which were important trading centres of the *Bilad Al-Zinj* and ports of anchor for Omani ships, where an exchange of goods took place[527].

From Mombasa the ships were obliged to take a parallel course along the African coastline in order to pass through the Zanzibar canal and make for the island of Zanzibar. The helmsman would steer the boat from Mombasa to the island of Wasin close to Mombasa along a watercourse well known to the boats and which linked it to Zanzibar[528]. Zanzibar was familiar to the Omanis as a prominent trading centre and they knew the distance to this island and to the islands surrounding it; and they were familiar with its natural geography and the commodities it supplied[529].

Al-Mas'udi refers to an island which was an important destination for the Omani ships which plied the East African trade. This was the island of Qanbaloo of which he says: 'Omani mariners cross this bay (the Berbery Bay) to the island of Qanbaloo in the *Bahr Al-Zinj*,' and again: 'The Omani sailors who traverse this sea (*Bahr Al-Zinj*) are Arab Azd and their destination in the *Bahr Al-Zinj* is the island of Qanbaloo to which we have referred'[530].

Al-Mas'udi describes the island of Qanbaloo thus: 'It is a populated island having among its inhabitants Muslims, though their language is *zinji* (African).

They took over this island at the end of the Ummayyad and beginning of the Abbassid States. From here to Oman is a distance by sea of around 500 *parasang* at the conjecture of sailors, though they do not say whether this is the direct distance or that of the actual crossing'[531]. Al-Mas'udi's particular interest in Qanbaloo was probably because it was the last station he visited before the return voyage to Oman. The precise location of Qanbaloo is still the subject of argument between scholars, even though Al-Mas'udi has furnished us with several geographical bearings in relation to the island which was a common destination of Omani merchant ships. And yet we have no final certain position for it, particularly as there are many islands off the East coast of Africa bearing all or some of the characteristics attributed to it by Al-Mas'udi[532].

The English Orientalist Spencer Trimingham attempted to study the texts furnished by Arab geographers regarding the island of *Bilad Al-Zinj*, starting with Al-Mas'udi and taking in Ibn Hawqal, Birzek bin Shahrayar and Al-Bayrouni in search of information from Al-Idrisi, Yaq'ut and Ibn Said and arrived at the following brief summary: as is clear from the maps of the first geographers and the accounts of travellers to East Africa, it is possible that Qanbaloo is a residence for foreign comers in an island off the coast of *Bilad Al-Zinj*. This island might have been Pemba, Zanzibar or Mafia, but not Madagascar[533].

Our study of the texts by Arab geographers on *Bilad Al-Zinj* leads us to suport what Trimingham said about the island of Qanbaloo. We even propose that this island was Zanzibar, the biggest island off the coast of *Al-Zinj*, due to the fact that it was the most important political as well as commercial Islamic Arab centre in the area[534].

Omani ships sailed through the sea of *Bilad Al-Zinj* south of Zanzibar towards the city of Kilwa, which was a significant political and commercial centre from the fourth century AH/tenth century AD until the arrival of the Portuguese in East Africa[535].

The third stage of the crossing by Oman ships in East Africa began with their departure from Kilwa towards 'Safala'. Al-Mas'udi is the first geographer to record the arrival of the Omani merchants in Safala. although he himself did not reach this area, Al-Mas'udi depended on the Omani sailors who provided him with a description of its features. He says' Those people (the Omanis) end their voyages on the sea of *Zinj* when they arrive at Qanbaloo, as we have aforementioned, and at the district of Safala and Waq Waq'[536]. About Safala, he says, 'it was the farthest extremity of *Bilad Al-Zinj* and it was to here that the Omani's ships were headed. This was their final destination'[537].

The journey to Safala was the last stage of the voyage of the Omani ships as is clear from the account of Al-Mas'udi. It is known that the trip to Safala was undertaken with the purpose of acquiring the most precious of all the commodities of East Africa - gold. Safala was known as the 'land of gold and ore'[538], and the Omanis would load as much gold as their ships could carry for the journey back.

The most important city of Safala was Tahanta and the first cities of Safala that the traveller encountered after leaving *Bilad Al-Zinj* were Ganta and Dandama, the latter of which was the last post of the *Bilad Al-Zinj* according to Al-Idrisi[539], while Ibn Said referred to the last post as Danmuta[540].

The district south again of the *Bilad Safala*, known to some Arab geographers by the name Waq Waq, was outside the radius of Arab trading activities. The reason for this was simple if we read Al-Idrisi[541] who says that in Waq Waq were 'two miserable towns, thinly populated in consequence of the strictures of their livelihood and wretchedness of their subsistence. Their land is devoid of gold and they have neither trade nor boats nor beasts of burden'. Apparently the district of Waq Waq was not a destination of any concern to the Omanis as they found there none of the things which they had travelled to obtain, so they did not bother themselves to sail any further than Safala. The Omani boats would return from Safala bearing gold and other merchandise to Oman, travelling the same route by which they had come.

Commodities Bartered

A discussion of the bartered commodities is a fundamental element of any history of trading contacts between Oman and East Africa. From the start we should acknowledge that Arab geographical and maritime sources have given us a living picture of the principal elements of Omani commerce with the East African coast. We know from these sources something of the variety of products provided by East Africa and from this we can gather with some certainty that Arab trading activity, including that of Oman in the great trading centres of East Africa, was considerably greater than the records suggest[542].

One of the most important East African commodities and one greatly coveted by the Omani merchants was gold, and gold was without question the pre-eminent and costliest commodity in the chart of goods exchanged between these two regions. Gold was then and still is the commodity that nations will scramble to obtain in order to boost their economic and political base. The Omanis were conscious of the importance of East Africa as a foothold for the supply of this precious metal and they made their best efforts to secure it and to bring it to those countries which expressed a demand for it.

Al-Mas'udi refers clearly to the mines of Safala and the Omanis' rush to get to them. In his account of the inhabitants he says: 'Their places of habitation extend as far as Safala which is the furthest extremity of the *Bilad Al-Zinj*. To this place are directed the Omani and Sirafi boats for it is the final destination at the nether part of the *Bahr Al-Zinj*. And so also the remotest part of the *Bahr Al-Zinj* is Safala and the remotest extremity (beyond) this is Waq Waq. These lands are rich in gold and marvellous things'[543].

Two centuries on we have Al-Idrisi[544] confirming the existence of gold in the Safala district, saying: 'The city of Danmuta is at the extremity of Safala and in this city is found gold dust in the same quantity as Safala'. Ibn Battuta in the eighth century AH/fourteenth century AD in an effort to pinpoint for the merchants the whereabouts of the gold-bearing districts explains: 'The gold is brought down into Safala from Yufi. Between Safala and Yufi in the land of *Al Leemi'yeen* is a march of one month and from Yufi the gold dust is brought down to Safala'[545]. And though Ibn Battuta does not describe for us the location of Yufi or whether it is a province of Safala, nevertheless we may surmise that the goldmines were situated in the heart of Africa and that Safala was no more than a collection point for the gold which was brought down from the interior. We cannot agree with Trimingham who goes on to state that Yufi was in Waq Waq[546], the simple reason being that most of the Arab works[547] confirm the presence of gold in Safala and that the district of Waq Waq was an impoverished one of no concern to Arab merchants as we have outlined above.

As gold remained a principal basis of mercantile contact between Oman and East Africa we find the Omani navigator Ahmed bin Majed giving special emphasis to the district of Safala in the naming of one of his compositions *Al-Arjouza Al-Safaliya* (Poem of Safala). Elsewhere he delineates the borders of the district of Safala along with its cities and ports[548]. Ibn Majed also describes precisely the goldmines of Safala which he says were a month's journey due west of the city of Safala in a region submerged in water (rivers). He estimated the distance of the Safala goldmine as being a march of seven days[549]. From all of which Ibn Majed interprets the importance which the Omanis attached to the gold of East Africa.

There was another commodity for which Oman's merchant fleets sailed to East Africa and which was in great demand in the markets of the Arab Islamic world. This was ivory, and East Africa was its principal and most abundant source in the Middle Ages. Says Al-Mas'udi[550]: 'Elephants are extraordinarily plentiful in the wild in *Bilad Al-Zinj*. None of them are tamed and the *zinj* have no use for them in war or any other activity. Instead they kill them for their tusks and it is from their land that the elephant's tusks come'. What interests us about the ivory trade is that the Omanis had a monopoly of the trade in East Africa whence they loaded the ivory for shipment to Oman and from there to the market centres of India and China, where it was used in the manufacture of chess and backgammon pieces and fine ornamentation because of its quality and size[551]. The foremost sources of supply of ivory to the merchants of East Africa were Mogadishu, Zanzibar, Kilwa, Safala and most of the coastal cities; and to some of these market cities the trade in ivory surpassed that of gold[552].

Iron was another bulwark of the trade between East Africa and Oman. It was available throughout the *Bilad Al-Zinj* and its trade was a mainstay along with gold of the livelihood of the inhabitants of these districts. Safala had an abundance of good quality iron. Al-Idrisi notes that iron was the commodity in greatest demand by East Africa's merchants in his own time (sixth century AH/ thirteenth century AD)[553].

Fragrances and aromatics of good quality, the most significant of these being ambergris, were in the forefront of the products purchased by the Omanis from the *Bilad Al-Zinj*. Ambergris was widely known in the Arab markets and was carried across to Oman and on to the other districts of the Arabian Gulf. Its sources of supply - Malindi, Mogadishu and Zanzibar - were destinations for the merchant ships seeking this precious commodity and it is likely that the owners of the Omani merchant fleets knew the places where ambergris was collected and the special methods used by the coastal dwellers of East Africa in collecting it[554].

We find in the chart of goods exchanged between Oman and East Africa skins, in particular the skins of the African tiger which were of a particularly high quality and smoothness and strength. The most important East African export centres for these skins were Malindi and Mombasa. The inhabitants would carry the skins down to the coast and the shipowners from Oman and elsewhere would come forward to make their purchase[555]. The island of Qanbaloo mentioned by Al-Mas'udi was one of the foremost trading posts with which the Omanis dealt in the purchase of tigerskins[556].

East Africa was also a prime source of a variety of precious and greatly desired timbers such as ebony, sandalwood, teak and the like. The Omanis carried these woods to Oman specifically for use in the construction of ships[557], the main supply centres being Mogadishu and Zanzibar[558].

Of the goods carried by the Omani boats to East Africa it appears that these did not command the attention of the writers of the Middle Ages, most probably because such were so well known to the merchants and travellers as for them to see no need to note them down. Al-Habib Al-Junhani[559] points out that agricultural products were the most important of Oman's exports to the districts with which its merchants traded. If we rely on the writings of the Arab geographers we find that Oman's prime agricultural exports were dates and a variety of fruits, wheat, barley and rice, saffron, frankincense, aromatic plants and rose blooms. It is certain that Omani merchants carried these goods with them on the passage to East Africa, along with goods imported from India and China such as cloth, copper utensils and glassware[560].

Some Navigation and Mercantile Systems on the Passage from Oman to East Africa

A proper examination of the navigational and mercantile practices required in pursuit of Oman's trading activities with East Africa would be wide-ranging and many-faceted. Nevertheless we will attempt to outline the main points.

The lengthy sea crossing to East Africa undertaken by Omani boats demanded a knowledge of the trade route, the calling points along the way, and the production centres to which they led. This was something with which the Omanis were thoroughly acquainted as we outlined previously.

Oman's trading relationship with East Africa required of the Omanis a knowledge of the navigational patterns and astronomy of the region. Moreover the merchants travelling in East African waters were required to know the measurements/calculations which had to be followed in planning the passage along with the nature of the route in terms of water depths, a knowledge of the ebb and flow of the tides, of the peninsulas and headlands and mountains along the route. There were Omani mariners who specialized in illustrating these matters for the merchants, of whom the most outstanding were the navigators Ibn Majed and Suleiman Al-Mahri who had an intimate knowledge of navigation and astronomy which served Omani merchants sailing to East Africa.

Oman's merchants and mariners also had a knowledge of the factors governing the merchant voyage between Oman and East Africa. They steered a course ahead of the monsoons of which Al-Mas'udi[561] said: 'The sailors who mounted these seas knew at any time which way the winds were blowing and this they had learnt from custom and experience inherited orally and through practice'.

It is known, as we pointed out above, that the Omanis greatly exploited the geographical location of their homeland in their use of the monsoon winds on the passage to East Africa. In winter, when the north-east wind was blowing, they found the best time for the merchant sailing ships to go out from Oman to the East African coast. In summer, the south-westerly prevailing wind sped them along the homeward journey to Oman[562].

The direct passage from Oman to East Africa took no more than three or four weeks. However the mandatory stops along the way where the merchant ships rested and an exchange of goods took place extended the length of the voyage. Over and above this the sailing ships were obliged to wait for a period of two months in East Africa for the first sign of the south-westerly wind which would carry them home to Oman. This interval was sufficient for the merchants to carry out their various commercial activities in East Africa. And so the entire outward and return voyage to East Africa took between six and eight months in all[563].

Apparently the winds and eddies off the East African coast varied from one place to another, and so the seasons for travelling to the various districts were different. The Omanis fixed a precise season specific to each district and city along the East African coast for the merchant passage[564]. Moreover the seasonal voyages were governed by tidal factors as well as rains and winds, and the Omani shipowners required a knowledge of all of this if they were to arrive safely to their desired destinations in East Africa[565].

The Omani merchants and the sea captains of the ships which plied the East African trade route were well aware of the perils which they faced on the sea journey. The first of the hazards to be faced was the gigantic swell of the *Bahr Al-Zinj*, which evidently struck terror into the hearts of the sailors. The Omanis called the waves on this heaving sea 'blind waves' by which they meant that they swelled to a mountainous height and sank low as valleys. They did not break or foam and the Omanis described them as 'frenzied'[566]. These frenzied waves attacked the Omani ships time and again - but even this did not deter them from their unbroken history of trade with East Africa[567].

It is worth commenting that most of the African merchants travelled by Omani boats, of which Al-Mas'udi[568] remarks: 'The Omanis were Arab Azd, and it was these who owned the ships which traversed the *Bahr Al-Berbera* and the *Bahr Al-Zinj*'. Al-Idrisi clearly says of this also[569]: 'The *zinj* do not have boats of their own but Omani and other ships call into the islands of the Africans and buy and sell their wares there'. Ibn Al-Wardi also confirmed this saying: 'They (the *zinj*) do not have boats but the Omani boats call in there'[570]. This testimony is adequate for us to infer that Omani ships monopolized the trade of East Africa as a consequence of the Africans not owning their own ships.

The ships owned by the Omanis and which carried the trade between Oman and East Africa required management. They needed sailors, *nakhoudha*, oarsmen and repairsmen. It is very likely that most of these crew, in particular the *nakhoudha*, who were the proxy owners of the ships consisted of Omanis[571]. We find in the Arab sources of the Middle Ages the names of a number of these Omani *nakhoudha* who specialized in the East African crossing and who were acquainted with the mysteries and terrors of these waters. There was Yazid Al-

Omani, *nakhoudha* of the *zinj*[572], and Ja'far bin Rashed who went by the name of Ibn Lakis. This latter was one of the sea captains and celebrated *nakhoudhas* of the gold run[573], and Mohammed Al-Omani and Ismailawaih bin Ibrahim bin Mardas[574].

The Omanis' relationship with the ships was not confined to the realm of ownership and management. It was they who built the ships in Oman, which has been famous from ancient times for its ship-building activities. The timber they needed they imported from East Africa and India, and Oman had specialist cadres of ship-builders who excelled at their craft[575]. The ships used in the waters of East Africa were built from wooden planks and they had triangular lateen sails set fore and aft . In building the ships destined for the East African crossing, the Omanis followed the prevailing tradition for boats built to cross the Indian Ocean, i.e. they were stitched with coir woven from the fibre of the coconut palm. No iron nails were used in the making of these boats, and this was because of the many rocks in the Indian Ocean. A ship held together by nails would be shattered on striking such rocks while the stitched timbers lent the boat flexibility[576]. Al-Mas'udi[577] ascribes the stitching to the fact that iron joins would fail because the ocean waters would rust them. So the Omanis would stitch the ship's timbers with coco fibre and then coat them with grease and lime.

Oman's East African merchant trade had many aspects, from ownership to repair and management of ships. We now take a brief look at the nature of the work of the men who served on the Omani boats on the East African crossing. Some of them owned the boats and took personal charge. Some merely managed them. A navigator would be hired to captain a ship for one or more voyages for a recognized and agreed sum which was based on the length of the voyage. The navigator had a crew who were classified into 12 ranks, each of which was associated with a specific duty[578]. The long crossing to East Africa which took more than six months to complete was organized in the form of a trade caravan as a form of protection from the perils and terrors along the route[579]. These caravans would contain as many as 16 boats in all[580].

Another form of mercantile activity practised by the Omanis in East Africa was the method of 'silent' gold trade which they employed in obtaining the gold of Safala. We will let Ya'qut tell us how this was done in his own words: 'The story of these (the inhabitants of Safala) is as we have related about the lands of gold dust (*tabr*) in the south of the *Maghreb*; that is to say goods are brought to them which the merchant leaves down. Then off he goes elsewhere, and when he comes back he will find in its place the value of everything he has brought. And the *zinj* know the value of the good gold'[581].

Thus we know that the gold barter trade in Safala was run in the same manner as that of the 'silent' gold trade in West Africa as described by Ya'qut. In short the barter trade which occurred between the merchants and the gold suppliers took place without a word spoken between them or a sight of one another.

Another of the trade practices pursued on the coast of East Africa involved the use of guides and agents who assisted merchants arriving at the trading posts. The assistance was in the form of outfitting quarters for them for the duration of their stay, storing their goods and facilitating the sale of the goods which they had brought with them and the purchase of goods for the return journey[582].

From the continuity of this commercial exchange between the East African coast and Oman in the Middle Ages we can be certain that the Omanis were encouraged in the practice of their merchant activities by a variety of natural, geographical, political and religious incentives. These activities led them to a thorough and intimate knowledge of the sea routes to East African trading centres and of the specific difficulties of these waters so that they could avoid them where possible, and allowed them to gain access to the exotic products of East Africa with which they were thoroughly acquainted. And they used these same Omani ships which had monopoly of the transport of goods and wares of East Africa to Oman whence they would redistribute them to other markets of the known world to meet the demand for them there, to carry many and diverse commodities from these markets back to East Africa. With them travelled aspects of the many civilizations they encountered and these they brought to the inhabitants of East Africa. Oman-East Africa contacts continued at this intensity and resulted in many Omanis settling in the cities of East Africa where they exercised in the first instance their commercial activities and later their political aspirations and in due course came to rule many of the coastal districts of East Africa for a lengthy period of time.

Notes for Part Three

[1] El Sayed Abdul Aziz Salem, *History of the Arabs before Islam*, Alexandria, 1973, p60. Here we have a scholar who places the destruction of the Ma'rib Dam at the middle of the sixth century AD. This historical placement is incorrect. (Compare Abdul Rahman Al-Aani, *Oman in the First Islamic Age*, Baghdad, 1977, p43 and Farouq Omar, *op. cit.,* p26.)

[2] Al-Bilathuri, *Futuh Al-Buldan*, published by Dr Salaheddin El-Mungad, section one, Cairo, 1956, p17.

[3] Phillips, *Oman : a history*, 1971, pp5-6. See *Kitab Kashef Al-Gumah*, p211f.

[4] Al-Awatbi, *Genealogy of the Arabs*, taken from Farouq Omar, *The Arabian Gulf in the Islamic Ages*, p26.

[5] *Al-Asuar'* (plural *'Assaour'* and *Asawirah*), Persian commander skilled in archery. It would seem that they were a distinguished army corps of cavalry or high command. See Al-Firouzabadi, *The Comprehensive Dictionary* under *'sura'*.

[6] Amer bin Ali bin Umair, *The Ancient Civilization of Oman*, p34.

[7] Ibn Hazm, *Jamharat Ansab Al-Arab* (The Genealogical Ancestry of the Arabs), p384. It should be noted that both Abi Zaid Al-Ansari and Amr bin Al-A'as Al-Sahami carried the Prophet's message to Abed and Gaifar, the sons of Julanda.

[8] Al-Bilathuri *Futuh Al-Buldan*, p93. See also Ibn Saad, *Al-Tabaqat Al-Kubra* [The Great (Upper) Classes], Cairo, 1358 AH, vol. 2, p27; Mohammed Rashid Al-Aqili, *The Role of the Arabian Gulf in the Islamic Conquests*, p153.

[9] Al-Bilathuri, *op. cit.,* p92.

[10] Ibn Al-Kelbi, *Genealogy* , p216; and Ibn Hazm, *Arab Genealogy,* p384.

[11] Al-Asma'i, *History of the Arabs before Islam* p87-p2114, and Khalifa bin Khayyat, *Siffat Jezirat Al-Arab (*History of Kalifah bin Khayyat) vol. 1, p2114.

[12] Ibn Rusta, *Al-Aa'ilaq Al-Nafisah* (Personal Relations),p206; Al-Isfahani *Al-Aghani* (The Songs), vol. 14 p300.

[13] Al-Ya'qubi, *Tarikh* (History), 1 pp232-233; and Ibn Durayed, *Al-Ishtiqaq*, p497.

[14] Khalifa bin Khayyat, *Kitab Al-Tabaqat* (The Book of Classes), p220.

[15] Saleh Al-Ali, *Socio-Economic Organizations in Basra in the First Century of the Hegira*, p324-325.

[16] Al-Asma'i, *History of the Arabs before Islam*, p87.

[17] Ibn Al-Kelbi, *Genealogy*, p203; and *Arab Genealogy*, p367.

[18] Khalifa bin Khayyat, *The Classes*, 10 p478; Al-Mas'udi, *Al-Tanbia wal-Ashraf*, p320; and

Arab Genealogy, p367.

[19] *Genealogy* , p203; and *Arab Genealogy*, p384.

[20] See Abdul Rahman Al-Aani, *Oman in the First Islamic Ages*, p48.

[21] Musa'b Al-Zubeiri, *Ancestry of the Qureish*, p13; and *Genealogy*, p12; and *Mu'jam Ma Istajam*, 1 pp46-7.

[22] *Al-Muhabbar*, p168.

[23] *Mu'jam Ma Istajam*, 1/p91.

[24] *Mu'jam Al-Buldan*, 3/p22.

[25] *Jamharat Al-Lugha* (Assembling the Language), 2/p9; and *Lissan Al-Arab* (The Arab Tongue), 3/p100.

[26] 1/p82 and see Al-Aani, Oman in the First Islamic Ages, p51.

[27] Al-Bakri, 1/p48, 1/p82

[28] See his account and biography in, Ibn Hayyan, *Kitab Al-Thiqat*, vol.13, p407; Ibn Na'im, *Dala'il Al-Nubowa* (The Signs of Prophethood), p76; Ibn Abdul Birr, *Al-Isti'ab*, vol.13, p1344; Ibn Al-Qairani, *Agreed Genealogy*, p134; Al-Samaani, *Ancestry*, vol. 5, p161; Ibn Al-Atheer, *Assad Al-Ghaba* (The Lion of the Jungle), vol. 5, p6; *Al-Labbab fi Tahthib Al-Ansab* (The Essence of Genealogical Revision), vol. 3, p81; Al-Dhahabi, *Tajrid Isma' Al-Sahhaba* (Inventory of the Names of the Companions), vol 5, pp704-5; Al-Zarkali, *Al-Aa'lam* (Notification) , vol. 6, p124; Omar Ridha Kahala, *Mu'jam Qabail Al-Arab* (Lexicon of the Arab Tribes), vol. 3, p1024.

[29] *The Rabi'a Al-Ta'ioun Family*, p17.

[30] *Early Arab History*, p48.

[31] *The Rabi'a Al-Ta'ioun Family*, p18.

[32] *Marasid Al-Atala'a*, vol. 2, p729.

[33] *Dala'il Al-Nubowa* (The Signs of Prophethood), p76.

[34] *Ibid.*, p76.

[35] *Kashef Al-Ghumah* (Third and Thirtieth Sections).

[36] *Al-Isti'ab* (Comprehension) vol. 3, p1344' *Al-Ansab* (Genealogy), vol. 5, p161.

[37] *Assad Al-Ghaba* vol. 5, p6; *Al-Labbab fi Tahthib Al-Ansab* vol. 3, p81; *Tajrid Isma' Al-Sahhaba* vol. 5, p4; *Al-Thiqaa*, vol. 3, p407.

[38] *Genealogy*, vol. 5, p161.

[39] See biography in, *Tarikh Baghdad* (History of Baghdad), vol. 11, p418; *Genealogy*, vol 5, p161; *Tahthib Al-Tahthib* (Revising the Revision), vol7, p294-6; *Al-Kashef fi Maarafa man lahu Ruwaiya fi Al-Kutub Al-Sitta*, vol 2, p280.

[40] See biography in, *Al-Kashef fi Maarafa man lahu Ruwaiya fi Al-Kutub Al-Sitta*, vol. 1 p 45 Tahthib Al Tahthib vol. 1, p23.

[41] Near Tartous.

[42] *Dala'il Al-Nubowa* (Signs of Prophecy), p.76; Al-Isti'ab, part 3, p.1344. *Asad Al-Ghaba* (The Lion of the Forest), part 5, p.6.

[43] *Ath-Thuqaat* (The Trustees), part 3, p.407.

[44] *Al-Isaba*, part 5, p.704.

[45] *Al-Isti'ab*, part 3, p.1344.

[46] *Taj Al-A'arous* (The Bride's Crown) Vol. 9, p.345.

[47] *Asad Il-Ghaba*, part 5, p.6.

[48] *Kashef Al-Ghumah*, section 33, *ibid.,* p.324-6.

[49] It was said as (Tajar) and (Bajar). In another story it was (Bajr) and (Najr) as mentioned in the *Asad Al-Ghaba*. But in *Al-Assnaam* (Idols) book p.63. the word (Bajar) was mentioned. Ibn Duraid said, it is an idol worshipped by the Azd and their neighbours Taye and Qudha'a during Al-Jahilya. They referred to him as (Bajar) and maybe (Bajir) as written in *(Jamharat - Allugha,* part 1, p.209). Ibn Al-Atheer had mentioned in his book *Fi Gharib Al-Hadith (The Strange in the Sayings)*, part 1, p.63, that the name was (Bahar) and he said some people mentioned the name (Bejar), (part 1, p.61). He also pointed out that Mazin used the name (Bajer) as an idol worshipped by the Azd during Al-Jahilya. See, *Lisan Al-A'arab (*The Arab Tongue*)*, vol. 1, p161.

[50] *Dala'il Al-Nubowa,* p.76. Asad Al-Ghaba, part 5, p.6.

[51] *Ibid.,* p.76., *ibid.,* part 5, p.6.

[52] This is what the *Kashef Al-Ghumah*(section 33) pointed out. But p.76 of *Dala'li Al-Nubowa and Asad Al-Ghaba*, part 5, p.6, the story was -(A man called Ahmed asked any person he met with to accept Allah's Messenger.....etc.)

[53] *Dala'il Al-Nubowa*, p.76.

[54] *Al-Ansab* (The Lineages), part 5, p.161.

[55] Most of the sources which pointed out these poems.

[56] Al-A'araj is near At-Taif and the beginning of Tihama. It is 78 miles (125 kms)from al-Medina. It is the land of Hatheel, but not Al-A'araj between Mecca and Al-Medina. Al-A'araj

is an outward sign between Mecca and Al-Medina....*Mu'jam Al-Buldan* (Atlas of the Countries) part 4, p.98-9. Al-A'araj also is a place in Yemen between Al-Mahaalib and Al-Mahjam, *Marasid Al-Ittila'a* (Watching Observatory), part 2, p.928.

57 Al-Falaj, victory and winning.

58 as mentioned (disagree).

59 Al-Nahj, depreciation.

60 The poems pointed to the signs of prophecy, p.76., *Al-Isti'ab,* Part 3, p.134., *Asad Il-Ghaba,* part 5, p.7.

61 *Al-Isaba,* part 5, p.705.

62 Al-Mira, Food, Al-Khafq, Camel, Adhilf, sheep.

63 Ibn Ruzaiq, *Al-Fet'h Al-Mubeen,* p73-4.

64 *Ibid.,* p.75.

65 Ibn Hushaam, *As-Sira Al-Nabaweya* (The life of the Prophet) part 4, Cairo, 1936, p.254. See also, Mohammed Hamid Allah, *Nabi Al-Islam* (The Prophet of Islam), part 1, Paris, 1979, p383.(in French).

66 Ibn Hushaam, *ibid.,* part 4, p254.

67 Al-Bilathurri, *Futuh Al-Buldan* (Conquests of the Countries), Cairo, 1956, p.87.

68 Unknown Author, (*The History of Oman*), Edited by Said Aashor, Sultanate of Oman, 1980, p40 and p259.

69 Al-Tabari, *The History of Messengers and Kings,* part 3, critically edited by Abu Al-Fadh Ibrahim, Cairo, 1960, p.103; See also Al-Ya'aqubi (The Book of History), part 2, Al-Najaf 1258 AH, p.62.

70 *Ibn Khaldoon* (Book of Considerations...), part 3, Beirut, 1965, p.788.

71 These letters were mentioned by Al-Sheikh Saif Bin Hamoud Al-Bataashi.

72 *Khalifa Bin Khayaat,* (Book of History), critically edited by Akram Dhiyae Al-Omari, part 1, Al-Najaf, 1967, p.84.

73 *Ibn Sa'ad, (*The Big Classes*),* Part 2, Cairo, 1968, p.27.

74 Dr Mohammed Rashid Al-Oqaili, *The Arabian Gulf During the Islamic Eras,* Amman, Jordan, 1983, p61.

75 Ibn Sa'ad, *ibid.,* part 2, p114.

76 Dahlan, *The Life of Prophecy and the Effects of Mohammedism,* part 2, p.166.

77 *Ibid.*

78 Anon., *Stories and Events that Happened in Oman.* p.40.

79 Anon., *The History of the People of Oman,* p259; Al-Salimi, *The Tohfat Al-'Ayian in the Life of the Omanis,* part 1, p.40.

80 *ibid.,* p.43.

81 Sarhan bin Said Al-Azkawi Al-Omani, *The History of Oman,* p.38-9.

82 Means the fighters who ride camels and horses.

83 Sarhan bin Said Al-Azkawi Al-Omani, *The History of Oman,*p.39.

84 *Ibid.,* p.40.

85 These were a branch of the Azd who migrated from Yemen when the Ma'rib Dam burst - to the north-west of the Arabian peninsula and parts of El-Sham where they lived at a watered spot there known as Ghassan, so they were referred to as the Ghassan Azd. There they managed to create a state, the Ghasasina State, which they ruled up to the coming of Islam. Jafna was the grandfather of the Ghasasana clan. See Dr Hassan Ibrahim Hassan, *Political History of Islam,* vol. 1, pp47-8 and references, 2nd ed., Cairo, 1948.

86 Sarhan bin Said Al-Azkawi Al-Omani, *History of Oman,* p40. *Stories and Reports of Oman,* p41.

87 Both previous references, same pages.

88 See Al-Salimi, *Tohfat Al-'Ayian,* vol.1, pp51-7. We note that Al-Salimi refers to the narrative of the historian Ibn Al-Atheer in his work *Al-Kamel.* In respect of the *Riddah* movement in Oman he says, 'It was all groundless without foundation and only God knows'; Al-Salimi, *The Tohfat Al-'Ayian,* vol.1, p57. See also Sayeda Kashef, *Oman at the Dawn of Islam,* p32-3.

89 See Al-Salimi, *The Tohfat Al-'Ayian,* vol.1, p55f.

90 Al-Salimi, *The Tohfat Al-'Ayian,* vol. 1, p69-70.

91 Abdul Rahman Al-Aani, *Oman in the First Islamic Ages,* Baghdad, 1977, p27.

92 Khalifa bin Khayyat, *Kitab Al-Tarikh,* vol.1, p91.

93 Al-Dhahabi, *The History of Islam and the Class Elite,* vol. 2, Cairo, 1367 AH, p81.

94 Farouq Omar Fawzi, *History of the Arabian Gulf in the Middle Islamic Period,* Baghdad, 1985, p85.

95 *Ibid.,* p86.

96 Khalifa bin Khayyat, *op. cit.,* vol. 1, p300.

97 Farouq Omar Fawzi, *Introduction to a Study on the Origins of Omani History,* Baghdad, 1979, p32.

98   Julfar, The city of Khasaba close to Oman. (Ya'qut, *Mu'jam Al-Buldan*, vol. 2, p622). This city was wiped out and its still surviving ruins lie close to what is today Ras Al-Khaimah in the UAE. (See Al-Salimi, *Tohfat Al-'Ayian,* Dar Al-Kutub Al-Arabi Press, Cairo, p18.

99   See Al-Salimi, *Tohfat Al-'Ayian*, vol .1, p52.

100   Dr Said Abdul Fattah Aashour and Dr Awad Mohammed Khalifat, *Oman and Islamic Civilization*, p27.

101   See Humaid bin Mohammed bin Ruzaiq, *Al-Fet'h Al-Mubeen fi Sirah Al-Sadah Al-Busaideen*, p213; and Sarhan bin Said Al-Azkawi Al-Omani, *History of Oman*, p40, *Stories and Reports of Oman*, p41; *History of the Omani People*, by an unknown author, p47.

102   Al-Tabari, *op. cit.,* vol. 5, p166. For the reign of Ibn Amr and then Ziad bin Abia see also Al-Tabari, *op. cit.,* vol. 5, pp212/6.

103   Al-Aani, *op. cit.,* p87.

104   Abdul Amir Daksan, from 'The History of Oman in the Ummayyad Period', article in *The Arabian Gulf* magazine, no. 1, University of Basra, 1973, p140.

105   See Khalil Shaker Hussein, 'The Issue of the Vacant Seat of Power after the abdication of Maawiya bin Mazid until Marwan bin Al-Hakam took power', article in *The Arab Historian* magazine, no. 28, 1986. p108f.

106   Ibn Al-Atheer, *op. cit.,* vol. 4, p204.

107   Abdul Amir Daksan, *The Ummayyad Caliphate*, Beirut, 1973, p53f.

108   Ibn Khaldun, *op. cit.,* vol. 3, p314.

109   Abdul Amir Daksan, from *The History of Oman in the Ummayyad Period*, p137.

110   Daksan, *The Ummayyad Caliphate*, p241.

111   Al-Siyabi, *op. cit.,* p185. Al-Salimi, *Tohfat Al-'Ayian*, p74.

112   Abdul Amir Daksan, from *The History of Oman*, p140f.

113   Abdul Amir Daksan, from *The History of Oman*, p140.

114   Humaid bin Mohammed bin Ruzaiq *Al-Fet'h Al-Mubeen fi Sirah Al-Sadah Al-Busaidiyeen*, London, 1871; Al-Azkawi, *Kashef Al-Ghumah Al-Jama'a Li Akhbar Al-Umma*, paper 1-2, British Museum, ref. 8067, and paper 336 - S.B. Miles, *The Countries and Tribes of the Persian Gulf*, London, 1966, p50.

115   Abdul Amir Daksan, *Oman in the Geographical Writings of the Third and Fourth Centuries Hegira*, Congress of Studies of the East Arabian Peninsula, Qatar, 1976, p386; Farouq Omar, *Introduction to a Study on the Origins of Omani History*, p13.

116   Ibn Asaker, *Tarikh Medinet Dimeshq* (History of the City of Damascus), vol.4, pp167/186, taken from Daksan from *The History of Oman in the Ummayyad Period,* p140.

117   Al-Siyabi, *op. cit.,* p185.

118   Al-Salimi, *Tohfat Al-'Ayian*, p74.

119   Al-Siyabi, *op. cit.,* pp186-7.

120   *Ibid.*, p188.

121   Al-Salimi, *Tohfat Al-'Ayian*, p74-5.

122   Daksan, from *The History of Oman*, p142.

123   Al-Siyabi, p190

124   See Ibn Ruzaiq, *Al-Fet'h Al-Mubeen* p216; and Al-Azkawi Al-Omani, *Tarikh Oman*, p 42; Unknown author, *History of the Omani People*, p50; *Stories and Reports of Oman*, p44; Al-Salimi, *Tohfat Al-'Ayian*, vol. 1, p 59.

125   *Op. cit.,* same pages.

126   See Ibn Ruzaiq, *Al-Fet'h Al Mubeen* p221; and Sarhan bin Said Al-Azkawi Al-Omani, *Tarikh Oman*, pp 42-3; Unknown author, *History of the Omani People*, pp50-1.

127   Ibn Qutayba, *Al-Maarif*, Cairo, 1969, p399; Abu Al-Farag Al-Isfahani *Al-Aghani* vol. 2, Cairo, 1972, p75. Ibn Hazm believes his name was Salem bin Siraq. See *Jamhara Ansab Al-Arab*, Cairo, 1982, p367

128   *Al-Aghani*, vol. 2, p76; Ibn Hajar, *Al-Isaba*, Beirut, 1328 AH, vol. 4, p108

129   Ibn Khalakan, *Waffiat Al-'Ayian*, Beirut, vol. 5, p358.

130   Saif bin Hamoud Al-Batashi, *History of the Commander Al-Mahlab*, pp13, 22.

131   Ibn Hajar, vol. 4, p108. There is another account in *Al-Aghani* that the appelation Abu Safra came from the fact that he used to lighten (the colour of) his beard. See, *Al-Aghani*, vol. 2, p76.

132   Ibn Abdul Birr, *Al-Isti'ab*, Beirut, 1328 AH, p109.

133   Nur Al-Din Al-Salimi, *Tohfat Al-'Ayian*, vol.1, p53f.

134   Ibn Saad, *Al-Tabaqat*, vol. 2, pp114-5.

135   Al-Bilathuri, *Futuh Al-Buldan*, p93.

136   Al-Awatbi, *Al-Ansab*, vol. 2, p121..

137   Ibn Khalakan, *Waffiat Al-'Ayian*, vol. 4, pp323, 329.

138   Al-Salimi, *Tohfat Al-'Ayian*, p45.

139   *Ibid.,* p43.

140   *Al-Aghani*, vol. 2, p76.

[141] *Al-Ansab*, p123; *Tohfat*, p46.

[142] Bani Umran of the Azd tribe, descended from Amr bin Adi bin Haretha bin Amru bin Amer (See Al-Ya'qubi, *Tarikh*, vol. 1, pp203-204.

[143] *Al-Ansab*, p122.

[144] *Tohfat Al-'Ayian*, p46.

[145] Ibn Khaldun, *Tarikh*, Beirut, 1986, vol.2, p989; Al-Tabari, *Tarikh*, vol.3, p176-7.

[146] Ibn Khal, *Al-Khalifa Othman*. Cousin of Caliph Othman and ruler of Basra at the age of 25 after the discharge of Abu Moussa Al-Ashaari (Ibn Aatham, *Al-Futuhat*, vol.1, p336.)

[147] *Al-Ansab*, p125; *Tohfat*, p48.

[148] Cf. *Al-Ansab*, p125-6.

[149] *Al-Ansab*, p125; *History of Al-Mahlab*, p25.

[150] Ibn Khalakan believed that Al-Mahlab was the youngest son of Abu Safra. He was born two years before the death of the Prophet (*Waffiat*, vol. 5, p351).

[151] Al-Nuwairi, *Nihayat Al-Irb*, vol. 20, p266.

[152] Al-Bilathuri, *Futuh Al-Buldan*, p531.

[153] Al-Ya'qubi, *Tarikh*, vol. 2, p222.

[154] *Nihayat Al-Irb*, vol. 20, p267; Al-Tabari, *Tarikh*, vol. 5, p251. He tells this story in his account of the events of the year 50 .

[155] Al-Tabari, *Tarikh*, vol. 2, p305.

[156] Al-Bilathuri, *Futuh Al-Buldan*, p508.

[157] Al-Ya'qubi, *Tarikh*, vol. 2, p252; Ibn Aatham, vol. 3, p157-9.

[158] Al-Ya'qubi, *Tarikh*, vol. 2, p252.

[159] Ibn Aatham, vol. 3, p159

[160] Al-Tabari, *Tarikh*, vol. 5, p545.

[161] *Nihayat Al-Irb*, vol. 20, p513.

[162] *Waffiat Al-'Ayian*, vol.5, p351; *Nihayat Al-Irb*, vol.20, pp323-4.

[163] Ibn Aatham, vol. 3, p201; *Nihayat Al-Irb*, vol. 20, p323-4.

[164] Al-Ya'qubi, *Tarikh*, vol. 2, p264-5.

[165] Al-Tabari, *Tarikh*, vol. 5, pp615-6; Ibn Aatham, vol. 3, p202.

[166] Al-Ya'qubi, *Tarikh*, vol. 2, p265; Al-Nuwairi, *Nihayat Al-Irb*, vol. 20, p324.

[167] Ibn Al-Atheer, *Al-Kamel*, vol. 4, p196

[168] *Ibid.*

[169] *Al-Mubarrad, Al-Kamel*, p226.

[170] *Al-Mubarrad*, p227.

[171] *Ibid.*

[172] Al-Homeiri, *Al-Rawdh Al-Mi'tar*, Beirut, 1983, p248.

[173] Ibn Al-Atheer, *Al-Kamel*, vol. 4, p197; *Nihayat Al-Irb*, vol. 20, p325.

[174] *Al-Mubarrad*, p233.

[175] Ibn Aatham, vol. 3, p206.

[176] *Al-Mubarrad*, p235.

[177] Al-Yahmad are Azd and the Farahid are an offshoot of them (*Al-Mubarrad*, p236).

[178] Al-Tabari, *Tarikh*, vol.5, pp621. Al-Tabari finishes the story saying, Some of his soldiers returned to the battle and after a time came back to (Al-Mahlab) saying, 'O Aba Alqimmah, the battle is getting tougher!!'

[179] *Al-Rawdh Al-Mi'tar*, p248; *Al-Mubarrad*, p234.

[180] Al-Tabari, vol. 5, p618.

[181] *Al-Mubarrad*, p235.

[182] *Al-Rawdh*, p248.

[183] *Al-Rawdh*, p248; *Al-Mubarrad*, p240.

[184] *Al-Kamel*, vol. 4, p196-200.

[185] Al-Ya'qubi, *Tarikh*, vol. 2, p264-5.

[186] Al-Nuwairi, vol. 21, p44.

[187] Ibn Aatham, vol. 3, p220.

[188] Al-Nuwairi, vol. 21, p45.

[189] Ibn Kathir, *op. cit.*

[190] Ibn Aatham, vol. 3, p318.

[191] Ibn Khaldun, vol. 3, p68.

[192] Cf. Al-Nuwairi, vol. 21, p46-8.

[193] Ibn Aatham, vol. 3, p326.

[194] Al-Tabari, vol. 6, p112; *Al-Kamel*, vol. 4, p275.

[195] Al-Tabari, vol. 6, p119; Al-Nuwairi, vol.20, p525.

[196] Al-Tabari, vol. 6, p127;

[197] *Ibid.*; Al-Nuwairi, vol. 20, p527.

[198] Cf. Al-Tabari, vol. 6, p158-9; Al-Nuwairi, vol. 21, p127; Ibn Khaldun, vol. 3, p80; Ibn Kathir

Al-Bidaya, vol. 8, p348.

[199] Cf. Al-Tabari, vol. 6, p187f.

[200] Ibn Aatham, vol. 3, p406.

[201] Al-Tabari, vol. 6, p169; Al-Nuwairi, vol. 21, p147.

[202] Bashr bin Marwan, brother of the Caliph Abdul Mulik bin Marwan. He was *Wali* of Kufa for his brother Abdul Mulik (cf. Al-Tabari, vol. 6, p196).

[203] Al-Nuwairi, vol. 21, p169.

[204] *Ibid,;* p149.

[205] Ibn Aatham, vol. 3, p418.

[206] Al-Tabari, vol. 6, p196.

[207] Ibn Aatham, vol. 3, p422.

[208] *Al-Kamel*, vol. 4, p366.

[209] Al-Tabari, vol. 6, p204.

[210] Al-Nuwairi, vol. 21, p214.

[211] *Al-Mubarrad*, p266.

[212] Ibn Aatham, vol. 4, p14.

[213] Al-Tabari, vol.6, p210.

[214] Karzon is a city in Persia between the sea and Shiraz (cf. Ya'qut, *Mu'jam Al-Buldan*).

[215] Cf. Al-Nuwairi, vol. 21, pp151-2.

[216] *Al-Kamel*, vol.4, p390; Al-Nuwairi, vol. 21, p153.

[217] *Al-Kamel, ibid.*

[218] Al-Tabari, vol. 6, p213.

[219] Al-Nuwairi, vol.21, p154.

[220] Al-Tabari, vol.6. p301.

[221] Ibn Aatham, vol.4, p14.

[222] *Al-Mubarrad*, p273; *Al-Rawdh*, p248.

[223] Al-Tabari, vol.5, p618.

[224] Cf. Ibn Aatham, *Al-Maarak*, vol.3, p23f; *Al-Mubarrad*, p272f.

[225] *Al-Mubarrad*, p277.

[226] Ibn Aatham, vol.3, p213.

[227] Ibn Aatham, vol.4, p30.

[228] Al-Nuwairi, vol.21, p155.

[229] Ibn Aatham, vol.4, p41

[230] Al-Tabari, vol.6, p313.

[231] Ibn Aatham, vol.3, p45.

[232] *Ibid.,* p42.

[233] Al-Ya'qubi, *Tarikh*, vol.2, p275;

[234] *Al-Mubarrad*, p292-3

[235] Al-Tabari, vol.6, p304.

[236] At the foot of the Tabaristan mountains (cf. Ya'qut, *Mu'jam Al-Buldan*); Al-Tabari, vol.6, p211.

[237] Al-Nuwairi, vol.21, p156.

[238] Cf. Ibn Aatham, vol.4, pp47-8.

[239] Al-Nuwairi, vol.21, p157

[240] Ibn Aatham, vol.4, p50.

[241] Al-Tabari, vol.6, p304.

[242] Cf. Al-Tabari, vol.6, p309f; Al-Nuwairi, vol.21, p159f.

[243] *Al-Mubarrad*, p294; Al-Mas'udi, *Murooj,* Beirut, 1986, pp185-6.

[244] Ibn Aatham, vol.4, p56.

[245] Al-Nuwairi, vol. 21, p158. Basra was known as 'Al-Mahlab's Basra' because he protected the city from the Kharijites. The Kufites used to call the Basrans 'Al-Muhalab's servants' for the same reason and because of the Al-Mahlab family's control and influence over that city. The Basran poet Al-Hassan bin Hani' wrote, 'And every Basran knows that nobility is bound by hazard. In Al-Mahlab the Omani Azd have among them a man to make them proud'. (cf. Al-Hamdani, *Mukhtasar Kitab Al-Buldan*, p122; *Waffiat Al-Aayian*, vol.5, p351).

[246] Al-Tabari, vol.6, p319; *Al-Kamel*, vol.4, p448.

[247] *Al-Kamel*, vol.4, p448.

[248] Al-Nuwairi, vol.21, p268.

[249] Ibn Aatham, vol.4, p58.

[250] Al-Nuwairi, vol.21, pp21, 201.

[251] Al-Khotal, *Kura Fi Ma Wara'a Al-Nahar* (cf. Ya'qut, *Mu'jam Al-Buldan*).

[252] *Al-Kamel*, vol.4, p453.

[253] Al-Nuwairi, vol.21, pp21, 201.

[254] Al-Tabari, vol.6, p326.

255   *Ibid.,* p338.
256   *Ibid.,* p351.
257   *Al-Kamel,* vol.4, p475.
258   Ibn Aatham, vol.4, p89. The poet Nahar bin Tawasa'a Al-Tamimi lamented him in the
      following verse,
      'No more to conquer lands nor grow in wealth
       With Al-Mahlab has died generosity and the open hand'.
259   Cf. Al-Tabari, vol. 6, p355.
260   Cf. Al-Nuwairi, vol. 21, pp239f.
261   Al-Tabari, vol .6, p370. It was said that Ibn Al-Ash'ath when he withdrew went to stay with
      Ratbil, the Turkish king who had struck up a friendship with Ibn Al-Ash'ath when the latter
      refused to go to war against him. His armies went on to engage Al-Hajjaj (Cf. Al-Tabari, vol.6,
      pp370-1; Al-Mas'udi, *Al-Tanbiya Wal Ashraf,* p287.
262   Al-Nuwairi, vol. 21, p251.
263   Al-Tabari, vol.6, p371.
264   Al-Nuwairi, vol. 21, p252.
265   Saad bin Abi Waqqas, when Hassan told him of Al-Mahlab's heroism in the campaign in
      Khorasan an the time of Maawiya said, 'Allah, do not humble him and may You increase his
      wealth and progeny'. And it was said that what all of Al-Mahlab's good fortune was a conse-
      quence of this prayer. cf. *Al-Ma'arif,* p242, *Al Ansab,* pp128-129.
266   Al-Nuwairi, vol. 21, p253.
267   Al-Tabari, vol.6, p397.
268   *Waffiat,* vol. 6, p278.
269   *Ibid.,*pp288-9; Al-Nuwairi, vol. 21, p264.
270   Al-Tabari, vol.6, p395.
271   *Waffiat,* vol.6, p289.
272   Al-Tabari, vol.6, p371.
273   *Ibid.*
274   Ibn Aatham, vol.4, pp145f.
275   Al-Tabari, vol.6, p396; Al-Nuwairi, vol.21, p265.
276   *Waffiat,* vol. 6, p288-9.
277   Al-Tabari, vol. 6, p488; Al-Nuwairi, vol. 21, p316.
278   Ibn Aatham, vol. 4, pp158.
279   Al-Tabari, vol. 6, p452.
280   *Waffiat,* vol. 6, p294.
281   Cf. Al-Tabari, vol. 6, p452-3.
282   Ibn Aatham, vol. 4, p187.
283   Al-Nuwairi, vol. 21, p343.
284   Al-Ya'qubi, *Tarikh,* vol. 2, p295.
285   Al-Tabari, vol.6, p506. *Al-Ansab,* vol. 2, p148.
286   Cf. *Al-Kamel,* vol. 5, p23; Al-Nuwairi, vol. 21, pp344f.
287   *Al-Kamel,* vol. 5, pp22-4.
288   Al-Nuwairi, vol. 21, p346.
289   Cf. details of the Al-Mahlab family's invasions during this period in Al-Bilathuri, *Futuh Al-
      Buldan,* pp412f; Al-Ya'qubi, *Tarikh,* vol. 2, p296.
290   Al-Bilathuri, p412-5; Al-Homeiri, *Al-Rawdh Al-Mi'tar,* p2160-1.
291   *Al-Kamel,* vol. 5, pp48-9; Al-Nuwairi, vol. 21, p363.
292   *History of Mosul,* p3.
293   *Al-Kamel,* vol. 5, p71; *History of Mosul,* p8.
294   Ibn Aatham, vol. 4, pp245-6.
295   *Al-Kamel,* vol. 5, p76.
296   Al-Mas'udi, *Al-Tanbiya,* p294.
297   Al-Tabari, vol. 6, p592; Al-Nuwairi, vol. 21, p286.
298   *Al-Kamel,* vol. 5, p85.
299   Ibn A'atham, vol. 4, p249, Al-Tabari, vol. 6, p 593.
300   Al-Tabari, vol.6, p592; *Al-Kamel,* vol. 5, p75.
301   Al-Ya'qubi, *Tarikh,* vol. 2, p341.
302   Al-Ya'qubi, *Tarikh,* vol. 2, p345; *Al-Ansab,* vol.2, pp156-157, Al-Tabari, vol.7, p458; Al-
      Bilathuri, p.451.
303   Al-Bilathuri, *Futuh Al-Buldan,* p432; Al-Ya'qubi, *Tarikh,* vol.2, pp134, 161.
304   Al-Bilathuri, *ibid.,* p32.
305   Cf. Khalifa bin Khayyat, *Kitab Al-Tabaqat* p197; Ibn Hazm, *Jamharat Ansab Al-Arab;* p266
      Ibn Hajar, *Al-Isaba,* vol. 1, p271.
306   Barous, the present location of which is not known except that there is a port there by the name

of Baruj on the coast of Kagarat which was mentioned by Ahmed bin Majed in his book, *Al-Wafa'id Fi Asul Al-Bahr Wa Al-Qawa'id*, p452. See also, Al-Humaidi, *Makran and Baluchistan from the Early Islamic Conquest down to Noisavne the Mongol*, Ph.D Thesis, Victoria University of Manchester, Department of Middle Eastern Studies, Faculty of Arts, June 1988, p283.

[307] Al-Bilathuri, *op.cit.,* p432. Al-Ya'qubi has a story in his *Tarikh* (vol. 2, p134) that Othman bin Abi Al-A'as was appointed by Abu Bakr, and this is a line which cannot be ignored; attributed by Al-Qadi Atthar to the writers, and only God knows the truth. See *Al-Aqd Al-Tathmin*, p35. However the contradiction is evident in the narrative of Al-Ya'qubi, cf. vol. 2, p138 and compare with Ali bin Hamed Al-Kufi *Fet'h Namah-I-Sind* - critically edited by by Dr Nabi Bakhash Balouj, Islamabad, 1403/1983, p27 notes.

[308] Al-Humaidi, *op. cit.,* p234.

[309] *Ibid.,* p237.

[310] Cf. as above on Banu Jadid.

[311] Cf. *Tarikh Khalifa bin Khayyat*, p205; and Al-Dhahabi, *Al-Ibar Fi Khabr Min Ghabr*, vol. 1 - a study critically edited by Salaheddin Al-Munjid, 2nd ed, Kuwait, 1984, p51; and Ibn Al-Emad, *Shathrat Al-Dhahab*, vol.1, Cairo 1250/1931-2, p53. See also Al-Humaidi, *Makran and Baluchistan*, p52.

[312] A district encompassing the mountainous regions west of Qasdar or Khazdar in present day Pakistan along with some of the western parts of the Kelat region in Pakistan. Its capital was Kaikanan or Kizkanan. See Al-Humaidi and see also the explanatory comments of Dr Nabi Bakhash Balouj on *Fet'h Namah-I-Sind* in English, pp42f, Al-Humaidi, pp218, 219.

[313] This is the well-known present day town in Pakistan of Gandava, capital of the Kachi region in Baluchistan.

[314] The exact present location of Benna or Betta is not known. Al-Bilathuri said it was between Kabul and Al-Miltan. Qadi Atthar says that Benna or Betta may have been the city of Nabkuhat in Pakistan though without giving any evidence of this. As to Lahore (Hore as noted by Khalifa bin Khayyat) or Al-Ahwaz as Al-Bilathuri described it, it is perhaps as Al-Qadi says, and we can agree with him if we accept the description of Al-Bilathuri, as being between Al-Miltan and Kabul - that is present day Lahore. See *Al-Aqd Al-Tathmin*, p89; Al-Bilathuri *Futuh*, p432; and the *Tarikh* of Khalifa bin Khayyat, p206; and Al-Humaidi, *op. cit.*, p250.

[315] Qadi Atthar, *Al-Aqd Al-Tathmin*, pp105-6.

[316] *Tarikh* of Khalifa bin Khayyat, p212. Compare with Al-Ya'qubi, *Tarikh*, vol. 2, p278; and Al-Bilathuri, *op.cit* , p22.

[317] *Fet'h Namah-I-Sind*, p59.

[318] *Ibid.*, p58 and see also, Al-Humaidi, *op.cit.*, p255; *Chachnama* - an English translation of *Fet'h Namah-I-Sind*, p64.

[319] Al-Bilathuri, *op.cit.*, p422; Al-Ya'qubi, *op.cit.*, vol.2, p278; and Al-Humaidi, *op.cit., loc. cit.*

[320] Ali bin Hamid Al-Kufi, *Fet'h Namah-I-Sind*, p59; and Al-Dhahabi, *Tarikh Al-Islam*, vol. 2, Cairo, 1368/1948, p372; and Ibn Khaldun, *Tarikh Ibn Khaldun*, vol. 3, 1391/1971, p94.

[321] Al-Bilathuri, *op.cit.,* p435.

[322] Qadi Atthar, *Al-Aqd Al-Tathmin*, pp121. Compare with Al-Bilathuri, *op.cit.*, p435; and *Tarikh* of Khalifa bin Khayyat, p277. See also Al-Humaidi, *op.cit.* , pp260-2.

[323] Al-Dhahabi, *Tarikh Al-Islam*, vol. 2, Cairo, 1368/1948, p372.

[324] Khalifa bin Khayyat, *Tarikh*, p278; Ali bin Hamid Al-Kufi, *Fet'h Namah-I-Sind*, p62; and *Chachnama*, p67; Al-Humaidi, *op.cit.*, pp262-2. See also S.B. Miles, *Countries and Tribes of the Persian Gulf*, 3rd ed. London, p54.

[325] Al-Humaidi, *op.cit.*, pp263-4.

[326] *Ibid.*, pp264-8.

[327] *Ibid..*, p436.

[328] Compare *Gag Namah*, also known as *Fet'h Namah-I-Sind*, p71.

[329] Al-Bilathuri, *op.cit.,* p41. Compare with Khalifa bin Khayyat, *Tarikh*, p318; and Al-Ya'qubi, *Tarikh*, vol. 2, p296. See Al-Qadi Atthar, *Al-Aqd Al-Tathmin*, pp176.

[330] Khalifa bin Khayyat, *op.cit.,* p322; Al-Bilathuri, *op.cit.*, p442; Ibn Hazm, *Jamharat Insab Al-Arab*, p246; and see Al-Humaidi, op.cit., p269.

[331] Al-Ya'qubi, *Tarikh*, vol2, p310-1; Al-Bilathuri, op.cit. p442; Al-Tabari, *Tarikh Al-Rusul Wa Al-Muluk*, vol. 6, pp600-3; and Al-Humaidi, *op.cit.*, p269.

[332] Al-Tabari, *op.cit. loc.cit.*; and Al-Qadi Atthar, *Al-Aqd Al-Tathmin*, pp181-3.

[333] Al-Tabari, *op.cit.,* p603; Al-Ya'qubi, *Tarikh*, vol. 2, p310-1; Al-Bilathuri, *op.cit.,* p442; and Al-Humaidi, *op.cit., loc.cit.*

[334] *Futuh Al-Buldan*, p442.

[335] *Tarikh Ibn Khaldun*, vol. 3, p79. Compare Al-Qadi Atthar, *Al-Aqd Al-Tathmin*, pp184

[336] Al-Tabari, *op.cit.,* vol. 6, p602. Compare Ibn Khaldun, *op.cit.,* vol. 3, p80.

[337] Al-Ya'qubi, *op.cit.*, vol. 2, p324; and Al-Qadi Atthar, *op.cit.,* p204. The sources relate that Abi

Uyayna bin Al-Mahlab and Othman bin Al-Mufadhal bin Al-Mahlab returned from the Turkish territories in the Caliphate of Hisham under an immunity granted to them by Assad bin Abdullah Al-Qasari the *Wali* of Khorasan (cf. Ibn Khaldun, *op.cit.*, vol.3, p80). What is certain is that the Al-Mahlabs enjoyed the good graces of the Abbassid Caliphs and among the family were princes, leaders and ministers in the course of a long association with the Abbassids.

[338] Al-Ya'qubi, *op.cit.*, vol. 2, p372; Al-Tabari, *op.cit.*, vol. 7, p512; Ibn Khaldun, *op.cit.*, vol.3, p187. See also Al-Qadi Atthar, *Al-Hind fi Ahd Al-Abbassiyeen*, Dar El Ansar, Cairo, 1399 AH, p15. Omar bin Hafas is traced here to Al-Mahlab bin Abi Safra.

[339] Ibn Al-Mo'tazz, *Tabaqat Al-Sha'raa*, p165, taken from Al-Qadi Atthar, *Al-Hind fi Ahd Al-Abbassiyeen*, p23. See also Fouad Sarakin, *Tarikh Al-Turath Al-Arabi*, vol. 2, part 4, translated from the German by Dr Arafa Mustafa, published by University of Imam Mohammed bin Saud, Riyadh, 1403 AH/1983 AD, p213.

[340] Khalifa bin Khayyat, *Tarikh*, p441; and Ibn Hazm, *Jamharat Ansab Al-Arab*, pp249-50.

[341] *Jamharat Ansab Al-Arab*, p350, Al-Qadi Atthar, *Al-Hind fi Ahd Al-Abbassiyeen*, p27.

[342] Al-Ya'qubi, *Tarikh*, vol. 2, p409; Al-Qalqashandi, *Ma'athar Al-Anafa*, vol. 1, critically edited by Dr Abdel Sitar Ahmed Farraj, 2nd ed., Kuwait, 1985, p200. See also Al-Humaidi, *op.cit.*, p274.

[343] Khalifa bin Khayyat, *Tarikh*, p463.

[344] Al-Bilathuri, *op.cit.*, p445. Compare Al-Ya'qubi, *op.cit.*, vol.2, p458; and Al-Qadi Atthar, *Al-Hind fi Ahd Al-Abbassiyeen*, p39.

[345] *Tarikh Al-Rusul Wa Al-Muluk*, vol.3, pp620-1; and Al-Ya'qubi, *op.cit., loc.cit.*

[346] Sayeda Ismail Al-Kashef, *Oman at the Dawn of Islam, p76.*

[347] Unknown author, *Kashef Al-Ghumah* manuscript no. 455.

[348] Salem bin Hamoud bin Shams Al-Siyabi, *Oman Across History*, vol.2, p230.

[349] Dr. Hussein Ali Al-Masri, *History of Political and Economic Relations between Iraq and the Arabian Gulf*, p124.

[350] Said Abdul Fattah Aashour *et al*, *Oman and Islamic Civilization*, p30.

[351] Shaker Mustafa, article in *Al-Dhikra Wa Al-Tarikh*, p245.

[352] Dr Farouq Omar, *The First Abbassids*, vol. 1, p252.

[353] Ibn Qutiba, *Al-Maarif*, p417.

[354] Al-Tamimi, *Manhaj Al-Ma'rij Li Akhbar Al-Khawarij*, manuscript no. 314.

[355] Unknown author, *Kashef Al-Ghumah Al-Jami' Li Akhbar Al-Umma*, manuscript no. 455.

[356] Ibn Al-Atheer, *Al-Kamel Fi Al-Tarikh*, vol. 4, p343.

[357] Unknown author, *Al-'Ayoun Wa Al-Hada'iq*, vol. 2, p63.

[358] Unknown author, *Kashef Al-Ghumah*, manuscript no. 456.

[359] Abi Mohammed Abdullah Al-Salimi, *Tohfat Al-'Ayian*, vol. 1, p65.

[360] *Ibid.*, pp73-4.

[361] Unknown author, *Qissas Wa Akhbar Jarrat Fi Oman*, p49.

[362] Wendell Phillips, *Oman: a history*, London 1967, translated into Arabic by Mohammed Amin Abdullah, p22.

[363] Sarhan bin Said Al-Azkawi, *Tarikh Oman*, p50.

[364] Abu Mohammed Abdullah Al-Salimi, *Tohfat Al-'Ayian*, vol.1, p84.

[365] *Oman Across History*, vol. 2, p39-40.

[366] Nur Al-Din Al-Salimi, *Tohfat Al-'Ayian*, Maktabat Al-Istiqama, Muscat, vol.1, p115.

[367] *Ibid.*, vol.1, pp138-40.

[368] To see the admonitions referred to cf. Nur Al-Din Al-Salimi, *Tohfat Al-'Ayian*, vol.1, pp140-9.

[369] *Oman Across History*, vol. 2, p84.

[370] *Al-Aqd Al-Tathmin*, p233.

[371] *Oman Across History*, vol. 2, pp105-8.

[372] Al-Salimi, *Tohfat Al-'Ayian*, vol. 1, p178.

[373] Al-Istakhri, *Al-Masalek Wa Al-Mamalek*, p27.

[374] Unknown author, *Kashef Al-Ghumah Al-Jami' Li Akhbar Al-Umma*, manuscript no. 463.

[375] Sarhan bin Said Al-Azkawi, *Tarikh Oman*, p61.

[376] Unknown author, *Kashef Al-Ghumah Al-Jami' Li Akhbar Al-Umma*, manuscript no. 465.

[377] Ya'qut Al-Hamawi, *Mu'jam Al-Odaba*, vol. 8, p86.

[378] Al-Azkawi, *Tarikh Oman*, p61.

[379] Al-Mas'udi, *Wa Murooj Al-Thahab*, vol. 1, p167.

[380] Ibn Al-Jawzi, *Al-Muntazzam*, vol. 6, p145.

[381] Dr Farouq Omar, *An Introduction to the Sources of Omani History*, p43.

[382] Ibn Ruzaiq, *Al-Fet'h Al-Mubeen* , p238.

[383] Unknown author, *Qissas Wa Akhbar Jarrat Fi Oman*, pp67-8.

[384] Unknown author, *Tarikh Ahl Oman*, manuscripts no. 296, 302.

[385] Dr Farouq Omar, *An Introduction to the Sources of Omani History*, p46.

[386] Unknown author, *Tarikh Ahl Oman*, manuscript, p69.

[387] Dr Farouq Omar, *An Introduction to the Sources of Omani History*, p46.
[388] *Ibid.,* p47.
[389] Dr Mohammed Rashid Al-Aqili, *The Arabian Gulf in the Islamic Ages*, p204.
[390] Ibn Khaldur., *Al-Ibar*, vol. 4, p198.
[391] Dr Ahmed Shalabi, *Encyclopaedia of Islamic History*, vol. 7, p310.
[392] Dr Mohammed Rashid Al-Aqili, *op.cit.,* p206.
[393] Ibn Khaldun, *Al-Ibar*, vol. 4, p199.
[394] Ibn Maskawiya, *Tajareb Al-Ummam*, vol. 1, p323.
[395] Al-Suli, *Akhbar Al-Radhi Billah Wa Al-Muttaqi Lillah*, p244.
[396] Ibn Al-Atheer, *Al-Kamel*, vol. 6, p292.
[397] Ibn Maskawiya, *Tajareb Al-Ummam*, vol. 2, p46.
[398] *Ibid.,* p144.
[399] Al-Qartabi, *Dhiyul Tarikh Al-Tabari*, p343.
[400] Ya'qut Al-Hamawi, *Mu'jam Al-Odaba*, vol. 9, pp124, 126.
[401] Al-Tanukhi, *Nishwar Al-Muhadhera*, vol. 1, pp347-8.
[402] *Ibid., loc.cit.*
[403] Ibn Al-Atheer, *Al-Kamel Fi Al-Tarikh*, vol. 2, p17.
[404] Ibn Maskawiya, *Tajareb Al-Ummam*, vol. 2, pp217, 232.
[405] Ibn Al-Atheer, *Al-Kamel Fi Al-Tarikh*, vol. 7, p57.
[406] *Ibid.,* p157.
[407] Abu Mohammed Al-Salimi, *Tohfat Al-'Ayian*, vol.1, p221.
[408] Al-Thaalabi, *Yatimat Al-Dahar Fi Mahasen Ahl Al-Asr*, vol. 2, p320.
[409] Abu Shaja'a Al-Rawaz Rawardi, *Dhail Tajareb Al-Ummam*, vol. 3, p100.
[410] Hilal Al-Sabi, *Tarikh Hilal Al-Sabi Al-Madhayel Ala Tajareb Al-Ummam*, vol. 4, pp414, 415.
[411] Ibn Al-Atheer, *Al-Kamel Fi Al-Tarikh*, vol. 7, p254.
[412] Ibn Al-Atheer, *Al-Kamel Fi Al-Tarikh*, vol. 8, pp19-20.
[413] Ibn Khaldun, *Tarikh Ibn Khaldun*, vol. 3, p146.
[414] Ibn Al-Atheer, *Al-Kamel Fi Al-Tarikh*, p20.
[415] *Ibid,*
[416] *Ibid.,* vol. 8, p55.
[417] Sarhan bin Said Al-Azkawi, *Tarikh Oman* taken from *Kashef Al-Ghumah Al-Jami' Li Akhbar Al-Umma*, p74; Abdullah bin Humaid Al-Salimi, *Tohfat Al-'Ayian Bi Sirat Ahl Oman*, vol.1, p303; Khalfan bin Jumai'yel Al-Siyabi, *Silk Al-Darrar Al-Hadi Gharrar Al-Athr*, vol. 2, p577, Salem bin Hamoud Al-Siyabi, *Oman Across History*, vol. 3, p93.
[418] This is Al-Mahlab bin Abi Safra, known as Abi Said. Al-Sayed Hamad bin Saif Al Busaidi says that the Al Busaid tribe from whom are descended the Said Family who constitute the present ruling family of Oman trace their ancestry to Al-Mahlab; thus it is evident that the Ateik tribe have ruled Oman from the sixth century of the Hegira up to today, as this reign was followed by the Nabhan, Ya'ruba and then the Said family. See Hamad bin Saif Al Busaidi, *Kitab Al-Mu'jaz Al-Mufid Nubtha Min Tarikh Al Busaidi* p7-10; and Salem bin Hamoud Al-Siyabi, *Oman across History*, vol. 3, p140.
[419] Abu Al-Abbas Mohammed bin Yazid Al-Mubarrad, *Nisb Adnan Wa Qahtan*, p33; Salma bin Muslim Al-Awatbi, *Al-Ansab*, vol. 2, pp117, 120. Abdullah bin Humaid Al-Salimi, *Tohfat Al-'Ayian Bi Sirat Ahl Oman*, vol.1, p303; Mohammed bin Abdullah Al-Salimi, *Oman's Renaissance*, p92. Salem bin Hamoud Al-Siyabi, *Asaaf Al-'Ayian Fi Ansab Ahl Oman*, pp116-8.
[420] Ahmed bin Said, *Diwan Al-Sitali*, pp443-4.
[421] *Diwan Al-Nabhani*, pp216, 232.
[422] Moussa bin Hussein bin Shawal, *Diwan Al-Kithawi*, p25.
[423] Abdullah bin Humaid Al-Salimi, *Tohfat Al-'Ayian Bi Sirat Ahl Oman*, vol. 1, p303;Salem bin Hamoud Al-Siyabi, *Oman Across History,* vol. 3, p 86. Mohammed Rasheed Al-Aqili, *The Ibadhis in Oman and their Relationship with the Abbassid State in the First Era*, p37; Dr Farouq Omar, *An Introduction to the Origins of Omani History*, p50-1; Abdullah Abu Azza, research study under the heading, *Oman's Relations with the Caliphate in the First Half of the Fourth Century AH*, pp162-3.
[424] See, *Diwan Al-Sitali*, p261, eulogizing Sultan Aba Mohammed Nabhan bin Oman bin Mohammed Ibn Omar bin Nabhan in the year 474 AH.
[425] *Ibid.,* p37. Aba Abdullah Mohammed bin Omar expresses his condolences on the death of his father in 501 AH.
[426] *Ibid.,* p273. He eulogizes Sultan Aba Al-Hassan Thahal bin Omar and greets him on his return from the *hajj* in 559 AH.
[427] It is unlikely that an ordinary human being would at this great age have the spontaneity and agility of mind required of the poet.
[428] *Tarikh Oman* taken from *Kashef Al-Ghumah,* p72.

[429] Sarhan bin Said Al-Azkawi, *Tarikh Oman* taken from *Kashef Al-Ghumah*, pp72, 74.

[430] Humaid bin Mohammed Ibn Ruzaiq, *Al-Fet'h Al-Mubeen Fi Sirat Al-Sadah Al-Busaidiyeen*, p250.

[431] Lorimer, *Gazetteer of the Gulf-* historical section, vol. 2, p629, (taken from Badger); *Ibid.*, geographical section, vol. 5, p1701. See also Zambawar, *Muj'am Al-Ansab Wa Al-Usar Al-Hakima Fi Al-Tarikh Al-Islami* (Encyclopaedia of Genealogy and Ruling Families in Islamic History), vol. 1, p194; Miles, *The Countries and Tribes of the Persian Gulf*, pp229-31; Ahmed Shalabi, *Islamic History and Islamic Civilization*, vol. 7, pp242-5; Published results of Seminar on Omani Studies, vol. 1, pp139-40.

[432] Al-Sitali, *Diwan Al-Sitali*, p211; Al-Nabhani, *Diwan Al-Nabhani*, pp36-7.

[433] *Diwan Al-Sitali*, p23; *Diwan Al-Nabhani*, pp22-3. See also, Ibn Battuta, *Rihlat Ibn Battuta*, pp181-2; Abdullah bin Humaid Al-Salimi, *Tohfat Al-'Ayian Bi Sirat Ahl Oman*, vol. 1, p303; Salem bin Hamoud Al-Siyabi, *Oman across History*, vol. 3, p97.

[434] Abu Bakr Ahmed bin Said Al-Kharousi Al-Sitali, *Diwan Al-Sitali*, pp46, 283-7.

[435] Mohammed bin Abdullah Ibn Battuta, *Rihlat Ibn Battuta*, pp181.

[436] Al-Nabhani, *Diwan Al-Nabhani*, p213.

[437] Suleiman bin Suleiman Al-Nabhani, *Diwan Al-Nabhani*, pp171-2, 187.

[438] The Al-Rayyes clan, An Omani tribal offshoot of the Tay'a whose tribal homeland is Fazah near the city of Luwa in the Batina district of Oman, where this large tribe has a long history. The Hodan are Omani Azd who take their name from Al-Hodan bin Shams and their tribal homeland is the Dhahira district in the west of Oman. See Al-Ya'qubi, *Al-Ansab*, vol. 2, p243; and Al-Sitali, *Isaaf Al-'Ayian Fi Ansab Ahl Oman*, p158; Al-Sitali, *Diwan Al-Sitali*, pp51.

[439] Ibn Ruzaiq, *Al-Sh'a'a Al-Shai'Billam'an Fi Dhikr A'imat Oman*, p73; Abdullah bin Humaid Al-Salimi, *Tohfat Al'Ayian*, vol. 1, p305; Salem bin Hamoud Al-Siyabi, *Oman Across History*, vol. 3, p102.

[440] Al-Azkawi, *Tarikh Oman* taken from *Kashef Al-Ghumah Al-Jami' Li Akhbar Al-Umma*, p74; Hamid bin Mohammed Ibn Ruzaiq, *Al-Sahifa Al-Qahtania*, vol. 2, p339 of photocopied manuscript; unknown author, *History of the Omani People* - an investigative study by A.D. Said Abdul Fattah Aashour, p97; Abdullah bin Humaid Al-Salimi, *Tohfat Al'Ayian bi Sirat Ahl Oman*, vol. 1, p304.

[441] Abu Suleiman, Mohammed bin Amer bin Rashed Al-Mawuli, *Qassas Wa Akhbar Jarrat Fi Oman*, photocopied ms. p31; Ibn Ruzaiq, *Al-Sh'a'a Al-Shai'a Ballim'an Fi Dhikr A'imat Oman*, p73.

[442] *Al-Shurat* plural of which the singular is *al-shari* (the purchaser and the person who sells himself (or bows allegiance) into the service of Allah and His gratification. See *Al-Mu'jam Al-Wasit*, p481, derived from the Quranic *Aya*, 'And there is the type of man who gives his life to earn the pleasure of God' (*Surat Al-Baqara, Aya 207*); and again, 'God hath purchased of the Believers their persons and their goods; for theirs (in return) is the Garden (of Paradise)' *Surat Al-Tawba, Aya 111* (English translation by A. Yusuf Ali).

[443] *Sirat Abdullah bin Mudad*, p38.

[444] Sarhan bin Said Al-Azkawi, *Tarikh Oman* taken from *Kashef Al-Ghumah*, p72.

[445] Miles, *The Countries and Tribes of the Persian Gulf*, p142; Arnold Wilson, *History of the Gulf*, p45.

[446] Abdullah bin Humaid Al-Salimi, *Tohfat Al-'Ayian*, vol. 1, p319.

[447] Salem bin Hamoud Al-Siyabi, *Oman Across History*, vol. 3, p104.

[448] Sarhan bin Said Al-Azkawi, *Tarikh Oman* taken from *Kashef Al-Ghumah* p74; Ibn Ruzaiq, *Al-Sh'a'a Al-Shai'aBilim'an Fi Dhikr A'imat Oman*, p71; *Al-Fet'h Al-Mubeen Fi Sirat Al-Sadah Al Busideen*, p247; unknown author, *Tarikh Ahl Oman* - an investigative study by Dr Said Abdel Fattah Aashour, p99.

[449] Ibn Ruzaiq mentions him in *Al-Sh'a'a Al-Shai' Billim'an Fi Dhikr A'imat Oman*, p74 under the name Abi Al-Hassan Rashed bin Khamis bin Amer Al-Azdi, but in his other book, *Al-Fet'h Al-Mubeen Fi Sirat Al-Sadah Al-Busaidiyeen*, he calls him Abi Al-Hassan Abdullah bin Khamis bin Amer Al-Azdi and this is the name which was taken from him by the Orientalists and those who in turn used them as a source.

[450] Zambaru, *Mu'jam Al-Ansab Wa Al-Usrat Al-Hukima Fi Al-Tarikh Al-Islami* (Encyclopaedia of Genealogy and Ruling Families in Islamic History), vol1, p194; Hussein Mu'nis, *Atlas of Islamic History*, p209; Donald Hawley, Oman and its Renaissance, p27.

[451] Abdullah bin Humaid Al-Salimi, *Tohfat Al-'Ayian*, vol. 1, p320.

[452] A descendant of Imam Al-Salt bin Malik Al-Kharousi Al-Yahmadi.

[453] Ibn Ruzaiq, *Al-Fet'h Al-Mubeen Fi Sirat Al-Sadah Al-Busaidiyeen*, p258; *Al-Sh'a'a Al-Shai'Billim'an Fi Dhikr A'imat Oman*, p79.

[454] Hamamet, a village in Wadi Bani Ruwaha known today as Mas Al-Jinaah.

[455] Salem bin Hamoud Al-Siyabi, *Oman Across History*, vol3, p107.

[456] Sarhan bin Said Al-Azkawi, *Tarikh Oman* taken from *Kashef Al-Ghumah* p74; Abdullah bin

Humaid Al-Salimi, *Tohfat Al'Ayian*, vol. 1, p321.

[457] *Al-Sh'a'a Al-Shai'aBilim'an Fi Dhikr A'imat Oman*, p79; *Al-Fet'h Al-Mubeen Fi Sirat Al-Sadah Al-Busaidiyeen*, p257.

[458] *Mu'jam Al-Ansab Wa Al-Usrat Al-Hukima Fi Al-Tarikh Al-Islami*, vol. 1, p194.

[459] *Al-Sh'a'a Al-Shai'Billim'an*, p77.

[460] Al-Azkawi, *Tarikh Oman* taken from *Kashef Al-Ghumah* p74; Ibn Ruzaiq, *Al-Sh'a'a Al-Shai'Billim'an Fi Dhikr A'imat Oman*, p79; Al-Salimi, *Tohfat Al-'Ayian*, vol. 1, pp225-6; Al-Siyabi, *op.cit.*, vol. 3, p116.

[461] Ahmed bin Majed, *Kitab Al-Fawa'id Fi Usul Al-Bahr Wa Al-Qawa'id* (published photocopy of ms.) p70-b.

[462] the word *from* in italics is added by the authors, i.e. this is not found in the source.

[463] Ibn Majed's style is weak because he wrote in the colloquial and not in classical Arabic.

[464] Al-Azkawi, *Tarikh Oman* taken from *Kashef Al-Ghumah* p75; Ibn Ruzaiq, *Al-Sh'a'a Al-Shai'Bilim'an Fi Dhikr A'imat Oman*, p79; Al-Salimi, *Tohfat Al-'Ayian*, vol. 1, pp326; Al-Siyabi, *Oman across History*, vol. 3, p116.

[465] Al-Azkawi, *Tarikh Oman* taken from *Kashef Al-Ghumah* pp75, 76; Ibn Ruzaiq, *Al-Sh'a'a Al-Shai'Bilim'an Fi Dhikr A'imat Oman*, p81-3; *Al-Fet'h Al-Mubeen Fi Sirat Al-Sadah Al-Busaidiyeen* pp258-9; Al-Salimi, *Tohfat Al-'Ayian*, vol. 1, pp327; Al-Siyabi, *Oman Across History*, vol. 3, pp116-9.

[466] *Diwan Al-Sitali*, pp214-5.
Allah granted the people of the faith all they desired if they would strive against injustice and the tyrant
The Persians came in a great horde assembled in strength with their troops
And sought to enslave and overwhelm the truth but the truth was triumphant
And they were thrown back and dissipated abroad one and all.

[467] The kingdom of Hormuz, founded by Mohammed Al-Daghastani on the coast of Karman it became a conquest of the rulers of Karman. Its king was the abovementioned Mahmoud who was the twenty second king in the dynastic succession. His rule commenced in 641 AH/1243 AD. Present day Hormuz is an island at the entrance to the Gulf close to the coast of Iran. The Europeans named the Strait after it, though it would have been more appropriate to name the strait the Strait of Musandam.

[468] Ibn Mudad, *Sirat Abdullah bin Mudad*, p66; Al-Azkawi, *Tarikh Oman* taken from *Kashef Al-Ghumah*, p73; Mohammed bin Amer Al-Mawuli, *Qissas Wa Akhbar Jarrat Fi Oman*, photocopied ms. p31; Ibn Raziq, *Al-Sahifa Al-Qahtania*, vol2, p338; Miles, *The Countries and Tribes of the Persian Gulf*, p140.

[469] Ibn Mudad, *Sirat Abdullah bin Mudad*, p66; Ibn Ruzaiq, *Al-Sh'a'a Al-Shai'Billim'an Fi Dhikr A'imat Oman*, p72.

[470] Al-Azkawi, *Tarikh Oman* taken from *Kashef Al-Ghumah*, p73; Mohammed bin Amer Al-Mawuli, *Qissas Wa Akhbar Jarrat Fi Oman*, photocopied ms. p31

[471] *Mann*, a unit of weight measuring 4 kgs. See Al-Ghassani, Results of Seminar on Omani Studies, vol1, p260.

[472] Ibn Ruzaiq, *Al-Sirah Al-Qahtania*, vol. 2, p338.

[473] Said Awadh Ba Wazir, *Features of the History of the Arabian Peninsula*, p168.

[474] Qalhat, Ibn Al-Atheer mentions that Qalhat was under the control of the Kingdom of Hormuz from the seventh century of Hegira (thirteenth century AD) See, *Al-Kamel Fi Al-Tarikh*, vol. 12, pp303-4.

[475] Ibn Ruzaiq, *op.cit.*, vol. 2, p339, photocopied ms., *Al-Sh'a'a Al-Shai'Bi llim'an Fi Dhikr A'imat Oman*, p72-3; *Al-Fet'h Al-Mubeen Fi Sirat Al-Sadah AlBusaidiyeen*, p248.

[476] The city of Bahla, Oman's best-fortified city, surrounded by high walls on every side which enclose its streets and cultivations. It contains the renowned fort which has been listed in recent times in the Unesco World Heritage Series.

[477] Ibn Mudad, *Sahifa Abdullah bin Mudad*, p67; Al-Azkawi, *Tarikh Oman* taken from *Kashef Al-Ghumah* p72-3; Mohammed bin Amer Al-Mawuli, *Qissas Wa Akhbar Jarrat Fi Oman*, photocopied ms. p31; Ibn Ruzaiq, *Al-Sahifa Al-Qahtania*, vol. 2, p338. Al-Salimi, *Tohfat Al-'Ayian*, vol. 1, pp304-5; Miles, *The Countries and Tribes of the Persian Gulf*, p141.

[478] *Al-Sh'a'a Al-Shai'Billim'an Fi Dhikr A'imat Oman*, p71; and *Al-Fet'h Al-Mubeen Fi Sirat Al-Sadah Al-Busaidiyeen*, p247.

[479] Ibn Mudad, *Sirat Abdullah bin Mudad*, p68; Mohammed bin Amer Al-Mawuli, *Qissas Wa Akhbar Jarrat Fi Oman*, photocopied ms. p32.

[480] Ibn Mudad, *Sirat Abdullah bin Mudad*, p68; Mohammed bin Amer Al-Mawuli, *Qissas Wa Akhbar Jarrat Fi Oman*, photocopied ms. p32-3.

[481] Abu Bakr Ahmed bin Said Al-Sitali, *Diwan Al-Sitali*, 173-7.

[482] *Ibid.*, pp341-4.

[483] *Ibid.*, pp344-7.

[484] Al-Azkawi, *Tarikh Oman* taken from *Kashef Al-Ghumah* p72.

[485] Proceedings of the Seminar on Omani Studies (The Role of Oman in Building the Civilization of East Africa), *op.cit.*, vol. 5, pp282-305. A research study presented by J. Kirkman entitled *The Early Islamic History of Oman in East Africa.*

[486] Al-Azkawi, *Tarikh Oman* taken from *Kashef Al-Ghumah* p72; Ibn Ruzaiq, *Al-Fet'h Al-Mubeen Wa Sirat Al-Sadah Al-Busaidiyeen,* p260.

[487] Al-Azkawi, *op.cit.,* pp83-9; Abdullah bin Humaid Al-Salimi, *Tohfat Al'Ayian Bi Sirat Ahl Oman,* vol. 1, pp337-43; Salem bin Hamoud Al-Siyabi, *Oman Across History,* vol. 3, pp147-56.

[488] Al-Azkawi, *Tarikh Oman* taken from *Kashef Al-Ghumah,* p93; Al-Salimi, *Tohfat Al'Ayian,* vol. 1 pp347-8; Al-Siyabi, *Oman Across History,* vol. 3, pp166-7.

[489] *Sahih Al-Bukhari,* vol. 2, pp143-4; Rabi'a bin Habib, *Al-Jami' Al-Sahih,* vol. 1, p85; and Muslim, *Al-Jami' Al-Sahih,* vol. 3, p66.

[490] J. Kirkman, 'The Early Islamic History of Oman in East Africa', *Report of Proceedings of Seminar on Omani Studies,* Sultanate of Oman, 1980, pp47-4.

[491] Ignatius Kratschkovski, *History of Arab Geographical Literature,* Arabic translation by Salaheddin Othman, Cairo, 1965, vol.1, pp183-5.

[492] Basil Davidson, *Africa in a New Light,* Arabic translation by Jamal Ahmed, Dar Al-Thaqafa Printing, Publishing & Distribution House, p215.,

[493] See, Abu Abeed bin Abdul Aziz Al-Bakri, *Al-Masalek Wa Al-Mamalek,* photocopied ms., Library of Higher Studies, Faculty of Arts, Baghdad University, no. 1260; Abu Abdullah Mohammed bin Mohammed Al-Sherif Al-Idrisi, *Nozhat Al-Mishtaq Fi Ihtiqaq Al-Afaq,* photocopied from copy , Oxford; ms. no. 15 - Geography in Library of the Iraqi Science Collection; Abu Al-Hassan Ali bin Moussa bin Said Al-Maghrabi, *Kitab Al-Jughrafia* - an investigative study by Ismail Al-Arabi, Beirut, 1970.

[494] Abu Al-Hassan Ali bin Al-Hassan bin Ali Al-Mas'udi, *Murooj Al-Thahab Wa Maadan Al-Jawhara* - an investigative study by Mohammed Mohieddin Abdul Hamid, Cairo, 1964, vol.1, pp107-8.

[495] Abu Abdullah Mohammed bin Ahmed Al-Maqdisi, *Ahsan Al-Taqasim Fi Maarafat Al-Aqalim,* Leiden, 1906, p35.

[496] Abu Al-Qassem Mohammed bin Ali Ibn Hawqal, *Surat Al-Ardh,* Beirut, p44.

[497] Emadeddin Ismail bin Mohammed bin Omar, known as Abu Al-Feda, *Taqwim Al-Buldan* - an investigative study, Mak Kokin Dislane, Paris, 1840, p99.

[498] The Sultanate of Oman, Ministry of National Heritage and Culture, *Oman and its Maritime History,* 1979, p92.

[499] Dr Jamal Zakariya Qasim, *Oman in East Africa,* Report of Proceedings of Seminar on Omani Studies, 1986, p81.

[500] For further details on the Julanda clan see, J.C. Wilkinson, *The Banu Julanda in Oman,* Sultanate of Oman, Ministry of National Heritage and Culture, 1982.

[501] *Ibid.,* p17.

[502] Al-Azkawi, *Tarikh Oman* from *Kashef Al-Ghumah Al-Jami' Li Akhbar Al-Umma* - An Investigative Study, by Abdul Majid Hassib Al-Qeissi, Oman, 1979, p43.

[503] *Ibid.,* vol. 5, p276.

[504] Abdul Rahman Zaki, *Islam and the Muslims in East Africa,* Cairo, 1965, vol. 1, pp71-7.

[505] Shashou Farah bin Humaid, Al-Baqeri Al-Lamawi, p9, translated from Swahili into English and published by William Hichens, Bantu. See also, Studies, Khawla Shaker Al-Dijili, *Arab-Islamic Relations with the Coast of East Africa,* unpublished PhD thesis, Faculty of Arts, Baghdad University, 1980, p77.

[506] This ruler is sometimes referred to as Ishaq Al-Sawahili. See Kirkman, *op.cit.,* p283.

[507] See A. Werner, 'The History of Patta', *Journal of African Society,* vol, London, 1914-5, p153; N, Chittick, 'A New Look on the History of Patta', *Journal of African History,* vol. X, no. 3, 1969, p376; cf. also Al-Dijili, *op.cit.,* p85.

[508] Qassem, *op.cit.,* p85.

[509] Kirkman, *op.cit.,* pp283-4.

[510] Dr Raft Ghanimi, *Oman's Role in Building the Civilization of East Africa,* Report of Proceedings of the Symposium on Omani Studies, 1986, vol. 3, p151.

[511] Qassem, *op.cit.,* pp82, 85.

[512] Abu Ali Ahmed bin Omar bin Rusta, *Kitab Al-Aa'ilaq Al-Nafisah* Leiden, 1891, p86; Abu Bakr Ahmed bin Mohammed Al-Hamdani, known as Abu Al-Fiqih, *Mukhtassar* (Abridgement of) *Kitab Al-Buldan,* Leiden, p11.

[513] Cf. Al-Mas'udi, *op.cit.,* vol.1, p318; Suleiman Al-Tajer, *Akhbar Al-Sin Wa Al-Hind* from *Min Rihlat Al-Arab,* Beirut, 1974, p22; George Fadlo Hourani, *Arab Seafaring in the Indian Ocean in Ancient and Early Medieval Times,* translated by Al-Sayed Ya'qub Bakr, Cairo, 1958, pp229-30, Princeton 1981.

218

[514] Cf. Al-Mas'udi, *op.cit.,* vol. 2, p6.

[515] Ahmed bin Majed, *Thalathat Azhar Fi Maarafat Al-Bihar* - an investigative study by Theodor Shoumoufki, translated by Mohammed Mounir Mursi, Cairo, 1969, p44.

[516] Cf. Al-Mas'udi, *op.cit.,* vol. 1, p11; Al-Bakri, *op.cit.,* vol. 1, ms. 67-a.

[517] The Berbery district consists of the northern and eastern coasts of Somalia and is known as the Benader Coast (*benader* being a plural of *bander*, a seaport or commercial district).

[518] *Murooj Al-Thahab*, vol. 1, p107.

[519] Cf. Al-Mas'udi, *op.cit.,* vol. 1, p107-8; Ibn Said, *op.cit.,* p81; Ahmed bin Majed, *Kitab Al-Fawa'id Fi Usul Al-Bahr Wa Al-Qawa'id* - an investigative study by Ibrahim Khouri and Azza Hassan, Damascus, 1971, p272.

[520] Cf. Al-Mas'udi, *op.cit.,* vol. 2, p6; Shehab Al-Din Abi Abdullah Ya'qut Al-Hamawi, *Mu'jam Al-Buldan,* (Dar Al-Sader, Dar Beirut, 1955-59), vol. 3, p442; Zakaria bin Mohammed bin Mohammed Al-Qazzouini, *Athar Al-Bilad Wa Akhbar Al-Ibad,* Dar Sader, Dar Beirut, 1960, p62.

[521] *Murooj Al-Thahab*, vol. 2, p6.

[522] *Al-Jughrafia*, p82.

[523] Ibn Said, *op.cit.,* p84.

[524] Ibn Battuta, *Tohfat Al-Nadhar Fi Ghara'ib Al-Amsar Wa Aja'ib Al-Asfar-* an investigative study by Ali Muntassar Al-Kitabi, Beirut, 1979, vol. 1, p279-80. See also Mohammed bin Abi Taleb Al-Ansari Al-Dimeshqi, known as Sheikh Al-Rabwa, *Nakhbat Al-Dahr Fi Aja'ib Al-Birr Wa Al Bahr,* Leipzig, 1923, p269.

[525] Ibn Majed, *Thalathat Azhar*, p27.

[526] *Ibid.,* p29.

[527] Al-Idrisi, *Nozhat Al-Mushtaq*, ms. 52; Ibn Battuta, *op.cit.,* vol. 1, p283; Ibn Majed, *Thalathat Azhar Fi Maarafat Al-Bihar*, p30, where he describes the anchorage of Mombasa as large and deep enough to receive ships into port.

[528] Ibn Majed, *Thalathat Azhar Fi Maarafat Al-Bahar*, p31.

[529] Ibn Majed, *Al-Fawa'id*, p229.

[530] *Murooj Al-Thahab*, vol. 1, p107-8.

[531] Al-Mas'udi, *op.cit.,* vol. 2, p98.

[532] Dr Sabah Ibrahim Al-Sheikhli, 'Trade Relations between the Arabian Gulf and East Africa', *Al-Wathiqa* magazine, no.7/13, July 1988, p177.

[533] S. Trimingham, 'The Arab Geographer and the East African Coast' in, *East Africa and the Orient,* ed. by Chittick and Rotary, New York, 1975, pp129-30.

[534] See Ibn Majed, *Al-Fawa'id*, p229.

[535] See Jamal Zakariya Qasim, *The Arab Colonization of East Africa,* Faculty of Arts Yearbook, Ain Shams University, vol. 5, 1967, pp292f.

[536] Al-Mas'udi, *op.cit.,* vol. 1, p108.

[537] *Ibid.,* vol. 2, p6.

[538] Al-Idrisi, *op.cit.,* ms.7.

[539] *Nozhat Al-Mushtaq*, ms.60.

[540] *Al-Jughrafia*, p85.

[541] *Nozhat Al-Mishtaq*, ms.7.

[542] Kawthar Abdul Rasoul, 'Studies in the Recent Migrations to Africa', *Faculty of Arts Yearbook,* Ain Shams University, vol. 13, 1973, p260.

[543] Al-Mas'udi, *op.cit.,* vol. 2, p6.

[544] *Nozhat Al-Mushtaq*, ms.70.

[545] Ibn Battuta, *op.cit.,* vol. 1, p283.

[546] Trimingham, *op.cit.,* p20.

[547] Al-Mas'udi, *op.cit.,* vol. 2, p6; Al-Idrisi, *op.cit.,* ms.70; Ibn Majed, *Thalathat Azhar*, pp44-5.

[548] Ibn Majed, *op.cit.,* pp38, 42-5.

[549] *Ibid.,* p42.

[550] *Murooj Al-Thahab*, vol. 2, p6.

[551] *Ibid.,* vol. 1, p150.

[552] Ya'qut, *Mu'jam,* vol. 5, p173.

[553] *Nozhat Al-Mushtaq*, ms.34, p52.

[554] Al-Mas'udi, op.cit., vol. 1, p163.

[555] Al-Missiu Jiyan, *Historical, Geographical and Trade Documents on East Africa,* abridged into Arabic by Youssef Kamal, Cairo, 1927, p107.

[556] *Murooj Al-Thahab*, vol. 1, pp107-8, vol. 2, p98.

[557] *Ibid.,* vol. 1, p163.

[558] Ya'qut, *Mu'jam,* vol. 5, p173. Sheikh Al-Rabwa, *op.cit.,* p162.

[559] *The Role of Oman in International Trade in the First Islamic Era,* Seminar on Omani Studies, 1986, vol. 3, pp64-5.

[560] Kirkman, *op.cit.*, p286; Davidson, *op.cit.*, p11.

[561] *Murooj Al-Thahab*, vol. 1, p112.

[562] Dr Jamal Zakariya Qasim, *The Historical Origins of Arab-African Trade Relations*, Alecso Publications, Institute for Research and Studies, Cairo, 1975, p49.

[563] *Oman A Seafaring Nation*, p94.

[564] See Ibn Majed, *Thalathat Azhar*, pp40, 50-1.

[565] See Ibn Majed, *Al-Fawa'id*, p328.

[566] Al-Mas'udi, *Murooj Al-Thahab*, vol. 1, p107.

[567] Birzek bin Shahrayar, *op.cit.*, p116.

[568] *Murooj Al-Thahab*, vol. 1, p107.

[569] *Nozhat Al-Mushtaq*, ms.53.

[570] Sarajeddin ibn Al-Wardi, *Kharidat Al-Aja'ib Wa Faridat Al-Ghara'ib*, Cairo, 1334, pp49-50.

[571] Dr Abdul Rahman Abdul Kerim Al-Aani, *The Role of the Omanis in Islamic Navigation and Trade*, Sultanate of Oman, Ministry of National Heritage and Culture, 1981, p15.

[572] Birzek, *op.cit.*, p150.

[573] *Ibid.*, pp173-4.

[574] *Ibid.*, pp172-3, 128-30.

[575] R. Coupland, *East Africa and its Invaders*, Oxford, 1938, p21.

[576] Ibn Battuta, *op.cit.*, vol. 2, p99.

[577] *Murooj Al-Thahab*, vol. 1, p163.

[578] Ibn Majed, *Thalathat Azhar*, pp101-2.

[579] Al-Mas'udi, *op.cit.*, vol 1, p107-8.

[580] Birzek, *op.cit.*, p161.

[581] Ya'qut, *Mu'jam*, vol 3, p224.

[582] Ibn Battuta, *op.cit.*, vol. 1, p279-80.

PART IV

The Unique Character of Oman

Studies Presented and Summarized in this Part

The Modern History Madrassah *(School of Thought) in Oman: its methods and approach,* by Prof. Tariq Nafi Al-Hamadani, Baghdad University.

The Omani Library, by Sheikh Muhanna bin Khalfan Al-Kharousi, Sultanate of Oman.

The Omani Fortifications, by Engineer Said M. Saqlawi, Sultanate of Oman.

Oman at the Outset of Islam, by Prof. Sayeda Ismail Kashif, Ayn Shams University, Cairo.

The Omani Library, by Prof. Abdul Mon'im Mohammed Hussain, Ayn Shams University, Cairo.

Omani Architecture in Islamic Ages, by Prof. Ghazi Rajab Mohammed, Baghdad.

Maritime Oman, by Prof. Youssef Nu'aisa, Cairo University.

The Omani Navigators Masters of the South Seas in the Islamic Period by Prof. El-Sayed Abdul Aziz Salem, Alexandria University.

Oman and its Trade with the Far East and East Africa in Islamic Periods, by Prof. Sahar El-Sayed Abdul Aziz Salem, Alexandria University.

The Political Capital Cities of Oman, by Prof. Ahmed Shalabi, Cairo University.

Ibadhism

Ibadhism in Basra

Ibadhi thought reverts in the first instance to the religious and political factors embodied in the induction of Abdullah bin Wahb Al-Rasebi by some of the Companions and followers who contested the rule of Ali bin Abi Taleb in Shawwal 37AH/657 AD[1]. The actual founding of Ibadhism can be traced to the first century of the Hegira in Basra, making it the oldest of the Islamic orthodox rites. Abdullah bin Ibadh Al-Tamimi, who is counted its originator, was a contemporary of Mu'awiya who died at the end of the Caliphate of Abdul Malik bin Marwan.

Abdullah bin Ibadh concerned himself with political, ideological and military matters as well as organization and strategy, with a view to founding an Islamic state which would be reliant on the precepts of the Holy Book, the *Sunnah* and the *Sirahs* of the Orthodox Caliphs. In his home were to be found students who included the students of Jaber bin Zaid and their helpers[2].

The Tamim tribe, from whom Abdullah bin Ibadh came, was one of the most powerful and numerous tribes in Basra at the onset of Islam. Abdullah participated with Ibn Zubair in the defence of the Ka'ba against the army of Yazid bin Mu'awiya. On his return to Basra, he became embroiled in a disagreement with Nafi' bin Al-Azraq Al-Khariji on account of the latter's extreme views[3]. This we can infer from the letter Abdullah bin Ibadh sent to Abdul Mulik bin Marwan in which he clearly washes his hands of Naf'a (founder of the Azariqites), saying: 'As to the leader of the *Khawarij* (Kharijites), Ibn Al-Azraq, we are through with him and his excesses and his zealotry and his exaggerated strictures; he treats innocent Muslims as infidels. These ideas of Naf'a's are inconsistent with the first principles of Islam for they judge innocent Muslims to be idolators'[4].

Abdullah bin Ibadh was not an advocate of force and discouraged the use of weapons against the authorities of the time, being content to pursue the instruction of his followers and to communicate with them clandestinely. Several of the sources credit Abdullah bin Ibadh with being the founding thinker and organizing force behind Ibadhism[5]. There are those however who attribute the sect's origins to Jaber bin Zaid Al-Omani.

Jaber was born in the village of Farq near Nizwa in Oman between 18 and 22 AH/639-642 AD and migrated to Basra as a young man to broaden his studies. He was to become one of the leading lights of Islam in the first century AH. He studied under Abdullah bin Abbas, Aisha and Ibn Omar[6] and gained a consummate knowledge of the Qur'an, Hadith and Islamic Law. Most of his adult life was spent at Basra and in the latter half of the first century he produced his splendid encyclopaedia, *Diwan Jaber*. His activities were not confined to jurisprudence and the pursuit of knowledge, nor indeed to teaching and writing. He devoted his considerable energy towards restoring the Islamic State to the orthodoxy of Abu Bakr, Omar and Othman, in the splendour of his early Caliphate, and Ali bin Abi Taleb before the arbitration. He spurred his students to work for the establishment of a Just Imamate founded on the true principles of Islam. When Jaber died his student Abu Ubaidah Muslim bin Abi Karima Al-Tamimi Al-Basri carried forward his message of faith and policy and set about organizing the Ibadhi Movement which had prevailed in Oman, the homeland of Jaber bin Zaid. In this way the Imamate became established there[7].

Whether the founder of Ibadhism was Jaber bin Zaid or Abdullah bin Ibadh, and irrespective of whether the one was the founder and the other the follower, Ibn Ibadh died during the Caliphate of Abdul Mulik bin Marwan and it looks as though after his death the Ibadhi movement abandoned its dialogue and theological discussion with the State and went underground, resorting to the tactics of *Kitman*, or clandestine pursuit of its goals. Jaber bin Zaid himself played a significant part in organizing his following along these lines. Despite the secrecy of Jaber's activities, however, Al-Hajjaj bin Youssef sensed the threat of Ibadhism to the security of Ummayyad rule in Basra, for he viewed Jaber as capable of turning the Basran masses - over whom he commanded great influence - against the State; and he sought a means to avert the danger posed by Jaber. He banished him to Oman - and in doing so inadvertently cemented the bonds between Jaber and his own people, amongst whom he propagated his ideas and principles. Contact between Oman and Basra was strong and uninterrupted; and so the seed planted by Jaber was nurtured and developed until it would culminate in the establishment of the Ibadhi Imamate, at first in Yemen and the Hadramaut and subsequently in Oman itself[8].

Here we should point out, before we speak of the appearance of *Ibadhism* in these countries, that it was not then known as Ibadhism (a description which did not become attached to the rite until the third century AH). The adherents were variously referred to as the *'Muslim Group'*, or the *'Muslims'* or the *'People of the Call'*. They themselves approved of the appellation *Al-Muhakkimah*, for they scorned the arbitration of men in (matters of) faith, saying: 'God alone is judge'. They were also known as the *'Righteous Ones'* or the *'Wahbia'* after Abdullah bin Wahb Al-Rasebi.

The Ibadhis were also known as *Al-Shurat* (the Purchasers) from their saying: 'We have purchased ourselves for the religion of Allah, and so we are Al-Shiraa'; or in line with the Qur'anic *Ayya*:

God hath purchased of the Believers
Their persons and their goods
For theirs (in return)
Is the Garden (of Paradise):
They fight in His Cause,
And slay and are slain:
A promise binding on Him

In Truth, through the Law,
The Gospel, and the Qur'an
And who is more faithful
To His Covenant than God?
Then rejoice in the bargain
Which ye have concluded:
That is the achievement supreme[9].

Ibadhism in Yemem, Hadramaut and Oman

Yemen and Oman entered the sphere of influence of Islam and the emerging Islamic State in Medina during the lifetime of the Prophet. The Yemenis and Omanis participated in the Islamic conquests which stretched the boundaries of the Arab-Islamic State to China in the East and France in the West.

Here an important question presents itself: Why did Yemen and Oman subscribe to Ibadhism? And when did this occur? The manifestation of *Al-Shurat* arose out of inconsistencies of an economic and social nature in the formative days of Islam; and it was in the nature of a rebellion against the Qureishi aristocracy assuming political and economic authority over Arab society. They (the dissenters) gave expression to certain ideas which in time grew to become Ibadhism. It first manifested itself in Basra, whence it spread to the Arabian peninsula, including Yemen and Oman.

It is likely that Jaber bin Zaid Al-Azdi, the Ibadhi scholar, was the founder of this rite and that it was he who enabled his successor Abu Ubaidah to expand it[10]. Al-Awatbi mentions two names amongst the propagators of Ibadhism: Munir bin Al-Nir Al-Riyami, one of the four *ulemas* who brought the message from Basra to Oman[11]; and another of the four *ulemas*, 'Mohammed bin Al-Mu'alla Al-Fajhi from Oman, this latter being one of the Bani Al-Sokoun bin Ashras bin Kindah, it was said, and the first to establish an Ibadhi government in Oman'[12].

The first open Imamate in Yemen was declared by *Taleb Al-Haq* (Seeker of the Truth) Abdullah bin Yahya Al-Kindi in 129 AH/746 AD. It was not altogether successful in meeting its objectives, but served as a necessary exercise for what would transpire in Oman. It is enough here to note the participation of Julanda bin Mas'ud and Hilal bin 'Attia in this experiment and Julanda was soon to declare the second openly manifested Imamate in the Arabian peninsula, specifically in Oman[13].

The truth is a number of crucial factors acted to place Yemen and Oman in the front line of the endeavour to reverse prevailing corruption and oppression, and they became the centre of the Ibadhi sphere of influence, assisted by their distance from Damascus, capital of the Ummayyad State.

Modern historical research methods would not entertain the notion of a school of thought or politics emerging without looking for the grounds in which it was nourished. So what was it that gave rise to the emergence of Ibadhism in Yemen and Oman and led to thousands of casualties in defence of the demand for truth and justice and equity? The answer to this question lies in the fact that Yemen and Oman were not insulated from the events that wracked the

Ummayyad Caliphate. We have two important documents which give us an idea of the nature of circumstances in Yemen and Oman under the Ummayyads (40-132 AH/660-749 AD).

The first document is embodied in the content of a letter from the Caliph Omar bin Abdul Aziz (99-101 AH/717-719 AD) to his *Wali* (provincial governor) in Yemen in which he says:'You have written to me to say that you have arrived in Yemen and that you have found its populace oppressed by *kharaj* (land tax) with which they are burdened irrespective of harvest or blight, or of whether they live or die. Praise the Lord... Praise the Lord... Praise the Lord Almighty'[14].

The second document is represented in the writings of Al-Bilathuri taken from Omar bin Abdul Aziz also. Al-Bilathuri says: 'Abu Al-Hassan Al-Mada'ini told me citing Mubarak Ibn Fadhala, saying that Omar bin Abdul Aziz wrote to Addi bin Artaa Al-Fazari, his agent in Basra. So - to our topic: I wrote to Amr bin Abdullah (telling him) to distribute what he found in Oman by way of date and grain tithes amongst its poor. He replied that he had asked your agent before him about this food and dates, and he said that he had sold it and given you the proceeds. So return to Amr what your agent in Oman has given you as the value of the dates and grain so that it may be disposed of in the manner as you have directed, *Inshallah*[15]'.

These two documents portray the populations of Yemen and Oman in a wretched state at the time of the Ummayyads, aware of the widening social gap between the rich and poor. It was not long before Oman and Yemen became stages for rebellion and demands for social reform, an end to oppression and the removal of the abnormal situation as portrayed by the Ibadhi Imam Abdullah bin Yahya Al-Kindi in a diatribe against the Ummayyad Caliphate in 129 AH when he gave vent to his anger: 'I have seen in Yemen outrage, despotism and vile deeds perpetrated against the people'. He incited his followers, declaring that they could no longer watch what was going on nor expect patience to yield results[16], and gave directives to declare openly the *Dhuhour* Imamate in Yemen.

Declaration of the First *Dhuhour* (Open) Imamate in the Arabian Peninsula 129 AH/746 AD

Shibam in 129 AH/746 AD became the home of the Ibadhi leadership and in a violent revolt against the Ummayyad Caliphate the Imam Abdullah bin Yahya seized control of the Hadramaut and cast out the Ummayyad prefect. He consolidated his position there and established security and stability, showing special care for the poorer classes. He won the backing of the cities of Abin, Lahej and Sana'a. When he moved on the Yemeni capital, Sana'a, a bloody battle was engaged with the Ummayyad *Wali* in which the latter was defeated and Sana'a opened its arms to the Ibadhi Imam and became his capital and centre of operation[17].

The historian Ibn Qassem (Yahya bin al-Hussein who died in 1100 AH/1688 AD) tells us that the term of the Imam, which lasted 16 months, was distinguished by its many merits, while Abdullah bin Yahya was an exemplary and just ruler[18]. He was also a gentle and compliant leader and in this won the hearts of the Yemeni masses and proved that there was no fundamental discrepancy between the *Shurat* Ibadhi rite and that of the Sunni community[19].

Oman was not isolated from this first wave of Ibadhism in the south of the Arabian peninsula. Al-Awatbi alludes to the strength of the Yemeni-Omani relationship which enabled Ibadhism to become established in the two countries: '... Abdullah bin Yahya Al-Shari who was known as *Taleb Al-Haq* - he it was who turned to Abi Hamza Al-Mokhtar bin Auf Al-Azdi; and Abu Hamza marched to him from Oman and then Abu Hamza set out from there with a troop to the Hijaz. He conquered Mecca and Medina, where he made his celebrated sermon from the Prophet's pulpit. And Abdullah bin Yahya ruled over all of Yemen and banished all vestiges of Ummayyad rule from there'[20].

Abu Hamza describes the cohesiveness of Ibadhism under the leadership of Abdullah bin Yahya thus: 'We heard a call to the truth and to the path of right-eousness and from scattered tribes we accepted the call, each one of us on a single camel, with our goods and ourselves, sharing by turns a single cover, a small and feeble band (of followers)'[21].

From the eloquent sermons of Abdullah bin Yahya Al-Kindi and his military commander Abu Hamza Al-Mokhtar Al-Azdi who had seized Mecca and Medina[22] can be seen the urgent need for the huge responsibility assumed by them. Abdullah says: 'It is the mercy of God that in every period He has spared for us a residue of learned men who will guide those who have strayed from the path of righteousness, who can face threat and bear pain with fortitude, who will die martyrs for the truth as they have done from time immemorial'[23].

Abu Hamza illustrates the politics of the Ummayyads 'who enslaved to themselves the servants of God and appropriated His possessions. They are misguided men who oppress with a heavy hand; distrustful, they bend the law according to their whim and kill to satisfy their anger. Misguided in their oblig-ations, they are again misguided in their impositions'[24]. Under their rule 'the rich grew richer and the poor poorer'[25]. Of their revolutionary goals he says: 'We did not leave our homes and possessions out of discontent or for useless diversion, nor in search of power. Rather we saw that the light of truth had been extinguished and the righteous were tortured or slain and life in this land, for all that it offered, had become intolerable to us'[26].

He adds that their revolution bore the political mark of the stand against the tyranny and oppression of the imams and kings. In a sermon to the citizens of Medina he says: 'O people of Medina the people are of us and we are of them, excepting the idolators and the polytheists, the unbelieving Christians and Jews and despotic Imams'[27]. Explaining their programme he declared: 'Since we have triumphed we will accord everyone his rights'[28].

Notwithstanding the high ideals and just demands of the revolutionaries their revolt failed in face of the grim brutality of the Ummayyads and Yemen was subjected to a military onslaught the like of which was not matched in brutality throughout the time of the Ummayyad oppression.

So the youthful aspirations of the Ibadhis were thwarted in Wadi Al-Qara and the remnants of the movement took refuge in Medina from whence they subsequently went on to Mecca. When Abdullah bin Yahya's forces set out from Sana'a to augment the defenders of Mecca, the Ibadhis were defeated and their honourable commander slain[29]. Abdullah bin Yahya encamped with his troops at a spot midway between Tabala, Bisha and Jerash, where a pitched battle was fought with the Ummayyad army; whence Abdullah withdrew to

Jerash and there fought courageously to the end. He fell in action in the attempt to halt the southwards advance of the Ummayyad commander Ibn Atiah Al-Sa'di[30].

The Ummayyad army was resisted in Sana'a, Al-Jand, Al-Ma'afar, Lahej and Abin. And though the army succeeded in reaching the Hadramaut, the determined resistance of the Shibamis severely hampered the progress of the Ummayyad army, forcing the Ummayyad commander to sue for a truce with the new Ibadhi Imam Abdullah bin Said who succeeded Abdullah bin Yahya on the latter's martyrdom in 130 AH/747 AD[31].

In all likelihood Abdullah bin Yahya's tactical errors had much to do with easing the path of the Ummayyads to victory in their various campaigns. It would have been more astute for Abdullah to withdraw his troops from Wadi Al-Qara, Medina and Mecca to a location to which he could retire in his hour of need. For example, if he had withdrawn his forces under their commander Al-Mokhtar from Mecca - after the defeat at Wadi Al-Qara - to Bisha or Jerash he could have united the resistance front against the Ummayyads and reversed the course of the campaign.

Ibn Atiah Al-Sa'di, the commander of the Ummayyad army, believed that his sins would not be requited and, when he was captured by the Yemenis in Jawf[32], pleaded for his life, asking to remain their captive. But they reminded him of his ill-deeds: 'Avaricious in life, you killed *Taleb Al-Haq* (Abdullah bin Yahya), Abu Hamza, Bajla and Abrahah and they wasted no time in putting him to death. They dispatched his head to the Hadramaut where it was displayed in Shibam[33], as a reminder of its victories and to proclaim that it was a centre of Ibadhism capable of fortitude and resistance in the face of tyranny.

However we view the outcome the Ibadhi Revolt had succeeded by 129-130 AH/746-747 AD in inserting the penultimate nail in the coffin of the Ummayyad Caliphate, which finally collapsed two years later.

Ibadhism entrenched itself successfully in Yemen and Oman and before long became formalized in the government of these two states, enabling the Ummayyads to subdue it for a while. In North Africa, meanwhile, the march of Ibadhism progressed apace and culminated in the foundation of the Rustumiya State in 160 AH/776 AD which maintained strong connections with Oman. Here we are led to ask which factors contributed to the rise of Ibadhism in North Africa. And what were the origins of the powerful bond that formed between the Rustumiya State and Oman?

Ibadhism in North Africa and its Relations with Oman

Factors Leading to the Emergence of the Ibadhi Rite in the Arab *Maghreb*

The Ibadhi body of ideas found wide support amongst the Berbers in appealing to their partiality for justice, equity and liberty. In the *Maghreb* the ground was well prepared for the reception of Ibadhi ideas, for here as well as in many other of the Islamic countries, the people were distressed by the effects of tribal strife between the Qaisis and the Yemenis. The Arabs of the Islamic Conquests who had settled in the *Maghreb* were Yemenis who rallied around Moussa bin Naseer when he was *Wali* up to 96 AH/714 AD. In that year the Caliph Suleiman bin

ATLANTIC
OCEAN

Algiers

Tahart

Wahran

Togert

Ghardaya

Jebel Nafoussah

Gharian

Mazda

MEDITERRANEAN SEA

ARABIAN GULF

Sohar

Muscat

Nizwa

GULF OF OMAN

OMAN

BAHR AL-QALZAM
(Red Sea)

GULF OF ADEN

Extension of the power of the Ibadhi Imams from Oman to North Africa.

Abdul Mulik removed[34] Moussa bin Naseer and appointed Yazid bin Mohammed Al-Qarshi, a Qaisi, as *Wali*, whence the latter at the instigation of the Caliph set about exterminating the family of Moussa. He pursued them relentlessly, harrassing them and seizing their possessions: Abdullah bin Moussa was captured, fined an extortionate sum, and subsequently tortured to death[35].

Under the *Wilaya* of Yazid bin Abi Muslim (101-103 AH/719-721 AD), Yemeni stock rose once again and it was Yazid bin Mohammed's turn to face prison and torture in vengeance for what he had inflicted on his Yemeni predecessor. Bishr bin Safwan[36] succeeded as *Wali* on the death of Yazid bin Abi Muslim. This man was an extremist and continued the relentless pursuit of the Qaisis, appointing before his death Naqash bin Qart Al-Kalbi Al-Maghrabi to carry forward the abasement of the Qaisis.

The Caliph Hisham bin Abdul Mulik (105-125 AH/723-742 AD) now assigned Ubaidah bin Abdul Rahman Al-Qaisi *Wali* of the *Maghreb* . This man set himself the task of tracking down the agents of Moussa bin Naseer until he had extirpated them thoroughly; and so the trials continued through the term of Abdullah bin Al-Habhab who took over in 116 AH/734 AD.

Over and above their preoccupation with tribal warfare, successive *Walis* competed to collect funds for the gratification of the Caliph on the one hand and to purchase support and satisfy their greed on the other. Expeditions were dispatched to the far quarters of the *Maghreb* to pillage and loot and these expedition forces were composed in large part of Berbers.

Meanwhile the Berber population chafed under the vile treatment of the Ummayyad agents who oppressed them with their extortionate demands to the extent that they believed their country to be a war zone, despite the fact that

The Ibadhi Imamate in Oman and North Africa.

229

they had adopted Islam in line with the policy of the Ummayyad Caliphate[37]. When Omar bin Abdul Aziz took over as Caliph (99-101 AH/717-719 AD), he assigned Ismail bin Ubaidallah bin Abi Al-Mahajer, *Mawla* (the slave) of the Bani Makhzoum, *Wali* of the *Maghreb*[38] in an attempt to define the boundaries of the *Wali's* power and to restore Berber trust in the Caliphate.

The Caliph instructed his *Wali* to abolish the *jizziya* (the tax on non-Muslims under Muslim rule) in respect of all Berbers who adopted Islam and to desist from enslaving their women. He directed him to declare the villages the possessions of their owners after taking a fifth so that they might gather their crop and pay the known *kharaj* on this. Moreover the Caliph was careful to assign to Ismail bin Ubaidallah the task of mediating between the chieftains and warlords as well as collecting *kharaj* and *sadqat* or alms tax with a view to ending the arbitrariness and tyranny of the tax collector. This policy however was to end with the death of the Caliph himself[39].

Yazid bin Abdul Mulik assumed the Caliphate[40], and Yazid bin Abi Muslim was his *Wali* in 102 AH/720 AD. He bore down heavily on the Berbers and reversed the reforms of his predecessor, reintroducing the *jizziya* on Muslim converts with a view to obtaining more funds for the Caliph and to avoid having to pay higher wages to the Muslim troops. He exceeded all bounds in his treatment of the Berbers to the extent of tattooing his Berber guard, the man's name on his right hand and the word 'guard' on his left[41]. Ubaidah bin Abdul Rahman succeeded him in this brutal policy.

Matters worsened further under the ruthless excesses of Ubaidallah bin Al-Habhab[42] who conscripted armies to plunder the Berbers and confine them in the far reaches of the *Maghreb*. Terror and misery stalked these areas. He appointed his son Ismail to Tangier and with him he brought Omar bin Abdullah Al-Miradi who if anything aggravated the situation further. Omar bin Abdullah regarded the Berbers as booty and Muslims or not he treated them like slaves. These were the grounds which led to the Ummayyads being regarded with such hatred and contempt by the *Maghreb* Berbers and which generated a climate well suited to the rise of Ibadhism[43].

The Ibadhis developed in two directions, the one complementing the other. First was the theoretical-political group, whose primary objective was to explain their ideology, as attested to in the exchange of letters between Ibn Ibadh and his opponents, and which cast light on the Ibadhi attitude to their adversaries as well as their philosophy and political thinking. After Ibn Ibadh, this viewpoint became institutionalized in the Ibadhi School of Basra. Its leaders were those who occupied themselves with the teaching of Ibadhi doctrine to their adherents and to writing on aspects of this subject. The second direction was practical in nature and its adherents went forth against the Ummayyads in the hope of acquiring a real power which would promote Ibadhism. They urged society to behave in accordance with the principles of Ibadhism, under the tutelage of the first group[44].

Certainly the Ibadhis of North Africa succeeded in establishing Ibadhi societies which subsequently transformed into Ibadhi states. The most renowned of these was the Rustumiya state which arose in Tahart in 160 AH/776 AD and took in most of the central and distant territories of the *Maghreb*. It was to be expected that links would develop between this state and

Oman before they set up their state at Tahart. This relationship developed further during the reign of this state which lasted for 136 Hegira years. And though it died away in 296 AH/908 AD, Oman's links with Ibadhism in North Africa did not falter and vestiges remain still. We must now examine the story of this relationship.

Oman's Relations with Ibadhism in North Africa

The Growth of This Relationship[45]

Islam burst forth from the Hijaz into the world beyond and within a brief few years had found its way to the distant corners of the earth. Three decades later fault lines were manifesting in Islam's united front and amidst the coming turmoil emerged a group who called themselves the '*Muslim Group*' or the '*Righteous Ones*' or the '*People of the Call*' whose inspired leader in the view of their contemporaries was one of their Imams, Abdullah bin Ibadh (d. before 86AH/705 AD)[46]. So the group became known as the *Ibadhis*. Ibadhi sources are agreed that the Imam was Abdullah bin Ibadh but the founder and support of the group it was said was Imam Jaber bin Zaid Al-Azdi Al-Omani (d. 93 AH/711 AD)[47].

Imam Jaber bin Zaid was of Omani origin but the sources declare him to have selected Basra as his home and it was there that he sent out his call. Basra at this early stage already had Azdi and Tamimi *quartiers*, which much resembled the atmosphere of Oman itself. All of the *ulema* of Oman at this time were either in transit between Oman, Basra and Al-Haramein (Mecca and Medina), as were the *Maghrabis* between Basra and Al-Haramein. In due course Basra's star would set and Oman and Hadramaut and Khorasan would rise to become centres of Ibadhism.

The question which concerns us here is the means by which the *Maghrabis* made contact with Imam Jaber bin Zaid, whose correspondence containing the call (to Ibadhism) is not available for our perusal today, with the exception of some documents in the vaults of the Barouni Library in Gerba (in Tunisia)[48].

Regrettably, an examination of these few remaining letters of the Imam[49] does not give us even the smallest clue; and this is the case also with the rest of the Ibadhi and non-Ibadhi sources available to us which were translated for Imam Jaber bin Zaid. This is largely due no doubt to the period of rigorous secrecy at the outset of the emergence of Ibadhism, surrounded on every side by the agents of the Ummayyad State, such as Zaid bin Abih, his son and Al-Hajjaj (the notorious *Wali* of Basra).

It would not be farfetched to assume contacts between the Imam Jaber and some of the *Maghrabis* and perhaps time will yield up some such texts which will throw light on the clandestine circumstances of this stage.

Our hypothesis of a continuity of contact is based on the substantial leap forward made in the first stage of the reign in Basra of the Second Imam, Abi Ubaidah Muslim bin Abi Karima, immediately after his release from Al-Hajjaj's prison following the latter's death (95 AH/714 AD). It is hard to believe that such dramatic progress could have taken place without some preliminary development.

It is widely held that all of the Islamic groupings sensed the winds of freedom with the accession of the Fifth Orthodox Caliph Omar bin Abdul Aziz (99-101 AH/719-720 AD). The Ibadhis were quick to dispatch to him their delegation, incorporating the 'First Squadron', which was contemporary with the Imam Jaber bin Zaid and which consisted of Ja'far bin Al-Simak, Abu Al-Hurr Ali bin Al-Hassin Al-Anbari, Al-Hattat bin Al-Kateb, Al-Habbab bin Kulaib, Abu Sufian Qanbar Al-Basri and Salim bin Zakwan[50].

In this context the Ibadhi sources mention the first visit of a *Maghrabi* to the power centre of Ibadhism, Basra. It must be logical to assume that reports of Ibadhism had reached him before this, particularly since Egypt was familiar with Ibadhism from the very outset. The first Egyptian sheikh mentioned by Al-Shamakhi was Ibn Al-Yas'a, along with Aba Is'haq Ibrahim Al-Masri and Issa bin Alqma Al-Masri[51].

The visitor whose journey is cited was Ibn Mughtair Al-Nafoussi Al-Jinawni and he is described as a learned jurisprudent and *mufti* (expounder of law), whose learning had been gained from Abi Ubaidah Muslim. He was followed by the abovementioned five[52]. After their arrival he abstained from being the Mufti.

It is clear that the journey of Ibn Mughtair preceded that of Salma bin Sa'ad whom the Ibadhi sources consider to have been the first to bring the call to Ibadhism to the *Maghreb*. It is most likely that this voyage was at the turn of the first century of the Hegira. It is hard to put a precise date on this journey which was without a doubt after the year 95 AH/714 AD - the year that Imam Abi Ubaidah left prison - as the sources do not mention that he met the Imam Jaber bin Zaid.

Al-Shamakhi tells us that Ibn Mughtair abstained from being the *Mufti* when the learned band came, since he had acquired his knowledge from Abi Ubaidah before matters had been clearly formulated whereas the five had learned from him after many of his interpretations had been established[53]. The journey took place at an early date; that is to say during the term of Imam Abi Ubaidah.

From the basements of Basra with the endorsement of the Omani Azdis, Abi Ubaidah continued to pursue the task of spreading the call to orthodoxy in the extremities of the Ummayyad sphere of influence - in Yemen, Oman and the *Maghreb*, a task made more urgent because of the declining fortunes of the Ummayyads.

Certainly Salma bin Sa'ad was energetic in spreading the call and bore aloft the banner of justice, collaborating with Ibn Mughtair in this mission at Jebel Nafoussah. He travelled to Kairouan, the 'capital of Africa', where he worked on putting together a compilation of knowledge from source, after the wisdom of four learned colleagues: Abdul Rahman bin Rustum (of Persian origin), whom destiny brought to Kairouan with his mother's husband; Assem Al-Sidrati from Sidrata west of Awras; Abu Dawud Al-Qabli Al-Nafazawi from Nafazawa in the south of Africa; and Abu Darrar Ismail ibn Darrar Al-Ghadamsi from Ghadams south of Tripoli. From Basra they were joined by Abu Al-Khattab Abdul Aa'la Al-Ma'afri, an Arab from Yemen. It was this group who brought the gift of religious learning to the *Maghreb* as all of the Ibadhi sources agree.

Salma bin Sa'ad bin Ali bin Assad Al-Hadrami Al-Yemeni's dearest wish was that the call of Ibadhism would be heard in the *Maghreb* but for a single day from dawn to dusk and he did not care if he lost his head afterwards if he were to have this wish[54]. He was indeed to have his desire for the call was welcomed among the Berbers and was heard in the distant periphery of the *Maghreb*. This was due in some part to the composition of the missionaries who included a student from the central *Maghreb*, another from the lower *Maghreb* and a third from Libya, along with Ibn Rustum who was of Persian origin but reared in Kairouan.

Before this learned band could carry out the plan of their Imam, the first stirrings of the influence that Abu Ubaidah's *madrassah* would wield were felt when Abdullah bin Mas'ud Al-Tajibi, leader of the Ibadhis and their chief spokesman in Tripoli, led a revolt against Elias bin Habib, *Wali* of Tripoli, by his brother Abdul Rahman bin Habib, *Wali* of Kairouan. Elias survived and Al-Tajibi was put to death in 127 AH/745 AD.

The Ibadhis were not extinguished however and presently Al-Hareth bin Talid Al-Hadrami was put forward in 131 AH/749 AD along with his magistrate Abdul Jabbar bin Qais Al-Maradi and delegated to the *Maghreb* from Yemen after the defeat of *Taleb Al-Haq's* revolt in 130 AH/748 AD. However Abdul Rahman bin Habib was quick to sense the menace posed by this Imamate to his sovereignty and had recourse to ruse when force failed to make an impression. His plot consisted of the murder of both men in which the sword of one would be found embedded in the corpse of the other. This took place in 132 AH/750 AD and one of the outcomes of this tragedy was a split in the ranks of the *Shurat* between those who regarded both men as innocent, those who wavered in their opinion and those who turned their backs on them.

As the dispute between the factions gathered pace in Tripoli, they considered taking the advice of their Imam in the *Mashriq*; and though we do not have access to the text of the letter which was dispatched in this regard other than the name of the messenger to Imam Abi Ubaidah, we did manage to secure a copy of the reply from Basra[55]. This letter overflows with expressions of friendship and brotherhood between the two sides, for the *Maghrabis* when they were in disagreement on some matter of concern never hesitated to dispatch a delegation to their Imam as the first authority and one whose word would be heeded by the populace[56]. Equally the Imam Abu Ubaidah was never slow to give counsel and to examine issues presented from any and every quarter as was the mandate of his creed. And indeed the *Maghrabis* empathized with the agonies of the *Mashriqis* and rejoiced in their gladness and success[57].

Abu Ubaidah's message to the *Maghrabis* moreover did not fail to remind them that the key to victory in spreading the message in the *Maghreb* was to repudiate everything which could be a source of difference and to embrace everything which helped bring people together; in this affirming the judicious view that the correct course of action was to call for outward reticence and inward forbearance by those who would contest one another; this, he told them, had been made clear to him from experience. Any departure from this behaviour constituted a deviation from the way of the Muslims: 'That which we desire of you and ask of you is that you be among the seekers after knowledge, and that no one repudiate another overtly, for (such) is between him and his God ... Go back to what you were and desist from this argument for your own benefit. Beware of exaggeration and departure from the Way of Allah; and there are those of you who might say: If I do my duty then I need not be concerned, for Allah will prevent me from transgression and spare me from exposure to repudiation. And God will grant us success and He will protect us and you if we are faithful'[58].

This letter did indeed reach the *Maghreb* and a curtain descended over this episode. In other words the Imam's counsel served its purpose well; it healed wounds and reconciled adversaries so that they were enabled to elect another Imam. He was Ismail bin Ziad Al-Nafoussi and the year was 132 AH/750 AD. In the same year, however, the forces of Abdul Rahman bin Habib were able to wreak a terrible vengeance on the Ibadhis, the Imam was killed and *Kitman* returned.

Into this interval came the Imamate of Julanda bin Mas'ud bin Gaifar in Oman 132-134 AH/750-752 AD, launched with the sanction of Imam Abu Ubaidah, as confirmed by a correspondence between them which is still in existence[59]. The sources do not tell us how this news was received in the *Maghreb*, but we can be sure that it was a powerful incentive to another Imamate; now that the banner of wisdom in the period immediately following was to be found in the environs of Basra where, if the accounts are to be believed, it was to remain between 135 AH/763 AD and 140 AH/758 AD.

 Ibadhi strategy succeeded in terms of maintaining contact between *Mashriq* and *Maghreb* during this difficult period; and if the Imamate declined in Oman to suffer extinction under the rule of a tyrannical regime, the collapse of the Ummayyad Caliphate and rise of the Abbassids enabled the *Maghreb* to revive *Al-Dhuhour* and once again enjoy an open Imamate.

A directive from the Imam Abi Ubaidah launched the Imamate of Abi Al-Khattab Abdul A'ala Al-Ma'afri (140-4 AH/758-62 AD) in Tripoli. With this happy event justice returned and integrity prevailed once again. The reverberations were felt as far as the *Mashriq* where the Ibadhis were greatly heartened and there were widespread hopes that the *Maghreb* would provide an Imam for all the Muslims.

Certainly the messengers were getting through and also the messages between the centre of Ibadhism, the centre of the Imamate in Tripoli and the various centres of Ibadhism in Oman, Yemen and Khorasan. This happy state was not to last however, and the Imamate of Abi Al-Khattab was not to prosper for long. Four years had not gone by when a brutal attack by the Abbassids left Jebel Nafoussah and its community devastated and with it the principal stronghold of Ibadhism in Libya.

We have at our disposal a letter on the subject of *Zakat* sent by Abi Ubaidah to the *Maghrabis* in response to an enquiry by Sheikh Ismail bin Suleiman Al-Maghrabi who was probably a colleague of the Imam Abi Al-Khattab.

The opening remarks of this letter are adequate to demonstrate to us the openhearted friendship between the Imam in Basra and the *Maghrabis*:

We have received your letter with news of the great reward with which God has blessed you, by which your word became one and your problem was resolved, though your opponents are many among you. Yet I swear that no matter how many they are, they will not outnumber those who were before them and who lived amongst your predecessors. So follow the example of

*your predecessors and you will prevail over them easily, whatever their
number. We urge God to assist you and grant you success in all your affairs
and to protect us and you and to bring victory to us and you and all of the
Muslims and to recover the hearts of the faithful and dispel their anger.*

*I swear that we were happy to hear how you discharged this matter of yours,
though we knew about it already. May God Almighty grant you assistane
and bless you with prosperity. Your letter contains many matters and I see
that I will have to answer these. Some I may answer easily, and others I must
answer at length and in the interests of what is best for your community, and
in a manner more suited to your affairs and more welcome to your hearts.
May God grant us his favour and help us succeed in His desires*[60].

Relations between Oman and Ibadhi North Africa are Maintained Across the Centuries.

The Second Century AH/Eighth Century AD

After the death of Abi Ubaidah Muslim, Al-Rabee bin Habib (75-175 AH/695-
792 AD) assumed office in Basra. While Oman remained in the hands of
despots, the *Maghreb* saw a *Difa'* Defense Imamate installed in 145 AH/763
AD and the election of Abu Hatem Al-Malzouzi. The struggle wore on between
this Imam and the Abbassids until he was murdered in 155 AH/772 AD along
with one of his learned assistants, Assem Al-Sidrati.

From here on the sources are tight-lipped on relations between *Mashriq* and
Maghreb, for both sustained the same agony in the endeavour to obtain justice
and be rid of the Abbassids who yearned to have mastery over the peripheral
regions of the Caliphate from which the Ummayyads had been ousted. This
reticence was not to suggest that the relationship between the two was
suspended; but the history of this period has issued such as we have it from mere
cracks here and there, particularly in relation to the revolutionary movements
who destroyed their texts every time their enemies prevailed over them.

What transpired in 160 AH/777 AD was the dawn of a new age in the central
Maghreb in the competent hands of Abdul Rahman bin Rustum who on his
return was authorized by the Imam Abu Ubaidah, on account of his great
learning, to formulate legal opinions both on matters that he had heard from him
and others; whereas Abu Al-Khatib was directed to judge only between matters
that he had heard from him; and Abu Darar was directed not to give an opinion
at all, neither on what he had heard from the Imam nor any other matter[61].

The *Mashriqis* were overjoyed after they received the news of the declaration of the Imamate in *Maghreb*. The new Imamate received moral as well as
material aid from the Omanis whose conditions could not allow them to declare
their own Imamate. Specifically, the Omani aid came from Al-Rabee. The
sources are all in agreement that those who presented the aid decided that they
could not deliver it unless they were assured that Abdul Rahman was faithful to
the religious instructions in every aspect of his life. So when they found him on
the roof of his house fixing the damage to it they knew that he was true to the
example of the Orthodox Caliphs and the Righteous Imams and they gave him
what money they obtained and he used it to consolidate the State[62]. Then the

Mashriqis gave him an additional sum of money, but he did not hesitate to return it saying: 'Go back with your money for its owners are in more need of it than we - for we are on ground which has been appropriated by justice and they are in a land which has been conquered by iniquity - so that they may use it to protect themselves, their possessions and their religion'[63]. This caused the *Mashriqis* to be even more impressed with the Imam Abdul Rahman. 'They were moved by his asceticism and by his anticipation for the afterlife. Every Ibadhi recognized his Imam and they came to him with their letters and with their counsel'[64].

Al-Shamakhi's account suffices as evidence of the line of trust which existed between *Mashriq* and *Maghreb*: 'Every Ibadhi recognized his Imam'. There is no doubt but this state of affairs was echoed in Oman and amongst the great sheikhs who were the Imams of Basra. It had its good effect, particularly in view of the fact that the situation was still deteriorating there.

Abdul Rahman's fame spread throughout the *Mashriq* to the extent that the *Mashriqis* had a saying that went: 'There is none more learned in sparing the blood of the *Ahl Al-Qibla* (Muslims) in our time than Abdul Rahman bin Rustum in the *Maghreb* and Aba Yazid Al-Khawarzemi'. Al-Shamakhi refers to this saying: 'God knows but do not go forward into bloodshed except with the *fatwa* of one of these two men, from the abundance of their wisdom, piety and restraint'[65].

The Imam Abdul Rahman bin Rustum died in 171 AH/788 AD and the Shura Council moved to elect his son Abdul Wahab as Imam for his abundance of good qualities; but strife broke out between his followers and critics whose rejection of this Imam was supported with two specious arguments. The first of these stated that an Imam had no right to defy an instruction without obtaining the counsel of the Muslims; and the second that no man would be accepted as Imam if a more learned Muslim than he existed[66]. Here they took refuge in the good opinion of the *Mashriqis*: 'The Muslims were reconciled with those who did not wish disunion amidst the ranks with Ibn Fandain[67] and they wrote to their brothers and *ulema* in the *Mashriq* so that they they might act in accordance with what they advised'[68].

Sure enough the message got to Mecca and the case was referred to the Imam Al-Rabee bin Habib and his companions. They confirmed with guidelines that the Imamate was intact and withdrawal from the contract futile. Whereupon they denounced the Imam for certain actions and it was established for them that he was not in fact responsible for these actions[69].

It is not for us to go into what happened after this in the way of factional strife and of the expressed desire of Shu'aib bin Al-Maarouf to support them after he had himself declared a *fatwa* on the legitimacy of the Imam Abdul Wahab's Imamate though there were others more learned than he declaring the Imamate to be intact and withdrawal futile, as a result of which Rabee pronounced repudiation of him[70].

The unshakeable relationship continued in the term of Imam Abdul Wahab with the centre of Ibadhism in the *Mashriq*. And when this Imam while he was at Jebel Nafoussah wished to undertake the pilgrimage to Mecca his *ulema* protested, but on finding him insistent they advised him to take counsel with the *Mashriqis*. So he sent a Nafoussi man from Tamzada[71] to Al-Rabee bin Habib and to Ibn Abbad Al-Masri[72] to seek the advice of the Muslims. Al-Rabee replied thus: 'One such as you who devotes himself to the affairs of the Muslims and bears the burden of their trust and who fears for his life, it were better that he send someone to fulfil his *Hajj* and spare his life. Ibn Abbad replied: "Such a one is under no obligation to carry out the *Hajj*, for it is a condition of carrying out the *Hajj* that the route be safe'[73].

And in truth for all the breadth of his wisdom the Imam had no option but to heed the opinion of the *ulema* of Nafoussah and the opinion of the source of the *fatwa* in the centres of Ibadhism in the *Mashriq* and he was in consequence relieved of the obligation of carrying out the *Hajj*.

Contacts and gifts were exchanged between the two parties. Imam Abdul Wahab sent a gift to Al-Rabee valued at 12,000 dirhams or dinars. The gift reached Al-Rabee and he purchased with it appliances and dispatched them with his brother to Tahart and the Imam directed the merchants of the city to purchase for him his everyday needs - this was done, and a good deed it was too[74]. With each of these delegations came correspondence and *fatwas* and the like which were universally applicable to Muslims.

We should not fail to mention the extent of scientific contact and the desire for books, so that 'Imam Abdul Wahab sent a thousand dinars to his brothers in Basra with which to purchase books for him; and on receiving the thousand dinars they purchased its value in paper and they copied onto it 40 loads of books'[75].

During this time also Abu Ghanem Bishr bin Ghanem Al-Khorasani (second/eighth century) was sent to them from the *Mashriq* and although he was not Omani he was one of the leading personalities of the Orient. He had studied at Basra. acquiring his knowledge from the students of Abi Ubaidah, from whom he also transcribed his books. In one of the most important of these, *Al Mudawanah*, he recorded the sayings of the students of Abi Ubaidah on jurisprudence and narrative and on their differences. He transmitted this account on visiting Tahart. A copy was stored there with Amrous, but fortunately another copy was made. This is the copy which survived in the *Maghreb* after the library known as *Al-Ma'souma* in Tahart was burnt with all its contents[76].

Thus was Tahart and its Al-Ma'souma Library enriched with a flood of books from the *Mashriq*, including the *Tafseer* (interpretation) of Imam Abdul Rahman and of his *fatwas*, along with the *fatwas* themselves and other texts and correspondence. These were no haters of wisdom; on the contrary they were eager to secure copies of these books and though Al-Ma'souma was later burnt, these remaining copies are still in existence and even to this day they crop up here and there from time to time.

The arrival of delegations to the Imam's capital at Tahart accelerated. They came on missions of observation or in search of benefit, reflection or retreat. On this the sources, citing the work *Seyar Nafoussa* by Maqaren Al-Baghtouri (sixth/twelfth century)[77], relate the following: 'A party of men from the *Mashriq* came visiting in the time of Imam Abdul Wahab and they selected from Tahart the Imam and his *vizier* Aba Abdul Ali Al-Samah and they selected from Nafoussah Aba Mardas...'[78]. We do not know which country this delegation came from, but the purpose of the visit we can infer from examining the status of the *ulema* of the *Maghreb*, which led to the visitors' citing their preferences for one over the other, and choosing the ones they did, an activity which demanded close observation and scrutiny and comparison through testing.

All of which points to the free intermingling of learning at this time with visitors from the *Mashriq*. Al-Shamakhi recalls this: 'The sheikhs of Nafoussah would visit the Imam (Abdul Wahab) and they would sit down with him if he was on the mountain. If Abu Mardas (a contemporary of Al-Sidrati) came forward the Imam would stand up for him. He was short of stature. One of the *Mashriqis* inquired: "Why does The Imam esteem this man"? One who overheard him replied how there was "none more sublime than he who dignified the angels and I do not know of a man like this one apart from one in the *Mashriq* and this one is slightly superior to him..." And after a discussion those present declared that they knew of no-one in either *Mashriq* or *Maghreb* to compare with this savant'[79].

It is evidence of this kind that enables us to believe what the available sources tell us of the relationship between the *Maghreb* and Oman at the time of the Imam Abdul Wahab. In the time of this Imam, events took place in the *Mashriq* the most prominent of which was the death of the Imam Rabee, though we do not have at our disposal an account of the effect this had on the *Maghrabis*. Then the Just Imamate returned to Oman from 177-208 AH/794-824 AD, first in the person of Imam Mohammed bin Abi Affan (177-179 AH/794-796 AD). Although this Imam was discharged from office for failing in the example he set in his latter years, the Omani biographies are strenuous in their praise of his successor, Imam Al-Warith bin Ka'b Al-Kharousi (179-192 AH/796-808 AD), and nothing but good is recorded of the latter's successor, Imam Ghassan bin Abdullah Al-Fajhi (192-208 AH/808-824 AD)[80].

The Third Century AH /Ninth Century AD

With the death of the Imam Abdul Wahab in 208 AH/824 AD, his son Aflah bin Abdul Wahab was installed to serve for half a century until 258 AH/872 AD; when the Rustumiya State reached a pinnacle of glory. His term coincided with the Era of the Second Imamate in Oman, and paralleled the successive reigns of three Imams:

* Imam Abdul Mulik bin Humaid (208-226 AH/824-841 AD).
* Imam Al-Muhanna bin Gaifar Al-Yahmadi (226-237 AH/841-852 AD).
* Imam Al-Salt bin Malik (237-273 AH/852-887 AD)[81].

These times were characterized by great luminaries in various parts of the Islamic world whose zeal, fervour, learned debates and writings made a strong impression in the *Maghreb* and Oman.

The most outstanding event was probably the acquisition by Nafath bin Nasr Al-Nafoussi, a student of Aflah, of the *Diwan* of Jaber bin Zaid, the Ibadhi Imam, for the *Maghreb*, having copied it, displaying both shrewdness and foresight, from the sole copy which was kept at the time in the safe of the Abbassid Caliph[82]. Unfortunately, having succeeded in this great undertaking, he would subsequently dig a hole and bury the book at a time when he was involved in a dispute with the Imam. Abu Zakaria says that he buried the book 'out of envy, outrage and malevolence'[83].

The sources furnish us also with the call of the Imam Aflah to study the books of the righteous in general and in particular that of Abi Sufian Mahboub bin Al-Raheel Al-Omani (second half of the second century AH/eighth century AD): 'You are enjoined to study the books of the People of the Call, in particular that of Abi Sufian Al-Omani'[84]. It is well known to any scholar of Ibadhi observance that this book of Abi Sufian's was the indispensable textbook of both *Mashriq* and *Maghreb* for acquiring a knowledge of the origins of the Ibadhi rite and of its first *ulema*. It was the work of those who gained their knowledge from Abi Ubaidah and Al-Rabee.

Mahboub played a formidable part in bringing together *Mashriq* and *Maghreb*. In the words of Ibn Salam: 'Mahboub sojourned in Mecca, and he maintained tents known as Mahboub's campsite at Mona during the season of the *Hajj* . For the three days of the *Tashriq* (the three days following the Day of Immolation) and after *Eid Al-Adha* (The Feast of Sacrifice), behind the great mound of stones cast by the pilgrims when first they come in from Al-Muzdalafa west of Mona, and west of the three rocks behind the steep incline of Mona, these campsites were the destination place of Omani *Hajjis*'. Elsewhere Ibn Salam notes that in the neighbourhood[85] of Mecca were '150 men of whom 25 were Omanis'.

This bond of trust continued under his son Mohammed bin Mahboub bin Al-Raheel (d. 3 Moharram 260 AH/29 October 873 AD), who was chief among the Ibadhi *ulema* after his father. He resided at Mecca and there met Amrous bin Fatah, one of the *ulema* of Nafoussah in 283 AH/896 AD, a meeting the importance of which the sources did not cease to emphasize in terms of intellectual exchange, saying: 'They recalled that Amrous and his companions set out for the *Mashriq* to execute the *Hajj*. On reaching Mecca they found there Mohammed bin Mahboub and went in to him, only to find him in council with his companions. They greeted him and he, delighted to see them, ushered them in and showed them great respect without knowing the individuals in the party. When they had settled down in the consultation seats Amrous asked Abu Abdullah about a certain matter and Ibn Mahboub said: "If Abu Hafas is around these parts, it has to be he who asks this question and none can answer save he". They said to him: "It is he who asks". Ibn Mahboub when he knew it was Amrous, welcomed him with great respect and honour and requested him to come closer to him. Amrous then came to questions of bloodshed, one after the other, until Ibn Mahboub said: "These are among the concealed matters of wisdom, not manifest to a heap of ignoramuses". At this Amrous said to his companions: "Memorize the question and I will memorize the answer for you so that we can make available to our brothers what we have memorized". This they did and when they reached their homelands Amrous said to them: "Out with what you have taken the trouble to learn". And they said: "We remember nothing but your saying: Memorize the issues so that we can reply to our brothers". At which Amrous recited it case by case to the last word'[86]. This story needs no commentary to confirm the depth of knowledge of the great scholars and the bonds of culture and learning that existed between the Ibadhism of the *Maghreb* and *Mashriq*.

After his sojourn at Mecca Mohammed bin Mahboub moved on to Oman to continue his propagation of wisdom, to experience the situation of the Imams there and to give counsel to them clearly that succession (in the Imamate) belonged to the man most qualified, else he should be disavowed. Mahboub was the most outstanding party consulted on the induction of Imam Al-Salt bin Malik in 237 AH/852 AD and he was granted the position of magistrate at Sohar by a member of the Raheel family from 249 AH/864 AD until his death in 260 AH/873 AD. To him was attributed a book on jurisprudence in 70 volumes and his *Sirah* to the people of the *Maghreb*, a handwritten document of 26 medium sized folios rendered in clear *Mashraqi* script which treated 53 matters posed by the *Maghrabis* to Sheikh Mohammed bin Mahboub. The reply to these matters was rendered individually after the necessity for a rearrangement of the *Sirah* was recognized. It demonstrates the superior state of affairs prevailing amongst the *Mashriqis* and *Maghrabis*: 'I have written to you and before me Muslims generally and specifically of the excellent circumstances and perfect ease of living and cohesion of views, and we thank God for all of this. It gratified me to read in your letter that you are in good form and circumstances. God has blessed you in His design. We have asked Him to grant you and us all of His favours for our Lord is great in His response'[87]. He then went on to give his response to the matters raised in their letter.

The *Sirah* itself requires close study for what it offers on issues of politics and law in which the author relies for guidance on the Holy Book and the *Sunnah* and on the stands taken by Ibadhi Imams and *ulema*.

Meanwhile Amrous Ibn Fateh was zealous in his scientific endeavours. We learned above that he retained custody of the writings of Abi Ghanem when their author left these in his charge. With his wealth of learning he stood with Abi Mahdi Al-Nafoussi against the views of Nafath Al-Makhalafa, he of the buried *Diwan* of Imam Jaber. This latter was magistrate to the *Wali* of Imam Abdul Wahab, one Abu Mansour Al-Yas. He was judicious in his verdicts and was killed by Al-Aghalibah in the battle with Manu in 283 AH/896 AD. No writings of his have come down to us apart from *Al-Dainouna Al-Safia* and it was confirmed to me on a visit to Wadi Mizab that this book was the first section of a book on jurisprudence after a manuscript deposited in the Dar Al-Talamith Library in the city of Ataf[88].

Over and above this Sheikh Nasir Al-Marmouri[89] tells us of Sheikh Abi Ishaq Ibrahim Atfish (d.1386 AH/1966 AD)[90] that an investigative study was conducted by a team of 70 *Maghrabi* students of Sheikh Abi Mohammed Abdullah bin Mohammed bin Barka (third century AH/ninth century AD)[91], author of a book of jurisprudence entitled *Al-Jami'*[92]. He was known as the '*Maghrabi* Sheikh', and the students were from different parts of the *Maghreb*, with the exception of Wadi Mizab as it still subscribed to the old insular research methodology[93].

We have here the *Sirah* which was directed by a number of Muslim jurisprudents to the Imam Al-Salt bin Malik (237-273 AH/852-887 AD) and we are inclined with the author of *Al-Seyar Al-Omaniya* to the belief that it was from the *Maghrabis*, even though the writers stated frankly that they withheld their names in order that the message should be Allah's unadulterated counsel: 'What prevents us from identifying ourselves to you is no more than a fear that there may be amongst you some who would be upset at this knowledge to the extent of opposing and rejecting the message'[94]. This caution was a direct consequence of the severity of the opposition to the Imam Abdul Wahab.

Whatever the source of the letter it gives a view of the cohesion of the Ibadhi parties, for it came with an urge towards harmony at a time when the authors felt that the movement was in danger of breaking down. Hence their warning: 'Be on your guard against conflict and strife and manoeuvring and differences and division...'. It showed also the limitations of the power of the Imam and his obligations, in particular the rules of leadership and withdrawal and the taking of a stand.

Finally the authors of the letter conveyed their willingness to go forth against their opponents if the letter did not work: 'All we desire from our action is the pleasure of Allah for all that He knows of our goal to strengthen Islam and elevate the Way of Allah in your country. So choose to avoid bloodshed and adopt the counsel we have given you, (or) we are ready to fight you if you are prepared for this... And all power is to Allah'[95]. The closing comments clearly indicate the goodwill of the authors in resolving the disunion and reconciling the adversaries.

After the death of Imam Aflah matters went into decline and the influence of the Rustumiya Imamate gave way to the Ubaidiyeen in 296 AH/909 AD. Affairs in Oman came to grief also following the successive Imamates of Rashid bin An'Nadhar Al-Yahmadi (273-277 AH/887-891 AD) and Imam Azzan bin Tamim Al-Kharousi (277-280 AH/891-894 AD); and reports of relations between the *Maghrabis* and *Mashriqis* become scant, other than what we have from Abi Al-Yaqdhan's anonymous trip to the *Hajj* and the Abbassids' notification of this and his imprisonment by them in Baghdad. He was later released to succeed to the Imamate in 261-281 AH/875-995 AD. He assumed the burden of many issues of doctrine, the most important of these being contained in his letter on the origin of the Qur'an, which Al-Baradi borrowed for his book *Al-Jawaher*[96].

Al-Shamakhi tells us of two calamities which befell the Ibadhis: 'The battle of Manu was after the battle of Ibn Thor who descended on the Omanis from Bahrain in the year 280 AH. He was an agent of Motadhid and the Caliph of Oman was Azzan bin Tammim'[97].

Such were the shadows of the events which were to convulse the very heart of Ibadhism in both east and west; and although Oman managed to return to an interval of *Dhuhour*, in the *Maghreb Kitman* remained - and does so to this day - after a number of failed rebellions almost succeeded in eradicating Ibadhism altogether.

The system of *'Azaba* took hold in the *Maghreb* in place of the Imamate and by this means contact with the *Mashriq* Ibadhis was maintained, that is to say those in existence in Oman, for the Ibadhis of Basra, Kufa, Mecca, Medina, Khorasan and Egypt had been exterminated.

The sources offer us no reports of east-west relations in the following centuries except for scraps here and there which bear witness to the existence of friendly bonds between Oman and the *Maghrabi* states where the Ibadhi rite was becoming extinct, that is at Jebel Nafoussah, Gerba, Wadi Mizab and Warjalan.

We bring you this brief report in chronological order always hoping that new texts will come to light which will clarify matters further. It is not rational to suppose that just one single encounter should occur over the period of a century, particularly given that the Ibadhis, as much as the rest of their Muslim brothers, were solicitous in performing the *Hajj* - indeed acutely so. All sources share the view that the Ibadhis of Jebel Nafoussah were remarkable pilgrims who would set out in a caravan with their women and children on the long journey to Mecca. On one such caravan it was recorded that 300 male infants were born, not to speak of the female births and the pregnant women who did not give birth on the journey and the men accompanying all these women. Bihaz Ibrahim comments on this in his account: 'This report if it is true and if it tells us nothing else, tells us of the importance accorded the *Hajj* by these people'[98].

Fourth Century AH/Tenth Century AD

Matters deteriorated during the fourth century AH and the Ibadhis instigated two revolts against the Ubaidiyeen. These were the revolt of Abi Yazid Mukhallad bin Kaidad in 336 AH/947 AD and that of Abi Khazrighla bin Zaltaf in 358 AH/969 AD. The first revolt came close to threatening the Ubaidi throne and the second failed. The brief rise of Abi Khazrighla bin Zaltaf (d. 380 AH/991 AD) and Abi Nuh Said bin Zanghil (fourth century AH/tenth century AD), both men of erudition well versed in theology, did not last. Muizzlidinillah (319-365 AH/931-975 AD) the Fatimid ruler, took the first of these as an escort to Egypt, fearful for him and in celebration of his learning.

No record of contact between Oman and the *Maghreb* follows this period when matters descended into a sink of despair. There was a brief interval represented in the Imamate of Said bin Abdullah bin Mohammed bin Mahboub (320-328 AH/932-939 AD) after which persecution returned to Oman. No doubt the contacts were few and *Kitman* ensured that these few went unreported. At all events only one single report has survived to tell us that Ibn Al-Jum'a, a sheikh of the Muslims, received a merchant arriving in Tozar from the *Mashriq* who was very learned. Abu Rabee Suleiman bin Zarqon (fourth century AH /tenth century AD) assisted him and they then went down together to Sijilmasa where they remained for several years. In Sijilmasa, he studied the religious sciences in the company of the great scholar Rifqat Abi Yazid Mukhallad bin Kaidad and Ibn Al-Jum'a died there.

So who was Ibn Al-Jum'a? And from which country of the *Mashriq* did he come? The sources are not of any assistance to us, not even furnishing us with his full name, in an excess of caution and circumspection. So Ibn Al-Jum'a remained active in commerce despite the vast reaches of his learning and the books he carried with him and the texts state that he counselled Abi Al-Rabee with them when destiny brought them together[99].

The Fifth Century AH/Eleventh Century AD

We know from the course taken by events that Sheikh Faseel bin Abi Massawar (fifth century AH/eleventh century AD) when he became convinced of the impossibility of reviving the Imamate openly in the fifth century AH, called on his student Abu Abdullah ibn Abi Bakr Al-Farasta'i (440 AH/1049 AD) to establish the fundamental principles of *Kitman* and to lay down the system of the learning circle of the type commonly known as the *'Azaba* (celibates/bachelors) system.

Abu Abdullah applied himself to this task after some initial reluctance and he established the rules of the system known by the Ibadhis as the Lesser Imamate. It arranged comprehensively the pattern of daily life for Ibadhis lacking only the definition of boundaries, with emphasis on the stimulation of the sciences and on the strengthening of the bonds of faith between the citizens of the (Ibadhi) community[100].

And so even in spite of deteriorating circumstances the Ibadhi library managed to preserve its heritage as the following report from Abi Al-Abbas Ahmed bin Bakr Mohammed bin Bakr Al-Farasta'i (d. 504 AH/1111 AD) demonstrates: 'I was reading about Sheikh Saadoun and (found) the slaughter of the uncircumcized sanctioned. He mentioned two opinions but did not attribute them. So I went inside his *Diwan* (council). There was at Jebel Nafoussah a *Diwan* which incorporated many written works, and I was obliged to study for four months, not sleeping except between the morning (first) call to prayer and the dawn prayer. The *Mashriqis* pondered on all of these compositions which approached 33,000 volumes in total, all of them written by the Ibadhis and most of them were useful to read'[101].

It is clear from this account that if the visits declined in number, writing remained the best line of communication between the *Mashriqis* and the *Maghrabis*. Abu Al-Abbas continued to research his cherished objective in the Ibadhi heritage of *Mashriq* and *Maghreb*. He was perhaps more accommodating of the *Mashraqi* writings for they took for the most part the form of compilations which were not shy of presenting a variety of views on the issue of unity where the *Maghrabis* leaned towards arrangement and selection and condensation.

And though affairs were deteriorating also in Oman with the exception of the period of the *Shiraa* Imamates of Khalil bin Shadhan (407-425 AH/1017-1034 AD) and of Imam Rashid bin Said Al-Yahmadi (425-442 AH/1034-1054 AD), the encounter between west and east proceeded as was customary in the Holy Cities. As Nasr bin Sijmiman Al-Nafoussi described: 'He encountered the Imams of Oman in Mecca and asked them about pleasure and discontent, he and his Nafoussi companion, and they said both of them were deeds. And they asked about the Qur'an and were told it was created'.

Al-Shamakhi refers to this report and says: 'This implies that the *Mashriqi* and *Maghrabi Wahbias* (Ibadhis) are in agreement that pleasure and discontent are both deeds except for those who were outside this unanimity. They were in agreement also about the creation of the Qur'an except for those who were outside the unanimity for some of the Omanis were opposed on the matter of the Qur'an, over and above the Iraqis, Egyptians, Meccans and *Maghrabis*. And Ibadhism and some of the *Maghrabis* remained at variance on the matter of pleasure and discontent'[102].

This report shows the *Mashriqis* were capable of disagreeing with the *Maghrabis* and they would excuse one another. There is a question which concerns us however and that is: Who were these Omani Imams? And when precisely did this encounter occur? It is difficult to make suggestions with any degree of certainty. The importance of presenting this encounter and the extent of the dialogue between the two parties is based on the fact that it treated of a precise theological issue on the nature of pleasure and discontent and whether they were features of essence or performance, a matter which baffled the theologians. The matter of the creation of the Qur'an was a test which occupied minds throughout the Islamic world. The two prevailing attitudes in the above-mentioned issue in the context of the Ibadhi school did not cause a convulsion between east and west nor ruffle the warmth of ages of goodwill between them.

Sixth Century AH/Twelfth Century AD

Warjalan's star rose in the sixth century AH and celebrated a proliferation of scholars and theologians, amongst the most famous of whom were Abu Ammar Abdul Kafi (before 570 AH/1174 AD), Abu Ya'qub Youssef bin Ibrahim Al-Warjalani (d. 570 AH/1174 AD), Abu Ya'qub Youssef bin Khalfoun and many others[103]. The biographies of these scholars say nothing of a relationship with the Omanis and perhaps this is because Oman was at the time suffering under the yoke of the First Nabhan dynasty.

How pleasant it is to read Abu Ya'qub Al-Warjalani's account in his poem *Al-Hejaziya* which ran to 215 verses on his encounter during the season of the *Hajj* with some Omanis, though he does not pause to tell us whether this was at close or distant quarters[104]. And despite his incessant wanderings we do not learn if he visited Oman. The same is true of his sheikh Abu Ammar who was content with living in Tunisia while he acquired his scholarship; we do not know if he visited Oman or if an Omani visited them there.

Al-Warjalani participated actively in arranging a book of *Mashriqi* Tradition which is a work of major importance in Ibadhi thought, a veritable pillar of the school of Ibadhi Hadith, deemed by them to be the most authentic book after the Holy Book itself. This Tradition is the *Musnad* of Al-Rabee bin Habib Al-Farahidi Al-Omani, in which the Hadith were not arranged. Abu Ya'qub arranged them after the jurisprudent classification and in this way the book became transformed into a *Jami' Sahih* or legally valid compilation. A work such as this is clear evidence of the complementary relationship between the various wings of the Ibadhi School.

Ibn Khalfoun was, we hear, at loggerheads with the jurisprudents of his day for his inclination towards the writings of the dissenters, and the sources note that he expressed his penitence in an encounter en route to the *Hajj* with Sheikh Yakhlaf Al-Temijari, the grandfather of Al-Darjini, the author of *Al Tabaqat*: 'Whenever he was accused of something he repented and apologized'.

The rest of the journey was described by Al-Shamakhi thus: 'We passed glad times with him to the House of God and there we came upon our brothers the Omanis, in the company of their jurisprudent Najiah bin Najiah, who had come with them to perform the *Hajj*. No *Maghrabi* ever executed a more satisfying *Hajj* than we did on that occasion. Every time I brought up an issue to him either in his house or elsewhere one of the three *faqihs* would be there and he would ask him and he would be satisfied. We returned and Abu Ya'qub was much taken with him'[105].

If we know nothing of the jurisprudent Najiah bin Najiah nor of what discussions went on between the two delegations we nevertheless are certain that the dialogue was greatly beneficial in that it included an exchange of books and news and this was a feature of all encounters during the *Hajj* season and other such occasions.

The Seventh Century AH/Thirteenth Century AD

Matters continued thus into the seventh century while Warjalan's star gradually declined. We are told nothing of the relations between the two peripheries except for one item of news which had a distant effect on the recording of the Ibadhi *Sirah* in the *Maghreb* and its connection with its early *Mashriqi* roots. This item concerns the reason behind the compilation of the book *Tabaqat Al-Darjini* (Darjini's Classes). It had not been the intention of this man to write a book of biography until he found himself furnished with source references and the explanations of the citizens of Gerba, in surrender to the wishes of their Omani brothers. Al-Baradi tells the story of the book in his *Jawaher*: 'Some of the *'Azaba* told me that the reason Abi Al-Abbas wrote the book was because when Issa bin Zakaria arrived at the *Hajj* from Oman with his books: Ibn Wassaf's *Hall* and the *Jami'* of Sheikh Abi Al-Hassan and the *Jami'* of Ibn Ja'far[106] and others, his brothers said to him: "They have directed to us a letter concerning a biography of our early adherents and the glorious deeds of our antecedents in the *Maghreb* from the time our school became part of it. But news of them and their effects were hidden from us over a great period as their difficulties increased". So he sought the counsel of the 'Azaba and jurisprudents in Gerba at the time and those skilled and high born; and he declared their brothers' request and described the book enjoined on them and they listened. And they did not know of anyone other than Abi Al-Abbas Al-Darjini who could undertake this compilation and they asked the above mentioned *Hajji* to oblige them'[107].

It is difficult to pin down the names of the sheikhs of Oman during this era for they are not listed, the more so because we know nothing about Al-Haj Issa bin Zakaria save what we can glean from the context - that he was from the island of Gerba, that he was not an *ulema* but was an avid advocate of the propagation of wisdom and himself bore this responsibility amply. It is most probable that this was the time of the two sheikhs who resided during the seventh century AH in Gerba, and these were Saleh bin Najm Al-Maghrawi and Abu Mohammed Abdullah Al-Sadd Ghayani[108]. When these two sheikhs had become famous along with their following on the island, Abi Al-Abbas Ahmed Al-Darjini, one of the teachers on the island, was chosen; and the abovementioned Haj Issa was diligent in supplying him with whatever information could be gathered from Oman as well as what could be gleaned from Gerba with a view to producing the book.

The book *Tabaqat Al-Darjini* constituted a compilation of the biographies of the Ibadhi sheikhs and no scholar of this domain can ignore it. Written in an exemplary literary style, it is free of the gibberish that is found in the *Sirah* of Abi Zakaria Yahia Ibn Abi Bakr Al-Warjalani (sixth century AH/twelfth century AD) and some commendable additions were made.

This is then another example of the cultural exchange between the Ibadhis of Oman and the *Maghreb*, derived from their need to preserve the record of their ancestors for they contain examples for those who wish to find them and accounts of the progress of a community. I do not imagine that this was the only encounter between the two sides in the whole length of the seventh century, but it is the only one documented.

Eighth Century AH/Fourteenth Century AD

Towards the middle of the eighth century, to be exact on 27 Dhul Qa'da 731 AH/1331 AD, the celebrated *Maghrabi* traveller Ibn Battuta arrived in Oman to observe events there. Al-Salimi in *Tohfat Al-'Ayian* describes the visit to us with his comments amongst which the most well known is his regrets that Ibn Battuta had come at a time when the country was oppressed. He said: 'His arrival in Oman was at the time of the Bani Nabhan and his description of them is not a handsome one. Would that he had visited at the time of the Just Imams, when he would have seen other than he did, when truth, clarity, nobility, conscience and glory were the qualities that he would have observed and the sentiments of charity and graciousness'[109].

Without going into the events of this trip, for fear of diverging too much from our subject viz. the common bond of Ibadhism, suffice to recall the lecture which was given by Professor Abdul Hadi Al-Tazi in Oman in 1978 entitled: 'Historical Contacts between the *Maghreb* and Oman' (he refers in particular to the far *Maghreb*, with some reservations as to the occasional exaggerations)[110].

In the second half of this century Sheikh Abu Al-Qassem Al-Baradi has concerned himself with counting Ibadhi writings, thereby confirming the wealth of Omani and *Mashraqi* writing which has enriched the written heritage of the *Maghreb* in a study entitled: 'And these are the Compositions of our Friends the *Mashriqis*'. *Al-Musnad*, Al-Rabee's book of Hadith; Abi Al-Hassan's *Jami*', this being one of the collection of books which Sheikh Abu Moussa Issa bin Zakaria Al-Yarasni brought to the island of Gerba from Oman[111]; *Al-D'aa'im Al-Asl*, of which he remarks: 'Some of our Omani friends told me in Mecca in the year 75 of the many verses which there were in this book in Oman and it is this book which we have now in our hands'[112].

Of another book he says: 'Another contemporary work mentioned is that entitled *Kashef Al-Ghumah fi Akhtalaf Al-Ummah* of which no equal exists in the literature of the faithful. I had assigned a group of companions from Mecca to copy it'. This letter is strong evidence of the links between the *Maghrabis*, *Mashriqis* and Omanis in general and confirms that the dialogue continues; for all relate back to one school and all endeavour to enrich it with their writing or interpretation or in completing a work where the author has abandoned it.

The historian Al-Baradi did everything he could to communicate all of the written compositions that came his way and which distinguished in arrangement and classification the work of Jebel Nafoussah and the *Mashriqis* from that of the *Maghrabis*. This methodological clarification facilitates matters for the reader. While dealing with this great task Al-Baradi takes care to name with admirable objectivity as many of the books of whose existence he was aware, irrespective of whether or not he had personally seen them.

We find him apologizing strenuously for the book *Kashef Al-Ghumah* not having arrived even though the Omanis had undertaken to dispatch it to him in the month of the *Hajj* 776 AH/1375 AD. However he made his pilgrimage in 775 AH/1374 AD and we know from the Barouni Manuscript in relation to this book that it did arrive later in Gerba and bears the introductory note: 'This book *Kashef Al-Ghumah* written by our Omani writer friends and which we have sent from Mecca in 775 AH/1374 AD and to which we have devoted our hearts'[113].

From his mention of the title of the book we know that it was not that of Sarhan bin Said Al-Azkawi the full title of which is *Kashef Al-Ghumah Al-Jami*'

Li Akhbar Al-Ummah (twelfth century AH/eighteenth century AD). It looks as though they are in agreement on the matter for a great part of Al-Azkawi's book details the topic of differences in the community.

We can no longer avoid the need to put in place a precise comparative study on the *Mashriqi* and *Maghrabi* writings to show how they complement one another in demonstrating different aspects of a single viewpoint.

The Ninth and Tenth Centuries AH/Fifteenth and Sixteenth Centuries AD

There is an absolute dearth of information on the relations in the ninth century of the Hegira, and on up to the appearance of an important poem in the tenth century by the Omani poet Mohammed bin Abdullah Al-Aghbari containing 84 verses extolling the people of the *Maghreb* in Gerba, Jebel Nafoussah, Warjalan and Wadi Mizab. A number of citizens and some learned scholars are mentioned by name in this eulogy, suggesting a close acquaintance with the affairs of the *Maghreb*. The Ibadhis studied it and we are inclined to think that the poet was either thoroughly familiar with the books of biography relevant to this region or else that he managed to visit it in person. If the latter then perhaps the visit was to Jebel Nafoussah; for he speaks of it at length while he is brief about the rest. This poem is an important historical document[114] in its illustration of the extent of Oman's acquaintance with the affairs of the *Maghreb*. We would have been happier if these verses had turned their attention on some of the sheikhs of Oman at this time and on some of the sheikhs of the *Maghreb* and their mutual contacts.

In the same century, in 973 AH/1566 AD, Sheikh Abdullah bin Omar bin Ziad bin Ahmed Al-Bahlawi Al-Omani, in an ode[115] consisting of 272 verses to his *Maghrabi* brothers, describes amongst other matters: the superiority of the Ibadhis and their scholars in the *Maghreb* and *Mashriq* and his partiality to their common traits; the features that distinguish the Ibadhi rite from rival sects, along with a description of some of the controversial issues that divide them, root and branch. And though the language of this long poem is rather worn in some places, it nevertheless shows the desire of the author to confirm the *Maghrabis* in their faith by giving an account of its splendid history and of the collaboration of its *ulema* in establishing unshakeably the principal, funda-mental and legal foundations of the faith on a basis of Qur'an and Sunnah.

Eleventh Century AH/Seventeenth Century AD

In the eleventh century AH the Second Nabhan dynasty came to a close to make way for the Ya'ruba Just Imamate, news of which victory reverberated throughout the *Maghreb*. We have been fortunate in obtaining a copy of the letter of congratulation which was sent by the *Maghrebis* on the installation of Imam Nasir bin Murshid Al-Ya'rubi (1024-1050 AH/1616-1641 AD)[116]. The letter was sent to Oman by the *Maghrabi* scholar Ibrahim bin Abdullah Al-Shamakhi Al-Yafarni Al-Ibadhi.

From the letter we can extrapolate something of their feelings of longing for a similar return in their region:

Our hearts go out to you and our being takes joy in the mention of you and our souls yearn to see you, and how can it not be thus. Allah says: "On those who believe and work deeds of righteousness will the Most Gracious bestow love (Surat Mariam, 19/96)". And the Prophet said that those who love one

another for the sake of Allah shall rest on platforms of musk in the shadow of the throne on a day when there is no other shade but this. And he said that whoever has loved a people, he shall be with them on the Day of Judgment.
We are gladdened by this Hadith *and there is no doubt but our longing for you increases day by day and our love with the passage of the months and years. It is constantly renewed and no language can describe it nor any man express it. We have been separated from you by deserts and barbarians, by water and jungle and the ocean deep and a hungry rabble. We have encountered powerful dreads and awesome barriers; and if by any means we could be enabled to salute your just succession and rich reward and deserved success we would have come with flying feet to share your joy. But let us say to you, may time allow us to witness your noble visage and the growth of our faith through your efforts and may our souls all benefit from its triumph.*

If this letter shows anything it demonstrate the extent of the good relations between the Ibadhis of *Mashriq* and *Maghreb*.

Justice flourished in Oman under the Ya'ruba. The Imam Bal'arab bin Sultan ruled for 13 years years of stability from 1091-1104 AH/1681-1693 AD, and during this time facilitated the visit to the region of a *Maghrabi* scholar, one Sheikh Omar bin Said bin Mohammed bin Zakaria Al-Gerbi Al-Ibadhi. The visitor was overjoyed to see justice manifest and the support enjoyed in the state for the Sunnah, but noticed that there was little regard for the seats of learning. He did not hold back on his advice and provoked the Imam by directing him to pay more attention to knowledge and education.

Sheikh Al-Salimi transcribed this advice into his *Tohfat Al-'Ayian*[117]. It is an important historical document insofar as it demonstrates the *Maghrabi's* amazement at the flourishing circumstances of Ibadhism in Oman. It notes the beneficial effects of educational centres in protecting the heart of a nation and gives the example of such schools being maintained in Gerba, despite its harsh circumstances. It confirms that the great scholar of the age at Gerba was Sheikh Abu Zaid bin Ahmed bin Abi Sitta[118]; it named the most important affairs of some of the Nafoussans and some of the Gerbans and the Bani Muss'ab and it spurred the establishment of schools in every fort throughout the country, where great care was afforded to both teachers and students as the precious resources of the nation.

Al-Salimi confirms that the Sheikh's counsel had a tremendously positive effect and was to be the launchpad of a scientific renaissance personally directed by the Imam from his base at Jibrin Fort. 'It was said that out of this school graduated 50 *ulema*, all of them of the status of orthodox judges and muftis'[119]. Meanwhile education became mandatory throughout the country. Limitations of scope compel us to end our account at this point - in the hope that we will be able to return to an analysis of the texts available to us relevant to the following centuries, in particular the period spanning the thirteenth and fourteenth centuries when for instance communications flourished once again with the celebrated Imam Sheikh Mohammed Atfish (1332 AH/1914 AD). But this correspondence alone merits an independent study[120].

Cultural & Scientific Movements in Oman Since the Beginning of Islam

From the very beginning of the Islamic period, Oman's contribution to Islamic civilization was evident in every field of human endeavour: in science, politics and economics and in its most notable and valuable legacy to mankind, the recording of scientific knowledge.

The student of civilization will be aware that the Islamic nation was and is in the vanguard of the quest for knowledge, as witnessed by the treatises on every major art and scientific subject left to us by Muslim scholars. The Omanis not only contributed much and from the earliest days of Islam to this search for knowledge; they were the first to be concerned with the studies of doctrine and language while making a simultaneous impact on science, art and literature.

They helped set the foundations of the expanding edifice of Islamic civilization and breathed life into the accumulating body of wisdom and learning which was to enrich mankind. The Omanis excelled in scholarship and wisdom, ignoring geographical, ideological boundaries in these pursuits which they shared with savants from within and without the known Islamic world.

To study Oman's heritage is to be made aware of the great many scholars and writers Oman has produced and of the wide net they cast in their scholarship, always returning to the Holy Qur'an and Hadith as reference and guide for their thought.

In Basra, in the first centuries of the Islamic era, the Omanis played a fundamental and prominent role in generating new ideas and communicating these to the far corners of the Islamic world. Wisdom they likened to a bird 'who laid her eggs in Medina, hatched them in Basra and flew to Oman'[121].

Historians, writers and biographers all make reference to Oman's many writers and their works, the most outstanding of these being in jurisprudence and Hadith, language and literature, history and biography. A number of schools specializing in these disciplines played an important part in enriching culture and thought both in Oman and beyond.

The Omani School of Islamic Doctrinal Science
(Law, the Holy Qur'an, *Hadith* and Theology)

There is considerable evidence that from the dawn of Islam - and continuing up to modern times - that Omanis have been involved in the science of jurisprudence and Hadith, pioneering this work from the first century of the Hegira (seventh century AD). A brief summary of the most important of the schools or *Madrassahs* follows.

Encyclopaedia of Islamic law from Oman.

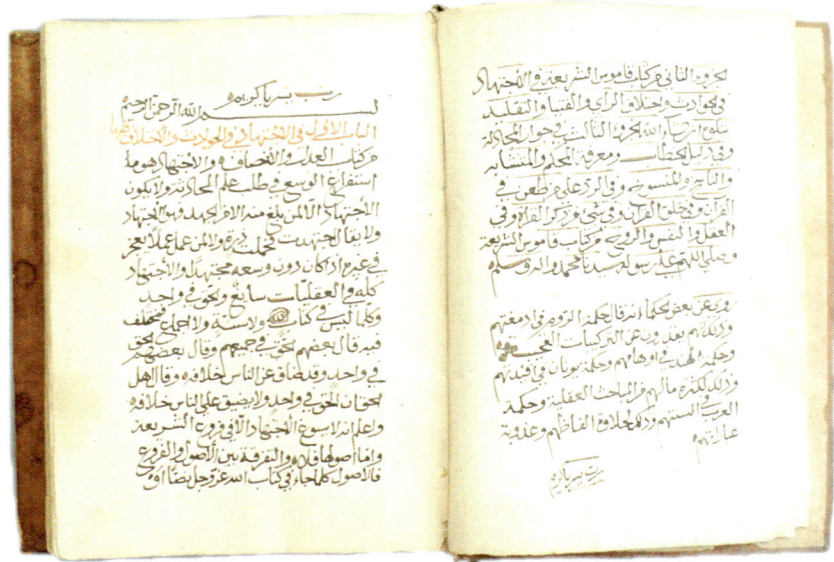

In the first century of the Hegira the ongoing links between Medina and Oman were very strong, most of the Azdi Medinans acknowledging connections with the Azd of Oman. Many Omanis settled in Medina itself. Some were Companions of the Prophet, among these Sohar bin Al-Abbas Al-Abdi, mentioned by Ibn Nadim in his book *Al-Fahrest*. Sohar recorded three major *Hadiths*, as noted by Ibn Hajar in his work *Al-Asaba fi Tamayyez Al-Sahhaba*. He also composed an anthology of proverbs which Ibn Al-Nadim described as a legendary work in its field.

In the second half of the first century of the Hegira the Jaber bin Zaid Al-Azdi Al-Omani *Madrassah* was established in Basra, the first of its kind. Many Omanis assembled here to study with the master, returning home to propagate the religious wisdom and knowledge of doctrine and law which they had learned.

Jaber bin Zaid was born, as we know, before the end of the Caliphate of Omar bin Al-Khattab, that is between 18 and 22 AH[122] (639 and 642 AD) in the township of Farq in the *Wilaya* of Nizwa in Oman. Jaber was from the tribe of Amr bin Al-Yahmad, a prominent Azdi tribe in Oman to whom the illustrious Banu Kharous are also related. He was known as Abu Al-Sha'tha, after his daughter of that name, whose tomb is to this day renowned in Farq.

Jaber bin Zaid began his education in his native Oman before travelling to Basra to further his studies in jurisprudence, for this city was a major centre of learning in the Islamic world at this time, having strong geographical, cultural and human links with Oman since these were first traced by Utbah bin Ghazwan at the time of Omar bin Al-Khattab. He was deemed among the foremost citizens of Islam and Abdullah bin Al-Abbas - or Al-Bahr - was one of his greatest teachers, a man proud of the student who had attained such depth of scholarship in his studies of the Holy Qur'an, Hadith and *Shari'a*. Jaber also transmitted the wisdom of Aisha, Mother of the Faithful, and of Anas bin Malik, Abdullah bin Omar bin Al-Khattab and other Companions of the Prophet.

Though Abu Al-Sha'tha spent his working career in Basra in the time of the Ummayyad Caliphate, when the hand of Al-Hajjaj bore down heavily on political life, he nevertheless applied himself to his religious mission and encouraged his students to pursue the ideals of the Just Imamate, founded as it was on fundamental Islamic teachings and principles. He prepared an encyclopaedia which was known popularly as the *Diwan* or *Diwan Jaber* during the second half of the first century AH. It was said that the Caliph Abdul Mulik bin Marwan and his sons seized the book and banned its distribution. The Abbassids did likewise[123]. *Diwan Jaber* was a substantial work in which Jaber put down the Hadith he had heard from the Prophet's Companions along with his views on interpretation and jurisprudence.

During the reign of the notorious *Wali* Al-Hajjaj bin Youssef, Abu Al-Sha'tha was banished for a time to Oman, precisely when or for how long the sources do not indicate. He died in Basra in 93 AH/711 AD, having delivered his teaching to innumerable students[124], who brought it back with them to their homelands. This included the many Omanis who had sought his wisdom in Basra and returned to Oman in the spirit of the holy teaching: 'Let a group of men pioneer the teachings of God, so they can preach to the people what they have learnt'. Many of these were learned *ulemas* , foremost amongst them being *ulema* and 'Grand Sheikh', Basheer bin Al-Munthir Al-Nizwi from Nizwa. He was one of the Bani Nafi tribe, descendants of Sama bin Lu'ai Al-Qartini, grandfather of the Bani Ziad who are settled in Oman. Second in importance was Al-Munir bin Al-Nir Al-Ja'alani Al-Riyami of the Bani Hadhrami Al-Riyami. Third was Moussa bin Abi Jaber Al-Azkawi of the Bani Dhaba of the Bani Sama bin Lu'ai. He was leader of the *ulema* who had pledged allegiance to the Imam Al-Warith bin Ka'b Al-Kharousi. Fourth was Mahboub bin Al-Raheel bin Saif bin Hubira of the Bani Makzum who went by the name of Abi Sufian, and the fifth was Mohammed bin Al-Ma'ala Al-Kindi of the Fassah clan from

Wadi Al-Sahten in Rustaq.

Sohar Al-Abdi and Jaber bin Zaid were not the only Omani jurisprudents of the first century AH. There were others, among them Salim bin Zakwan Al-Hilali who published his views on the *Wilaya* (succession) and other issues of law. This man was a student of Jaber and a leading *Mujtahid* or trusted legal theologian.

The second century of the Hegira produced more prominent Omani *ulema*, Rabee' bin Habib Al-Farahidi Al-Azdi, a Basran Omani, being one. He hailed from Batinah and went to Basra on a mission of scholarship, for the premier learned men of Oman at that time were resident in Basra. There the young Al-Rabee' met the Imam Abu Al-Sha'tha (Jaber bin Zaid). It was said that the body of jurisprudential thought had come from three men: Abu Abidu, Abi Nuh and Dhamam bin Al-Sa'ib Al-Omani.

Al-Rabee' bin Habib spent most of his life in Basra acquiring wisdom and later passing it on, returning at the end of his life to Oman. He died in 170 AH/786 AD[125]. His book *Al-Jami' Al-Sahih* has been reprinted many times, most recently in Jerusalem in 1381 AH/1961 AD. The Egyptian National Library in Cairo contains a manuscript *Musanid Al-Rabee'* (Al-Rabee's Chain of Transmitters) under the reference 28512B. This manuscript was arranged by Abu Ya'qub Youssef bin Ibrahim Al-Warjalani[126], a sixth century AH/twelfth century AD North African *ulema*, and interpreted in recent times by the *ulema* Nur Al-Din Al-Salimi and it is deemed by the Ibadhis a major source work on the Prophet's Hadith.

Another second century scholar was Abu Safra Abdul Mulik bin Abi Safra who compiled the noted *Jami' Abi Safra* containing Hadith confirmed by Jaber bin Zaid. Abi Safra's transmission source was Sheikh Al-Rabee bin Habib whose source was Sammam bin Al-Sa'ib from Jaber bin Zaid.

Abu Safra was with the Sohar School of Jurisprudence headed by Sheikh Mahboub bin Al-Raheel as mentioned previously. This school drew students from all over Oman. Amongst its many students were his sons Mohbar and Mohammed and the abovementioned Abu Safra Abdul Mulik bin Safra; Moussa bin Ali and Azzam bin Saqr, along with his grandson Abdullah ibn Mohammed bin Mahboub and Abu Al-Mo'thir Al-Salt bin Khamis Al-Kharousi, all of these among the foremost thinkers and savants of Oman.

In the third century AH schools of jurisprudence emerged in a major way in Oman. A leading *Madrassah* of the time was that of Moussa bin Abi Jaber at Izki, which produced a large number of distinguished *ulemas* and scientists from Nizwa and Sija, including bin Ghilan Al-Sijani and Suleiman bin Othman Al-Aqari Al-Nizwi and others. Writing was at its peak, with many writers and authors in religion and jurisprudence producing significant works, among these:

- *Jami' Abu Ali fi Al-Fiqh*, a treatise on doctrine in two volumes by Sheikh Moussa bin Ali.
- A book on doctrinal sources written by Sheikh Muhammad bin Mahboub Al-Raheeli in 70 volumes, it was referred to in *Al-Jawaher* (The Jewels) by Abu Al-Qasim Al-Baradi and was highly regarded by this eighth century *ulema.*
- Four valuable books in doctrinal studies and beliefs by Sheikh Bashir bin

Mahboub:

    i.   *Al-Khazana* (70 Vols.)

    ii. *Al-Moharba*

    iii. *Al-Tawheed* (Oneness of God)

    iv. *Al-Bustan*

- Two books by Sheikh Abu Al-Mu'tamar As-Salt Bin Khamis Al-Kharousi, one on history and the other on doctrinal studies entitled: *Al-Bayan Wa Al-Burhan* (The Clear Evidence).

- Another legendary work was the many-volumed *Jami' Ibn Ja'far*, by Abu Al-Azhar bin Mohammad bin Ja'far Al-Azkawi (the first edition of which was printed in Oman by the Ministry of National Heritage and Culture in three volumes).

- Among the works of another third century theologian, Abu Al-Hawari were:

    i.   The major work *Jami' Abu Al-Hawari* (a book in two large volumes - now reissued in five volumes).

    ii. The book of *Al-Deraya* (Enlightenment), explaining five hundred *Ayas* or verses concerned with the administration of justice (currently in print).

    iii. A letter of reply to the Ibadhis of Hadramaut on doctrinal matters.

    iv. A work of jurisprudence by this theologian has been lost and is not now available to scholars.

The art of collective writing grew at this time with the Omanis pioneering the collective compilation of an encyclopaedia. This was the time of Imam Ghassan bin Abdullah (192-207 AH/808-822 AD) and a typical example was *Kitab Al-Ashiakh* (The Book of the Sheikhs) written by a number of learned Sheikhs during a sojourn at Dama, now Al-Seeb. This work extended to many volumes, some of which have been lost, and was written along the lines of a modern encyclopaedia.

In the fourth century AH, *Ulema* Abu Mohammed Abdullah bin Barka Al-Selim Al-Bahlawi established from his own funds his celebrated *Madrassah Al-Darh* in the city of Bahla. From this school graduated the most distinguished of Oman's *ulema* of the era including Abu Al-Hassan Al-Bessiwi, as well as 40 *ulemas* and jurisprudents from *Al-Maghreb* (North Africa) along with many others. Among its illustrious teachers were Abu Malik Ghassan bin Mohammed bin Al-Khodar Al-Salani, Abu Marwan bin Suleiman bin Mohammed bin Habib and Imam Said bin Abdullah bin Mohammed bin Mahboub.

At the same time the Omani library was flourishing, adding to the stockpile of Islamic books numerous valuable works on doctrinal matters, Islamic trans-actions, regulations, and *fatwas* or legal opinions. Foremost amongst these was the body of writing of *Ulema* Abu Mohammad Abdullah bin Barka as follows:

- *Al-Jami' fi Asul Al-Fiqh* (2 volumes), one of the most important and frequently reprinted extant works on doctrinal science.

- *Al-Taqayyed*, a record of Sheikh Abi Malik Al-Salani's pronouncements on the diverse founding principles and philosophies of nations.

- *Al-Ta'aruf*, a study of social customs and traditions.

- Annotation of *Jami' Ibn Ja'far*
- *Al-Mawazana* (Book of Analogy).
- *Al-Mufsidat* (The Book of Wrongdoings).
- *Manthourat Abi Mohammed* (The Prose of Abi Mohammed).
- *Kitab Al-Iqleed* (The Key)

Another *ulema*, Sheikh Abu Said Mohammed bin Said Al-Kadmi al-Na'bi, enriched the Omani library with many valuable manuscripts, among these:

- *Kitab Al-Istiqama fi Al-Wilaya Wa Al-Bira'a* on the merits of straight dealing in government, a printed work.
- *Kitab Al-Mu'tabar fi Al-Fiqh*, (The Ideal in Doctrinal Studies), an encyclopaedic reference work of significance of which only two volumes now remain out of nine. These have been made available in print by the Ministry of National Heritage and Culture of Oman.
- *Kitab Al-Jami' Al-Mufid*, a collection of *fatwas* (legal opinions) in two volumes also printed by the Ministry of National Heritage and Culture of Oman.
- *Kitab Ziadat Al-Ashraf*, a manuscript in four volumes written after the manner of the *Kitab Al-Ashraf* of Ibn Al-Munthir Al-Nisaburi, and one of the most valuable extant works in its field.

The scholar Abi Said Al-Kadmi Al-Na'bi was a prominent theologian and his school opened its doors to students who came from afar in search of learning. Here the controversy surrounding the Imamate of Rashed bin Al-Nathar and the removal of the Imam Al-Salt bin Malik were debated heatedly and in depth, resulting in the emergence of the two factions, the Nizwani and Rustaqi respectively. The Imam Abu Said succeeded in facing down and subsequently reconciling the two parties and establishing his position and views after the long and bitter struggle which had torn these two opposing factions. His resolution of this matter he committed to writing in his treatise *Kitab Al-Istiqama* - and the door finally closed on the strife between the Nizwanis and the Rustaqis.

Abu Qahtan bin Khaled bin Qahtan Al-Hajari also belonged to this era; his celebrated book on religion and jurisprudence was issued in two volumes under the title *Al-Jami' fi Usul Al-Din wa Al-Fiqh*.

In the fifth century AH /eleventh century AD we find more eminent Muslim scholars enriching the Islamic libraries and *madrassahs* with many significant works of scholarship and law. The most illustrious of these *ulema* were:

Abu Al-Hassan Al-Basiawi, who wrote:
- *Jami' Abi Al-Hassan Al-Basiawi* book (in four volumes, printed by the Oman Ministry of National Heritage and Culture). This book is written after the manner of Abi Mohammed's book on the origins and principles of doctrine.
- *Mukhtasar Al-Basiawi* (Al-Basiawi's Concise Works) (also published by the Ministry of National Heritage and Culture).
- *Suyugh Al-Ni'am* (still in manuscript form).

- *Kitab Al-Muqtassid* on Religion and Doctrinal Rules
- *Kitab Al-Sirah Al-Kebira* (The Great Biography)
- Numerous other letters.

Abu Zakaria Yahya Bin Said:
- His important book was *Al-Aydah fi Ahkam Al-Qadaa*, a leading work on judicial verdicts (published by the Oman Ministry of National Heritage & Culture of Oman in four volumes).

Najad bin Ibrahim Al-Manahi, whose books include:
- *Haqai'q Al-Adla* (Facts about Evidence) (5 volumes)
- *Al-Irshad* (The Guide Book)
- *Al-Hawala* (The Book of Transformation)
- *Kitab Al-Sirah* (The Biography)

Said bin Quraysh, whose book *Al-Aydah* (Clarifications) exists in three volumes.

Mohammad bin Ibrahim Al-Kindi, author of three works.
- His major work *Bayan Ash-Shar* on Theology and *Shari'a* (72 volumes) is a comprehensive encyclopaedia encompassing the pronouncements of the progressive scholar on the subject of *Shari'a* (Islamic Law). Al-Kindi transcribed these sayings with great precision and conscientiousness and presented this vast work to Oman's Islamic library as an invaluable source reference for scholars. This *opus* has been issued in print by the Ministry of National Heritage and Culture of Oman.
- His famous epic poem *Al-'Abiriya* on the subject of asceticism and spiritual counsel and the description of and longing for paradise which was interpreted by Mohammed bin Youssef Atfish.
- *Kitab Al-Naghma* (The Melody), a poem.

The scholar Al-Kindi had studied at a well-known *Madrassah* of his time, the *Madrassah* of Abi Ali Al-Hassan bin Ahmed bin Mohammed Al-Nizwi, who came from a wealthy family in Al-Aqar. This school turned out many learned scholars, as did its near neighbour, the *Madrassah* of Sheikh Saleh bin Waddah, author of *Kitab Al-Basra* (The Book of Basra). This latter taught many distinguished theologians, among them the eminent Mohammed bin Ali bin Abdul Baqi Al-Aqari Al-Nizwi and Ahmed bin Khalil Al-Sijani, author of *Kitab Al-Ayjaz* (The Book of Conciseness) and other learned jurisprudents who composed many scholarly works and carried the issues of their day.

A third *Madrassah* opened in the fifth century, that of Abi Ali who was the judge of Imam Al-Khalil Shathan who ruled Oman in or around 406 AH /1015 AD. Abi Ali Al-Qadi established his *Madrassah* at Al-Aqar in Nizwa where it was soon crammed with students and scholars. The ethos was ascetic and, though many students from affluent backgrounds came to study there, their money was not accepted. This school produced many fine scholars in the time of Al-Khalil bin Shathan.

The sixth century AH/twelfth century AD found yet more schools being founded by distinguished *ulemas* who also bequeathed a rich legacy of written works, among them:

Mohammed bin Moussa Al-Kindi, who wrote:
- *Al-Kifayya* (Sufficiency) a comprehensive work in 51 volumes, now lost as
- *Jalaa Al-Basa'ir* (The Book of Visions), on the subject of asceticism and spiritual counsel.

Ahmed bin Abdullah Al-Kindi, whose works are as follows:
- *Al-Musannaf* (42 volumes) published by the Ministry of National Heritage and Culture of Oman.
- *Al-Jawhari Al-Mukhtasar* on the science of philosophy and logic.
- *Al-Takhsis* on government and disavowal.
- *Al-Tas'hil* on religious duties.
- *Al-Ahtidaa* a history of events in Oman.
- *Al-Tayseer* a grammatical book.
- *Al-Thakhira* a book of theology.
- Other documents and letters on varying topics.

By the seventh century AH /thirteenth century AD we find the following prominent contributions to the growing Omani library of Islamic works:

Othman bin Abdullah Al-Asam, who left the following books:
- *Al-Taj* (The Crown), a book of jurisprudence in 51 volumes which has unfortunately been lost to us.
- *Al-Noor fi 'Ilm Al-Tawhid* (Light in the Science of the Oneness (of God))
- *Al-Basira* (The Vision) on worship and conduct.
- *Kitab Al-Ahkam* (The Book of Religious Rules).
- *Kitab Al-Anwar* on doctrinal sources.

Mohammed bin Said Al-Qalhati, who wrote *Al-Kashef Wa Al-Bayan* (2 volumes), in print.

After the seventh century AH many *Madrassahs* emerged to teach jurisprudence and doctrinal science in Oman. One of the most famous of these was the Ya'ruba, established inside the Jibrin Fort during the Ya'ruba dynasty (the rule of Imam Bal'arab bin Sultan Al-Ya'rubi, eleventh century AH/seventeenth century AD). The most distinguished *ulemas* of the day graduated from this school, chief amongst them the scholar Khalaf bin Sanan Al-Ghafari, the scholar Mohammed bin Abdullah bin Jum'a bin Ubaidan, and the poet Al-Habasi Rashed bin Khamis. This celebrated Ya'ruba *Madrassah* was the Jewel in the Crown of that era after Imam Nasir bin Murshid. Its influence was far-reaching and extends to this day.

The era of these religious and legal *Madrassahs* continued into the time of the Al-Busaidi, among them the *Madrassah* of the blind scholar Habib bin Salem bin Mohammed Ambusaidi, who had sought learning from an early age. Many leading magistrates and *ulemas* benefited from this man's wisdom. It was during the Imamate of Imam Ahmed bin Said Al-Busaidi and the school was at

Al-Aqar in Nizwa. Next door to it was the *Madrassah* of *Ulema* Abi Nabhan Ja'id bin Khamis bin Mubarak Al-Khalili Al-Kharousi who dedicated his large mosque, *Masjid Al-Hashaa*, to the teaching of his students whom he paid for, being a man of substantial means. Students flocked from towns and villages to study with him. Occasionally he would relocate to the surrounding villages such as Al-Alia, Badi and Al-Awabi. Amongst his pupils was his son the *Ulema* Nasir bin Abi Nabhan who was renowned for his wisdom and asceticism, as well as Sheikh Said bin Mohammed bin Rashid bin Basheer Al-Kharousi, Hassan Darwish, the celebrated astronomer of the Al-Shoh clan, and the blind Sheikh Mansour bin Mohammed bin Nasir bin Khamis Al-Kharousi, who annotated the *Lammiah* of Ibn Al-Nadhr in *Manasek Al-Hokm*, pointing to his encompassing skills in law, language and letters.

The students of the scholar Abi Nabhan bin Ja'id bin Khamis Al-Kharousi were many also, as were his writings, the most significant of which were:

Kitab Al-Diqaq (The Book of Rigours) and *Kitab Al-Masajed Wa Al-Madaress* (The Book of Mosques and Schools); a book on the succession of Imams and one on fasting and allegiance, an interpretation of the definitions of *halal* and *haram* in animal (flesh), a volume on jurisprudence in the form of question and answer; a commentary on his poem *Hayat Al-Mahaj fi Al-Solouk*; (The Inner Life in Matters of Conduct); an encyclopaedia of jurisprudence from fundamentals to issues of loss of faith; an abridgement of *Al-Nahaj fi Manasek Al-Hajj* (The Right Way in the Rites of Pilgrimage); a book on Sanctity; a biography of the kings of old *Moqtada Al-Nosah wa Al-Irshad* (The Need for Guidance and Counsel); *Maqalid Al-Tanzil Li'idrak Haqa'iqih Bal-Ta'weel* (The Keys to Revelation in the Attainment of its Truths through Interpretation), an encyclopaedia of many parts. This book may be found in the library of the Ministry of National Heritage and Culture executed in the handwriting of the author. His other books include one on alchemy, one on the principles of fortified houses and *Al-Maghanem fi Al-Khalas min Al-Madhalem* on the benefits of excising iniquity, also handwritten by the author. This latter book is in the library of Sayyid Mohammed bin Ahmed Al-Busaidi. Also by this author is a book on medicine; and a collection of verse entitled *Nafa'is Al-Aqban* in the poetry collection of Abi Nabhan; a book of grammar and a book on morphology and scholastic theology.

In the thirteenth century AH/nineteenth century AD, Sheikh Nasir bin Abi Nabhan School of Jurisprudence grew to prominence, after incidents in the village of his father Sheikh Abi Nabhan, when his priceless library was gutted and its contents of more than 6000 books looted. Only a few of these were spared. Following this calamity Sheikh Nasir resolved to make his home in Muscat and there he founded his school at Darsait, later transferring to Bosher. Students flocked here and soon his reputation based on his skills, wisdom and personal sacrifice in the higher interest of learning had penetrated afar. This was in the time of Sultan Said bin Sultan. The most outstanding *ulema* graduated at his hands, among them the scholar and magistrate Said bin Khalfan bin Ahmed bin Saleh Al-Khalili and the blind scholar Muhanna bin Khalfan bin Mohammed Al-Busaidi, along with the poet historian and jurisprudent Humaid bin Mohammed bin Ruzaiq, his inseparable friend.

There is no doubt but that scholarship flowered in Sheikh Nasir's day and the time he spent at Muscat. Later he moved to Zanzibar amongst the retinue of Sultan Said bin Sultan and there he put his learning and wisdom to good use, benefiting large masses of people. He had not long more to live however, and died in Zanzibar in 1263 AH/1847 AD. This great savant was, like his father before him, eminent in scholarship and prolific in his writing which embraced a vast body of books and scholarly treatises, among them: *Haq Al-Yaqin* a book in five volumes; *Al-Jawab* (The Answer); and *Al-Ikhlas Linour Al-'Ilm* (Allegiance to the Light of Science and Redemption), which is contained in the library of Mohammed bin Ahmed Al- Busaidi; *Nuthum Al-Solouk illa Malik Al-Muluk* (Comportment to the King of Kings), an annotation of Ibn Al-Faredh's *Al-Thai'a*; *Kitab Mubtada' Al-Asfar* (The Commencement of Journeys); *Al-Tahthib*, a book of instruction; *Al-Kashef fi 'Ilm Al-Harq* (Discovery in the Science of Combustion); *Al-Safa Al-Musfa* (Cloudless Serenity); *Ghaiyat Al-Muna* (The Goal of Destiny); *Al-Ma'arej fi Al-Ziarej; Al-Risa'il Al-Masawna fi Al-Israr Al-Maknawna; Al-Maknawna fi Ashkal Al-Masawna; Mustaghraq Al-Ashwaq fi 'Ilm Al-Awfaq; Rawdhat Al-Uloom fi 'Ilm Al-Horouf wa Al-Nujoum; Dorrat Al-Afaq fi 'Ilm Al-Harouf wa Al-Awfaq; Kitab Nayl Al-Ashraf Alla Al-Horouf wa Al-Awfaq; Aja'ib Al-Afaq fi Ghara'ib Al-Awfaq; Kitab Qabas Al-Anwar wa Jami' Al-Asrar; Al-Kanz Al-Bahar fi Sharh Horouf Al-Malik Al-Dhaher; Muntaha Al-Karamat fi Asrar Al-Riadhat; Al-Ma'arej; Risalat Al-Awdha'; Taraf Al-Altaf; Al-Sirr Al-Khafi fi Al-Shekl Al-Alfi; Al-Sirr Al-'Ali fi Khawas Al-Nabat Baltadbir Al-Sawahili; Al-Sirr Al-Mo'atham; Al-Tanbih; Al-Risala Al-Fawz; Al-Risala Al-Medidia; Salamat Al-Hal*. These works treated of a wide diversity of subject matter, from elucidations of Islamic law to worship, linguistics, astronomy and plant life.

The scholar Said bin Khalfan Al-Khalili, who opened the doors of his school in the same century, left us six books of his own composition, including a major work on morphology *Kitab Maqalid Al-Sarf* (The Key to Morphology).

Many noted scholars studied under this sheikh and magistrate. One was the Imam Azzan bin Qais Al-Busaidi and his son Sheikh Ahmed bin Said, as well as Sheikh Juma'a bin Khusaif Al-Hina'i and Sheikh Rashid bin Aziz Al-Khoseibi, who instructed Sheikh Said and his son Ahmed. The lectures were held in the Sama'il Mosque which was the leading *madrassah* of its time. Sama'il was never devoid of scholars, who published their letters and learning in the king's quarters in that city while the school continued to graduate scholars, jurisprudents and literary men.

The most famous of the *madrassahs* at the outset of the fourteenth century AH was that of Sheikh Nur Al-Din Al-Salimi, who gave up most of his life to the quest for knowledge and science until he became teacher to all of the *ulema*. Students came in quest of knowledge from all over Oman. His greatest efforts went into the creation and classification of the sciences and the teaching of students who absorbed his wisdom to become luminaries themselves and ensure that the *madrassah*, despite its relative youth, wielded a commanding influence.

This venerable scholar bequeathed a rich legacy of work to the library of Omani authors, covering a breadth of interest, from the fundaments of religion and jurisprudence to history and the Arabic language. Some noteworthy works were: *Madarej Al-Kamal wa Ma'arej Al-Amal*, arranged and annotated (18 volumes); *Anwar Al-Aqul fi Usul Al-Din; Bahjat Al-Anwar*, interpretations of

Anwar Al-Uqul; *Mashareq Al-Anwar, Anwar Al-Aqul*, and *Al-Jami 'Al-Sahih* (3 volumes); *Jawhar Al-Nitham* (in 2 volumes); *Tohfat Al-'Ayian bi Sirat Ahl Oman* (2 volumes); *Al-Manhal Al-Safi fi Al-'Arudh wa Al-Qawafi; Talqin Al-Subian fima Yalsam Al-Insan; Bulugh Al-Amal fi Al-Naha*w, on aspects of religion, biography and grammar.

In the fourteenth century AH the torch passed to the *Madrassah* of Imam Mohammed bin Abdullah Al-Khalili in Nizwa. From this great school issued more than 40 judges, as well as jurisprudents, men of letters, writers, scribes and savants. By this time there were academies in almost every province of Oman, in Bahla, Hamra, Rustaq, Al-Awabi, Wadi Al-Ma'awil, Nakhal, Sama'il, Ibra, Al-Qabil, Badiah, Al-Mudhaibi and Sinaw.

The rule of the Ya'rubas and of the Al-Busaidis were each characterized by patronage of learning and this climate nurtured schools which produced *ulemas* and creative writers. We have not dealt comprehensively with the developments of these two dynastic eras for fear of exceeding the scope of this work, of the vast wealth of original, interpretative and creative work, exemplified by the following small selection: Ahmed bin Khalil Al-Sijani's *Al-Ayjaz* and Mohammed bin Ibrahim Al-Shajebi's *Miftah Al-Sharee'ah*, both works of jurisprudence; *Marahim Al-Qoloub fi Manajat Al-Mahboub*, a sermon by the same Mohammed bin Ibrahim Al-Shajebi Al-Kindi; *Misbah Al-Dhalam* by Al-Ruqaishi; *Al-Hal wa Al-Isabah* by Ibn Wassaf; *Manhaj Al-Talebin*, by Sheikh Al-Shaqsi in 21 volumes, reproduced in print by the Oman Ministry of National Heritage and Culture; *Jawahir Al-Athar* by Sheikh Jum'a bin Ali Al-Sayeghi in 14 large volumes; *Qamoos Al-Sharee'ah* in 92 parts, currently being published by the Oman Ministry of National Heritage and Culture so that scholars may have access to its benefits; *Al-D'aaim* by Sheikh Ahmed bin Al-Nathar, who also wrote on the *Tawhid* or Oneness of God, and on jurisprudence, history and letters. These books however were burnt by one of the Nabhan rulers after he had executed the author. *Al-D'aaim* was the only book of this man's prodigious

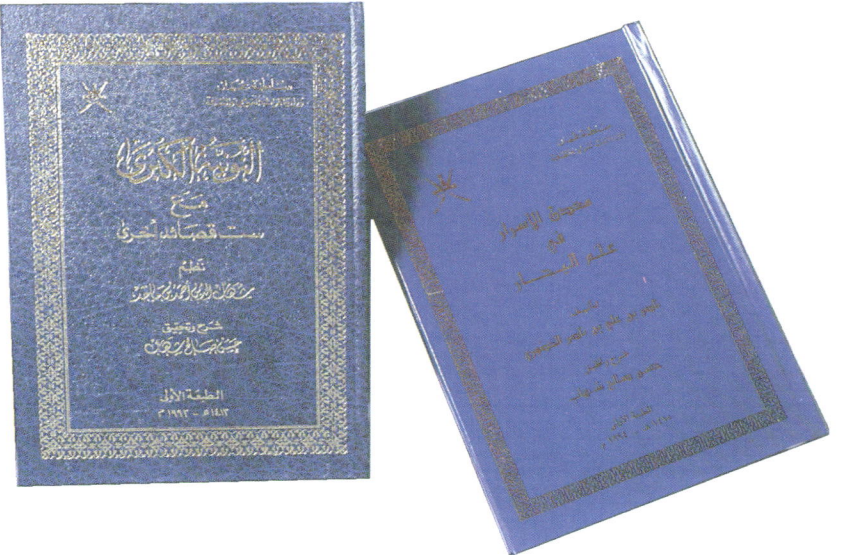

Omani books.

writings to survive the holocaust. Other works were Sheikh Saif bin Nasir bin Suleiman Al-Kharousi Al-'Ariqi's *Jami' Arkan Al-Islam*; and *Manhaj Al-Talebin wa Balagh Al-Raghebin* in 22 volumes, authored by Sheikh Khamis bin Said bin Ali bin Saud Al-Shaqsi; *Al-Jawahir* by Sheikh Salem bin Said Al-Sayeghi in 15 volumes; *Kitab Lubab Al-Athar* by Sheikh Muhanna bin Khalfan Al-Busaidi, of which 14 volumes have been published; *Al-Akhbar wa Al-Athar* by Sheikh Salim bin Abdullah bin Rashed Al-Busaidi (2 volumes); *Tadhkirat Al-Hukam fi M'ana Al-Da'awa wa Al-Ahkam* by Sheikh Suleiman bin Mubarak bin Ali Al-Busaidi. There were many other *ulemas* who produced significant compositions, among these: Sheikh Nasr bin Salim bin 'Udayim Al-Rawahi, whose prolific output included: *Nithar Al-Jawhar fi Al-Athr; Kitab Al-Nisha'h Al-Mahmoudia; Al-Nour Al-Mahmmedia; Al-Nafas Al-Rahmani; Kitab Al-Futoohat Al-Samadiyah; Kitab Al-Sualat; Kitab Al-'Aqida Al-Wahbia*; a book on *Tawhid*; *Al-Mandhoum fi Al-Solouk wa Al-Ilheyat wa Al-Tawsulat*; another volume on dirges and brotherhoods, and one on his poetic arrangement of *Al-Istinhadh bi Hoquq Allah* (Awakening to the Truth of God). He was an outstanding poet and a luminous scholar.

Sheikh Mansour bin Nasir bin Mohammed bin Saif bin Mohammed bin 'Adi bin Fares Al-Farsi Al-Fanjawi, Judge to the Imam Al-Khalili and prolific author whose collected works included *Al-Durrar Al-Manthoura*, an interpretation of Sheikh Nasir bin Salem's *Al-Maqsoura*; *Riyadh Al-Azhar; Al-Durrar Al-Behiya; Taqrib Al-Athhan; Al-Ghaya Al-Quswa; Ghayat Al-Awtan; Somout Al-Fara'id; Ghayat Al-Ajtihad Madah Khair Al'; Al-Ibad Al-Rahman fi Thobout Khalg Al-Qur'an; Minnat Al-Rahman fi Iqamat Al-Jum'a fi Ahd Al-Sultan; Al-Nassa'ih fi Ahkam Al-Jawa'ih* and *Al-Durr Al-Nadhid fi Ma'rifat Al-Tawhid*.

These examples demonstrate the surpassing excellence of Oman's contribution to science and a tradition of scholarship which extends back in time to the very dawn of Islam and continued uninterrupted up to the present day.

Oman's star rose to a high point of science and erudition in the first century of the Hegira and the Omani Library commenced its accumulation of what would become a substantial and unrivalled collection of works in Hadith, interpretation, jurisprudence, history, literature and the other fields of learning. No student of Islamic civilization or of the refinements of Islamic culture can claim to have executed his task if he has not spent time acquainting himself fully with the history and development and contents of this magnificent library; in order to be aware of the great contribution and service of the *ulema* and scholars of Oman to Islamic culture, by means of their exploratory writings in every branch of learning.

Undoubtedly, there is still an abundance of evidence to be uncovered by the diligent researcher of Oman's rich and diverse heritage of knowledge, as transmitted by the authors we have mentioned and others besides. But for all that, much of Oman's legacy of authorship was lost forever in the wars and traumatic events which convulsed Oman and the Islamic region - for the Ummayyads and after them the Abbassids, the Fatimids and other powerful enemies of Ibadhism did what they could to extirpate all vestiges of its legacy.

Meanwhile such Ibadhi source writings as did survive ridicule and destruction are for the most part handwritten and not accessible to scholars. The fact is that Oman from the earliest days of Islam was home to a rich pool of writers, scientists and legal experts, of thinkers, philosophers and social strategists, soldiers and merchants.

Oman continued to give and take from the pool of knowledge, interrupted only by periods of internal strife or when its sovereignty was usurped by outside powers. Its legacy was not confined either to Oman itself and the region of Islamic influence, but extended also to the Far East and North Africa. It cannot be ignored that Oman has been a beacon and stronghold of the Islamic faith and of Arab-Islamic brotherhood and a forward citadel of Arabism and Islam.

The Madrassah of the Arabic Language, its Science and Literature

If the Omanis were prolific in the second century AH in their contribution to Hadith and jurisprudence, they outstripped all rivals in the field of language in the person of the outstanding genius of the Arab and Muslim world, Al-Khalil bin Ahmed Al-Farahidi Al-Azdi Al-Omani (100-170 AH/718-786 AD).

Al-Khalil bin Ahmed grew up in Widam Al-Sahel at Al-Musin'ah on the Batinah coast in Oman, later travelling to Basra where he would become its leading luminary. He pioneered the studies of prosody and poetic metre and became the premier teacher of language in Iraq. He outshone all others in many fields of learning, and was to become a hallmark of generations of Omani scholars[127].

The third century AH saw the rise of two great scholars, one the poet and luminary Abu Bakr Mohammed bin Al-Hassan bin Durayed (223-321 AH/838-933 AD). Ibn Durayed grew up in Oman and divided his time between Basra, Persia and Baghdad. He was first among the savants of his time in language, poetry and Arab genealogy, and succeeded to the position of Al-Khalil bin Ahmed in language, introducing many new ideas. Popularly known as 'scientist of the poets and poet of the scientists', when he died it was said that the science of language died with him. Although he lived most of his life in Iraq and died there, nevertheless Al-Mas'udi always referred to him as Omani. Ibn Durayed wrote many books, among them *Kitab Al-Jamhara* and *Kitab Al-Ishtiqaq*, both on linguistic subjects, the latter one of the most important source works on the subject of linguistic derivation, along with other useful texts[128].

The other Omani savant was the great man of letters Abu Al-Abbas Al-Mubarrad (210-286 AH/825-899 AD). Born and reared in the township of Maqa'is between Saham and Al-Khaboura on the Batinah Plain in Oman, he moved to Iraq where he soon outstripped his peers in the subjects of grammar and language. Amongst his rich output of writings were the celebrated *Al-Kamel fi Al-Adab* and *Kitab Al-Rawda, Kitab Al-Muqtadhab* and others[129].

Aba Al-Munthir, Salma bin Musallam Al-Awatbi Al-Sohari, upheld the tradition of Omani excellence with works which included a volume on the Arabic language entitled *Kitab Al-Ibana*, a leading work in its field.

Oman was celebrated for its poets from the pre-Islamic era. Malik bin Fahm was an example, along with his sons and others[130]. These were among the poets who lived at the turn of the pre-Islamic era and they attached themselves to the

Prophetic mission at its outset. Mazin bin Ghadhuba Al-Sa'adi Al-Sama'ili Al-Tay Al-Omani, a reciter of poetry which had come down from historical sources[131], migrated to Medina in the early days of Islam, where he became a Muslim and returned to Oman to propagate the faith.

Amidst the gloom of the traumatic events which troubled Oman under the Ummayyads and Abbassids, much of Oman's poetic inheritance was lost. Some survived, as we know from history and literature[132] and the comments of Thabit Qutna Al-Ataki[133]. As noted above, Ibn Durayed was a poet and man of letters who gave expression to the events that happened in Oman in two poems written after the Rawda incident at Tanouf which occurred during the civil strife in Oman following the removal of the Imam Al-Salt bin Malik (273 AH/886 AD). Al-Awatbi recalled these two poems and Al-Salimi recorded them from him[134].

At this time and in this century the reciting of poetry was not the monopoly of Omani men. There were women poets also, most notably the woman known as Al-Zahraa who composed a lengthy appeal in verse to the Imam Al-Salt bin Malik exhorting him to attack the Abyssinnians who had taken over her island home of Socotra. The Imam complied, arriving with his fleet and a tremendous army which came ashore and inflicted a crushing defeat on the invaders[135].

Some Imams were poets such as Imam Rashed bin Said Al-Yahmadi who succeeded to the Imamate after the death of Al-Khalil bin Shathan in 425 AH/1033 AD. The author of *Al-Ansab* recorded this and from him Nur Al-Din Al-Salimi brought this Imam's poetry to us in the form of an epic poem describing the events which arose out of the rebellion of some of the tribes against him[136].

When the Nabhans succeeded to power, the poet's stock rose and the market for verse spread. Many of the Nabhan kings were poets, among them Suleiman bin Mudhaffar Al-Nabhani whose *Diwan* or collection consists of love and war poems, and others. There were adept poets who extolled the Nabhan kings, among them Abu Bakr Ahmed bin Said Al-Sitali who wrote a substantial collection in this genre[137].

At the time of the Ya'ruba dynasty poetry reached a pinnacle, especially after the Ya'rubas had gained a series of victories over the Portuguese and succeeded in ousting them, and then pursuing them as far as Africa and the Indian Ocean. The poets celebrated these great victories, among them Khalfan bin Sinan bin Khalfan bin Uthaim Al-Ghafri who described the triumphs and conquests of the Imam Sultan bin Saif in a long poem relayed by Al-Salimi in his *Tohfah*[138]. Sheikh Mohammed bin Mas'ud Al-Sarmi did likewise in a long poem describing the march of this Imam to Bata and its conquest[139].

In the time of the Imam Bal'arab bin Sultan bin Saif lived the illustrious poet Rashid bin Khamis Al-Habasi, who was born in the village of Ain Bani Sarekh in the province of Dhahira in Oman in 1089 AH/1678 AD. Having lost his sight as a child the young Rashid moved to Jibrin after the death of his father and was raised there by the Imam Bal'rab who treated him with kindness. He learned the Qur'an and studied grammar, morphology and language, developing into a great and skilled poet. He lived to a great age and ended his days at Nizwa. Over his lifetime he wrote many poems in praise of Bal'arab and of his brother the Imam Saif bin Sultan who succeeded him as well as a description of the fort at Jibrin[140]. The Imam Bal'arab bin Sultan was a poet and this was no doubt the basis of his encouragement of poetry and poets[141].

The poets continued through the Ya'ruba era to recite verse in the lyric and elegiac mode. On the death of the Imam Saif bin Sultan the poets lamented him in lengthy poems, among them one by Mohammed bin Saleh Al-Muntafaqi Al-Basri which has been relayed to us by Al-Salimi. This latter tells us that whereas he has not managed to master all of it he can furnish a large chunk of 64 verses which he (Al-Salimi) classes as both elegant and profound[142].

The rise of the poetic medium continued through the rule of the Al-Busaidis. Some of the sultans were reciters and lent their support to poets and writers. Sayyid Said bin Al-Imam Ahmed bin Said, who ruled Oman after the death of his father, was a reciter of verse as confirmed by Al-Salimi in his *Tohfah*[143]. Another was Al-Sayyid Hilal bin Al-Imam Ahmed bin Said (d.1236 AH). The poets of this era were many - Sheikh Amr bin 'Addi bin Amr bin Mohammed Al-Batashi (d. 1317 AH/1899 AD), Sheikh Said bin Musallam bin Salem Al-Bahri Al-Sama'ili (d. 1372 AH/1952 AD), Sheikh Suleiman bin Said bin Nasr Al-Kindi Al-Nizwi (d. 1379 AH/1959 AD), Hamoud bin Mohammed bin Said Al-Kharousi (d. 1352 AH/1933 AD), Sheikh Jum'a bin Selim bin Hashel Al-Khanjari Al-Harethi (d. 1387 AH/1967 AD), Sheikh Abdul Rahman bin Nasir bin Amer Al-Riyami Al-Azkawi (d. 1374 AH/1954 AD), Sheikh Mohammed bin Saif bin Abdullah Al-Saadi Al-Sama'ili (d. 1365 AH/1946 AD), Sheikh Abdullah bin Suleiman bin Abdullah bin Saadallah Al-Nabhani (d. 1352 AH/1933 AD), the skilled physician Said bin Rashid bin Musallam Al-Farsi Al-Sama'ili (d. 1367 AH/1947 AD), Sheikh Saif bin Salem bin Hashel Al-Maskari (d. 1343 AH/1924 AD), Sheikh Ahmed bin Abdullah bin Ahmed bin Saleh Al-Harethi (d. 1346 AH/1927 AD), Sheikh Mohammed bin Issa bin Saleh bin Ali Al-Harethi (d. 1366 AH/1946 AD), the scholar Ahmed bin Said bin Khalfan Al-Khalili Al-Sama'ili (d. 1324 AH/1906 AD), Sheikh Said bin Hamad bin Amer bin Khalfan Al-Rashedi Al-Sinawi (d. 1314 AH/1896 AD), and many many others who gave us innumerable collections of poetry - *Diwan Al-Maawli*, *Diwan Al-Nabhani* and the *Diwans* of Al-Bahlani, Ibn Shaikhan, Al-Khalili, Ibn Ruzaiq and Ibn 'Araba, all of these printed. Many others have not yet been reproduced but contribute to an overall portrait of literary and cultural vigour which characterized Oman from the earliest days of Islam and survived undimmed into this century.

The Omani School of History, its Methodology and Direction

In the early centuries of Islam Oman was less concerned with history than it was with language and religion and there are few books on history from this period, only one solitary book in the first five centuries to be precise. This was the book of Salma bin Musallam Al-Awatbi Al-Sohari. Even this was, strictly speaking, more a work of genealogy than of history in that it traced the roots of the Arabs of the south and in particular of the Azd of Oman and their role in settling and developing the Imamate there. This book supports some of the Omani biographies and interpretations contemporary with it such as the *Sirah* of Shabib bin Attia Al-Omani, who lived in the first half of the second century AH. He was an Ibadhi Imam after the fall of the First Ibadhi Imamate in 134 AH/751 AD at the hands of the Abbassids; and the *Sirah* of Abi Mu'athar Al-

Salt bin Khamis who was a contemporary of Muhanna bin Gaifar (237 AH/851 AD), who witnessed the installation of Al-Salt bin Malik (237-273 AH/851-886 AD); and the *Sirah* of Abi Al-Hassan bin Mohammed Al-Bessiwi who lived in the third century AH also and saw the collapse of the Second Ibadhi Imamate in 280 AH/893 AD. He wrote a *Sirah* about this event which he called *Al-Hujja 'ala Man Abtala Al-Su'al fi Al-Hadath Al-Waq'i bi Oman* and these *Sirahs* and interpretations were useful historical documents, though limited in scope to one aspect of this history[144].

Sheikh Muhanna bin Khalfan Al-Kharousi, who was a member of a committee reviewing this book, mentioned a number of other not inconsiderable *Sirahs*, though none of them are very useful in recording the history of Oman, being specifically concerned with the Imamate and the internal squabbles of the Omanis on this matter and pay no attention whatsoever to culture. These *Sirahs*, collected by Sheikh Muhanna, consist mostly of letters from *ulemas* to Imams correcting them in certain matters or clarifying points of doctrine for application at the level of politics, government or faith. Other of the *Sirahs* constituted collections of letters to other Ibadhi groups outside Oman, in the Hadramaut, Yemen or Africa, for the same purpose.

Amongst these many *Sirahs* were that of Al-Munir bin Al-Nir Al-Jaalani to Imam Ghassan; the Sirah of Abi Sufian bin Al-Raheel to the people of Oman on the matter of Haroun bin Al-Yamani Al Shi'i: the *Sirah* of Abi Sufian Mahboub bin Al-Raheel to the people of the Hadramaut; the *Sirah* of Haroun bin Al-Yamani Al-Shi'i to the Imam Muhanna bin Gaifar on the matter of Mahboub; of Abi Al-Hawari Mohammed bin Al-Hawari to the Hadramautis and another to the Omanis; Abi Bakr Ahmed bin Omar's *Sirah* on the rules of warfare and Hashem bin Ghilan's to the Imam Abdul Mulik bin Humaid; of Wa'il bin Ayoub on matters of orthodoxy and of Ahmed bin Mohammed bin Saleh on the incidents at Nizwa.

The following five centuries, from the sixth to the end of the tenth AH, are clouded in darkness, for the Omanis have left us practically nothing in the way of a historical report. The only information we have is from the works of their Ibadhi brothers in North Africa such as the *Seyar Al-'Aima wa Akhbaruhom* which is popularly known as *Tarikh Abi Zakaria* (Abu Zakaria's History) (d.471 AH/1078 AD); Al-Warjalani's *Sirah wa Akhbar Al-'Aima* (Biography and Reports of the Imams) (570 AH/1114 AD) and Al-Darjini's *Tabaqat Al-Ibadhia* (The Ibadhi Classes) (d. around 670 AH/1271 AD); *Jawaher Al-Muntaqa'a*, which completed matters not fully covered in Al-Baradi's *Tabaqat* (eighth century AH); *Al-Seyar* by Al-Shamakhi (d. 928 AH/1521 AD). These books were translated from the work of orthodox Ibadhis in Basra and North Africa. Some of them elaborate on the struggle between the Ibadhis and the Ummayyads and Abbassids respectively and are little concerned with the history of Oman, mentioning only what relates directly to the *ulema* and Imams. It should have been a priority for the early Omanis to write down in detail the history of their country, government and civilization for posterity, but this they did not do. Sheikh Nur Al-Din Al-Salimi puts the reason in a nutshell in his *Tohfah:* 'History is not the task of the companions (of the faith). On the contrary these were preoccupied with the institution of justice and the transmission of religious learning and with demonstrating what had to be demonstrated for the benefit of the masses, for this was of the highest importance. Thus they do not have a collective *Sirah* nor a comprehensive history'[145].

So the Omani writers of old during the government of the Imams concerned themselves with recording matters of religious doctrine and law and they have bequeathed us a vast legacy in these topics, though not in other areas. This dearth of secular writing had another cause. The rule of the Imams was not continuous or uninterrupted; other internal or external powers frequently seized control. These the Imams and their followers deemed tyrants and usurpers and they refused to commit to the record any description of these rulers or of their office[146]. Perhaps it was that a single government occupied the seat of power uninterrupted for several centuries, but the writings of the past give us no inkling as to what went on one way or the other. We have as an instance the Nabhan dynasty ruling Oman for around five centuries and yet we have no record of them apart from that of the the poet laureate Al-Sitali whose *Diwan* makes reference to a few of their names and deeds[147].

The Omanis when they did write about the Imams of the Middle Islamic Period did not do so in the manner of the detailed report, but rather furnished us with a rudimentary table of the ruling succession - no history, no civilizational context. The non-Imam rulers did not even get this peremptory treatment because they were deemed oppressors and unworthy of being recorded at all[148]. Or perhaps the Omanis in the Islamic period we speak of did write, but we have no books to prove that they did, apart from those of the Omani historians Ibn Ruzaiq and the author of *Kashef Al-Ghumah* as well as Al-Salimi, Al-Siyabi and a few others in recent times. There is no question but strife and civil war as well as invasion by outsiders with all that attended these by way of destruction and conflagration were in the greatest part responsible for the loss of these books. Suffice it to say that some of the narratives describe a fire in Rustaq as having devoured a library of 9000 books[149].

All of this contributed to a dearth of source references on the early history and civilization of Oman. This scarcity was the obvious cause of the deficiencies in histories written by Omanis at a later stage. By deficiencies we allude to two problems: there is no sequential chronology of Oman's rulers, neither Imams nor sultans, from the arrival of Islam and up to the Portuguese occupation. The second inadequacy concerns the failure to record the cultural history of Oman in a comprehensive manner such as would cover all of its diverse facets and which are vital to any clear and beneficial understanding of this people and their culture[150].

The Omanis under the Ya'rubas energetically narrated and recorded their history, generating much written material, including some covering the period back to the start of the eleventh century AH/seventeenth AD. This proliferation of writing continued in the centuries following until it had come to constitute a formidable historical record unrivalled in its coverage of Oman's modern period, this despite the fact that much of Oman's historical documentation was destroyed or burnt during civil and tribal strife, especially in the eighteenth century. Al-Azkawi, writing in that century, confirms this: 'Many books were burnt then which were without equal in Oman'[151]. He reckons that in all around 9073 handwritten manuscripts, went up in flames[152].

Today all we have are a few remaining books on the history of Oman, and a few manuscripts dispersed about the libraries of the world and in Oman itself. Meanwhile, there is a developing interest in recent years in the assembling of Oman's scattered heritage and its revival through publication. Today scholars have access to many historical manuscripts; and so our study can move on to an examination of the nature of these Omani writings and their historical method.

The scholar who closely examines Oman's modern history will notice an underlying common denominator, for historical events are recorded after the understanding of the Ibadhis, that is to say the prevailing orthodoxy in Oman from the very origins of this rite and up to date. In the Ibadhi context religious learning was given a status and wielded an influence not accorded it by the other rites. Such support helped to define the framework within which books of heritage in general and history in particular were written.

Omani history books, numerous though they are and irrespective of their age were limited in scope to recording the circumstances and events of Ibadhi society in Oman or, as these books describe it, the 'history of the existence of Islamic communities' in the south-east corner of the Arabian peninsula. The Omanis documented this history in great detail insofar as it was closely bound up with these communities. Outside this limited framework, events were not seen as being of any importance or worth documenting.

Thus Omani historians did not concern themselves with a record of events other than those having a direct bearing on the districts within the jurisdiction of the Imamate. No incident, for example, which occurred on the eastern coast, in particular during the Portuguese occupation of the coastal region, was recorded by these historians. As to events which took place outside Oman, even where these were directly linked to occurrences within, they were either referred to in the most cursory fashion or ignored altogether[153].

If we look at Oman's recent contribution to the writing of history and to the impetus behind this revival, we find that all of the output in this field is written after the Ibadhi view. This is true of the works of the seventeenth century and even on up to the end of the turn of the twentieth century. Abdullah bin Khalfan bin Suleiman, more commonly known as Ibn Qaisar, author of *Sirat Al-Imam Nasir bin Murshid*, began his book at the request of a number of sheikhs and *ulemas*, among them Sheikh Mohammed bin Saif Al-Wali and Sheikh Nasir bin Thani bin Jum'a bin Hilal, who asked him to 'undertake a *Sirah* of the Imam and that I should mention in it the compilation of the *Sirah* of his life which was completely devoted for the sake of God and I liked what they asked and consented to their requests'[154].

It is clear from the composition of this book, which counts as one of the oldest Omani histories commissioned in modern times, that it was written in the eleventh century AH/seventeenth AD, that it arose out of the directives of a group of pious scholars with the purpose of preserving the *Sirah* of Imam Nasir bin Murshid Al-Ya'rubi (1624-1649), who is remembered for his long *jihad* against the Portuguese and for his indefatigable struggle to free Oman from their grip, as well as his work in building up the defensive forces and unity of the country.

This book nevertheless enjoyed great respectability, for it furnished us with valuable information on this Imam, particularly in that it was written during his lifetime. Many Omani historians after him benefited from this book of Ibn Qaisar's, a point we see clearly if we compare him with the works of Al-

Azkawi and Ibn Ruzaiq. It is worthy of comment that Ibn Qaisar's book only occasionally gives us an account of the wars of Imam Nasir bin Murshid against the Portuguese. In this it resembles those Omani works of history which concerned themselves solely with internal affairs or such events only as occur within the areas controlled by the Ibadhi Imam[155].

The book *Kashef Al-Ghumah Al-Jami' Li Akhbar Al-Ummah*, attributed to Sarhan bin Said Al-Azkawi who lived in the eighteenth century AD, refers in its introductory pages to the goal for which the book has been written: 'I was inspired by the importance of compiling the material for this book and summarizing and arranging it and I welcomed the task even though it is possible that I am not competent to execute it. For I have observed that the greater part of the populace of our time are ignorant of the origins of their noble creed ... and they do not read the books of their antecedents'[156]. Clearly the author is anxious to protect the Ibadhi legacy in Oman, for the shortage of books on this topic and the low regard in which the scholars held it. In another context Al-Azkawi further explains Ibn Qaisar's goals: 'Nothing remains for the people of Oman but the memory of their history and what they find recorded in the *Sirahs* and Traditions; and now the learned classes are diminishing and oblivion is setting in'[157].

Omani books.

Kashef Al-Ghumah is a book of history encompassing the history of the Arabs before and after Islam up to an abrupt ending in 1728. As such it is the principal if not the first source for Oman's history. Later historians have taken from it. And yet the prime purpose of the author was to answer the Ibadhi call and dispel some of the mystery surrounding his sect, as is stated in his introductory remarks: 'I have put together this book and ... I have presented it in the style of a narrative, while it contains within the true message of the faith. For the people do not care to hear the latter, but are much taken with the stories. I have acceeded to their desire to listen, in the hope that they will thereby come to know the principles of their faith and recognize the truth of the righteous'[158].

It is clear that Al-Azkawi, as indicated in the text, drew a veil over his intent in writing the book, the search for a definitive rendering of Ibadhism. However he chose the narrative method in the writing of history for he believed that this method was more accessible to the reader. At any rate a number of later Omani historical works took their information from *Kashef Al-Gumah* such as Al-Ma'awali's *Qissas wa Akhbar Jarret fi Oman* (Stories and Reports of Occurrences in Oman); Ibn Ruzaiq's *Al-Fet'h Al-Mubeen* and Al-Salimi's *Tohfat Al-'Ayian*.

There are two books in existence which are almost certainly original copies of *Kashef Al-Ghumah*. The first is *Qissas wa Akhbar Jarret fi Oman* by Abi Suleiman Mohammed bin Amer bin Rashid Al-Ma'awli and the second is *Tarikh Ahl Oman* (History of the People of Oman) by an unknown author. The only difference between these three books is that *Kashef Al-Ghumah* stops at 1140 AH/1728 AD, whereas *Qissas wa Akhbar Jarret fi Oman* goes on a little further, to 1159 AH/1746 AD and the history by the anonymous author continues beyond this again - up to the end of the eighteenth century to the days of Sultan bin Ahmed bin Said, i.e. to 1215 AH/1800 AD[159].

The similarities between the three books suggests that Al-Ma'awli and the unknown author respectively sourced their information principally from Al-Azkawi's *Kashef Al-Ghumah*, indeed copied verbatim his report on the history of Oman up to the end of *Kashef Al-Ghumah* in 1728, then added information probably taken from other sources.

The book *Al-Fet'h Al-Mubeen fi Sirat Al-Sadah Al-Busaidiyeen* by Humaid bin Mohammed bin Ruzaiq was written in response to a request by Al-Sayyid Hamad bin Salem bin Sultan bin Al-Imam Ahmed bin Said Al-Busaidi to Ibn Ruzaiq to relay to him what he knew from his own memorization and the recollections of others about the ancestry of Imam Ahmed bin Said, his *Sirah* and his kingdom, and the *Sirah* of his offspring and their affairs in Oman and elsewhere[160].

Ibn Ruzaiq arranged his book in three sections, the first on the genealogy of the Omani Azdi Al-Busaidis; the second an account of their various branches and descendants, and the third an account of the Azdi Imams of Oman and their affairs, from Al-Julanda bin Mas'ud to the noble Al-Busaidi Imam, Ahmed bin Said Al-Azdi Al-Omani Al-Ibadhi[161]. Ibn Ruzaiq says elsewhere: 'If our purpose in (preparing) this book was to document the biography of Imam Ahmed bin Said and his descendants, it seems proper that we should proffer an account of the Omani Imams as a whole to increase our understanding and to learn something new, that the Yemeni Omani Azd were a great and consequential people'[162].

In Ibn Ruzaiq's declaration that his goal was not to portray the biography of the Imam Ahmed bin Said alone, but along with it the history of the Ibadhi Imams in Oman, he shares the view of contemporary Omani historians representing the modern school of history in Oman.

Al-Fet'h Al-Mubeen is the primary source for the history of the Al-Busaidis in the period from 1741-1856 AD, not least because its author Ibn Ruzaiq was a contemporary of the period of history of which he wrote. Born at the end of the eighteenth century, he died in 1875. He and his family had close links with the Al-Busaidi family, giving him the advantage of greater acquaintance with his subject matter and direct access to information on their history and the major circumstances of their reign. This book is given additional weight over its predecessors by the inclusion of a number of texts and agreements concluded between the Imam Nasir bin Murshid and the Portuguese, along with letters exchanged between them. This is a departure of great historical importance, for prior to this such information was available only from Portuguese sources.

Ibn Ruzaiq wrote a number of books on the history of Oman of which the one of greatest interest to us, apart from his *Al-Fet'h Al-Mubeen* there is *Al-Shua' Al-Sha'i Billama'an fi Thikr A'imat Oman*[163], for it was this book which established the historical method followed by Ibn Ruzaiq; a measure of its influence on the Ibadhi *ulema* of which he was one is found in his declaration: 'When a number of colleagues asked me to put together a poem on the names of the Rightly Guided Imams of Oman, and requesting that I explain it concisely and usefully or provide a simple explanation which would not require much knowledge, my response was to comply with his directive and I did so with humility in regard for his status'[164]. So the book is actually no more than a collection of poems or verses arranged by the author who describes by this means the historical events which took place in Oman. Amongst them is the history of the orthodox Ibadhi Imams, from Imam Julanda bin Mas'ud to the time of Imam Sultan bin Murshid Al-Ya'rubi.

Tohfat Al-'Ayian bi Sirat Ahl Oman by Nur Al-Din Abdullah bin Humaid Al-Salimi is counted among the principal references by all the modern schools; and though the author had lost his sight by the age of 12 and died before he reached 40 in 1332 AH/1914 AD, the work is deemed amongst the most significant on Oman's history. Al-Salimi wrote more than 22 books, some of which are no less important on the subjects of Ibadhi jurisprudence than *Tohfat Al-'Ayian* is on history.

This great savant had an exceptionally vigorous output, and this was not unconnected with the valuable legacy of original thinking he inherited from his predecessors and nineteenth century contemporaries amongst the Ibadhi *ulema* of Oman. At any rate if we remain aware of this formidable background in the study or evaluation of Al-Salimi's ideas and works, we find that most of it can be reduced to the execution of a single purpose: the revival and strengthening of the past spirit of Ibadhi thought among the Omanis[165].

Al-Salimi in the introduction to *Tohfat Al-'Ayian* refers to his goal in writing this book and to the historical and ideological method he has employed:

'History is not the task of the companions (of the faith). On the contrary these were preoccupied with the institution of justice and the transmission of religious learning and with demonstrating what had to be demonstrated for the benefit of the masses, for this was of the highest importance. Thus they do not have a collective *Sirah* nor a comprehensive history; and so I looked closely at the possible books on *Sirah* and Tradition and history and I wrote what I could on Oman and its Imams'[166].

A close examination of this text along with other texts presented in the book elicits the following:

- Certain issues relevant to the history of Oman were discarded because the Omanis, in Al-Salimi's view, 'are not preoccupied with history and thus most of the reports of the Imams are absent'; how much more so then with regard to others?[167]
- The documentation of historical events is not given in an independent manner but is present in the biographies of the Imams and the discussion of religious issues such as precepts and so on.
- Religious matters, in particular those relating to the history of the Ibadhi Imams, was given special emphasis by Al-Salimi who was an Ibadhi. He says: 'Justice and precedence in Oman were what most spurred me to write such Traditions of the Ibadhi Imams as I could stand over, by which those

who are ignorant of them can know their *Sirahs* and by which those who seek their Tradition might be bound, given the dearth of material in this area'[168].

- Al-Salimi was determined to pursue the scientific method to assemble and classify historical material; and so he travelled the length and breadth of Oman investigating every scrap of historical information to include it in his work in a testimony to the precision of his data and its importance in the study of Oman's modern history.

Notwithstanding Al-Salimi's comments in *Tohfat Al-'Ayian* it remains the most important work of the 50 years up to the turn of the twentieth century, for it added new information to its predecessors while not differing from them in adaptation or portrayal. On the contrary, in pursuing the manner of the modern Omani school of history it was open to the influence of Ibadhism and Ibadhi jurusprudential thought in the documentation of history.

Principal Directions of Modern Omani Historical Writing

The Ibadhi Imams not only influenced the documentation of Oman's heritage, they had a major impact on state policy throughout the Islamic period. The Omani state experienced many periods of tribal upheaval, some generated by internal unrest, some by foreign invasion. So where did Omani historians stand in the recording of these events? It would appear that a number of directions were pursued by historians, ranging from a reluctance to report certain events to longwindedness in their accounts of others. This is what we will now attempt to portray in this part of the study, under three headings.

The Stand on Internal Events and Civil War in Oman

The Imamate reached the peak of its power in the eleventh century AH/seventeenth century AD. This was followed by a period of political turmoil brought about when the Nabhan tribe seized control of Oman at the end of the twelfth century AD. So when the historian turns to the history of the Nabhan period between the thirteenth and fifteenth centuries AD he finds no known historical source for his information. And yet the absence of a written history covering this period of Oman's past does not mean that the history of these rulers is of no value; but the Nabhan did rule by a different stick and were viewed as tyrants. The Ibadhi historians therefore make no reference to them, neither those who were their contemporaries nor those writing in the following centuries[169].

Attempts to revive the Imamate in Oman were renewed in the fifteenth century but these attempts were premature and the Nabhan kings conscripted the Bani Hilal tribe to protect their interests. The Omanis however rallied around the Imam Nasir bin Murshid who was elected from one of the tribal offshoots of the Nabhan, that is to say the Ya'ruba, with a view to expelling the imposters and defeating the Nabhan who were allied with them[170].

From the start of the fifteenth century new sources became available to cast some light on the return of the Ibadhi Imams in Oman, even though these sources in pursuing their purpose did not focus their attention strictly on the subject of the Imams, but rather on the search for indicators of national unity in the context of the Imamate. Such is the case with Ibn Qaisar, who wrote about the Imam Naṣir bin Murshid in the first half of the seventeenth century. He was followed by other Omanis who wrote about local history, memoirs and biography.

If we now turn to the position of the Omani sources on the internal situation under the Nabhan rulers and the civil wars under the Ya'ruba, we find without exception that they are judgmental in their accounts and apologetic in reporting the destruction for which these wars were responsible. As Al-Azkawi points out, on their account 'a great part of the ordinary citizenry, along with sheikhs and jurisprudents of Oman were injured, as well as pious, ascetic and learned men'[171]. In his treatment of this important subject Al-Azkawi does not differ greatly from *Kashef Al-Ghumah* on the actual events which led to the outbreak of civil war. This view is also applicable to Ibn Ruzaiq, who follows the line of Al-Azkawi in adding some information gleaned from other sources.

Al-Salimi is the only Omani historian who attempted to take up a position on the roots of the civil war, a matter traceable to the election of Imams who were neither qualified nor competent, in defiance of Ibadhi principle. He said: 'Wickedness echoed throughout Oman and the people became restless and agitated; the leaders sought to turn the state into an inheritance, at variance with the directives of their learned peers. Ignoring retribution they allowed bigotry to march in their hearts'[172].

Views on the Portuguese and Persian Invasions

Omani authors differed in their views on the Portuguese invasion, though not the Persian. The former they ignored altogether or reported only in the most cursory fashion, while the latter was rendered in great detail. What then was behind these two very different treatments? And whatever it is is it significant in the context of our study of the modern school of history in Oman?

The fact is that the Portuguese invasion took place at the start of the sixteenth century, that is approximately a century and a half before the first Omani history written after the modern method, if we consider this to be Ibn Qaisar's *Sirat Al-Imam Nasir bin Murshid*. Thus Omani historians when they came to record the circumstances of the Portuguese invasion found nothing to convey distinction on this nation, in particular since the Portuguese had won speedy victories in the Gulf region including Oman as a result of their military superiority; for they had modern ships and weapons. So the historians deliberately declined to record these events[173], particularly given that the Imamate was on the point of collapse at this time.

The Persian invasion on the other hand occurred around the latter half of the eighteenth century and its events were either contemporary or in the recent memory of the Omani historians who wrote about it and who found in the climate of the people at the time a desire to cast out the invader and unify the country.

Proceeding along these lines we notice Omani historians withholding detail in respect of long periods of the country's history - often centuries at a time - thus avoiding coverage of what might be found unsavoury by the Omanis, as was the case with regard to the Portuguese occupation of the coast. Meanwhile many of these historians frequently gave free rein to their pens in expressing their sentiments about certain events, reflecting their pain and distress at the internecine strife which invited outside intervention.

Periods of occupation always tended to be blind links in the chain of history and here we have a historical phenomenon not confined to a particular country or time. In describing such periods the Omani historians did not pass up an opportunity to disparage the occupation and denounce the circumstances which had given rise to it or ensured its continuation. Such was the case in the early part of the seventeenth century when tribal strife accelerated to a point where Umair bin Hamyar in 1025 AH/1616 AD was roused to seek the assistance of the Portuguese in Hormuz against his own people. No doubt but this was a shortsighted and irresponsible course of action and the Portuguese were quick to exploit his naivete, arriving with their fleet to bombard the coast until they succeeded in taking Sohar. This enabled them to consolidate their military grip and seize control of Muscat's trade, for Sohar was the most prominent of Muscat's trading ports at this time[174].

Circumstances were repeated when in 1150 AH/1737 AD Saif bin Sultan lent assistance to the Persians against his rivals in the Imamate and this dangerous conduct led to an invasion by the Persians. Nader Shah, who occupied the Persian throne at the time, harboured expansionist ambitions in the Arab Gulf region as well as a hostile intent against Oman which possessed a powerful fleet. He thus found this a propitious occasion to pursue his plans for mastery of the Gulf and proceeded to invade Oman. The Persian invasions were not to achieve their objective of subduing Oman in view of the valiant resistance put up by the Omanis; despite recurrent attempts in the period from 1150 to 1157 AH/1737-1744 AD. During this period the Omani sources tell us of the annihilation and torture wrought by the Persians on the populace[175]. The Persian army which came to the aid of Saif bin Sultan against his adversaries tightened its grip on the affairs of state and, having seized Muscat, proceeded to attempt the occupation of the whole country. So Saif bin Sultan's appeal to the Persians for assistance to further personal aims was a topic of loathing to all Omani historians. Says Al-Salimi: 'Few of the people of Nizwa were saved; and Saif bin Sultan must bear responsibility for many crimes committed in this (debacle), for he led their enemies to them...'[176].

The most outstanding example we have of the abuse and contempt felt by Omani historians was a letter by an anonymous author - furnished by Ibn Ruzaiq in *Al-Fet'h Al-Mubeen*[177] - to Saif bin Sultan after he had contacted the Persians to ask for their help: 'It has come to the point that a band of Persians have arrived at Khorfahan in the company of some of their insolent brethren. This is a terrible disaster for us and for you, and a curse of fate, for if they triumph they will exceed all bounds, and if they outnumber you they will subject you to wretched torture. They will slaughter your sons and rape your women, praise the Lord. Are you asleep or awake? Or has the devil possessed your hearts? You write your dispatches to them and you send them an invitation and ask them to help you! Do you not know what they did in Bahrain? They murdered men and seized their ships. What has become of you? What has happened to your judgment that it should fail you so badly in how you have chosen to act?'

If the periods of occupation represent grim aspects of Oman's history there were important other aspects to these times as agreed and documented by all of the historians. The selection of Imam Nasir bin Murshid to the Imamate in 1034 AH/1624 AD was one such, along with his efforts to curb the power of the Portuguese, efforts which would culminate in the final defeat of this influence in 1060 AH/1650 AD. The heroic resistance put up by the Omanis in face of the Persian forces in 1150 AH/1737 AD and their expulsion by Imam Ahmed bin Said Al-Busaidi in 1157 AH/1744 AD was another. These events impressed historians and found common cause amongst them irrespective of their various departure points.

Nasir bin Murshid was elected Imam of Oman in 1034 AH/1624 AD after a long period in which Oman was engulfed in violent civil wars. This Imam, after strenuous efforts, succeeded in uniting the country under his leadership and after engaging the Portuguese, who were entrenched in the ports and coastal areas, in a skirmish, he managed to wrest from them control of the ports of Qalhat and Sohar and encircled Muscat. But he was destined to die before he had liberated the rest of the country from the occupier.

These accomplishments of Nasir bin Murshid on the road to unity and rebirth in Oman and the victories he visited on the Portuguese were what excited some historians, in particular Ibn Qaisar in *Sirat Al-Imam Nasir bin Murshid*, to write about his triumphs in such hyperbolic terms.

Later historians after Ibn Qaisar - Al-Azkawi, Ibn Ruzaiq and Al-Salimi - were no different in their approach to Imam Nasir bin Murshid, except perhaps in their endeavours to tone down the language of overstatement and adulation which informed Ibn Qaisar's comments on the Imam, in order to create a more credible account of his reign.

We noted above the Omani historians' reluctance to record the events of the Portuguese occupation; now in their coverage of the term of Imam Nasir bin Murshid they began to document events in elaborate fashion, for they had become a source of pride. And while they did not pursue the progress of the victories over the Portuguese in the Arabian Gulf, they did follow the course of their rout in India and East Africa[178].

Historians now sensed the wind of victory rising and hastened to place on the record everything they saw worthy of note. Al-Salimi, for instance, transcribed for us a letter from the Portuguese to Imam Saif bin Sultan dated 1109 AH/1697 AD which incorporated threats and intimidation directed at the Imam. The latter was not fazed by the threats and responded with vigour. An extract from the Portuguese letter gives a sense of their menace: 'Know that we are the soldiers of God, creatures of his displeasure, who deal harshly with those who bring down His anger. No compassion have we for sceptics nor tears for mourners. God has stripped our hearts of mercy. So woe unto those who do not heed our commands'. And the Imam replied:'God has stripped your hearts of mercy and this is your vilest sin ... who adheres to fundamentals shall not be concerned with side issues ... We are the faithful, and shame shall not separate us from you nor admit to us doubt or uncertainty... our steeds cross land and sea, our concerns are lofty.... and while you say that your hearts are as mountains and your numbers as sand: The butcher is not mindful of the numbers of sheep....if we live we live blissfully, and if we die we die martyrs to our faith'[179].

There are many noble aspects to Oman's resistance to the Persian invasion in the period 1150-1157 AH/1737-1744 AD and their ultimate victory over them at the hands of the Imam Ahmed bin Said Al-Busaidi who succeeded in ousting the Persians from Oman and was elected Imam in 1157 AH/1744 AD.

Imam Ahmed bin Said was *Wali* of Sohar at the time of the Persian invasion. One of the effects of this invasion was to fire the Omanis' national spirit and to cause them to seek out a strong leader who would save them and their country from the Persian army. They rallied around the Imam Ahmed bin Said in Sohar which became a centre of national resistance, and under his leadership succeeded in withstanding the Persians until they could inflict a final victory on them. Imam Ahmed bin Said's term represented a high point in the history of Oman and historians were not slow to give it due credit, not least of them Ibn Ruzaiq, whose *Al-Fet'h Al-Mubeen* was written specifically to glorify these events.

Here we might aptly mention the testimony of Rudolph Said-Ruete the German who carried out research in Oman to demonstrate the extent of Arab identification with and fealty to their leaders when they sensed in them sincerity and patriotism and heroism. He said: 'One of the Arabs' outstanding traits is their fondness for acts of bravery and the public standing of their heroes. They do not hesitate to rally round their leaders and to confer on them the title of Imam. And they are just as quick to abandon them and the religious status which they themselves accorded them and transfer their allegiance, without remorse or pity or conscience, to another who might better achieve for them their patriotic goals. So it is no surprise to find that Ahmed bin Said, besieged in Sohar, was yet master of Oman and all recognized him as their chieftain and leader'[180].

Omani Historians and the Events of the Arab Quest for Self-Determination

Notwithstanding his remarks quoted above on the documenting of internal events by Omani historians, in particular those relevant to the orthodox Ibadhi Imams, yet they did not on occasion extend to episodes involving the Imams that occurred outside Oman. One record which would be important to obtain would be that of the help given by Imam Ahmed bin Said to Basra during its siege by Karim Khan in 1189 AH/1775 AD and the subsequent breaking of the siege as we described previously.

In view of the good effects of this assistance, it was decided to pay an annual subsidy from the Basra Treasury to Imam Ahmed. This subsidy according to Ibn Ruzaiq continued up to the time of Sayyid Said bin Sultan[181].

So we can see how most of the writings were influenced by the Ibadhi rite; and this is what gave Oman's modern school of history its distinguishing trait of being thoroughly versed in its method and direction. The writings in the other disciplines of doctrine, language and letters took on the appearance of being also of a school or schools in full command of their disciplines, as we have seen, attesting to the pedigree of the thought and culture of Oman and its people and of the abundance of its scientific heritage from the earliest days of Islam.

Architecture and Fortifications in Oman

The story of the architecture and fortifications of Oman demands examination in that a knowledge of this aspect of its culture gives us access to a facet of Oman's history which has continuous links from the dim past up to the present day. Oman's civil architecture, that is its palaces, mosques and schools; and military architecture in the shape of citadels, forts and towers, are the product of history, geography and other factors relating to Oman's natural environment.

We described Oman's geographical bearings and the significance of these in the first section of this book; and how location contributed to Oman's prominence as a station on the sea trading route to the Orient and to its becoming a crosslink between the Arabian peninsula and Africa, India and other countries. This spurred the Omanis to attain mastery of the craft of seamanship until Omani mariners were known in the remotest ports and its merchants were in constant contact with the other sea merchants of the world. Oman was not merely a link between these worlds; it was a trading juncture for merchants from every part of the world, an entrepôt where trade was transacted and goods exchanged[182] so that it was said: 'Who seeks to trade let him go to Oman or Aden or Egypt'[183].

Oman and the rest of the Gulf continued to experience a golden age with the growth of Islamic navigation up to the fifteenth century AD, when the Portuguese discovered the sea passage around the Cape of Good Hope which brought them to the shores of the Indian Ocean and the Gulf of Oman[184].

The policies of Portugal in this region were responsible for many outbreaks of war and tribal friction and these assisted the intruder in his dismantling of national unity, enabling him to seize and maintain a grip on the coastal regions for more than a century and a half; until the spirit of the Omanis was roused to find common cause against the enemy. United, the Omani resistance cast out the Portuguese in 1060 AH/1650 AD and their other strongholds outside Oman fell in 1100 AH/1689 AD[185].

To the attractive attributes we have mentioned, add the fact that Oman is the second largest state in the Arabian peninsula, with spectacular coastal plains which extend for 1700 kms, as well as oases and villages distributed here and there among the mountains of the interior. Its climate varies from hot and dry in the interior to hot and humid on the coast to moderate in the Jebel Al-Akhdar region. The southern district meanwhile is distinguished by green mountains and prevailing monsoons[186].

These factors were to have a strong bearing on the way in which Omani society developed and on its relations with the world around it - and on the development of the style and nature of the buildings constructed by the Omanis over the centuries[187].

From its earliest recorded history Oman was a land coveted by others and the object of an ever-recurring struggle between international powers, and so it was inevitable that Oman would have military installations and suitably constructed fortifications[188].

This society, with its high level of national consciousness and civilization, owned military installations which demanded that they be defended against attempts to overcome them. It became imperative that the Omanis build fortifications which would enable them to withstand the dangers that surrounded them. With the growth in the manufacture of high quality construction materials in the region and the increasing use of quarried stone, it was inevitable that a sophisticated workforce of masons and craftsmen would be built up. These skilled masons were conscious of the requirements and experienced in the practice of their craft. Amongst them must have been specialists in many related skills - masons and carpenters, plasterers, ironsmiths, engineers and the like.

We can thus infer that the exercise of building forts and citadels in Oman has left it with a vast heritage, the early roots of which go back to the pre-Christian era; and this inherited tradition is still interacting dynamically with developments in architecture today. Behind all new departures in architecture lie the inherited traditions which gives Oman's buildings their unique quality and style.

The development in architecture has been an unbroken one from earliest times, though there were periods when there was less innovation than might have been expected. These periods were in the nature of an intermission when the architectural movement gathered strength, or rested between surges forward, or attained maturity in some aspect. The Omanis were ever interested in the development of the architectural movement and kept abreast of trends abroad, always seeking new input to add to their considerable existing knowledge.

Support in this endeavour was always to be found in a return to Oman's vigorous history, and the architectural movement in Oman was fuelled in a positive way by every archaeological discovery announced, whether in Oman itself or in other districts in the region. Many civilizations flowered in Oman at various times, and all were coveted by other civilizations in the region who exerted stringent efforts with the goal of suppressing the culture and independence of Oman by dragging it into the arena of struggle. An example was to be found in the struggle between Samharam and Shabwa as described in archaeological inscriptions[189], or Magan's struggle with the Assyrians[190] and various contests with the Persians and others[191]. All of this spurred the Omanis to build strongholds to enable them withstand the dangers threatening them and with this assistance they were enabled to overwhelm their enemies. Omani history, ancient and modern, is replete with such examples.

On this basis then the fortified protection of Oman's settled population was an obligation of the highest order. Fortification, therefore, was one of the focal points of the architectural movement in the early colonies; the citadel or fort came to occupy a prominent place in the design of cities, in recognition of the vital role it played over other types of structure in protecting the interests of its immediate environs, disappointing the hopes of those with a mind set on conquest and preventing any thought that such a goal would be easily achieved.

Discoveries at Bat in Ibri district allow us to deduce the existence of a variety of fortified structures, some circular, some beehive in shape, others in the nature of strongholds which have been dated to the third millenium BC. These latter were of a tower formation having a diameter of up to 20 metres. Archaeologists believe that these towers were as much as 10 metres high[192].

The Omanis used stone in their early constructions, in particular the construction of strongholds, going back to the earliest times. Phoenician remains in Carthage displayed similar thinking in their fortified buildings, which they had constructed from huge square angled blocks so that they could be laid one above the other without recourse to mortar. They brought this method with them to other cities which were under Phoenician control, such as Cicilia and Sur (Tyre) and this construction style is identical to that identified at Bat in Ibri in Oman[193]. The stones used in building the fortifications at Bat were not random blocks but showed evidence of the use of stone quarried in Oman. The block measurements as recorded by archaeologists - that is 1 x 1 x 0.8 metres and 2.5 x 3 x 0.5 metres - adds to the conviction that the science of masonry had reached a level of which we hope new discoveries will offer us greater knowledge. It would be particularly interesting to come across some of the construction materials, such as wood, stone and marble, which it is known Magan used to export to Sumer and Kuli. It would not be surprising then if we were to find that Omani fortifications, citadels, strongholds forts and walls, date back as far as the pre-Christian era and continued to be a feature of the pre-Islamic era and later the age of the Caliphs, then the Nabhan, the Ya'ruba and other historical periods right up to the twentieth century[194].

Through all of these times and arising out of the natural, social and economic circumstances previously alluded to, the Omanis were obliged to build forts and strongholds the length and breadth of the country. Their citadels were their most formidable architectural monuments in evidence, and even today are a lofty reminder of the ancient roots of this mighty people, with their able tradition and honourable history.

There is not a spot in this vast territory which does not show a citadel here and a fort there; and each citadel and fort tells a tale of civilization and of the Arab Islamic heritage. Oman has more than 500 towers and defence strongholds going back to the Islamic age, not including the citadel of Rustaq and Bahla which were built before Islam. Three citadels only were built by the Portuguese, the rest were built by the Omanis themselves, despite claims by many that they were Portuguese constructions[195].

The most celebrated citadel in Oman at present is the Jibrin Fort, built by the Imam Bal'arab bin Sultan at the end of the seventeenth century at a distance of 208 kms from Muscat; and Al-Hazm fort which was built by the Imam Saif bin Sultan bin Saif Al-Ya'rubi at the start of the eighteenth century, 159 kms from Muscat. These two citadels are masterpieces of engineering and design and contain many interesting defence features as well as ornamental embellishments on walls, ceilings and gun openings[196].

During the Islamic age the Omanis built many civilian structures, including mosques and government buildings, as well as forts and citadels. The remains of these buildings are visible monuments and clear testimony to the prosperity and advanced knowledge achieved by the Omanis in this domain. The buildings varied in scale and shape in line with the natural, social and political circumstances and the requirements prevailing when they were built. Omani engineers were presented with the challenge of successfully resolving architectural problems and devising appropriate solutions.

In order to demonstrate something of the formidable standard of Oman's architecture and fortification and to gain a grasp of the art of building and architecture as shown by the Omanis and how it reflected their environment, lifestyle and history, we should take a look at some of the citadels and forts and towers built by them in a more or less chronological sequence. Historians tell us that the oldest of Oman's forts is the one at Bahla.

Bahla Fort.

Bahla Fort

Some historians believe that Bahla Fort which rises 150 metres above the plain in the Oman's heartland was built 1500 years before Islam. This would date it to the first millenium BC. They then go a step further to declare that it was erected by Nebuchadnezzar before he marched on to Mesopotamia to found his empire[197]. If we accept the date of construction indicated, for reasons supported by the closeness of the district of Bahla to the district of Bat and its location within a radius of influence of this civilization, then given the dates we have for Nebuchadnezzar's reign, we cannot attribute the construction of this fort to his time. There is another view, that it was built in the era of Malik bin Fahm Al-Azdi[198]; while others believe that the north-eastern portion of the citadel is the part which predates Islam. This latter is the most sensible view, for Oman prior to Islam and back as far as the first Arab migrations was a society of colonies settled around water springs and flood valleys[199]. Moreover this thesis does not contradict the proposed date of construction, for the Arab migrations began in the pre-Christian era and continued in a steady outpouring to the various surrounding districts[200].

What is agreed is that the wall which was built with the fort has not been preserved and that it bears little resemblance to the structure that existed before the time of Islam, having been modified and added to repeatedly. It is claimed that the south-easterly fortification was built by the Nabhan kings at the start of their reign in the eighth century AH. There are two aspects to this theory. While it could find corroboration in the historical factors and events which took place in this district, making it a likely possibility, there is not much hard evidence to support the argument. Moreover, and this is the other aspect, the Nabhan kings were in power for at least two centuries before this date (eighth century AH)[201].

The Bait Al-Jebel building located in the corner nearest to the north was built in the last part of the twelfth century AH/ eighteenth century AD, i.e. in the age of the Al-Busaidi Imams, while the new building in the south-west corner was built in the mid-thirteenth century AH/nineteenth AD[202].

Sohar Fort

Some historical accounts ascribe the construction of the Sohar Fort to the time of Oman bin Qahtan and others to the time of Malik bin Fahm Al-Azdi[203]. It is considered to be one of the latter's most important monuments. Yet others attribute it to Al-Julanda bin Al-Mustakbir. This fort was known as the citadel of Sohar, suggesting that it was built before Islam: and perhaps we can lend weight to this view if we recall the historical significance of Sohar as an important metropolis on the coast of Oman and one of the celebrated markets of the Arab region in pre-Islamic times[204]; and again if we consider its location in relation to the former Persian Empire. We know that Abd and Gaifar, the sons of Julanda, made Sohar, along with Tu'am, their centre of government. And surely there must be a mark somewhere in the architecture of this fort to remind us that Amr bin Al-Aas, envoy of the Prophet Mohammed, was received there in the year 9 AH/630 AD. Other historians of architecture say that Imam Warith bin Ka'b Al-Kharousi built the fort on the rubble of an old fort in 179 AH/750 AD; and this view does not contradict the previous one[205].

Sohar Fort.

Archaeological discoveries at the fort in 372 AH/983 AD point to the presence of an emerging culture in this district[206]. The historian Al-Hamdani mentions the Ghorab Fort in Dhofar in the course of his discourse on the coastline of Oman, saying that it was built before Islam. This gives additional support to the proposition that many of these forts, Sohar and Ghorab among them, were built before Islam[207].

There are those who say that the Portuguese built this fort after they had begun their occupation of Oman[208], while others tend to the view that the Hormuzis built it before the Portuguese; for Sohar was one of the coastal cities under their control. This latter view shows something of an Islamic influence, for the Islamic period encompassed the time of Al-Warith bin Ka'b and on up to the Hormuzi age. It is hard to give any credence to the first view, since Sohar was under the rule or control of Mohammed bin Muhanna Al-Hodeifi Al-Busaidi who with the assistance of the Nabhans resisted Portuguese attempts to occupy Sohar from within this very fort[209].

This fort was probably modified and added to several times by the Arabs and the Portuguese[210]. In all likelihood the design principles of this fort were borrowed by the Portuguese in the construction of their military installations in the Gulf region[211]. The north-west tower is considered to be the only one which bears a resemblance to its original form. The Imam Nasir bin Murshid Al-Ya'ruba made several modifications to this fort in 1024 AH/ 1640 AD, though we do not know to which part or the nature of the work involved. Imam Ahmed bin Said added other towers in 1147 AH/ 1747 AD and these were renewed by the *Wali* Mohammed bin Ahmed bin Hilal in 1320 AH/ 1902 AD. It was renovated during the reign of Sultan Said bin Taimur in 1378 AH/ 1958 AD and underwent repairs under H.M. Sultan Qaboos bin Said .

Rustaq Fort.

Rustaq Fort

It is believed that this fort was built during the Sassanid period, although no precise date[212] is available. One indication is the fact that it was known as *Kisra* fort. The truth is that this term came from a linguistic corruption; for the fort was constructed in the district of Qasra and this became, in some of the Omani dialects, particularly that of the north, *Kasari* , where a 'K' replaced the 'Q'. So the notion that it was built in the Sassanid period is not founded on a logical and consequently acceptable basis. Oman at that time enjoyed a measure of political freedom which allowed it to ignore the influence of the Persians, a fact which rendered them free to embrace Islam without feeling obligated to pay heed to the reaction of the Persians. On the contrary the Omanis invited the latter to embrace Islam. If one were to accept the view of Persia as an empire whose influence extended as far as Yemen (on which the Sassanid origin of the fort is based) this would be to ignore the influence and significance of the Arabs; and we are confident that Oman before the coming of Islam was under the rule of Abd and Gaifar, sons of Julanda bin Al-Mustakbir[213].

The fort was renovated in 50 AH/670 AD and the Ya'ruba added the Al-Rih Tower and the Al-Ahmar Tower. Again the height was raised in the time of Imam Saif bin Sultan Al-Ya'rubi in 1104 AH/ 1668 AD. Imam Ahmed bin Said added the Al-Hadith Tower and wall and numerous fortifications. Al-Sayyid Said bin Ibrahim did more structural work to it in 1320 AH/1902 AD and it was repaired in the time of Sultan Faisal bin Turki in 1324 AH/1906 AD.

Nakhal stronghold.

Nakhal Fort

This fort was erected on a promontory at a height of 200 metres and some date it to the pre-Islamic age. What would lead us to accommodate this view is the fact that the fort was renovated in the time of Yahmads in 200 AH/ 815 AD, confirming its prior existence. Those who hold this view give it the same approximate construction date as Rustaq Fort and perhaps also Sohar[214].

Another view attributes its construction to the Imam Al-Salt bin Malek[215] who ruled Oman as Imam for 35 years (237-273 AH/ 851-886 AD). The fort, however, would have been built before the Imam took office and in his time was the product of additions to a predecessor[216].

This fort was repaired a number of times and additional structures were added by various rulers of Oman over the ages. The Nabhan rulers renovated it, as did the Ya'ruba in 1000 AH/ 1591 AD. Sultan Said bin Sultan added a wall and towers and the existing gate in 1250 AH/ 1834 AD[217].

Nizwa Fort.

Fort and Citadel of Nizwa

This fort was built in the territory of Nizwa in 225 AH/ 845 AD[218], and it was said that the builder was Imam Al-Salt bin Malik in 237 AH/ 851 AD who built it close to the old mosque.

If we consider the two dates we see that the fort was built about 12 years before the Imam Al-Salt bin Malik took office. Accepting the authority of Omani history from the time of Malik bin Fahm, we believe that this city along with other Omani cities witnessed a progression of events throughout the course of Oman's history and thus it would seem most likely that the fort was built at a time prior to the date mentioned and may even predate Islam.

This fort was renewed in the time of the Imam Nasir bin Murshid Al-Ya'rubi in 1034 AH/1624 AD, though the Imam Sultan bin Saif Al-Ya'rubi built the great citadel, unique in the stronghold architecture of Oman and perhaps of the entire region. Its construction dates to 1059-79 AH/ 1649-68 AD[219], the actual construction work occupying a full twelve years.

Another history dates the construction to 1062 AH/1651 AD, that is during the time of the Imam Sultan bin Saif bin Malek[220], adding that it was built in the period between 1059 AH/1649 AD and 1074 AH/1663 AD[221]. Yet another view places the construction in the decades following this, that is 1081-1091 AH/1670-1680 AD[222].

Bait Al-Fulaij Fort

Bait Al-Fulaij Fort is considered to be a prototype of the stronghold palaces of the quadrangular diametrical axial format, that is to say they consisted of two opposite corner towers on a northwest-southwest diametrical axial path.

It was said to have been built on the rubble of an ancient Arab fort at a time before the foundation of the Ya'ruba state[223]. It is not possible to say with certainty what the date of its construction was; but this fort saw important events in Oman's history including those that took place between the Omanis and the Persians in 1156 AH/1743 AD under Saif bin Hamad Al-Ya'rubi, *Wali* of the Imam Sultan bin Murshid Al-Ya'rubi[224]. Again Mohammed bin Khalfan, *Wali* of Muscat in the time of the Imam Said bin Ahmed, made it his base after the death of Al-Sayyid Hamad the son of Al-Imam Said in 1207 AH/1792 AD[225].

Bait Al-Fulaij Fort.

We are inclined to believe that the fundamental architectural principle of this type of fortification was that of the ancient Arab fort which we mentioned - with several modifications to suit the strategic aims of the Ya'ruba and Al-Busaidi rulers who succeeded them.

Its construction was not novel in the sense of the fort of Ruwi or the octagonal tower at Barka Fort which were built by Al-Sayyid Hamad bin Said[226] or Al-Rawiya Fort which was built by Al-Sayyid Sultan bin Ahmed[227]. Nor can it be attributed to the Al-Ya'ruba; it was probably built earlier than their time. This fort was used for defence purposes and its site gave it an advantage in this respect. It was an advance base for Matrah and Darsait specifically and for Muscat and the roads leading to it generally. Evidence of the hostilities which would have revolved around this fort and to which it would have been subjected are found in the design of the building itself, with its towers, gunslits and cannon platforms.

The fort was also used as a residence, Al-Sayyid Said bin Sultan having taken it as a country retreat[228]. Once again evidence of this is gained from the design of the building which incorporated bedrooms, reception rooms and other civil rooms. This inclusion of a residential function resembles many of the other stronghold homes or palaces of Oman such as Jibrin, Hazm, Bait Al-Nu'man, Al-Fulaij and others.

Bait Al-Fulaij Fort was a focus for the attention of many rulers who added Arab architectural decoration to the buildings. The walls were treated with ornamental plasterwork and the ceilings painstakingly embellished. The wooden joists holding up the ceiling were inscribed and painted; there were carved doors and windows with latticework outside. Perhaps the name Bait Al-Fulaij (House of Falaj) as well as Husn Bait Al-Fulaij (Fort of House of Falaj) came from its dual military and residential functions.

The strategic view has evidently played a part in the design of this fort which was subjected to adjustments and alterations at various intervals. Its use as a defence fort increased its importance and it remained a base for the leadership of the armed forces up to 1398 AH/1978 AD[229].

After this date it was transformed over a period of time into a museum of the armed forces and it was opened officially under H.M. Sultan Qaboos bin Said in December 1988.

Jalali Fort (Kout Al-Sharqi)

This fort is sometimes called Kout Al-Jalali or Kout Al-Sharqi. Some say this word is not of Arabic origin and suggest that it is Portuguese, derived from the Portuguese word *fort*. The Portuguese referred to the western citadel (Al-Mirani) as Fort Capitan, or 'seat of the commander'. It is said that originally this fort was known as San Jao and probably the name came from one of its commanders[230]. It could also of course derive from the English word *court* meaning seat of government or of the

Jalali Fort in Muscat.

magistrates; or even from the term *curtain wall* describing the fortification, after a distortion in the dialect. Or it may have come from the Arabic *kouth* in the form of a metaphor, this word meaning a four-leaved plant[231]. This citadel has several towers and a linguistic corruption could realistically give *kout*. We are not inclined to give much weight to this latter derivation and if we accept it as a metaphor for the form, we cannot accept it as a metaphor for the fort's defence function which was of the first order. We are more inclined to accept it as having been derived from one of the the western language sources. However the Arabic *koud* meaning a pile or heap is the most likely if compared with the pronunciation *kout* after some distortion.

Opinions differed as to the construction and reason for the construction of this fort. There are those who believe that it was built in 995 AH/1587 AD after the Portuguese had reclaimed Muscat with the purpose of taking control of all Oman by means of the seizure of its seaports[232]. The Jalali part of the name it is said comes from the occupation of this fort by the Persian commander in 1150 AH/1737 AD. Another view however is that it goes back to its construction, that is to the year 994 AH/1586 AD. A third view informs us that it was built in 997 AH/1588 AD[233].

At any rate this fort was built on the rubble of an older structure which is thought to have been a group of observation posts; these possibly took the form of towers erected by the citizens of Muscat. Perhaps this stronghold was demolished by the fires of Albuquerque who described the town as 'densely inhabited'. This suggests to us that the population would require the stability and continuity which would be provided by the presence of secure fortifications. Albuquerque did not take his drastic step until negotiations had failed[234]. We are inclined to support the view that the fort was built on the ruins of an old building. The negotiations referred to and their subsequent failure imply the presence of a resistance force which saw itself as equal to the aggressors and capable of taking them on and withstanding their strength from the ensconsed defences of forts and citadels. So the most likely supposition then would be that the Portuguese rebuilt what they had destroyed, alert to the value of this strategic monument and its importance in defence. In the reconstruction they would have turned to the design features of the Sohar citadel[235], using their long military experience, which is evident in the architecture of the citadel.

This fort was a subject of great interest to several Omani rulers. The Ya'ruba preserved it and renovated it sometime between 1068 and 1070 AH/1657 and 1659 AD, that is in the time of the Imam Sultan bin Saif bin Malik Al-Yar'ubi who died in 1190 AH/1776 AD[236]. The *Wali* Khalfan bin Abdullah in the time of the Imam Ahmed bin Said also made renovations in 1168 AH-1170 AH/1754-1756 AD, i.e. approximately a hundred years later[237]. Sultan Turki bin Said carried out repairs in 1285 AH/1868 AD, adding the western rooms[238], and it was renovated again by H.M. Sultan Qaboos bin Said to consolidate and strengthen it along with the additions introduced in 1401 AH/1981 AD.

Al-Mirani Fort (Kout Al-Gharbi)

As controversy marked the interpretation of the name of the Jalali Fort so also with the present fort of which it was said that the name was derived from the

Portuguese *almirante* or admiral[239]. It was said also that the Portuguese called it *Fort Capitan*. The prevailing view is the one given, that it was called *almirani* in a reference to one of the Persian commanders who occupied Muscat in 1150 AH/ 1737 AD, and to whom Imam Saif bin Sultan Al-Ya'rubi had appealed for help[240]. It is thought that this fort was built on the remains of an old building and that it was an observation post for the protection of the city, sharing in this respect the purpose of the Jalali Fort; and that King

Al-Mirani Fort.

Philip of Spain who conquered Portugal in 986 AH/1578 AD or 988 AH/1580 AD as reported by Dr Soad Maher, ordered it to be built. It was finished in 996 AH/ 1587 AD[241] and it was said to have been built on the rubble of an older building[242]. The Portuguese are known to have improved it, supporting the notion that it was not an original structure but the result of the development of an older structure which probably had proved inadequate to the circumstances then prevailing. This fort bears all the hallmarks of having had a military function which was developed to suit the requirements of the district it defended.

The date of construction again has historians divided, some ascribing it to 996 AH/1588 AD[243] and others to 998 AH/1590 AD[244]. The difference in the dates is slight and we can be content with it; it may be due simply to a printing error or error of transmission.

Just as the Jalali Fort was cared for and conserved by the Ya'ruba, this fort also gained its share of attention and care from these rulers. It was renovated in 1080 AH, that is in the time of Imam Sultan bin Saif, in recognition of its structural function and in deference to its defence role and strategic value.

Imam Ahmed bin Said appointed his *Wali* Khalfan bin Abdullah as his agent to carry out renovations between 1168 and 1170 AH/1754-1756 AD. This was the same period in which the renovations of the Jalali fort were taking place[245], according to a plan for the overhaul and maintenance of the forts of Oman. This occurred in the term of Imam Ahmed bin Said, when repairs and renovations were undertaken at a number of famous forts.

On the orders of H.M. Sultan Qaboos bin Said, the fort was renovated and its facilities enhanced in 1395 AH/1975 AD[246].

The façade of Matrah Fort shows how well the design is tailored to local features.

Matrah Fort

Matrah Fort

This is sometimes called Kout Matrah after the fashion of the other two forts mentioned, Jalali and Al-Mirani; and sometimes it is called the Portuguese fort[247]. This is a clear reference to the Portuguese and probably its circumstances were similar to that of the two other forts in Muscat.

The Portuguese were accustomed to refer to Matrah as *Makara* possibly a corruption of the word *maghara* or *maqaar* (dwellings or quarters). The second interpretation is more acceptable as the fort was used for a habitation or seat. This interpretation is an Arabic one in essence, for *maqaar* is the plural of *maqar*. It would also permit us to encompass the meaning of Matrah (place or seat) while not departing from the meaning of a 'citadel.' Perhaps this fort was named by the local citizenry.

Matrah Fort is believed to have been built in 986 AH/1578 AD that is ten years before the Al-Mirani Fort[248] and eleven years before Jalali. This precedence would imply that Matrah and its fort were more important than Muscat. We believe, however, that they were both built in the same year as the Al-Mirani Fort with the purpose of strengthening their fortifications and that the difference in the dates is the result of an error in transmission. The date was probably 986 AH/1578 AD, this being the year in which the Jalali Fort was completed. Or the building commenced in this year and was completed in 996 AH/1587 AD. Matrah did not at any time supercede Muscat in importance from a strategic point of view as far as the Portuguese were concerned; as testified by the number and variety of fortifications in Muscat which drawings from this period show clearly[249].

At any rate this fort, along with some others came in for special attention. Matrah was one of the important trading centres of Oman and the maintenance of its fort by means of repairs and renovations was an obligation imperative for its safety and defence. Oman's Ya'ruba and Al-Busaidi rulers took pains to maintain it, and in execution of the orders of H.M. Sultan Qaboos bin Said the Ministry of National Heritage and Culture repaired it once again in 1400-1401 AH/ 1980-1981 AD[250].

Jibrin Fort

The townland of Jibrin is now in the jurisdiction of the *Wilaya* of Bahla in the interior of Oman. Jibrin and Jabra'il have at their root the word *jabr* or force[251], from which we can assume that the fort was built with this idea in mind. If the concept of force contradicts the concept of choice then the word must be understood in the sense of 'prevention.' The prevention of fragmentation means the preservation of unity; and this interpretation of force contains a sense of loftiness and grandeur.

The townland of Jibrin is distinguished by healthy cultivation, in particular wheat and grains, and has water brought to it by *aflaj*. In this context the interpretation 'unity and peace and the call (of Islam)' in respect of the word *jabr* is the one in which we can have most faith. Moreover one of the functions for which the stronghold or stronghold castle was built was residential and the meaning we have chosen would also be more in harmony with this designation and with the deep and interlocking relationship and shared history of the townland of Jibrin and its fort. Perhaps the townland was named after the fort, though it was more likely the other way round; and this again is supported by the belief that it was built on an older foundation[252].

The references are agreed that Jibrin fort was built by the Imam Bal'arab bin Sultan Al-Ya'rubi, though they differ as to the date. There are those who say it was built in 1081 AH/1670 AD or 1082 AH/1671 AD[253], and others who say it was built in 1086 AH/1675 AD, basing this on the date given on the inscribed arch leading to the staircase going down to the vault[254]. Of those who say the date of construction was 1081 AH/1670 AD[255] some claim that Imam Bal'arab added a wing in 1112 AH/1700 AD[256]. It is worth mentioning that some of the references place the reign of the Imam Bal'arab in the period 1091-1104 AH/1680-1692 AD[257] and Sheikh Nur Al-Din Al-Salimi says the Imam was elected in 1091 AH/1679 AD[258] although another historian says 1090 AH/1679 AD[259].

All this ambiguity in the historical record is attributable in the first instance to a lack of precision in the transmission and recording of events, as well as confusion in evaluation of both the length and the starting date of the reign; and it occurs again in respect of the Imam's death and the end of his term of office. If we make a comparison between the version of Nur Al-Din, Sheikh Abdullah bin Humaid Al-Salimi, that he held office in the period 1091-1104 AH/ 1680-1692 AD and that of Enrico d'Errico that the construction of the fort took place in 1112 AH/1700 AD, we observe a difference of around eight years between the Imam's death and the construction and would have to conclude that the fort was built after he had passed on. And yet we have all of the source references agreeing that the Jibrin fort was built by Imam Bal'arab.

Jibrin Fort.

The construction date given by Donald Hawley, that is 1080 AH/1669 AD, differs from Nur Al-Din's date (of Bal'arab's accession) by 11 years; inferring that the fort was built 11 years before the Imam took office. However if we compare this with his (Nur Al-Din's) account elsewhere - in *Kashef Al-Ghumah*- we find him explaining that the fort was built some 30 years before this. Certainly this revisionist approach to the dating of events, accessions and accomplishments makes it imperative that a light be turned on this whole issue and that dates be verified by carefully pursuing them through all of the references, comparing notes and making adjustments, if we are to put an end to confusion and debate; this should be done without delay.

It looks as though this fort underwent several alterations. Historians and in particular archaeologists say that its original design was quite different from its present appearance and that it was subjected to a many-phased construction process, suggesting an ongoing construction operation[260]. They propose that a part of it was added later for defence purposes. Others say that no alteration of the basic structure occurred. Perhaps external additions were made within the confines of the surrounding wall. To accept the first view would be to have gained an added dimension to the development of architectural thinking in the course of the phased process. Indeed this is the type of process that informs present day urban and structural planning. Moreover the practice of adding to and extending structures was quite common in many Omani buildings, including the various stronghold buildings: Rustaq, Sohar, Jalali and Bahla citadels; and in the castle forts such as Al-Nu'man and similar style residences we find that this is a normal construction pattern. Among the inspirational architectural features of this building is the fact that its facades are not symmetrical but were each composed individually.

Some historians ascribe its construction to its residential significance over and above its value as a fortress from which to repel hostile assaults[261]. It is most probable that the thinking behind this structure involved an awareness of the importance of having forward bases scattered about the various parts of the country as is the case at present with Hazm and other forts.

Al-Nu'man House.

Fat'h Al-Busaid

Al-Hazm Fort.

It is recorded that the Imam Bila'rab bin Sultan funded this fort from private means as did the Imam Sultan bin Saif in the building of Hazm fort. The Ministry of National Heritage and Culture completed repairs to this fort in 1404 AH/1983 AD.

Al-Nu'man House

Al-Nu'man House was built on the rubble of an older structure which was once the seat of the *Walis*[262]. Its construction is attributed to Imam Saif bin Sultan around 1103-1104 AH/1691-1692 AD[263], although these dates correspond to the last two years of his brother Imam Bal'arab bin Sultan's reign (d 1104 AH/1692 AD), implying that it was this Imam who built the house and that his brother Saif bin Sultan undertook the planting of a great number of trees around it, *viz.* 300 date palm seedlings and 600 coconut palms[264].

It is possible that the construction operation did not begin in the reign of Imam Bila'rab as a complete project, but that walls and towers were added to it and that he was content with carrying out some repair work. What can be understood from the word 'rubble' is that the previous building had been demolished or crumbled away as a result of human or environmental factors. We can perhaps also understand from it that a part of the structure was still in existence, whether this be in the shape of walls or merely foundations, and it was to the vestiges of this basic structure that the repairs and additions were carried out.

The Imam Ahmed bin Said also renovated it and added new towers and extended the walls. These additions we can interpret in the case of the walls as meaning either an extension of the length or a raising of their height. He also refurbished its gardens from which we gather that he added to them and revitalized them[265].

Al-Hazm Fort

Al-Hazm means strain or stress and the verb Hazm means to brace or make firm[266]. Perhaps the name Al-Hazm was given to the fort with the intention that it would carry this assurance of purpose and hold fast against the enemy. Perhaps this purpose illuminated its distinctive design and the presence of the defensive fortifications which were added to it in the form of towers, secret pathways, defensive walls, apertures and gun platforms.

The fort and village are linked in both name and purpose, for the village is called Al-Hazm village. Perhaps the fort took its name from the village if the latter were there first or *vice versa*. It is an outstanding architectural monument and supports the evidence of the Omani's high perceptivity and the advanced state of his architectural thinking and civil engineering skills. Almost all of the references agree that it was built by the Imam Sultan bin Saif who occupied the Imamate in the period 1123-1131 AH/1711-1718 AD[267]. A substantial sum of money was spent[268] on building activity and in particular the building of this fort. Some sources date the construction to 1126 AH/1714 AD[269], and others to 1120 AH/1708 AD, the latter attributing their version to an inscription over the main entrance door. Others place the construction in the year 1121 AH/1709 AD[270] and yet others 1708 AD[271]. If the ruling term of the Imam was seven years[272] starting in 1123 AH/1711 AD and ending in 1131 AH/1718 AD as all of the Omani sources agree, then we cannot accept that the fort was built in 1120 AH/1708 AD as was claimed, nor indeed in the alternative 1121 AH/ 1709 AD. We also note a lack of precision in the conversion of the Islamic to Christian dates in the records furnished to us by the references, though most of them ascribe the building of the fort to 1126 AH/1714 AD, and this we can probably trust. It was said that the Imam Sultan bin Saif funded the building from his own pocket and from the *waqf* (Islamic charitable trust) and was buried inside it.

This fort underwent a number of additions, sharing in this respect much with the Al-Nu'man House and Jibrin Fort and others. Ibrahim bin Qais added a number of claybrick buildings in 1318 AH/1900 AD[273]. This fort would benefit from an exhaustive study from an archaeological and engineering point of view of every aspect of it insofar as it represents a good prototype of the genre from which might be learned much about the thinking which informed its design and ensured its continuity of purpose and form.

Buraimi Fort - Al-Khandaq Palace/Al-Khandaq Fort

This fort is called the Buraimi Fort because it is situated in the *Wilaya* of Buraimi. It is one of the frontline forts of Oman which were prominent in the military history of the country. Its other title, Al-Khandaq, comes from the fact that a wide ditch or trench measuring 7.5 metres and having a depth of around 3 metres once surrounded it and its rampart fortifications. The name Al-Khandaq Palace derives probably from its having been used as a palace residence, as were Jibrin, Al-Nu'man House and Hazm Fort and others like them which were built as stronghold castles with an official aspect to their function. It is thought that Sultan Said bin Sultan commissioned it and this is supported by the presence of cannon bearing his name, dated 1258 AH/ 1842 AD[274].

So with Buraimi Fort and the other forts and citadels we have discussed so far; merely a few of the many which abound throughout Oman. If we have given some attention to the dates when these forts were constructed and reviewed some of the architectural features which characterize them, these features must now guide us to an examination of the basis from which this military architecture developed in Oman.

The Foundations of Omani Military Architecture

The approach taken to military defence by Oman revolved around a number of central principles and on a legacy extending back in history to pre-Islamic times, in particular to the fourth millennium BC, and continuing through landmarks in the pre-Islamic era, the age of the Caliphs and the sixteenth-seventeenth centuries up to today.

The various legacies combined to weave a strategic approach to defence which was not attributable to a single specific factor but rather was the product of all of the elements necessary and vital to the furnishing of strength in the sense that is intended by Almighty God in the Qur'an.

The elements from which the military architecture of the Omanis was fashioned are many. First among them must be Oman's own history, for it provided a living focus for the creation of an approach to defence. This history has accumulated a rich and significant fund of military experience gained from Oman's long succession of struggles and wars, in its interior and on its plains, coasts, deserts and territorial waters; and even those territories which Oman subdued, stretching back to the civilization of Umm Al-Nar - as was revealed in the remains of ancient fortifications found in the Bat district in the present day *Wilaya* of Ibri, dating to the fourth millennium BC. The existence of evidence of a variety of fortifications, including a fort, wall and stronghold, imply that experience was being gained even then in this field. There was then the war waged by the Sumerian King Naram Sin against King Manium, king of Magan[275], and the events which transpired between King Shabwa and King Samharam and the Azd wars with the Persians in the time of Malik bin Fahm and his successors[276]; and on to the Islamic era when the Omanis were prominent in the ranks of the Islamic armies[277] and as commanders, such as Al-Muhalab bin Abi Sufra and his sons, to whom was delegated the war on the oppressors of the Islamic State[278]; to the Imams who disdained the mastery of the Ummayyads, such as Al-Julanda bin Mas'ud[279] and the resisters of the pirates, such as Imam Ghassan[280] and their withstanding of the Abbassids in one of the great battles fought near the Dama (Al-Seeb) Fort in 280 AH/ 893 AD in the time of the Imam Azzan bin Tamim al-Kharousi[281]; to the military activities of the Omanis in India in the days of Imam Al-Salt bin Malik which gave victory to the *Muslims*; and again the repulsion of the Persians from Sohar prior to the Portuguese occupation; and their refusal to yield to the Portuguese in 913 AH/1507 AD before they had fought a staunch resistance in the cities of Sohar, Muscat, Sur and Quriyat[282]; to the firing of the spirit of resistance which enabled the Omanis to overcome[283], defeat and pursue the Portuguese; then to build their fleet which granted them success in resisting the Persians in the Gulf[284]. And so it was also with the attempts of the other foreign countries such as France and Britain and Holland to establish relations with Oman[285].

The Omanis' history of wars and battles was a consequence of their unwillingness to submit to oppression, whether this was political, social or economic in nature. Their internal feuds in the shape of civil wars which recurred throughout the country's history arose principally from their tradition of facing the enemy and confronting evil (Who assaults you unjustly, assault him in return).

This fighting which the Omanis endured gave them valuable military skills the central focus and first principle of which was defence, and this in turn led to the erection of a great number of forts, fortifications, defence walls and towers.

The second element was Islam and this was a most important aspect of the defence approach. The shock operation (*raw'*)[286]had its origins in the *Muslims'* willingness and readiness to withstand invasion and their fiery spirit of resistance. This was a particular characteristic of their opposition to the Ummayyads, the Abbassids, the Persians, the Portuguese and others. Patriotism is the third factor in the defence approach and even today is deemed one of the most crucial factors in military thinking. Nationalism had a powerful impact on both military objectives and high command. An instance is when the Omanis rallied in support of the Imam Nasir bin Murshid who adopted a policy of national unity and subdued every means to its achievement.

The level of cultural and intellectual development prevailing are elements of the Omani approach to defence which cannot be ignored. They proceed directly out of its vast social heritage and were responsible for the Omanis' attaining control of their own destiny by such knowledge as they had gained from historical events. It was this cultural and intellectual heritage also which armed the Omani to move forward and, grasping the effects of confrontation, to learn to deal more effectively with events and to avoid it for happier pursuits. Many travellers mention this about Oman, among them Ibn Jubair[287], Ibn Battuta[288], Marco Polo and Corviro de ma Farinma. Before them the Arab geographers drew attention in their narratives to the marks of civilization shown by the Omanis, Al-Maqdisi, Al-Kalbi and Ya'qut, and others among them. Modern states are conscious of the importance of this in the process of understanding the mechanics of war and their use of every endeavour to raise military potential and ability. International contact is an element in defence thinking and Oman has kept abreast of all of the military equipment used throughout the world and by maintaining its relations with India, Persia and the Western nations[289] has managed to avail in a major way of their technological developments in the manufacture of weapons and to import and use these. As the use of arrows advanced to guns and cannon this affected the architecture of war and defence; instead of the slit openings used by archers, fort embrasures were modified to accommodate gunfire, their cannon platforms were modernized and a new military manufacturing industry grew up for this purpose as well as for the outfitting of an updated fleet.

In this context we cannot simply hand over credit for the military expertise gained by the Omanis to the Portuguese as the writer E. d'Errico[290] has done; no more than we can close our eyes to the undeniable impact made by the latter. The Omanis were prepared by the circumstances of their history to relate to them as an equal force, giving as much as they took. Donald Hawley believes that Western writers are wrong in attributing many of the fortress buildings in Oman to the Portuguese. On the contrary the Portuguese built very few of them, most having been constructed by the Omanis themselves[291]. Dr Soad Maher maintains that the Portuguese borrowed the designs of the old Omani strongholds such as Sohar Fort during their occupation of Oman[292]. Briton Busch says that the Westerners benefited from the architecture of Arab Eastern-style towers in Andalucia during the Crusades[293]. The witnesses we have reviewed in this

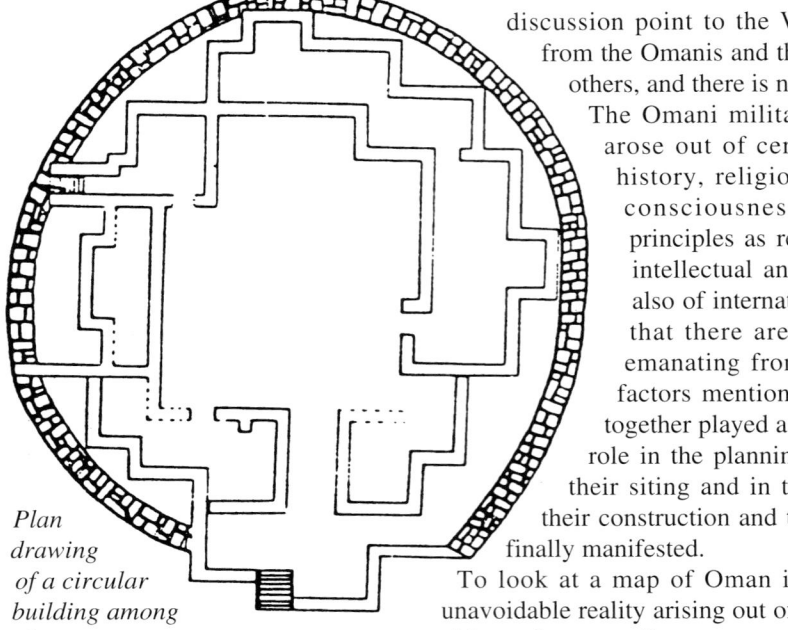

Plan drawing of a circular building among the monuments of Bat at Ibri, c. 3000 B.C.

discussion point to the Westerners having taken from the Omanis and the Omanis from them and others, and there is no shame in that[294].

The Omani military or defence approach arose out of certain fixed principles of history, religion and tribal or national consciousness, and other variable principles as represented in the level of intellectual and cultural awareness and also of international contact. We believe that there are other complex matters emanating from the fixed and variable factors mentioned and that these factors together played a significant and prominent role in the planning of the fortifications, in their siting and in the manner and nature of their construction and the design and shape they finally manifested.

To look at a map of Oman is to see immediately an unavoidable reality arising out of its multiplicity of coastal cities and metropolitan centres, set at intervals all the way from the far north to the eastern extremity and then down to the south. These cities constitute access points to the country from the sea coast. Their respective importance is bound up with their position in relation to the centre of events at any time. Amongst these cities are Sohar, Sur, Quriyat, Khasab, Barka, Marbat, Salalah, Muscat and so on, all of them seaports.

Another type of access point exists on the western and north-western sides - landports these - the most important of them being Buraimi and Ibri. On the whole the seaports are more numerous than the landports and that is to be expected given the length of Oman's coastline and because it has been the line of contact with other civilizations from time immemorial. Moreover the western and north-western borders of Oman are inhabited by desert and are not densely settled. Perhaps in the future excavations will show that civilization visited these regions too[295].

General Jamal Mahfoudh believes that the idea of building the ports goes back to the time of the Caliph Omar bin Al-Khattab when he ordered the construction of a number of cities in which the *Muslims* would reside with their families during the expanding wave of Islamic conquest[296]. The Ummayyads and Abbassids maintained the procedure. Omani cities however go back to pre-Islamic times and were not the product of this notion, for many civilizations had visited them prior to this. Moreover these cities by their economic activities were to remain important access points to Oman's interior from a military point of view, being the equivalent of forward strategic bases which demanded fortification by means of citadels and strongholds to enable them to withstand their enemies and maintain their independence. Topography was the primary factor for consideration in selecting the location of a city's fortifications and in the case of the coastal cities which were hemmed in by mountains to the rear the strongholds were built atop mountains and rocky prominences, such as at

Muscat, Matrah and Quriyat, Sur and Daba. In this and in the manner of their defence and control they were distinguished from others. The coastal cities which lacked the advantage of a mountain backdrop sited their fortifications on sandy outcrops at a slight elevation above sea level, such as Sohar and Suwaiq, this circumstance being shared by Barka, Al-Musan'a, Salalah and other well-known forts on the coast and its *wilayas*. Yet others were built on coastal headlands and tongues of land such as the Ras Al-Hadd fort and the Raisout Fort.

The statement that the coastal strongholds are for the most part sited on mountain peaks[297] is something of an overstatement and this is compounded by an absence of clarity. Mountain peaks and rocky outcrops were used for the siting of fortifications in the cities of the eastern district such as Ibra and Al-Mudhairub, or of the interior district such as Sama'il and Bahla and others. This was also found to be the case at the site of the ancient remains in Bat. Another popular location for a fortification was the junction of main roads in busy districts. In this category would fall the forts and citadels of Nizwa, Barkat Al-Mawz, Awabi and others.

So the Omanis exploited the steep mountain inclines in building fortifications as they used them (for other purposes) in the areas of cultivation. Thus evolved a type of semi-fortified or semi-military architecture which is almost unique to Oman, at least in this region. This led to the construction of a type of graduated fortification as exemplified in the houses of the Jebel Al-Akhdar in particular. We believe that the use of this type of building for residential purposes superceded its military use[298].

At Jaalan the siting of the fortifications was dictated by the need to protect the centre and surrounds of the cities as well as other broad or specific purposes, and so a number of forts and citadels were built at the Jaalan of the Bani bu Hasan and the Jaalan of the Bani bu Ali, as well as Al-Qabil, Azki, Buraimi and Ibri. The latter two cities are amongst Oman's most significant inland trading centres on its western and north-western borders.

Not least among the factors we must consider are the water springs and flood waters of the *wadis*; indeed these were among the most crucial factors in the selection of stronghold sites and water has remained a most insistent factor through the ages and up to the present day. The *Muslims* were made aware of its vital significance at the battle of Badr and it became a factor of first consideration in strategic planning; and so it remains in the twentieth century, when every power understands the value of attaining control over the supply of

Fortified city walls.

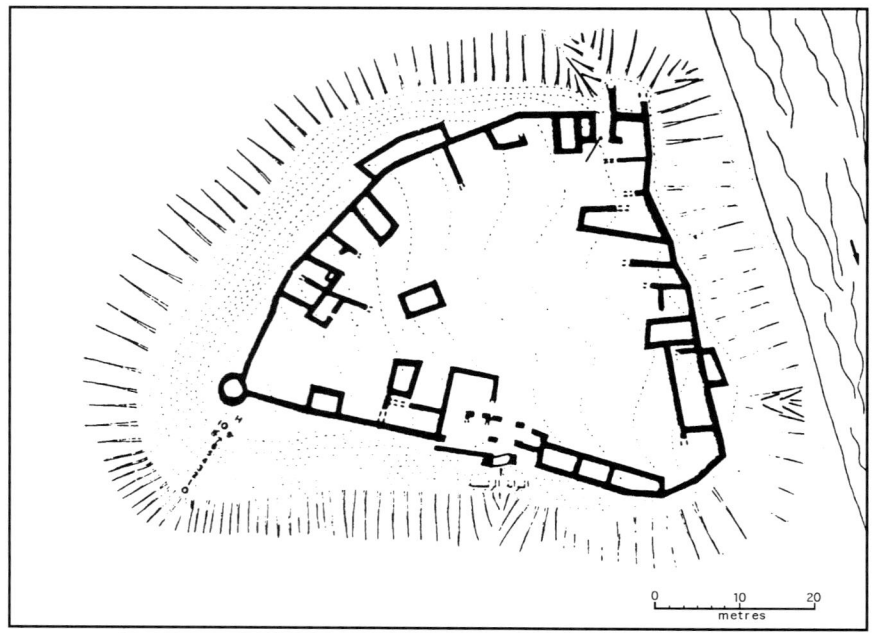

water. Consequently some of Oman's forts and strongholds were constructed close by water springs or flood valleys, among them Al-Awamer citadel on the Wadi Halfeen in the Sharqiyah (Eastern) district[299], the Madha Fort at the juncture of Wadi Sahna and Wadi Madha, Bidbid Fort at the head of the Sama'il valley, and Al-Rawiya Fort and others[300].

There are a number of fortifications which were built without any reference to topography in their task of protecting cities and their resources. Rather they were built at intervals in the manner of forward strategic bases with the function of shortening supply and communications lines for an army fighting at a distance from its principal base which would be at the district capital such as Rustaq or Nizwa. These advance bases constituted a forward line of defence from which to sap the enemy's strength and assess their capability and in this way assist the main army defending the town. This principle has been adopted by the most modern armies where we see a multiplicity of lines from a first to a second (forward base) to a third and so on. We believe that forts such as Hazm and Jibrin were built with this purpose in mind. Hazm Fort lies in an intermediate setting assisting the north of Batinah as represented by Sohar in one direction and the south of Batinah as represented by Barka and Musana'a in the other direction. Jibrin Fort meanwhile offers backup to Al-Dhahira in one direction and Dakhiliya in the other. The roots of this military concept go back to the Islamic era[301].

The constituent forms evident in the design and construction of Oman's strongholds arose from a finite number of formats which recurred more or less in all buildings; some were encountered in other local buildings such as old residences, mosques, old schools and the customs offices.

As a result of the study we made of a considerable number of buildings and fortifications in different parts of Oman it became clear to us that they can be

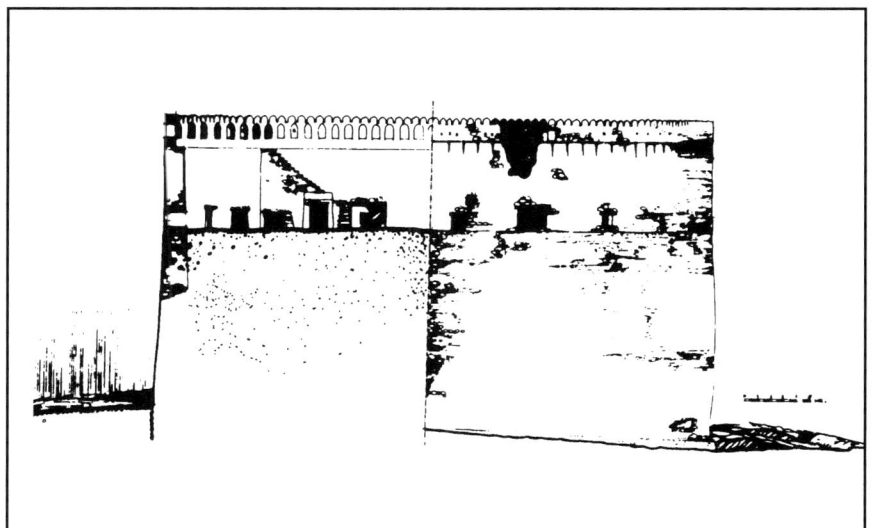

The main facade of Nizwa Fort: an example of an isolated round building

summarized under five categories of shape: rectangular, amongst them Barkat Al-Mawz, Al-Rawiya, Al-'Araqi etc.; square (Quriyat, Ras Al-Hadd, Bidbid etc.); circular, the most famous of which is Nizwa; oval, exemplified in the shape of the main tower at Rustaq Fort; and finally triangular, of which the most obvious example is the fort of Al-Seeb, which is thought to be Portuguese[302]. The discoveries at Bat have given us two fortification designs which were probably typical of the time. These were triangular and circular in the shape of a large tower[303]. We suspect that the geography of place and local topography played some part in determining the shape of the structure to be built, a not unnatural phenomenon in civil engineering and architecture; and the claim that the triangular design owes its existence specifically to a cost-saving endeavour is not entirely justifiable for it must be self-evident that any money spent on fortification will have strength as a primary goal to be achieved by whatever the means and this would be the practice anywhere in the world.

Over and above the design shapes which we were able to study because there are examples of them still standing; thus allowing us to establish prototypes and classify the various forts as we have done above, there are other varieties of fortification in the form of buildings, trenches and walls which may be graded for instance as follows:

- **Forts:** such as the Jalali and Al-Mirani Forts, along with Matrah, Bahla, Ibri, Nakhal, Rustaq and Sohar etc.
- **Towers:** such as the tower of Nizwa Fort and the towers of Ibra, Al-Mudhairub and Muscat etc, some of which were corner (towers) or were oval or square in shape. Others were polygonal and for the most part were an important constituent element of the fort or stronghold.
- **Strongholds:** Al-Awabi, Al-Khandaq, Buraimi, and Barkat Al-Mawz etc.
- Stronghold castles: Jibrin, Al-Hazm, Al-Nu'man House, Al-Jeriza House, Bait Al-Fulaij, Bait Al-Sama'il Al-Safali, Al-Falaij etc.
- **Stronghold Houses:** such as Al-Bait Al-Kebir (the large house) and other

Defensive Trenches.

residences in Ibra Al-Uliya, Bait Al-Sodour, Bait Buma and others again in Ibra Al-Sufla, and Bait Habra in Wadi Al-Ma'awal, along with the houses in the Jebel Al-Akhdar and the southern region and Sur and Al-Mudhairub, Al-Qabel and others throughout Oman[304].

• **Walls:** including those built in cities (such as the walls of Muscat and Sohar and the like), and around citadels and strongholds - this being a feature of most fortified buildings; and standalone walls fortified by corner towers, sometimes just one accompanied by ammunition stores. The Batinah district is the district most noted for these walls[305]. Some walls form part of the fortification of a castle, a fortress, a palace or a well-protected house. Its height would not be more than two thirds the height of its towers. However, the width varied, sometimes reaching 2 metres. The materials used in the construction and design also varied.

• **Trenches:** In the past, trenches were used to protect Sohar city and the city of Muscat. The Omani people used trenches to protect their cities long before the arrival of Islam and may have learned this technique from the Persians. The Arabs in Mecca and especially in Medina were not familiar with this type of protective trench, however, there was some allusion to it in the advice sought out by Salman Al-Farisi from the Messenger, during the invasion of Uhud[306].The southern Arabs, especially in Yemen, had used this kind of protective device and the Omanis acquired the technique as part of their historical heritage. Having learnt the technique in Yemen, they put that knowledge to good use when they emigrated to Oman. Trenches were used to protect some Omani cities, and were also part of the protective mechanism for castles and fortresses. Al-Buraimi Fort, aptly known as Husn Al-Khandaq, i.e. the Trench Fort, is considered to be the most famous of these structures. Trench construction varied in terms of depth and width. Coating materials for the trenches were also different and would depend on the function of the trench, its geographical importance and the availability of materials. None of these trenches have been built on the top of mountains or other elevated sites; the reason being that the natural protection afforded by the heights was better than that in the plains and valleys. The castles and the forts built in the flatter areas were surrounded by high walls, reaching 30 metres in Salalah, or 22 metres at Jibrin, and 12 metres at Al-Hazm. High walls were also built around forts and castles at Al-Batinah, Ja'alan, Al-Qabil and in Al-Dhahira provinces. By and large such high walls did not exist in the castles and fortresses built on elevated sites, as in Al-Dakhilya province.

There are many designs and architectural variations in the construction of Oman's forts and citadels. For instance, floor-levels differ from one castle to another. The ceiling height over each floor-level is also different: the height of the ceiling depended on the size of the area to be covered and protected. High ceilings also helped to cool the air within the castles.

The towers on these forts and citadels were sometimes sited at the four corners of the building, as at the fortress of Madha and the castle of Ras Al-Hadd. Towers were also located on diagonal corners, as at the forts at Jibrin, Al-Awabi and Barkat Al-Mawz. The towers could also be built on the corners of one of the parallel lines, as in the Bidbid fortress, or just on triangular three corners, as on As-Seeb (which is known as the Portuguese fort) and the old Bakra fort. Some of the forts had only one tower which was usually located on

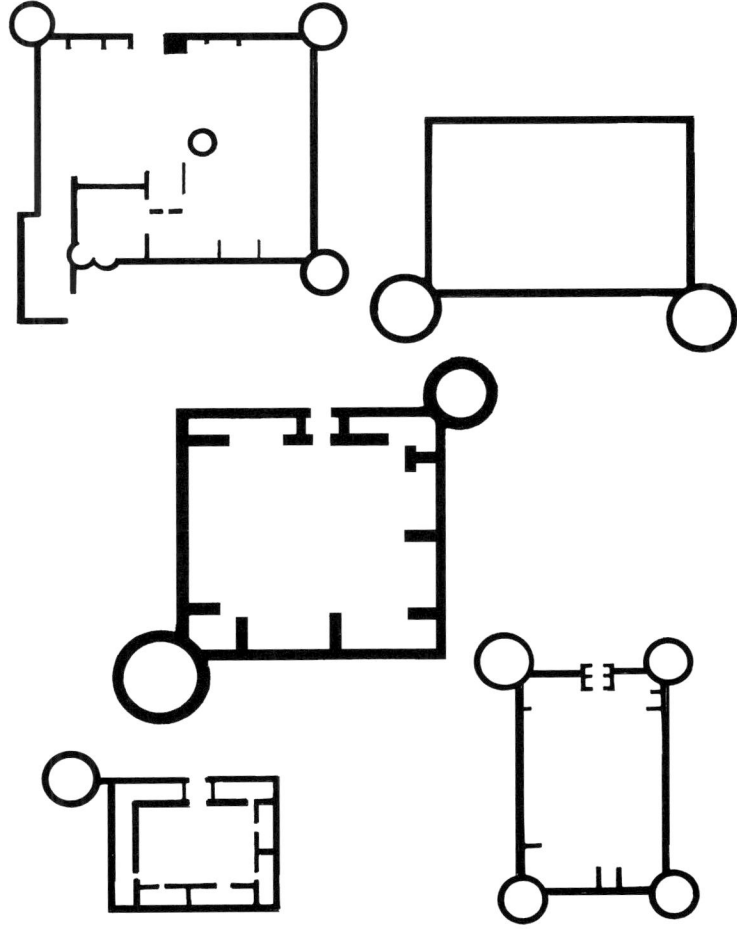

a corner as in the Araqi fort. But Nizwa is the only castle which differs from all the other citadels and forts: it is a huge tower constructed as a castle.

Those forts built on elevated sites would be designed according to the topographical nature of the location. The towers would also be constructed according to the topography. The castles of Muscat, Matrah, Al-Jalali and Al-Mirani are the most obvious examples of such forts.

Many of the walls of these forts were built in the manner explained above. But some had their own design characteristics as can be seen on the walls surrounding certain cities. The towers on these walls, also constructed on the corners, were built at a specific distance from each other. The wall surrounding Sohar city is typical of this type.

From our brief examination of Oman' forts and citadels, we can conclude that the design and construction methods used in the erection of these buildings varies considerably. In each case, the rationale behind construction dictated these variations.

Five plan drawings of construction patterns in the fortification of towers.

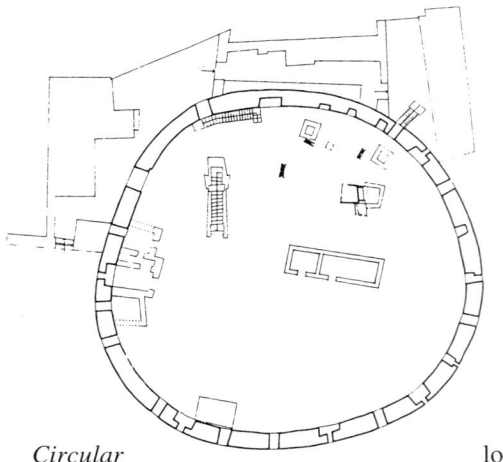

Circular fortification: Nizwa fort in Oman's interior.

Circular Castles and Fortresses

Circular castles and forts are among of the characteristic building designs used by the Omanis. Castles were built in this way because of defence requirements which necessitated the kinds of design and materials used in the vaults, for example.

The castle at Nizwa is the most famous round castle in Oman. We have already mentioned that Imam Sultan bin Saif bin Malik Al-Ya'rubi (1059-1100AH /1649-1688AD) built this castle to protect the city and surroundings. The castle with a diameter of 27 metres and a height of 34 metres took 12 years to build at this strategic location. It has seven doors, and its wall has fortifications and defence positions to launch arrows, fire and burning liquid. Inside are ammunition and food stores[307].

The secret behind the construction of round forts and castles is defence, i.e hindrance of an attack by the enemy. Since there are no corners on the building, the enemy would find it difficult to hide and the guards could watch the whole area around the fortress. This building design would also be resistant to high winds and storms which would be deflected as soon as they hit the wall. The amount of materials used in this kind of design would also be less than those used in other designs. The Omani people were aware of the advantages of such forts and castles long before the arrival of Islam, having built cities 3000 years BC[308]. Round- shaped towers were added at one corner of the castles at a higher level than the walls, in order to acquire a high degree of surveillance and control. More than one tower was often constructed in order to control all sides of the fortress, as was the case with Jibrin's fort: two large towers were built across from each corner, where control of all sides could be maintained[309].

The design and construction of forts and citadels encompassed two defensive elements which were common to many forts in Oman and elsewhere[310], especially the fort at Nizwa. The first such defensive feature, the battlements, was situated above the walls, the second, long, narrow vertical slits, on different parts of the wall itself. The battlements were to be found above the entrance to the fortress which was surrounded by a parapet constructed on strong pillars. On the floor of this balcony and in the parapet several openings were strategically placed for firing arrows and spraying burning liquids on the attackers. This kind of defence design had been known in Syria, a long time before Islam, and it was from there that these Arab defence constructions had spread all over the region. The most obvious example during the Islamic era was at the Arabian Hira Palace, at the beginning of the second century Hegira[311]. This type of structure continued to be built over forts and citadels during the Islamic era. Europeans, having learned these defence designs, reconstructed them in Europe in different historical periods.

The second type of defensive feature consists of long, narrow vertical slits in the walls themselves through which arrows could be fired and burning liquid sprayed on the attackers. These vertical openings are readily seen on the Al-

Ukhaidhar fortress in Iraq. The defenders could very easily manoeuvere behind these openings, without fear of being hit by the enemy's arrows from without. Some of the openings were false to increase the enemy's confusion when they discovered that their arrows were not able to go through. The castle of Nizwa had such false defences, and the floor at the top of the castle also had an outward slope to allow the defenders to see and direct their weapons more effectively. This kind of defensive design is very common on Islamic castles. The other horizontal defence openings, already mentioned, are situated on the fort's entrance roof, through which the burning liquids would be sprayed over the assailants, from above. We can also see on the side of Al-Hazm castle a huge water tank which was used to put out any fires lit by the enemy on the wooden doors.

The Inner Open Ward
The inner open ward or bailey was completely under surveillance by the defenders from the castle's gate and battlements. The open ward is one of the main featuress in the construction of Omani mosques, castles and houses. Very clear evidence of this is seen in Jibrin fort which was built by Bal'arab bin Sultan bin Saif (1100-1123 H/1688-1711 AD). Jibrin fort is one of the most elegant fortresses in Oman[312]. The inner open bailey, the breathing space of the whole construction and the main source of light, is surrounded by beautiful buildings and walls. This type of open space is also found at Barkat Al-Mawz[313] and in many of Nizwa's city mosques[314].

From the early stages of history, eastern peoples made wide, open courtyards a feature in all their buildings[315]since they were a natural method of lessening the harsh environmental impact of both heat and cold. The central area of forts and citadels was used for the organization, distribution and mobilizing of all sorts of materials for the surrounding building units. It was also an open space for cool air to flow in and accumulate at night, only to gradually rise and disperse during the day time, in the heat of the sun, thereby ensuring a constant circulation of air which was vital to sustain the optimum temperature required for the long life of the construction.

The inner open ward was also important for the distribution of light, to absorb and disperse noise, and act as a natural filter for dust when the wind blew up. In addition, the buildings were constructed in two groups with two different orientations, determined by the nature and direction of the winds facing the two groups[316]. One group was used as a residential complex in summer, while the opposite buildings were occupied in winter.

The Wooden Ceiling
During the Islamic era, wood and timber were widely used in constructing ceilings. In the Middle Ages, Muslims extensively used timber to fashion ceilings since it was plentiful, light and easily used in construction. Omani artists and engineers transformed these ceilings into works of art of rare beauty, using colourful paint, the art of parquetry and decorative arches. Tenons and mortises were widely used and artistical work employing different kinds of spandrels and anaglyphs can be seen on most timber ceilings of houses and castles. Consoles, prets, friezes, rosettes, rose windows, fine art, flower and rose

shapes are still used on timber ceilings. Many types of tools for woodwork are used even today, such as planes, rabbets, ripsaws, wooden treadles, braces and bits[317].

Many timber ceilings are adorned with very fine, brightly-coloured paintings, the best example of which are to be found in the famous Jibrin Fort. The wooden doors are ornamented with brilliant artistical designs, the ceilings uniquely painted with water-colours. The mosque's ceiling and the ceiling of the residence of the Imam, as well as the ceiling in the guest room resemble art galleries[318]. The artistry was not confined to wood-work, engineering and painting, the buildings also demonstrate that the Omani people were highly competent Arabic calligraphers.

Gypsum and Wooden Screens

The climate in Oman is very harsh, and so the population invented various ways to soften the impact of the severe weather conditions on their daily life. The incorporation of many windows in the walls of their buildings is one of the most significant ways to reduce heat inside homes as well as castles. The flow of air through these windows helps to maintain cool air inside. Latticed and mullioned gypsum and wooden screens were put in place to cover the inner windows of the castles. The screens contain many apertures to reduce the heat from the sunlight and to allow a continuous passage of air.

The design of these screens is evidence of Omani Arab craftsmenship and artistry, living proof of their engineering ingenuity combined with an immense practicality. Arabic calligraphy of rare beauty, drawings and colourful paintings provided comfortable living in a peaceful and pleasant atmosphere. Many of these screens were crafted with coloured pieces. Only recently have scientists discovered that a combination of colours can cure some illnesses. We can now marvel at the cleverness of those people in the past who instinctively understood the role different colours played in improving the quality of life. Some research work has been done on Arabic and Islamic crafts in relation to these screens. These studies proved that the artistical work is based on a deep scientific knowledge of geometry and engineering[319].

The Omani people were able to procure the timber for the doors and windows from Oman where a variety of trees which can give solid timber suitable for making these windows were grown. In addition, Omanis were able to import many kinds of timber from India and Africa, using the sea routes to import the woods with which they kept the craftwork traditions going for many centuries[320].

The gypsum and timber windows were fixed on the upper parts of the upper floors of the castles, forts and houses. The reason was that these areas were exposed to the heat of the sunlight more so than the rest of the building. The lower parts would be covered with timber windows crafted to different shapes and designs, and the glass would be either white or transparent. In some cases a small, round window was built on top of the main window: this combination is widely used in Yemen.

In some parts of Oman many different types of window can still be seen. Some of these exquisite timber windows were built according to the decorative designs which Omani travellers brought from India and Africa[321]. Some of the imported designs are round or semicircular, or a combination of more than one design, like the windows of Jibrin fortress[322].

Timber screens were often made in sections, where one or two sections of the window could be opened to allow a certain quantity of air and sunlight to enter the rooms. At one stage it was common to erect a rectangular frame made of latticework which covers the window itself from outside, and has a wide base[323].

These beautiful windows reflected the fine art that was deep-rooted in Omani history, providing clear evidence that Oman's forefathers were brilliant craftsmen who worked hard and efficiently in all aspects of their lives[324]. This kind of timber window flourished all over the Arabian peninsula and in Iraq and Egypt. In Iraq they call it *shanasheel* and in Egypt it is known as *mashribyat*. Their function is the same as the Omani gypsum and timber windows. They are used to filter the dust from the air and to cool down the buildings during hot weather.

Western architects and engineers have learnt to appreciate the technical and aesthetic appeal of these windows[325], but they do not understand the practical benefits behind their beauty.

Mosques and Minarets

Omani mosques do not have very complex engineering designs and their architectural plans are not very sophisticated. Generally, they have open inner courtyards surrounded by porticoes[326]. Most of the mosques have this kind of design except for a few, which are slightly different. Ibn Battuta mentioned in his book that the mosque of Qalhat had its walls coated with semi-smooth tiles[327].

One of the main features of Omani mosques which may differ from those in other Islamic countries are the minarets. In Oman, and especially on the coastline, the minarets are simply small square constructions, sometimes round, usually with open windows on two floors. The *muethin* stands inside and calls for prayer. The ceiling of the minaret has an oval shape with a pointed end[328]. This type of minaret is reminiscent of Al-Gioshi Minaret built in Cairo by the Fatimids.

To call for prayer, the *muethin* could stand on the nearest roof next to the mosque, or could stand on the stairs built on the outside wall of the mosque. This situation existed in the mosque of the Messenger and in many mosques built during the early days of Islam[329].

Crenellations

This is another Arabic-Islamic architectural feature designed to be in harmony with the environmental conditions. The crenellations would be either incorporated in the design of the building itself or achieved through the use of certain building materials in construction. Historical evidence has proved that a combination of both aspects have been used for many centuries.

Crenellations have crowned the walls of many religious, residential and military forts for a very long time. The erection of a crenellation meant that the building had reached the final stage of its construction. There are quite a few designs for crenellations. Some of them are like stairs or leaves, they can also be square or rectangular, round or triangular, as well as many other types.

Crenellations, known as 'brides of the skies' [330], are a very familiar structure on mosques and forts. Erected on the top of these buildings, they were square-shaped, the upper part taking the shape of circles or triangles; these crenellations used to be coated with gypsum and bright coloured paints. Such crenellations can be seen erected over the walls of Jibrin fort and on most of the castles and forts all over the country. As already mentioned, they were also built over the walls of the mosques, minarets, towers and houses. The Omani designs are different from those in other Islamic countries.

Crenellations were erected primarily for aesthetic reasons, but many of them were also used as posts for defence against attackers. However, the origin of their construction was in climatic requirements since crenellations help to bring fresh air into mosques, castles and houses. We need to explain here the historical changes and developments that occurred in the design and construction of these crenellations. Some aspects of ancient Omani castle and fort designs have altered during contemporary times. Military requirements and strategy, in particular, has necessitated some changes in the original designs of the crenellations. Ancient and Islamic structural and architectural techniques have been improved in many ways, as in the forts and castles of Sohar, Ar-Rustaq, Al-Jalali and Al-Mirani. Such developments were necessitated by changing needs. Omani leaders, during the reign of Al-Ya'ruba committed themselves to take responsibility for achieving new developments, especially improvements in castles and forts. Such developments emerged as a result of long experience and because the methods and means of warfare, particularly as a result of the acquisition of rifles and cannons, changed dramatically. But traditional weapons, such as swords and the bow and arrow continued to be used: the introduction of new weapons did not completely negate the older ones. Both types of weapons were used side by side. However, on the eve of the twentieth century, traditional weapons gave way to new ones. Some traditional weapons, such as swords and machetes were retained by individuals only and within a narrow section of the population outside formal governmental institutions.

Today we are able to see the old narrow vertical defences used to fire arrows, side by side with the openings used by defenders armed with rifles, guns and cannons, whether on the battlements or inside the fortresses. This co-existence between the two generations of defence techniques can be seen especially at the forts of Jibrin, Sohar and Al-Hazm. The size, number, height and width of the fort's doors are also different. The galleries, porticoes and the underground and secret exits and entrances all had different designs at different historical periods. In the castle of Nizwa and the fortress of Al-Hazm, one can see today, how the openings for throwing burning liquids on the assailants were just next to the site for defenders who were carrying rifles and guns.

Some of the forts were constructed to withstand cannon fire, such as the castles of Muscat, Al-Jalali, Al-Mirani and Matrah. These castles contained the launching pads for guns and cannons. Such association between the old and new defence techniques also existed at the castle of Nizwa. The original design of Nizwa castle contained both systems, but because there was a plan set in motion to repair and renew the old castles of Ar-Rustaq, Sohar and Nakhal, amongst others, it was decided that new and dynamic erections should exist in these castles.

There was also a campaign to repair some of the fort's walls, while renewing the very old ones. Developments in the waging of of war and new thinking in how to protect and defend people and country had to be taken into account. Therefore, the height, thickness and the width of the walls had to be capable of serving new requirements. For example, soldiers and personnel had to be able to freely manoeuvre over the walls. These ideas were implemented whilst renewing the high walls of Nizwa castle. The walls of many castles had to be repaired and new Martello towers built on top of them. In most cases, the towers had to take the shape of half circles to allow the defenders to spread their fire over a wider range. This type of new development was incorporated into the castle walls of Sohar and Jaalan Bani bu Hassan.

Many fortress walls and buildings were topped with crenellations, some had new towers constructed on top of their entrances, as at the forts of Jibrin, Ar-Rustaq, Barkat Al-Mawz and the wall of Muscat. All these forts were equipped with the new phase of modern weapons and equipment.

The process of development was also directed at the stores and ammunition dumps which had to be upgraded from storing traditional and classical weapons to more modern ones such as guns, rifles, cannons and many other kinds of new ammunition. Such considerations were paramount during the planning process which underlay the renewal of the old buildings as well as the design and construction of new stores and dumps.

The types and shapes of the towers were very different from each other, the size of the tower depending upon its location. The diameters of some of them reached up to 6 metres, as seen in the case of Al-Afi fort. There is also a very big difference between the diameters of individual towers. For example, the diameter of the tower of Bait Al-Fulaij is 7 metres, Al-Awabi fortress - 9.6 metres; Ar-Rustaq castle - 11.9 metres, while the tower diameter of Nizwa castle reached more than 37 metres[331].

We have mentioned these examples to give the reader an idea of the development process which occurred in the building of the towers as a response to defence requirements. The bigger towers needed different thicknesses of roof and different sizes of pillars. Architects and construction engineers of course are well aware[332] that if the roof of the tower is required to be larger then its thickness must increase and the pillars must be enlarged and vice versa. All these calculations had to be based upon the weights and the range of movements over the roof and the vibration impact of firing cannons and guns.

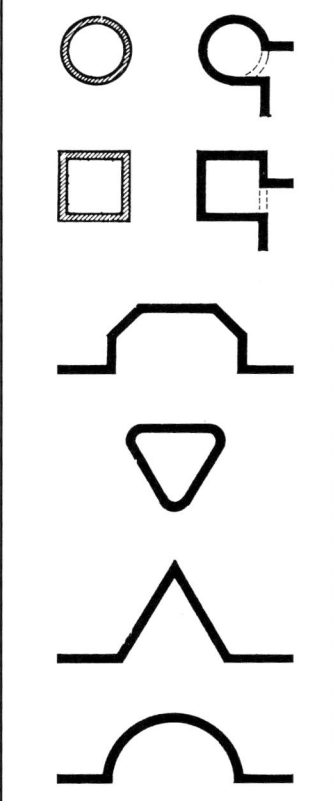

Tower shapes and their means of communicating with the fortifications.

The Omanis had developed engineering and construction acumen since the year 3000 BC which enabled them to meet these challenges. Likewise, the Arabs had the same knowledge when they were in Andalucia (Spain today)[333].

There was very little innovation as far as the trenches were concerned. However, we do know that the trenches were very well developed in Iraq during the reign of Haroun Al-Rashid in order to protect Baghdad. At this time the trenches were separated by high walls, as had been done by the Ummayyads before that[334]. The trenches in Oman were not improved as such, except those constructed around Khandaq fort in Al-Buraimi and those around Muscat which were paved with bricks[335].

The Omanis used various building materials for the construction of their citadels, forts and houses. Archaeologists and scientists in Oman have pointed out that ancient man in Oman built trenches with large stones, having cut them into symmetrical shapes with dimensions of 1x1x0.8 metres. They placed these one on top of the other without any gypsum, cement or mortar between them[336]. The Phoenicians had used this method to erect their buildings at Carthage[337]. The Omanis built with more than one kind of brick, e.g. square, rectangular, and some which were stoved. Coned (cut) bricks were particularly popular in the construction of round buildings and the different types of arches. The square bricks were used for buildings with corners and those that had sharp bends. Rectangular ones were used in both buildings, whether with corners or rounded.

At Al-Batinah, the walls of the castles and fortresses were built with bricks, while its towers were built with stones and quicklime[338]. The wall of Bahla was built with the same materials and followed the same construction method. The castles and fort in Jaalan also followed suit.

Building with small stones required the use of more gypsum and cement. The same would apply for different sizes of bricks. To join the bricks and small stones, they would have had to use mud and quicklime, with the possibility of coating the wall with gypsum. The quicklime was also employed as an insulation material against moisture and damp, because its fine, solid particles did not allow the water to be absorbed. The Omani environment provided the population with many kinds of materials which could be used in construction and building. Timber was one of those gifts. The trunks of date palms, coconuts, acacia and oak were used in the construction of roofs and to make windows, doors, supports and bridges across the ceilings. Timber was used in making steps, stairs, frames for the doors and windows and as separators between walls. It was also used as pillar and arch supports and to cover the floors of the halls and rooms[339].

The leaves of palm trees were extensively used in the embellishment of the walls and ceilings. Gypsum was always used to coat the walls from inside and out. Gypsum, in addition to its usage in construction was employed in Oman in pointing and embellishing the ceilings and the corners of the rooms.

We can see the beautiful artistry in the well protected palaces and large houses in Jibrin, Al-Hazm, Al-Bait Al-Kebir in Ibri and Bait Al-Sayyid Nadir, amongst others. In these houses, can be found first class art and embellishments on walls, ceilings, corners and on windows. Despite the intention to construct robust buildings which would withstand the heat and harsh environment, much attention was lavished on adorning palaces and houses, both inside and out.

Meanwhile, we can see the strength and toughness of the castles and fortresses of Nizwa, Ar-Rustaq, Al-Jalali and Matrah. Such differences were related to the function of the building whether a palace for residential purposes or a fortress for defence. Many researchers noticed the influence of Safavid architecture on the construction of Jibrin fort[340]. This is very evident in the pointed arches in the interior as well as the exterior of the building. It can be seen also on the bridge boards connecting the pillars.

Another suggested influence on Omani buildings and castles was Moghul architecture. Some people believe such influences are to be seen in the houses of Ibra and Muscat and claim that the connection was between Oman and the Moghul empire in India. With all due respect to such claims, we have to remember that the Safavid state was established in 888 H/1483 AD[341] and that the Ya'ruba state was established after a period of about one century. If we go back and study Arab architectural achievements, especially in Andalucia, and focus in particular on the pointed arches in Cordoba Mosque in Spain[342], we can see that the bridging technique between the pillars had also been used in Al-Azhar mosque in Cairo. There is no doubt that pointed arches, ridgepoles and tufting embellishments are all Islamic architectural features[343]. Muslims freely exchanged their architectural designs and engineering knowledge with others. This explains the existence of Moroccan arches and embellishments on many doors in Sur[344]. The same explanation can be given for the spread of embellishments and tufts on the doors and windows of the buildings in the southern region of Oman. The innovation process certainly had been based entirely on the Islamic philosophy and thinking. Therefore, we are sure that the claim that our architectural methods had been influenced by Western and African methods is incorrect. We do agree that there are mutual influences as a matter of give and take and as a natural development within international exchanges and relations. However, it is not possible to say that the Arabic architecture of Oman is completely and entirely copied from Portuguese house designs.

It must be said that the Omani castles and forts had more than one function. Some were used as schools and teaching centres, while others contained government offices and administrative centres for governors. Others were assigned to house lawyers and judges. A few of them had residential complexes for the chief of staff and his officers, or for government officials. In some cases they housed ordinary citizens especially during war and crises. Some of these forts were also used as army barracks. The forts at Jibrin, Al-Hazm and Ar-Rustaq encompassed schools, residential buildings, army barracks for defence purposes and government centres. Some forts were used for military purposes only, as is the case with the two castles of Al-Jalali and Al-Mirani and the defence walls of Al-Batinah and Jaalan.

Information on the functions of the castles and forts in Oman prompts us to ask the question - What are the designs and functions of contemporary buildings?[345]. We have seen the luxurious and magnificent buildings in Jibrin, Al-Hazm and the well guarded palaces of Sayyid Nadir and Al-Nu'man. These palaces were solely for residential and civil use. The craftwork and embellishments were obviously for civil purposes and their original designs envisaged peaceful functions only. This is obvious from their facade.

In the case of castles solely with military function, the facade and the general appearance of the forts which belie this function can be recognized at a glance. Crafted embellishments did not adorn these buildings, and even if they did, then the type of embellishments would be associated with the military function and would indicate strength and power. That is why we stated that there is a direct correlation between the functions of the castles, forts, buildings and their original designs.

We should state in this regard that the Omani environment nurtured all these buildings. The materials used for construction, as well as the geographical positions, all assisted these castles, forts, palaces and other buildings to withstand the harsh climate. The mountains, valleys and heights provided natural protection to those constructions. The castle of Nakhal is a very good example of the marriage between natural position and the architecture and engineering design of the castle.

The topography and the solid rocks supplied these castles and forts with power and strength, while the open plains gave the palaces of Jibrin, Al-Hazm and Al-Nu'man House magnificent views. The distribution of the buildings around the castles and palaces, together with the locations of the doors and windows, allowed sufficient light and air to enter the buildings. We are able to see such clever design in Bait Al-Fulaij fort, Bait Hubra and all other buildings which we have come across. All were provided with sources of water, whether through watercourses, canals or fountains, as in the castles and forts of the inner province, or artesian wells as at Al-Batinah.

All modern theories insist on the role and importance of the environment on the designs and engineering work of the buildings. The famous engineer, Mese van Dorda, believes that the dominant determining factor in the design of any building should be that it would belong to its own historical time. This should take precedence over all other factors, such as aesthetics[346]. Most Omani castles would fall into this category as the appearance of the building was a secondary

consideration. Omani castles and fort designs were based on the required functions of dynamic military thinking. The general characteristics of Omani palaces, castles and forts are that they are solid and firm in their construction whilst also having a good appearance and fitting in with the local environment.

From our study of the long history of Omani architecture and construction we can conclude that the process of design and building did not come out of a vacuum: it was rooted in the heart of Oman's history and the great civilizations that existed on this land. The various types of castles and forts built in Oman are one proof of the rich history of Oman. In our study, we introduced the reader to a few examples from our historical heritage, outlining the history behind the construction of some of the castles, palaces and forts. It must be stressed that these great constructions were not associated with particular historical periods or directly related to individual dynasties. It is our unique heritage that so many great civilizations flourished in Oman and that our architectural history does not spring from one civilization such as the Sumerians or Phoenicians and is not associated only with the Persians, for the Arab tribe of Julanda Azdi had a very significant architectural role[347].

The process of construction of castles and forts continued after the arrival of Islam. Many rulers were involved in the building of these structures: for example Imam Al-Warith bin Ka'b; Al-Salt bin Malik; Ghassan bin Abdullah and many others, including Al-Nabahina[348]. Al-Ya'ruba[349] and Imams and Sultans of Al-Busaid also played a significant role in construction and development. Each fort in Oman tells its own story from which we are able to learn much when following its historical development.

From this elucidation of the construction processes of Omani military defences and forts, and the rules and policies followed during construction, we can see that many features of these buildings had changed and developed, whether aspects of design or materials used in the construction. Every fort and defence structure needs to be studied and researched in detail. It is important to know the kind of building materials used, the designs, and the detailed plan of the stages of construction. Such studies will help us to understand all aspects of architectural and engineering development, information which would help us to serve our present government, as well as the local private sector.

Oman was one of the earliest countries in the region to develop defensive structures. Its history and the challenges it faced required the building of forts, castles, towers and palaces in many parts of Oman. Cities did not have the same defensive importance, although some are highly significant on a trade and business level whilst others were of significance from a political point of view, still others have scientific and historical importance. We mentioned already some aspects of these scientific and cultural centres. Some cities are politically and economically important also, because of their historical background. Each of these cities was a capital of Oman during one of its historical phases. This leads us to discuss the Omani political capitals.

Political Capitals of Oman

There were numerous centres of Islam within the region. In Iraq, for example, Kuffa was the initial capital for the Abbassid caliphate but their administrative centre moved from there to Heera, then Annbar and Hashimiya until they built Baghdad. The Abbassid ruler, Mo'tatham, preferred to live in Samara'a, which he turned into his political capital.

In Egypt, however, the first Islamic capital was Al-Fustat. But, during the reign of the Abbassids, the city of Al-Askar was built and turned into a capital. Upon his assumption of power, Mohammed bin Tawloon established the city of Al-Qatayei which was duly made into a new capital. Finally, the advent of the Fatimid kingdom in Egypt brought about the establishment of Cairo as the new capital of that Islamic nation.

With respect to Oman, on the other hand, Ibn Ruzaiq[350], the renowned historian, stated that when Imam Nasir bin Murshid came to power, the nation was very divided. Nakhal was ruled by Sultan bin Abi Al-Arab, Sama'il by Mani'bin Sinan, Samad Ash'Shan by Ali bin Qutn Al-Hilali, and Ibri by Mohammed bin Gaifar. Izki was ruled by the Bani Azra tribe, while the people of Al-Aqr were governors of Nizwa. Oman continued to be divided during the entire period of Al-Ya'ruba rule. When Ahmed bin Said was selected as Imam, he began by first taking Ar-Rustaq, then Sama'il, Izki, Nizwa and Bahla under his unified rule[351].

The location of the main administrative centre would move, according to which person was in power. Thus, a particular Imam might designate one city as the religious capital of the state whilst the Nabhani kings might take another city or cities as their political capital.

Let us take a brief look at the political capitals of the Omani state from its early phase to the present period.

Qalhat

Qalhat is an old Omani town located on the coast of the Gulf of Oman, north of Sur city. Ya'qut, a famous Arab geographer, described it as a port for most ships coming from India. Ibn Battuta[352], another notable Arab traveller, said it was a city of beautiful markets; and that its mosque was the best, with ornamented walls and a considerable height providing excellent views toward the sea and the port. Ibn Battuta emphasized the commercial importance of Qalhat, mentioning that its residents were mostly traders whose living was largely dependent on Indian Ocean trading. Thus, he maintained, the residents

Qalhat was the capital of Oman at the time of Malik bin Fahm and his dynasty.

would express their happiness whenever a commercial ship docked at the port. The area's rich fish resources were also mentioned by Ibn Battuta who preferred fish over all kinds of meat. He also commended the high morality of its emir, who was both decent and good-mannered, and with whom Ibn Battuta spent six days[353].

This town was not only an important commercial centre, it was also the first historical Omani capital to be known in the centuries prior to Islam. Malik bin Fahm immigrated with his Azd people from Yemen towards the end of the second century, in the aftermath of the great collapse of Ma'rib Dam. Soon after their arrival in Oman Malik bin Fahm took Qalhat as his political capital. There were several reasons for this choice: it was on the coast yet in a central location with respect to the rest of Oman; and Qalhat was seen as to avail Malik bin Fahm of fairly good communication with Yemen, the origin of his immigration and from where he could request support, should he need it, in order to assist him in his long-standing dispute with Persia.

Moreover, the location of Qalhat, close to the northern part of Oman which was previously controlled by the Persians, and who now used Sohar as their administrative centre, had provided Malik bin Fahm with an insight into Persian military strength. Reconnaissance was possible due to the accessibility of the coastal-route connecting Qalhat with Sohar, as well as the other Omani seaports[354].

In addition, Qalhat had good natural defences and formed a strong fortress, which was easily accessible by sea. It was a commercial centre of considerable significance. Ships from India, Dhofar and Yemen would regularly visit the port. Thus, the town's commercial and economic activity was stimulated. The combination of these factors no doubt helped to persuade Malik bin Fahm to select Qalhat as his capital before his subsequent penetration into the hinterland in order to settle conflicts with the Persians.

Furthermore, it is very likely that a key factor for Malik bin Fahm was that Qalhat was not under Persian control at that time, and therefore its people were in a better position to provide him with assistance and provisions in their mutual quest to expel the Persians from the northern parts of the nation. In fact, that was exactly what happened.

Malik bin Fahm entered Qalhat accompanied by 6000 members of his tribe. He defeated the Persians whose army was in the range of 40,000[355].Though Malik bin Fahm's courage should be acknowledged, this victory would never have been achieved without the assistance provided by the Arab inhabitants of Qalhat and other local people.

Malik bin Fahm and his men, using Qalhat as a spring-board, advanced to defeat the Persians in the Salut desert near Nizwa. The Persians were thus forced to retreat to Sohar and finally reached a truce under which they agreed to return back to their own country within one year. In addition to providing Malik bin Fahm with this firm agreement, they also paid a settlement fee[356].

Soon afterwards, however, the Persians breached the contract, since their king Darius was angered by the treaty which had been concluded by his deputy in Oman. Darius sent a large force to occupy Oman, but Malik bin Fahm, from his fortress in Qalhat, attacked these forces which were finally left with no choice but to return back to Persia. Following on this and other successes Malik bin Fahm was able to control the remaining parts of Oman and became known for his reasonable statesmanship[357]. Sheikh Nur Al-Din Al-Salimi further specifies his place of residence, stating that he used to reside in different places in the area between Oman and Yemen. But the main residence was in Qalhat on the Omani coast. From there he used to visit other places[358].

Whilst Malik bin Fahm maintained Qalhat, the capital of his kingdom, he used to reside for a while in other cities as well in order to investigate the conditions throughout the kingdom. Qalhat's role as his military fortress, a spring-board to attacking the Persians and to attaining independence, pre-empted its status as a political capital.

Thus, whilst Qalhat was the first Arab capital for Oman, there could have been be some other capitals, prior to Qalhat, in the history of Oman. Available historical literature, however, does not provide any clear information regarding earlier capitals, if any. Therefore Qalhat is of particular interest as the first Arab city to be designated by a king as his political capital at the end of the second century AD. It retained this status until power passed from Malik's clan to the Julanda tribe who replaced it initially with Tu'am, and finally with Sohar. This measure might have been taken for political and commercial considerations. With the advent of Islam, Sohar was the main city for Omani rulers from the Julandi clan. Thus, we may consider Sohar was the first capital for Oman in the post-Islamic era.

Sohar

Sohar is located some 145 miles northwest of Muscat[359]. Ibn Hawqal[360], an Arab historian, described Sohar as the major city of the nation, located on the sea and with a volume of trade and money that was immeasurable.

The historian Al-Istakhri, on the other hand, mentioned that Sohar was the oldest and richest Omani city and that there was no city along the coastline of the Persian Gulf to match its buildings and wealth[361].

Al-Maqdisi also stated that Sohar was a place with a mild climate, rich fruits and a major city in Oman. Its mosque on the beach had an attractive minaret; the city had fresh water wells and its people were rich in almost everything[362].

View from the battlements of Sohar Fort.

Researchers have confirmed that copper was extracted from a location near Sohar in the fourth century BC[363]. Copper continued to be extracted thereafter and Sohar prospered as an early smelting centre with mining workers constituting a significant portion of its population[364].

Aside from the copper industry, Sohar was an agricultural centre for the region. It used to produce a surplus of farm products such as palm dates and semi-tropical fruits. Several historians mention that Sohar was so productive in dates, banana and figs that there was a significant export business with farmers constantly expanding their operations[365].

Industrial and agricultural activities coupled with the coastal strategic location of the city combined to create Sohar's remarkable commercial importance. Trade with India and East Africa was intensified. Al-Istakhri and Ibn Hawqal agreed that Sohar was a global warehouse containing products from the four corners of the globe[366].

Sohar's political and cultural role, as well as Omani efforts to expel foreign occupation, provoked endless discussion. Of relevance in this regard were two letters from the Prophet Mohammed, the first to Omanis at large and the second was addressed to the two sons of Al-Julandi, Abd and Gaifar. A translation of the first letter reads:

Sohar was the capital of Oman at the time of the Bani Sulanda, immediately before the coming of Islam, and up to 177AH/739AD.

From Allah's Messenger to the people of Oman: I call upon you to testify that there is no God but Allah, that I am His Messenger and you should perform prayer, discharge the zakat and construct mosques.

A translation of the second letter reads as follows:

In the Name of God, Most Gracious, Most Merciful; from Mohammed, Allah's Messenger, to Gaifar and Abd, the sons of Al-Julanda: I call you to Islam; convert to Islam and be assured of your safety, for I am the messenger of Allah to all peoples to warn those who are alive so that truth prevails over disbelievers[367].

The Omanis were converted to Islam whereas the Persians in Oman rejected Islam altogether. Consequently, a war was waged between Muslims and Persians, in which the latter called for peace with an acceptance of the condition to ultimately withdraw from Oman.

Sohar thus became the first capital in Oman to voluntarily adhere to Islam and expel foreigners. The city was controlled by a *wali* (Muslim governor) appointed by the Prophet Mohammed and his successors. However, during the reign of the Ummayyads, Oman fell under severe pressure from certain caliphates. During the rule of Abbasids, however, its independence was restored once again. And, soon after, Sohar commenced its golden age with the recognition of Imam Al-Julandi bin Mas'ud in 750 AD as the first Imam of Oman[368].

Within a short period Sohar relinquished its political role as capital to the inland city of Nizwa. During the second Imamate, which was in effect from 793 AD, Sohar's importance was focussed on the commercial realm as a city deriving great significance from its geographical location on the Gulf of Oman. It remained the commercial capital of Oman for over seven centuries until the nation was occupied by the Portuguese.

Sohar Under the Portuguese

In the early sixteenth century the Portuguese invaded Oman following Vasco da Gama's successful rounding of the African Cape of Good Hope. With the discovery of this route, the traditional land-and-sea route between Europe and India could be replaced by a long, but continuous, sea-passage. The Portuguese were thus eager to establish centres for supplies and defensive purposes along the route. In this they were inexorably drawn towards Oman where they occupied Sur, Quriyat and, finally, Sohar in 1507 AD. The Portuguese naval commander opted for destruction of the Omani ships and an installation of bases and fortresses to strengthen his supremacy in a region of strategic significance and navigational importance[369].

Ya'ruba Struggle to Expel the Portuguese from Sohar

The Ya'ruba state, established under the leadership of Imam Nasir bin Murshid, ceaselessly confronted the Portuguese. In 1650 AD Imam Sultan bin Saif was able to expel the Portuguese from Oman. The nation thus became a unified state; but certain parts fell under the influence of Hormuz which was in turn governed by the Portuguese. In 1622, when Hormuz gained independence from the Portuguese, becoming part of the Persian empire, the Persians attempted to recapture the areas previously under Hormuz administrative control, the most important of which was Sohar. Imam Nasir bin Murshid waged war against them and was, consequently, able to extricate Sohar and Julfar (the present Ras Al-Khaimah)[370] from Persian control.

Freedom was thus restored in Sohar following a prolonged struggle. Although the Portuguese remained persistent in directing campaigns toward Sur and Quriyat, the Imam was determined to liberate them. Sohar became the stronghold of the Imam in his fierce struggle against both the Persians and the Portuguese[371].

Sohar was the headquarters of Ahmed bin Said, the founder of the Al Busaidi state, who was previously appointed as a governor of the town by Imam Saif bin Sultan. This was approximately in the last days of the Ya'ruba state when Ahmed as governor was gradually assuming the mantle of power and responsibility to establish Sohar as a centre from which Muscat and other ports could be controlled.

Sohar's International Status

Sohar was the strongest Omani fortress town to be recurrently used whenever the nation was threatened by foreign forces. At the same time, Sohar had become a well-known centre for maritime trading. Certainly, its unique location gave it an advantage over other ports in the region. As Al-Istakhri said: 'Products from the four corners of the globe could be found in Sohar, and its cargoes reached all commercial centres in the world'.

As we have already mentioned Sohar remained the capital of Oman for a considerable period of time. It was a significant centre so far as administration was concerned and close relations were maintained with Basra, India and Khorasan. Thus, even after Sohar had lost its role as political capital of the state, it nevertheless remained the economic centre of the nation. It was famous for its great historical castle.

Present day Sohar has experienced the benefits of modern development. There, one finds the renowned farms, 'Shams Oman' which were established in 1972 to accommodate many industrial, agricultural and animal production activities. Copper mining is yet another feature of Sohar where the copper factory is located. In addition there are several important educational and health institutions.

View of Nizwa

Nizwa

Nizwa is an important area, with outstanding Islamic architecture, located in the Dakhiliya area (the interior of Oman), some 180 kms from Muscat. A well-developed city, it has a long history of scholarship and learning, housing many institutes for higher education. Before we elaborate on Nizwa as one of the major cities in Oman, we will shed light on the city's position as an academic centre.

Nizwa as a City of Knowledge
Omanis gave Nizwa the nickname 'Centre of Islam' because it was the historical residence for several schools of Islamic jurisprudence. Muslim

scholars residing in the city were actively engaged in studying and writing on all aspects of Islam and many eminent scholars graduated from its institutes. Nizwa's mild climate helped to make it a comfortable place for scholars to live and work.

Nizwa was among the first Omani cities to embrace Islam. Thus, one finds mosques of a mixed blend of old and modernized architecture. For instance, Shawathna mosque was the first one in the city, dating back to 725 AD. There is also a huge mosque which is presently used as a school of jurisprudence and Islamic studies.

Many notable Omani clerics graduated from Nizwa's mosques. These included Imam Jabir bin Zaid Abu Al-Sha'tha, Imam Al-Salt bin Malik Al-Kharousi, Sheikh Mohammed bin Ibrahim Al-Kindi, Sheikh Bashir bin Al-Munthir and Sheikh Ahmed bin Abdullah Al-Kindi, to mention but a few names.

Nizwa the City of Fortresses

Nizwa is famous for its historic fortress which was built by Imam Sultan bin Saif (1649-1668 AD). The building process itself was said to take over 12 years. With a diameter of 37 metres, the fortress included fortified towers with some areas for praying and administration, as well as seven potable water wells.

The city has several other fortresses; Tanuf fortress, surrounded by three giant towers, is at the foot of Al-Jebel Al-Akhdar. Al-Raaida fortress, on the other hand, has a strategic location, giving access to the valley leading towards Al-Jebel Al-Akhdar[372].This particular fortress was built by Imam Ahmed bin Said and his son Hilal[373].

Nizwa was the capital city of the Imams, by tradition, since 177AH/792AD.

Other Features of Nizwa

Nizwa is famous for the manufacture of Omani *halwa* (local sweets). Perhaps the availability of red sugar in the city has been a catalyst in this regard. Nizwa is also renowned for its tanning and leather-work. In addition, the city has a handful of other crafts such as manufacturing gold and silver ornaments, swords and other traditional handiwork.

Since Imam Mohammed bin Abi-Affan established Nizwa as a capital in 793 AD, Omani imams preferred the city over other candidates for the position of political capital of the nation. Sheikh Salim bin Hamoud Al-Siyabi stated that 'Oman was repeatedly attacked by the Persians and by Indian pirates, and accordingly Muslims decided to make Nizwa the new capital of their state instead of Sohar. The officials in charge thought that Nizwa was better fortified and safer as their administrative base and it thus became the seat of the Imam, who would thereafter remain in the city, only departing from it for urgent reasons. During the reign of Imam Ghassan, Nizwa was locally referred to as the *Centre of Islam*'.

BAHRAIN

ARABIAN GULF

GULF OF OMAN

ARABIAN PENINSULA

Rustaq

OMAN

ARABIAN SEA

Ar-Rustaq

Ar-Rustaq was used as a capital by several imams, including Nasir bin Murshid, who assumed power in 1624, founding the Ya'ruba state in the new capital[374].

From Ar-Rustaq, Imam Nasir bin Murshid set forth on his campaigns to unify the nation. His attacks against the Portuguese and the Persians intensified and he was able to achieve considerable success. By the end of Ya'ruba rule, however, Ar-Rustaq was affected by a serious dispute among members of the ruling family. In 1737, as the conflict heightened, Saif bin Sultan bin Saif, one of the contenders, took exile in Persia where its ruler, Nadir Shah, found it convenient to assist Saif. The

Ar-Rustaq was capital of Oman during part of the Ya'ruba era and the beginning of the Al-Busaidi era.

Persians then invaded Oman, rapidly revealing Nadir's real intentions: i.e. that of serving their own narrow interests rather than extending any genuine help to Saif or Oman.

By the time the last Ya'ruba Imam died, Persia had occupied a considerable portion of Oman, including Muscat. In 1744 AD, however, Ar-Rustaq was home of one of the best political and military leaders of the nation: Imam Ahmed bin Said, the head of the Al-Busaidi dynasty which has held power since then. His restoration of independence, expulsion of the Persians, and his nation-wide rule, were all coordinated from Ar-Rustaq, his political capital and an economic centre of great significance. In fact, Imam Ahmed bin Said did his best to stimulate trade and commerce within the city. In this regard he struck a fair balance between the coast and the interior; and consequently, security and stability were greatly restored to the nation. Ar-Rustaq remained the capital city until after the death of Imam Ahmed, who was followed as ruler of Oman by his son, Said bin Ahmed bin Said[375].

The city was famous for its great fort, Al-Hazm castle and Bayadha mosque. The latter was a great institute from which several eminent scholars graduated. The city was also renowned for its Kasfa hot spring well.

In the past, Ar-Rustaq was a significant commercial centre for Jebel Al-Akhdar produce such as grapes, peaches, pomegranates, figs and apricots. People from the Al-Batinah region of Oman would also bring in their products to sell here, ranging from fishes to bananas and lemons. As a result, the city was more of a commercial capital than a political one.

Numerous industries sprang up in Ar-Rustaq, including the making of Omani *halwa,* silver-work for ornaments and hand-made *khanjars* or daggers, together with other traditional Omani crafts. Date-packing was always a feature of the city whilst today Ar-Rustaq has a date factory where processing of dates is carried out to a high standard.

View of the city of Muscat.

Muscat

According to Ibn Faqih Al-Hamadani (who died in 902 AD), 'Muscat is located some 200 *parasangs* from Siraf; it is a seaport from which ships navigate to India'[376]. Ibn Battuta, on the other hand, wrote about Muscat, describing it as, '... a city where the famous fish (diamond-heart) is abundant'[377].

The notable Omani historian Sheikh Salim bin Hamoud provided a somewhat brief account on Muscat, confirming that, 'it is a city which is the most important along the Arabian Sea. Its significance and position has been remarkable since the twelfth century Hegira when Portuguese occupied the city and built many fortresses. The kingdom of Oman took the city as its capital during the reign of Bani Nabhan. The situation remained so during the days of the great Ya'ruba rulers who were proudly religious. Al-Busaidi rulers, too, resided in the city and designated it as their capital. Thus, the city reached the point that it is at today'[378].

Since the second century Hegira, however, Muscat had a considerable role to play, alongside Sohar, so far as international trade was concerned but Sohar continued to enjoy the lion's share of this trade.

The renowned Arab navigator, Ahmed Ibn Majed, commented that Muscat 'is a famous port with no equal in the world. The city has several things which a person seldom finds elsewhere. On the tip of the port, furthermore, there is a high rock to be seen from far away. To the north-west, there is an elevated island called Al-Fahal which is an outstanding feature to be distinguished by the traveller by day or night.

'Muscat is the first Omani seaport to which many ships come for supplies. From Muscat, textiles, vegetables, edible oils and oilseeds can be bought. Moreover, when ships enter the port, they are safe from any winds. In Muscat, drinking water is clean; its people are decent and welcome foreigners'[379].

ARABIAN GULF

GULF OF OMAN

UNITED ARAB EMIRATES

✳ **Muscat**

KINGDOM OF SAUDI ARABIA

OMAN

ARABIAN SEA

YEMEN

Muscat has a number of unique features. Located on Oman's long coastline, it is well connected with areas of fertile lands. Seen from a distance, or from out at sea, it has a most attractive profile. A series of seemingly endless mountains provide a fascinating backdrop for a walled city flanked by two prominent castles.

Modern Muscat, however, is a city that is in process of rapid development. It has broad streets and large buildings, and remains one of Oman's key trading ports.

Sultan bin Saif Restored Muscat

When Sultan bin Saif was elected Imam for Oman in the aftermath of the death of his cousin Nasir, he paid great attention to completion of what his predecessor had started. Thus, he continued with the struggle against the Portuguese and was finally able to expel them in 1650, thereby liberating Muscat and Matrah.

An accurate description of the battle waged against the Portuguese was given by the historian, Ibn Ruzaiq:

Muscat has been capital of Oman since the early period of the Al-Busaidi era.

'When Imam Sultan bin Saif's cousin died and he took power, he had already spent a number of years fighting the Portuguese and was able to expel them from Muscat and Matrah'.

Muscat: the Capital of Oman

Indeed, when the Al-Busaidi state was established, the founder of this state, Imam Ahmed bin Said used Ar-Rustaq as his capital but his life was wholly divided between the former capital, Muscat to which he himself was previously a governor, and Ar-Rustaq, the centre for Muslim scholars and research. However, during the reign of his successor, Hamad bin Said (1779-1792), the capital moved once again to Muscat.

Muscat's Economy

The Irish surgeon Sir Peter Freyer visited Muscat and its bustling markets where products of various origins were sold. Such products included textiles, cotton, ornaments, utensils, meats and fish. Charleston, on the other hand, commented in his book, *Journeys through Arabia*, that, 'Muscat produces cheese, malt, lentil and grapes. It exports a large quantity of dates'. Whereas, G. T. Rinal mentioned that Muscat used to export frankincense, Arabic gum and silver[380].

Perhaps the most significant economic role Muscat played was as an entrepôt. In fact, the Gulf was in the midst of a network of sea routes linking India, eastern Asia, the Far East and Africa. By that time Muscat, due to its strategic location, was one of the most important ports on the Arabian Gulf. On a national level its significance was partly measured by the considerable revenues it produced for the nation.

It is clear that Muscat's location and products played a vital role in its historical prominence. It has been rightly commented that Muscat's influence in the Gulf was indisputable[381]. This influence was underpinned by the impressive fortifications of the city formed by numerous fortresses and castles.

Muscat: The City of Castles

Castles and towers are abundant in Muscat. They were erected on surrounding hills with the intention of providing security and surveillance over the city's main gates. Muscat still possesses a number of castles and fortresses which overlook the city from the sea side. Could it be that Muscat always felt vulnerable to attack from the sea?

There are two great castles: the western one, Al-Mirani, might have taken its name from a Portuguese admiral. The Portuguese, however, used to call this castle *Forte Captain* for it was the headquarters of their navy commander. The other fort, Al-Jalali, may be named after its builder.

Castles were originally used as rulers' residences but were also sometimes used as schools, libraries or even as cells for political prisoners so that they could be kept under the close scrutiny of the ruler.

Muscat Today

Present day Muscat merits a separate and elaborate study beyond the scope of this brief account. We should nevertheless mention that His Majesty Sultan Qaboos has been instrumental in bridging the gap between the past, present and future of the city. In fact, all Oman has been geared to preserve the original values of its Arab tradition, with an attempt to display such traditions without distortion or radical change. Thus, Oman has adopted modern civilization, benefiting from what it has to offer without permitting any adverse impact on basic Arab traditions and Islamic values. Muscat has been part of this trend, enjoying features which are briefly listed below.

- A coastline extending from Muscat to Matrah, providing the visitor with a sense of the prevalence of nature, combined with the capabilities of modern society;
- An efficient road system passing through the mountains so that what previously constituted lengthy journeys have now been shortened; and the capital's various districts are also well connected with each other;
- Several new villages, or the so-called Muscat suburbs have emerged. Among these are Sultan Qaboos City and Al-I'lam (information) village which accommodates the radio, television, mass media and a residential complex for the workers of the Ministry of Information. The new districts also include the diplomatic quarter, with its embassies and residences for diplomats; the industrial area with all its equipment and factories; a group of international

Contemporary view of Greater Matrah.

hotels, the most notable of which is Al-Bustan Palace Hotel which is a model of modern Islamic architecture; well equipped modern hospitals with the best available technology, including the Royal Hospital and the Sultan Qaboos University Hospital; an international airport at which the largest aircraft can land in safety; Sultan Qaboos Seaport which receives ships of various sizes and tonnage; Sultan Qaboos University, a well equipped centre for science and knowledge, which has been built to the highest standards, utilizing the latest technologies to assist researchers and students; a number of monuments located on several roundabouts in the capital. These are intended to express Oman's heritage and its uniqueness, as well as to indicate the need for conservation of such heritage.

This is but a brief account of the various features of Muscat, features that reflect Islamic civilization, in general, and the Omani heritage in particular.

Shipping and Omani Sailors

Omani Maritime Activity Prior to Islam

Oman experienced a considerable amount of maritime activity long before the advent of Islam. Its strategic geographic location, on the north-east of the Arabian peninsula, helped to ensure that Omani sailors achieved widepread fame for their sea-going skills since the earliest historical period. Indeed, the country's location between the outlet of the Arabian Gulf and entrance of the Indian Ocean, the main commercial sea route leading to the eastern coast of Africa in the west and to India, Malaysia and China in the east, played a large role in the development of Oman as a seafaring nation. Because of the difficulty in establishing land communication between Oman and its neighbouring regions like Bahrain and Hadramaut, the people of the country resorted to the sea.

Classical Arabia according to Ptolemy, c. 150 AD.

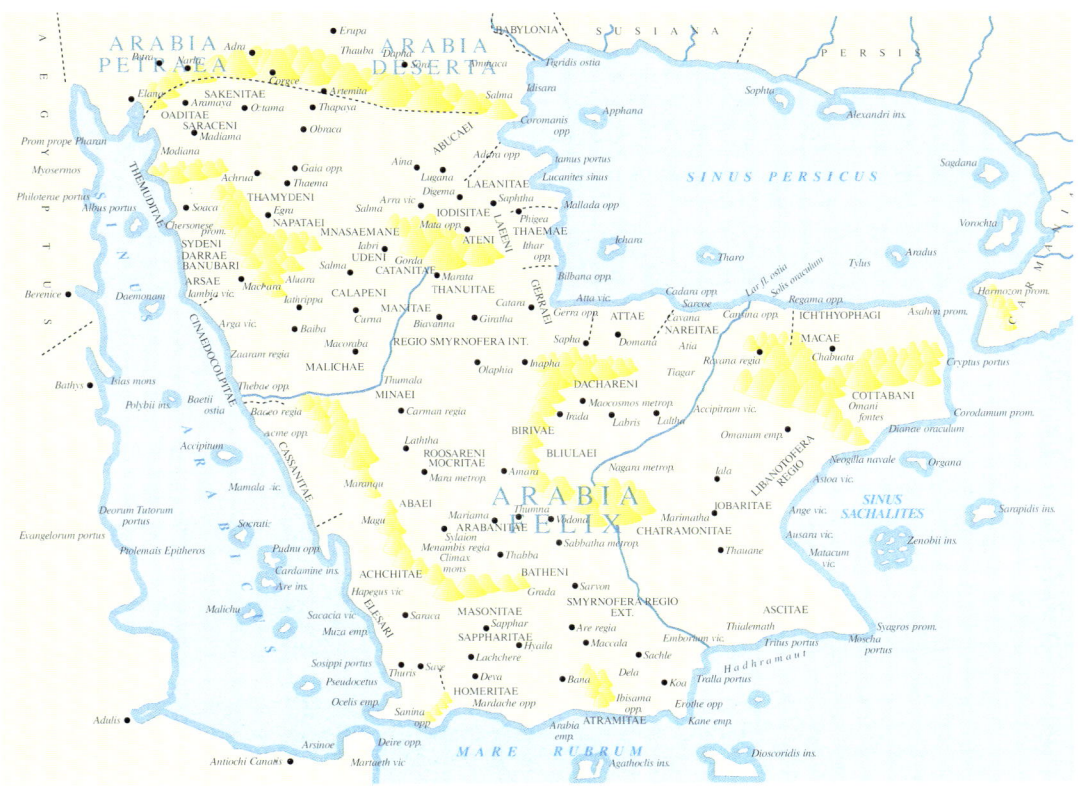

It is somewhat difficult to draw a clear picture of Omani sailors and their activities during the various periods of history due to a paucity of reliable sources, especially those related to ancient times. However, piecing together information gleaned from different places we have been able to establish an acceptable account of Oman's seafaring backgound. It should also be mentioned that Oman's political geography varied according to internal and external political situations.

Throughout their history Omanis have attempted to earn their livelihood from their own land and their coastal waters, as well as the coastal provinces of the Indian Ocean and the Red Sea. They exchanged information with visiting vessels and travelled to neighbouring regions themselves, all with a view to exploring prospects for trade or other forms of cooperation. Omani sailors were thus among the vanguard of ocean pioneers, learning from and teaching others whom they came in contact with. Their achievements go back to very early times when they were the first people to use the mast and sail as a means of boat propulsion.

Information inscribed on Sumerian and Akkadian tablets, dating back to 3000 BC, provides documentary proof of the existence of long-term trade with Mesopotamian countries. It is quite likely that they superceded the people of Mesopotamia and ancient Egypt in developing navigational skills and that they crossed vast area of sea, reaching unknown and dangerous areas, all in their quest to gain from their maritime experiences.

It is hardly surprising that the people of Oman were commonly known as pioneer navigators. About 4000 years ago, the Sumerians referred to Oman as Magan[382]. They also referred to the Omani ship-builders in the reign of Shulgi *circa* 2050 BC. Magan was known as place from where a variety of goods were obtainable including a number of transshipped items such as wood from India which was re-exported to other countries.

The geographical position[383] of Oman and the interest of Mesopotamian countries in it played an important role in its maritime activities. During this period between 2800-1800 BC, Oman experienced considerable social and economic development[384] and its maritime activities played, among others, a substantial role in this progress.

Continued overseas contacts were established and expanded over subsequent years and the process continued during the periods of the southern Arabian Ma'in and Sabaean cultures, around 1000 BC.

By the third century BC Oman already possessed the second largest fleet after that of Cordoba. It is even possible that at this time Oman's fleet was the strongest and the largest in the entire world[385]. The fleet undoubtedly provided the means to transport both people and goods between Ma'in, Babylon, Susa and India. With this flux of goods and people, flowed ideas and knowledge. The people from southern Arabia, for example, taught the Indians astronomy, philosophy, mathematics and astrology as well as exchanging fundamentals of civilization and intellectual development that predated the Hellenistic era by several centuries[386].

The geographical position of Oman was of central importance to this process. Oman lies between the Indian Ocean, Arabian Gulf, Red Sea, East Africa and the Arabian peninsula countries. Its mountainous interior slowed down serious contact between the country's coastal areas and its lower valleys, creating food shortages along the coast that could only be compensated by turning to the sea in search of food. Thus, the people resorted to the sea as their sole means of livelihood. In this sense, they resembled the Phoenicians who were based on the coast of the Mediterranean Sea.

Most human settlements along Oman's coastline depended primarily on the sea for their livelihood. Omanis were in need of a big mercantile fleet to achieve their goals. The Omani fleet represented, from the outset, the backbone of the country's economic life. It was multifunctional, involved with fishing, transportation, trade and protection of the country and its people (on the land as well as at sea). It would not be an exaggeration to say that Oman's power depended upon its maritime strength and *vice versa*.

The most dependable information about Omani shipping in ancient times emanates from the major victories of Alexander the Great (356-322 BC). These resulted in fundamental changes in the political and cultural landscape of western Asia. Although Alexander depended on Phoenician sailors in expeditions to the Red Sea and the Arabian Gulf, the Omanis played a basic and positive role in marine activities in the Indian Ocean and China Sea during this period.

Agatharchides, who lived in Egypt in 120 BC, wrote that 'the Omanis have arrived on the Indian coast'. Despite the surprising dearth of information in Ptolemy concerning ancient Oman, he does mention that the nobility and fame of the country - which were its source of pride - came from marine and navigational activities rather than from activities on the land. The Koshians in Oman depended greatly on overseas activities and they were considered the pioneers of navigation in the Indian Ocean. They were able to transport vital goods and products from the East to the western world through the Mediterranean and, thus they contributed to the development of human civilization'[387].

Regarding contacts between Omani sailors and China in ancient times, some indications can be found in Chinese books, written on this subject between 206 BC to 97 AD. We also know from the *Periplus of the Erythraean Sea*, written by an unknown author in the first century AD, that vessels hailing from a distant port of 'Omana', reached the southern shores of China during this period. The 'Omana' referred to could be an Omani harbour such as Sohar, Muscat or elsewhere. There was also a mention of a city called Ikleek near Ras Musandam. This could be the port of Qalhat near Ras Al-Hadd[388].

It should be mentioned that the Omanis possessed strong determination, enabling them to face the dangers and challenges associated with their lengthy journeys. Added to which they had considerable knowledge of the sciences of navigation and astronomy. There is no doubt that key elements of their culture and knowledge were communicated to other people during the early period of history. In addition, there is good evidence that they used big ships capable of transporting large consignments - an indication of their abilities in the sphere of boat-building.

There was considerably rivalry between Persia and Oman in the period preceding Alexander's invasion. This was particularly apparent during the reign of the Persian, Darius the Great (521-485 BC). The Persians did not confine themselves to that healthy commercial competition but attempted to expel

Omanis from the sea area. Despite this set-back, the Omanis, aided by their persistence and perseverance, were successful in restoring their international maritime role by 100 BC when their ships began sailing across the Gulf towards India. Although the Egyptian king, Ptolemy VII, is credited with discovering the direct sea route to India, depending on the trade-wind direction, the Omani pattern of maritime trading was hardly affected.

Between 50-200 AD, the Romans emerged as a dominant power and the Roman Empire boosted international maritime trading, with special emphasis on trade between the East and the West. Despite the growth of Roman influence, Omani naval vitality was not adversely affected. It was in fact strengthened since Omanis increased their peaceful trading activities, altering their traditional sea routes in order to visit Persian and Sind ports along the coastline as far as India, thus avoiding any potentially dangerous encounters with the Roman ships.

In 225 AD, the Persian Furthi Empire collapsed and a new Sassanian state replaced it. The latter adopted a completely different policy which encouraged shipping in the Gulf. The Sassanian state established a strong fleet, which proceeded to invade certain southern and eastern parts of the Arabian peninsula, provoking an inevitable dispute between the Omanis and the Persians. But the Omanis, under the leadership of Azd tribes, resisted the Persians and prevented their expansion efforts. Finally, and after some serious battles, the Omanis retaliated by invading Persia, occupying certain southern ports and coastal provinces.

The Arabs remained dominant over these coasts for a considerable part of the second century AD, all the third century and part of the fourth as well. Trading activities in the Gulf and the Indian Ocean were largely in Arab hands during this period[389].

Despite the fact that the Persians established certain military centres along the western coast of the Gulf[390,] Arab dominance was maintained and the Persian incursions were resisted. In the mid-sixth century AD, however, Arab waves of migration, particularly from the Yemen Azd tribes, instigated a weakening of the Persian presence on these coasts. Arabs, for their part, were able to control the Omani hinterland and they were, by then, the ultimate rulers of Omani territory[391]. Yet a Persian presence, at least along certain parts of the coast, supported a degree of commercial activity in the Gulf throughout the sixth century AD. Nevertheless, international conflicts over routes and ports of commercial importance imposed new challenges for Omanis. For instance, the long-standing dispute between the Axumite kingdom (in present day Eritrea) and the Persians was considerably escalated in the first quarter of the sixth century AD. In consequence of this conflict the Byzantine influence in the region was heightened since the empire supported the Axumites against the Persians. The Omanis were somewhat in the middle of this, left to wrestle against massive powers in both the southern and eastern parts of the Arabian peninsula. Despite the inevitable problems that this caused they maintained their maritime activity in the region.

In the remainder of the sixth century AD, however, a naval power composed of Persians, Abyssinians, Greeks and Somalis competed with the Omanis for influence in the marine sphere. Ships of this conglomerate of nations appeared with increasing regularity on the high seas resulting in the Omanis clashing with them. They particularly fought against the Abyssinian forces that were then occupying Yemen[392]. In addition, they battled against the Persians who did not hold such a strong trading position in the Gulf as the Omanis. Prior to Islam, however, trade was virtually dominated by Arab Omanis of the Azd tribe who travelled as far as the eastern coasts of Africa. Daba, on the Gulf of Oman, was flourishing as one of the most vibrant Arabian markets of the period[393]. Similarly, several locations along the coasts of Oman and Bahrain gained remarkable reputations. These locations were known as *Al-Khat*[394]. They imported spears and lances from India, and sold them to the arabs. These spears were known as *Al-Khati* spears[395].

Azd tribes were quite dominant in this area prior to Islam since the Persian presence was very restricted at that time. For instance, the prominent historian, Al-Bilathuri, wrote about the introduction of Islam in Oman without mentioning the existence of any Persian influence[396]. Yet another historian, Al-Tabari, indicated that following Oman's conversion to Islam, the Prophet Mohammed's representative obtained a punitive tax from the Magians[397].

However, these Magians, referred to by Al-Tabari were only a minority in Oman by then. They possessed no political, social or economic influence whatsoever. Thus, by the time of the introduction of Islam to Oman, the nation was an independent Arab country, governed by two brothers of the Julanda dynasty: Gaifar and Abd[398]. It is clear, therefore, that Oman's dominance in the Arabian Gulf region and its well-established control over this maritime area depended on its Arab people.

Omani Naval Efforts in the Islamic Ages

Oman's naval force played a significant role in the Islamic invasion of Persia during the reign of Caliph Omar bin Al-Khattab. In reality, Omanis were already in control of much of the Arabian Gulf. The governor of Oman and Bahrain, Al-Alla bin Al-Hadrami, had already crossed the Gulf to invade Persia, an act which aggravated Omar bin Al-Khattab, who (around 637 AD) finally ordered his own troops to invade Lar Island and to advance further to Kharj Island[399].

In 638 AD Al-Alla was removed from Oman and Bahrain and Othman bin Abi Al-A'ss Al-Thaqafi was appointed in his place. The real age of the Islamic invasions of Persia began from this time with Caliph Omar bin Al-Khattab requesting Al-Thaqafi to take his fleet across the Gulf in order to confront the Persian emperor. Al-Thaqafi, with an army of 3000 soldiers, mostly from the Azd, Najiah and Abd Al-Qais[400]tribes, went first to Ibn Kawan Island: a small strategically located Arab island which had a good supply of swords (the major weapon of the day). It's strategic location controlled routes leading to the Gulf, on one side, the Indian Ocean and the African ports, on the other. In addition, the island formed a useful rendezvous, relatively distant from the Persian forces gathered to the north of the Arabian Gulf.

Al-Thaqafi, supported by his naval and terrestrial forces from Oman and Bahrain, seized control of the island in 640 AD and immediately constructed a mosque, a gesture which encouraged Arab immigration to the island[401.] Meanwhile, Al-Thaqafi's forces fought a fierce battle with the Persians under the command of Shahruk on Qeshm island. Once again, Al-Thaqafi's army defeated the Persians, whose leader was killed, and he consequently took control of this island[402].

It is clear that Caliph Omar bin Al-Khattab, with unfailing intuition, master-minded the military coordination between the Basra garrison in Iraq and Al-Thaqafi's bases in Oman and Bahrain. This military cooperation was undertaken in a rather unexpected manner with a large number of Omanis translocating to Basra in order to participate in the campaign aimed at opening up Persia. Early successes included the occupation of Astakher by Omani and Bahraini tribes in 649 AD [403]

Al-Thaqafi and his Omani troops were, in fact, almost double the strength of the Persian defenders in Kamaran, a city invaded during the reign of Caliph Othman bin Affan[404].

However, Persia was not the only target of the Omani naval fleet in this age of conquests. Omanis played a vital role in the conquest of the Sind. Al-Thaqafi invaded the Indian coast near Bombay whilst his brother, Al-Mughayera, moved towards the mouth of Sind river in 636 AD[405]. In addition, Oman had an important part in combating Indian piracy during the Ummayad period. Al-Hajjaj bin Youssef Al-Thaqafi, ordered the commander of Oman to deal with the problem of piracy[406].

Omanis, mostly of the Azd tribe, participated in these naval activities, as well as in the Islamic campaigns to conquer the western parts of the Islamic world. Historical accounts confirm that Azd participated in the campaigns directed at Morocco and Andalucia. It was equally apparent that the Islamic leader Muawiya bin Abi Sufian greatly benefited from Oman's vast experience in his efforts to build an Islamic naval fleet. As we have seen, Omanis were quite famous for their sailing skills[407]. Prominent leaders of the time included the naval commander Julanda bin Abi Umayya[408], from the Azd tribes, who invaded Cyprus, Rhodes, Akritish and Arwad island, and Sufian bin Mujeeb Al-Azd who invaded Tripoli in 26 Hegira[409].

It is likely that Azd also participated in the establishment of the first Islamic naval fleet at Andalucia. This fleet was remarkably active between Morocco and Andalucia, at a time when the Ummayyads had not yet adopted an official naval policy.

Similarly, Azd were influential in trade and in order to illustrate this we should look first at the main navigational routes adopted by Omani ships, together with the most significant commodities they transported.

Sea Routes Used by the Omani Maritime Fleet

The first of these routes covered the Arabian Gulf, which is an arm of the Indian Ocean. In the past the Arabian Gulf was considered to be formed by three seas: i.e. the Persian Gulf, the Bahrain Sea and the Gulf of Oman. To the east, the Arabian Gulf was connected with a number of major ports within the Indian Ocean[410].

The Omani fleet followed several different routes to reach mainland China. Their vessels often called at the Persian Gulf ports such as Siraf and Basra where they would replenish their supplies and prepare for new voyages, either towards the Far East and China, or turning westwards after leaving the Gulf and heading towards East Africa's ports. The Omani ships sailed to these remote areas with the most basic of navigational aids: a form of simple telescope, certain wooden instruments, a knowledge and understanding of tidal and current patterns and an appreciation of seasonal variations in wind direction. Al-Istakhri, a notable and reliable historian, described such devices and natural aids as follows: 'The Persian Gulf is quite wide but with many narrow channels, the most difficult of which is that between Janaba and Basra. This winding inlet, called Khor Janaba, is a treacherous one that no ship can easily survive in rough weather. And there are numerous wooden posts, erected and lit at night, to guide vessels entering the Tigris'[411].

Al-Mas'udi confirmed this when he wrote: 'in the mouth of the Persian Gulf there are wooden signs, which are erected in the sea to guide boats sailing to Oman'[412].

In addition to the navigational difficulties posed by narrow tortuous channels, the Persian Gulf could also present some very rough seas with steep waves. Omanis had the measure of it however, understanding the seasonality of its sea-conditions which were influenced by weather patterns in the Indian Ocean. Since ancient times certain astronomical phenomena had been used in weather prediction. Geographers have written at some length on this subject; among them eminent Arab scholars such as Ibn Faqih Al-Hamthani, Ibn Rusta and Al-Mas'udi. The latter, in particular, said that, 'the Persian Gulf has rough weather with high waves interspersed with calm periods when sailing becomes easier; the calm period in the Gulf coincides with a reverse situation and a period of strong winds in the Indian Ocean which becomes extremely rough and overcast making it difficult for sailing. The most dangerous time to sail in the Persian Gulf is during autumn'[413].

Moreover, the Persian Gulf had many sea-facing cliffs bordering narrow passages or inlets, particularly close to Oman. Whilst such straits could be quite dangerous, the Omanis. with their vast navigation experience, were able to pass the most difficult of these which was commonly referred to as Al-Dardure and located quite close to Oman. Chinese navigators were unable to pass through this strait. Ibn Faqih described Al-Dardure as, 'a mountainous narrow where only small boats could sail, not those of the size of the Chinese ships'[414].

After the Gulf, and into the Indian Ocean proper, was the Sea of India, which was the largest of these peripheral seas[415]. Sailors knew little of this area, or its navigational features, but it was common knowledge that ambergris (a product of sperm whales) was quite scarce in this sea whilst it was relatively abundant along the African coast.

Between the Sea of India and the Bay of Bengal, there were approximately 1700 small islands, all of which were populated[416]. All these islands were under the command of a formidable woman who controlled a large army. The group of islands was commonly known as Dibayhat, the last of which was Ceylon (present day Sri Lanka)[417]. Here there was a mountain in which, according to legend, Adam first landed, and his footprints are still to be seen.

Ceylon was surrounded by other small islands in the Bay of Bengal; all of which were quite well acquainted with Omanis. The most important of them

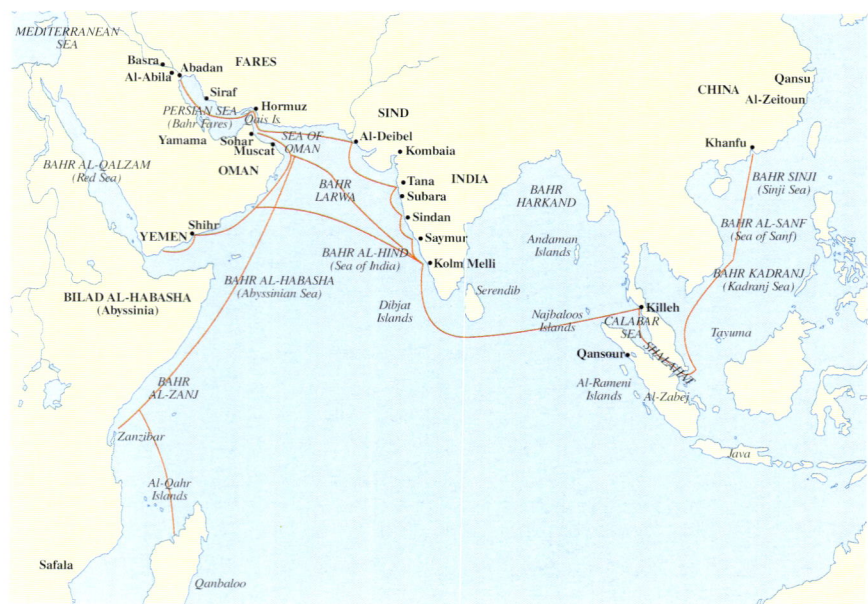

was Ramini Island[418], a populated island of 800 *parasangs* in area where there were good quantities of gold, camphor and coconut. Also elephant, rhinoceros and buffalo were abundant[419].

Ramini island was close to Gansur where the famous gansuri camphor was produced[420]. After that came the Andaman Islands which, according to Al-Mas'udi, were populated by unusual people 'that would come out naked to see ships sailing by them'[421]. These islands were considered to mark the end of the Bay of Bengal, from which point the fourth sea, known as Kilahbar, began. It is clear that the Omanis reached the Andaman Islands and beyond them into this sea.

Omanis were well-acquainted with the wealth of these distant islands, sailing there to collect minerals, ambergris and pearls. It was common knowledge that the archipelago had good supplies of ambergris, pearls, all sorts of corundum, minerals, silver and coconuts[422].

The sea of Kilahbar, or Kila, lay just beyond the Andamans[423]. In it there was the island of Kila (Sumatra), which was exactly located on the sailing route from Oman to China, straddling the Equator. The Arab famous historian Ya'qut described Kila as the major island in the Indian Ocean[424].

The Kila sea was characterized by shallow water and small islands[425]. Ibn Faqih, for instance, mentioned that there were several small islands where Lanj people lived. This was a nation which did not know 'any language, and whose people wear no clothes. They used to barter ambergris for small pieces of iron'[426].

The island was, in fact, a part of the kingdom of Zabij, to the east of India[427]. Here, the king was commonly called a Maharajah, or the king of kings[428]. On the other hand, the Silhat straits had several small islands, too. Ibn Rusta said that ambergris produced in these islands was of premium quality[429]. It seems clear that there was a direct navigational route linking Oman with these islands.

Beyond here, however, there was Krange Bay, an expansive shallow sea full of reefs and small tropical islands which enjoyed quite heavy rainfall. Then the Sinf Sea, where there was another Maharajah kingdom. The mountains in this area were probably volcanic. Al-Mas'udi described such mountains in vivid terms: 'their mountains have fire during the day and at night; in the day the mountains were reddish and black at night'[430].

The Sinf Sea led into the China Sea. Arabic references described the China Sea as a reef-strewn area with high waves. The fact that Omani traders reached this area indicates that they were well skilled in the arts of navigation and seamanship.

Turning now to the other major route, westwards from the Arabian Gulf, vessels sailed to *Bahr al-Zinj* which ended to the south at Qanbaloo Island. Indeed, Omanis reached the eastern coasts of Africa quite early. Al-Mas'udi commented that, 'Omani sailors would cross to the Qanbaloo Island in the *Bahr al-Zinj*. In this island, there live many Muslims among the pagans '[431].

Al-Mas'udi, in another location, said that, 'those Omani people who sailed to *Bilad al-Zinj* are from the Azd tribe. On board, during their voyage, they sing traditional sea-shanties'[432].

It is worth mentioning that Al-Mas'udi himself took this voyage from Sohar, accompanied by a group of sailors. In 304 Hegira, when Oman's ruler was Ahmed bin Hilal, he returned aboard a ship from Qanbaloo Island to Oman[433].

Whilst some researchers believe that the Qanbaloo Island mentioned in these texts was present day Madagascar, others believe that the authors are referring to the Comoros[434]. Regardless of its precise identification, Qanbaloo and Sohar were linked by a direct navigation route. But, as winds were sometimes very strong and severe, ships were often diverted to the nearby eastern coast of Africa[435].

Oman's role as a trading intermediary between East and West in the Islamc Ages.

Merchant Shipping Routes of Omanis in the Islamic Era

There were many routes of which two were of great importance:

The Maritime Route to the Far East

In its trade with the West, China focussed mainly on silk at that time. By contrast, India had goods ranging from spices to ambergris and other commodities. There were two marine routes to carry Chinese silk to the Islamic world and from there, in turn, to Europe. The first of these was a land route; whilst the other, the sea route, is of relevance to this study[436].

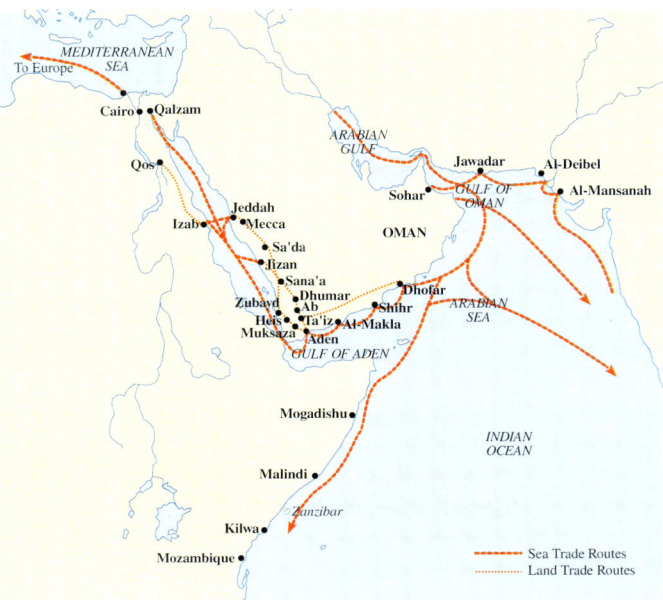

This shipping route was formerly extensively used by Omanis and by utilizing it as a means to carry Chinese silk to the West, Omanis were instrumental in the creation of a direct East -West link and there is no doubt that Omanis had vast experience of navigating this route. They were acquainted with all its setbacks, seasonal variations of currents and winds, together with all the islands, safe-havens and supply ports enroute.

Arabic references provide considerable details about this route. Ibn Khordathuba in his book, *Al-Masalek Wal Mamalek*[437] and Ibn Faqih, in his work, *Mukhtasar Kitab al-Buldan* are worth consulting in this regard[438].

Through the understanding gained from this literature, it is possible to briefly describe the voyage undertaken by Omani merchant seamen to India and China. Small ships would converge on Basra or Siraf, where they would unload their cargoes into larger vessels which would immediately sail to Sohar in Oman, and from there to Muscat. In Muscat ships would take on drinking water before commencing their journey to Kolham Mele on the southern coast of India. This part of the voyage, from Muscat to India, would usually take about a month. From India the ships would continue their voyage to Ceylon and thereafter depart the Sea of India altogether, crossing the Bay of Bengal in order to reach the Andaman Islands, whose people did not know Arabic and therefore the medium of communication with Omanis would be by sign language. From there they would sail towards a location known as Bitoma, where abundant drinking water could be obtained[439]. The sail to Bitoma took about ten days. From there, ships would sail to the Strait of Silahit (the present Strait of Malacca) then finally to the main Chinese port of Canton where they would stay for a while[440].

This main route had a branch, running from the Andaman Islands to Java. In addition, there was another navigational route directly linking the Arabian Gulf ports with the Sind (present Pakistan).

The route from Oman to the Far East was at the mercy of political change and upheaval in the countries through which it passed. Al-Mas'udi, for instance, maintained that the Chinese ships were accustomed to sailing to the Arabian Gulf until China fell into turmoil[441]. With the new unstable situation in China, the Chinese began sailing as far as the Andaman Islands, midway between China and Oman, where they could meet Arab traders. Al-Mas'udi commented: 'Andaman Island is approximately half-way. Arabian vessels go there to meet Chinese traders'[442].

The unrest referred to in China was the political instability that China suffered during in the dying days of the T'ang dynasty (619-907 AD). Chinese manuscripts record that, for two centuries, the kings of this dynasty had encouraged trade relations between their land and west Asia, Africa, Persia and Arabia as well as the Byzantine state[443]. Over 30 Arab envoys arrived there during the period 651-798 AD.

Chinese cities during the reign of T'ang dynasty had a considerable number of Arabs - traders who were extremely interested in silk, jewels and corundum. In Yang Zhou[444] alone, there were more than 1000 Arabs and Muslims[445] whilst Guang Zhou, had over 10,000 Muslims.

Chinese references confirm that Islam was widely introduced to China during the reign of T'ang dynasty and that the paper industry and silk cloth manufacture, later known in Europe and Africa, were originally introduced to

China by Arabs through communications established with them on their sea-trading routes[446]. Inevitable disputes occurred in the T'ang dynasty's latter days, resulting in a spate of military and social upheavals[447]. A socialist, popular revolution led to a radical change in the political landscape of the nation[448].

Al-Mas'udi, in particular, gave details of local conditions prior to the revolution: 'Yan Chu, an advisor from outside the ruling family, became powerfully influential in certain cities of China. He was an evil man, who collected criminals and prostitutes as supporters for his rule'[449].

Yan Chu was openly aggressive toward Omani merchants living in Chinese commercial cities. He took control of Canton, which was the main trade centre of that period[450], and killed a large part of its population, including Muslims, Jews, Christians and Magians. He is reported to have killed around 200,000 persons[451].

Yan Chu carried his bloody rampage to almost all the other Chinese cities but suddenly, and inexplicably, disappeared. Some claimed that he was killed after one of his savage battles; while others maintained that he was burned to death[452].

Due to these radical changes in the political landscape of China, and mainly as a result of the unprecedented turmoil affecting the nation, Omanis and other Arab traders stopped entering China's commercial ports and instead took to using the Andaman Islands as a commercial centre, at least until stability was to be restored. It was here that Arab, Indian and Chinese traders would meet to exchange their commodities. Within a relatively short time however, following the take-over of the Sung dynasty (960-1279)[453], China was once again a stable country.

As already mentioned, Oman enjoyed a flourishing trade with China during the reign of the T'ang dynasty and indeed Chinese historical literature paid just tribute to the role of Omani traders in invigorating trade in China during the first half of the sixteenth century (the Ummayyad rule). Many Omani merchants were mentioned as having played a vital part in boosting trade with China[454]. During the Sung dynasty, Omani and other Arab ships resumed visiting the Chinese ports following an interruption caused by political instability within China. Chinese historical literature, covering this period, offers descriptions of many Arab cities and ports as related by Arab navigators themselves. Oman, Bahrain, Iraq, Kish, Mosul, Mecca, Somalia, Zanzibar, Qanbaloo and Egypt were among the notable places given detailed description in Chinese history[455].

A Chinese manuscript belonging to the Sung family, a manuscript commonly referred to as the Sung-Chu (or the history of the dynasty), contained some generalized accounts about Arab lands. Arab names of cities, transliterated into Chinese, included Ma-Jun (which stood for Oman) and Ya-ra-ha-chi (which was the Chinese version of present Qatif in Saudi Arabia). Two remarkable expeditions to China were particularly mentioned as being undertaken by Omanis, with special emphasis on visits to the ruling dynasty. The first of these expeditions was carried in 1011 AD, under the leadership of an Arab commander named Abdul Qassim[456].

The second expedition, was led by Hashim bin Abdullah, who presented a gift to the Chinese emperor. The gift was said to include pearls, dates, rose-water, textiles and other things. China's emperor responded in a similarly generous manner[457]. Good commercial relations between Arabian merchants and the southern Chinese ports, in particular, remained strong throughout the era of the Sung dynasty, and even after the critical political changes following the shift in Caliphate in the Islamic world.

During the Ming dynasty in China (1368-1644) these relations were further strengthened. Certain Omani references spoke about an expedition undertaken by an Omani trader, Abu Obeida, to China in the mid-sixteenth century. This trader returned back with considerable quantities of frankincense wood[458].

Official Chinese records of the Ming ruling family confirm that the Chinese recommenced regular commercial voyages to the Arabian peninsula. Such trips included a journey carried out by a Muslim Chinese gentleman sent by Emperor Cheng-Zu (1402-1424). During the reign of the Emperor Xuan Zong (1425-1435), two notable expeditions were conducted to a number of Arab ports, including Oman[459]. It is clear from these and other records that commercial relations between China and the Arab world in general, and Oman in particular, were significantly strengthened.

During this period the status of individual ports fluctuated according to local and regional events. For instance, Siraf, on the eastern coast of the Arabian Gulf, dimished in commercial importance when it was put under the control of the rulers of Qais Island which took over its role[460].

Qais itself flourished in economic terms for less than a century, prior to entering a period of sharp decline and steady fragmentation, relinquishing its own position to Hormuz.

Omani cities tended to buck this trend since they had been able to maintain their significance over extended periods of time. Sohar, for instance, never relinquished its importance to any other city or port[461].

The Maritime Route to East Africa:

Omani trading routes[462] to East Africa began from Sohar or Muscat and tended to hug the shore, thus maximising their trading contacts with coastal communities enroute[463]. Omani vessels would sail as far as Safala on their East African voyages. Al-Mas'udi, in this respect, said, 'Safala is the furthermost place of the *Bilad al-Zinj* to which Omani and Sirafi boats would sail'.

It is likely that Omanis did not sail further than Saffala[464] because they would lose the benefit of monsoon winds once they passed Corrients, a mountain Arabs called *Mountain of Sorrows*; and also because of strong currents.

Among the islands reached by Omanis were Qanbaloo and Zanzibar[465]. They used to establish their own colonies in these islands in order to protect their commercial interests.

Commodities of Importance for Omani Traders

Omani vessels sailing to Africa, would usually carry the various products of the Arabian peninsula and goods from India and other Far Eastern sources. On the return voyage, they would load their ships with the diverse products available at East African ports.

The pearl was the most important export of Oman at the time. Al-Jahiz[466], a notable Arab literary figure and historian, gave fascinating details about the sorts of pearls Omanis exported to Africa, describing over a dozen classes of pearl. Omani vessels also transported ambergris from the coasts of Oman, as well as from Aden, Mukkha and Zeilla; dates from Oman and Basra; frankincense from Hadramaut; and leather from Aden's tanneries[467].

Omanis were also famous for trade in Omani copper[468], Yemeni alum, emeralds from Egypt and their native horses[469].

Chinese products imported by Omanis included silk, musk, frankincense, clay, sable and galingale. Other historians also mention gold, silver, pearls and silk brocade as the most significant Chinese exports[470].

Goods imported to Oman from India included cotton, gold, silver, frankincense, coconut, camphor[471], elephant tusks, perfumes, jewels, ambergris and pepper. From the Andaman Islands, they brought camphor, ivory and ebony.

From Africa, on the other hand, Omani traders would mainly bring ivory. This particular product was widely used by Chinese kings and aristocrats as well as by wealthy members of the Indian community. Omanis also carried aloe from Socotra, which lay on the route between Arabia and East Africa[472]. Chinese references state that numerous rhinoceros horns were imported to China from various parts of Asia but that the finest quality of all were those brought by Omani tradesmen from Zanzibar[473].

Initially the method used for exchanging goods was based upon barter but later Omanis adopted coins, and eventually paper money. In fact, China was the first country to use paper currency[474].

Omani and Bahraini sailors honed their navigational skills and maintained their reputation as some of the finest seamen of the Indian Ocean and the Arabian Sea. Sailing east to India and west to the eastern and southern coasts of Africa, they remained masters of the southern seas and leaders of trade in the Indian Ocean until the fifteenth century AD. The arrival of the Portuguese in the Indian Ocean changed all this however[475]. Ibn Majed, an Arab sailor and master navigator, was reported to have acted as a pilot for Vasco da Gama on his expedition from Malindi, on the East African coast, to Malabar; showing the Portuese captain the safe trans-oceanic route towards India. However, this has been contradicted by Dr Anwar Abdul Aleem, who believed that Da Gama's pilot was in fact a person with the name Kanaka[476].

Consequences of Maritime Trade Conducted by Omanis

As we have seen already Omanis played a crucial role as commodity brokers between the East and West. This role had significant cultural consequences since, in addition to their major contribution towards international economic development, they also played a major role on behalf of Islam as excellent examples of Islamic values and culture, communicating these principles to the people with whom they came in contact as part of their trading activities. Omanis were thus able to attract others to voluntarily convert to Islam. It is a tribute to the force of the message, and to the strength of their faith, that Islam spread so widely in such a short period, to south-eastern Asia, China and East Africa.

Due to their commercial activities as merchants, Omanis were involved in the economic prosperity of Egypt during various Islamic ages. This is particularly true of the Fatimid era. Under the Mamelukes, Egypt relied on spices imported by Omanis from their source locations in Asia and elsewhere, depending on them, both for domestic consumption, and for re-export.

In addition, the Omanis' role as trade coordinators between the eastern and western parts of the Islamic world enabled it to attract an increasing number of businessmen and scholars from Andalucia and elsewhere, causing an influx of visitors to Oman, and from it to other Arabian Gulf ports such as Abila, Basra and Bahrain. Thus, the Omanis certainly played a vital role in establishing strong cultural and economic links between the Islamic countries in the western and eastern parts of the Islamic world. A considerable number of Islamic scholars and philosophers from Andalucia eventually migrated to India and the Far East, seeking both their livelihoods and to learn from these communities.

Moreover, the Omanis' competence in trade and navigation was a real stimulus for new generations to excel in oceanography, astronomy and geography. A number of Omanis were conducting research in these fields at that time, making important contributions. We will now consider these matters in more detail.

The Peaceful Introduction of Islam in China and South East Asia

Muslim Arabs were first mentioned in Chinese historical literature during the period of the T'ang dynasty (618-907 AD). Some manuscripts mention the establishment of a state by the Prophet Mohammed in Medina in the seventh century AD. Researchers have confirmed that Islam was introduced to China during the time of Prophet Mohammed, when an Islamic three-person delegation arrived in China. Two members of this mission died immediately after arrival. The third one, however, was able to build a great mosque in China, which is still in existence today[477]. In 627 AD an additional mosque, named as Kuang Ta (or Medina's Minaret), was built in Canton.

Chinese sources state that the spread of Islam within their region was concentrated during the rule of T'ai-tsung (627-650 AD) with the arrival in China of a Muslim from the family of the Prophet, accompanied by 3000 migrants. Furthermore, there were certain diplomatic contacts between China's emperor and the third caliph, Othman bin Affan, during the early period of the Islamic State. The latter is reported to have sent an Arab delegation to China in 651 AD: a move which was generously accepted by the Chinese ruler[478].

Whilst it is clear that Islam was introduced to China from the early days of the Islamic state in Medina, its wide dissemination there can be attributed to the involvement and presence of Omani merchants during the first century Hegira. There was a large Omani community in China, most of whom were merchants; and, consequently, the spread of Islam in the region was closely linked with the degree of trading activities with Omanis, and *vice versa*. An Omani merchant would generally sail back and forth throughout the trading region, only making the trip back to his home country after a number of years[479]. His longest periods of residence in China were likely to have been at the main commercial centres such as Beijing or Canton.

We have recently identified some Omani traders who migrated to China. They include Abu Obeida Abdullah bin Al-Qassim, who lived in the first half of the second century Hegira, settling in China where he became a famous merchant dealing in frankincense. He lived there for a long period before finally returning to his homeland. Another Omani businessman, Al-Nadhar bin Memoun, who had formerly been living in Basra, took ship to China where he joined Al-Qassim. These two, along with about a dozen others, played a crucial role in the spread of Islam in China[480]. They usually married Chinese women and thus raised offspring with mixed Chinese and Omani origins: an instrumental factor in further boosting the spread of Islam in China. They also built mosques in a number of Chinese cities such as the grand mosque in Guang Zhou, which was probably constructed in 1009 AD[481].

With respect to India, on the other hand, Omanis participated in its exploration as early as the second century Hegira. As we have already noted, Othman bin Abi Al-A'as Al-Thaqafi, the governor of Oman and Bahrain, commanded a military fleet which approached the Indian coast. Meanwhile, in the year 15 Hegira, he ordered his brother Al-Mughayera to sail to Khor Deible near the estuary of the Sind river[482]. Omanis were also successful in confronting Indian pirates in Islamic coastal waters.

The Arab historian, Al-Mas'udi, who visited the Indian city of Siamur in 304 Hegira, gave detailed accounts of a large Muslim community, amounting to around 10,000 people from Siraf, Basra, Oman and Baghdad. On the other hand Al-Idrisi confirmed that most Arab inhabitants of India were Omanis and that they were greatly respected by the Indian rulers[483].

Omani merchants and seamen also played a key role in the spread of Islam in south-east Asia. They travelled as far as the Malaysian archipelago, particularly to the important port of Malacca on the Straits of Malacca[484]. Malacca itself prospered mainly due to the stability created by Arab merchants and the reputation it gained from the early Islamic ages. Since then, and to this date, the city has been a major centre along the western coastline of the Malaysian subcontinent[485].

Arab and Omani businessmen at that time were primarily living in the major cities and commercial centres where they were in a direct contact with the local people; a factor which helped to promote Islam in the region. In other words, a Muslim businessman was both a merchant and a teacher. Whenever he settled in an area, he would establish religious schools to teach the community in that particular place. An emphasis would usually be given to recital of the Holy Qur'an[486].

Muslims did not confine their efforts to introduction of Islam to the Malaysian archipelago, they also reached the East Indies. Historical records indicate that an Omani sheikh who lived in Sumatra was able, owing to his diplomacy and intelligence, to persuade its king to treat Muslims with great respect. In fact, the kings of this island were actually converted to Islam during the time of the Arab traveller, Ibn Battuta[487].

In Malaysia and Java, old Muslim cemeteries have been found with Arabic inscriptions on the graves. Among these, there is a grave of a woman who died in the Javan town of Gresik in 1082 AD. Malabar island was also known to Arab traders since the year 200 Hegira. Its king also converted to Islam and died during a journey back from a visit to Arabia; being buried in Dhofar[488]. Ibn Battuta mentioned that he saw three mosques that had Omanis as their full-time judge and cleric in the town of Vandarina, where he arrived in 1341 AD [489].

Omani Muslims in East Africa

As previously stated Oman was intimately connected with East Africa insofar as trade was concerned. Relations between the two regions were further consolidated due to the large increase in commerce associated with the establishment of several ports which were originally built by Omanis to serve their business. Going back as far as the first or second century AD, the author of the *Periplus of the Erythrean Sea* indicated that many Arabian boats used to arrive on the East African coast, from the Arabian peninsula, including Oman. The anonymous author of this ancient manuscript also commented on intermarriage between Arab traders and tribal Africans [490]. Ever since that time, East Africans have considered Omanis as their close relatives.

Perhaps the prevailing weather patterns in the Indian Ocean greatly assisted vessels sailing between East Africa and Oman. The north-westerly monsoon in winter would usually provide a free-wind for vessels sailing from Omani ports to East Africa whilst the south-westerly monsoon winds helped them on their return journeys, from African to Oman, in summer[491].

Omani merchants did not penetrate far from the African coastline prior to the emergence of Islam. During that early historical period, they were satisfied with settling along the eastern shores of the continent. Here, they continued to establish commercial centres, bartering Chinese and Indian goods, imported on Omani vessels, for ivory and gold which were freely available at that time in Africa[492].

With the advent of Islam, and the establishment of the Arab Islamic countries, the situation completely changed. Omanis experienced difficult political conditions during the Ummayyad and Abbasid periods and as a result many emigrated to East Africa, settling there permanently as economic refugees, creating their own Islamic communities.

It is well known that the Prophet Mohammed appointed Amr bin Al-A'as as his governor for Oman[493]. But when Abu Bakr assumed office, in the aftermath of the death of Prophet Mohammed, he allowed Omanis to rule their own country. This situation continued for a long period of time, until the reign of the Ummayyad caliph Abdul Mulik bin Marwan who appointed Al-Hajjaj bin Youssef Al-Thaqafi from Iraq. It was at this particular juncture in history that the first extensive migration of Omanis to East Africa took place since Al-Hajjaj was eager to extend his authority over Oman. He dispatched a series of missions against Oman but, Suleiman and Said, the sons of Abd Al-Julanda, who were the then rulers of Oman, were able to counter his campaigns, preventing any advances[494].

Despite the repeated defeats, and his persistent failure to control Oman, Al-Hajjaj kept up his efforts to take over the country. In 695 AD, he sent a large army to Oman which was eventually able to defeat Suleiman and Said[495]. The two brothers had had no choice but to sail to East Africa accompanied by their relatives. Apparently they settled in the region of the Lamu archipelago[496] and on Mafia Island near the estuary of Rufiji river as well as on Patta island to the north[497].

This was not however either the first or the last Omani migration to Africa. During the Abbassid era, the Abbassid rulers were keen to include Oman under their control. Their armies repeatedly attacked Oman, ransacking and destroying many of the important cities. For instance, Mohammed bin Nour, the leader of the army of Caliph Motadhid, conducted a vicious massacre in Nizwa. As a result, Omanis left the country in considerable numbers, in order to emigrate to East Africa[498].

Once again, in the early seventh century Hegira, a new wave of Omani emigration to East Africa commenced. This particular influx of migration had had a far-reaching effect on the region. It was mainly under the leadership of Suleiman Al-Nabhani, a prominent Omani leader of the time. He was warmly received on Patta island by the resident Arabs. He married a Swahili princess, daughter of King Is'haq of the Sherazi sect in the Kilwa kingdom. Immediately following this marriage, Is'haq relinquished the throne to his new son-in-law, Suleiman Al-Nabhani who became the first Arab ruler in East Africa. The Nabhani ruling family was able to annex almost all of the East African region within its territory by the turn of the ninth century Hegira. Their kingdom included Kismayu, Brawa and Mogadishu (in present day Somalia). The dynasty remained in power until 1745[499].

Due to Omani settlement of the eastern coast of Africa, Islam was widely, though gradually, spread among the Africans. Indeed, the Omanis role was of considerable significance in converting the various, diversified tribal communities of East Africa to Islam. Since intermarriage between the immigrants and the East Africans was on the increase, there was an intermixing of race and culture which had a deep-rooted impact on future generations. Intellectual, personality and physical charateristics of the new mixed generations were quite similar to those of Omanis. This new race of mixed origins became known as the Swahili race, speaking Kiswahili language and adhering to Islam. The commercial, ethnic, cultural and religious bonds that now linked Oman and East Africa had never been stronger[500].

Several studies have been conducted on the Kiswahili language; its dialects and its relations with African and Arabic languages[501]. From these it is apparent that Kiswahili, since its early formation, has been closely linked with Arabic. This link is quite clear in the vocabulary of the new language as well as in certain syntactic structures that it followed. Omanis played a key role in the spread of Kiswahili through the interior of Africa as well as along the eastern seabord of the continent. Some researchers have suggested that Arabs, including Omanis, living in the coastal cities and towns of East Africa were reluctant to use Arabic although it was widely understood among the elite. Instead, Kiswahili was the language of day-to-day communication. Neverthless, right up to the present day, Kiswahili uses the Arabic alphabet[502].

As we have already mentioned, prior to the emergence of Islam, Omani immigrants did not penetrate far into the interior of Africa. Following the introduction of Islam, however, they actively moved into the hinterland of the continent, spreading the teachings of Islam as they went. For instance, the Ethiopian tribe of Galla was converted to Islam. And in Somalia, too, Islam became quite prevalent at that time. In fact, the Arab immigrants, from Hadramaut, Yemen and Oman, practised their trading activities at the same time as teaching Islam[503].

The small states and kingdoms established by Omanis along the eastern coast of Africa thrived on both social and economic levels. The Portuguese themselves - although potential rivals of the Arabs in this region, during their great expeditions to Africa around the turn of the fifteenth century AD - made complimentary comments about the civilization that they discovered in East Africa.

The Portuguese navigator, Duarte Barbosa, for instance, wrote as follows: 'When the ships of Vasco da Gama reached Safala, they were surprised to discover that the African ports were as busy as bee-hives. They encountered well populated coastal cities, and a more widely based commercial realm than their own. They also learned that Arab navigators had sailed across the Indian Ocean on several occasions and that those Arab navigators were familiar with the most intricate details of the ports of this ocean. Their accurate information was carefully recorded on skillfully prepared charts which were at least as good as those that the Portuguese had developed for Europe'[504].

There were other economic and social effects of the Omani migrations to East Africa. Omani merchants exported the crops of the region to various parts of the Indian Ocean and up the Red Sea. African nationals brought slaves from the prisoners of local tribal wars to the Arab traders. Thus, black African elements came to represent an important element of the demography of the Arab Islamic countries. Some of these African Arabs became prominent leaders such as Kafour Al-Ekheshidi in Egypt. Others set off the famous revolt against the Abbassid state in Iraq[505] in the third century Hegira. The main activists of this revolt were Somalis and other black Africans. Their struggle against the Abbasids continued for 14 years.

Arabs helped to exploit the mineral resources in the coastal areas of East Africa, extracting gold, silver, copper and iron ore. Huge quantities of gold were taken back to the Islamic world from Safala in Africa (the city later became known as: 'Safala of the Gold').

Arab-style of architecture was quite conspicuous in East Africa with various engravings and decorative inscriptions following the Arabian and Islamic fashions of art[506]. By the end of the Middle Ages Islam was widely followed in the interior of East Africa, at a time when the Portuguese danger loomed on the horizon. Muslims tended to depart from the coastal cities and move into the hinterland in order to avoid persistent raids undertaken by Portuguese forces. This development greatly boosted the spread of Islam among the various African tribes of the interior[507].

Just as Omani merchants had a significant impact on the social, cultural and economic conditions of regions along the Indian Ocean, they also had an equivalent impact on nations bordering the Mediterranean Sea such as Egypt, Morocco and Andalucia.

Omani Trade and Its Impact on Egypt's Trade and Political Life
Omani traders acted as brokers between sellers of Indian, Chinese and southeastern Asian goods on the one hand, and the buyers of these goods in the Islamic Middle East and western Europe, on the other. Egypt, due mainly to its strategic geographic location, was a contact point for trade between the East and the West: a fact which was especially apparent in connection with trade in spices brought to Egypt from the Far East by Arab and Omani merchants and seamen, and from there transshipped to Europe.

Egypt had placed major reliance for its economic prosperity, ever since the Fatimid rule, on its status as a clearing house for spices. In the latter days of the Mamelukes, however, Egypt's economy was on the brink of a decline triggered by the Portuguese discovery of an alternative spice route, around the Cape of Good Hope. With the adoption of this direct sea route, avoiding Arabian territory and cutting out the Egyptian role, Egypt's economy suffered a telling blow[508].

Notwithstanding this set-back, Oman played a very significant role in bringing the East's produce, particularly spices, to the commercial centres in the Arabian Gulf, or to Aden, in order to be transshipped to Egypt via the Red Sea. These mercantile efforts directly contributed to the economic prosperity Egypt enjoyed towards the end of the nineteenth century AD. Two routes were frequently used in the delivery of spices from India and Malaysia, by Omani vessels, to reach the Egyptian traders in the Red Sea.

The first was that from Oman to Aden, a port which was throughout the Islamic Middle Ages a centre for embassies. Ships from India, China, Persia, Bahrain and Ethiopia would meet there. Goods from Egypt, brought by both sea and land, would also arrive in Aden. From there, two routes would usually be used, one by land: a mountainous route crossing the Yemeni plateau through Ta'izz, Ibb, Dhamar, Sana'a and Sadah and directly on to Mecca. The other one, a lowland road, eventually branched into two paths: one leading towards the coast which met the land route at Jizan; and a second one which would continue to run parallel with the coast until reaching some of the Red Sea ports frequented by Egyptian ships which used to lie at anchor, awaiting the arrival of the Indian spice caravans[509].

Some historians have pointed out that Muslims in Ethiopia played an important role in the transport of the Far East's produce to Egypt. They used to buy the goods from Omani merchants in Aden, and elsewhere, and carry them by land for considerable distances up to the Red Sea littoral where they met with Egyptian vessels. Some would even go to Suakin in the Sudan and from there across the desert to the Nile, and later by land or river boat to Cairo[510].

Alternatively Omani ships, loaded with spices, would divert from their course to East Africa, heading up the Red Sea for some distance until they liaised with Egyptian vessels. After transferring their cargoes the Omani boats would head back down the Red Sea and into the Indian Ocean[511].

Oman's Trading Skills and Their Effect on Relations with Morocco and Andalucia

Oman's reputation as being highly competent in both trade and seamanship in the Indian Ocean was a popular topic of conversation. People in Morocco and Andalucia were thus encouraged to forge contacts with the Islamic East, which was seen as the cradle of Islam and as a source of valuable goods. Oman played an important role in this bridge building and Morocco's relations with Oman were consequently strengthened thereafter.

The eminent Moroccan geographer Al-Idrisi gave detailed accounts of his visit to Oman. He wrote about Dhofar, Muscat, Nizwa, Sohar and Julfar. A reader of his book, *Nuzhat al-Mushtaq*, would certainly gain a good impression of Al-Idrisi's view of Oman but the geographer himself did not visit the country, but relied on second-hand information about it. Ibn Battuta[512], on the other hand, who also hailed from Morocco, personally visited Oman so his details about it are somewhat more accurate.

Scholars have pointed to numerous similarities between Omanis and Moroccans. In Morocco, they found a number of families which claim to be originally from Oman, including, among others, the Ghassani, Harithi, Zubaidi and Salimi families[513].

So far as Andalucia is concerned, journeys to the east formed prime challenges for both scholars and merchants. There are abundant references providing specific names of people from Andalucia who travelled to the Islamic East, either for knowledge or trade[514]. Oman and its various cities were among their primary destinations. The Andalucian trip to the Islamic East would usually be by sea, commencing from the south-eastern ports of Andalucia, such as Daniya and Marie, and across the Mediterranean Sea to Alexandria. From there to the Nile, using small boats, and south to the Red Sea. Vessels would then take travellers to Aden and finally to Oman, Basra, and Abla in the Arabian Gulf. Occasionally they would complete the journey to India or China. An alternative way for them to reach southern Arabia was by the land-route from Damascus to Iraq, and from there to the Arabian Gulf and the Indian Ocean[515].

The most important Andalucian products brought to the Islamic East were olive oil[516], mercury, brimstone, *kohl* (eyeliner) and textiles. Omani traders usually exported oriental goods such as jewels, Chinese silk and spices to Andalucia[517].

Omanis' competence in navigation and commerce underpinned achievements in the marine field in all its facets, including instrument design, astronomical records and so on. Numerous instruments, although of relatively basic capabilities, were employed by Omani sailors as navigational aids. These were mainly used to measure wind speed and direction, sea currents and tide. In reality, it was well-recognized that Muslim astronomers such as Mohammed Al-Kho'arizmi, Al-Bitani and Al-Bairouni were superior to their Greek counterparts in this field of human knowledge.

Ibn Majed, for example, wrote detailed notes on his sea voyages, correcting several previous errors and recording his vast experience and practices during his long career as a navigator. From the accounts given by Omani navigators, who had good experience of sailing on the Indian Ocean and the China Sea, it is clear that a sailor or a coxswain was usually very knowledgeable about all marine characteristics such as tides, seasonal currents and wave patterns on his route.

The Role of the Omani Naval Fleet in Omani History

Oman is a maritime nation situated adjacent to the open ocean. Traditionally, the majority of Omanis worked in fishing and the mercantile trade.This strong association with the sea played a key role in development of the Omani naval fleet and in ship-building. The latter activity will be discussed in the next chapter, whilst in this chapter we will shed light on the Omani naval fleet and its role in the history of Oman, especially during the Islamic era and beyond.

It is well known around the Arabian peninsula that the Omanis were early converts to Islam and that they were very sincere in their adherence to the faith. They did their best to uphold Islam and to expand the Islamic state, using their naval fleet in the Muslim cause[518].

Political circumstances created conflicts among the Arabs and Muslims, the difficulties commencing when when Ali and Mua'awiya disagreed with each other. The Omanis suffered tremendously for their support of the Muslim cause; incurring many casualties in battle and losing valuable resources. There was considerable antagonism directed towards them by both the Ummayyad and

Al-Khandaq Fort in Buraimi.

Abbassid dynasties. Oman's internal situation suffered as a result, as did its navy. Many Omanis left the country and emigrated to East Africa and other places[519].

During the reign of Abdul Mulik bin Marwan, Al-Hajjaj bin Youssef Al-Thaqafi was appointed as the Governor of Iraq. Al-Hajjaj dispatched a sizeable naval fleet to occupy Oman; his forces landing near Al-Jassa on the Omani coastline, surprising and outflanking the Omanis who battled the Al-Hajjaj forces at Wadi Hitat. After a few days, with the support of the naval and land forces, they managed to regain the initiative. Omani fighters killed the Ummayyad commander, and those who survived the conflict fled across the sea.

The Ummayyads attempted to invade Oman on numerous subsequent occasions. Finally they succeeded in defeating Said bin Abbad Al-Julandi who fled to Jebal Al-Akhdar, the green mountain. Omani forces counter attacked the Al-Hajjaj forces and destroyed the Ummayyad fleet in Oman's coastal waters whilst the rest of the Ummayyad army fled for their lives.

Following the Abbassid defeat of the Ummayyads, the capital of the Caliphate was transferred from Damascus to Baghdad, stimulating development of Oman's naval force. During Haroun Al-Rashid's reign, the Omani naval fleet reached a peak of capability. Thus, when, in 187 AH/802 AD, the Omani people refused to pay him tax, resulting in Haroun Al-Rashid sending a large naval forces to invade Oman, the Omani navy, together with the full support of its land-based army, defeated the Abbassid forces, killing their commander. Haroun Al-Rashid was enraged and sought revenge but his sudden death a short while later, followed by conflict between his two sons, Al-Amin and Al-Ma'moun, forestalled any new invasion attempt.

Imam Ghassan bin Abdullah Al-Yahmadi further developed the Omani naval forces, consolidating national security and prosperity. The task was undertaken without any major difficulties, with the exception of some internal differences between clans (such as those between the Nizari and Qahtani clans). Omani Imams countered the threats from Indian pirates who tried to prevent Omani ships from undertaking their trading missions. These pirates also attacked some of the Omani ports such as Daba, Julfar and the surrounding region. The Omanis organized a special task force, including a small naval fleet of very fast, small ships to challenge the Indian pirates. Their superior equipment and greater navigational skills put an end to Indian troubles, with the Omanis pursuing them right back to the Indian shores[520].

Between 225-7 AH/821-3 AD, Imam Al-Muhanna bin Gaifar Al-Yahmadi Al-Kharousi was inaugurated. During his period of power, trade and business flourished and the naval force and land army became very well organized. Oman's naval fleet contained 300 warships to challenge any foreign aggression[521]. It was held in absolute readiness, constantly patrolling and challenging any acts of aggression by foreigners attempting to invade Oman or attack its coastal settlements. During the reign of Imam Al-Salt bin Malik Al-Kharousi, 237-273 AH/857-881 AD, the Ethiopians attacked Socotra Island (an Omani Island at that time) and occupied it, killing the Omani Governor of the island. Imam Al-Salt prepared a very strong fleet, consisting of more than 100 ships, and attacked the Ethiopians, defeating them and liberating the island[522].

During the Al-Salt period, Oman's naval fleet comprised more than 300 strong and well-armed ships. The terrestrial and coastguard forces were also equipped with the most modern weaponry at that time[523].

In 331 AH/942 AD, the Carmathians controlled the entire Gulf area. Oman's navy attacked the Caramathian fleet, destroying it completely. Omani naval forces adopted a new and highly successful strategy in the naval clashes[524] which became the main battleground between the rival forces.

The Buwayhids organized a huge naval fleet in 355 AH/965 AD with the aim of conquering Oman. They bombarded the Omani naval fleet and in a surprise attack, destroyed 89 ships out of the entire fleet. The Buwayhids had hoped to conquer the entire territory of Oman but the Omani navy once again played the crucial role in defeating the aggressors and expelling them from the country. This battle, which took place in 431 AH/1019 AD, was a great victory for Oman, ending the Buwayhid occupation[525].

By the end of 650 AH/1252 AD, the Omani naval fleet was suffering the effects of years of mismanagement. Mahmoud bin Ahmed Al-Kusti, Emir of Hormuz, arrived in Qalhat and demanded that Oman's citizens should pay him land-tax. Kahlan rejected this effort at plundering the nation by telling him: ' Omani citizens are very poor, they do not have it to give away'. The Emir of Hormuz became incensed with the resistance to his efforts and raided Dhofar, escaping afterwards by sea with his booty[526].

Despite the relatively poor state of the Omani naval fleet during this period, it continued to function in Arabian and international waters; not facing any real threat to its maritime supremacy until the arrival in local waters of European ships. The better equipped naval ships of the Portuguese severely bruised the Omani fleet, causing considerable damage to the Omani military strength. It was during the reign of Imam Mohammed bin Ismail, commencing in 906 AH/1500 AD, that the Portuguese commander, Alfonso Pedro Albuqerque, led his forces on a scorched earth campaign along the Omani coastline, devastating the entire area between Ras Al-Hadd and Ras Musandam[527].

The Ottoman and the Mamelukes confronted the Portuguese in the Gulf, Red Sea and in the Indian Ocean. In the space of just a few years, by 914 AH/1508 AD, all those who had been challenging the Portuguese were in despair, and the erstwhile relatively stable trading conditions, both regionally and internationally, were turned upside down. Principal trade routes were diverted from the Gulf and the Red Sea to a new southern route, around the Cape of Good Hope.

The Portuguese gave little or no quarter, relentlessly pursuing their efforts to destroy all Omani ships and harbours; and burning cities. In 913 AH/1507 AD, for example, the Portuguese naval fleet bombarded Omani ships and sunk them at Khor Grama. They attacked the ports of Qalhat and Quriyat, murdering most of the citizens. After destroying 83 ships, they raided Muscat, burning its ships and ransacking the city[528]. They were merciless in their vengeance, killing civilians, and dismembering many of those who survived the initial massacres. The Omanis were weakened, their naval and mercantile fleets destroyed, commercial centres looted and the nation's infrastructure left in ruins. Caught between the rock and the hard-place, Omanis seemed to be doomed whichever way they turned, whether to resist against overwhelming odds, or to surrender. In both cases the likely consequences were death!

The Omanis resolved to conquer the Portuguese, or to die in the attempt. In the early eleventh century Hegira (1034 AH/1624 AD), Imam Nasir bin Murshid Al-Ya'rubi raised his leading banner; mustering land forces supported by strengthened Omani naval power, he regained control of Oman's coastal provinces provinces between Julfar and Dhofar[529]. In 1060 AH/1650 AD the Omanis bombarded the Portuguese boot camps in Muscat where many soldiers fled and over 700 became Omani prisoners. Imam Nasir raided Portuguese munitions depots in the city, capturing all their weapons[530]. The Omanis learnt many valuable lessons from their contact with the Portuguese; recognizing their own weakness within their navy, and identifying the strengths of the enemy's naval fleet. With these things in mind, they built bigger and better ships; and more of them - in order to double the size of the fleet so that it could match the power of the Portuguese enemy. The Al-Nabhan family lost their grip on power in the beginning of the seventeenth century, and the Al-Ya'ruba family came to rule Oman.

Al-Ya'ruba rulers realized that their power and strength lay in the naval forces and the united front of the people. Imam Saif bin Sultan Al-Ya'rubi endeavoured to build a very strong naval fleet to challenge the Portuguese. He was deeply aware of the crucial importance of uniting the disparate forces within Oman into a single national force, an achievement which his own strong leadership made possible.

In 1060 AH/1650 AD, following the overthrow of the Portuguese from Muscat, a new stage began in the history of Oman. The Omanis again started to expand their political and economic influence overseas, while the nation's regional interests once more extended across the Gulf in a pattern that was to continue for almost two centuries. It became, by international standards, an important political, trade and maritime centre. In all of this they depended upon their naval fleet which extended its pursuit of the Portuguese to the western parts of the Indian Ocean.

The Omanis decided to dismantle their traditional vessels and to replace them with modern and larger ones, similar in appearance to those of the Europeans. Most of these were built in India and were equipped with larger cannons[531]. Sultan bin Saif Al-Ya'rubi (1059-1091 AH/1649-1680 AD) continued the efforts of his predecessors in vanquishing the Portuguese. He attacked them on Mombasa Island and in 1080 AH/1669 AD pursued them as far as Mozambique. The gaining of the Fort of Jesus on the African shores was a landmark event in Omani history (1110 AH/1698 AD) and a crushing defeat for the Portuguese[532].

Over the following years Omani naval forces continued to oppose the Portuguese in a number of places. Step by step they regained lost territories, whilst the Portuguese retreated in fear, and the Dutch, taking advantage of the situation, bolstered their own presence in the Gulf. The Omanis, however, were not about to accept the replacement of Portuguese aggression with that of the Dutch. From 1107 AH/1695 AD onwards the Omanis resisted the rise of Dutch influence; attacking Dutch ships in the Gulf and Indian Ocean.

The situation worsened following Persian clashes with the Arabs. Arab sailors, who worked on the Persian ships, decided to mutiny and take control of their ships. The Dutch were unable to help[533] since the improved power of the Omani naval fleet was enough to defeat both powers: Dutch and Persian. Whilst the Europeans were concentrating on strengthening their power in India, Oman took advantage of their preoccupation by focussing on their own positions along the coast of East Africa and the islands of the Indian Ocean. They developed improved diplomatic, commercial and personal relations with many other countries; particularly in the fields of naval power and commerce.

The Omanis reached a high point of naval and economic power in 1112 AH/1700 AD; leading to consolidation and strengthening of their influence over a large area, across thousands of miles of the Indian Ocean[534]. Thus, at the beginning of the eighteenth century, the Omani naval fleet was stronger, larger, and better equipped than at any time in its past history. Commenting on this, Alexander Hamilton, in his account of the East Indies, published in 1727, observed that in 1127 AH /1715 AD, the Imam's naval force included one ship which was equipped with 72 cannons, two with 60 cannons on each of them, another ship carrying 50 batteries on board, 18 ships equipped with 12 to 32 cannons, and many boats carrying four to eight batteries. Hamilton noted that the Imam's naval might was legendary, spreading fear amongst the invading forces right up to the Red Sea[535]. In this regard, Miles commented that despite the Omani naval fleet having emerged and expanded in number, we know nothing about its real size. The only thing we do know is that some of its ships were built like those of Europeans, whilst the other section of the fleet was built according to Arab or Eastern designs. No one would deny that the weaponry and other equipment on board the fleet was of the first class, and designed to achieve two goals at once: one military and the other economic (trade, transport, fishing etc.).

The Al-Ya'ruba family, as we have seen, led Muscat's liberation campaign against the Portuguese. They built the greatest naval fleet ever assembled by a non-European country in the Indian Ocean and their influence reached all along the African coast. In 1133 AH/1720 AD, the Omani fleet was in control of Mogadishu, Mombasa, the Zanzibar Islands, Pemba, the entire Arabian Gulf, the Arabian Sea, the Indus Valley and the East Indian shores[536]. The Omani naval fleet had grown to the point where it was able to administer this extensive region and its military strength was sufficient to crush any internal rebellion by any province which endeavoured to split from the state[537].

Imam Ahmed bin Said Al-Busaid, the founder of Al-Busaidi dynasty, focussed on further strengthening the country's naval might[538]. In 1170 AH/1775 AD the Omani naval fleet had a major victory when the Omani battle cruiser *Ar-Rahmani* was able to break through a Persian blockade at the entrance of Shatt Al-Arab and to carry supplies to the besieged port of Basra. The Omani naval fleet managed to drive off the pirates up to the Malabar coast of India and destroyed them[539]. The number of fighters in Imam Ahmed bin Said's army was numbered between 15,000 and 20,000 infantrymen and 1000 horsemen[540].

As we have seen, the African trade had been controlled for some time by Oman's navy. Imam Ahmed now surprised many people by using his naval strength to extend his influence over numerous other powers that were involved with mercantile shipping in the Indian Ocean[541]. The extent of Omani influence at this time is indicated by the fact that its naval forces controlled the East African coast and the two cities of Makran and Shah Bahar on the Persian coasts; together with Qeshm Island in the Gulf. It transported all the cargoes from islands controlled by the French in the Indian Ocean to the Gulf and gained considerable profit from its dealings with France.

Whilst Oman was faced with some internal political problems, slowing down its general development for some time, the Al-Busaid family was very active in supporting its naval fleet in the Indian Ocean. They developed trade activities, especially in Muscat. Between 1164-1215 AH/1750-1800 AD this family encouraged merchant shipping, sending out naval forces to regulate shipping channels in the Gulf and to provide protection to the Omani mercantile fleet. It was this force that crushed the pirates, and made direct contact with the European and American ports such as London, Amsterdam and New York[542].

Local circumstances demanded that Oman maintain a strong naval fleet. Wars, conflicts, and pirate raids prevailed between the forces of the region and the Europeans. It was quite standard practice that a merchant or trader at that time would be an 'adventurer' carrying his wares in one hand and a weapon in the other. During that time, no one was able to differentiate between a battleship and a merchant ship and all vessels were well-equipped with different types of weapons. The reverse was also true, with even warships carrying their own commercial cargoes and being deeply involved in all aspects of business.

European travellers and the British East India Company provide us with valuable information about the Omani naval fleet and general commerce within the region. The British East India Company sent a letter at the end of the 1860s in which it explained, in detail, the situation and conditions existing in the Arabian Gulf, mentioning the capability of the naval forces of each regional power. The letter stated that the Imam of Muscat had six men-of-war, one ghurab[543] or corvette with 14 to 20 cannons on board and many small warships[544]. The letter also mentioned that the Omani merchant fleet in 1179 AH/1765 AD comprised over 50 ships, both large and small[545]. This fleet was able to sail every year to many ports, from Basra in the west to Malacca in the east. One of its better known voyages was the 'Coffee Fleet's' annual sailing. This used to bring coffee from Yemen to Basra, from where it was distributed to many countries in the Near East. Carsten Niebuhr visited the region in 1179 AH/1765 AD, recording in his diary that: '...the Omanis are among the best of the Arabs in navigation. They are sending 50 *tranki* ships every year with a full load of coffee to Basra'[546].

He also pointed out that the Omani war fleet comprised four large ships and eight small ones. The large ones were used in trade with East Africa during peace time and the smaller ones were used to provide protection to Omani ports and coastal provinces[547]. Over the course of the following three decades, the number of Omani merchant ships, and the size of the naval force, increased dramatically. At the same time the Europeans played a role in the build up, and support of, the Omani fleet. It is not difficult to find comments in eighteenth century documents which characterized the Omani ships as 'built similar to the European style'. The number of batteries of cannons, and the type of equipment on board Omani ships also provide an indication of the degree of European influence on the Omani naval fleet.

It is worth noting that the most significant developments and improvements in Omani ship-building techniques took place during the last decades of the eighteenth century, concurrent with the increased number of Omani merchant and naval vessels in active service. In addition to improvements in Omani ship-building, Oman's ports were extended, and new ones were built. Muscat, Sohar and Sur were the centres of the ship-building industry. Importation of timber and many other kinds of building wood from India had increased tremendously. In addition, Omanis were not content with their own ship products, so they also imported ships made by the Europeans. Such imports were either directly from European manufacturers or from European ship owners operating throughout Asian countries. The Omanis used the most developed Indian ship-building ports, including Bombay and Surat, to build some of their own vessels.

In the summer of 1189 AH/1775 AD, the traveller Abraham Parsons was in Muscat. He saw the Omani naval war fleet reprovisioning at this port, taking on board all necessary supplies, including munitions, and undergoing training exercises prior to heading up the Arabian Gulf towards Iraq in order to relieve Basra from the Persian siege. Parsons described the Omani naval fleet as containing no less than 34 battleships, four of them built in Bombay and equipped with 44 cannons. The fleet also contained five frigates and on board each were between 18 and 24 cannons. Other ships that were present included ketches and galeots. Each ship of this fleet was equipped with between eight and 14 batteries[548].

The reign of Sayyid Sultan bin Ahmed Al-Busaid, 1207-1219 AH /1792-1804 AD, provided the best example of these developments. The types of ships, their design and firepower all gained momentum. The merchant fleet in his time, was made up of 15 large ships, each handling a payload of between four and seven hundred tonnes. Hundreds more different sized ships belonged to the merchant fleet[549]. The large ships used to sail to Malabar, Malacca and Batavia; those of medium size travelling to East Africa, and the smallest sailing up and down the Arabian Gulf and Red Sea.

Sayyid Sultan bin Ahmed Al-Busaidi's naval fleet was very powerful and efficient. The leading corvette was named *Gunjana* and had a payload of 1000 tonnes. Such a large ship, with its massive payload, was unique among all the Asian and European ships. There were 32 cannons aboard, while the war fleet contained three ships of smaller size, each equipped with 20 cannons. All these vessels were designed according to European standards[550]. In addition, the fleet included more boats of smaller size, all of them equipped with the best weapons of their time.

Sayyid Sultan needed considerable financial resources to supply the needs of the country and its naval fleet. In order to raise the necessary revenues he imposed a trade tax on ships passing through the Straits of Hormuz in either direction. The new tax caused an outbreak of war to erupt between Oman and the newly established emirates with the Wahabi supporting the emirates. Following the invasion by the Egyptian Mohammed Ali Pasha's forces, and the occupation of Al-Dariyyah in the year 1234 AH/1818 AD, the Wahabi threat to Oman diminished.

In the nineteenth century, the Omanis decided to give greater consideration to their naval fleet. Without doubt, the strength of the Omani naval forces reached a new peak during the reign of Sayyid Said bin Sultan Al-Busaid, 1219-73 AH/1804-56 AD. The following table gives a clear idea of the Omani naval fleet during one period of Said bin Sultan's rule[551]:

Year	Name	Specification	No. of cannons	Payload /tonnes
1217 AH/1802 AD	*Taj Bex*	Naval ship	-	737
1229 AH/1814 AD	*Caroline*	Frigate	36	575
1234 AH/1819 AD	*Shah Aalam*	Frigate (181 ft x 41 ft)	56	1111
1237 AH/1822 AD	*Nusri*	-	-	164
1241 AH/1826 AD	*Liverpool*	Class 3 (180 ft x 48 ft)	74	1715
1249 AH/1833 AD	*Sultanah*	Naval ship	12	312
1250 AH/1834 AD	*Taja*	-	12	205
1251 AH/1835 AD	*Nusri*	-	-	179

As we have seen, the reign of Sayyid Said bin Sultan was accompanied by increased development in both the merchant and naval war fleet. Boat-building yards at the Omani ports of Matrah, Muscat, Sur and Shinas were the main centres for timber ship construction. Much of the required wood was imported from India and Java, whilst some local woods were also used, including date-palm trees which were used for building small ships. In addition to this home-based building Sayyid Said bin Sultan ordered a number of merchant and war ships to be built at the Indian ship-building centres, especially in Bombay. Among the most famous warships to have ever served with the Omani naval fleet are those mentioned in the above table, particularly ships such as *Taj Bex*, *Caroline*, *Shah Aalam*, *Liverpool*, *Sultanah* and *Taja*. In 1240 AH /1824 AD, Sayyid Said bin Sultan gave the large ship, *Liverpool*, as a present to the British King William IV. The British monarch then changed the name of the ship to *Al-Imam* as: a mark of appreciation to Sayyid Said bin Sultan. The warship *Sultanah,* which was the most powerful ship among the Omani naval fleet, was dispatched to the United States where it docked at the port of New York and carried gifts for the American President.

During the first half of the nineteenth century, the Omani mercantile and naval fleet dominated the Arabian Gulf and Indian Ocean. It was the second largest fleet after the British one, and maintained bases on the eastern coast of the Arabian Gulf, at Bandar Abbas, Jask, Shamel, Saiab, Lingeh, Qeshm Island, Hormuz and Larg. On the Omani coast, the bases were at the ports of Muscat, Matrah and Masirah Island. Oman also had naval bases on the African coast at Mombasa, Lamu, Kilwa, Marka, Mogadishu and Zanzibar. Sayyid Said bin Sultan's rule as Sultan of Oman lasted over half a century during which he administered a large state between the Arabian Gulf and the Indian Ocean. He used to travel between areas under his control in Oman and on the African coast, spending considerable time on his ships, watching over the countries of his wide empire.

In the latter years of his rule, he preferred to spend a large amount of time in Zanzibar, looking after the Omani estates on the African coast. He had very good relations with the chieftains of many African clans and the kings of many provinces and islands such as Madagascar. His naval force was the basis of his power. An American merchant visiting Zanzibar at the beginning of the 1830s gave a very good account of Omani naval fleet strength, mentioning that Sayyid Said had arrived in Zanzibar at the head of an impressive force, comprising a huge warship with 64 cannons, three frigates, each equipped with 36 cannons, and two smaller ships, each with 14 cannons. Moreover, 5000 soldiers had arrived aboard 100 ships. The Omani fleet was sufficiently strong and efficient to protect a vast area between Bandar Abbas and Zanzibar. In spite of a distance of more than 2000 miles between Oman and Africa, Oman's navy managed to protect all the areas under its control; including dozens of ports on the Arabian and African coasts and more islands across the Arabian Gulf and Indian Ocean. Thanks to Oman's protection hundreds of merchant ships sailed between India and south of the Arabian peninsula without any problems.

In 1256 AH/1840 AD, Sayyid Said bin Sultan sent the Omani ship, *Sultanah* to New York for a friendly trade mission. His ambassador, Ahmed bin Nu'man Al-K'abi, who travelled aboard this ship, was the first Arab diplomat to pay an official visit to the United States. The same ship visited London in 1258 AH/1842 AD, carrying Ambassador Ali bin Nasir, who presented his credentials to Queen Victoria. Historical documents also indicate that in 1266 AH/1849 AD the Omani warship *Caroline* with 36 cannons, visited Marseilles for a friendly trade mission on which it brought to the French port considerable quantities of Eastern merchandise.

In the mid-nineteenth century, the Omani armed merchant fleet exceeded a hundred ships of various carrying capacities. Each was equipped with between 10 and 74 cannons, in addition to hundreds of small merchant ships. It is worth mentioning that Sayyid Said bin Sultan spent his last days on board the ship, *Victoria*, sailing around the Indian Ocean. He died in 1273 AH/1856 AD, on a return passage to Muscat, while the ship was close to the Seychelles.

So what were the secrets of the magnificent success of Oman's naval fleet during the reign of Sayyid Said bin Sultan? Given the impressive advances in navigational science during his rule, most of which were of Omani or Arabic origins, there is little doubt that these skills played a key role in the great achievements of the period. Many centuries previously, long before the Portuguese, Dutch, English, French and German explorations of the Indian Ocean, Omani sailors discovered and explored Asian and African coasts. Omani researchers in nautical studies have written many books about the science and art of navigation. Works by the distinguished Arab scientist Ahmed ibn Majed and the Omani sailor, Suleiman Al-Mahri, were considered to be the standard references for all ship pilots and crews. Omani sailors acquired this vast navigational experience over many centuries with knowledge of the art of navigation being handed from grandfather to father to son, and so on, from generation to generation; whilst others picked up their knowledge by talking with, and working alongside, sailors in the Arabian ports, or those of India. Cultural and scientific exchanges took place between Oman and the Indian coastal states. There were also exchanges of knowledge and experience between these two areas in the field of ship-building. In addition, Sultan Sayyid Said bin Sultan invited many skilled naval architects from Britain, Holland, Portugal and France who supervised construction work in Bombay.

Omani ports were impressive and efficient, able to handle a wide variety of cargoes from their friendly trading partners. British, American, Dutch, French and German naval documents all refer to the excellent facilities provided by Omani port administrators. The hospitality and cooperation provided to visiting vessels by Sayyid Said bin Sultan, his sons and representatives, was frequently commented on.

The number of foreign ships which visited and docked in Omani ports during the reign of Sayyid Said bin Sultan was quite impressive. In 1250 AH/1834 AD, for example, 30 American merchant ships called in to Zanzibar port alone. The international importance of this port is indicated by the fact that the United States opened a consulate there four years before the British did so. In the year of Sayyid Said's death 1273 AH/1856 AD, Oman owned the largest mercantile and naval fleet in the entire region between the Arabian Gulf and the island of Madagascar; and its influence extended well into the Red Sea. Furthermore, the Omani fleet was already well known and respected at the Chinese ports as well as those in the Sea of Bengal.

Given the important part played by Oman's naval fleet in the economic and political history of Oman, it is worth considering the ship-building industry in Oman.This provided key support for the growth and development of the fleet, ensuring its strength and giving it the wherewithal to achieve its aims. Indeed, it has been of crucial importance in maintaining Oman's pre-eminent position throughout its history.

The Ship-building Industry in Oman

Most historians agree that the task of providing clear and concise sequential historical records on Omani ship-building is a difficult one, especially for the period prior to the arrival of the Portuguese in the Indian Ocean. They also agree that the evidence varies according to the different types of vessel, and to which particular elements of local design were preserved after the arrival of the Portuguese. There are however a few Arabic and Islamic historical documents, and other sources, primarily in the form of personal diaries, which describe the development of Omani ships. Some of these craft spanned the advent of Islam. Additional documents, discovered elsewhere in the Indian Ocean and Gulf region, provide an insight into the history of Omani ship-building[552].

The western part of the Indian Ocean, from Ceylon up to East Africa was considered to be one cultural region and was therefore studied as one geographical unit. The classical, traditional vessels were not confined by national boundaries, and thus some evidence from western India may provide better examples of Omani ship-building than the evidence which came from the Gulf region[553].

In order to examine the history of Omani boat-building and design, we can focus our studies within certain geographical limits. It is important to distinguish the Omani craft from those vessels plying the Mediterranean on the one hand, and those that sailed west of the Indian Ocean on the other. From a temporal perspective, we must also differentiate between the ships that were present prior to the arrival of the Portuguese and those constructed after their arrival, even though the later vessels drew in part from designs of earlier classic models. In this chapter, we shall take a look at the historical development of Omani ship-building, and we shall then have some insight into nomenclature, architectural and construction aspects and the final stages of ship-building, including some knowledge of the industry itself.

The Development of Omani Ship-building

The distinguishing features of the Arabian vessels in the Indian Ocean prior to the emergence of European influence were as follows:
- The use of fibre and ropes, instead of nails, for fixing the joints and sewing the planks of the ship.
- The use of triangular shaped sails which set fore and aft, instead of the square-rigged sail.
- The two ends of the ship were of the same shape.

These three characteristics can still be seen on the remains of Omani classical ships like the *boum,* the *badan* and other kinds of traditional boats. However, all three characteristics can only be seen in the design of the *sambuq*[554]. The hulls of all these ships were made from coconut wood and teak timber[555] which was imported from India. Teak was highly regarded for its solidity and the later use of iron nails made the hull strength more resistant to harsh environments. Theophrastus, who lived around 300 BC, described teak timber as follows :'At the Tylos Islands (Bahrain), on the Arabian coast, a type of timber was used in constructing their ships. It is very strong and is not affected if thrown in sea water. Such timber will stay in the water for more than 200 years without being damaged. Out of the water, it deteriorates much faster than if in the water'. George Fadlo Hourani, comments as follows: 'because this kind of timber does not exist in the Arabian Gulf, then this teak wood is certainly imported from India'[556].

The Arabs also used to import coconuts and coconut palms from India and its islands. They even went to Indian locations to build their ships whilst the Laccadive and Maldive islands were very important locations for Arab boat-building and sail making[557]. Abu Zaid Hasan Al-Sirafi, in the second section of his book *News of India and China,* written during the third century Hegira/ninth century AD, pointed out that: 'The Indian people used to travel to the islands [i.e. Maldives and Laccadives] around them to grow coconut trees. The Omani people went to the same islands together with their carpentry tools. They cut down these trees, dried them, stripped off the leaves and spun a yarn from the bark which they then use to sew together the planks, thus building a ship. They used the same wood to make a mast; from the leaves they weave the triangular sails, coconut bark is used for making ropes. After they thus built their ship, they loaded it with coconuts and sailed to Oman, selling their merchandise on arrival. Thus it is that, from this tree alone, so many articles are convertible to use, as suffice not only to build and rig out a vessel, but to load her when she is completed, and in a trim to sail' [558].

An Omani merchant sailing ship.

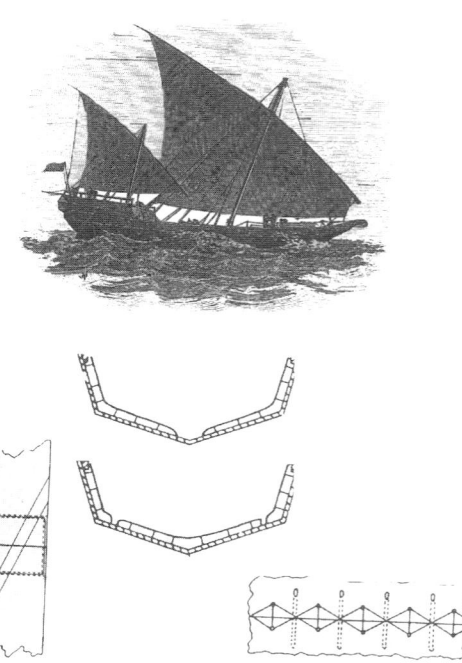

The Omani people used other solid, strong timber to build their ships and sails, like mimosa and *Acacia nilotica* trees which were available in Oman. Other people in the Arabian Gulf used to import their supplies of timber from other places[559]. The framework of the ship would be built according to standard procedure with the main supporting keel laid down first and then horizontal planks would be fastened on both sides of the keel with fibre ropes. The planks would be sewn with fibre and thus held very tightly together. Carvel construction was used, i.e. the boards were sewn edge to edge rather than overlapping. European ship-building favoured the clinker-built method with planks overlapping each other but this method was not practised in the Indian Ocean before the sixteenth century[560]. The fibre ropes were threaded through holes bored at regular intervals along the edge of planks which were then held together in this manner, i.e. by rope-sewing rather than by nails.

Abu Zaid Al-Sirafi described these methods of building Arab ships in the second section of *News of India* which, as we have mentioned above, was written eleven centuries ago[561]. There were numerous reasons for using ropes rather than nails on the western side of the Indian Ocean before the fifteenth and sixteenth centuries. There is both practical and scientific justification for this technique, whilst other explanations which have entered into traditional folk-lore were based on myths. The Byzantine historian Procopios, writing in the sixth century AD, provided an explanation of why these ropes were used instead of nails to fasten together ship's planks. He believed that the Greek and Roman ship-building method (in which they used metal nails) was costly and time consuming. According to him Omani ship-builders preferred to use cord which was made of cheap and plentiful coconut fibre[562]. Procopius compared this ancient Omani method with that used by the Sumerians in 3000 BC[563].

Discussing these points in his book, *Oman A Seafaring Nation*, its author, Wiliam Facey, comments that: 'Iron technology was at least as developed, and probably more so, in Iran and India during Greco-Roman times as in the Greco-Roman world itself'. When Marco Polo, the famous Venetian traveller, visited Hormuz in the seventh century AH/thirteenthth century AD, he mentioned the lack of iron in the area as the reason why the Omani ship-builders used fibre cordage and wooden trenails rather than iron nails[564]. Another explanation was that timber was so hard and solid, the nails would crack it. Hourani rejected this claim by writing: 'teak timber is very flexible and nails will not crack it if they are used' [565].

Arab geographers like Al-Idrisi (493-560 AH/1100-1165 AD) and Ibn Jobair (540-614 AH/1145-1217 AD) believed that fibre and cordage provided a safer means of construction than nails. They claimed that sailing vessels with flat bottoms were more flexible and safer, and that if an accident occured to the ship, grounding on rocks for example, it would survive better than if nails were used on it. They believed that the Red Sea's prolific coral reefs were one of the numerous reasons why many sailors preferred cordage to nails in their ship-building industry.

Al-Ma'sudi (346 AH/956 AD) mentioned another reason for the use of fibre rope in ship-building. According to him the water of the Red Sea affected the iron nails of the ships, and this is the reason behind the usage of ropes instead of nails. Covering the ships with fat and tar also helped. Dr. Anwar Abdul Aleem believed that Al-Ma'sudi probably had the right explanation for the use of ropes instead of nails. He said that the sea water would rust the iron nails, and this was why the Greeks coated their nails with lead. Recent discoveries of Greek and Roman ships on the sea bed of the Mediterranean revealed that copper nails were used in their construction. The ancient Egyptians used the method of overlapping to join the edges of the boards, and used nail shaped timber to attach the planks, in addition to sewing with fibre cord[566].

Bhoja, the famous Sanskrit writer, mentioned that 'there were magnetic rocks on the sea floor pulling ships with metal parts to their death'! This myth was repeated in many books later on, causing some writers to refute it[567]. One popular storyteller employed this myth in the book *Arabian Nights*. The French version (translated by Galan) records that Scheherazade recounted an event on the fifty-third night; whilst the Cairo published script refers to the fourteenth night. Whichever is 'correct', the story tells of magnetic mountains in the sea pulling out the nails from ships, dismantling them and causing them to founder[568].

Dr Hussein Fawzi explained the story of the 'magnetic mountain' as a kind of powerful sea current which dragged the ships suddenly towards the rocky shores and crushed them. Many sailors and even some passengers wrongly explained such accidents as caused by rocks on the coast itself, rather than the force of the current which did the actual damage[569].

The framework of the ship would be shaped so as to make it very solid and to withstand the forces of the current and the storms. The builders started the next phase of construction which was called caulking (closing all the holes and gaps, both inside and outside). The entire surface was covered by a mixture of tar and heavy fats, usually derived from whales[570], or else coated with a mixture of lime and wax[571]. In this regard, Abu-Zaid Al-Sirafi, in one chapter of his book, *News of India and China* wrote: 'if the fishermen catch one whale, they cut it into many pieces, dig a ditch, and throw the parts in it until the thick oil leaks out. They collect the fat and sell it to the ship's owners who mix the oil with some other stuffs and use it to coat the surfaces of their sails to fill the holes. They sell the rest of the whale and make even more money'[572].

Al-Idrisi was more specific when he mentioned in detail the ship-building industry: 'In the Indian Ocean, the fishermen catch small whales, cut them into pieces, and cook them in big pans. They collect the liquid fat, this kind of oil was very famous in Yemen, Aden, Persia, Oman and all around the Indian and China Sea. It was the main material used to coat their ships. and was used also to protect the ships hull from woodworm'[573].

The Omanis sailed their vessels for considerable distances. Many ships sank as a result of the timber planks loosening. Even if the affected ship did not actually sink, the sailors had to continuously bail water from the scuppers in order to keep it afloat.

Water sometimes leaked through the gaps between planks, because they were not coated on both faces[574]. In the fourth century of Hegira, the writer Birzek Shahrayar Al-Nakhitha Al-Zam Hormuz made a number of observations in his book, *The Wonders of India*. He recounted many stories of sinking ships. The seventh Sinbad voyage of the Arabian Nights was based on these accounts of seven ship-wrecks.

The arrival of European vessels in the region at the start of the sixteenth century stimulated a new phase in development of the ship-building industry. Iron and other metals replaced the fibre and cordage. However, some dockyards remained unaffected by the introduction of iron and steel into the ship-building industry. They continued to use wood-chisels, carpentry tools, knives, drills, hammers, saws, adze, and penknives. Omani ship-builders worked from eye, not depending upon the formal application of engineering principles or design plans. They relied only on their previous experience and their ancestors' knowledge.

Ship-building at Sur.
An ancient craft.

The Omani ship-building profession, which thrived in many parts of Oman, such as the Sur boat-yards, was based on family traditions[575]. The same double-ended vessels, with sewn planks, were very popular on Omani waters for over 200 years. This class of Omani vessel, with its proven record of success, was basically unaffected by European ship-building influence. Many Omani ship-builders used to decorate their vessels, adding a personal touch with paintings of flowers, stars and many other artistic shapes, using numerous different colours. A great number of people were skilled in these fine arts, applying their art not only to their ships but also to doors and windows of their houses.

The only steering system on these ancient and early Islamic vessels was the side rudder or steering oar. During the thirteenth century AD, the stern rudder appeared simultaneously in Europe and the Gulf. The Arabs were the first to invent the aft rudder which was controlled by ropes: a system that was continued on the Omani *badan* and *baqarah* [576] right up to recent times. Meanwhile the Egyptians used these rudders on their Nile-based sailing vessels up to the thirteenth century Hegira/nineteenth century AD.

'Mast' was the original name used to describe palm tree trunks, confirming this tree's importance in ancient boat-building. During the Middle Ages, the Arabs along the coast of the Arabian peninsula made the masts for their vessels from coconut tree trunks or teak trees. These were sometimes very tall, depending in the total length of the ship. Modern Arabian vessels may have 50 yard masts, as pointed out in the book *Wonders of India*[577].

All these references underline the long history of the Arabs in ship-building around the Indian Ocean[578].

Sails were made primarily from date palm leaves, coconut palm leaves and cotton. During the thirteenth century Hegira/nineteenth AD, the Omanis grew a great number of palms around Sohar and Majis on the Al-Batinah coast. They had cultivated them as sail-making materials long before the Portuguese arrived. Cloth material was imported from India. Omani ships used to carry at

least two sails on board, one for stormy weather and night sailing whilst the other was for calm day sailing. There was no reefing system in order to reduce sail size in stormy weather[579].

Arabian vessels used the lateen sail. A number of maritime historians described the sail's shape as similar to the fins of fish, following a typically triangular outline[580]. The sail was usually the same length as the vessel itself and attached both fore and aft. The ancient Mediterranean world used square-rigged square sails. The practice was continued among the Indian fleet for a considerable period of time, and they are recorded in use there during the seventh century AD. It seems clear therefore that the triangular lateen sail was an Arabian invention, based upon an adaptation of the square sail. There is general agreement among historians that the sail passed through the following four stages:

- The square sail: this sail was widely used throughout the ancient world and was still in used on *sambuqs* in Aden up to very recent times, together with triangular sails. It was used in the Omani region until 1210 AH/1796 AD[581]. The square sail, whilst remaining quite stable in heavy seas, was inefficient for sailing into the wind. It was necessary to develop a type of sail which could be used for sailing close-hauled and which could provide manoeuvrability in channels and narrow passages for example.
- Some improvement was introduced by setting the square-sail in a fore and aft rig, dipping towards the front to form a balance lug. Such sails were used

in countries where they had to navigate through rivers and narrow waterways and they differed from those used in the open seas and oceans.

- The third stage in development was to shorten the luff (fore part of the sail) and heighten the leech (aft edge of sail) in order to capture more wind. It was this development that led to the appearance of the triangular or lateen sail. Such sails are still very popular among sailors in the western Indian Ocean. The historian George Hourani held the view that the triangular sail, which played a major role in development of human civilization, was introduced into the Mediterannean region by the Arabs. Without the lateen, the epic ocean voyages by great travellers would not have been possible[582]. Clowes mentioned in his book, *The Sailing Ships*, that during the year of 802 AH/1400 AD, all the ships in the north depended entirely on favourable winds. They were unable to sail against the wind and did not even attempt to do so. However, before 905 AH/1500 AD, they were able to sail on longer voyages and to cross oceans, which in fact, led to the explorer Columbus discovering America, the rounding of the Cape of Good Hope by Diaz, and the opening of trade routes to India by Vasco da Gama[583].

- The fourth development, which occurred at some time before 287 AH/900 AD, involved a design change to the cut of the sail so that the fore part was brought into a point, thus creating a triangular sail.

The Arabs carved stones and made holes in the middle of them for the ropes to pass through and used them as anchors for their ships. They even carved big blocks of timber and filled the innards with molten lead. They used metal anchors long before the Mediterranean nations[584]. Small life-craft and *huris* were carried aboard larger vesssels. The book *Wonders of India* states that these small life-boats were used for rescue missions with the smallest ones able to carry four people while the medium ones could rescue up to 15 people and the largest of all could accomodate up to 33 people. This book also mentioned that lifeboats were used to tow a grounded vessel off the reef after the sailors had thrown everything overboard, lightening it to enable the stricken boat to float free of the sea bed[585].

The Arabs also transported small vessels or built them on board their main ship before setting sail. This is how the Omanis sold their craft to Yemen during the reign of Briblos in the fifth century AD[586]. The Arabs checked their ship thoroughly before each voyage to ensure the passengers were safe. Evidence on these precautions is recorded by the traveller Ibn Majed in his diaries and books. He mentioned the written rules of safety, including the instruction to 'investigate and examine the vessel very carefully when hauled out and to record any faults or indications of possible problems[587]. It was also said to be important to check the navigational and sailing equipment and all parts of the ship which were critical for the safety of passengers, sailors, cargo and the ship itself. Example of this equipment included navigational items, astronomical tables, astrolabe, *kamal*, (traditional Arabian instrument for measuring latitude), compass, safety equipment, sundial, vane, plumb-line and log (for estimating speed and thus distance travelled). Ibn Majed summarized the procedures in a few lines:

Before setting sail, refurbish the equipment,
Check stowage of cargo and stores,

Service the astrolabe, and other navigational aids,
Consider the voyage as a serious mission
Not a pleasure-trip.

Ibn Majed focussed very clearly on safety at sea. With regards to the compass position, he says: 'we depend on the magnet, because we cannot work if we do not know the direction of the poles'. He insisted on checking the compass position since he regarded this as the most important instrument on board. He pointed out that the compass should not be placed in position by the ship-builder. He also insisted that the anchor be dropped in a safe place, recommending the use of chain in stormy conditions. This was evidence that the sailors of his time were already familiar with iron chains. The rudder was also a point of concern: 'check all instruments and tools, especially the rudder, every hour', he wrote. In another book he commented: 'I did not write this book before going through 50 years of first-hand experience. I never let the pilot of the ship out of my eye, nor even his replacement'.

He urged all sailors to thoroughly check their vessels before sailing and warned them not to postpone any repairs, no matter how small they might seem. He advised sailing in clement weather as much as possible, instructing the crew not to take on more than the safe loading of passengers or cargo[588].

We will now turn to the customs and traditions in boat construction. A goat was slaughtered on the first day of building a vessel. As the final touches were put to the completed boat, the local people, men, women and children celebrated. Women spun cotton ropes and the men caulked the ship to protect it from any leakage through the ship's hull[589]. Such customs existed up to 1980.

Omani boat-builders were skilled in constructing a variety of vessels, and knowledgable on a wide range of designs and building methods. Their business was dictated by the needs and orders of the mercantile community. In order to provide an adequate picture of the Omani boat-building industry we must take a look at the various types of vessels that formed the Omani fleet.

Types of Omani Ships

As we have mentioned, there were many types of craft made in Oman. A ship's function determined the appropriate type and design. Some were designed and built to cross oceans whilst others were made for fishing in local waters. The operational range was a major factor in determining the appropriate form and dimensions of the required ship. Some functioned only in the Gulf whereas others sailed between Oman and the southern region of the Arabian peninsula. Other boats were confined exclusively to the Omani region. Oman, without doubt, was the centre of navigation in the Gulf and Indian Ocean. As they reached the end of their working lives, some of these ships were laid-up, whilst others received a new lease of life as the recipients of new developments, such as various types of engines. Many old vessels were rebuilt and put back into service. The following are some of these types:

- **Al-Baghlah** or **Al-Shuwai'i** were the most popular ships the Omanis produced during the thirteenth century Hegira/nineteenth century AD. This

Omani fishing trawler.

Drawing of a baghlah *from Paris: Souvenirs de Marine 1299 AH/ 1822 AD. Baghlah in Arabic means 'mule'.*

design continued to operate during the first half of the fourteenth century Hegira/twentieth century AD. With an overall length of up to 135 feet, it was the primary cargo vessel in Oman and the Gulf area with each ship's payload between 150 and 400 tonnes. The large ones had copper-coated hulls and carried three masts. They also had high poop-decks and quarter galleries, with the transom stern carrying five windows whose frames were often elaborately carved and colourfully painted. The last vessel of this type was built in Sur in 1371 AH/1952 AD. Such ships were used mainly for extended voyages.

- **Al-Qanjah** is not too dissimilar from *Al-Baghlah*. Indian influence is evident in its design but its distinguishing feature is the stem-head ornament which consisted of a small rounded projection with three concentric circles, surmounted by a three-leafed crest. It was a beautifully decorated vessel with works of art, painted pictures and engravings on its side. Like the *baghlah*, the *qanjah* had a square, galleon-type, stern with five windows but it was less elaborately carved and decorated.

It is important to note that this type of ship had the same masts and rigging as *Al-Baghlah*. The city of Sur was the ship-building centre of *Al-Qanjah*. All these ships have now disappeared except for two which are beached at Matrah and Sur. The payload of *Al-Qanjah* was between 150 and 300 tonnes and the vessels measured 75 and one 120 feet in length. Like *Al-Baghlah*, they were used for ocean passages.

- **Al-Boum:** This type of ship gradually replaced *Al-Baghlah* during the present century. It became the main passenger and cargo ship for the Omanis in the Indian Ocean. The *boum* lacked the high transom stern of the previous two types and both bow and stern were pointed. They cost less to build than the previous vessels and *Al-Boum* has retained its design since before the Portuguese entered the Indian Ocean at the beginning of the sixteenth century, right up to to the present day. The payload of this type of vessel was between 74 to 400 tonnes and it was between 50 and one 120 feet long and between 15 and 30 feet wide. Its stem-post was straight and there were pictures painted on the side of the ship in black and white, similar to the 'eyes' painted on ancient craft. Although not as finely decorated as the *baghlah* the stern was sometimes decorated with a carved rosette or some paintings. The rudder is operated by a yoke steering gear. There was an additional sail carried on a mizzen mast, aft of the main mast.

- **Al-Sambuq:** This was the most frequently seen Arabian sailing vessel in Oman, the Gulf and the Red Sea. It was the oldest and most prestigious ship built in Oman. The earliest ones were built in Dhofar. Its main characteristic is the low, pointed, sleek, curved bow and a higher square stern, rendering a most attractive overall appearance. Sur was a famous centre for building this type of vessel and construction continued there until at least 1380 AH/1960 AD. These Sur-made *sambuqs* were much larger in comparison to the similar design in the Gulf and were used for long distance passages as merchant ships with a payload of between 20 and 150 tonnes. They were about 80 feet long and not elaborately decorated on the hull, except for some blue and painted decoration at the stern. *Sambuqs* were traditionally used for pearling, although in later years they began to be used as a passenger and cargo vessels. One of its main features was the unusual length of the stem piece which extends underwater resulting in a relatively short keel. This feature improved manoeuverability, permitting *sambuqs* to sail in water shallower than many other vessels could contend with.

  The sewn *sambuqs* of Dhofar are one of the earliest Omani sailing vessels. Both ends were of similar shape and no nails used on the bodywork. They still used the old square sail and therefore represented a direct link, in boat building terms, with the period prior to the Portuguese. These boats had most attractive lines and the hull was made from mango wood imported from the Malabar coast of India. They were between 25 and 40 feet long, with a relatively small rudder and a few oars, with a single sail. Used for fishing, between four and eight crewmen worked on them.

- **Al-Jalibut:** This type derived many of its features from European vessels and was similar in appearance to the British naval 'jolly boat'. Its name reportedly stems from the Indian coastguard boats, the *gellywatte* which in turn derived their name from the Portuguese *galeota* or galley *Al-Jalibut* was also used as a pearl-diving vessel in the Gulf, whilst in Oman it was used for cargo transport, especially from Sur. Occasionally it was used as a fishing boat, but more recently it was favoured for transport along the coast. About 50 feet long, it had a payload of between 40 and 75 tonnes and carried a single mast and sail. The rudder fixing was unusual in that the hinges were attached directly to the transom instead of being connected to a separate timber joined to the stern post as it was in all other ships.

- **Abubuz:** This was a small cargo boat similar to the *sambuq* but of a larger size. A modern craft, with an inboard-engine, its hull shows signs of European influence in design. It was not a popular craft and its production was halted in Sur more than 25 years ago.
- **Ash'Shuwai'ee:** derives its name from the Indian language, being of similar design to a particular type of Indian fishing boat. It was loaded on board an *Al-Baghlah* to be used for passenger transport or for rescue missions and was not dissimilar to the small Gulf *sambuq*, except in size. Suitable for a variety of inshore used, it carried a maximum of 15 tonnes and had a transom stern and generally a curved stem.
- **Al-Badan:** This was the best known Omani craft, used for fishing and passenger transport along the coast. It served the local people's needs exceeding well. Its long, low, straight hull was distinguished by a recurved clipper bow, while the stern carried a conspicuously high rudder-post to which the rudder itself was attached by lashings. *Al-Badan* had no deck but was lined with thatched straw and palm tree leaves. It had a slope on both sides and was lighter at the stern. Bamboo and date-palm trees were the main materials used to build this type of ship. Its single sail was uniquely fixed in a vertical fashion in the middle of the ship. At the beginning of this century, metal nails replaced rope-sewing of the planks as a method of construction for these vessels, confirming the vessels long history. One of the most important features of this boat was its flat bottom which allowed it to sail near the coastline while horizontal.
- **Al-Bateel:** This ship was used for a long time, up to the beginning of this century, as a coastal cargo vessel. It also had a small diving area. Its outer hull was decorated with fine inter-linked carvings and it was faster than other boats of its size, and because of its high speed was used for fighting purposes during various wars. In the thirteenth century AH/nineteenth century AD these boats were often equipped with cannons. It was one of the most beautiful craft not only of

A sewn fishing badan *from the 1250s AH/ 1830s AD, and (bottom) a cargo* badan. *Both drawings were made in Oman and originally published in Paris' work on the subject of Omani boat construction.*

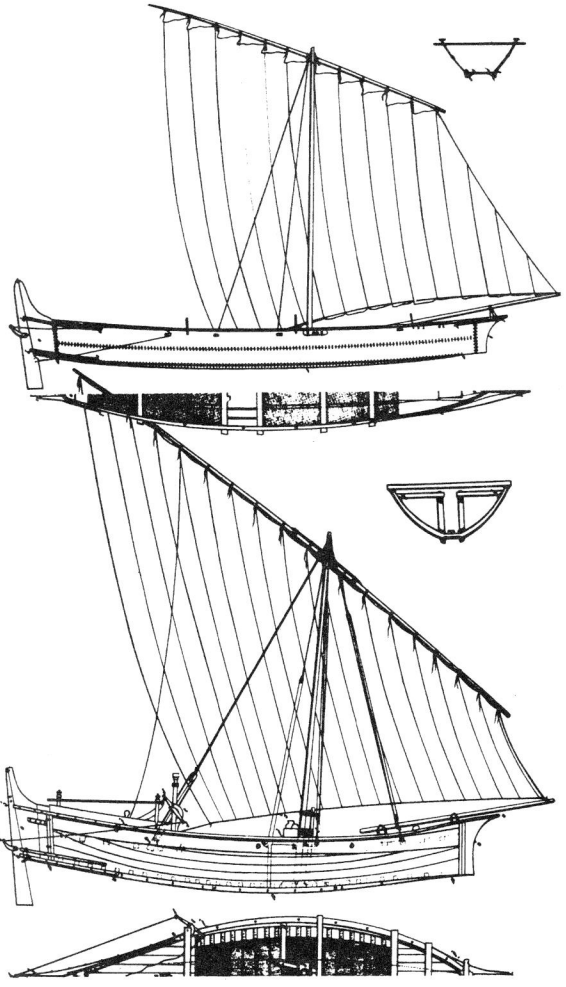

Omani ships but of Arabian ships as a whole. At the bows it looked like an Arabian fiddle whilst its raised poop deck and high stern post were equally distinctive features. Its payload exceeded 200 tonnes and it was more than 75 feet long. It had two, and in a few cases three, sails. The *bateel* is no longer seen in Oman.

- **Al-Baqarah:** Between 25 and 35 feet long, sometimes called *Al-Shahuf,* this is not greatly dissimilar to *Al-Bateel.* The only differences are seen on the bow and stern with the intricately carved and painted stem piece being very straight, unlike *Al-Bateel.* Its sternpost, while as high as the *bateel's,* lacks projections. Generally, it is smaller than *Al-Bateel.* This is a vessel that is still in use today in Oman, remaining popular, especially at and near Ras Musandam, where they are used for fishing. Stitching is still used in construction of this type of boat in Oman.

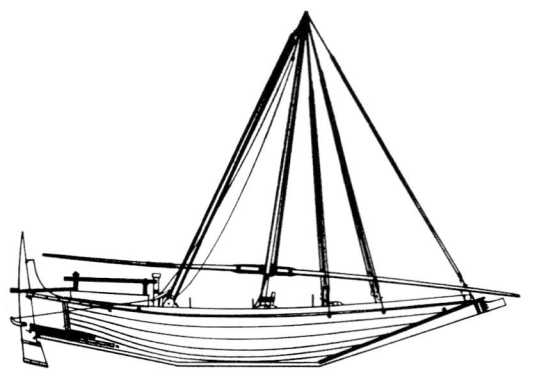

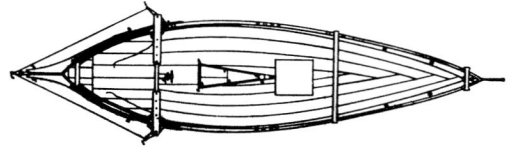

- **Al-Huri:** This small canoe-shaped craft, with a length of between 10 and 20 feet, was made from mango tree-trunks imported from the Malabar coast. The *huri* is used as a fishing boat and for cargo transport over short distances and may be paddled, sailed or propelled by small outboard engine. It is fairly narrow and fishermen are wary of it, because it is relatively unseaworthy in stormy currents. *Al-Huri* is an Indian word and the Omani citizens in Al-Batinah area still call many small boats *Al-Huri.*

Drawings of a Baqarah *with rope steering gear from the 1250s AH/ 1880s AD.* Baqr *in Arabic means 'cow'.*

- **Al-Shashah:** is a craft with ancient origins. It is a small boat, about 10 foot in length, constructed by binding together bundles of date palm sticks. Sometimes coconut timber and its fibre are used in construction. *Al-Shashah* accomodate one or two people and are quite buoyant but only last for two or three years.

- **Al-Mashuwah:** is not a popular boat in Oman. As its Arabic name indicates, the shape of the hull is more or less rectangular. It is around 25 feet in length and can be used for carrying passengers, cargo, or both. Its transom stern is square-shaped while the stem is straight, curved or vertical. It has no deck and oars are the usual means of propulsion, although they can also be fitted with a mast and sail. Many people in Oman use the name *Al-Mashuwah* to describe any small boats with a square transom and no deck, even aluminium craft of this shape.

- **Al-Ramath or Al-Rams:** is a type of catamaran-like raft used for fishing along the Batinah coast, and by the islanders from Socotra who used to visit Al-Batinah and Muscat. It was made from three long tree trunks, arranged with the central one longer than the two outer ones, and lashed together with coir. Propulsion was by a double-ended paddle.

- **Al-'Uwaisiyyah:** was like *Al-Badan,* and used for long distant passages. It had two sails and a payload of between 20 and 100 tonnes. Around 45 feet long, it had a width of 10 feet. No longer in use, a few skeletons of this type of boat are still to be seen around Al-Batinah.

- **Al-Zaima:** was the same size as *Al-Bateel* but was primarily used near the coastline.
- **Al-Zawariq:** many Omani boats like *Al-Badan*, *Al-Bateel*, *Al-Baqarah* and *Al-Shahuf* were known as *Al-Zarwariq*. Some of the western visitors who visited Oman called these boats *garookuh* as an altered pronunciation of the Arabic. The term also refers to larger vessels, used for fighting, as well as certain fishing boats.
- **Al-Dhow:** is a general term for a larger traditional Arabian vessel.
- **Al-A'abra:** is a general term for a small boat using oars.
- **Al-Junk:** is an old type of vessel used to travel between Oman and India during the fourth century Hegira. The famous Arabian traveller Ibn Battuta saw this type of vessel while docked on the Indian coast.
- **Al-Danga:** is an Indian built craft, with a very specially designed bow, which is very different from the *boum*.
- **Al-Ghurab:** is one of the oldest war-ships known in the region. Its colour is black because it must be coated with black tar. A number of European authors refer to it in their writing. Cordage is extensively used in building this vessel which is very close in form to the Omani *Al-Zawariq*
- **Al-Za'ameem** or **Al-Za'aimat:** was a very old type of Omani vessel of which no trace survives.
- **Al-Barsha:** there are two types of this vessel; one is big and the other is small and they were of Italian origin (Barqa). Powered mainly by oars, they were used in sea-battles and as cargo ships. They carried many cannons on board.
- **Al-Shathaat** and **Al-Gharaf:** were two very similar types of fast ships that were used to drive off the pirates during medieval times.

The above list[590] gives an idea of the great variety of vessels that were constructed in Oman. The vast majority were built according to ancient traditional methods. This situation continued until the arrival of the Europeans to the Arabian Sea and the Gulf. European ships were stronger than those built in the Gulf region, because they used nails and metals in the construction. The Omanis and the Arabs realized the importance of nails and metals in shipbuilding and therefore followed the Europeans in the use of nails. The Omanis thus managed to construct larger and stronger vessels which enabled them to fight the Portugese colonial ships[591]. Omani craftsmen had little difficulty in copying the European ship design and by the end of the eighteenth century, the Omani naval fleet contained many vessels of European design equipped with modern cannon. Most of these ships were built at Omani shipyards like Matrah and Sur, but a number were built at yards in India[592] about which little is known.

The ship-building industry was functionally based and purpose oriented, with vessel design depending upon whether the ships were for passenger transport, trade and cargo, coastguard service, fishing, defence, or for more than one job. Several different types of vessel could be used to carry out a particuar function.

A ship designed for defensive purposes might be fitted out for hurling missiles or firing cannons, landing marines, carrying coastguards, fighting pirates, engaging in a battle against the enemy's naval force, or as a support ship.

Each ship had its own crew and operators depending on the type of mission for which she was designed. An ocean-going vessel would have 25 to 40 crew including a captain, sailors, first officer, navigator, book keeper, engineer, cooks and many other service people.

Many of these maritime workers carried Indian and Persian names in Oman and Omanis used many Persian expressions to identify seamen, tools or parts of the ship, for example: *Al-Balang* is derived from the Persian word *Balank* which means a room; *Al-Daftar* which means the navigation signs. The *Day-Daban* means controller and frontier and *Alkhun* means the dot on the compass whilst *Al-Rahmani* meant the sailing procedures.

The Omani sailors gave the name *Al-Mua'alim* (teacher) to the best sailor of a ship, whether it crossed the ocean or sailed near the coasts. The position of *Al-Mua'alim* (pilot or navigator) was even higher than that of the captain *(nakhouda)*. *Al-Mua'alim* is sometimes called the president or master.

As we have mentioned, the majority of navigational experts on the Indian ocean were Omanis, Gulf Arabs, Hormuzians, Indians, Shulians or Africans[593]. All ships required very complex management. Crews included boatswain or mate *(sarhang)*, helmsman *(sukkani)*, clerk or keeper of accounts *(karani)* , ship's owners or their representatives, together with seamen *(babriyah)* , maintenance and repair workers and others. The Omani navigators worked on board many ships, travelling across the seas and oceans, eventually reaching China, India and the Gulf.

Early Omani sailors did not sail very far from the coasts and depended upon navigation by sight of land. Later on they started to define their route according to the locations of the stars which they knew very well. Among them were first class astronomers. During the reign of Al-Mamon and after the science of astronomy had developed dramatically [594] the Omanis benefited a considerably from their knowledge and understanding of this science. They used the compass from a very early time, developing it by dividing it into certain segments and certain lines based on geometrical science. There were 15 known stars fixed on the compass to show their rising time and location in the sky and the exact time of their setting. They fixed the direction of north and south and used many Persian words for the compass sections. *Al-Qutb Aljah* recorded the locations whilst *Al-Rahmani* was a book of nautical instructions containing information on latitudes of ports of call. There were many geographical and astronomy related symbols and navigation rules which guided and directed the sailors to follow certain routes. Sailors were able to consult their navigational and sailing books for the right course and for safe voyages[595].

History reminds us that so many Omani sailors had to have a high standard of scientific knowledge to operate and navigate ships and entire fleets. In the maritime world, the Omani people since medieval times and right up to the present, have made epic voyages and navigated across the oceans.

Omani sailors gradually commanded all the maritime professions, serving on board many different ships and learning the trade as they went, moving from one position to a higher one, and from menial work to the most scientific and complex management. Some of them reached an advanced standard to command large vessels and to become *nakhoudas*.

At this stage we might ask the question: did the Omani naval fleet depend on transport and trade only? Or did they follow another path in their attempt to find a living?

In actual fact, they did more than that. They became actively involved in the pearling and fishing industries. Fish were considered a good source of nutrition for human beings, as well as having many other uses.

We do not have very thorough information on the pearl-diving during ancient and medieval times, but for the more recent era excellent records have been preserved. Oman's pearl divers ranged over the pearl banks from the northern Gulf, in Kuwaiti waters, right down through the Gulf and back into Oman, a distance of over 330 miles. The area was renowned for its rich pearl fisheries from early times.

At the height of the fishery an estimated 3000 - 5000 vessels were involved in pearl diving in the Arabian Gulf with between 27,000 and 40,000 men employed in the fishery. The richest pearling banks were close to the Bahrain islands whilst the second best area was off Oman. Over 1500 Omani vessels were engaged in pearling.

Omani pearl divers generally dived to between 25 and 50 feet, but sometimes up to 100 feet in search of pearls which were classified into three kinds. *Al-Mahly* was one of the best known pearls.

Parsons wrote in his diaries in 1189 AH/1775 AD that the pearl harvesting technique had been relatively disorganized in the past. But during his time the industry developed and witnessed some improvements during the nineteenth century[596].The fishing industry was, however, a different story. Omanis had been experts in this field for many centuries. With so many fishing areas within the Omani waters, and with Omani agriculture relatively poorly developed, the people of Oman used to consider the sea as their main source of food. Oman's coastline is very long and contains a great variety of marine-life. Not surprisingly Oman became very famous for its rich fishing grounds whilst fishing became the most important industry in the country. Fishermen developed a wide range of techniques for catching the different kinds of fish, including a large number of sharks. There were four basic areas for fishing, each of which required a particular technique; i.e.open sea areas; inshore fishing grounds; surface fishing and deep-water fishing.

In each case the methods differed, whilst their suitability depended on the seasons and the migration of fishes. Fishing boats used to leave their harbours and anchorages in the early morning and return back in the evening. Some used to start their mission in the early evening and return to their home-bases in the morning. Fishing techniques varied from one place to another according to the types of fish sought, the nature of the coastline, and the depth of the water[597].

Omani fishermen harvested great quantities of fish supporting a strong market, locally, regionally and internationally. Before 1255 AH/1839 AD for example, the Omani fish traders exported fish skins and sea-shells to China, and later on to Europe, to be used in a variety of industries. Ambergris, a product derived from certain whales, was collected for use in making valuable perfumes. Blubber was used locally and exported to many countries[598].

From Omani maritime history, and from what has been mentioned above, we can conclude the following:

- Oman's strength depended on the strength of its naval force and internal unity. Its naval power was proportional to the degree of national unity and cohesion. At times of national unrest, the naval force was also affected.
- Oman's lengthy history has been dominated by the strength of its maritime fleet. As is well documented, it was an important source of wealth, contributing to the prosperity and welfare of the Omani people. This economic contribution took place through its involvement in trade and transportation of cargo, both nationally and internationally, as well as through fishing and the pearling industry.
- Omani citizens residing along the coast established contact with many foreigners, leading to a healthy exchange of experience and knowledge.
- The Omani people defended their independence with great determination, demonstrating considerable firmness in protecting their high moral values and principles, as well as their national territory and its people.
- Omanis were very brave and resolute in their resistance towards the invaders. On the other hand they suffered a great deal, were faced with many dangers, and traversed the seas and oceans for their livelihood. They carried Arab culture and Islamic religion to many parts of the world, reaching places of great civilizations where Islam was previously unknown, whether in Africa or Asia.
- Oman's maritime activities, its great ocean crossings, its command over and control of the surrounding seas, especially the Indian Ocean, continued right up to recent times.
- Oman's people, even without many industrial resources, were able to achieve great success in establishing a versatile ship-building industry.
- Omanis worked hard to develop navigational science, producing some strong naval fleet commanders, both in the past and present, for both Oman and the rest of the Arab world.

In short, we can state that the development of the Omani naval force closely tracked that of its economic and political history.

Notes for Part Four

[1] Bakir bin Said, *Islamic Studies in the Fundamentals of Ibadhism*, p19.
[2] Bakir bin Said 'Awashet, *Ibid.*, p24.
[3] Al-Tabari, *Tarikh Al-Rusul wa Al-Mulouk*, vol. 5, p568.
[4] Bakir bin Said 'Awashet, *op. cit.,* p25.
[5] Abdul Qader bin Taher Al-Baghdadi, *Al-Farq bain Al-Firaq*, p82.
[6] Sherif Yahya Al-Amin, *Mu'jam Al-Firaq Al-Islamiya*, p14; Al-Baradi, *Al-Jawaher Al-Muntaqah*, p234.
[7] Al-Sama'ili, *Izalat Al-W'athaa*, pp2-3.
[8] Dr. Mohammed Rashid Al-Aqili, *The Arabian Gulf in the Islamic Era*, p129.
[9] Surat Al-Tawbah, Ayah 111.
[10] Al-Isfahani, *Al-Aghani*, Al-Taqaddum Press, Egypt, 1323 AH, vol. 20, p97; Al-Baghdadi is of

the view that the Ibadhi sect arrived in Yemen immediately after the battle of Al-Naharwan (38 AH). See *Al-Farq bain Al-Firaq*, Dar Al-Ifaq Al-Jadida, Beirut, 4th ed., 1980, p61; see also Wilhausen, *op. cit.*, p106 and Mahmoud Ismail, *op. cit.* , p22.

[11] Al-Awatbi, *Al-Ansab*, Ministry of National Heritage and Culture, Sultanate of Oman, 1981, p234.

[12] *Ibid.*, p378.

[13] Ahmed Obeidli, *Kashef Al-Ghumah*, p131.

[14] Ibn Abdul Hakam, *Sirat Omar bin Abdul Aziz*, 5th ed., Dar Al-Ilm lil Malai'yeen, Beirut, 1967, p123.

[15] *Futuh Al-Buldan*, Dar Al-Kutub Al-Ilmiya, Beirut, 1978, p88.

[16] Al-Isfahani, *Al-Aghani*, vol. 20, p97; *Kashef Al-Ghumah,* pp242-4.

[17] Khalifa bin Khayyat, *Tarikh Khalifa*, a study by Akram Dhiyya, 2nd ed., Dar Al-Ilm lil Malai'yeen, Beirut, 1977, p5384; Al-Shateri, *op. cit.,* vol. 1, pp125-7.

[18] *Ghayat Al-Amani fi Akhbar Al-Qutr Al-Yamani*, a study by Said Abdul Fattah Aashour, Dar Al-Kitab Al-Arabi, Cairo, 1968, vol. 1, p124.

[19] Wilhausen, *op. cit.,* p107; for further information on Ibadhi views see Al-Shahrastani, *op. cit.,* vol. 1, pp180-82.

[20] *Al-Ansab*, p378.

[21] Ibn Abd Rabbo Al-Andalusi, *Al-Iqd Al-Ferid*, a study by Mohammed Said Al-Arian, Al-Maktaba Al-Tujaria Al-Kubra, 1053, vol.2, p200; Nayef Maarouf, *Adabiyat Al-Khawarij fi Kitab Diwan Al-Khawarij*, Dar Al-Messira, Beirut, 1st ed., 1983, pp287-8.

[22] *Tarikh Khalifa*, p385; Al-Isfahani, *Al-Aghani*, vol. 20, p97ff.

[23] Al-Isfahani, *Al-Aghani*, vol. 20, p98; Nayef Maarouf, *op. cit.*, p98.

[24] Nayef Maarouf, *op. cit.*, p384-5.

[25] *Op. cit.,* 287.

[26] *Op. cit.,* 287.

[27] *Ibid.,* p288.

[28] *Tarikh Khalifa*, p397.

[29] *Ibid.,* pp393-4.

[30] *Ibid.,* p394.

[31] *Tarikh Khalifa*, p394; *Al-Aghani*, vol. 20, p97ff.

[32] *Tarikh Khalifa*, p395.

[33] Al-Isfahani, *Al-Aghani*, vol.20, p113; Bawzir, *Landmarks of the History of the Arabian Peninsula*, Al-Subban Est, Aden, 3rd ed., 1966, p259

[34] Served as Caliph from 96-99 AH/714-717 AD.

[35] See Al-Kindi, *Al-Wulah wa Al-Qudah*, pp66-7.

[36] Ruled Egypt before Yazid bin Abdul Mulik in 101 AH/719 AD, then Yazid's credentials were presented outlining his appointment over Africa in 102 AH/720 AD, then Hisham bin Abdul Mulik was appointed over Africa up to his death in Kairawan in 109 AH/727 AD; see Al-Bilathuri, *Futuh Al-Buldan*, p274, (revised with commentary by Radwan Mohammed Radwan, Egypt, 1959; Al-Kindi, *Al-Wulah wa Al-Qudah*, p70-71

[37] Ibn Abdul Hakam, *Futuh Afriqia wa Al-Andalus*, pp106-118, Algiers, 1942; Dr Saad Zaghloul, *Tarikh Al-Maghreb*, pp232-4; Dr Mahmoud Ismail, *Al-Khilafah wa Al-Khawarij*, pp28-9, Dar Al-Awda, Beirut, 1976; Mohammed Ali Dabbuz, *Tarikh Al-Maghreb*, vol. 2, 2nd ed., Issa Al-Babi Al-Halabi Press, Cairo, 1964, pp170, 207, 216, 231, 232, 234-5.

[38] Al-Bilathuri, *Futuh Al-Buldan*, p273.

[39] Ibn Abdul Hakam, *op. cit.*, p108; Al-Bilathuri, *op. cit.*, p273; Dr Saad Zaghloul, *op. cit.*, pp235-6, 238; Dr Mahmoud Ismail, *op. cit.*, pp29-30.

[40] Yazid bin Abdul Mulik bin Marwan assumed the Caliphate after the Caliph Omar bin Abdul Aziz in 101 AH/719 AD and died in 105 AH/723 AD. See Al-Siouti, *Tarikh Al-Khulafaa*, p247, a study by Mohammed Mohieddin Abdul Hamid, 1st ed., Cairo, 1952.

[41] Al-Bilathuri says that when Yazid bin Abdul Mulik ruled, Yazid bin Abi Muslim, the slave of Al-Hajjaj bin Youssef ruled over Africa and the *Maghreb*. He took on Africa in the year 102 AH. His escort was Berber and he tattooed them on the hand with the word 'guard'. This vexed them and they banded together in a resolve to assassinate him; and on his going out one evening to make the evening prayer, they assassinated him in his oratory. See *Futuh Al-Buldan*, pp273-4.

[42] Hisham bin Abdul Mulik appointed him as *Wali* over Africa in 116 AH/734 AD and was killed in 123 AH/740 AD. See Ibn Abdul Hakam, *Futuh Afriqia wa Al-Andalus*, p120.

[43] *Ibid.,* p118; Dr Mahmoud Ismail, *Al-Khilafah wa Al-Khawarij*, p30; Mohammed Ali Dabbuz, *Tarikh Al-Maghreb Al-Kebir*, vol2, p219.

[44] Al-Sama'ili, *Izalat At-W'atha*, pp64, 65, 83-100; Al-Sama'ili, *Al-Haqiqa wa Al-Majaz*, p41, Sultanate of Oman, 1980; Rifaat Fawzi Abdul Mutallib, *Al-Khilafah wa Al-Khawarij*, 1st ed., Cairo, 1973, pp22-3.

[45] We do not wish to go into more detail about the political situation than is necessary to convey the meaning. This subject is fully treated in the sources to which reference is made.

[46] Abdullah bin Ibadh who died before 86 AH/705 AD, 'Imam of the achievers and support at the outbreak of dissent'. He withdrew from *Al-Muhakkimah* in 64 AH/683 AD in Basra; Al-Jaabiri, *Al-Bu'd Al-Hadhari*, 52, note 47.

[47] Jaber bin Zaid (d. 93 AH/711 AD), Omani by origin, Basran by residence; Ibadhi Imam; thoroughly versed in the knowledge of his day; Al-Jaabiri, *Al-Ba'ad Al-Hadhari*, 52, note 44.

[48] The Al-Barouni Library is in the Homat Al-Hashan quarter on the island of Gerba and contains the best collection on the Ibadhi heritage.

[49] Amr Al-Nami discovered these letters in the Barouni Library and extracted this from the handwritten manuscript which we are in the process of studying .

[50] Abu Al-Abbas Ahmed Al-Shamakhi (928/1522), *Kitab Seyar Al-Mashayekh*, Cairo, 1301, pp98, 123.

[51] *Ibid.,* p122.

[52] *Ibid.,* p143.

[53] *Ibid.,* pp143-4.

[54] *Ibid.,* p98.

[55] Sheikh Salim bin Ya'qub copied this letter during his sojourn in Egypt without mentioning its source (Notebook No. 2). We are fortunate to have a copy of this, for Mubarak Al-Rashedi extracted the letter in appendix I of his thesis, pp674-9.

[56] Mubarak Al-Rashedi, *Imam Abu Ubaida*, Master's thesis, p679.

[57] *Ibid.,* p676.

[58] *Ibid.,* p679.

[59] *Ibid.,* p327.

[60] *Ibid.,* pp594-5.

[61] Al-Shamakhi, Al-Seyar, p129.

[62] *Ibid.,* p140.

[63] *Ibid.,* p141.

[64] *Ibid.,* p141.

[65] *Ibid.,* p146.

[66] *Ibid.,* p162.

[67] Yazid bin Fandain (second century AH/eighth century AD), one of the candidates to the Ibadhi Imamate from the group whom the Imam Abdul Rahman had advised in the role of mediator. He rebelled against Imam Abdul Wahab as leader of the opposition movement; Al-Jaabiri, *Nazam Al-'Azaba*, pp153, 155.

[68] *Ibid.,* pp146-7.

[69] *Ibid.,* p147.

[70] *Ibid.,* p148; Farahat Al-Jaabiri, *Al-Bu'd Al-Hadhari* Al-Alwan Al-Haditha Press, Sultan Qaboos University, Oman 1408/1987, p106, note 43.

[71] An elevated castle situated at 637 metres in an ancient village in Jebel Nafoussah west of Jado in the district of Fassato (today's village of Tamzada); Mohammed Hassan, *A Study of Al-Shamakhi's Seyar*, part of PhD project discussed at Faculty of Arts History Department, Tunis, 1979, ref. 530.

[72] Ibn Abbad Al-Masri (second century AH/eighth century AD), a jurisprudent mufti in Egypt and scholar who was a student of Abi Ubaida; Ibn Salaam, *Bed' Al-Islam*, p159.

[73] Al-Shamakhi, *Al-Seyar*, p110.

[74] *Ibid.,* p161.

[75] *Ibid.,* p162.

[76] Al-Shamakhi, *Al-Seyar*, p228; Al-Jaabiri, *Al-Bu'd Al-Hadhari*, p105, note 40. Cf. also 'Amrous's remarks.

[77] Muqarran Al-Baghtouri (sixth century AH/twelfth century AD), one of the *ulema* from Jebel Nafoussah who undertook the documenting of the Ibadhi *Sirahs*. The work was completed in *Seyar Nafoussah* in 599 AH/1203 AD. Al-Shamakhi also makes reference to this in *Al-Seyar*, pp244, 245. This book was lost until Sheikh Salem bin Ya'qub came upon it and it remains in his library in manuscript form.

[78] Al-Shamakhi, *Al-Seyar*, p165.

[79] *Ibid.,* p175.

[80] Abdullah Al-Salimi, *Tohfat Al-'Ayian bi Sirat Ahl Oman*, a study by Ibrahim Atfish, Al-Shebab Press, 2nd ed., 1350 AH, vol. 1, p89-109.

[81] *Ibid.,* vol. 1, pp109-180.

[82] Abu Al-Abbas Ahmed Al-Darjini, *Tabaqat Al-Mashayekh Al-Maghreb*, a study by Ibrahim Talai, Al-Baath Qastantiniya Press, Algiers, vol. 1, p81.

[83] Abu Zakaria Yahya bin Abi Bakr Al-Warjalani, *Kitab Al-Sirah wa Akhbar Al-A'ima*, a study by Ismail Al-Arabi, Maktaba Al-Watania Publications, Algiers, 1309 AH. 1979 AD, p96.

84   Abu Al-Qassem Al-Baradi, *Risalat Ta'leef Ashabna*, appendix to Abi Ammar Abdul Kafi's *Mu'jaz*, a study by Ammar Al-Talebi, National Printing and Distribution Co, Algiers, 1398 AH/1978 AD vol. 2, p284. Abu Sufian Mahboub bin Al-Raheel was an authoritative source for the *Sirah* of whom it was said that very little in the *Sirah* of the Prophet or of the Muslims after him escaped his knowledge. He was one of those who wrote *Akhbar Ahl Oman*. Al-Jaabiri, *The Cultural Dimension*, p108, note 47.

85   Ibn Salaam, *Bed' Al-Islam*, p109.

86   Al-Darjini, *Tabaqat*, vol. 2, p324.

87   *Al-Seyar Al-Omania*, pp188, 145-6.

88   Al-Jaabiri, *The Cultural Dimension*, p109, note 52.

89   Al-Nasir Al-Marmouri was born in the city of Qarara in Wadi Mizab where he was a pupil of Sheikh Bayoudh Ibrahim. Later he left to pursue his studies and lived among the Omanis in Cairo, where he was commissioned to supervise a scholarly project. He subsequently returned to Qarara, when the Omanis dispatched a troupe of their young students to study in the Wadi. He is a member of the Azaba Council, an expert in the history of the Ibadhi antecedents, and a much travelled man.

90   Abu Ishaq Ibrahim Atfish (d. 1386 AH/1966 AD). Originally from Yasjan in Wadi Mizab, he studied with the leading Imams, then left during the French occupation first for Tunis and then Cairo. There he spent time at the National Library Manuscript Department where he studied many of the Ibadhi books and other material; Al-Jaabiri, *The Cultural Dimension*, p84, note 147.

91   Abu Abdullah Mohammed bin Barka Al-Bahlawi Al-Omani (third/ ninth century). We do not have much information on his man except that he was an *ulema* from Oman. To him is attributed *Al-Jami'* which is popularly known as *Ibn Barka's Jami'*. In this he pursued a methodological style which was clear in its elucidations of matters of jurisprudence arising out of the Holy Book, Sunnah and opinion. This *Jami'* was published by Issa Al-Barouni in two volumes in 1971.

92   *Ibn Barka's Jami'*, of which we noted that Issa Al-Barouni published the manuscript form. The first edition was printed in Beirut in 1971 and the Ministry of National Heritage and Culture in Oman reprinted it (undated).

93   We know that the villages of Wadi Mizab were founded by Abu Abdullah Mohammed bin Bakr Al-Farasta'i (d, 441 AH/1049 AD) at the start of the fifth century. See note 11 of this study.

94   *Al-Seyar wa Al-Jawabat li Ulama wa A'ima Oman*, a study by Ismail Kashef, published by the Ministry of National Heritage and Culture in Oman, Dar Ahiaa Al-Kutub Al-Arabia, 1406 AH/1986 AD, vol. 1, p231. The above *Sirah* is on pp186-232. Note, we have relied on the manuscript copy of the *Sirah* and this is from p380 to 403. The study did not undertake an analysis of the letter, merely transcribing the text, p186.

95   *Ibid.*, p232.

96   Abu Qassem Al-Baradi, *Al-Jawaher Al-Muntiqaa*, completing the unfinished *Tabaqat* of Al-Darjini, Cairo, 1302 AH/1885 AD, pp183-200.

97   Mohammed Hassan, *A Study of Al-Shamakhi's Seyar*, p168. The issue was analysed thoroughly in the margins.

98   Bihaz Ibrahim, *ibid.*, p391.

99   Al-Shamakhi, *Al-Seyar*, pp229-30.

100   See Al-Jaabiri, *Nazam Al-'Azaba*.

101   Al-Shamakhi, *Al-Seyar*, p424.

102   Mohammed bin Hassan, *A Study of Al-Shamakhi's Seyar*, p378. See Farahat Al-Jaabiri, *Al-Bu'd Al-Hadhari*, pp240 and 344-396.

103   Amr Khalifa Al-Nami, *Malamih 'an Al-Haraka Al-Ilmiya fi Warjalan*, a lecture delivered to the Islamic Forum at Warjalan, Al-Isala magazine, Algiers.

104   Sheikh Salim bin Ya'qub had a copy in his own writing of this *Hijazia*. From the margin notes it would seem that he relied on several copies. Private collection, Ghizan, Gerba.

105   Al-Darjini, *Al-Tabaqat*, vol. 2, p498; Al-Shamakhi, *Al-Seyar*, p446.

106   Copies of these books are to be found in the Barouni Library. They are not the originals, but rather transcribed copies. The Ministry of National Heritage and Culture have printed them all. Mohammed bin Wassaf Al-Omani's (seventh century AH/thirteenth century AD) annotation of Ibn Al-Nazar Al-Omani's book *Al-D'aim* (sixth century AH/twelfth century AD), a study by Abdul Moneim Amer, Issa Al-Babi Al-Halbi Press, 1982, in 2 vols; Abu Al-Hassan Al-Bessiwi (fifth century AH/eleventh century AD): *Jami' Abi Al-Hassan Al-Bessiwi*, Jeridet Oman Press, 1984 in 4 vols; Mohammed bin Jaafar Al-Azkawi (third century AH/ninth century AD): *Jami' Ibn Jaafar*, a study by Abdul Moneim Amer, Aissa Al-Babi Al-Halbi Press, Cairo, 1931, in 3 vols. All of these books are on the subject of jurisprudence except for the first which is on doctrine (an interpretation of Al-D'aim).

107   Al-Baradi, *Al-Jawaher*, p11.
108   Farahat Al-Jaabiri, *Nidham Al-'Azaba*, pp203, 295.
109   Al-Salimi, *Al-Tohfah*, vol. 1, p310 and The Trip, vol. 1, pp309-19.
110   See proceedings of the Symposium on Oman Studies, vol. 3, pp209-43.
111   See previous account of Al-Darjini's composition.
112   Umm Wajbyi, *Bihasab Al-Jamal*.
113   Farahat Al-Jaabiri, *Nidham Al-'Azaba*, pp296.
114   Copies arranged by Sheikh Salim bin Ya'qub from the handwritten script of Sheikh Qassem bin Yahya Al-Wirani Al-Lajimi Al-Gerbi in Jumada Al-Awla 1354 AH in Cairo. See notebook no 1, p32-34 in his library at Ghizan, Gerba.
115   This *Makhamas* is in 22 pages and was photocopied for us by Suleiman Al-Bakli from the village of Yasjan in Wadi Mizab. It is written in clear *Maghrabi* script.
116   The handwritten letter was copied by Sheikh Salem bin Ya'qub in Cairo, notebook no. 2, pp84-88.
117   Al-Salimi, *Al-Tohfah*, vol. 2, pp79-82
118   Farahat Al-Jaabiri, *Al-Bu'd Al-Hadhani*, p157.
119   Al-Salimi, *Al-Tohfah*, vol. 2, p83.
120   We would like to express our extreme gratitude to our brothers in Wadi Mizab. When we wrote to them requesting documents for the purpose of our study, they supplied us with copies of everything they had in their possession and went on to give us every assistance possible.
121   Al-Salimi, *Tohfat Al-'Ayian*, vol. 1, p66.
122   Al-Baradi, *Al-Jawaher Al-Muntiqaa*, Cairo, 1884, p155.
123   Al-Shamakhi, *Kitab Al-Seyar*, Cairo ed., 1301 AH, p70; and Mohammed Ali Dabbuz, *Tarikh Al-Maghreb Al-Kebir*, Cairo ed., 1963, vol. 3, pp138-49; and Al-Siyabi Al-Sama'ili, *Asdaq Al-Manahej fi Tamayyez Al-Ibadhia in Al-Khawarij*, p59.
124   Salim Al-Siyabi, *Azalat Al-W'atha' 'an Itba'a Abi Al-Sha'tha*, pp13-32 plus references.
125   Sayeda Kashef, *Oman fi Fajr Al-Islam*, p67 plus references.
126   Al-Warjalani, *Kitab Al-Dalil wa Al-Burhan*, Hijra ed., Al-Barouni Press, Cairo, 3 vols, Cairo 1306 AH.
127   Rajab Mohammed Abdul Halim, *The Omanis, their Navigation, Trade and Propagation of Islam*, Muscat, 1989, pp39, 40. Prepared by Dr Rajab Mohammed Abdul Halim.
128   *Ibid.,* p40.
129   *Ibid.,* p40.
130   Nur Al-Din Al-Salimi, *Tohfat Al-'Ayian*, vol.1, pp22, 34, 37, 39.
131   *Ibid.*, vol.1, pp53, 55, 56.
132   Al-Tabari, *Tarikh*
133   Nur Al-Din Al-Salimi, *Tohfat Al-'Ayian*, vol.1, pp59-60.
134   *Ibid.,* vol.1, pp234-9.
135   *Ibid.,* vol.1, pp166-8.
136   *Ibid.,* vol.1, pp204-6.
137   *Ibid.,* vol.1, pp352, 376-7.
138   *Tohfat Al-'Ayian*, vol. 2, pp61-64.
139   *Ibid.,* vol. 2, pp73-5.
140   *Ibid.,* vol. 2, pp76-8.
141   *Ibid.,* vol. 2, p94.
142   *Ibid.,* vol. 2, pp101-4.
143   *Ibid.,* vol. 2, p173.
144   Rajab Mohammed Abdul Halim, *The Omanis, their Navigation, Trade and Propagation of Islam*, Muscat, 1989, pp6, 7.
145   Nur-Al-Din Al-Salimi, *Tohfat Al-'Ayian bi Sirat Ahl Oman*, Muscat, 1981, vol. 1, p4.
146   *Ibid.,* vol. 1, p294.
147   Ibid., vol.1, p352.
148   Ibid., vol.1, p353.
149   Said Aashour, Awadh Khalifat, *Oman and Islamic Civilization*, Muscat, 1987, p228.
150   Rajab Mohammed Abdul Halim, *op. cit.,* p9-10.
151   Sarhan bin Said Al-Azkawi, *Tarikh Oman*, citing *Kashef Al-Ghumah Al-Jam'a Li Akhbar Al-A'ima*, a study by Abdul Majed Hassib Al-Qaissi, Sijl Al-Arab Press, 1980, p11.
152   Mohammed bin Abdullah Al-Salimi, *Nahdat Al-'Ayian bi Hurriyat Oman*, Cairo, p45; see also J. C. Wilkinson, 'Interpretations/Biographies of the Omani Ulema from the Ninth to the Fourteenth Centuries AD' in, *Oman - History and Scholars*, translated into Arabic by Mohammed Amin Abdullah, 1980, p41.
153   Wilkinson, *ibid.,* pp33-44; see also Dr Farouq Omar, *An Introduction to the Study of Omani History*, Baghdad, 1979, pp18-9.
154   Abdullah bin Khalfan bin Qaisar, *Sirat Al-Imam Nasir bin Murshid*, a study by Abdul Majed

Hassib Al-Qaissi, 1977, p13.

[155] Ibn Qaisar, *ibid.,* scholar's introduction, p7.

[156] Al-Azkawi, *op. cit.,* p90.

[157] Al-Azkawi, *op. cit.,* p97.

[158] *Ibid.,* pp9-10.

[159] *Ibid.,* p4.

[160] Humaid bin Mohammed bin Ruzaiq, *Al-Fet'h Al-Mubeen fi Sirat Al-Sadah Al-Busaidiyeen,* a study by Abdul Moneim Amer, Mohammed Mursi Abdullah, Sijl Al-Arab Press, 1977, p1.

[161] Ibn Ruzaiq, *ibid.,* p2.

[162] *Ibid.,* p213.

[163] An investigative study of this book has been published by Abdul Moneim Amer, 1978.

[164] Taken from Farouq, *op. cit.,* p103.

[165] Wilkinson, *op. cit.,* p76.

[166] Nur Al-Din Al-Salimi, *Tohfat Al-'Ayian bi Sirat Ahl Oman,* annotated and corrected and printed by Abu Ishaq Ibrahim Atfish Al-Jaza'iri, Al-Shebab Press, Cairo, 2nd ed, 1350, vol. 1, p3.

[167] Al-Salimi, *ibid.,* vol. 1, p304.

[168] *Ibid.,* vol.1, p3.

[169] Wilkinson, *op. cit.,* p74-5.

[170] Wilkinson, *ibid.,* p76; Omar, *op. cit.,* pp24-5.

[171] Al-Azkawi, *op. cit.,* p112.

[172] Al-Salimi, *op. cit.,* vol. 2, p112.

[173] Suleiman Mohammed Al-Ghannam, *The Portuguese Presence in Local Omani Sources, Sources of the History of the Arabian Peninsula,* Riyadh University Press, 1979, vol. 2, p116.

[174] Al-Azkawi, *op. cit.,* p91-2; Ibn Ruzaiq, *Al-Fet'h Al-Mubeen* pp254-5; see also Ayesha Ali Al-Siyar, *The Ya'ruba State in Oman and East Africa,* Dar Al-Qods, Beirut, vol. 1, 1975, pp41-3.

[175] Al-Azkawi, *op. cit.,* p141; Al-Ma'awli, *op. cit.,* p157; Ibn Ruzaiq, *Al-Fet'h Al-Mubeen,* pp336-7.

[176] Al-Salimi, *op. cit.,* vol. 2, p142.

[177] Ibn Ruzaiq, *Al-Fet'h Al-Mubeen,* pp335-6.

[178] Al-Azkawi, *op. cit.,* p113.

[179] Al-Salimi, *op. cit.,* vol. 2. p106-7.

[180] Rudolph Said Reute, *The Sultanate of Oman during the Reign of Al-Sayyid Said bin Sultan (1791-1856),* translated by Abdul Majed Hassib Al-Qaissi, Basra University Press, 1983, pp42-3.

[181] *Ibid.,* pp370, 438.

[182] Ministry of Information, Sultanate of Oman: *Oman in the Eyes of the World,* Muscat, 1987, vol. 2, p 188.

[183] Al-Maqdisi, *Ahsan Al-Taqasim,* Leiden, 1906, p35.

[184] Madiha Ahmed Darwish. *The Sultanate of Oman in the Eighteenth and Nineteenth Centuries,* Jeddah, 1982, pp 34-55.

[185] *Oman in the Eyes of the World,* vol. 1, p 171; Darwish, *op.cit.,* pp 24-6.

[186] Ministry of Information, *Oman 1986,* p 16; *Oman in the Eyes of the World,* vol. 2, p25.

[187] *Oman in the Eyes of the World,* vol. 1, p170.

[188] Oman in the Third Millennium before the Christian Era', *Turathna* series no.41, publication of the Ministry of National Heritage and Culture.

[189] Donald Hawley, *Oman,* Stacey International.

[190] *Ibid.*

[191] Sarhan bin Said Al-Azkawi, *Kashef Al-Ghumah Al-Jami' Li Akhbar Al-Ummah* - An Investigative Study by Ahmed Obeidli, Cyprus, Dilmun Publications.

[192] *Journal of Oman Studies* - Selections from the First and Second Volumes, p145; Mohammed Abu Al-Mahasen Asfour, *Phoenician Cities,* Dar Al-Nahda Al-Arabia, Beirut, 1975, 1976, Ministry of National Heritage and Culture.

[193] Madeleine Horus Miawan, *History of Carthage,* Beirut - Paris.

[194] Donald Hawley, *Oman.*

[195] *Oman in the Eyes of the World,* vol. 2, p188.

[196] *Oman in the Eyes of the World,* vol. 2, pp190-1; Hawley, *op.cit.,* pp32, 33, 124.

[197] Major Hilal bin Mohammed bin Ahmed Al-Busaidi, *History of the Forts and Citadels of Oman,* 1988.

[198] *Ibid.*

[199] Salim bin Hamoud Al-Siyabi, *Oman Across History,* vol. 1, Ministry of National Heritage and Culture, 1986.

[200] Paper of the Ministry of National Heritage and Culture, *Bahla Fort.*

[201] *Ibid.*

202 *Ibid.*

203 *Ibid.*

204 Al-Qalqashandi, *Nihayat Al-Irab Fi Maarafat Ansab Al-Arab*, Dar Al-Kutub Al-Aalamiya, Beirut.

205 *Forts and Citadels of the Sultanate of Oman*, 1985.

206 Dr Soad Maher, *Proceedings of the Symposium on Oman Studies*, vol. 2, Ministry of National Heritage and Culture publication, 1980.

207 *Ibid.*

208 *Ibid.*

209 Sarhan bin Said Al-Azkawi, *Kashef Al-Ghumah*- An Investigative Study by Ahmed Obeidli, Cyprus, Dilmun Publications.

210 Abdullah bin Humaid Al-Salimi, *Tohfat Al-'Ayian*, vol. 1, Dar Al-Tali'a, Kuwait, 5th ed., 1974.

211 Dr Soad Maher, *Proceedings of the Symposium on Oman Studies*, vol. 2, Ministry of National Heritage and Culture publication, 1980.

212 Paper of the Ministry of National Heritage and Culture: *Sohar Fort*.

213 *Forts and Citadels of the Sultanate of Oman*, 1985.

214 *Ibid.*

215 Paper of the Ministry of National Heritage and Culture: *Nakhal Fort*.

216 Sarhan bin Said Al-Azkawi, *Kashef Al-Ghumah* - An Investigative Study by Ahmed Obeidli, Cyprus, Dilmun Publications.

217 *Forts and Citadels of the Sultanate of Oman*, 1985.

218 Paper of the Ministry of National Heritage and Culture: *Nizwa Fort*.

219 *Ibid.*

220 *Ibid.*

221 Major Hilal bin Mohammed bin Ahmed Al-Busaidi, *History of the Forts and Citadels of Oman*, 1988.

222 Dr Soad Maher, *Proceedings of the Symposium on Oman Studies*, vol. 2, Ministry of National Heritage and Culture publication, 1980.

223 Ibn Ruzaiq, *Al-Fet'h Al-Mubeen Fi Sirat Al-Sadah Al-Busaidiyeen*; Major Hilal bin Mohammed bin Ahmed Al-Busaidi, *History of the Forts and Citadels of Oman*.

224 Salim bin Hamoud Al-Siyabi, *Oman across History*; Major Hilal bin Mohammed bin Ahmed Al-Busaidi, *History of the Forts and Citadels of Oman*.

225 Ibn Ruzaiq, *Al-Fet'h Al-Mubeen*; Major Hilal bin Mohammed bin Ahmed Al-Busaidi *History of the Forts and Citadels of Oman*.

226 Ibn Ruzaiq, *Al-Fet'h Al-Mubeen*.

227 Nur Al-Din Al-Salimi, *Tohfat Al-'Ayian*, vol. 2, 5th ed

228 Major Hilal bin Mohammed bin Ahmed Al-Busaidi, *History of the Forts and Citadels of Oman*.

229 *Ibid.*

230 Donald Hawley, *Oman*, Stacey International.

231 Collected authors, *Al-Mu'jam Al-Wasit*, vol2, 2nd ed., Dar Ihya' Al-Turath, Beirut.

232 *Oman A Seafaring Nation*, Ministry of Information publication.

233 Dr Soad Maher, *Proceedings of the Symposium on Oman Studies*, vol. 2, Ministry of National Heritage and Culture publication.

234 Aisha Ali Al-Sayyar, *The Ya'ruba State in Oman and East Africa*, Dar Al-Quds, Beirut.

235 Dr Soad Maher, *Proceedings of the Symposium on Oman Studies*, vol. 2, Ministry of National Heritage and Culture publication.

236 Sarhan bin Said Al-Azkawi, *Kashef al-Ghumah* - An Investigative Study by Ahmed Obeidli, Cyprus, Dilmun Publications.

237 *Forts and Citadels of the Sultanate of Oman*, 1985.

238 Paper of the Ministry of National Heritage and Culture, *Jalali Fort*.

239 Donald Hawley, *Oman*, Stacey International.

240 *Oman A Seafaring Nation*, Ministry of Information publication, 1979.

241 Donald Hawley, *Oman*, Stacey International.

242 Major Hilal bin Mohammed bin Ahmed Al-Busaidi, *History of the Forts and Citadels of Oman*, 1988.

243 *Oman A Seafaring Nation*, Ministry of Information publication, 1979.

244 Dr Soad Maher, Proceedings of the Symposium on Oman Studies, vol. 2, Ministry of National Heritage and Culture 1980.

245 Paper of the Ministry of National Heritage and Culture, *Al-Mirani Fort*.

246 *Forts and Citadels of the Sultanate of Oman*, 1985.

247 Paper of the Ministry of National Heritage and Culture: *Buraimi Fort*.

248 Mohammed bin Abdullah Al-Salimi & Naji Assaf, *Oman - History Speaks*, Damascus, 1963.

249 *Ibid.*

250 Paper of the Ministry of National Heritage and Culture: *Matrah Fort*.
251 Mohammed bin Bakr bin Abdul Qader Al-Razi, *Mokhtar Al-Sahah*, Dar Al-Hilal Books, Beirut.
252 Major Hilal bin Mohammed bin Ahmed Al-Busaidi, *History of the Forts and Citadels of Oman*, 1988.
253 Visitors' Guide Series, Ministry of National Heritage and Culture.
254 Major Hilal bin Mohammed bin Ahmed Al-Busaidi, *History of the Forts and Citadels of Oman*, 1988.
255 Donald Hawley, *Oman*, Stacey International.
256 *Journal of Oman Studies*, Second and Sixth Volumes, Ministry of National Heritage and Culture publication.
257 Mohammed bin Abdullah Al-Salimi & Naji Assaf, *Oman - History Speaks*, Damascus, 1963.
258 Abdullah bin Humaid Al-Salimi, *Tohfat Al-'Ayian*, vol. 1, Dar Al-Tali'a, Kuwait, 1964.
259 Sarhan bin Said Al-Azkawi, *Kashef Al-Ghumah* - An Investigative Study by Ahmed Obeidli, Cyprus, Dilmun Publications.
260 *Journal of Oman Studies*, Second and Sixth Volumes, Ministry of National Heritage and Culture publication.
261 Paper of the Ministry of National Heritage and Culture, *Jibrin Fort*.
262 Paper of the Ministry of National Heritage and Culture, *Al-Nu'man House*.
263 *Forts and Citadels of the Sultanate of Oman*, 1985.
264 Major Hilal bin Mohammed bin Ahmed Al-Busaidi, *History of the Forts and Citadels of Oman*, 1988.
265 Major Hilal bin Mohammed bin Ahmed Al-Busaidi, *History of the Forts and Citadels of Oman*, 1988.
266 *Oman A Seafaring Nation*, Ministry of Information publication, 1979.
267 Paper of the Ministry of National Heritage and Culture, *Matrah Fort*.
268 Mohammed bin Bakr bin Abdul Qader Al-Razi, *Mokhtar Al-Sahhah*, Dar Al-Hilal Books, Beirut.
269 Sarhan bin Said Al-Azkawi, *Kashef Al-Ghumah - An Investigative Study* by Ahmed Obeidli, Cyprus, Dilmun Publications.
270 Donald Hawley, *Oman*, Stacey International.
271 *Forts and Citadels of the Sultanate of Oman*, 1985.
272 Major Hilal bin Mohammed bin Ahmed Al-Busaidi, *History of the Forts and Citadels of Oman*, 1988.
273 E. d'Errico, *Journal of Oman Studies* , 6/1.
274 Hilal bin Mohammed bin Ahmed Al-Busaidi, *op. cit.*
275 Mohammed bin Abdullah Al-Salimi & Naji Assaf, *Oman - History Speaks*, Damascus, 1963.
276 *Forts and Citadels of the Sultanate of Oman*, 1985.
277 Lt. Col. Sir Arnold Wilson, *History of the Gulf*, Ministry of National Heritage and Culture publication.
278 Salma bin Musallam Al-Awatbi, *Al-Ansab*, Ministry of National Heritage and Culture publication.
279 Dr Naf'i Tawfiq Al-Aboud, *The Family of Al-Muhallab bin Abi Sufra*, University Press, Baghdad.
280 Abu Jaafar Mohammed bin Jarir Al-Tabari, *Tarikh Al-Muluk Wa Al-Ummam,* Beirut.
281 Sirhan bin Said Al-Azkawi, *Kashef al-Ghumah* - An Investigative Study by Ahmed Obeidli, Cyprus, Dilmun Publications.
282 *Ibid.;* Abdullah bin Humaid Al-Salimi, *Tohfat Al-'Ayian*, vol. 1, Dar Al-Tali'a, Kuwait, 1984.
283 *Ibid.*
284 *Oman A Seafaring Nation*, Ministry of Information publication, 1979.
285 Sarhan bin Said Al-Azkawi, *Kashef Al-Ghumah* - An Investigative Study by Ahmed Obeidli, Cyprus, Dilmun Publications; Abdullah bin Humaid Al-Salimi: *Tohfat Al-'Ayian*, vol. 1, Dar Al-Tali'a, Kuwait, 1964.
286 *Oman A Seafaring Nation,* Ministry of Information publication, 1979.
287. Gen. Jamal Mahfoudh, *The Arab Art of War in pre-Islamic and Islamic Times*, Encyclopaedia of Arab Civilization, Arab Institute for Studies and Publishing, Beirut.
288 Mohammed bin Abdullah Al-Lawati Ibn Battuta, *Rihlat Ibn Battuta* or *Tohfat Al-Nadhar Fi Ghara'ib Al-Amsar Wa Aja'ib Al-Asfar*, Beirut.
289 Jacqueline Byrne, *Discovering the Arabian Peninsula*, Dar Al-Kitab Al-Arabi, Beirut.
290 Lt. Col. Sir Arnold Wilson, *History of the Gulf*, Ministry of National Heritage and Culture publication.
291 E. d'Errico, *Journal of Oman Studies* 6/2, Ministry of National Heritage and Culture publication.
292. Donald Hawley, *Oman*, Stacey International.

[293] Dr Soad Maher, *Proceedings of the Symposium on Oman Studies*, vol. 2, Ministry of National Heritage and Culture publication, 1980.

[294] Burton Page, *The Tower in Islamic Military Architecture*, Dar Al-Maafif Al-Islamia Books (6), translated, Dar Al-Kitab Al-Libnani, Beirut.

[295] Beatrice de Cardi, *Study of the Monuments of Oman*, Turathna series, no. 39, Ministry of National Heritage and Culture publication.

[296] Gen. Jamal Mahfoudh, *The Arab Art of War in pre-Islamic and Islamic Times*, Encyclopaedia of Arab Civilization, Arab Institute for Studies and Publishing, Beirut.

[297] Dr Soad Maher: *Proceedings of the Symposium on Oman Studies*, vol. 2, Ministry of National Heritage and Culture publication, 1980.

[298] Beatrice de Cardi, *Study of the Monuments of Oman*, Turathna series, no. 39, Ministry of National Heritage and Culture publication.

[299] Dr Soad Maher, *Proceedings of the Symposium on Oman Studies*, vol. 2, Ministry of National Heritage and Culture publication, 1980.

[300] *Ibid.*

[301] Major Hilal bin Mohammed bin Ahmed Al-Busaidi, *History of the Forts and Citadels of Oman*, 1988.

[302] Gen. Jamal Mahfoudh, *The Arab Art of War in pre-Islamic and Islamic Times*, Encyclopaedia of Arab Civilization, Arab Institute for Studies and Publishing, Beirut.

[303] Major Hilal bin Mohammed bin Ahmed Al-Busaidi, *History of the Forts and Citadels of Oman*, 1988.

[304] Turathna series, no. 39, 42, Ministry of National Heritage and Culture publication; *Journal of Oman Studies*, Second Volume, Ministry of National Heritage and Culture publication.

[305] *Journal of Oman Studies,* Second and Seventh Volumes, Ministry of National Heritage and Culture publication.

[306] *Ibid.*

[307] *Oman in the Eyes of the World,* 2nd ed. p 190; Hawley, *op. cit.,* p 31, 124.

[308] Hawley, *op. cit.,* p136.

[309] Hawley, *op. cit.,* p32.

[310] *Oman in the Eyes of the World* , 2nd ed. pp 190-1.

[311] K.A.C. Creswell, 'Fortifications in Islam before 1250 AD', *Proceedings of the British Academy,* No.38 (1952), p91

[312] Hawley, op. cit. , p124.

[313] Hawley, *op. cit.,* p128.

[314] Ibn Battuta, *The Voyage of Ibn Battuta,* Beirut, 1964, p271.

[315] Intwan Mortcat, *Art in Ancient Iraq* translated, Baghdad, 1974, p200.

[316] Ghazi Rijab Mohammed, *Environmental Impact on Arab Architectural Designs,* (in press).

[317] Hawley, op.cit., p160-1.

[318] Hawley, op.cit., pp 36, 128.

[319] Hawley, *op. cit.,* p127.

[320] Hawley, *op. cit.,* p 118.

[321] Hawley, *op. cit.,* p 121.

[322] Hawley, *op. cit.,* p 35.

[323] C. Rathjens, *Jewish Domestic Architecture in Sana'a,* Jerusalem 1957, p42; Hawley, *op. cit.,* p112.

[324] M.S. Dimand, *Islamic Art,* translated, Cairo, 1958, p110; Abu Al-Ghada Ibn Kuthair, *The Beginning and the End,* Beirut and Riyadh, 1966, ch.14., p298.

[325] L.T. Bilbas, 'The Islamic Spanish Buildings', translated, *The Magazine of the Egyptian Institute for Islamic Studies,* Madrid, 1st. Ed., 1953, p125-7.

[326] Ibn Battuta, *The Voyage of Ibn Battuta,* p271.

[327] *Ibid.* p271.

[328] Hawley, *op. cit.,* p170-1.

[329] Hawley, *op. cit.,* p169

[330] Hussein Mu'nis, 'The Mosques', in *The World of Knowledge,* ch.37., 1981, p145-7.

[331] Major Hilal bin Mohammed bin Ahmed Al-Busaidi, *History of the Forts and Citadels of Oman*, 1988.

[332] Donald Hawley, *Oman,* Stacey International.

[333] Burton Page, *The Tower in Islamic Military Buildings,* The Islamic Publishing Press, 6, Beirut, Lebanon Book Store.

[334] Dr. Khalid Jasim Al-Janabi, *Arabic and Islamic Military Organisations During the Ummayyad Era,* Freedom Press, Baghdad.

[335] Major Hilal bin Mohammed bin Ahmed Al-Busaidi, *History of the Forts and Citadels of Oman*, 1988.

[336] *The Journal of Omani Studies*, 2nd. ed., Turathna series, no.42, published by The Ministry of

National Heritage and Culture.

[337] *Ibid.*

[338] *As-Sarouj*, a type of building material. Tar would be one of its components.

[339] *Al-Samim: pl. Sama.* The *Sama* is a type of material made from the leaves of date palm tress. Used to cover the ceilings and floors of rooms.

[340] Shawqi Dhayf, *The History of Arab Literature During the Time of the States and the Emirates,* vol. 5, Cairo, Dar Al-Hilal.

[341] Dr Mohammed Abdul Wahab Khallaf, *Islamic Cordoba During the Eleventh Century AD, the Fifth Hegira,* Tunisia, The Tunisian Publishing House.

[342] Tawfiq Ahmed Abdul Jawad, *The History of Architecture and Art* (3), *The European and Islamic Middle Ages,* Cairo, The New Art Press.

[343] Donald Hawley, *Oman,* Stacey International

[344] Major Hilal bin Mohammed bin Ahmed Al-Busaidi, *History of the Forts and Citadels of Oman,* 1988.

[345] Dr. Muhsin Zahran, *The Philosophy of Design* The *Art and Critics of Architecture Towards Contemporary Changes,* Cairo, Dar Al-Hilal.

[346] Dr Mohammed Hammad. 'Mese Van Dorda, The Pioneer of Positive Architecture', *The Great Engineers and their Works.* (3), Cairo, 1st ed.

[347] *Castles and Forts of the Sultanate of Oman,* 1985.

[348] Abdullah Bin Nasir Al-Harithi, *Banu Nabhaan in Oman and the Economic Situation in their Time,* M.A. Thesis. College of Literature, University of Cairo, 1990.

[349] Major Hilal bin Mohammed bin Ahmed Al-Busaidi, *History of the Forts and Citadels of Oman,* 1988.

[350] Humaid bin Mohammed bin Ruzaiq, *Al-Fet'h al-Mubeen fi Sirat Al-Sadah Al-Busaidiyeen,op. cit.*

[351] *Ibid.,* p 349.

[352] *Mu'jam al-Buldan* (Atlas of Nations), Beirut, 1957, vol. 4, p393.

[353] *Travels of Ibn Battuta* (in Arabic), Beirut, 1987, p 284.

[354] Salem ibn Hamoud Al-Siyabi, *Oman Across History,* Muscat, 1986, vol. 1, p 86.

[355] Nur Al-Din Al-Salimi, *Tohfat Al-'Ayian,* Muscat, undated, vol. 1, pp 22-24.

[356] *Kashef Al-Ghumah Al-Jami li Akhbar Al-Ummah,* anonymous, edited by Ahmed Obeidli, Delmon Publishing, Cyprus, 1985, pp 213-217; see also Al-Salimi, *op. cit.,* pp 23-28.

[357] *Kashef Al-Ghumah, op. cit.,* pp 218-222.

[358] Al-Salimi, *op. cit.,* vol. 1, p 33.

[359] Proceedings of the Omani Studies Symposium, vol. 1, p 272.

[360] *Surat Al-Ardh,* p 44.

[361] *Al Masalek Wal Mamalek,* p25.

[362] *Ahsan At-Qassim fi Marifat Al-Aqalim,* vol. 5, pp 338-339.

[363] Malallah bin Ali Habib, *Glimpses of Oman's History* (in Arabic), p 3.

[364] Andrew Williamson, *Sohar in History,* p 28.

[365] *Ibid.,* pp 11 and 32.

[366] Williamson, *op. cit.,* pp 19-23.

[367] The two letters had been included in an Omani anonymous transcript, which was edited by Said Ashour and given a new title, *Tarikh Ahl Oman,* p 40.

[368] *Oman A Seafaring Nation,* Ministry of Information publication, p 34.

[369] Stephen and Handt, *Arab Civilization,* p 396.

[370] George Percy Badger, *History of the Imams and Sayyids of Oman from AD 661-1856,* the introduction, New York, 1963.

[371] The Proceedings of the Omani Studies Symposium; vol. 2, p 38.

[372] *Sultanate of Oman, Development Progress in the Interior and Central Regions* (in Arabic), p 19.

[373] *Ibid.,* p 23.

[374] Said bin Ali Al-Mughairi, *Jahinat Al-Akhbar fi Tarikh Zanzibar,* p 199.

[375] Ibn Ali, Mallalah, *Glimpses of Oman's History* p. 24.

[376] *Kitab Al-Buldan,* p 117.

[377] *Travels of Ibn Battuta,* vol. 2, pp 210-211.

[378] *Oman Across History,* vol. 1, p 62.

[379] *Ibid.,* (edited excerpts) p 12.

[380] *Oman Across History,* pp 74, 31 and 43, respectively.

[381] *Oman A Seafaring Nation.*

[382] See *Oman A Seafaring Nation,* (former) Ministry of Information and Culture, Oman, 1979, p. 9.

[383] See G. F. Hourani, *Arab Seafaring in the Indian Ocean in Ancient and Early Medieval Times.,* translated into Arabic by Yacoub Bakr, Cairo, pp. 27-29. Princeton 1981.

[384] In fact, the Arabian Gulf comprises the sea area and the shores enclosed by its opposing coasts. The body of the Gulf is thus divided into the Arabian Gulf and the Gulf of Oman extending to the Arabian Sea. These two gulfs, however, constitute a continuous basin reaching north to the Iraq delta and southward to the Indian Ocean and East Africa. Thus, Oman is at a confluence of nations and on one of the oldest maritime routes, a fact that has had a deep-rooted impact on the entire region, from Asia to Africa.

[385] S. B. Miles, *The Countries and Tribes of the Persian Gulf,* Sultanate of Oman, 1982, p. 24.

[386] Hourani, *op. cit.,* p. 42. Also see: Abdul Rahman Al-Ani, *The Role of Omanis in Islamic Navigation and Trade to the End of the Fourth Century Hegira*, Ministry of National Heritage and Culture, 1986, p. 4.

[387] Miles, *op. cit.,* pp. 25 and 27.

[388] Hourani, *op. cit.,* pp. 48 and 52.

[389] Isam Sakhnini, *Arab Expansion along the Eastern Coasts of the Arabian Peninsula,* p. 87.

[390] *Ibid.,* p. 89.

[391] *Ibid.,* p. 89.

[392] Abdullah Al-Salimi and Naji Assaf, *Oman -History Speaks* (in Arabic), Damascus, 1283 Hegira, pp. 80-81.

[393] Yaq'ut Al-Hamawi, *Mu'jam Al-Buldan*, vol. 2, p. 435.

[394] *Ibid.,* vol. 2, p. 378; see also Al-Homeiri, *Al-Rawdh Al-Mi'tar* p. 220.

[395] Sakhnini, *op. cit.,* p. 90.

[396] Al-Bilathuri, *Futuh Al-Buldan*, vol. 1, pp. 92-93.

[397] Al-Tabari, *Tarikh al-Ummam wal Muluk,* vol. 3, p. 139.

[398] Farouq Omar Fawzi, *The Arabian Gulf in the Early Islamic Ages,* p. 44.

[399] Farouq Omar Fawzi, *Arabs in the Eastern Arabian Gulf Regions,* p. 71.

[400] Al-Bilathuri, *op. cit.,* vol. 2, p. 476.

[401] *Ibid.*

[402] Al-Tabari, *op. cit.,* pp. 213-214.

[403] *Ibid.,* vol. 5, p. 55.

[404] Al-Bilathuri, *op. cit.,* p. 384; and see also Fawzi, *op. cit.,* p. 74.

[405] Al-Bilathuri, *op. cit.,* vol. 3, p. 530; see also Obada Kuhailah *Arabs and the Sea*, p. 49.

[406] Al-Bilathuri, *op. cit.,* vol. 3, p. 534.

[407] Al-Thaallabi, *Thimar Al-Quolob fil Mudhaf wal Mansub,* Cairo, 1908, p. 423.

[408] For further details on the invasion of Rhodes in 672 AD, see Al-Bilathuri, *op. cit.,* vol. I, p. 278; for details on the invasion of Akritish in 675 AD, see Al-Bilathuri, *ibid.,* p 279.

[409] *Ibid.,* vol. 1, p 150f.

[410] Al-Ma'sudi, *op. cit.,* vol. 1, p. 149; and Said Abdul Aziz Salim, 'Marine Trade in the Arabian Gulf in the early Islamic Era', a paper presented to Qatar Conference convened in 1976, vol. 1, p. 400.

[411] Al-Istakhri, *Al-Masalek wal Mamalek*, p. 30.

[412] Al-Mas'udi, *op. cit.,* vol. 1, p. 149.

[413] *Ibid.,* p. 147; see also Ibn Faqih, *Mukhtasar Kitab Al-Buldan*, p. 8; and Ibn Rusta, *Al-Aa'ilaq Al-Nafisah*, p. 86. But, to get further details on the risks and difficulties facing trade in the eastern part of the Arabian peninsula, see Ahmed Al-Toukhi, *East of the Arabian Peninsula*, pp. 92-99.

[414] Ibn Faqih, *Mukhtasar Kitab al-Buldan*, p. 11; *Silsilat At'Tawarikh*, p 100. Al-Mas'udi records that it was called *Dardure Musandam* and *Abi Hijra.*

[415] Al-Mas'udi, *op. cit.,* vol. 1, p. 150.

[416] Ibn Al-Faqih, *Mukhtasar Kitab Al-Buldan*, p 13; *Silsilat At'Tawarikh,* p 5, 186-7, Al-Mas'udi, *Murooj Ath-Thahab,* vol. 1, p 151; Al-Maqdisi, *Ahsan At'Taqasim,* p 13.

[417] Ibn Faqih, *op. cit.,* p. 13; and *Silsilat At'Tawarikh,* pp. 5, 186 and 187.

[418] Ceylon is the biggest island in the Bay of Bengal. From its shores, ambergris and pearls were sought. Many reference confirm this particular fact. For accurate details, however, see Ya'qut Al-Hamawi, *Mu'jam Al-Buldan, Silsilat At'Tawarikh* and Al-Hamiri, *Al-Rawdh Al-Mi'tar,* p. 313.

[419] Ibn Al-Faqih, *Mukhtasar Kitab Al-Buldan*, p 10.

[420] Al-Mas'udi, *op. cit.,* vol. 1, p. 152; see also, *Silsilat At'Tawarikh,* pp. 7-8.

[421] Al-Mas'udi, Murooj Ath'Thahab, vol. 1, p 152.

[422] *Silsilat At'Tawarikh,* p. 7.

[423] Al-Mas'udi, *op. cit.,* vol. 1, p. 153.

[424] Ya'qut Al-Hamawi, *op. cit.,* vol. 4, p. 478.

[425] Al-Mas'udi, *op. cit.,* vol. I, p. 153.

[426] Ibn Faqih, *op. cit.,* p. 12.

[427] *Ibid.*

[428] Ibn Rusta, *op. cit.,* p. 138.

429 *Ibid.*
430 Al-Mas'udi, *op. cit.,* vol. 1, p. 153.
431 *Ibid.,* p. 107.
432 *Ibid.,* p. 108.
433 *Ibid.,* p. 108.
434 *Ibid.,* p. 128; Obad Kuhailah, *Arabs and The Sea,* p 57.
435 *Ajaib Al-Hind,* p 38.
436 For further details about the land road, see Nicole Ziyada, *Geography and Arab Expeditions,* p. 220 and on.
437 Ibn Khurdathuba, *Al-Masalek wal Mamalek,* pp. 64-72.
438 Faqih, *op. cit.,* pp. 11-13.
439 *Silsilat At'Tawarikh,* p 15-21.
440 Kuhailah, *op. cit.,* p. 60.
441 We have already mentioned that the expression, 'Chinese ships 'is used extensively in the Arab historical literature to mean the Arab and Islamic commercial ships designated to the Chinese route. This fact can be further verified in Yajima Hkoichi, *Maritime Activities of the Gulf Population and the Indian Ocean World in the Eleventh Century,* pp. 55-56. O. Kuhailah accepts this opinion with respect the Arab trade prior to Islam. But, however, in the post-Islam era, Kuhailah agrees with Al-Mas'udi that Chinese ships had rarely visited the Arabian Gulf.
442 Al-Mas'udi, *op. cit.,* p. 140.
443 Yajima Hkoichi, *Marine Activities,* p. 55 - China Handbook Series - History (Translated by Dun J. Li), p. 59.
444 Ibn Khurdathuba, *op. cit.,* p. 70.
445 China Handbook Series, History, pp. 57-59.
446 *Ibid.,* p. 59.
447 For further details about such political turmoil, see: Marwyn S. Samuels, and Carmencita Samuels, *Islam in the Southern Seas:* ,The Impact of Arabian Gulf Merchants in the South China Sea, Tenth to Nineteenth Centuries, pp. 68-69 (A study presented to Qatar symposium in 1976).
448 Kuhailah, *op. cit.,* p. 63.
449 Al-Mas'udi, *op. cit.,* vol. 1, pp. 137-138.
450 Canton was a big city on the bank of a relatively big river, about six to seven days from the South China Sea. Ships of traders from Basra, Siraf and Oman as well as from Indian ports, would sail up-river to Canton. In this city, though, there was a diversity of peoples - Muslims, Christians, Jews and Magians. (Al-Mas'udi, *Murooj Al-Thahab,* p. 138).
451 *Ibid.,* p. 138.
452 *Ibid.,* p. 139.
453 Five dynasties ruled China from 907 AD, when T'ang dynasty collapsed, until 960 AD. Since 960 AD, however, a new state of stability was ushered in by the advent of Sung dynasty which remained in office to 1279.
454 Abdul Aziz Salim, *Maritime Trade in the Gulf in the Early Islamic Era,* p. 409.
455 Yajima Hkoichi, *op. cit.,* p. 56.
456 *Ibid.,* p. 57.
457 *Ibid.,* p. 58. Obada Kuhailah, also based on Chinese references, depicted another Omani expedition undertaken by Sheikh Abdullah. This person was later called Kin Yateo by the Chinese; he lived in Canton for several years in the eleventh century AD. He was quite close to the Emperor Shen Zong (1067-1085), who appointed him a mayor of the foreigners' district in the city. The Emperor gave him a gift of a magnificent white horse. Sheikh Abdullah returned to Oman in 1072. (These details can be found in Kuhailah, *op. cit.,* pp. 63-64).
458 Abdul Aziz Salim, *op. cit.* p. 410.
459 Kuhailah, *op. cit.,* p. 66.
460 Yaq'ut Al-Hamawi, *Mu'jam Al-Buldan,* vol. 4, p. 422.
461 Ibn Battuta, *Travels,* p. 273.
462 Mediterranean ships were different from those sailing the Indian Ocean or the south Asian seas. The former were made of pieces of wood, nailed together. Whereas Omani ships were made without nails, but sewn with cords made from the outer bark of the coconut tree, as was the case in the old Egyptian boats. See Al-Masudi, *op. cit.,* vol. I, p. 147; *Silsilat At'Tawarikh,* p. 176.
463 Kuhailah, *op. cit.,* p. 55.
464 Al-Mas'udi, *op. cit.,* vol. 2, p. 7. Safala is a Semitic term found in Arabic and Hebrew which means the low land. See Al-Sir Sidahmed Al-Iraqi, 'The Islamic Civilization Features in the East African Coast in the Middle Ages', *Journal of Africa* published by the Islamic African Centre in Khartoum, Sudan, April 1986, p. 102.
465 Kuhailah, *op. cit.,* p. 55 and further.

[466] Al-Jahiz, *Al-Bayan wel Tab'yeen,* vol. 2, p. 17.

[467] Ibn Hawqal, *Surat Al-Ardh*, p. 49.

[468] Al-Mas'udi, *op. cit.,* vol. 1, p. 112.

[469] Ibn Battuta, *Travels*, p. 36.

[470] Faqih, *op. cit.,* pp. 16 and 215.

[471] *Ibid.,* p. 35.

[472] Al-Mas'udi, *op. cit.,* vol. 2, pp. 7-8.

[473] *Aja'ib Al-Hind,* p. 49.

[474] Kuhailah, *op. cit.,* p. 53.

[475] *Ibid.,* p.235.

[476] Anwar Abdul Aleem, *Navigation and Oceanography,* pp. 132-136. It is worth noting that Obada Kuhailah followed Abdul Aleem in his assertions, yet without referring to him. (See Kuhailah, *op. cit.,* pp. 79-82.)

[477] Ibn Khurdathuba, *Al-Masalek wal Mamalek,* p. 153.

[478] Badawi Abdul Latif Awad, 'The Role of the Gulf Arab in the Spread of Islam in South-east Asia', a paper presented to Qatar Symposium in 1976, p. 230.

[479] *Ibid.,* p. 231f.

[480] Oman was faced by a problem created by the prolonged absence of Omani traders from their homeland, a fact which had its implications with respect to payment of *zakat* (the Islamic form of tax on personal income). Imam Muhanna bin Gaifar (226-237 Hegira) designated the governor of Suhar to collect *zakat* from traders. (Kuhailah, *op. cit.,* p. 46).

[481] *Ibid.,* p. 62. See also Ahmed Al-Tookhi, *The Eastern Arabian Peninsula*, p. 88.

[482] Ibn Battuta, *Travels*, p. 633 and what follows.

[483] Ibn Rusta, *Al-Aa'ilaq Al-Nafisah*, pp. 135-136.

[484] Al-Mas'udi, *op. cit.,* vol. 1, p. 210.

[485] Kuhailah, *op. cit.,* p. 63.

[486] Badawi Awad, , *op. cit.,* p. 225.

[487] *Ibid.,* pp. 225-226.

[488] Kuhailah, *op. cit.,* p. 65.

[489] *Ibid.,* p. 65.

[490] Ibn Battuta, *op. cit.,* p. 564; for more details see p 256f of the same book.

[491] Amin, M. Mohammed, 'Development of Afro-Arab Relations in the Middle Ages', chapter in the the book on *Afro-Arab Relations* issued in 1977 by the Arab Research and Studies Centre, p. 45.

[492] A. Mohammed Al-Hajri,'The History of Omani-African Relations', a paper presented to Qatar Symposium in 1976, vol. 1 of the Proceedings, p. 774.

[493] Al-Hajri, *op. cit.,* p. 775; and see also Kuhailah, *op. cit.,* p. 53.

[494] Ibn Saad, *Kitab Al-Tabaqat Al-Kubra*, vol. 2, p. 27. See also Saida Kashif, *Oman in the Dawn of Islam*, p. 24.

[495] A. Abdul Hadi Al-Atta, 'Islam on the Western Coasts of the Red Sea', an article published in the *Journal of African Studies*, the Islamic African Center in Khartoum, issue 3, April 1987, p. 47.

[496] Al-Hajri, *op. cit.,* p. 777; and see also Fawzi, *op. cit.,* pp. 124-125.

[497] As'Sir Sidahmed Al-Iraqi, 'The Features of Islamic Civilization on the East African Coast in the Middle Ages', a study published in the *Journal of African Studies*, the African Islamic Centre in Khartoum, issue 2, p. 83.

[498] Kuhailah, *op. cit.,* p. 51.

[499] Al-Hajri, *op. cit.,* p. 777.

[500] Kuhailah, *op. cit.,* pp. 52-53; see also Amin, *op. cit.,* pp. 49-50.

[501] Sayyid Hamid Heraiz, *Arab Influences in the Swahili Culture in East Africa,* Al-Jeel Publishing House, Beirut, p. 188.

[502] The prominent scholar Sayyid Hamid Heraiz mentioned that Kiswahili has 19 dialects. He also named Arab poets who had written verses in Kiswahili.

[503] *Ibid.,* p. 129.

[504] H. Ibrahim Hassan, *The Spread of Islam and Arabicism in the Region Beyond the Sahara*, 1957, p. 12. See also Al-Shattir Busaili, 'The Sudan of the Nile Valley and Islam', *The Journal of Egyptian History* , issue 2, 1949, p. 39.

[505] Al-Hajri, *op. cit.,* p. 778.

[506] Al-Mas'udi, *op. cit.,* vol. 4, p. 194.

[507] Amin, *op. cit.,* p. 52.

[508] *Ibid.*

[509] Isam el-Deen Abdul Ra'oof, *Yemen in Islamic History since the Early Dawn to the Establishment the Prophet's State*, 1982, p. 260.

[510] *History of Yemen*, edited by Dr Hassan S. Mahmoud, pp. 40-42. See also Farouq Osman

Abbaza, *Aden and the British Policy in the Red Sea*, 1976, p. 27.

[511] This probability has been further confirmed by certain Arab sources such as Mameluke kings, including Sultan Gilawoon, who had ordered his officers to properly deal with traders coming from the Far East to encourage them to bring more spices to Egyptian ports in the Red Sea.

[512] Ibn Battuta, *op. cit.,* p. 271 and what follows.

[513] Abdul Hadi Al-Tazi, *Historical Relations between Morocco and Oman*, Ministry of National Heritage and Culture, Oman, issue 22, p. 21.

[514] Abdul Aziz Salim, 'Andalucia's Trade with Iraq and the Arabian Gulf in the Ummayyad Era', a paper presented to a symposium held in the United Arab Emirates on the status of the Arabian Gulf in the period of the Ummayyad state, 1989, p. 61.

[515] Salim, *op. cit.,* p. 64. Al-Maqdisi, *op. cit.,* pp92-3

[516] Abu Abdullah Al-Zahri, *The Geography Book* (in Arabic), edited by M. Haj Sadiq, p. 89. And see Salim, *op. cit.,* pp. 67-68.

[517] *Ibid.,* p 69f.

[518] George F. Hourani, *The Arabs and Navigation in the Indian Ocean,* Dar Al-Kitab Press, Cairo, Arabic translation by Dr Yaqoub Bakr, p101-2. English edition, Princeton Univ. Press 1951.

[519] Hourani, *op. cit. supra,* pp.106 and 175.

[520] S.B .Miles, *Countries and Tribes of the Persian Gulf*, London 1966, p78, p81-2; Abdullah bin Mohammed Al-Salimi, and Ghassan Naji, *Oman- History Speaks,* p134, Damascus, 1283 AH/1963 AD; Salim bin Hamoud bin Shamis Al-Siyabi, *Oman Across History,* vol. 2, p141 and p152, Al-Aarab Sigil Press, 401 AH/1980 AD.

[521] Al-Siyabi, *op. cit. supra* 152; Al-Salimi, *op. cit. supra*, p135.

[522] Al-Salimi, *op. cit.,* p137.

[523] Al-Siyabi, *op. cit., p*152, and pp. 205-207.

[524] Miles, *op. cit.,* p124, p112-3.

[525] Miles, *op. cit.,* p113, pp.122-4.

[526] Al-Salimi, *op. cit.,* p149.

[527] Miles, *op. cit.,* p147.

[528] Miles, *op. cit.,* p141, p151-2

[529] Al-Said Amin, *The Arabian Gulf in its Political History and Contemporary Development* , Dar Al-Kitab Al-Arabi, Beirut, no date, p30.

[530] Miles, *op. cit.,* p193.

[531] Robert Geran Landen, *Oman's Path and Fate,* p50-2.

[532] Ayesha Al-Sayyar, *op. cit.,* p81.

[533] Miles, *op. cit.,* p213-4.

[534] Al-Salimi and Ghassan Naji, *op. cit.,* 154.

[535] Between 1164-1215 AH/ 1750-1800 AD, ' there were fifteen ships of western design, of square shape, at Muscat city alone. Three small ships and two hundred and fifty ships with sails, most of them large, were used for cargo and transportation, their payload was also large. In addition to one hundred ships used to operate at the Port of Sur, there were also many other types of ships all over the Omani ports'. See R. G. Landen, *op. cit.,* p57.

[536] Al-Sayyar, *op. cit.,* p81.

[537] Miles, *op. cit.,* p242 and p244.

[538] In his reign, the Omani naval fleet contained 15 ships of European design, 74 battleships, five frigates and many other types of ships designed according to European standards. During peace time, the Omani naval fleet operated profitable trade routes. This fleet was able to carry 20,000 men on board. Imam Ahmed bin Said loved the sea. See Landen, *op. cit.,* p66.

[539] Ahmed Qasim Al-Boraini, *The Seven Emirates on the Green Coast.* p125.

[540] Jacqueline Byrne, *The Discovery of the Arabian Peninsula: Five centuries of Science and Adventure.*, pp 284 , 385, Arabic translation by Qala'agi Qadri, Dar Al-Kitab Al-Arabi, Beirut, Al-Nahdha Books, Baghdad.

[541] Fred A. Hold, *The Political Conflict in the Arabian Peninsula*, Arabic translation by Saghia, Hazim and Mahyo Said, Beirut, Ibn Khaldoon Press, April 1978, p94-5.

[542] Al-Salimi and Ghassaf Naji, *op. cit.,*p165 and p194.

[543] *Al-Ghurab* is an Arabic word. This kind of ship was very popular during the sixteenth, seventeenth and eighteenth century around the coasts of Malabar, the Arabian Gulf and the Red Sea. In actual fact, there are many types and designs of this ship. Some of them were small, while some others were large. But in general, it was known that that *Al-Ghurab* was a big ship with three sails on board. See Habib Zayyat, *The Dictionary of Ships and Boats in the Islamic World*, Al-Mashriq Press, Beirut 1949, p254.

[544] India Office, Factory Records, Letters from Bussra, Gambroon, etc., Letters from Bussra, vol. 21, September, 1769.

[545] Lorimer, *op.cit.* ,p416.

[546] C. Niebuhr, *Travels through Arabia and other Countries in the East*, (trans into English by

Robert Heron) Edinburgh. *Al-tranki*: It was a popular ship used in the Arabian Gulf in the first half of the eighteenth century. Operated by both oars and sails, it was used in sea battles and for the transport of both passengers and cargo. This type of ship has now disappeared.

[547] Lorimer, op.cit. p416-7.

[548] Parsons, *op.cit.*; a ketch is a ship with two masts, whilst a galliot is smaller than a frigate.

[549] Lorimer, *op.cit.* ,p435.

[550] *Ibid.*

[551] *Oman A Seafaring Nation,* p77.

[552] *Oman A Seafaring Nation,* p107; G. F. Hourani, *Arab Seafaring in the Indian Ocean in Ancient and Early Medieval Times.*, Arabic translation and editing by Dr Al-Said Yaquob Bakr, The Anglo-Egyptian Bookshop, 1958, p240. English edition Princeton, 1951.

[553] Hourani, p241.

[554] *Oman A Seafaring Nation,* p107.

[555] *Saj* without stress on the letter 'j'; The origin is *sak* in the Al-Parkrit language, and in the English language, Teak, which is derived from Kake of the Dravidian language of north and middle India. It was associated with sanskrit or with one of its branches. See *Arab Seafaring in the Indian Ocean in Ancient and Early Medieval Times*, p244.

[556] *Ibid.,* p245.

[557] *Ibid.,* p247.

[558] Reinaud, *Relation des Voyages par les Arabs et les Prians dans l'Inde et a la Chine dans le IXE Siecle,* Paris, 1845. Arabic translation p130-1.

[559] *Oman A Seafaring Nation,* p156.

[560] *Arab Seafaring in the Indian Ocean in Ancient and Early Medieval Times*, p248.

[561] *India and China News,* p87-8.

[562] *Oman A Seafaring Nation,* p108.

[563] *Ibid.,* p,110.

[564] *Ibid.,* p108.

[565] *Arab Seafaring in the Indian Ocean in Ancient and Early Medieval Times,* p306.

[566] Anwar Abdul Aleem, *Navigation and Marine Science of the Arabs,* The World of Science series, The National Council for Culture and Art, Kuwait, 1979, p85-6.

[567] *Arab Seafaring in the Indian Ocean in Ancient and Early Medieval Times,* p255.

[568] Youssef Al-Shahroni, *Sindbad in Oman*, The Egyptian General Committee for Books, Cairo, 1986, p157.

[569] *Ibid.,* p213.

[570] *Arab Seafaring in the Indian Ocean in Ancient and Early Medieval Times,* p159.

[571] '*Navigation and Marine Sciences,* p84.

[572] *News of India and China,* Arabic text, p140-1.

[573] 'Quotations from *Arab Seafaring in the Indian Ocean in Ancient and Early Medieval Times,* p159.

[574] *Arab Seafaring in the Indian Ocean in Ancient and Early Medieval Times,* p254.

[575] *Oman A Seafaring Nation,* p156.

[576] *Ibid.,* p112.

[577] *Wonders of India,* p70.

[578] *Ibid.,*p91.

[579] *Arab Seafaring in the Indian Ocean in Ancient and Early Medieval Times,* p365; and *Oman A Seafaring Nation,* p113.

[580] *Wonders of India,* p58; Al-Mas'udi, *Murooj Al-Thahab*; The Lebanon's Book Press, 1982, p94; *The News of India and China*, Sofaj Print Edition, Arabic Script, p10.; Jean Sauvaget, *Relation de la Chine et de l'Inde Redige en 851*, Paris, Societe d'edition les belles lettres, 1948.

[581] *Oman A Seafaring Nation,* p114.

[582] *Arab Seafaring in the Indian Ocean in Ancient and Early Medieval Times,* p272.

[583] Clowes (gsl), *Sailing ships*, London, 1930, p53.

[584] *Arab Seafaring in the Indian Ocean in Ancient and Early Medieval Times,* p62.

[585] Barzak Bin Schhehrayar Hormuzi Al-Ram, *Wonders of India,* edited by Youssef Al-Sharoni, Riadh Al-Rees Press for Books and Publications, London, 1990, p71.

[586] *Arab Seafaring in the Indian Ocean in Ancient and Early Medieval Times,* p263.

[587] Ibn Majed, p105; and *Navigators and Marine Sciences of the Arabs,* p215.

[588] *Ibid.,* notes 35 and 36, p107 and p216 respectively, See also Youssef Al-Sharoni, *Sindbad in Oman, Ahmad Bin Majed: a Great Omani Sailor* p49.

[589] *The Proceedings of the Seminar of Omani Studies'* The Ministry of National Heritage and Culture, Sultanate of Oman, 1980, vol. 4, p112.

[590] In this final part of our study, we are dependent mainly on chapter fourteen of *Oman A Seafaring Nation,* p117-152.

[591] Aisha Al-Sayyar, *The State of Al-Ya'ruba, p* 66-7.

[592] *Ibid.,* p68.

[593] Shihab Hassan Saleh, *The Art of Navigation of the Arabs',* Dar Al-A'awda Press, Beirut, 1982, p53.

[594] During the eighth and ninth century many Persian, Indian and Greek books had been translated to Arabic, and before 215 AH/830 AD Ali bin Isa wrote books on the Astrolabe and Astronomy. During the following centuries, many great Muslim astronomers became very well known, See Hourani , *op. cit.,* p275-6.

[595] Hourani, *op. cit,* 278-9.

[596] S.B. Miles, *The Countries and Tribes of the Persian Gulf.* London 1919, repr. 1966. p343; and Parsons' Diaries. Based on information collected by Miles from the documents of Wilson, Wellstead, Anicok and Pelly, during the nineteenth century.

[597] Miles, *op. cit.,* p327-8.

[598] Miles, *op. cit. ,* p330-4.

PART V

Oman in Modern Times

Studies Presented and Summarized in this Part

The Expulsion of the Portuguese from Oman: First of the Arab Victories in Contemporary Times, by Dr Mohammed Al-Suroji, Alexandria University.

The Omani Role in Ending Portuguese Domination, by Dr Lufti Ja'far Faraj, University of Al-Mustansiryah, Iraq and Dr Mohammed Ali Al-Dawood, Arab Historians Union.

Al-Ya'ruba State: Between National Unity and Conquests Overseas, by Dr Mohammed Arab Sabir, Sultan Qaboos University.

The Emergence of the Al-Busaidi State, by Dr Mustafa Aqil, Qatar University.

The Establishment of the Al-Busaidi State . . . Causes and Consequences, by Dr Abdul Latif Al-Rumayhi and Dr Fouad Sihab, Bahrain University.

Oman's Relationship with East Africa in Modern Times, by Dr Mohammed Altae Sana, Arab Historians Union.

Omani Assistance to Basra between 1775-6, by Dr Tariq Nafi Al-Hamdani, Baghdad University.

Omani-Franco Relations in the Second Part of the Eighteenth Century, by Dr Salih Mohammed Ala'abid, Baghdad University.

Omani-American Relations during the Nineteenth Century, by Dr Raf'at Ghunaimi Al-Sheikh , Al-Zaqaziq University, Egyptian Arab Republic.

Omani Trade and Navigational Development in the Arabian Gulf and Indian Ocean, by Dr Mohammed Ali Al-Dawood, Arab Historians Union.

Britain and the Partition of the Sultanate of Muscat-Zanzibar in the Light of British Documents, by Dr Jad Mohammed Taha, Ayn Shams University.

A Study of the Partition of the Ottoman Empire, by Dr Mustafa Abdul Qadir Al-Najar, Arab Historians Union.

Omani Foreign Relations 1871-88, by Dr Samir Mohammed Taha, Asiot University, Egyptian Arab Republic.

Omani Naval Superiority and its Impact on Foreign Relations During the Reign of Al-Ya'ruba, by Dr Arab Mohammed Sabir, Alazhar University.

The Civilizing Influences of Oman on East Africa, by Dr Ibrahim Al-Zain Sughairoon, Sultan Qaboos University.

Focus on Some Omani Cultural Influences in East Africa, by Dr Abdul Fattah Hassan Abualiah, Imam Mohammed bin Saud University, Riyadh.

Omani Trade and Maritime Development in the Arabian Gulf and Indian Ocean, by Dr Mohammed Ali, Iraq.

Trade and Maritime Development during the Reign of Al Busaidyeen, by Dr Abdul Amir Mohammed Amin, Iraq.

Establishment of the Al-Ya'ruba State
and Imam Nasir bin Murshid's Efforts to Unite the Country

The Appearance of the Portuguese in the Waters of the Indian Ocean and Their Occupation of Oman's Coastal Provinces

The Islamic and Arab world was exposed to a massive wave of early European colonization to the East towards the end of the fifteenth and the beginning of the sixteenth century. Following the ending of the Arab presence in Andalucia, hostile and fanatical Portuguese who were at the forefront of this wave aimed to chase the Arabs along north and west Africa. They planned to attack them in their homelands, and to control the trade routes. The Portuguese King in his letter to Pope Paul in 911 AH/1505 AD explained his military crusading attitude, stating that he was not only determined to destroy the Mamelukes' trade, but that he would do his utmost to fight for the sake of Christianity, and that Mecca would be targeted by his guns and soldiers [1].

During the first decade of the sixteenth century, the Ottoman State was the only Islamic power which was capable of challenging the Portuguese. The Ottomans engaged in fierce fighting on the eastern front of Europe, achieving numerous victories. The Portuguese, however, succeeded in making their way to eastern waters where the Islamic powers in the Indian Ocean and the Arabian Gulf were facing their own internal problems. The Mamelukes decided to take up the challenge because they had been badly affected by the Portuguese presence: the Venetians, had suffered huge economic losses as a result of the detour around the Cape of Good Hope at the southern tip of the African subcontinent. The Mamelukes' naval fleet, therefore, engaged the Portuguese.

The war along the Indian coastline proved to be an unequal one. In the area of Dio, the Mamelukes suffered a crushing defeat in 1509 causing them to withdraw from the fighting. They were particularly angry because the Muslims of west India failed to provide adequate and timely support for the war effort. Following their conquest of Egypt, the Ottomans inherited the great Mameluke wealth and the mantle of protecting the Islamic world from Portuguese threats and actions fell to them. They tried to prevent the Portuguese from surrounding the Arabian peninsula, following Portuguese control of the right arm of the Arabian Gulf.

The Portuguese were very anxious to penetrate westwards and to colonize the left flank of Arabia: the Red Sea. However, the Ottomans were determined to retain control of the Red Sea because of their huge wealth in Egypt and the Arabian peninsula. In line with Mameluke military strategy with regards to the Red Sea, they assigned it an even higher priority than their domination over the Gulf.

The Portuguese, meanwhile, having succeeded in conquering the Indian shores, set about implementing their planned strategy of surrounding the Arabian peninsula from the east. It was with this in mind that they colonized some of the islands in the Arabian Gulf and began their attacks on Oman.

During the fifteenth century, Oman passed through an unstable period because of the predominance of internal dissent. Taking advantage of this disarray, the Portuguese conquered Oman's seashores. They were very much aware of the strategic importance of Oman and also knew the importance of other ports in Arabia and East Africa which formed important first staging posts on voyages to India. The Portuguese navigator and explorer Vasco da Gama discovered, in the year 904 AH/1498 AD, the vital importance of this area, leading to Portuguese influence in Zanzibar and surrounding islands such as Pemba and Mafia[2]. The first military campaign led by Alfonse Albuqerque arrived in Oman in the year 913 AH /1507 AD. Oman's large trading vessels and fishing boats were attacked and set on fire, whilst Muscat, Sohar, Sur and Quriyat were occupied.

The Portuguese used many harsh methods to strengthen their control over Oman, terrorizing the Omani people, cutting off the noses and ears of many leaders in Muscat and burning Muscat, Qalhat, Tiwi, Darsait and Julfar[3]. The Portuguese set up a trade centre in Goa on the western coast of India which later became, in the 915 AH/1509 AD, their most important base in the Indian continent. They extended their influence even further to the east, reaching the Spice Islands (Indonesia and Malaya). For the next 100 years, they managed to control 100 per cent of the spice trade with Europe, establishing strong links with the biggest trade station they ever built, in Molucca[4].

The invasion of Oman formed part of a master plan, affecting the whole region, in which economic and religious factors were interrelated. The plan was masterminded by the Portuguese commander Alfonso Pedro Albuqerque in order to destroy the Islamic presence on the eastern seas, their stated goal being to destroy the monopoly which the Arab's had gained over trade. The plan aimed to control all trade with the East through the Indian Ocean by means of controlling its exits. Within this overall strategy they were very anxious to control the Red Sea, the Straits of Molucca and the Arabian Gulf. Their intention was to redirect the Arab trade route towards the Cape of Hope. Thus, the Portuguese invasion of Oman was a major step aimed at strengthing their control over the Gulf and guaranteeing a secure source of fresh drinking water and food supplies for their bases. At the outset, it was not so easy for the Omani people to defeat the invasion. Arriving with a huge armada armed with daunting fire power, the local people were ill equipped or prepared to face the Portuguese campaign and had little chance of withstanding such aggressive and determined attacks[5].

Following their invasion of Oman in 1507, the Portuguese penetrated into the Gulf in the year 914 AH/1508 AD. Their commander, Pedro Albuqerque, invaded the Island of Hormuz, and forced the prince to pay what they referred to as a fine. In addition, the Portuguese authorities imposed an annual tax to be paid by the local people[6].

The Portuguese suspected that the Persians were determined to control Hormuz. Despite the fact that the Portuguese king was friendly with the Persian

Shah, the king's commander, Pedro Albuqerque, invaded the island for the second time, raising the Portuguese flag, and breaking the hold that its kings had enjoyed over Indian Ocean and Red Sea trade for approximately two and a half centuries[7]. The Portuguese invasion did not cease with their establishment of control over the entrance to the Arabian Gulf, they pressed on with their military attacks against the rest of the Gulf states, occupying Bahrain and the surrounding countries up to Kuwait[8]. Increasingly, however, they were challenged by the English and the Dutch.

English and Dutch Roles in Gulf Waters and their Influence on the Decline of Portuguese Power

Since the early sixteenth century and up to 1060 AH/ 1650 AD, the Portuguese were the dominant force in Oman. The Al-Ya'ruba family managed to challenge the Portuguese and expelled them from their defences in Muscat and Matrah[9]. This success resulted from the determination of the Omani people to liberate their land. In their defence of national interests the Omanis utilized the cut-throat competition between the English and the Dutch on one side and the Portuguese on the other. They became, in the first half of the seventeenth century, one of the strongest naval powers in the region, and in the entire western Indian Ocean, able to defeat and put an end to Portuguese domination.

Towards the end of the sixteenth century, England became one of the strongest naval powers in Europe. England coveted the wealth and resources of the East, and as such was in direct competition with the Portuguese[10]. *Edward Banouentour* was the first English warship to visit Zanzibar in the year 1000 AH/1591 AD. Nine years later, that visit resulted in the formation of the English East India Company[11] which was established by royal decree of 1009 AH/1600 AD. In due course the company became the prime source of trading with Europe and was closely interlinked with the British navy.

The East India Company began its activities in the Arabian Gulf region by selling English wool to Iran in exchange for silk. The Persians and the English merged their own mutual interests to attack the joint Portuguese forces. This Anglo-Persian threat reached its peak in the year 1032 AH /January 1622 AD when its attack on Hormuz[12] inflicted considerable damage on the Portuguese. The English also, this time together with the assistance of the Dutch, succeeded in eradicating Portuguese competition when an Anglo-Dutch naval fleet, consisting of eight ships defeated the Portuguese fleet near Hormuz in the year 1035 AH /1625 AD[13].

Having sailed into the Gulf and Arabian Sea for the first time at the beginning of the seventeenth century, the Dutch were already a force to be reckoned with. Following their successful joint operation with the English against the Portuguese navy near the entrance of the Gulf, they commenced their trading activities in the eastern seas. This placed them in severe competition with the Portuguese, who began to suffer from this new rivalry. As time passed Portuguese influence weakened[14].

The Dutch became Europe's most important power and played a key role in the seventeenth century decline of Portuguese influence on the eastern seafront:

a process that began with the establishment of the Dutch East Indian Company in 1011 AH /1602 AD. In a short period of time, they managed to become the main rivals to the Portuguese in the spice trade[15].

Dutch trade interests in the Indian Ocean and Arabian Gulf were not the only reason for challenging the Portuguese. The closure of the Portuguese port of Lisbon to Dutch trade, the annexation of Portugal by Spain in 988 AH /1580 AD, the attacks on Dutch ships in Europe, all these factors together with steep price increases of eastern goods by the Portuguese (especially the price of spices) were the main contributing reasons to increasing the tension and the conflict between the Dutch and the Portuguese[16]. These factors also prompted the English to cooperate with the Dutch in order to destroy Portuguese interests.

In the end, Anglo-Dutch cooperation led, during the first half of the seventeenth century, to a weakening of Portuguese influence. But neither of these powers gained similar power and influence to that which the Portuguese enjoyed during the sixteenth century. This is partly explained by the sharp increase in commercial rivalry between the English and the Dutch[17]. Opposition by the local peoples against the influence of foreign forces also contributed to the deepening conflict between the two powers.

As Portuguese influence declined quite a few countries managed to free themselves from foreign control and in 1032 AH /1622 AD the Portuguese lost Hormuz. They also lost control over the Arabian Gulf waters and the Omani Arabs took that opportunity to build up their forces with better equipment and to expel the Portuguese occupiers from their country. The establishment of the Al-Ya'ruba state in Oman in the years 1034-1157 AH/1624 -1744 AD[18] heralded the decline of Portuguese influence.

The Establishment of Al-Ya'ruba State and Imam Nasir Bin Murshid's Efforts to Unite the Country

The Al-Ya'ruba state was established in the year 1034 AH/1624 AD. Many conditions contributed to its rise including the degree of suffering resulting from political turmoil towards the end of the Nabhan era which lasted five centuries with its peak in the first three. On the eve of the fifteenth century, signs of fundamental weakness appeared, leading to a decline, the main cause of which was a division of Omani territory into small weak kingdoms. This fragmentation contributed to the state's ultimate demise. Omani archives show that Nabhan history had some glorious moments, periods of strength when some distinguished leaders ruled Oman, Falah bin Mohsen being the most famous of these[19].

A major contributing factor to the decline of the Omani state in the Nabhan era was the awarding of positions as local or regional rulers to dishonourable elements who violated the dignity and rights of the people. Justice and moral values were forgotten and a selfish spirit prevailed. The real nail in the coffin of the Nabhan state was that its people were acutely aware of the system's failure. They were looking for leaders who could bring about much needed improvements to their lives. But their rulers became increasingly oppressive towards their own people who became increasingly unhappy and frustrated. Angered by the seemingly endless bloodshed and waste of resources the Omani people elected Abu Al-Hassan bin Amer Al-Azdi as their new leader. The next Imam chosen by the people was Omar bin Al-Khattab Al-Kharousi who managed to gain Al-Nabhan wealth[20].

However, the power of Al-Nabhan had not yet fallen. Suleiman bin Suleiman bin Mudhaffar Al-Nabhani fought against Imam Omar Al-Kharousi, and Oman entered another stage of severe civil war. Mohammed bin Ismail, who had the support of the people, became Imam between 906-937 AH/1500-1530 AD. A highly respected leader, he was able to defeat Suleiman Al-Nabhani. Nevertheless, this defeat did not bring an end to the rule of Al-Nabhani. The situation deteriorated further, and the people becoming divided with each tribe following their own chieftain. A new strong leader, Imam Barakat bin Mohammed bin Ismail, rose to power, although disturbances had destabilized the whole country which was split into many smaller districts, ruled by chieftains and sheiks who were pitted against one another. The Portuguese took advantage of Oman's disarray to establish their new military base at Hormuz.

Whilst the well-organized Portuguese strengthened their positions, the Omanis became steadily weaker. Thus the Portuguese were able to establish control over the entrance to the Arabian Gulf. They occupied Sohar and Muscat, along with many other Omani ports, and became the dominant power in the Indian Ocean and the Arabian Gulf. They targeted all the Arab and Islamic forces. However, Muslims and Arab forces did not unite to face the common enemy but fought between themselves. The Ottomans attacked the Persians, succeeding in occupying their capital city. The Mamelukes joined forces with the Venetians in an attempt to defeat the Portuguese. The rest of the Arab forces in the Gulf, such as the Al-Jobour, Al-Nabhani and the Kingdom of Hormuz were engaged in their own battles, often aimed at annexation of neighbouring states. Thus, instead of uniting against the common enemy, they contributed to their own ineffectiveness. The Portuguese were the beneficiaries of this division and rivalry among the Gulf states, encountering little resistance in entering the Gulf and spreading their influence in Oman. It was the beginning of a historical period during which Oman was once more fragmented into many small weak entities. Oman's sea shores, starting from Sur, Muscat, Sohar and up to Julfar remained under Portuguese occupation.

A new era for Oman began under the leadership of Nasir bin Murshid whose efforts resulted in uniting all the Omani forces. The Portuguese on the other hand continued to occupy more Gulf territory.

Nasir bin Murshid's Efforts to Unite the Country

The beginning of the seventeenth century brought several changes to the Arabian Gulf area. First there was the establishment of the British East India Company which enjoyed considerable support and influence, managing to secure part of Portugal's maritime business, thus breaking its trading monopoly in the Arabian Gulf. The Company convinced the Persian Shah Abbas to coordinate their campaigns to expel the Portuguese from the Gulf. They succeeded in expelling the Portuguese from Hormuz in 1032 AH/1622 AD, when the Meenab Treaty was signed by both sides[21]. The expulsion of the Portuguese from Hormuz was a major turning point. The Omanis, for their part, intensified their efforts to dislodge the European forces whilst the Portuguese displayed extra vigilance in the face of the combined attacks on their vessels by British and Persian navies. Muscat was one of the Portuguese strongholds. In the second decade of the seventeenth century, the first Imam of the Al-Ya'ruba State, Nasir bin Murshid, took control and Oman now had a leader who was capable of understanding the dimensions of the problem. He possessed a real talent for political analysis, both on national and regional levels. Appreciating the magnitude of the task which he faced, he carefully evaluated all aspects of the situation. It was clear that it would not be easy to defeat the Portuguese and the problem could only be solved through a very strongly united national effort. This could only be achieved by vigorous attempts to unite the Omani tribes.

Imam Nasir bin Murshid was raised in the Rustaq area. In actual fact, he also started his struggle in this area. He and his followers went to conquer Al-Rustaq Fort where his cousin Malik bin Abi Al-A'arab Al-Ya'rubi lived and governed. Within a short time they surrounded Imam Nasir and conquered the fort[22]. Despite this success it remained clear to Imam Nasir that the enemy occupying the Omani coast was well prepared for any attack. Unless he was able to unite Oman and its people into a single fighting entity, it would be very difficult, if not impossible, to liberate the country. It was therefore unwise to declare open war against the Portuguese while the country was still divided[23]. The goal of national unity was the one thing that could prove a successful rallying cry, gaining the support of all the clans who passionately believed in the expulsion of all the Portuguese.

All the Omani archives mention the importance of Sheikh Khamis bin Said Al-Shaqsi who was very much respected by the people of Al-Rustaq. He supported Imam Nasir from the beginning in all his efforts[24], lending his assistance to the fighting forces during the course of uniting the country. Many religious and clan leaders who were also anxious to see the country united, also lent their support. So too did the Al-Yahmad clan who provided many resources and soldiers for the war effort. Such help was vital for the war of liberation and the control of the entire area of Al-Rustaq. The military leadership considered the national interest as the supreme goal, taking precedence over all others. The village of Nakhal provided one example of this great effort, against all the odds, to achieve national unity. Despite the fact that it was owned by the uncle of Imam Nasir bin Murshid, Sultan bin Abi Al-A'arab, it was the first area to be surrounded, and occupied, by Imam Nasir's forces; Abdullah bin Said Al-Shaqsi becoming its *Wali*[25].

The war between Imam Nasir and some of the local chieftains was characterized from the beginning by swift and severe fighting. This decisive action helped to foster a belief in both the importance and achievability of unity. The people supported Imam Nasir's leadership and followed his orders. The movement for national unity took on such fervour that many chieftains competed in supporting Imam Nasir since the greater their loyalty to him, the stronger they became. They were each looking for the day when they could defeat their common enemy and become victorious. Imam Nasir's just campaign for national liberation and unity brought great victories to his people. When the inhabitants of Nizwa, a most important strategic centre, asked Imam Nasir to unite with them he went to the town and discovered that some of its leaders were not so happy with such a union and went so far as to openly declare war against him. He returned to Al-Rustaq and a few days later, a delegation from Sama'il, led by its leader Mani' bin Sanan Al-Umairi, declared their allegiance to Imam Nasir. Since Nizwa remained a strategic priority in Imam Nasir's plans, he left Sama'il to return to the Al-Rustaq region, taking control of those areas that supported his leadership.

These campaigns revealed one vital element in that it became clear that it was the aim of Imam Nasir to prevent any bloodshed. He was, therefore, using his wisdom and diplomatic skills to convince the nearby chieftains and kings to accept the union along with him. He did not resort to war unless it was imposed on him and unless it was necessary for the interests of the entire people. His great victories would have been impossible without the support of most of the clans, especially when he went to conquer Nizwa. He was such a humane leader, that he did not kill his opposition if they agreed to leave their land [26] in Aqar. They became refugees in Sama'il which was under the control of Mani' bin Sanan. Mani' gave his assurance to Imam Nasir that he would not fight him, but later events proved that he was not prepared to keep his promise and was looking for any opportunity to harm Imam Nasir. In the expectation that the war could be prolonged, Imam Nasir would regularly assign one of his followers to be in charge of each recently conquered fort or small area before he carried on to subdue another area and his planned mission was implemented. By strict adherence to this rigorous policy, he attained great influence. A just man, he drew many people to work under his leadership[27].

Imam Nasir's mission was complicated by the fact that so many small kingdoms were established on a tribal basis. It was very difficult to differentiate between a clan and the government[28]. Rule was in the hands of the chieftains who gave themselves titles of king or prince without any historical justification. The concept of a central unified, nation-state was not accepted by the clans at that time. Nizwa's importance to Imam Nasir's central plan caused him to consolidate his victory, waiting for a considerable period before continuing with his campaign. He was also keen to prevent any further bloodshed, hoping, with some justification, that other chieftains would accept his leadership peacefully. Indeed, the inhabitants of Manah, Samad Ash'Shan, Ibra and all Al-Sharqia accepted his call. All except Sur and Quriyat which were now under Portuguese occupation[29].

The striking element of Imam Nasir's strategy was that he would wait for some time following the conquering of a new area. His aim in this was to give an opportunity to other chieftains to join him. It also provided an opportunity to regroup and reorganize his troops and to improve and consolidate his control over each newly conquered region. It was a wise policy with great benefits on all levels. However, despite all these efforts, Imam Nasir was faced with rebellion from the Al-Dhahira area.

This rebellion reached the point where Imam Nasir's enemies set out to kill him. Calling upon all his loyal clans, he appointed Sheikh Khamis bin Ruwaishid to lead his troops. The ensuing battle was a particularly fierce one in which Ja'id bin Murshid (brother of Imam Nasir) was killed[30]. Omani documents show that the Al-Dhahira rebellion was the most serious situation ever faced by Imam Nasir: many of his soldiers were killed, while some of his clan's supporters withdrew from the battle following a pre-emptive attack by Al-Dhahiran forces. Imam Nasir decided to take over command of the battle-field, leading his forces by himself. He succeeded in bringing the situation under control and gave a considerable boost to his army's morale. They fought very bravely, especially at Ibri, Husn Al-Fubbi and all of Al-Dhahira. Proof emerged that the conspiracies of Nasir bin Qutn were behind the rebellion: Nasir bin Qutn himself surrendered following the fall of his fort and Imam Nasir agreed to forgive him.

The Al-Dhahira situation settled down but Al-Jobour were afraid of the continuous growth of Imam Nasir's state and felt extremely threatened by him. They influenced some of the clans in the area and tried to unite as many tribes as possible to fight Imam Nasir[31]. However, the Imam became aware that Al-Jobour were planning to assassinate him. A conspiracy was also planned by some clans who declared war against Imam Nasir resulting in the bloodiest battle ever fought by him against his enemies. Al-Jobour's forces were defeated and a great number of their soldiers were killed. Al-Azkawi described the battle as follows: 'a large number of the enemy's soldiers were killed, they were not even able to bury them. They put seven or eight bodies together in one grave'[32].

Following Imam Nasir's defeat of Al-Jobour he adopted a new policy leading to the conclusion of the war. He sent out a few brigades to engage in skirmishes against some of the rival clans while the major battle was under preparation, directed towards another area. This policy was followed, especially as Imam Nasir came nearer to gaining overall control of Oman. Under the command of Mohammed bin Ghassan Al-Nazwi, he dispatched troops towards Al-Jaw near Al-Buraimi, then to Liwa village where Al-Jobour were living. Al-Jobour attacked Imam Nasir's army whenever they found the smallest opportunity[33].

Controlling the Al-Jaw area was a relatively easy operation compared to Liwa which proved to be much more difficult. Imam Nasir had great difficulty conquering it because it was so well protected. Mohammed bin Ghassan Al-Nazwi demanded the support of the clans near Sohar who were seeking victory for Imam Nasir's forces, and planning for a major battle against the Portuguese in Sohar. Liwa was defeated after one week's siege. Sohar then became the next most practical objective.

Imam Nasir bin Murshid, in 1059 AH/1649 AD, was able to unite Oman and protect it, to a large extent, against foreign attacks. His mission to unite the country provided the inspiration that the country was seeking[34]. Confronted by major, seemingly intractible, problems on both fronts (i.e the coastal region and the interior of the country), by the time of his death, in 1059 AH /April 1649 AD, this most unique of all the Ya'ruba Imams, had succeeded in uniting the Omani clans under a single flag. His era was the richest and most colourful throughout the period of Al-Ya'ruba rule and his work in the interests of national unity provided a foundation for every victory achieved later on against the Portuguese.

As we have seen, from 1034 AH /1624 AD until the death of Imam Nasir bin Murshid in 1059 AH/1649 AD, Oman lived through severe civil wars, but the period of conflict had now ended and a new stage of unity began under the leadership of a central government. The period wherein Oman was partitioned into tiny kingdoms under the leadership of weak kings was thus also brought to a close. The divisional leaders had not taken their responsibilities for the well-being of their people seriously, hence their states were weak and their efforts were not directed towards the well-being, unity and strength of their country. Imam Nasir bin Murshid made the utmost effort, and the ultimte sacrifice, in his epic struggle to unite the country. His great contribution is still considered as a vital part of the heroic struggle that helped to create the Oman of today.

The Role Of Al-Ya'ruba in the Defeat of Portuguese Influence in Oman and East Africa

Imam Nasir bin Murshid achieved national unity, but the final elimination of the Portuguese on the Omani coastline demanded more and better resources than he had available to him during his own life. The conventional methods used by Al-Ya'ruba to bring an end to the civil wars were insufficient to defeat the Portuguese. Imam Nasir bin Murshid's battles for national unity had been land-based. However, the Portuguese controlled the seas, fighting naval battles. Their ships were impressively designed and built, drawing upon experiences gained from their voyages of discovery. Their colonial policy thus depended primarily upon the occupation of many coastal cities, forts and defences and they did not venture far into the interior because they were unable to provide sufficient soldiers to do so.

Al-Ya'ruba understood their enemy's ability when they considered the skills and resources they needed to sail all the way to Oman from Europe. Oman was a maritime nation that engaged in fierce battles in order to sustain its position. The Al-Ya'ruba utilized their naval fleet in order to protect their economic interests and built vessels for both commercial and military fleets, copying designs and technologies of the most advanced countries at that time. They learnt a lot from the British East India Company, establishing very good relations with it long before their interests clashed[35]. Indeed, Imam Nasir bin Murshid's naval fleet defeated all the local rival forces before he turned to fight the Portuguese, pursuing his efforts until the final liberation of Sur and Quriyat which took place under the leadership of his cousin, Sultan bin Saif Al-Ya'ruba[36].

The liberation of Sur and Quriyat was by no means an easy task, the imbalance between the two conflicting forces was quite considerable. National unity was still a long way from being achieved. The burden of expelling the Portuguese was so heavy that it necessitated better coordination and under-standing. By 1622 the Portuguese had recovered from their expulsion from Hormuz and the clans were engaged in bitter in-fighting in a bloody civil war. Rapprochment between the Portuguese and the British East India Company introduced a new political situation. From early 1044 AH/1634 AD[37], this new found friendship strengthened, leading to closer cooperation between Britain and Portugal, especially following the Portuguese independence from Spain in 1050 AH/1640 AD[38].

International and local political factors thus forced the Omani people to suffer under unfavourable and brutal conditions. Their success in achieving national unity, combined with their religious belief, provided the strength for them to carry on in their struggle. They were willing to sacrifice lives and wealth for the sake of defeating the Portuguese, a characteristic that was lacking among the Portuguese who hid behind their defences within the Omani ports. Any researcher into the struggle of Al-Ya'ruba against the Portuguese will realize the importance of national unity as a religious and political issue. That was exactly what Imam Nasir bin Murshid had believed in, and struggled to achieve. As a divided nation, conflicts and hatred reached such a level that they harmed the country and lowered its high sense of values, all for the sake of personal gain. Imam Nasir bin Murshid was deeply conscious of this fact. He believed that the cornerstone for any significant achievement lay in national unity. Without this, all efforts would count for nothing and the people would find themselves in complete disarray. As a result of pursuing such an honest policy, the internal situation strengthened considerably and Imam Nasir bin Murshid's forces regained the upper hand in their struggle against the Portuguese along the coastal regions.

Sohar formed a central plank of Al-Ya'ruba's strategic policy. They besieged the city, while the Portuguese remained within their defences and forts. The Portuguese responded with intensive cannon fire directed at the Omani positions. The situation developed into a prolonged siege causing Imam Nasir to construct his own fort opposite the Portuguese one.

From the year 1050 AH/1640 AD, Imam Nasir bin Murshid's policy of national unity began to bear fruit. Thus, when news of the siege of Sohar reached the clans, they encouraged their young people to join in the construction of the new fort. The people of Liwa, Bat and the whole area around Sohar answered the call for help in the construction of the castle. A brigade led by Khamis bin Said Al-Shaqsi arrived in Muscat by order from Imam Nasr[39]. While the Omani people laid siege to Sohar, the brigade engaged in fighting with the Portuguese and disturbed their plans in both Sohar and Muscat. Such operations helped to prepare a series of very effective offensives against all the Portuguese defences[40].

In 1053 AH/1643 AD, Imam Nasir bin Murshid seized the city of Sohar and completed the fortress in front of the Portuguese castle. A certain amount of support was provided by the British, who supplied a number of modern vessels, ammunition and gunpowder, assisting them in their military offensives against the Portuguese bases[41]. British assistance to Oman did not, however, match the Portuguese capabilities, but when the British signed the Treaty of Meenab in 1032 AH /1622 AD, they provided the Persians with huge supplies for the liberation of Hormuz. Al-Ya'ruba fought their war under different circumstances, relying primarily on their own resources, with no outside help. The Omani people intensified their struggle following Portugal's independence from Spain[42].

The Anglo-Omani relationship did not bear fruit during the reign of Imam Nasir bin Murshid, but during the rule of Imam Saif bin Sultan that relationship improved dramatically. We cannot agree with the suggestion that the English played a major role in the Omani-Portuguese conflict. This was proposed by a European academic, Boxer, who concluded that the English were sympathetic to the Omani struggle against the Portuguese, basing his assumption on the religious conflicts that existed between the English and the Portuguese. He also stated that the monopolistic policies pursued by the Portuguese were against the interests of the British East India Company[43]. Another researcher into the history of the Gulf, put forward an opposite view, pointing out that the English were very upset by the increased power of Oman. Such power was considered to be against their future interests[44]. The agreement signed by England and Portugal, in their treaty of 1072 AH /1661 AD tends to support this latter conclusion[45].

It was illogical that the English would stand side by side with the Omanis, while they knew that Omani power was against their interests. Commercial operations of the British East India Company weakened the Portuguese grip on trade. This created an opportunity for Al-Ya'ruba to double their own military and trading activities and to gain a competitive edge. They also improved their ships through contact with the English, Dutch and even with Portuguese ships. Omani naval development, no doubt, was a cause of concern to the English. Mr Branguin the representative of the British East India Company in Bandar Abbas, expressed his worries by saying: 'The Omanis will be disastrous to India, in the same way as the Algerians were to Europe' [46]. In addition, relations between the English and Al-Ya'ruba deteriorated with the English ships becoming targets for Al-Ya'ruba vessels. The Governor of Madras wrote to the Company head office asking for more ships and soldiers to confront the Omani attacks[47].

It is important, in this regard, to ask one question. If Al-Ya'ruba became a threat to the English, then why did the English not challenge them? The answer to this question would seem to be that the English were preoccupied with establishing their influence in India. They were also engaged in the War of Devolution against Spain. By the end of the seventeenth century, the Omani naval forces reached such strength that the idea of opposing it was fraught with danger. Al-Ya'ruba's struggle against their competitors persisted for a considerable period during which a range of different political attitudes prevailed. The most difficult and dangerous time was the era of Imam Nasir bin Murshid who fought for strong national unity, and he spent a great deal of time and energy in achieving it. He utilized all available resources in an efficient manner, including political dialogue. Such policies were employed in 1058 AH /31 October 1648 AD. By the time of his death[48], the number of areas under Portuguese control had diminished to Muscat, Matrah and a fortress in Sohar[49]. Imam Nasir tried to recapture these two cities, sending out an army under the command of Massoud bin Ramadhan to liberate them. He managed to reach Matrah and besiege it, while an epidemic of the plague hit the area, terrifying the Portuguese[50].

The siege did not, however, result in the liberation of Muscat and Matrah, but instead led to a cease-fire and an agreement which was, for the most part, in Oman's favour[51]. The signing of this agreement was a test of power for the two parties with the Omanis realizing how weak the Portuguese had become. In the meantime, Imam Nasir bin Murshid needed time to evaluate the situation and regroup his forces.

On the other hand, the Portuguese had felt a sense of relief, especially since they had signed an agreement with the English, even though they had engaged in a war with the Dutch[52]. The Omani people believed that they were close to liberating their country from 140 years of occupation. By the time of Imam Nasir bin Murshid's death, the Omani people were close to their final goal.

Plan of Muscat dated 1669 taken from the Dutch Work Alam Al-Arabi *(The Arab World), Leiden University Library.*

Their struggle and sacrifice had reached Julfar (Ras al-Khaimah). The Portuguese occupied one of its forts, whilst the Persians, under the leadership of Nasrud'deen Al-Farisi, occupied a second one[53].

Omani historical documents state that Nasud'deen Al-Farisi cooperated with the enemies of Imam Nasir bin Murshid and this led to the Al-Ya'ruba plan to liberate Julfar. Ali bin Ahmed mounted a campaign based on a surprise attack and a quick siege. As a result of this strategy, the defenders of Julfar were not able to respond promptly. Omani forces strengthened their attacks and the Portuguese, in turn, wanted to seek safety at their fort in Muscat. Consequently, all opposition forces began to collapse in face of the Al-Ya'ruba onslaught. After each victorious mission, another front was opened to more victories.

Following the death of Imam Nasir bin Murshid, in 1059 AH/April 1649, Sultan bin Saif, who supported Imam Nasir, took up the banner of *jihad*. He was a very experienced commander who had led military operations under the guidance of Imam Nasir. He frequently visited Muscat in order to collect the taxes which were owed by the Portuguese. Sultan bin Saif was thus a natural nominee for the succession and the country desperately needed a new leader who would continue the progress which was started by Imam Nasir bin Murshid. As the new Imam, Sultan bin Saif set about making preparations for the final offensive to destroy the Portuguese. He realized that timing was the most important factor in the final assault. He also knew that the size of the Portuguese garrison had been reduced, owing to demands on manpower for the Portuguese campaign in India[54]. The Portuguese mistakenly believed that the death of Imam Nasir would bring an end to Omani attacks against them in Muscat and Matrah. Within a few days Sultan bin Saif departed for Tawy-er-Rula, near Matrah, where he pitched camp as the main base for the major offensive against the Portuguese. The Portuguese entrenched themselves inside their forts and behind the defensive barricades, aiming their cannons in all directions. They were quite well prepared, with a defensive moat around the high walls and watch towers in the mountains overlooking Muscat and Matrah. From these towers, the Portuguese launched heavy fire at the Omani forces[55].

The war was fought on nearly equal footing. The Omanis were unable to enter Muscat or Matrah whilst the Portuguese were unable to counter the Omanis. Both armies used hit-and-run tactics. The war was prolonged, and Sultan bin Saif became frustrated and contemplated stopping the siege, especially when some of the clans decided to withdraw their troops. Then an unexpected occurrence altered the course of events. Arabs from the outskirts of

Muscat[56] gave Imam Sultan bin Saif a very crucial tip-off which enabled Imam Sultan to enter the city. The new intelligence described the true situation inside the city, especially at the end of 1059 AH/December 1649 AD which was the time of Christmas and the New Year. It was observed that Portuguese vigilance was at its lowest at this time, and there was little awareness of the enemy.

Arab observers were able to by-pass the security guards and enter the city of Muscat[57]. They saw everything, and brought back their detailed information to Imam Sultan bin Saif. The Imam's forces promptly occupied Al-Jilali fort where the Portuguese surrendered[58]. A similar situation arose in Matrah and the Portuguese were left with only two ships. They were covering Muscat, but the Omanis eventually managed to capture both of them. By the time that the Portuguese received news of the defeat it was too late. A large naval fleet from India arrived when it was all over and the Portuguese garrisons and forts had been surrendered to the Omanis[59]. The Portuguese suffered many casualties, the majority of their soldiers being killed and the Indian-based attempt to save Muscat came to nothing. By the end of 1063 AH/1652 AD, all that was left of the Portuguese in the Gulf was their representative on the East Coast.

The Portuguese did not lose hope in recapturing Oman's coastline. They brought more support to their centre in Kanj and they opened negotiatations with the Persians in order to obtain permission to establish a trade centre on Hanjam Island. Persian terms were excessive, and the Portuguese promptly rejected the Persian offer[60]. Lorimer's view of this Portuguese rejection was that he believed that the Portuguese main interest lay in taking the Arabian shores. They did not try to negotiate with the Arabs in this regards[61].

The Omanis in the meantime, continued to chase the Portuguese, even to their refuge at their trading post in Kanj. They chased the Portuguese up to India and East Africa. Trade routes between the trade centres at Kanj, East Africa and India thus became very difficult for the Portuguese to operate under this Omani control. The Portuguese, therefore, decided to withdraw from Kanj for good[62], marking their departure from Oman and the Gulf.

The expulsion of the Portuguese from the Gulf was regarded as another high point in the heroic struggles of Oman's history. Not only did the Omanis manage to attack the Portuguese on their own shores but also in the Indian Ocean: in the water and on the land. The Portuguese centres in India suffered tremendously from the Omani strikes. Bombay in 1072 AH /1661 AD, Dio in the years 1079 AH/1668 AD, 1081 AH/1670 AD and 1086 AH/1676 AD. The battles stretched up to the western Indian Ocean, where the Portuguese and the Omanis engaged in bloody battles for the control of East Africa[63]. The people of Zanzibar had close religious and family ties with the Omanis and asked Sultan bin Saif to assist them in expelling the Portuguese from their country. However, the Portuguese did not immediately retreat from Zanzibar.

Upon Sultan bin Saif's death his son succeeded to the leadership of Oman and established Oman's naval force. This controlled all the East African shores, so that from Mombasa up to Kilwa fell under Omani control. In 1110 AH/1698 AD, the Omanis conquered Mombasa and then entered Pemba, Zanzibar, Patta and Kilwa. Mozambique was the only country that resisted the Omani Arab fleet, and it stayed under Portuguese control until the twentieth century[64].

The Portuguese tried unsuccessfully to recapture the lost naval centres. In

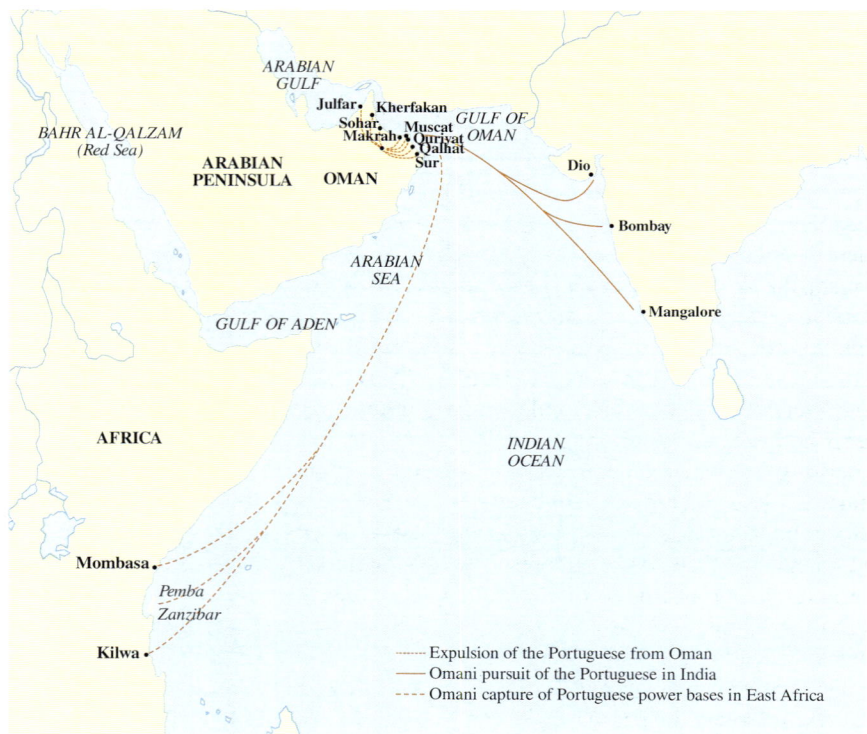

Expulsion of the Portuguese from Oman
Omani pursuit of the Portuguese in India
Omani capture of Portuguese power bases in East Africa

1142 AH /1729 AD, they attacked Zanzibar and Muscat in one coordinated campaign. But the Portuguese had now been defeated once and for all. Their hope of returning to the Arabian Gulf and the Indian Ocean was dashed yet again[65]. Omani influence extended from the south of the Arabian peninsula and East African shores in the west, up to the shores of the Sind Valley to the east.

During this period Muscat became the main entrepôt of the Arabian Gulf and one of the most important ports in the entire region. Its influence reached the central African lakes on the western side and extended to Kinj Delta[66]. Oman itself rose as the new power to replace Portuguese domination. Omani ships patrolled in search of the enemy's ships in the Arabian Gulf and the Indian Ocean[67] causing English and Dutch ships to increase their defences against the Arabs of Oman[68]. The British Ambassador, resident at that time 1106 AH/1694 AD in Bandar Abbas, expressed his fears of the growing forces in Oman: 'They will prove to be a big disaster in India, just like the Algerians in Europe'[69].

The Safawi rulers had pointed to the superiority of the Omanis during this period. They wrote a memorandum to the French government stating that: 'they [the Omanis] enjoy an important geographical location which allows them to control the Gulf, and this explains why the Omani forces, with more than 30 boats, could capture so much booty'[70].

The Al-Ya'ruba victories caused considerable upset to the Persians who were looking for control of the Gulf in order to take the place of the defeated Portuguese. This is why, on many occasions, the Omanis confronted the Persians and defeated them. Persian trade suffered greatly and so they attempted to obtain support from the European powers. Their aim was to eliminate Omani competition and so they asked the English to help them to achieve this goal[71]. However, the English did not respond positively to the Persian request because they were worried that their economic interests would be marginalized.

During the reign of Louis XIV, Persia approached France culminating in a treaty signed in 1119 AH/1707 AD. This treaty contained some secret aspects. The French, for example, promised the Persians that they would help them if they invaded Muscat. In fact the French, much the same as the English, were unhappy with what might happen to their economic interests if they helped the Persians. Despite the intense diplomatic efforts carried out by the Persians together with the signing of a new treaty with France in 1127 AH/1715 AD, the Afghan invasion of Persia in 1135 AH/1722 AD resulted in turmoil in Persia. The French decided not to implement the treaty which had been signed a few years before the Afghan invasion.

Portugal reached the conclusion that the period of Arab weakness was at an end. All their attempts to defeat Al-Ya'ruba had failed. If they continued to pursue present policies, then they stood to lose all their bases and influence on the Indian and East African shores. They attempted a military collusion with the Persians in an attempt to defeat Al-Ya'ruba. Sultan bin Saif had already realized the danger of this new situation. This is why he moved very quickly to attack the Portuguese and defeat them.

He divided his naval fleet into two, each going in a different direction; one to East Africa where he succeeded in conquering Mombasa in 1110 AH/ 1698 AD. It was the first stage towards control of the Green Isle and Kilwa[72]. The second part of the fleet headed towards India and managed to destroy the Portuguese commission in Mangalore on the Indian shore[73]. The fall of Mombasa, at the hands of Al-Ya'ruba, was considered to be a great step in the history of Islam. It was a well known fact that the presence of the Portuguese in East Africa and India allowed them to spread their Catholic beliefs. The influence of Al-Ya'ruba not only put an end to the spread of Catholicism but also forced the Portuguese to leave all the shores of north Delgado. Al-Ya'ruba, therefore, succeeded in ending Portuguese domination and influence. Their strategic centres on the African and Indian shores were eliminated by Al-Ya'ruba.

The English historian Coupland mentions that in the early eighteenth century the Omani naval fleet had reached its zenith. Their naval force was superior to all others in the region and was successful in many campaigns. The English and Dutch fleets did their best to avoid any contact with the Omani navy. Whether they were European traders or those from the Arabian Gulf and the Indian Ocean, all respected the Omani forces[74].

In 1130 AH/1718 AD, during the reign of Sultan bin Saif the Second, Oman succeeded in creating well-balanced international relations. These were reflected in the respect shown by Europeans towards Oman's sovereignty. Many European countries sought friendly relations with Oman. The economic success of Al-Ya'ruba state combined with its naval strength were part of the natural development of the state's power and formidable influence in all the eastern seas. Unity of the Omani people and their role in commercial development created the conditions of economic security, under the shadow of justice and dignity. Al-Ya'ruba achieved these successes following the collapse of Portuguese influence and the breakdown of their trade monopoly in the region.

It is important to explain the reasons behind the fall of Portuguese influence in Oman and the Arabian Gulf. The following are the main causes of Portugal's demise in the Gulf:

- Portuguese imperialism depended on military bases to protect the route between India and Portugal. However, the Portuguese did not penetrate deeply into their colonial territories since they lacked the necessary manpower and their Empire was so vast that they were unable to protect the whole area. To maintain a strong Empire, they were dependent upon sustaining a very strong naval fleet. When their naval force weakened, they lost everything.

- The first wave of Portuguese imperialism was fuelled by a thirst for invasion of other countries in order to exploit their wealth. They did not face strong resistance and were soon joined by many other European powers such as Britain, Holland and France which entered the race with the Portuguese for the booty that was to be gleaned. In their turn, the Portuguese were overwhelmed by the competition and thus lost the trade battle.

- The Omanis benefited from the favourable international situation. Cut-throat competition between the Portuguese on the one hand, and the Persians, English and Dutch on the other, contributed to the weakening of the Portuguese. Most of the European powers wanted to expel the Portuguese from the Gulf. The Omanis thus found themselves in a very good position to attack the Portuguese, and to defeat them.

- The Portuguese followed a vicious and oppressive policy in dealing with the people of their colonies. They exploited the wealth and resources of these countries, resulting in a determination by the inhabitants to rid themselves of their domination.

- The Omanis gained great confidence, especially after the establishment of a strong naval force. They realized that the battle between them and the Portuguese would be at sea. This was the real reason behind the preparation and organization of a strong naval fleet. They trained a large number of naval forces which enabled them to destroy the strongest Portuguese bases in the Gulf and the Indian Ocean.

- Imam Nasir bin Murshid pioneered the unity of the Omani people. Without this unity, the country's supreme interests could not be attained. In order to reach his objective, Imam Nasir engaged in bloody wars against all those who opposed the unity of the country, as described above.

- The Omanis devoted considerable attention to their agricultural sector as a vital element in their overall policy. They established and developed a drainage system and introduced a variety of crops and plants from East Africa which helped to support the economy.

- Al-Ya'ruba developed commerce and resisted the kind of trade monopoly pursued by the Portuguese. Arabian Gulf trade became part of the international trade movement leading to significant economic advancement for Oman.

- The Arabic and Islamic cultures were rooted in the hearts of the Omanis.

They loved their heritage which enhanced national values and helped to expel the enemy. As we have seen, many factors assisted in the elimination of the Portuguese. Whether Portuguese influence was in Oman or on East African shores or the Indian Ocean, the Omanis, during the reign of Al-Ya'ruba, were the main movers in the elimination of Portuguese domination which had lasted for up to one and a half centuries.

Having considered the reasons for Portugal's demise in the region, we should also understand the significance of the expulsion of the Portuguese from Oman. The entire region has enjoyed the benefits derived from forcing the Portuguese to leave the area.

These results can be summarized as follows:

- Oman's success in being the sole force to drive the Portuguese out from its territory boosted national morale. The Omanis learnt where their strengths lay and what they were capable of achieving. Furthermore, they participated in naval activities across the Gulf, especially from the middle of the seventeenth century up to the end of the second half of the nineteenth century.
- The Omanis embraced the principles of free trade by rejecting Portuguese monopolistic policies. Oman's economy began to rapidly expand, resulting in a growth of its influence and power in the region and in East Africa.
- The Persians were very keen to supplant the role of the Portuguese in the region and dreamed of becoming the masters of the Gulf. The British helped the Persians for a number of reasons, primarily because of the interests of the British East India Company in Persia. The second reason was that the Persians helped the British to defeat the Dutch in the Gulf. In addition, the Arabs did not form any Arab organizations, which could have engaged in direct relations with the British. But then the Persians received the support of the imperial powers who were hoping to colonize the Gulf and they entered the battle against the Omanis.
- The Portuguese community in Oman, and in the Arabian Gulf in general, helped the Arab powers to assert their control over the Gulf[75]. Such leadership became very clear in the eighteenth century.
- On the eve of the expulsion of the Portuguese from the Gulf, many political groupings emerged on the western shores of the Gulf. The Utoob and their branches appeared in Kuwait, Qatar and Bahrain.

So many changes followed the departure of the Portuguese from the Gulf. National unity, which was achieved by the pioneers of Al-Ya'ruba, became the cornerstone of the great victory. Many achievements occurred during the reign of early Al-Ya'ruba and their subsequent Imams. The first of them was Bal'arab bin Sultan bin Saif.

Imam Bal'arab bin Sultan [76]:

In 1091 AH/mid- December 1680 AD, Imam Bal'arab bin Sultan was inaugurated. His declared policy was *pro patria*. He built the city of Jibrin and constructed its drainage system. Land was reclaimed and the famous Jibrin fortress was constructed with great engineering skill. Imam Bal'arab chose the fortress as his office and residence, at the same time building a school within the defense complex to teach science and general knowledge.

The first few years of Imam Bal'arab's reign were marked by a continuation of the stability and growth experienced under his father's Imam Sultan bin Saif's, rule. Imam Bal'arab maintained the country and the state as it was under his father, continuing with the mission of construction and development. Towards the end of his rule, his brother Saif bin Sultan, demanded his resignation. Following that demand, divisive weakening factors began to take their toll on the country. Things began to deteriorate, especially in the manner of choosing the country's Imam during Al-Ya'ruba reign. The Omani people suffered greatly from the conflict between the elected Imam and his brother Saif. The latter opposed the Imam who left Nizwa and went towards the north[77]. After some time, Imam Bal'arab returned to Nizwa but found that the people who had begun to support his brother Saif bin Sultan prevented him from entering the city. He then went to Jibrin where Saif had laid siege to his fortress. The chieftains realized that the Imam was unable to deal with his brother. Accepting the status quo they inaugurated Saif bin Sultan bin Saif bin Malik who became the Imam following the death of his brother Imam Bal'arab bin Sultan. The new Imam followed the path of his predecessors and fought the Portuguese in East Africa and India.

Omani historical documents show that this inauguration was instigated to prevent any serious threat to the state. The people were afraid that Imam Saif might retaliate if they opposed his inauguration. Following his accession to power, Imam Saif took control of all Oman's fortresses and castles. Only Jibrin fortress, where Imam Bal'arab lived, refused to surrender. Imam Saif bombarded the fortress and all his attempts to break down its defences failed. The Imam's soldiers fought very bravely and killed many of the attackers. The chieftains and the advisors decided to mediate between the two brothers, demanding that the two brothers resign if they wanted to stop the bloodshed. However, Imam Bal'arab and his brother refused to stop the fighting and the chieftains warned both of them that if the siege continued, they would return to their own regions. The conflict continued, however, until the death of Imam Bal'arab in the year 1104 AH/1692 AD, when Imam Saif bin Sultan gained power and control over the whole land.

Imam Saif bin Sultan (known as *Qayd Al Arth* or Bond of Earth):

His full name was Saif bin Sultan bin Saif bin Malik. Following the death of his brother, he was officially installed as leader and pursued the policies of his predecessors. Some Omani documents point out that after the death of Imam Bal'arab, Saif's inauguration was reconfirmed. The religious leaders forgave him for fighting his brother. Sheikh Al-Salimi thought that the first inauguration was not valid because he rejected the recognition of his brother's leadership. Whilst continuing on the path set by previous Al-Ya'ruba Imams, Imam Saif managed also to improve on policy and continued to fight against the Portuguese in East Africa and India. He made considerable strides in strengthening the army and naval fleet and developed strong military strength to fight the Portuguese and any foreign power that opposed him.

One of the historical documents mentions that his army contained 90,000 horses when it entered India. The number of ships within the Omani naval fleet exceeded 100. The most famous ships of that fleet were *Al-Falak*, *Al-Malik* and *Ka'b Raas*. The big ships were equipped with 78 cannons, whilst the smaller ships contained only eight to ten cannons. With such a great force, Imam Saif took control of the Green Isle and Patta in East Africa, expelling the Portuguese from those areas.

Imam Saif established major infrastructural projects in Oman, including several new *falajs*. More than fifteen *falajs* were established, such as Falaj Al Barakah and Falaj Al Bazeeli in Al-Dhahira, Falaj Al-Hazm and the Falajs of Ja'lan Bani bu Hassan. He also deepened many *falajs*. In addition, Iman Saif improved the agricultural sector and increased crop production such as wheat and barley. He was directly involved in supervising some of the agricultural processes, and also extended vegetable and sugar cane production. He planted a large number of date trees, mango and other fruit trees, as well as perfume plants, plants such as saffron and *wars* (a local plant used to colour clothes), whilst honey bees were introduced for the first time. The state owned a large area of well developed agricultural land by which national revenues achieved a great economic boost.

Imam Saif bin Sultan died during Ramadhan in 1123 AH/1711 AD. Under his influence Oman accomplished the greatest period of stability in its history. The country extended its borders beyond the Arabian peninsula. It also owned a great military force, one that was stronger than that of any of the European powers who were active in the region. The Omani forces regained strength similar to those of earlier Arab-Islamic forces. Imam Saif bin Sultan therefore, was called *Qayd Al-Aarth*, or Earth's bond. This expression means that the Imam had to protect the state property, both inside and outside the state owned lands. With such a system, the welfare of the people and stability were improved dramatically. Following the death of Imam Saif bin Sultan, his son, Sultan bin Saif was inaugurated.

Imam Sultan bin Saif the Second

His full name was Sultan bin Imam Saif bin Imam Sultan bin Saif bin Malik bin Abi Al-A'arab Al-Ya'rubi and he was inaugurated in 1123 AH /1711 AD, following the death of his father. The religious leaders forgave him for having rejected the decision to inaugurate his brother as the Imam. They suggested that they would not make any final decision, no matter how minor, or what issue was involved, until the religious leader pronounced his decision. He accepted those conditions and served his country and people extremely well. He constructed the Al-Hazm fort and moved the capital there. His move to Al-Hazm was not intended to copy his predecessors but had strategic connotations, linked to Persian expansionary policies in the Gulf. The Persians were making an effort to pick up the pieces that had been dropped by the Portuguese and were thus keen to restrict Omani influence in the area. Al-Hazm, commanding a strategic position between the coast and interior, was a stronghold for Imam Sultan and a frontline defensive position to protect Oman and the region in general.

The Liberation of Bahrain

One of Imam Sultan bin Saif the Second's most significant achievements was the liberation of Bahrain from the Persians who were in occupation of the island. In order to achieve this, he first strengthened his grip on the islands at the entrance to the Gulf, sending reinforcements to the islands of Larg, Al Qeshm and Hormuz. He also maintained a tight grip on some of the important Persian citie,s such as Lingeh and Bandar Abbas, and organized a large contingent led by Al-Sheikh Hamyar bin Saif bin Majed. Following their arrival in Bahrain a fierce battle took place, marked by gruesome scenes and heavy mortalities but bringing to an end the Persian presence in Bahrain and thus curtailing their influence in the Gulf. In Bahrain, Imam Sultan constructed the greatest fort ever built in the area: A'arad fort. Prior to his death, the Omani presence reached out through the Arabian Gulf, to Indian shores and as far as East Africa; even to some Arab countries on the Red Sea which fell under Omani influence.

Imam Sultan died in his Al-Hazm fortress in 1131 AH/1718 AD, after more than seven years of great achievement. His death was a disaster for national unity, the state of Al-Ya'ruba, and the general public.

The End of Al-Ya'ruba State and the Split in National Unity

Following Sultan bin Saif the Second's death (in 1131 AH/ 1718 AD) Oman entered a stage of decline with population divided into two camps. Al-Ya'ruba and the general public wanted Saif bin Sultan to be inaugurated even though he was still a young boy, while on the other side, the religious leaders were in favour of Muhanna bin Sultan bin Majed Al-Ya'rubi[78] who was trusted by the dead Imam, and was also his son-in-law. Sheikh Al-Salimi described him as follows: 'He was the right man to be the Imam, and even though his knowledge was not so deep, he was willing to learn and asked questions, and did not decide on any important issue until after he had consulted with the religious leaders'[79].

The general public had been impressed by the unique personality of Sultan bin Saif but his son, Saif, was not the right man to be inaugurated as the Imam since he was too young to lead prayers. Given these difficult circumstances one was bound to ask how this boy could become the Imam of Muslims? But many people were not prepared to heed their religious leaders' advice. Instead they gathered in crowds, brandishing their weapons and declaring their loyalty to the youngster. Wishing to prevent bloodshed, religious leaders felt that they could solve the problem by inaugurating a different Imam.

The religious clerics did not openly support Muhanna bin Sultan. The judge Adi bin Suleiman Ath'Thuhli suggested a compromise, but in actual fact, it was a hidden conspiracy. Bringing the young boy (Saif) before a huge Muslim crowd, the judge declared: 'Saif bin Sultan is in front of you'[80]. Given such a regal demonstration, the announcement was interpreted by the people to mean 'the boy will be your Imam!'. This calmed a very tense atmosphere and left the religious clerics with the view that they had the power to decide who should be the Imam. A meeting was held with Muhanna bin Sultan at Al-Rustaq fort together with many chieftains and leaders and, in the same year as the death of his father-in-law, Imam Sultan bin Saif, in 1131 AH/1718 AD, Muhanna was declared as the true Imam.

Imam Muhanna did his best to satisfy the religious leaders, not issuing any decree without thorough consultation with them. He focussed on development of the economic sector, establishing a new trade policy in which Muscat became a tax-free port where customs tariffs were abolished. Trade and business doubled, which naturally led to an economic boom but the regime was short-lived with a new rebellion brewing. After only one year of his reign, the people of Al-Rustaq and Al-Ya'ruba demonstrated their resentment at the *fait accompli* with which they had been presented.

Ya'rub bin Imam Bal'arab bin Sultan led the protestors and secretly entered Muscat. The governor, Sheikh Massaoud bin Mohammed Al-Sarmi Al-Riyami, and perhaps Ya'rub, were in secret collusion with the people of Muscat. At that time, Imam Muhanna was in Al-Bazeeli at Al-Dhahira, outside the capital where he was told about the new development and the presence of Ya'rub in Muscat. Returning to Al-Rustaq, enroute to Muscat, with the intention of expelling Ya'rub from the city, he was met with little support from the people. Moreover, many of them raised their weapons against him. When Imam Muhanna realized that most of the people had betrayed him, he wanted to leave Al-Rustaq fort without fighting, asking them to spare his life and the lives of those with him in the fort. However, his opponents captured him while on his way out of the fort, tied him up together with his followers and one of his cousins and then murdered them in a brutal fashion. In this tragic way, in 1133 AH/1721 AD, Imam Muhanna lost his life and ended his reign.

Ya'rub was very cavalier in his approach, breaking his promises and going back on his word with regard to saving the life of Imam Muhanna and his followers. Religious clerics and the clan leaders denounced his notorious behaviour, considering him an unjust ruler and hated oppressor. Matters had gone too far for Ya'rub to command the real loyalty of the highly respected religious leaders and the chieftains. Ya'rub requested their forgiveness, and sought their support, but to no avail. Judge Adi Bin Suleiman Ath'Thuhli came to the rescue of Ya'rub who defended himself during the case which had been presented before the court. He justified his action by saying that it was legitimate to resist Imam Muhanna since he believed that the young Saif bin Sultan had the right to inherit the Imam's position.

Ya'rub decided that he would prevent any bloodshed taking place if anyone other than Saif bin Sultan was inaugurated. To unite the nation, he decided to move swiftly and implement his plan. According to the historian Al-Salimi, writing in 1134 AH/1721 AD[81], Judge Adi accepted the reasoning of Ya'rub and decided to dismiss the case against him, offering forgiveness. Sheikh Al-Salimi pointed out that his assertion was supported by the fact that the religious leaders inaugurated Ya'rub as the rightful Imam. On the other hand, Sheikh bin Razik said that Ya'rub was not the Imam. The right Imam was Saif bin Sultan, but Ya'rub took the position as Imam, because Saif bin Sultan was still a child[82]. It seems clear that, in view of Saif's age, Ya'rub was his trustee. Following his conferring as the Imam he settled in the city of Nizwa.

The religious leaders now found themselves in an awkward situation since the entire people of Al-Rustaq refused to accept Ya'rub, either as Imam, or as trustee. Finally, they wrote to Bal'arab bin Nasir (Saif bin Sultan's uncle) and expressed their wish for Saif bin Sultan to be their Imam. This was behind all the attempts to dismiss Ya'rub Bal'arab. A bloody power struggle was underway during which Bal'arab bin Nasir forced all the opposing clans to respect and confer Saif as their Imam. However, this was not the end of it since the conflict deepened further, with the nation being split between supporters of Ya'rub bin Bal'arab and those who demanded that Bal'arab bin Nasir should be the only trustee to Saif bin Sultan.

It was the beginning of a prolonged period of instability in Oman. The people were divided into two camps: the Hinawi and Ghafiri, with a tribal split following the same pattern. Mohammed bin Nasir Al-Ghafiri, chieftain of the Al-Ghafiri, was inaugurated as the Imam of Oman and fought Ya'rub bin Nasir in the name of Saif bin Sultan. During a fierce battle at Sohar, Mohammed bin Nasir Al-Ghafiri was mortally wounded. Saif bin Sultan finally achieved his majority, and in 1140 AH/1727 AD was inaugurated as the only Imam. Much was expected of Saif bin Sultan, who was now a strong youth who had lived through difficult times before reaching maturity.

These traumatic events had caused division within the country with many people taking the wrong direction. Saif bin Sultan became a symbol of hope for the population when he was inaugurated and assumed the job of Imam. They loved him and looked forward to a very long time with him as their leader. Unfortunately, however, Saif bin Sultan proved to be a bitter disappointment because he lacked real power and was unable to fulfill the role of a statesman who could unite the people and create national stability. During his period, Al-Ya'ruba fragmented and indulged in internecine clashes like never before[83]. Oman's history books describe how the new Imam ignored his duties behaving in a manner that was not in keeping with his position. Many Omanis protested against his poor conduct and the religious leaders were the first to oppose him, withdrawing their support and isolating him. Finally, they nominated Bal'arab bin Hamyar in 1145 AH/1732 AD as the new Imam[84].

The Persian Invasion of Oman

Saif bin Sultan was removed from his office and replaced by Bal'arab bin Hamyar. Saif appealed for help to the Baluchis of Makran, and with their help he fought Bal'arab who defeated him. He officially requested Nadir Shah, the Persian king, to send an army to help fight his rivals. Nadir Shah was the first Persian ruler to build a naval force in the Arabian Gulf, led by the commander Latif Khan. This commander was very anxious to control the Arabian shores of the Gulf and was ready to send his army to invade Oman and keep it under Persian government control[85].

Nadir Shah accepted Saif's invitation and organized a naval force and directed the army to occupy Oman. He made considerble preparations for his mission to invade Oman, supervising all the preparations and organizing a team to study the geography and topography of the region, in order to provide all the necessary information to the Persian forces. Nadir Shah's intention was to invade Oman and Bahrain and put them under the complete control of Persia and then to dominate the entire Gulf region[86].

In 1150 AH /14 March 1737 AD, Latif Khan, set sail with his Persian forces for Oman in a fleet comprising four huge ships, two middle-sized ships and many other small ships and boats. Saif bin Sultan discovered later, that these forces did not invade Oman to assist him, but to put Oman under Persian domination. During this time, some of the clans' chieftains mediated between Saif bin Sultan and Bal'arab bin Hamyar. The condition for this mediation was that Bal'arab should resign his post in favour of Saif for the sake of putting an end to the bloodshed and saving Oman from the Persian occupation[87].

For the second time, Saif bin Sultan became the Imam of Oman. He assigned Sheikh Ahmed bin Said Al-Busaidi (the founder of Al-Busaidi state) as a governor of Sohar. Saif bin Sultan, again misused his position and did not follow the Islamic Shari'a. The Muslim leaders wanted him to resign and replace him with Sultan bin Murshid Al Ya'rubi as a new Imam in 1154 AH/1741 AD. Saif bin Sultan did not accept their ruling and again asked the Persians to send their army to assist him. Saif promised the Persians that he would recognize their domination of Oman if they sent him the military assistance he required. The Persian commander Mohammed Taqi Khan agreed to send more military support from Iran, in return for Saif bin Sultan's recognition of Persian dominance and for duties and taxes payable to Persia if they helped him to sustain his grip on power in Oman[88].

Saif bin Sultan trusted the Persians when they said that they were assisting him in the first place. In actual fact, they arrived in Oman to achieve their dream of expansion and control of the entire region.

Saif bin Sultan had called on the Persians to intervene against his own people[89] and the Omanis lost their trust in him: all except some of his followers. Imam Sultan bin Murshid headed to Sohar, to stand side by side with its Governor Ahmed bin Said Al-Busaidi, to fight Nadir Shah's forces.

For over one century Oman had enjoyed considerable economic growth and prosperity under the leadership of the Al-Ya'ruba family. But the exploits of the recent leaders, combined with their misconduct, helped to put an end to the state. Imam Sultan bin Murshid died at Sohar fortress as a result of injuries incurred in battle alongside Ahmed bin Said against the Persians. The deposed Saif bin Sultan, died shortly after the death of Imam Sultan.

Saif blamed himself for the criminal acts he had committed and realized that the Persians had not come to assist him, but to occupy Oman. He was very saddened by what he did but it was too late to admit his faults. Ahmed bin Said was left to continue the fight against the Persians while they besieged Sohar and Muscat[90].

The Persians besieged Sohar for nine months but Ahmed bin Said, its governor, succeeded in resisting the invaders in spite of their supplies being almost exhausted. Persian forces bombarded the city day and night with heavy cannons[91]. In 1155 AH/July 1742 AD, Ahmed bin Said, losing hope of any supplies being delivered to him by the Omani clans, was forced to sign a cease-fire agreement between the two parties: i.e. the Persians and the Omanis. Some local and foreign documents considered this agreement to be a surrender to Persia, but in reality it was a victory for the Omanis. Ahmed bin Said signed this agreement for the following reasons:

- To stop the spilling of Muslim blood: mainly because ammunition, food and all other necessary supplies ceased to reach the forces.
- In preparation for the reorganization of the fighting forces to be ready for the next confrontation and for the final push to liberation.
- The death of Imam Sultan bin Murshid had created a vacuum in the leadership; Ahmed bin Said found that Al-Ya'ruba family would not be able to run the state and he was very worried that a family feud would occur as a result of this political vacuum at the same time as he was fighting the Persians.
- To reunite the Omani cities and provinces which became semi-states and tiny Emirates[92] since he wanted to face the Persians as one strong united front.

Ahmed bin Said strengthened his position and guaranteed the support of the Omani clans. In addition to this, the Persian government officially recognized him as the governor of Oman when he became the main signatory of this treaty. In this way, Ahmed bin Said became the supreme leader of the liberation movement against the Persians. The Omani sheikhs felt that the situation in Oman had deteriorated and needed a very strong Imam to unite the country, especially since the Ibadhi belief did not allow more than one Imam for the state.

Following the death of Saif bin Sultan, many of the Omani leaders tried to revive the Al-Ya'ruba state. The sheikhs and Omani chiefs assembled together in Nizwa and decided, in 1157 AH/1744 AD, to inaugurate Bal'arab bin Hamyar Al-Ya'rubi. Many Omani cities announced their support to the new Imam, including Bahla, Nizwa and Izki, in contrast to other cities that abstained from accepting the new Imam. There was however little time for this Imam to consolidate his position since before long most Omanis had deserted him[93].

Due to these events, Ahmed bin Said's star rose very high. All the chieftains and the Omani clan leaders supported him since they all sought the liberation of their country from the invaders and were very anxious to establish peace and prosperity[94].

As far as Persian-Omani relationships were concerned Saif bin Sultan's death created some difficulties for the Persians since he was their ally. Internal events in Persia also interceded, causing the government of Nadir Shah to withdraw some of their forces from Oman in order to face some of the problems within their own country. This helped Ahmed bin Said, who was a first class politician, to achieve his ambitions. Although the Omanis felt very uneasy with the support offered to the Persians, they realized in the end that efforts were being made behind the scenes to liberate the country from the Persians. Ahmed bin Said was finally inaugurated in 1157 AH/1744 AD, following the liberation of Oman. Humaid bin Mohammed bin Ruzaiq had this to say: 'When Ahmed bin Said became the Imam of Oman, and the people were hoping for the best, a new twist in the situation occurred. In 1157 AH/1744 AD, the chiefs of Oman and the people of Ar-Rustaq decided to inaugurate Abi Hilal the great Imam Ahmed bin Said bin Mohammed Al-Busaidi Al-Azadi Al-Omani Al-Istiqami of the Ibadhi sect[95].

The inauguration of Imam Ahmed bin Mohammed bin Said Al-Busaidi, on the downfall of the Al-Ya'ruba state (which had been established under similar circumstances by Nasir bin Murshid in 1034 AH/1624 AD) marked the birth of the Al-Busaidi state.

Omani Naval Supremacy and Its Effect on Foreign Affairs in the Epoch of the Ya'ruba

The Omani Navy During the Era of the Ya'ruba

At the beginning of the sixteenth century the Portuguese empire had begun to diversify its naval strike-force in the east, both in respect of its awesome range – from the coast of Portugal to Calicut on the western coast of India – and its mastery of the most powerful and intrepid fleets.

Two Arabian states – the Ya'ruba in Oman and the Sa'di Sherifs of Marrakesh – were fated to dream of putting an end to that great imperial force. Certainly, the British historian Robert Landen was right when he made a connection between the collapse of Portuguese influence in the Gulf and the mortal blow which befell them in *Wadi al-Makhazin* in August 1578[96].

If there is one strategic feature by which the Ya'ruba state was distinguished then it certainly was as a naval power, since geographical location, a constant factor in the making of history, combined to make it a natural focus of such power.

Al-Ya'ruba's inclination towards the sea was a strategic necessity since their lands were bounded by the Arabian Gulf to the north, the Arabian Sea to the south, the Gulf of Oman to the east and the vast Empty Quarter desert to the west. The desert was always a constant immutable presence to the rear, playing a background role in the story of Oman, whereas the sea was very much to the forefront, forming and fundamentally underlining every aspect of Omani history.

The Imams of Al-Ya'ruba, whether at the height of the dynasty's power or even at its weakest times, were able to focus on the essence of Omani history, the conjunction of sea and dry land, grasping the danger and importance of their location. It is striking that life in the shadow of such danger is not necessarily evil, rather it is often reckoned to be a healthy phenomenon. From early on the element of danger sharpened the national consciousness, increasing national and religious vigilance, as well as removing any possiblity of obscurity or ignorance of the external world.

The Ya'ruba were fully aware that a dangereous enemy lurked in ambush for Oman ready to push it mercilessly towards the desert because in Oman lay the root of power and the key to the region. Throughout this strategic struggle certain fundamental invariables were established, defining a dynasty which perfected the art of balancing between all competing powers in the Gulf, or setting them to contend with one another; that took the form of Oman's forging alliances with one of the rival states against the threat of another state.

As a result of all these considerations the Ya'ruba plunged into the life of the sea, became inextricably linked with it, and succeeded to a tremendous degree in forming a powerful naval force which was able to extend its influence across the eastern seas, so that the Omani navy towards the end of the seventeenth century had become the dominant power in the Indian Ocean[97].

In particular, the Ya'ruba realized the importance of developing their ships. The coasts of Oman were always renowned for ship-building, however, the Ya'ruba were not content with local ships such as the *Huri*, the *Baghlah* and the *Sambuq*. Instead they made many improvements, taking advantage of the tremendous progress which had overtaken European ships. A decade or two into the sixteenth century the Omanis took to building their ships in Malabar with nails, from where they were transmitted to Europe. The Omanis retained the lateen sail, resembling the fins of a fish.

Generally, most of the battles which the Omanis embarked on against the Portuguese during the era of Nasir bin Murshid took place on land with the aim of liberating the cities and coastal areas of Oman. Modern research based on Portuguese and Dutch documents highlight Nasir bin Murshid's desire to control Oman's foreign trade[98].

Apparently, the Omani navy were not completely in control until after the liberation of Muscat, when the Omani fleet took to pursuing the Portuguese navy along the Indian and African coasts. At the same time, following diplomatic negotiations between Sultan bin Saif and the English and Dutch, the Omanis were able to replenish stores, gunpowder and provisions. For that reason, the Portuguese suffered crushing defeats during their attempts to reconquer Muscat, the most important occasion being the attempt of 1652. The Portuguese suffered other setbacks at that time, particularly when they lost a convoy of merchant ships in a storm while it was *en route f*rom Malabar to the north. At the same time rumours circulated that the Dutch had made an alliance with the Imam Sultan bin Saif and that they were collecting taxes on shipping in the Gulf on his behalf. Even though these rumours were false, they do indicate that commercial society in the Gulf had grasped the extent of Oman's ambition to take the place of the Portuguese, and the probability of European support for those ambitions[99].

It is interesting that as soon as Imam Sultan bin Saif succeeded in liberating Muscat in 1649 the Omani navy hurried to launch even more fierce attacks on Portuguese strongholds in India in order to throw the Portuguese defences into confusion. The period 1650–52 witnessed much Omani naval activity which disturbed the Dutch and the English. This cannot be explained only in terms of Sultan bin Saif's ambitions for the navy, it seems also to have been based on Imam Nasir bin Murshid's assumption that it was essential for the fleet to reach this strength, which had already taken it a decade or two to achieve. Apparently, the use of modern European ships, whether through purchase or hire, was the significant new factor in the reign of Imam Sultan[100].

Important developments in the Omani navy at this time were as follows: complete reliance on modern ships and the employment of highly developed cannons with the same capacity as European cannons; the use of huge ships on the European model, some of which were built in India and others bought from the Dutch after the Ya'ruba had benefited economically from repeated attacks on Portuguese positions in India. Bombay was the chief focus of incessant attacks by the Ya'ruba who levied customs duties reckoned at 17.5 per cent on many regions, e.g. Goa, Briyalore, Mitfaloo, and Batikaloo, which gave them abundant returns. This they used in the development of their ships and in the acquisition of the most modern weapons, which had not existed in any great abundance in the era of the Imam Nasir bin Murshid[101].

Remarkable economic development took place in the era of Sultan bin Saif, trade blossomed and new naval strength facilitated the establishment of fortresses and fortifications in Nizwa, Jibrin, Al-Rustaq and Al-Hazm which compelled the Dutch to try to improve their relationship with the Omanis. The Dutch director (Hendrick Van) sent a letter from Bandar Abbas to the Imam of Oman in 1665 proposing co-operation against the Portuguese and the establishment of a centre for the Dutch Company in Muscat[102].

The Imam Sultan bin Saif responded positively to this communication by establishing commercial and economic co-operation and the Company undertook to study the possibility of creating a centre in Muscat. However it appears that Persia exerted considerable pressure with the aim of preventing Dutch-Omani co-operation. Indeed Persia actually contemplated occupying Muscat with the help of the Dutch, a move which Holland rejected, preferring not to get entangled in military actions against the Ya'ruba who were fortunate to have a great measure of respect in Dutch circles.

As the English historian Coupland confirms, by this stage Oman's naval strength had become so strong, in the Indian Ocean as well as the Gulf, that the English and Dutch fleets were in fear of it[103].

A Dutch mission undertook in 1666 to visit a number of Arabian cities. According to the report of this mission which was particularly interested in military fortifications: 'Muscat is a city surrounded by walls upon which are cannons firmly fixed and pointed towards the Gulf, and in which there are three fortresses close to the coast. On the eastern side of the city there is a fortress called *Maughubalwan*, and on the western side a fortress (Muscat) joined to which at the base of the mountain there is a citadel in which there are stone steps leading to the fortress. At the foot of the mountain there are two citadels one of which is called 'Saint Anthony'. There are between eight and nine lookout posts on the mountain'.

Omani naval development was to a striking degree, throughout the second half of the seventeenth century, a practical realization of the economic growth enjoyed by Omanis during this period. The end of the Portuguese presence in Oman is considered to be the actual end of the policy of monopoly which had afflicted the Arabian Gulf and the Indian Ocean since the beginning of the sixteenth century and from which the decline in the movement of commerce sprang. Some foreign sources intimate that it was not possible that such amazing naval progress by Oman could spring from ships manufactured in Oman alone, or even as a result of craft bought from the English and the Dutch; there were certainly other souces: Surat in India was an essential centre for manufacturing the ships which the Omanis used; others were constructed in Nahr as-Sind (the river of Sind), still others were built in places which were unknown to the English and the Dutch[104].

Apparently it was not an easy matter for the Omani fleet to reach the strength at which European ships were intimidated and the process absorbed a tremendous amount of time and effort. Finance was a primary inhibiting factor, as was internal unrest which would surface even when the state was at its most powerful.

According to a contemporary Dutch report from the time of Sultan bin Saif, i.e. 1674, the Portuguese fleet executed a manoeuvre close to Muscat. The report records that Omani preparations to repulse this manoeuvre consisted of the mustering of three or four large square-sailed ships, two sailing-ships, and nine or ten small ships. The total firepower of all these ships amounted to 90-95 cannons, the majority of which were light gauge. The report records that the Omanis did not have a permanent navy to man these ships: they called on sailors from fishing vessels and from some merchant navy vessels when they needed them, in addition to a number of Baluchis upon whom they were completely dependent as able soldiers and crew[105].

Wilmsohn compiled this report on behalf of the Dutch Company when it entrusted him with the task of visiting Oman and studying possible areas of economic co-operation. Wilmsohn was utterly amazed at the Omanis' lack of permanent naval crews, for during times of peace the sailors would turn to the practice of their trades and when duty called they went off to their military duties. This was completely the opposite of what happened on European ships which had crews committed to working on them exclusively whatever the situation. Perhaps that doubled the difficulty of the task which the Ya'ruba had undertaken, as they built with one hand and carried weapons in the other, a phenomenon unknown to Europeans.

Another source of astonishment for the Europeans was the contrast between the equipment and the gauge of the cannon on the Omani and Portuguese ships, for the Portuguese ships were more modern and their cannons were of a larger gauge. In spite of that the Omanis with their modest capabilities were more daring and self-sacrificing than their Portuguese opposites.

This was possibly a consequence of the sincere motives with which the Omanis fought, since struggle for their religion and homeland was a path to victory or martyrdom, noble motives in an era in which religion was a fundamental force among ordinary people as well as governments. This was in contrast to the Portuguese forces who were deceived by the Papacy and with whose lives and destinies the governments of Portugal traded.

Imam Sultan bin Saif (1648–79), through extraordinary skill, expelled the Portuguese from Muscat and pursued them along the coasts of India and Persia, inflicting crushing defeats on them, whilst succeeding at the same time in making an economic and commercial haven of Oman. The port of Muscat became the centre of trade in the Arabian Gulf and the Indian Ocean, similar to a free zone where ships arriving from the Yemen, East Africa and the coasts of India could anchor, their merchandise transported to Hasa, Bahrain, Qatar and Basra. Dates, coffee, cotton textiles and rice were basically the backbone of that commerce. According to an independent report, Muscat was the most important commercial city in the region. The same report confirms that the security engendered by Sultan bin Saif's rule was one of the main reasons for the Omani success[106].

With the death of Sultan bin Saif[107] his son Bal'arab bin Sultan bin Saif was appointed to the Imamate. He preferred not to stay in the capital Nizwa and transferred his residence to Jibrin where the remains of his uniquely-constructed fortress can be seen today. Some European accounts mention that his full-brother Saif rose in rebellion against him in 1689. Those accounts ascribed the disagreement between the two brothers to Bal'arab's aversion to war and his undertaking to make treaties – whose conditions were unfair to the Omanis – with the Portuguese. Bal'arab allowed them to open an agency in Muscat, granted the head of the agency a salary from the Imam himself, and built a fortress for them in Khasab when they requested it, in exchange for a welcome for Omani ships visiting Portuguese ports in India and a committment by the Portuguese to pay customs duties in Muscat. Saif bin Sultan conducted the front-line of opposition by rejecting co-operation with the Portuguese and he occupied the fortresses of Muscat and Jibrin and gained control over the situation to his own advantage after the death of his brother Bal'arab[108].

No mention is made of the cause of this conflict between Bal'arab and his brother Saif. However, Bal'arab was a man who loved peace and rejected war. It is said that he encouraged scholars and poets and he showered them with gifts[109].

Numerous contemporary testimonies and historical accounts describe Omani naval strength during the era of Saif bin Sultan, so much so that Bruce wrote: 'The strength of the Arabs in Muscat with respect to defences and manpower was tremendous. It was to such a degree as to terrify the Europeans. Every indication assures us that they will come to control all of the Gulf'[110]. Dr Freyer, who visited the Gulf in the time of Saif bin Sultan, mentions that the Omanis had gained awesome naval capacities and that their naval activities threatened Bandar Abbas to such an extent that the Persians asked the English navy to remain to protect the city and they agreed to their request. These events led to Captain Brandon[111] forecasting that the Omanis would become a plague in India as the North Africans had been in Europe[112].

The last decade of the seventeenth century witnessed ten desperate Portuguese attempts to place their foot firmly in the Gulf. In 1690 they tried to make contractual agreements with the government of Basra; however they were not very pleased with the results. In the following year they tried to prepare an expedition to support the Persians in an attack on Muscat, but the Persians gave up and changed their minds about the agreement. They tried to occupy Hormuz and to establish secure ties with the Persians but the English and the Dutch frustrated the attempts. In 1695 they themselves tried to occupy Hormuz but the Omani fleet counteracted them and scattered their attempts[113].

Lockyer mentions, in a detailed description of Muscat which he had visited: 'I saw an Arab crew in the port of Muscat and learnt that they were Omanis. I saw one of the Omani ships and it was equipped with approximately 70 cannons and guns. I learnt that the smallest ship was equipped with about 20 cannons and guns. I knew that the Omani fleet had undertaken to capture one of the richest ships of Calcutta which was under the command of Captain Murvill and, in spite of the actions of the Omani fleet against the English ships, the English companies which owned these ships did not undertake any contrary action against the Omani Arabs'[114].

The Omanis believed that the Portuguese presence along the coast of Persia was a direct challenge to Oman. For that reason in 1695 an Omani fleet arrived at Bandar Kanj and took possession of the Persian and Portuguese ships anchored in the port. Oman's primary aim was to not to make Muscat a pivot of local commerce in the Gulf and to curtail the role of Bandar Kanj; in fact the Omanis believed that a Persian-Portuguese treaty would entail a Portuguese attempt to control Muscat, which was what had motivated Saif bin Sultan to take the initiative and attack, regarding attack as the best means of defence.

The Portuguese were convinced of the importance of co-operation with Persia, particularly after the Omani attacks on Bandar Kanj. The immediate result was that the Omanis divided their fleet into two sections, one of which sailed to the African coast to destroy the Portuguese settlement in Mombasa, and the second set off and destroyed the Portuguese agency in Mangalore on the Indian coast. The Portuguese attributed the Ya'ruba's victories over them to the weapons and support which they received from the English in Bombay, also claiming that most of the Omani ships were under the command of English officers and that they flew the English flag[115].

The truth is that the Portuguese administration tried to spread this popaganda, but its authenticity was never established whether on the part of the English or the Dutch, nor throughout this period do writings of foreign explorers allude to it. In addition, the English fleet itself was a target of the Omani navy and there were many clashes between the two fleets both in the time of Sultan bin Saif and the time of Saif bin Sultan.

In spite of the fact that the Portuguese fleet had greater capabilities, the Omanis relied on the element of surprise and comprehensive military planning. They would watch the movement of their enemy extremely minutely and eagerly.

Throughout the last years of the seventeenth century the Persians made desperate efforts to create a Dutch-Persian fleet which would attack Oman. Because the Shah, the Dutch claimed, was preoccupied to a considerable extent (with his wives) and his excuses were illogical, the Dutch disregarded this arrangement, from which derives the noticeable decline in Dutch-Persian relations. The Persians were therefore eager to strengthen their relations with the Portuguese at the beginning of the eighteenth century, seeking their support in an attack on Oman. In fact, six ships reached Persia, and it would appear that the Persians played down the significance of this assistance. These ships suffered from many difficulties because many of their sailors were forced to retire[116].

Most sources dealing with the Gulf's history during this period agree that with the ending of the seventeenth century, more particularly beginning in the year 1694, Iman Saif bin Sultan was active in waging war on the Portuguese in the Indian Ocean where he attacked the seat of the Portuguese in Baseen as he also attacked the coast of Gujurat and the port of Bombay. The biggest battle was at the island of Salist where the Omani forces became involved in a violent struggle with the Portuguese defences and inflicted a defeat on them which threw the Portuguese into confusion[117].

On the coast of East Africa, the greatest victory which the Omanis achieved was their success in overthrowing the Fort of Jesus in Mombasa in 1698 and, following that, their command of Pemba, Kilwa and Zanzibar, until they completely expelled the Portuguese from all their bases to the north of Mozambique and this region became one of Oman's dependencies[118].

In our opinion, what helped the Ya'ruba to achieve this naval supremacy was that the policies of the European states during the period which followed the decline of Portuguese control were not based on the politics of commercial monopoly as the the Portuguese had been, instead they turned their attention to the foundation of commercial companies, the establishment of colonies and the creation of empires. In the commercial field, there was now room for local elements, which had long been active, to work in the shadow of new mutual competition until the powers were alerted to the significance of this course of action. Intent on securing their lines of communication with India, they entered into relationships with those local powers and these relationships were not to their benefit[119]

The fact is that European explorers and chroniclers were particularly concerned about the remarkable supremacy which the Omani navy had attained during the eras of Sultan bin Saif and Saif bin Sultan and they set out to discover the factors which had helped the Omani navy attain this degree of power. Some mention that the Imams of the Ya'ruba were able, thanks to their friendship with some of the rulers of India, to guarantee the imports of timber needed to build ships. The Ya'ruba concluded a number of treaties with the ruler of the Bajwa region of India; perhaps that is what drove John Malcom to believe that the best way of putting an end to Omani naval power was to cut the link between Oman and the rulers of India[120].

The full extent of Omani naval strength reached in the era of Al-Ya'ruba can be gleaned from the writings of Hamilton in which he discusses the Omani navy and mentions that it was composed of hundreds of big ships with different gauges of large and small cannon[121].

The explorer Fraser added that: 'It is imperative that we do not provoke the Omanis since we will gain nothing after that but blows meted out to us'[122]. Just as the explorer Bruce wrote about the events of the year 1695 that 'the Arabs of Oman will gain the leadership and authority in the Arabian Gulf', similarly Colomb discussed the supremacy which the Omani navy had reached during the era of Al-Ya'ruba[123].

Even if some of these writings have a measure of exaggeration they still reflect to a great degree the enormous power which the Omani navy had attained, and which had contributed to a great degree to the international balance of power not only in the Arabian Gulf but also in the Indian Ocean. The English historian Coupland reports that the Omani navy at the beginning of the eighteenth century had come to excel every other naval power to such a degree that the English and Dutch fleets were afraid to confront the Omanis. It is sufficient to say that this fleet was able to bring all of these successful operations to fruition and to fill European hearts with terror whether in the Gulf or in the Indian Ocean. Coupland expressed his astonishment at the superiority which the Omanis achieved[124].

Miles said that effectively leadership of the Indian Ocean had gone to Al-Ya'ruba and their ships had come to strike terror into the Europeans for a century and a half[125].

Many European sources treat the subject of Omani naval activity during the era of Al-Ya'ruba as if it was a type of piracy, completely neglecting those deviant actions and inhuman practices which the Portuguese committed in the seas of the East. It seems likely that this bias is due to the European powers' complete failure to acknowledge Arabian political administration in the Gulf and their refusal to apply the term 'state' to them. For that reason these sources did not distinguish between the collective opposition of Al-Ya'ruba who were endeavouring to retain their dominance in the area and between those who practised individual acts of piracy. It is striking that piracy is counted as a patriotic act if it was committed by the Europeans, but if it was committed by the Arabs or the Muslims then it become piracy for the purpose of plunder and spoils.

England indulged in naval operations of a piratical nature when it commissioned naval adventurers such as Cavendish, Francis Drake and others to practise piracy against Spain – and the astonishing thing is that these pirates were honoured by Queen Elizabeth I and granted honorific titles in consideration of their undertaking glorious national deeds. Just as the Atlantic coasts teemed with piratical operations so the Indian Ocean saw much of them. However, it was Omani naval exploits that the European states feared, not European pirates. The European states were propelled into uniting into a single bloc, in spite of the competition between them, with the aim of weakening Omani naval power. A number of treaties were signed, perhaps the most important being the treaty of 1700 between England, France and Holland which divided up the naval regions in which each had to preserve the safety of shipping. The French selected the Arabian Gulf, the Dutch chose the southern shores of the Red Sea[126], and the English the southern Indian seas. The latter is proof that the English didn't help the Omanis in their struggle with Portugal as some Portuguese sources claimed.

In the meantime although Persia was bent on inheriting the mantle of Portuguese colonial influence the Ya'ruba were taking the opportunity of internal disruptions within Persia in order to ensure their control and supremacy over the waters of the Gulf[127]. Despite Persia's boast that it was the deciding power occupying the void after the defeat of the Portuguese the Ya'ruba's opposition remained and Bandar Abbas became an Omani target.

Persia resorted to the English and Dutch for help but the English were not over-enthusiastic about the Persian proposal and the British Company did not have any desire for a military involvement in the affairs of the Gulf because of its need to use its own forces in the administration and reinforcement of its interests in the Indian sub-continent. At the same time it wanted to prevent the Dutch benefiting from the critical development of the Persian-Omani situation. Nevertheless, Muscat's trade flourished remarkably and Omani merchant ships had come to traverse the Arabian Gulf and the Indian Ocean to such an extent that the representative of the English Company in Basra wrote to the management of the Company affirming that Muscat had become the one of the most prominent local forces in the Gulf and that its ships had come to control its trade thus necessitating the creation of a British agency in Muscat[128].

At the same time Persia tried to persuade the Dutch to strike at Omani interests in the Gulf by every means possible including the occupation of Muscat. However their attempts failed and Holland itself remained aloof from involvement in military actions with no guaranteed outcome.

In Isfahan the Persians discussed the issue of Omani ambitions with the

French ambassador. France proposed that if the Persians agreed to expel the Dutch and the English from their lands then the French would attack Muscat, thereby reversing the decline in Persian trade. However, realizing that the French were not powerful enough for this mission, the Persians did not support the proposal[129].

Persia tried every conceivable method to weaken Oman and put an end to its naval power. Despite their lack of faith in the French offer, they had given up all hope in the English and the Dutch and so Persia renewed its connection with the French. Discussions ensued concerning the ratification of certain clauses of the treaty, perhaps the most important of which was that the French undertook to send a fleet to help Persia to occupy Muscat[130].

The Shah made some rather weak attempts to urge France to fulfil its promise and a Persian envoy travelled to France and met Louis XIV conveying to him the difficulties the Persians faced from the Omani navy. He implored him to fulfil the Persian-French treaty in exchange for the agreement of the Persian government to France's conquest of Muscat, since the treaty had also affirmed the commitment of Persia to find some method of expelling states competitive to France from the lands of Persia.

In August 1715 another treaty was concluded in which it was stipulated that the French were to be exempt from all duties and that there was to be no limitation on the volume of their trade. This treaty also went unratified because the Shah was unhappy that there was no reference in the text to the formation of a Persian-French alliance with the aim of occupying Muscat. The treaty was finally ratified when French ships arrived in Bandar Abbas in 1721. However, France began to reconsider the situation in the light of its own interests. Because of internal unrest in Persia and the ensuing Afghani invasion in 1722, it actively pursued a relationship with Muscat and the development of its trade with Oman.

The international situation in the region was becoming increasingly complex since the Omanis doubled their attacks on Persian coasts at the same time as the English and Dutch had become indignant at Persia because of its opportunistic stance. Oman also renewed their diplomatic efforts. Commercially, Bandar Abbas declined and all Shah Sultan Hussein could do was to revert to their arrangement with the Portuguese.

Oman benefited from the decline in the international situation in the region and began to direct severe blows against Persian interests. The Omanis launched wide-ranging attacks against Bandar Abbas, sacking the two cities and capturing Persian and Portuguese ships. The Omanis also multiplied their attacks on Bahrain which the Persians controlled, but the Omanis suffered great losses in the beginning which Dutch documents reckon at a thousand men[131].

In 1717 the Omanis repeated the attempt on Bahrain, this time seizing the fortress after a siege which lasted a month. Their forces also subjugated fortresses on the islands of Qeshm and Larg and they took control of the ports of southern Persia, thereby preventing the Persians from using the waters of the Gulf. This caused tremendous turmoil in English and Dutch circles, especially after Hormuz fell into the hands of the Omani navy. So the Dutch sent a message warning the Ya'ruba of the result of a decline in the commerce of Bandar Abbas.

In February 1718 a meeting between the Omanis and the Dutch took place in

Hormuz which had come under Omani control: the ship *Haringtuyn* had been on its way home from Batavia (Djakarta) to Bandar Abbas and when it put in its foodstuffs were exhausted. Some of its crew decided to take a small sailing boat to Larg to buy something there. One of the Omani ships called on them to stop in Hormuz believing that they were Portuguese. The crew were removed to the Omani army camp in Hormuz where they were presented to an Omani officer who received them hospitably and provided them with the water and food they needed.

That crew sent a full report to their government on this unusual event which left a favourable impression on the Dutch who preferred co-operation with the Omanis and rejected all Persian pressure aimed at weakening the Omani navy. What is interesting in this report is the detailed description of the Omani forces garrisoned on the island of Hormuz which the Dutch crew estimated at a thousand men who took turns to guard the island, in addition to the cannons mounted everywhere, manned by men of a high degree of alertness and preparedness.

Persia exhausted every means of propaganda to establish an Anglo-Persian or Dutch-Persian alliance to attack the Omani navy and finish it off. Writings of contemporaries to these events affirm the Persian efforts and the contrast of the Persian stance with the position of the Omanis who were characterized by sincerity and respect, particularly in dealings with people of other religions and the freedom to establish religious practices. Hamilton mentioned that the Arabs of Oman launched attacks against the Portuguese colonists on the Indian coasts, sacking cities and towns. However, he insisted that they did not kill defenceless people or children, and they used to treat their prisoners generously as opposed to the Portuguese who used to treat their prisoners brutally. Hamilton added that the Omanis used to grant their prisoners similar provisions to those they gave their own troops[132]

In the light of the foregoing perhaps it is appropriate to affirm a number of facts:

- The strong link between the Omanis and the sea; it is interesting to note that all of the great exploits which the Omanis carried out were successful when they made use of natural geographical factors.
- Perhaps the era of the Ya'ruba, in spite of its shortness, is one of the golden ages of Omani history. The Ya'ruba were able to make use of their long cultural heritage by virtue of the fact that their land had played a leading role in the movements of human history and that therefore through the ages they had vied for positions of power. This experience enabled them to take advantage of competition between international rivals in the Arabian Gulf and Indian Ocean as they their persisted in their attempts to liberating their territory.
- The Imams of the Ya'ruba grasped the strategic importance of the sea. They therefore set about developing their naval potential based on the tremendous advances which had taken place in the manufacture of European ships, of whatever power. They did not confine themselves to purchase or hire since they undertook to manufacture their own ships, both at home and in Indian ports, making such improvements as baffled the European powers of the time.

- The Omanis were extremely skilful at playing one international power off against the other and they gained tremendous experience in dealing with rival European powers which afforded them the opportunity of realizing their strategic aims. That was probably one of the foremost factors in their political and economic success.
- The sense of Omani national security had expanded beyond geographical limits, since the Omanis had taken to launching attacks on their enemies on the Persian coasts and in the Indian Ocean, reaching as far as East Africa which provoked both European and local powers. The Omani-Persian struggle was a natural result of this new direction in Omani politics.
- If it could be said that Omani coastal cities had recorded a glorious page in the history of Oman throughout the periods of the Portuguese-Omani struggle, then the Arabian Gulf and Indian Ocean certainly recorded numerous resplendent pages covering almost a century, proving that the Omani navy – as is confirmed by all historians – had reached such a strength that the European powers had come to fear it and avoid coming into contact with it.

Adroit Diplomacy in the Era of Al-Ya'ruba

Al-Ya'ruba grasped the importance of exploiting their traditional capabilities by means of their capacity to confront the greatest naval powers in the Arabian Gulf and the Indian Ocean. The Imam Nasir bin Murshid succeeded in creating a new class of ships with streamlined hulls, using the tremendous developments which European navies had attained, square sailed, and built with planks fixed with nails.

The capacities of Al-Ya'ruba are shown in their tremendous ability to exploit the international rivals in the seas of the east and in their grasping the importance of balanced relations with the European powers who had appeared in the Arabian Gulf during the second half of the seventeenth century.

According to some sources, Nasir bin Murshid established relations with the English in 1645. Whereas he used to impose economic strangulation on the Portuguese, he demanded that the East India Company send an envoy to negotiate. The Company commissioned Philip Wylad to travel to Sohar where he achieved the ratification of a treaty with the Imam Nasir bin Murshid which gave the English the right to freedom of trade in Muscat and the practice of their religion[133].

In spite of the fact that this treaty did not provide the results hoped for because of the growth of Dutch interests – the British East India Company could not compete at that time – yet it is counted as the practical beginning to a string of treaties of friendship and commerce which were concluded between Oman and the British East India Company.

The Ya'ruba dynasty was distinguished by the fact that they were able, with remarkable skill, to take advantage of all possibilities, both on land and at sea, forging policies with such strategic depth that Oman was destined to be the sole Arabic power in the region of the Gulf able to confront all foreign and regional ambitions.

Apparently, the Imams of the Ya'ruba perceived the challenges facing them in such a way that they took upon themselves the responsiblity of liberating all of the Arabian coasts not only from Portuguese but also from Persian influence. So in 1718 Saif bin Sultan prepared a naval campaign to liberate Bahrain from the Persians who had been dominant there there for more than a century[134]. At the point at which Anglo-Dutch rivalry reached a peak, in the middle of the seventeenth century, the Omanis were able to earn the trust of the two rival powers.

The Imams of the Ya'ruba grasped the importance of benefiting from each of the rival powers in order to realize their political and economic goals. Apparently the Imam Sultan bin Saif (1649-79) had clearly understood the need for a balance of power. For this reason, he saw no harm in promoting his relations with the English at a time in which the British East India Company were urging the importance of English co-operation. The Imam Sultan bin Saif received Colonel Rainsford in his capacity as a deputy of the Company (1659) and the negotiations resulted in the granting to the English of one of the citadels in Muscat on the condition that the number of soldiers in it should not exceed one hundred, and that the Imam should share the customs duties with the English[135].

When this treaty was not fulfilled in accordance with English aspirations in the Gulf and especially because Dutch pressures prevented its implementation, Sultan bin Saif was provided with an opportunity to change his mind and avoid the danger of relinquishing a fortress in Muscat to one of the greatest foreign powers. This was a policy which the Imams of the Ya'ruba were intent on until the end of their dynasty, in appreciation of Omani interests and avoidance of the arena of international rivalry.

One explanation for Sultan bin Saif's change of mind about implementing the treaty of 1659 was the tremendous superiority which the Dutch had attained over the English in the period 1654-84 when the Dutch wrested away most economic activity in the Gulf. The treaty of 1659 with the Omanis was basically an act against growing Dutch activities whose peak was reached in 1664 when the Dutch became the first power in trade in an important region such as Bandar Abbas.

When Dr John Freyer visited Bandar Abbas in 1677 he found that the Dutch absolutely controlled the trade in spices and had been skilfully able – which brought pressure to bear on their English opponents – to monopolize this trade to such a degree that at one time they were forced to burn four ship-loads which they owned in order to force Persian merchants to accept their prices for the cargo of the remaining two ships. Dr Freyer estimated that their exports of velvet, raw silk and Persian carpets, apart from gold and silver, each year exceeded 50,000 tuman[136].

British diplomacy had fastened on establishing strong relations with the Ya'ruba and attempting to take one of the Omani citadels as a zone of support against the threat of Dutch interests in the Gulf generally. So, it is interesting that whenever Dutch-Persian relations strengthened then the English turned to Oman in an attempt to realize a sort of balance of power, which the nature of commercial and political rivalries between the English and the Dutch required.

Generally, the refusal of the Imam Sultan bin Saif to implement the treaty of 1659 was not to blame for strained Anglo-Omani relations and in particular the

English employed methods of adroit diplomacy to safeguard their threatened interests in the region.

The British position is impossible to explain except in the light of the volume of British interests in the region, even if that did not prevent the agent of the British Company in Persia from comparing the naval activities of the Ya'ruba in the Gulf to the movement of Arabian *jihad* along the North African coast when he said, 'The Omanis will become a plague in India as the North Africans were a plague in Europe'[137].

If the British position had been defined by the nature of British interests in the region then the Omani position was also defined by the nature of the Portuguese-Omani struggle. If the Ya'ruba had realized a noted military success which was remarkable to the rival European powers then that depended on an outstanding effort of Omani diplomacy in an attempt to make use of all factors. Anglo-Omani relations in that period were viewed by the Ya'ruba as a method of deciding the struggle with the Portuguese.

Anglo-Omani relations grew strikingly in the era of Sultan bin Saif (1649-79). In the light of amicable relations between the Omanis, the Dutch and the English, the Portuguese-Omani struggle intensified and the Omanis began to pursue their enemy in the Indian Ocean and along the African and Indian coasts to such a degree that in 1694 the Imam Saif bin Sultan concentrated his military operations, exploiting his strong relations with the two rival opponents (the English and the Dutch). The Omanis succeeded in launching sudden attacks on the Portuguese in India where they attacked their base in Baseen. Similarly other Omani groups succeeded in launching comparable attacks on the coast of Gujurat and on the port of Bombay. The battle for the island of Salist was one of the most successful of these operations when the Omanis descended upon the island, engaged the Portuguese defence and inflicted a crushing defeat on them[138].

On the African coast the Omanis took the Fort of Jesus in Mombasa in 1698, and subsequently Pemba, Kilwa and Zanzibar until they were eventually able to gain complete control over all the Portuguese bases to the north of Mozambique, these regions becoming a part of the Omani possessions[139].

It is interesting that the number of Omani victories dismayed the European powers in the Arabian Gulf and the Indian Ocean to such a degree that the Portuguese were convinced that the cause of the successive Omani victories was to be found in English and Dutch military support. Not only that but the Portuguese went to even greater lengths in promulgating the unlikely claim that Omani ships flew the English flag and that English officers commanded them[140].

It may be possible to explain the Portuguese accusation in the light of the Omani capacity for transactions with the English and the Dutch, whether from the point of view of the success the Ya'ruba had in exploiting the rivalries which existed between the two of them, or their ability to ignore either side if it suited them, at other times making use of their advanced weaponry; or indeed even accentuating the mutual incompatibility which existed between the English, Dutch and Portuguese, as well as the capacity of Omani diplomacy to benefit from the tensions created by such mutual incompatibility; an opportunity they exploited just as frequently as their military operations in the Arabian Gulf and the Indian Ocean.

Boxer, one of the dependable researchers, believes that there was mutual good will between the English and the Omanis which he attributed to the fact that the English were Anglicans, unlike the Portuguese who were greatly attached to Catholicism. In addition, the Portuguese left a bad reputation behind them because of their monopolistic policies, their enthusiastic avowal of which greatly damaged British interests. Boxer adds that the English did not give a great deal of assistance to the Omanis even though some English personnel did work on the Omani fleet. However, these were individuals acting as a matter of personal choice. Their help was sought as crew for the Omanis but that was done remotely from the British East India Company and without the knowledge of the British Government[141].

Along with our respect for Boxer's viewpoint we believe that the good-will which the English showed the Omanis was a tactical good-will with the aim of furthering their political and economic interests. The English stance is best understood in the light of the turmoil which beset British circles because of the rise of Omani power. There was a treaty in 1661 between Britain and Portugal – which was crowned by the marriage of King Charles VIII (of Scotland, II of England) to Catherine of Bragança – one of whose clauses stated that the English would hand over Muscat to the Portuguese if they were ever in a position to control it. In addition to the fact that Anglo-Omani relations did not remain favourable for long – since the Omanis frequently attacked English ships, forcing their crews to participate in attacks on Portuguese bases – a report from the British East India Company in Bandar Abbas affirmed that the Omani fleet was impeding the Company's trade. The agent of the Company in Bandar Abbas acknowledged that the Omanis were hampering the commercial activities of the British Company and causing it great losses[142].

Very often confrontations took place between Omani and English fleets, for example when an English ship was sailing to Bombay and the Omani fleet blocked its way, a scuffle occurred in which 11 English sailors were killed and double that number were wounded[143].

Scuffles similar to this happened on many occasions without being ordered by the Ya'ruba Imams. Many of them occurred for reasons connected to each particular situation, but most of the ships, especially merchant ships, were not defined by any particular relationship since the Gulf and the Indian Ocean were a living arena for many ships regardless of their identity. Many sources dealing with this period note the desire of the Ya'ruba Imams not to clash with the English, yet that did not prevent clashes which aroused the resentment of the English without leading to an announcement of open hostilities. The settlement of each occurrence was accomplished in the light of the Anglo-Omani relationship of mutual understanding.

Saif bin Sultan's eagerness to avoid hostilities with English ships did not prevent Omani sailors in 1697 from forcing the English ship *London* to take part with them in one of their military operations against Portugal. The English who resisted were treated roughly, shackled and placed on the deck of one of the Omani ships[144]. When the Imam Saif learnt of this incidence he dealt harshly with the crew and announced the dispatch of compensation to the English. However, the English seized one of the Omani ships which in turn angered the

Imam Saif. He confiscated the ship *London* and challenged the English to repeat the action[145].

These circumstances provoked a reaction within British circles but relations did not deteriorate further. The English contented themselves with strengthening their fleet and resuming the restoration of their fortresses in Bombay against a repetition of the Omani attack. The English could do nothing but rely on defensive measures because of their preoccupation in India with other colonialist powers. They wished to avoid a military confrontation with the Ya'ruba at all costs.

Even though the Omanis wished to bring about balanced relations with the English they also desired to establish good relations with the Dutch who had shown considerable good-will to the Omanis during their struggle with the Portuguese, at the time when Dutch commerce was prospering which was contemporary with the liberation of Muscat from the Portuguese presence in 1650.

In appreciation of the Dutch attitude the Imam Sultan bin Saif (the First) presented a project which would facilitate the transport of goods for the Dutch across Omani lands to Basra instead of Jambarun, particularly because Shah Abbas the Second had gone to great lengths in imposing taxes on Dutch trade[146]. In spite of the improvement in Dutch relations with Persia and the revival of Jambarun as an important commercial centre for the Dutch, Dutch-Omani interests continued to improve daily.

At the same time as the Omanis liberated Muscat, Portuguese-Persian negotiations focussed on the leasing of one of the Persian bases to Portugal and the Shah offered the Portuguese the island of Hanjam[147]. However the negotiations did not reach a definite conclusion. It may be that the Portuguese preferred one of the bases on the Arabian coast to help initiate the recapture of Muscat, which the Portuguese had seriously relied on remaining in their hands. The king of Portugal had showed great seriousness (1649) about Muscat's remaining under the control of his forces and he demanded that they direct every effort to guarding and protecting it. He also demanded that Arabs should be prevented from residing there and advised his forces to establish a new port in Bandar Abbas as a starting point for the securing of Muscat[148].

It was difficult to go back and it was impossible for the Omanis to retreat from the desperate struggle to have Muscat remain free particularly as they had put everything they had into developing their strength, just at the same time as the Portuguese fleet was breathing its last.

The Italian explorer Petro Delafali noted the decline in the level of organization in the Portuguese navy and in the morale of the troops. He compared it, in spite of his good-will for his Catholic brethren, with the level of organization in the Dutch and English ships. In addition, Portuguese historians themselves summed up the factors in the collapse which afflicted Portugal in a short phrase: 'Our downfall springs from the way that our eminent people have contempt for their inferiors, and from the greed of the lower classes, a greed which blinds them to the claim which the country and glory make on them. The Portuguese can retrieve what they lose, but they are incapable of preserving it, and that is the main point'[149].

Generally, the English exulted in the disappearance of the Portuguese from the arena of competition, yet they were faced with the rivalry of the Dutch whose influence increased daily. Beginning in 1650, Dutch rivalry took to threatening the British Company's interests and in 1652-53 the Dutch sent 15 ships to Bandar Abbas whose total value was estimated at 120,000 British Guineas. They were able to sweep away English commerce in spite of the Shah's insistence on not treating them equally with the British with respect to commercial privileges.

It appears that the Dutch had succeeded in recovering their strong commercial links with Persia since the opening of the port of Bandar Abbas to Dutch ships was restored in 1664 subsequent to the meeting between the Shah and the Dutch representative in Isfahan[150].

The Omanis had succeeded in remaining neutral with respect to the Dutch with the purpose of putting an end to the Portuguese, yet Dutch-Omani relations did not go as far as an alliance, rather the reverse is true, since the Omanis felt that the Dutch were eager to go it alone and assume the mantle of the Portuguese as far as Gulf trade was concerned. They were not prepared to exchange Dutch influence for Portuguese, especially since their fleet had begun to cruise the Indian Ocean and the Arabian Gulf causing a great amount of alarm in foreign companies.

It may be that increasing good relations between the Dutch and the Persians upset the Omanis. In any case, at the end of the seventeenth century, the Omanis were making repeated attacks on Dutch ships. The Dutch began to turn their attention towards the Omanis who were also launching surprise attacks on the Persians who, in turn sought help from the Dutch.

Dutch support for the Persians in their struggle with Al-Ya'ruba did not prevent the Omanis from inflicting repeated defeats on the Persians who threatened their commercial interests in many Persian regions. This propelled the Dutch into advancing the treaty of 1705 which stipulated the protection of Persian shipping as recompense for many of the provisions which the Shah saw as unfair to his commercial interests. The Shah preferred to co-operate with the English and, in spite of all that, the Dutch remained, retaining their commercial centre in Bandar Abbas while Anglo-Persian relations began to flourish quite remarkably.

The Ya'ruba preceived that Persia wanted to advance its regional interests in the Gulf at the expense of the Omanis who alone were able to defeat the Portuguese. The matter went as far as the Persians seeking the assistance of the English or the Dutch. Persia was able to realize its objectives because the British East Indian Company considered such aid to be in the interests of the Company in Persia. In addition, the English and the Persians drew closer together in the time of Shah Abbas the Great on the basis of Persia's assistance to the English in their struggle with the Dutch.

It is interesting that although Persia was attempting to replace Portuguese colonialism in the Gulf it found itself in confrontation with the Ya'ruba who took advantage of the internal disturbances to which Persia was exposed so that they could assume for themselves control and supremacy as the price for the sacrifices they had made in their struggle with Portugal[151].

The Persians were fearful to such a degree that they sought help from the Dutch. When they were assured that they were unable to protect them they turned to the English. In 1695 the Persian government tried to persuade the

English East India Company to participate with them in attacks on Muscat in exchange for granting the English in Muscat the same concessions from which they had benefited in Bandar Abbas[152]. However, the Company was not over-enthusiastic about the Persian proposal because of its strained circumstances in India. They were also fearful of involvement in a struggle with the Omanis whose outcome was not guaranteed.

Sources dealing with this period inform us that Muscat at the end of the seventeenth century had realized such commercial and economic growth that representatives of the English East India Company in Basra, Baghdad and Bandar Abbas sent a message to the management of the Company assuring them that Muscat had become one of the most prominent local forces in the Gulf and that its ships had begun to cruise the Gulf and the Indian Ocean. Both Haford and Samuel Manister urged the Company to establish an agency in Muscat where the Company was represented by some native Omanis[153]until the start of the eighteenth century. Persia did not despair of invoking the help of the European powers in its bid to occupy Muscat. In the wake of the failure of its attempt with the English and the Dutch it decided to have recourse to France at the time of Louis XIV. A treaty, under which France would aid Persia to take Muscat in addition to numerous secret clauses, was ratified in 1708[154]. However, its execution was delayed to an appropriate time. Persia tried to exert pressure on France to begin military operations. France, for its part, found many reasons for delaying until, in 1721, Omani diplomacy was able to improve relations with France and increase trade through its colonies on the island of Mauritius. The French position was probably influenced by internal disruptions in Persia and the consequential invasion by Afghanistan in 1722, all of which totally undermined Persia's influence in the Arabian Gulf.

Having eliminated the ruling Safavid family and assumed power, Nadir Shah tried to strengthen Persia's situation in the Gulf by forming a navy, an entirely novel experience for Persia. Nadir Shah's primary aim was to finish off the power of the Ya'ruba. Circumstances in Oman during the Imamate of Saif bin Sultan the Second encouraged Persia, since internal dissension had reared its head for the first time in Oman and Nadir Shah did not hesitate to respond to the Omani Imam's request for help.

A Persian expeditionary force embarked from Bandar Abbas at the beginning of the month of April 1737 under the leadership of Latif Khan, disembarking first at Ras Al-Khaimah. During the years 1737-38 the Persians swept over all of Oman and Muscat[155]fell into their hands. Following this, the dynasty rapidly declined, a phenomenon which is not often repeated in the lives of states and dynasties.

The age of Al-Ya'ruba represents an exceptional period in Omani history with respect to the speed with which the Ya'ruba family in the space of two decades assumed power, their capacity to take advantage of the factors of success, their reuniting of the nation and their supreme capacity to resist their opponents both internally and externally. The collapse of the dynasty commenced with the same alacrity, dissension having arisen and the population having divided into opposing camps.

However, fate determined that a disciplined, extremely courageous man should emerge from the chaos, basing his opposition in the city of Sohar which was used as a symbol for the whole country, in order that the age of Al-Ya'ruba might come to an end but that Oman might remain as a vibrant country.

The Omani Presence in Africa During the Time of the Ya'ruba

If there is one particular quality which distinguishes Oman during its long history, its periods of victory and defeat alike, it is that it was a pivotal point, both in its times of expansion or regression – it was always a centre of power and the heart of a region. Certainly this essential quality – containing striking contradictions – stems originally from geographic roots which together form the history of Oman, which itself has played an active role in history of mankind.

The history of any country can only be fully appreciated through an understanding of its strategic nature, as espoused by the famous Arab geographer, Jamal Hamdan, who, when defining the strategic features of typical geographic regions, maintains that the ideal geographic situation coincides with the ideal natural place, that is, in a harmonious relationship[156].

A description of the geographic situation of Oman together with its natural setting fits, to a large extent, the essence of this analogy – for the people interact with their geographical environment in an harmonious fashion, and water and dry-land correspond with each other to form together a harmonious chain which, seen as a whole, explains all the stages of history as a precise interrelationship and as an interaction which may be measured.

Since the dawn of history, the Omanis have gone to sea and have viewed it as a means of livelihood and life itself. The monsoon trade-winds of the Indian Ocean have been an important influence in the movement of Omanis towards the coast of East Africa – for when the north-easterly trade-winds gather force in the middle of December until the end of February each year, the Omani triangular-shaped, single-sailed boats would set out on their steady journey to the African coast.

Between April and September, the south-westerly trade-winds begin to blow and propel these boats once more on the journey home – a distance of 2000 miles over the Indian Ocean. The Omani sailors and traders have made use of these winds for at least 3000 years, through long periods of history. It must be emphasized that the ground had been laid for the Omani presence in East Africa by many explorers who reached the area in the distant past, founded trading centres, established towns and interacted with the African environment: this brought Arabic and Islamic influences throughout the region from Ra's Jurdafun in the north to the Gulf of Delgado in the south – a region to which the Arabs gave the name the *Zinj* coast.

It is difficult to define precisely the beginnings of the Omani presence in East Africa although it has been established that the Ummayyad and Abbassid periods were full of vigorous Islamic activity there – confirming that a strong Arabic presence had preceded this development: the Omanis had gone there singly and in groups over long periods of time, colonization and trade continuing almost uninterrupted; with the passing of time they mixed with the Africans, married their women and established important centres of trade[157].

Historical sources indicate that important Omani emigrations resulted in settlement of the African coast during the time of Abdul Mulik bin Marwan, and the Omanis founded a number of African towns such as Malindi, Zanzibar,

Mombasa, Lamu, Kilwa and Patta[158].

With the beginning of the sixteenth century, because of the political situation in Oman and especially the separation of the coast from the interior (which represents an exceptional state of affairs in Omani history), the East Coast of Africa witnessed waves of emigrants at the end of the Nabahina period: a number of the Nabahina kings (601 AH) who had left Oman after the collapse of their rule at the beginning of the sixteenth century emigrated to the African coast and made the island of Patta their new home; particular mention should be made of the fact that they had found a large number of Omanis on the island who had taken up residence there before them and who made their guests welcome. One of the Nabahina kings married a daughter of the Swahili ruler of the island whose name was Is'haq– the ruler voluntarily ceding rule of the island in place of his son in-law. The Nabahinas continued to rule the island and succeeded in stimulating a great economic revival, often enabling them to extend their influence to Malindi, Kilwa and Mombasa. It was during their rule that trading activity flourished and Arabs, Indians and Persians flocked into their towns – until the Portuguese arrived and began to seize the African towns in quick succession. According to the Swahili report of Bwana Kayteen Sultan of Patta, Mohammed IV sent for help from the Sheikhs of Hadramaut against the Portuguese in 1574, although an Arab historian specializing in the history of the Gulf rejects this, pointing out that the Sultan of Patta's request for help was to the Imams of the Ya'ruba and not to the Sheikhs of Hadramaut[159].

The Omanis had long colonized the African coast and had become part of the fabric of society such that the level of culture and civilization, the degree of sophistication and order and the trading activity attained by African towns such as Lamu, Patta, Malindi, Mombasa and Kilwa – according to the eye-witness accounts of Arab and foreign travellers – was remarkable. Al-Mas'udi who visited the African coast in the fourth century of the Hegira confirms that the Arab emirates extended from Mogadishu in the north to Safala in the south[160].

Many European historians specializing in the history of East Africa have praised the civilizing influence of the Arabs of Oman – their manner of living, the diffusion of Arabic and Islamic culture and the features of the towns marking their Arabic identity. The round-trips of Barbosa may be counted among them: he visited the African coast in 1518 and recorded the surprise of the Portuguese at what they witnessed, flourishing towns and cultured societies – together with a thriving trade with the Far East, India and Persia – just as he recorded his impression of the clear contrast between the West Coast of Africa and the East Coast.

Barbosa states: 'Hardly had Vasco de Gama's ships reached Safala in East Africa than they were astonished by the unexpected: sailors crossing the waves of the sea, the quays bustling like bees' nests and extremely well developed coastal towns; the men were possessed of a profound knowledge of the Indian Ocean's routes, of a fine knowledge of its ports, had well-charted maps no less instructive than those of the Europeans and inhabited thriving towns whose activity was not inferior to that of the towns of Portugal and plied a prosperous sea-trade in gold, pearls, leather, cotton cloth, among other things ...'. The Portuguese in fact found a world of trade which was more extensive than their own and richer than in their own territories – to the extent that even the Arab boats were larger than those of the Portuguese[161] .

The Portuguese arrived on the coast of East Africa in April 1498, extending their hegemony over it during the first years of the sixteenth century. The Muslims failed to avert the threat they posed because of the division within the Arab coastal kingdoms and the lack of co-operation between the major Islamic powers, namely those of the Mamelukes and the Ottoman empire.

In the middle of the seventeenth century, the Ya'ruba state had gained considerable experience in their struggle with the Portuguese which enabled them to liberate all Omani territory. Indeed men such as Sultan bin Saif[162]concentrated on three main factors:

- The first of these was the attention he paid to the connection between water and dry-land: he based his judgement on the geographic and historical realities, comprehending that these realities confirmed that any disconnection between the dry-land and the water was to be considered an exceptional state of affairs in the history of Oman and that whenever they occurred, a time of decline began; moreover, the opposite is also true such that whenever there is interaction between water and land, a period in which wars and victories are prevalent begins. It may well be that the geography formed a kind of challenge to the Omanis, a challenge imposed on them by the particularly difficult geographical situation.
- The second is that the Imam bin Saif, and before him Imam Nasir bin Murshid, recognized the real importance of the means which were born of this challenging situation – namely the means to mount the most devastating attacks, coming as they did, mostly via the sea. Moreover, the only means available to the enemy proceeding from Europe was by ship.
  It was because of this that the Omani ships and their subsequent development became a necessity imposed by the situation and the severe challenge to this situation. The remarkable thing is that in no more than three decades, beginning from the time of Nasir bin Murshid in 1624 to half-way through the fifth decade of the same century, the Omani navy developed in such a way that it commanded the respect of all the naval powers fighting in the Arab Gulf and the Indian Ocean. The Imams of the Ya'ruba were aware of this natural strategic situation – from which a certain truth derived, namely, that Oman was an amphibious force with one foot on dry-land and the other on the water. It was because of this that, to a great degree, sea power was augmented by land forces. Oman was, however primarily a sea power by the very nature of the situation although no time was wasted in becoming, by the nature of the situation also, a land-force. The call of the sea, however, always had a stronger influence than the attraction of the land-base – which made the Omani people a civilizing defensive force. Moreover the sea was the only means of effecting the migrations which continued uninterrupted during long periods of Omani history. It is for this reason that we note that the Ya'ruba Imams reintroduced this perception of strategic factors into the history of Oman and so their activity and their victories were correspondingly remarkable.
- The third of these is that the Ya'ruba Imams' understanding of national security surpassed by far the traditional understanding of the matter. It may

well be that their experience with the Portuguese had given them a new vision of things which went far beyond their land borders. Therefore their success in pursuing the Portuguese and in waging war against their forts and castles on the Persian coast and in West India may be seen as an active expression of this understanding of national security. Thus their subsequent ventures against the West African coast and their struggle against the coastal islands and towns was, on the one hand, out of consideration for the security of Oman and on the other in order to save the Arab states – fearing, as they did, both for their Arab and Islamic identity.

At the beginning of the second half of the seventeenth century, Oman had freed itself completely from Portuguese hegemony. This prompted the inhabitants of East Africa to seek the help of their fellow countrymen and co-religionists: and so Oman turned its attention to Portuguese colonization in East Africa. Al-Ya'ruba were able to put an end to Portuguese hegemony there as they had done in both Oman and the Arab Gulf[163].

In my opinion Imam Sultan bin Saif, having liberated Muscat, was not simply responding to the call for help from his countrymen in East Africa as sources dealing with this time indicate that he was already intent on pursuing the Portuguese: therefore the invitation he received from the people of Mombasa coincided with his readiness to journey towards East Africa. A sudden Omani attack on Zanzibar and Patta took place in 1655, and the Omani navy was able to take a large number of Portuguese captive and to seize a number of war-ships and trading vessels; Zanzibar thus came under the total authority of Oman and its ruler agreed to pay the yearly *jizya* tax in return for protection against the Portuguese[164].

Omani assistance to East Africa continued and orders were issued to the Omani fleet besieging Bombay to make for Mombasa – whose inhabitants had sought help from Imam Sultan. The Omanis succeeded in besieging Mombasa for nearly five years (1660–65). Although the Portuguese were able to bring an end to the siege, the Omani navy began to open up new fronts in Bombay at the same time as Omani ships were setting out for the East African coast: this threw the Portuguese defence into confusion and they then began to attack the inhabitants, destroy their places of worship, raze their houses and burn their crops in a violent manner engendered by the destructive crusading sentiment.

Following the siege of Mombasa, Sultan bin Saif made his way to the islands of Pemba and Zanzibar and was able to free them from the control of the Portuguese – who were extremely angry by the inhabitants' co-operation with the Omanis. It was for this reason that the Portuguese commander Carerra mounted an attack on the civilian population of those islands in a manner devoid of even the most basic humanity. Despite this however, he was unable to stand up to the Omanis themselves: the latter inflicted several defeats on the Portuguese and during the second half of the seventeenth century, the Omanis were able to free all the Portuguese colonies in East Africa extending from the island of Socotra in the north to Delgado in the south[165].

The reality is, that the cooperation of the Africans with the Omanis was vital in bringing this conflict to an end. Neither is it a coincidence that the inhabitants of East Africa joined ranks with the Omanis – for historical reasons, the

Africans were very familiar with the Omani character, the exemplary conduct in everyday matters and strong cultural values of Omani sailors and traders having played a fundamental role in gaining the respect of the Africans.

This unfavourable comparison between the Portuguese and the Omanis seems to have been one of the main reasons for the Africans' preference for the Omanis. The latter did not claim to have a monopoly of any particular distinguishing feature but considered themsleves to be messengers of a civilization which was distinguished by noble human values. In addition, intermarriage between Omanis and Africans made the former a part of the fabric of this society, prompting – since the time of Sultan bin Saif (1649–79) – the integration of East Africa into Omani territory. Despite this however, the Ya'ruba Imams did not proceed along these lines believing their message to be a human and civilizing one and respectful too of the international balance of power at that time.

There is no doubt that the success of Al-Ya'ruba was connected to many factors, the first of which was, as already mentioned, the nature of the Omani character which earned the trust of the African nationals; other factors included the superiority of the Omanis, their capacity to learns the skills of the sea and to develop their ships, and their ability to absorb the advances which had appeared on European ships – together with the various provocative circumstances surrounding the policy of the Portuguese who used their monopoly as a means of subjugating the African peoples[166].

Sultan bin Saif was succeeded following his death in 1679 by his son Bal'arab bin Sultan who made an oath to free Mombasa or die – as the Portuguese had regained their hegemony over it following the return of Sultan bin Saif to Oman. In 1680 Bal'arab prepared a fleet composed of 28 boats and laid siege to Mombasa; the latter, however, was able to defy the Omanis because of its strong fortifications and the fact that Mombasa was one of the strongest Portuguese centres in East Africa. Bal'arab then looked to other Portuguese areas and so laid siege to Mozambique's fortress; the Portuguese defence, however, under the command of Gaspara de Soussa de Lacerda, was able to withstand the Omani siege.

According to many reports dealing with this subject, the Omanis began to dig a tunnel beneath the fortress intending to penetrate inside; this prompted the Portuguese defence to place charges which exploded with a tremendous force causing distress to the attackers who then refused to besiege the fortress[167].

It appears that the strife between Bal'arab bin Sultan and his brother Saif bin Sultan had repercussions on the struggle between the Omanis and Portuguese in East Africa to such an extent that the Portuguese regained their control over cities (which had been freed) like Malindi, Faza, Patta and Lamu. The Portuguese used every means to destroy society and the Portuguese commander took the Patta Mosque as a command centre and transformed many of the mosques to military bases. When, however, Oman was able to regroup at the end of the struggle between the two brothers Bal'arab and Saif, i.e. when Saif became the Imam of Oman, their military vigour returned and they made massive victories, the most important being their success in the capitulation of Mombasa on 14 December 1698.

Mombasa was among the most important fortresses relied upon by the

Portuguese. For this reason European historians believed that its fall into the hands of the Omanis marked the end of Portuguese supremacy in East Africa. It appears that it had occurred to Saif bin Sultan to keep on Mombasa as a major base in order to maintain his victories over the Portuguese; at least, this is what some have understood, namely that Saif was determined to establish an Omani empire on the rubble of the Portuguese empire. The weakness of his strength in Oman, however, caused him to disregard this project, thereby delaying for 1100 years the establishment of an Omani empire in East Africa until the reign of Said bin Sultan (1856–96)[168].

The fall of Mombasa marked the beginning of the expulsion of the Portuguese from the whole coast of Africa, and in 1699 the Omanis succeeded in freeing Pemba, Kilwa, Patta and Zanzibar. These defeats caused the Portuguese to again try to annex Mombasa and military expeditions arrived directly from Lisbon. These attacks were repeated at the beginning of 1699 and during 1702 and 1710 and perhaps the most dangerous attack came in 1728 when the Portuguese were able to regain Mombasa for two years because of the Omanis' preoccupation with their internal conflict – although the Omanis were able to unite again and recapture Mombasa.

In general the Ya'ruba took upon themselves the task of putting an end to the Portuguese presence along the African coast and by the end of the seventeenth century the Omani presence in the Indian Ocean had increased to such an extent that the towns to the north of the Delgado Cape gradually rejected Portuguese domination and succumbed to Omani rule. In this way they reaffirmed their direction towards Islam – something which is confirmed by the important point that the successful advance of the Omani Arabs was not the only important factor in bringing the Portuguese domination to an end in East Africa but rather that the significance of this advance was that it afforded the religion of Islam a propitious arena of action without constraint or barrier[169].

If we ponder on the motives of the Portuguese and their methods in the propagation of their Catholic teachings during almost two centuries, the active role played by the Omanis in enabling Islam to spread amongst the Africans will become clear to us. It is for this reason that many consider the fall of the Mombasa fortress in 1698 as an important landmark – not because of the bringing to an end of Portuguese hegemony but rather that it afforded a suitable opportunity for the spread of Islam amongst the Africans[170].

Although the Ya'ruba continually challenged Portuguese hegemony over the African coast and made great sacrifices in doing so, Omani control over the East African coast was not an active domination because of the internal problems reoccurring within the Ya'ruba state and the demands of the civil war. Despite this, however, Al-Ya'ruba were able to take over from the Portuguese and to appoint an Arab leadership along the African coast at a time when the state had expended most of its efforts in its struggle against the Portuguese and no longer had the strength to extend directly their hegemony in East Africa.

It was natural for the rulers who had come to power as vice-regents of the Ya'ruba in East Africa to take advantage of the weakness of the state and the atmosphere of anarchy and disunity: thus affording them the opportunity of taking power over the administrative regions for themselves alone. The transfer of rule from the Ya'ruba state to that of the Al-Busaid dynasty had a powerful reaction amongst the rulers of East Africa – since the latter had taken over the reins of power on behalf of the Ya'ruba state then what would prevent them from becoming independent in those regions they had taken over if that Ya'ruba state fell?

It is perhaps pertinent to state the opinion of some European historians who maintain that the slave trade became very active in East Africa during the Ya'ruba hegemony over the Indian Ocean[171]. We can say that the trade in slaves was a European invention undertaken by states and companies and that in the case of the Arabs – even if they did practise this trade – it was not with any great effort: in fact the furthest their African slaves reached was the Arabian peninsula and the coast of the Arabian Gulf. As for the slave trade in the west of the continent – which did not preoccupy the European historians in the same way as that in East Africa – it was based on a definite policy of exploiting this human wealth of Africa. To this end, many trading centres were set up where agreements were concluded, policy laid down and discord between the African tribes instigated resulting in the worst kind of exploitation known to man in modern times and the subjection of the African race to the harshest and most difficult of journeys as they were driven from West Africa to the plantations of the two Americas across the waters of the Atlantic.

Despite all this, European historians omitted this painful fact and poured all their anger onto the Arabs of East Africa. Indeed Coupland and others have attempted to make the Arabs responsible for the slave-trade in East Africa by saying that they were the mediators who supplied the Portuguese trading centres with the necessary number of slaves without mentioning any numbers or precise statistics to compare them with what was happening in West Africa.

There is also another aspect which appears in the European sources dealing with East Africa, namely that many have tried to play down the role of the Arabs and their cultural influence at the time of Al-Ya'ruba by saying that they were not interested in introducing agriculture and that their only concern was to satiate their appetite for gold, ivory and slaves.

It may well be that this European opinion was unaware of the reality of the situation – confirmed by European travellers who made visits to East Africa at the time of the Portuguese migration. The most important of these visits were the voyages of Barbosa who came to the African coast in 1518 and registered his surprise at the centres of trade and culture: he elucidated the role of the Arabs in the development of the African coast, mentioning a number of the centres of civilized life which attracted the attention of the Portuguese themselves[172].

It is natural for the Arabs to be preoccupied with trade in East Africa because it was *the* economic life-line at the end of the Middle Ages and at the beginning of modern times, although after the Omani hegemony established itself over East Africa at the beginning of the Al-Busaid dynasty, an interest in introducing many types of crops developed. This occurred in particular at the time of Sayyid Said bin Sultan who transformed East Africa into an agricultural society of the first order, especially regarding the culture of cloves – so much so that the islands of Pemba and Zanzibar began to supply the world with a major part of this crop.

Ahmed bin Said and the Establishment of the Al-Busaidi State

Persian Interference in Oman and the End of the Ya'ruba Period

After Saif bin Sultan died (in 1711 AD), his son Sultan bin Saif became the Imam and he continued the war against the Portuguese and the Persians in order to liberate Bahrain, Qeshm and Larg. However, when Sultan bin Saif died (in 1718 AD), the national unity of Oman was threatened, and civil war erupted again, lasting for the next 18 years. Subsequently, the tribes divided into two groups. Some supported the leadership of Saif bin Sultan, who was then a little boy, and others supported Muhanna bin Sultan because he had the necessary qualities to be an Imam; in contrast, Saif bin Sultan was not lawfully entitled to lead the people in prayer. In addition, some people believed that the granting of religious leadership to him contradicted custom and Islamic law. It should be noted that the *ulema* did not reject the notion that leadership could reside in the Ya'ruba family to whom Muhanna bin Sultan belonged, but they could not give their open consent to his leadership because of the offence this might give to some major tribes.

However, according to some sources the *ulema* brought the boy Saif in front of the Muslims crowd declaring 'amamukum'(meaning ' in front of you') which the crowd misinterpreted as 'imamukum' (meaning ' your leader '). This allowed the *ulema* to smuggle Muhanna bin Sultan into Rustaq fort without provoking opposition and they then declared him Imam in 1719 AD. Although Imam Muhanna bin Sultan worked extremely hard to bring justice to the country, he was strongly opposed. One of the opposition, Ya'arub bin Bal'arab forced him to give up his religious leadership and then killed him in 1720 AD. After that Ya'arub moved to another town, Nizwa, with the Imam (Boy) Saif bin Sultan. There, Ya'arub emphasized that he did not want the official leadership himself because it belonged to Saif bin Sultan, according to the majority opinion, but that he would take charge of Oman as custodian for Saif. However, even though he was in power, he ignored his responsibilities as custodian, causing his removal by Bal'arab bin Nasir who re-installed Saif as an Imam in his own custody in 1723 AD.

The first custodian (Ya'rub bin Bal'arab) made an agreement with Mohammed bin Nasir Al-Gafiri who circulated among the tribes campaigning for the opposition. That resulted in a civil war which destroyed the military and economic infrastructure of the country provided by the great Imams, such as Sultan bin Saif and Saif bin Sultan. These devastating circumstances forced Saif bin Sultan (The Second) to make a request to Nadir Shah in Persia seeking his help[173]. At the time Nadir Shah had just defeated the Ottoman maritime fleet in Basra and occupied Bahrain. These victories fueled his ambition to gain total control of the Arabian Gulf[174]. Nadir Shah realized that this was a good opportunity, to control Muscat and even the entire coast of Oman, which was the longstanding dream of the Persians. In response to Saif's request, Nadir Shah sent a large maritime expedition to Muscat, displaying the white Persian flag decorated with a red sword, under the command of Latif Khan (1737 AD). Saif bin Sultan joined his Persian alliance in Julfar. Together they moved towards Al-Buraimi, then Ibri where the Persians committed many atrocities. Saif resented the savagery of his ally and proceeded towards Muscat on his own[175].

However, after the Persian forces had overcome the resistance of Bal'arab bin Hamyar, the Persian commander, Latif Khan at once declared himself military governor of the whole of Oman, leaving no control to Saif bin Sultan who was busy fighting supporters of Bal'arab bin Hamyar. Many Omanis, especially scholars, who opposed the Persian interference gathered around Bal'arab at his base in Bahla. They wrote to Saif bin Sultan condemning his reliance on Persian forces[176]. Because the Omanis had established a very strong resistance in the face of the Persian invasion, the Persians were forced to seek logistical support and supplies such as ropes, anchors and sails, from English and Dutch factories in Bandar Abbas. They also sought the help of skilful European carpenters, because according to Dutch and English reports the two European factories in Bandar Abbas, were able to fulfil all the Persian needs. The same reports indicated that the Persians were paying bribes and taxes to some English and Dutch officials[177].

Imam Saif and Latif Khan soon fell out, indicating that the policy, Imam Saif had followed to strengthen his position was not a success. This became abundantly clear with the failure of the new Persian commander Taqui Khan to control Sohar and the destruction of the Persian garrisons by the Omanis in Bahla and Izki. At the same time, the Arab sailors mutinied on the Persian fleet. This devastating disaster forced Taqui Khan to retreat with his forces to Julfar (Ras Al-Khaimah) where he received the Persian reinforcements and then was able to capture Al-Dhahira province.

In February 1738 AD, a great battle took place between the Persian and the Arabian forces near Bahla. The Persians won a great victory opening the way to Muscat. At the same time, Imam Saif escaped to the Al-Buraimi province. There he expressed his sorrow and readiness to fight and resist the Persians. Having changed his attitude towards the Persians, the tribes rallied around Saif, but this national unity did not last long because some tribes chose Sultan bin Murshid as Imam. In these disturbing circumstances, the Persians tried to capture Muscat. According to Dutch sources, the Persians used a number of Dutch ships in the attack on Muscat[178]. Saif bin Sultan attempted to redeem himself by performing a heroic act. He therefore led the Omani resistance which displayed outstanding courage when they pursued the Persians across the Gulf. Saif then decided to continue the fight inside Persia itself. He therefore appealed to all Arabian tribes in the Gulf to supply him with combatants to enable him to fight in Bahrain and Bandar Abbas[179].

It appears that the success achieved by Imam Saif coincided with ruinous circumstances in Persia caused by widespread rebellion. These circumstances forced Nadir Shah to withdraw his forces from the Arabian Gulf and Oman in order to deal with his internal problems. The withdrawal of the Persian forces from Oman calmed the situation there, enabling Imam Saif to return. This provoked and angered most of the Omani people resulting in a revolt against Saif. The latter was removed and the leadership was given to Sultan bin Murshid, who went on to control Muscat and attack Saif in Barka. Saif escaped to Julfar (Ras Al-Khaimah), taking refuge inside the Persian camp. He then re-contacted Taqui Khan, asking him to deliver a letter to Nadir Shah seeking his help in regaining his leadership and promised to give the Persians the total control of Oman.

It appears that Saif bin Sultan did not learn a lesson from his previous experience when he had plunged his country into a civil war that exhausted most of its resources and had invited in a foreign invader. For the second time Nadir Shah order Taqui Khan to prepare a new expedition to invade Oman. The Persians succeeded in besieging Sohar. At the same time, the new Imam Sultan bin Murshid arrived to break this siege. However, this costly operation lasted for nearly seven months: both Persia and Oman suffered great losses and wasted considerable effort[180]. Some European sources from that period indicate that the English and the Dutch donated a huge quantity of supplies in support of the Persians. Some English ships even collaborated in besieging Muscat. Although Muscat was captured by the Persians, its forts stayed under Omani control, enabling them to inflict many severe defeats on the Persian forces[181].

Ahmed bin Said and the Liberation of Oman

The naked ambition of the Persians in Oman galvanized the Omani tribes into coming together in order to achieve a common goal. Perhaps, the Omanis learnt their first lesson that every one is a loser and there is no hope of liberating the country unless national unity is restored under one strong leader capable of making use of all the national resources of this large country and of motivating people to liberate Oman. The circumstances in Oman led to the appearance of a strict disciplined leader who played a very active role in the liberation of his country from the Persian occupation. This leader was Imam Ahmed bin Said Al-Busaid Al-Azdi who is regarded as the founder of the Al-Busaidi adminis-tration. As deputy of Sohar he played an important role in motivating national resistance to the Persians, his garrisons making great sacrifices in order to overcome and eliminate the Persian forces. Indeed Ahmed bin Said received such huge support from the Omani tribes that Imam Saif suspected a plot to overthrow his leadership. At that time, Imam Saif was in control of Muscat and based on his suspicions he gave the order to arrest Ahmed bin Said. The latter was called to Muscat but on his way Ahmed discovered the plot hatched by Imam Saif, and so returned home[182]. Soon after, Saif revealed his animosity to Ahmed bin Said by sending a naval fleet to attack Sohar. Although the combatants were unable to take Sohar, Ahmed bin Said preferred peace, and thus declared his loyalty to Imam Saif. Before he could send one of his children to Muscat as a guarantee of his loyalty to Imam Saif, circumstances changed extremely quickly, forcing Imam Saif to declare his withdrawal; the devastation brought to his countryside was revealed. Meanwhile the Persians continued their siege of Sohar and Imam Sultan bin Murshid died from the many injuries he received during this siege[183]. The deaths of the two competitive Imams enabled the deputy of Sohar, Ahmed bin Said, to become Imam.

It seems that Ahmed bin Said had a profound understanding of the balance that had to be achieved between the internal and external situations when he decided to negotiate a peace agreement with the Persians in order to reorganize the internal affairs of Oman. Some Omani sources add that the Persians requested the agreement in order to ensure their safe withdrawal from Sohar, after they found it impossible to capture it. However, some Persian sources deny this and emphasize that Ahmed bin Said had shown some flexibility with the Persians and so gained the trust of Taqui Khan, who withdrew from Sohar in order to instigate a revolution in Farstan against Nadir Shah while Nadir Shah was struggling in a fierce war against the Ottoman government.

However, whether it was the Persians or Ahmed who had requested the lifting of the siege around Sohar, the result was the same, the Persians were no longer in Muscat and Matrah. Persian garrisons took refuge in the two castles, Al-Mirani and Al-Jalali. This gave Ahmed bin Said the opportunity to get back to preparing for the total liberation of Oman from the Persian occupation. All Arabic and foreign sources agree that Ahmed bin Said was remarkable, possessing a resourceful and clever personality, which enabled him to strengthen his position throughout the interior in preparation for restoring national unity to Oman. Later he studied and came to appreciate his enemies' means. Firstly, he ignored the agreed tax payment; secondly, he left the soldiers of the Persian garrisons in Al-Mirani and Al-Jalali without salaries or supplies; lastly, to finish the siege, he waived custom tolls. This attracted trading ships to Barka instead of Muscat. These factors contributed to the weakening of the Persian garrisons who were suffering because of depleted ammunition stocks and the stoppage of their supplies and salaries[184].

The Persian force commander in Muscat, fully appreciating the danger of his position, wrote to the Shah requesting proper action. The Shah chose a man named Majed bin Sultan, a relative of Saif bin Sultan, the former ally of the Persians. Majed bin Sultan travelled to Tabreez where he met the Shah who agreed to appoint him as the governor of Oman under Persian authority[185]. Some Omani sources mention that gales capsized the ship in which Majed bin Sultan was travelling on his return to Sohar, and that he was later captured. The order of the Shah, which appointed him as governor of Muscat and Matrah, was then rescinded. Ahmed bin Said dispatched one of his assistants to the commander of the Persian garrison in Muscat as if he had been sent by Majed bin Sultan to surrender all Muscat's forts. The source regards this ruse carried out by Ahmed bin Said as more or less marking the beginning of Al-Busaid period and the end of the Ya'ruba period[186].

Omani and European sources differ very slightly about the details of this event, however both sources regard the date (24 June 1747 AD) as the date of the beginning of the decline of the Persian garrison in Muscat. A rumour spread claiming that Nadir Shah had been killed. This of course increased the despair of the Persian garrison. In August, around 200 soldiers arrived on the Persian coast, having run away after an ambush plotted by the Omanis which wiped out most of the garrison[187]. Whether the destruction of the Persian garrison took place in Muscat or in Barka, the result was the same in that Ahmed bin Said captured Muscat and Julfar province (Ras Al-Khaimah) was left, in which Rahmat bin Matar fortified himself and was declared by Nadir Shah to be a ruler of that city from 1740 AD.

The commentators differ concerning the date that Ahmed bin Said assumed the leadership. Ibn Ruzaiq did not define a particular date for this event, however it is understood from his writings that 1741 AD is the year Ahmed bin Said struggled with the Persians. Therefore, Ibn Ruzaiq regarded the struggle with the Persians as the starting point of the process to choose Ahmed bin Said as Imam; whereas an important historian, Al-Salimi, regarded 1158 AH /1745 AD as the year that Ahmed bin Said became Imam. Al-Salimi's commentary has logic on its side since he regarded 1744 AD as the year when the Persians were forced to leave Oman and Ahmed bin Said succeeded in getting rid of Bal'arab bin Hamyar, and it is the same year as the consent to the leadership took place. Another historian, Al-Azkawi[188], specified 1162 AH /1749 AD as the year that the consent to the leadership took place. Nevertheless, Ahmed bin Said was installed as an Imam after the death of both Imams. It is certain that Ahmed bin Said ruled Oman by himself from 1744 AD, which is the year we regard as the beginning of his leadership.

From the beginning, Ahmed bin Said realized the importance of restoring national unity. Therefore, he dedicated himelf to bringing unity to Oman, and to preparing it to play a major role in the history of the Arabian Gulf during the second half of the eighteenth century[189].

Even before he took on the mantle of leader Imam Ahmed bin Said was trustworthy, truthful, and very highly regarded by all who knew him. He had come from a pure Arabic family, most of whom worked in trade. He was also remarkably distinguished with a rare courage and bravery which attracted attention to him. These factors enabled him to be installed by Al-Ya'ruba as the deputy of Sohar state.

No one can deny the great efforts made by Ahmed bin Said in laying the foundations of government. It seems that the most challenging problem at the start of his period was the Al-Ya'ruba rebellion instigated by their loss of power. In addition some tribes rebelled in Al-Dhahira province. In dealing with these problems, Ahmed bin Said used force when necessary, but often he pursued an easy, flexible policy. He used marriages of convenience in order to establish closer relationships with opposing tribes, for example his marriage to Saif bin Sultan's widow[190]and a marriage into the family of the Sheikhs of Bani Al-Hilali with whom his relationship had strengthened since he was deputy of Sohar. He joined in alliance with the tribes of Bani Ka'b at Shatt Al-Arab and Al-Karoon river. He also looked after the strengthening of good relations with his country's neighbours, the resident Arab tribes, south of Persia and the Arabistan region. His relations with Bani Ma'n, to the east of Bandar Abbas, had also strengthened and prevented the attempts of Karim Khan Zand to control the area. His relations spread as far as India where he helped Shah Alam, the Mangulian emperor of India, in his fight against the pirates who were disturbing trade movements between Mangalore, on the western coast of India, and Muscat. This relationship was crowned with a treaty in 1766 AD which provided for the continuation of friendly relations and the opening of a consular house, later known as Bait Al -Nu'wab, for the ambassador of the Mangulie ruler[191].

It can be said that the country experienced for the first time in 20 years some kind of central government after Ahmed bin Said was able to unify the conflicting tribes. He immediately took the necessary steps to strengthen the foundations of the new government, by constructing and equipping the armed forces so that they would be equal to the challenges facing Oman. He modernized economic activities and organized a military and commercial maritime fleet. During his reign, Muscat became one of the most important commercial cities in the Arabian Gulf and its harbour became one of the most commercialized harbours, used even by European ships[192].

Indeed Oman progressed and prospered during the rule of Imam Ahmed bin Said, and Dutch and English reports admitted that Oman was the dominant power around the coasts of the Arabian Gulf and Indian ocean. These reports also proclaimed the cleverness and intelligence of Ahmed bin Said, particularly in his manner of dealing with his own population, his forgiving policy with foreigners, and the expansion of his control to East Africa. Risso admits that Oman is the only country which benefited from the trade decline in Bandar Abbas and the ruined circumstances of the Europeans in the Gulf during the second half of the eighteenth century[193]. A Dutch report, published in 1749 AD, pointed out that Ahmed bin Said's relations with the Arab Sheikhs along the Persian coast who were in possession of huge military means had improved to the point where he was able to make a treaty of alliance with them[194]. Thus, Ahmed bin Said was able to transfer the Omani-Persian war to Persian territories, resulting in a disruption to Persian trade movement, especially in Bandar Abbas which the Dutch wished to abandon. However, despite the conflict between the European powers in the Gulf, Ahmed bin Said furthered Omani interests against international competition in the Gulf without significant recourse to violence. We can say, if the Ya'ruba government was described as 'The maritime military government', then the Al-Busaid government is 'The maritime trade government'.

Ahmed bin Said was successful in forcing the Persians out of Oman and in overcoming the problems resulting from the Omani civil war. He gained the loyalty of the Omanis who collectively agreed to elect him as Imam in honour of the part he played in the liberation of Oman. Perhaps the circumstances in Oman as Ahmed bin Said came to power were very much similar to the circumstances prevailing during the establishment of the Ya'ruba government. At that time, Nasir bin Murshid confronted the separatists at the same time as he was fighting a fierce war against the Portuguese along the Omani coast, as did Ahmed bin Said when he confronted the tribes who opposed him whilst fighting a fierce war against the aggressive Persians. The improvement in internal affairs reflected very positively on the Omani struggle against Persia.

After Ahmed bin Said had liberated his country, he immediately began to take strategic steps that would ensure the continuation and stability of the government in Oman, such as the preparation of a well-equipped military force, the appointment of civil servant officials, and the re-organization of commercial activities in the country[195].

Arabic and European sources agree that the first eight years of Al-Busaid rule were a flourishing period. There were many factors which helped the Omanis to play an outstanding role. Firstly, they gained a great deal of experience and skill in commerce and navigation, as a result of the historical events, the strategic geographical location of Oman and its heritage. Secondly, Oman's harbours benefited considerably from the internal stability which Oman experienced during this time, any disruptions that occurred were mostly in Gulf harbours. Thirdly, Ahmed bin Said's personality contributed enormously to Oman's success at this time: he was extremely disciplined, upright and blessed with good judgement. In addition, he was highly respected and trusted by European powers. His advanced policies attracted and encouraged foreigners to establish commercial offices in Oman's cities, and particularly in Muscat which became in 1790 AD one of the most important Asian cities, according to a report written by the English East India Company. The report has offered reputable evidence that Muscat was running an active commercial enterprise in `excess of the combined trade of all the other cities in the Gulf[196].

External Relations of Al-Busaidi Government

The Relationship with East Africa

The first few years of Imam Ahmed bin Said's rule were not easy, mainly because of the disturbances within the country and the instability they engendered. Imam Ahmed bin Said found himself faced with external challenges which could not be ignored. One of these was the desire of some deputies, loyal to the Ya'ruba, to orchestrate the collapse of the government so that they could defect and form their own state. Take for example, the case of Mohammed bin Othman Al-Mazrui, who declared his independence from the Omani government, justifying himself by saying that Mombasa had been under Ya'ruba control and it had pledged loyalty to the Ya'ruba government, but since the latter had collapsed, it did not intend to continue its loyalty to Oman. Moreover, Al-Mazrui believed that since the founder of the new government had attained his position through personal effort[197] and ambition then what would prevent Al-Mazrui, a Ya'ruba deputy, from placing Mombasa under his authority[198].

Ahmed bin Said could not ignore this dangerous challenge to his authority by an unknown deputy such as Al-Mazrui. Since Imam Ahmed belonged to a respected merchant family, he understood clearly that the continuation of his authority in East Africa would grant Oman an outstanding commercial position. This, in turn, was vital in order to consolidate his authority in his own country. On the one hand Ahmed bin Said was faced with Al-Mazrui's disloyalty and his refusal to send taxes to the new Imam of Oman, on the other hand, he was fully cognizant of the difficulty in bringing military action against East Africa. In those circumstances, Ahmed decided to use all his wisdom and sagacity in order to put an end to this opposition and to prevent the dilution of his authority. Imam Ahmed sent six of his closest followers headed by Saif bin Khalaf to Mombasa. They presented themselves to Al-Mazrui, making credible claims that they were in opposition to Imam Ahmed. Some of what they said to

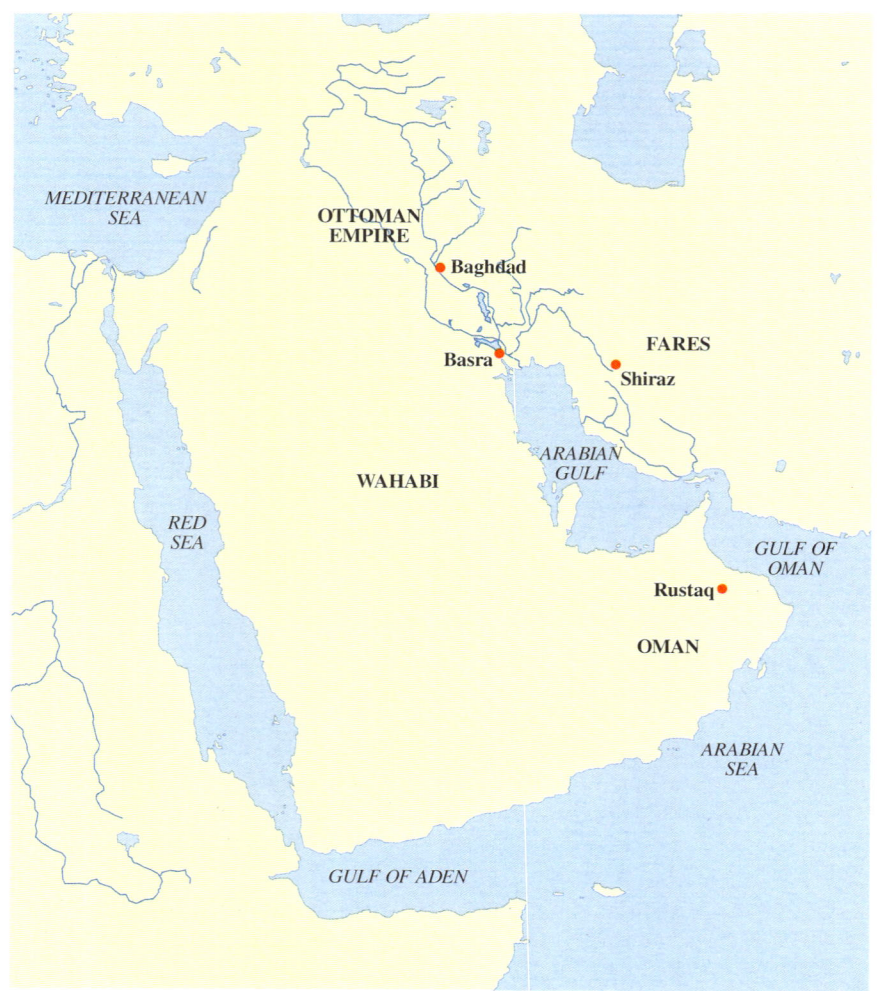

him was: 'We have opposed the Imam and come to you, we would like to join you and to do what you wish and your regard be our regard'[199]. After they were satisfied and confident that Al-Mazrui had trusted them, they asked him for permission to go to Kilwa and Pemba in order to gather their followers and supporters for the common cause, which was the resignation of Imam Ahmed bin Said. The day before they departed, they went to visit him in his castle to say goodbye, and Saif bin Khalaf used this opportunity to kill Al-Mazrui and the people with him in the castle[200].

Despite the success achieved by Imam Ahmed's men in extending the authority of the new government to Mombasa, the Al-Busaidi authority did not last long in this part of East Africa, because almost immediately, Ali bin Othman Al-Mazrui avenged his brother when he succeeded in assassinating Saif bin Khalaf, the Imam's deputy in Mombasa[201]. Ali also succeeded in regaining control of Mombasa, thus the Al-Mazrui family ruled this African city and led the opposition movement on the African coast against the Al-Busaid government. The rest of the cities in East Africa, except Zanzibar, avoided falling under the authority of Imam Ahmed bin Said. In Zanzibar, he appointed Abdullah bin Hamad Al-Busaidi as deputy[202]. Although Imam Ahmed bin Said's success was limited in East Africa, he had greater success in confronting Persia's aggressive desires.

The Relationship with Persia

Persia and Oman were in direct competition, each vying with the other for naval supremacy. It was well-known that Persia had tried many times in the past to limit the Omani naval forces. Persia sometimes relied on their own resources to weaken the Omani navy, and more frequently on the European powers[203]. After they had received military aid from the English East India Company, the Persians appealed to France, during the period of Louis XIV, seeking help to solve their problem. This Persian-French communication resulted in an agreement signed by both parties. One of its secret provisions was a proposed collaboration between the French maritime fleet and the Persian maritime fleet to colonize Muscat[204]. Although the agreement was not implemented, the Persians continued to offer attractive deals. At some stage, they even agreed to give Muscat with all its fortified strongholds to France and promised with all their capability to oppose all countries, rejecting French authority on the route to India[205]. The agreement also included custom's relief on all imports from and exports to France, and incentives to encourage Persian-French trade. The agreement was signed in 1134 AH /1721 AD[206] but the development of the situation in Persia, i.e. invasion by the Afghans, prevented France from getting any benefit from this agreement[207]. This weakened the Persians in the Gulf and Indian Ocean even more.

Nadir Shah tried, after he liberated his country from the Afghans, to strengthen the Persian position in the Gulf: firstly by exploiting Oman's internal difficulties, Oman being the primary power in the Gulf; secondly, by using aid provided by the European countries, such as England and Holland, who indeed contributed in the building of a very strong and modern Persian naval fleet. The Persian maritime fleet faced many difficult problems, during Nadir Shah's time. Firstly, he had depended on European aid in constructing it; secondly, Persia lacked experience and personnel skilled in the different types of seamanship. Therefore, the leadership was forced to recruit Arab seamen in order to staff their maritime fleet. However, many historians agree that Nadir Shah overcame these difficulties and persisted in building this modern maritime fleet in order to carry out his external policy. Thus, the power, of the Persian maritime fleet, was attached to a great extent with Nadir Shah's life. The assassination of Nadir Shah (in 1160 AH/1747 AD) coincided with the appearance of Imam Ahmed bin Said. Since the beginning of Imam Ahmed's reign, he had tried to strengthen Oman's role in the Arabian Gulf. Inevitably there was a head-on collision between Imam Ahmed's policy and the policy of the new Persian leader Karim Khan who succeeded Nadir Shah. Karim Khan followed Nadir Shah's policy, after he succeeded in strengthening his rule in Persia.

Karim Khan sent a letter to Imam Ahmed demanding an annual tax payment, claiming that Oman belonged to Persia. Imam Ahmed bin Said refused Persian demands. He declared, in a firm and self-confident manner that his country refused all Persian demands and sent this refusal in a tough letter to Karim

Khan Zand. The letter stated that Oman did not pay tax to any one, indicating that if Karim Khan insisted, he would have to take it by force[208]. Imam Ahmed did not let the matter go with only a strong letter, he planed to use force against his enemy if need be. Therefore he made an alliance with Persia's enemies, in particular the Turks[209], in order to destroy the power of Karim Khan Zand. Imam Ahmed played an active role in breaking the siege imposed around Basra by Karim Khan Zand[210]. In the honour of this action, the Ottoman Sultan Mustafa the Third rewarded Imam Ahmed with an annual payment to be paid from Basra bank[211] for his outstanding courage. Because of the weakness of his rivals in the Gulf region, and the death of Karim Khan, Imam Ahmed was able to restore Oman to its former position of strength and to revive the importance of Muscat trade in the region. Indeed, this new progress forced the European powers to try exceedingly hard in their attempts to control Muscat.

The Relationship with the European Powers

The international powers struggled for supremacy in the region. Thus it was not strange that the two superpowers (Great Britain and France) expended a lot of time and effort trying to control Oman in order to include it in their domain, because of its distinct strategic position. Imam Ahmed bin Said was aware of the European desire for colonization, so he planned his external policy on the principle of neutrality, a strategy which was very successful, particularly at the time when English-French relations were stable. However, this neutrality was at times severely jeopardized, especially during the Seven Years War (1170-1177 AH/1756-1763 AD) between England and France. During this period the ships of the two countries used to attack each other inside Omani territorial waters. In 1175 AH/1761 AD, Oman was in an awkward position when Count de Stane tried to take revenge on the British. He attempted to attack an English vessel inside Omani territorial waters in order to cause harm to English trade in the Gulf, ignoring Omani rules. Therefore, the deputy Khalfan bin Mohammed was forced to fire at the French ship *Boloni* to encourage it to retreat in an attempt to protect the English ship[212].

Despite the repeat occurrence of these awkward situations necessitating Omani fire against French ships on a number of occasions, this did not reflect in any way an Omani preference for the British as much as it reflected Omani attempts to protect its neutrality, especially since English ships commonly sailed inside Omani territorial waters. It is true that the British strengthened their position and gained the confidence of some local powers in the Arabian Gulf region, after the Portuguese and the Dutch had left. Imam Ahmed, as it seems and despite his understanding of the British special interest in the region, believed in the importance of friendly relations with France. One of the Imam's letters to the French, dispatched in the wake of shots being fired at a French ship, contained the following sentence of goodwill: ' I am a friend to the French'[213].

It should be mentioned that Imam Ahmed was the first to start commercial trade with Mauritius island and other regions which were all under French authority[214]. As a result of the progress in commercial relations[215] between Oman and French colonies in the Indian Ocean during that period, Imam Ahmed bin Said revealed his desire to open a French office in Muscat without any reciprocation. Imam Ahmed expressed his wishes to a French official saying : 'My country is your country and our friendship is even stronger than it was in the past'[216]. When this official visited Muscat, he found a very welcoming reception which influenced him to encourage his country to strengthen its relationship with Muscat in a report he wrote[217]. It seems the French government was not interested in establishing a commercial office in Muscat at the time. However, after the insistence of the French consul in Baghdad and Mauritius, the French government decided to open two consulates in Basra and Muscat. A letter, sent by the French Foreign Minister to the French consul in Baghdad, contained the following : 'The wishes of the Imam Ahmed in having a representative, your note on the benefit of rewarding His Majesty 's people in navigation and trade, and easing of the link with India, all of these made us decide to establish an official office in Muscat[218]. However, the circumstances, which France had to deal with before and during its revolution, prevented the establishment of this office from taking place[219].

The policy of neutrality, which was pursued by Imam Ahmed bin Said, contributed to strengthening the commercial status of Oman, and accordingly he permitted the ships of the superpowers to visit and trade in Omani harbours. No doubt all of these had contributed to the economy of the country. In addition, Oman's status increased when it sent immediate help to Basra in order to save it from Persian control. This needs to be explained in greater detail to fully appreciate the central role Oman played at that time in maintaining Arab cultural values in this part of the Arab world.

The Main Powers in the Arabian Gulf During the Second Half of the Eighteenth Century

Basra and Oman occupied an important political and commercial status in the Arabian Gulf during the second half of the eighteenth century, in comparison to the political and commercial status of Persia and its harbours. After the death of Nadir Shah in 1160 AH /1747 AD, Karim Khan Zand assumed the Persian throne in 1163-1193 AH/1750-1779 AD. He tried to restore to Persia the commercial and political stability which it had forfeited and he found that the only way to achieve this was by increasing the pressure on Basra and Oman. These two cities were experiencing great commercial and political stability in the Arabian Gulf at the expense of the Persian harbours. Karim Khan planned his policy with these two powers, in the light of this and many other issues. We will now survey the political, military and economic means of these three powers: Basra, Oman and Persia.

Basra
Basra was ruled by slave rulers from the middle of the eighteenth century, as was the case with Baghdad. These slaves had some local authority. Al-Bab Ali could not dispense with their services, even if he wanted to because deputies appointed by Al-Bab Ali were liable to be killed. As Olivie says: 'They do not dare to go to Baghdad, since they would be killed on the way or forced to withdraw soon after assuming power. All attempts to remove these

slaves were unsuccessful, because all whom the Sultan had sent lost their lives or were unable to complete their mission'[220]. That is why Baghdad and Basra to some extent were ruled independently of each other. However they were vulnerable to attack during Nadir Shah's reign which made the deputies of Baghdad think of unifying these two countries under Baghdad administration, and that is what Ahmed Basha and his successors did from 1162 AH/ 1749 AD. Thus, Baghdad and Basra became one country, Baghdad being regarded as the centre, and Basra was ruled by deputies appointed by the Baghdad administration.

Many deputies presided over Basra, but the best known one was Suleiman Agha. He was acting as deputy when Karim Khan tried to invade Basra in 1189-1190 AH/1775-1776 AD and he showed outstanding courage in defending Basra. Baghdad and Basra states were considered, during that time, to be the second power in the Arabian Gulf, and the only greater force, in quality and quantity, was Persia. The governor of Baghdad was easily able to raise and support a military force of 40-50,000 fighters. Besides the regular army, the Arab tribes throughout the country would provide 10-12,000 warriors. To do this they had to have peaceful relations with the governor and the governor was required to have enough money to pay them generously and regularly[221].

This situation suited the deputy of Basra, as he was not able to defend the city without the help of the Arab tribes resident on its outskirts. The best known tribe was Al-Muntafeq. He, therefore, sought their loyalty and friendship[222].

It is really astonishing that the powerful deputies of Baghdad and Basra succeeded in overcoming Persian invasions along their eastern borders, one after the other, whilst lacking a sufficient maritime force in Basra. This ensured that their role in the events and affairs of the Arabian Gulf was limited.

The maritime fleet of Basra consisted of 50 small military boats. This naval power was not able to protect safe navigation in the Shatt Al-Arab and the two rivers, Tigris and Euphrates, and the necessary naval protection was not available when Persian naval forces started to make an appearance at the outskirts of the city[223]. Despite all this, Basra was a very important commercial centre, regarded as one of the most important trade centres in the East. Indian goods were imported there and from it the goods were distributed to Persia, the Arabian peninsula, the Ottoman Empire and Europe. Also, Basra was an important centre, for the export of goods to India[224]. More importantly, there was an active commercial relationship between Basra and Omani ports during the second half of the eighteenth century which made Karim Khan think that the control of Basra would help him to dominate Omani trade movements and therefore all of Oman[225].

Oman

The other strong power, in the Arabian Gulf, besides Iraq and Persia, was Oman. Oman had achieved liberation during the second half of the eighteenth century, and was now free from the threat of Persian invasion. The Persian occupation had resulted, as it was mentioned before, in the appearance of a new leader who worked to regain the independence and integrity of the country, to regain its authority in the Arabian Gulf, and to achieve national unity. This leader was Imam Ahmed bin Said (1157-1198 AH /1744-1783 AD). He became well known after he confronted the Persians and forced them to withdraw from Oman in 1157 AH/1744 AD. Thus, he was rewarded and honoured for his work by being elected Imam. His leadership was the beginning of Al-Busaid's reign, the family that are still ruling Oman today.

As was mentioned before Oman was united during Imam Ahmed's reign. He made Rustaq the capital, and he controlled Omani cities, and appointed their governors himself. He ruled in a very disciplined manner, so he was able to achieve national unity. By these means he gained the respect of his people and their high esteem, leaving behind him a well-known and respected name. The people of Sohar were particularly loyal to their ruler. They gave him all the support he needed and they stood behind him in all circumstances, good or bad, that he faced when he took over the leadership[226].

Once Imam Ahmed bin Said had laid the foundations for national unity, he concentrated on regaining Omani domination in the Arabian Gulf, extending his authority to the north, south and east. In the north his authority extended along the Arabian Gulf for 300 miles; to the south, he controlled up to Bab Al-Mandab[227]. In the east, it extended up to the east coast of the Arabian Gulf[228]. The Persians, during Karim Khan's rule, were watching the Imam Ahmed activities with jealousy and envy; in particular, the actions which increased his authority and status inside his own country and along the Arabian Gulf. They used every opportunity to interrupt and interfere with his progress. This resulted in a direct conflict between the Imam and Karim Khan as we shall see.

We do not have an accurate estimate of the land or marine forces in the employ of Imam Ahmed bin Said, and most of what we have is speculative; as Ibn Ruzaiq emphasized when he asked his father about the number of the soldiers at the time of Imam Ahmed, his father answered him: 'Their number is huge and uncountable'[229]. However, the best estimate of the Imam's marine forces would be in the thousands. This can be deduced from comments of the Italian traveller Fenzinzo. He mentioned that the Omani Imams, one of them being Sayyid Said, were able to enlist between 15-20,000 land and marine troops and around 1000 cavalry[230]. The soldiers were, as pointed out by Niebuhr during his visit to Muscat in 1179 AH/1765 AD, armed with rifles, swords and axes, and they were receiving regular salaries from the Imam[231].

But the maritime forces of the Imam were the source of his fame in the Arabian Gulf region, sufficient to make his enemies reconsider any aggressive step in his direction. It is worth noting that the Imam's maritime power, which consisted of a huge number of large and small ships, was used for trade during peacetime. In wartime, large ships were requisitioned for the navy, which helped enormously in strengthening the fleet. Omani merchants used to contribute to the building and arming of these ships, because state revenue was not enough to fund such huge extra expenses[232]. Therefore, the Imam's maritime power became the equal of all other maritime powers in Arabian Gulf ports [233]. As proof of the huge increase in the Omani fleet, when Parsons visited Muscat (in 1775 AD) he said :'The effective striking power in the maritime fleet is not less than 34 large ships and a huge number of small boats' [234].

Since the second half of the eighteenth century economic activity had increased in Oman particularly in the commercial sector, whereby Muscat became one of the most important centres in the Arabian Gulf. These activities were due to three factors:

- The huge size of the Omani maritime fleet; the number of ships had increased during 1179-1189 AH/1765-1775 AD. Even Parsons was astonished by this maritime fleet and he wrote the following comment: ' Muscat is a very important trade city and it has a huge number of boats trading with Surat, Bombay and Java, along the Malabar coast and with Mukha and Jeddah in the Red Sea'[235].
- Imam Ahmed bin Said's encouragement of his people to trade with other countries; this resulted in an increase in trade contact with ports in the Arabian Gulf, with Indian harbours, and those in the Red Sea and East Africa[236].
- The advancement of trade in Muscat over the other harbours in the Gulf; this enabled the city to occupy a primary position in the importing and collecting of Indian goods and articles and their re-exportation. As an expert in Gulf history comments: 'There arrives in Muscat over half of all trade between India and the Arabian Gulf, and it is then distributed to its destination'[237].

Other factors had contributed to Muscat's important position, in particular, merchants had security and protection for their goods in the harbour at Muscat. The English traveller Parsons expressed his astonishment at the large amount of goods he saw stored safely in this harbour, when he said: 'There are, in the present time in 1189 AH/1775 AD, huge amounts of goods and articles piled in the street without any supervision or guard, because the stores cannot contain half of the existing goods, even though, we did not hear of any theft, accident nor any burglary of these goods whatsoever'[238]. Muscat was also regarded as a safe navigable harbour. Therefore, most ships, especially those belonging to the English East India Company, used to dock in this harbour in order to take on freshwater and other provisions, during their voyage between India and Basra[239]. The importance of this is very clear in the comment of the Italian traveller Fenzinzo, in which he said :'There is not a place in the whole coast of the Arabian Gulf, apart from Muscat, that could supply the ships with freshwater and food, and these two things are vital for life'. Perhaps trade in Muscat progressed because of its ability to provide these essentials[240].

Persia
Persia, ruled by Karim Khan Zand from 1163-1193 AH/1750-1779AD, was the greatest political power in the Arabian Gulf. Karim Khan, founder of the Al-Zandi dynasty in south Persia, benefited greatly from the external disturbances and tensions which affected Persia because of the contest for the throne after Nadir Shah's death in 1160 AH/1747 AD. However, he was able to eliminate his opponents one after the other. He then extended his authority to all districts except some of the remote regions. Shiraz was designated as the capital[241].

Even after Karim Khan had grabbed power in Persia, he was satisfied with the title of viceregent (vice-Shah), and he ruled with absolute authority, whereas the Shah, Ismail the Third, ruled in name only and he was virtually in Karim Khan's custody. Externally, this period was characterized by an unusual calmness and stability in comparison with other periods before and after him.

In a similarly aggressive manner to that of Nadir Shah, Karim Khan tried to colonize Iraq and Oman. This policy appears to have sprung from the desire of Persian rulers to minimize the internal threat from the more ferocious tribes by orchestrating threats to their authority. One way to achieve this was to keep these tribes busy with invasions and wars along the borders[242]. The Persian rulers had therefore to raise a huge military force, and in order to do this they had to depend mainly on manpower provided by tribes on the one hand and governors on the other. Perry estimated that the land forces numbered around 45,000, during Karim Khan's period. This, however, is a rough estimate, because tribal or local forces, brought together in wartime, could be more or less than this number[243]. To give an example of the size of a wartime force Karim Khan was able to raise an army consisting of 30,000 combatants when he planned to invade Basra in 1189 AH /1775 AD while at the same time his forces were carrying out military operations north of Iraq[244].

Although Persian maritime power was considerable during the Karim Khan era, it was not as strong as it had been during the time of Nadir Shah, because Karim Khan did not try to repeat Nadir Shah's experience and build a Persian maritime fleet in the Arabian Gulf. Instead, he tried to use the help of local maritime fleets which were on the east coast of the Arabian Gulf, or the ships of the English East India Company, in order to carry out any attempt at military operations[245]. By these means, Karim Khan was able to equip 30 ships armed with cannons to invade Basra, and these cannons were powerful enough to attack the city from the sea in order to support the operations of the combatants on land. Those ships entered Shatt Al-Arab waters in March and April 1189 AH /1775 AD, arriving on the outskirts of Basra at the same time as the land marine[246]. At the same time Karim Khan was furious because of the increase of the powers of Iraq and Oman which had risen to their peaks.

Political developments in Iraq and Oman were not the only reason for Karim Khan's discontent and hatred, the fact that both Oman and Basra were flourishing as commercial centres at a time when other ports were losing their importance was also highly significant. Because political disturbances had spread throughout Persia after the death of Nadir Shah, the agents of the English East India Company started to transfer their offices one after another from Persian cities to Basra and Oman, since these two countries were enjoying a huge commercial boom as a result of their political stability. The transformation of the trade entrepot activities, in the Arabian Gulf, from Persian cities to Iraqi and Omani cities, was one of many reasons for Karim Khan's aggressive policy.

Karim Khan's Policy in the Arabian Gulf and its Effect on Persian Arab Relations

Karim Khan's policy resulted in a decline in Persian-Arab relations during Karim Khan's time because he had tried to implement an expansionist policy, not only against Arab countries and the Arabian coast, in particular Oman and Basra, but also against the tribes and the Arab powers which were dominating the east coast of the Gulf.

Karim Khan's Policy Towards the East Coast of the Arabian Gulf

Before we talk about Karim Khan's policy towards the east coast of the Arabian Gulf, it must be mentioned that this region was under the rule of the Arab tribes which were known for their special seamanship and navigation. Three of these important tribes were heavily involved in the political events of the southern part of Persia during the 1870s. These three tribes were: Arab Bushehr, ruled by Sheikh Nasir Al-Makhtur, who were from the Omani Arab Al-Matarish. Secondly, Arab Bandariq, belonging to Arab Ziab on the Omani coast, who were resident towards the north of Bushehr. They also controlled Karj island, with other Arab tribes in Lingeh harbour and Heera island near Lingeh harbour. Finally, there was the Arab Bani Ka'b centred at Al-Dourak[247]

These tribes were directly related to western coastal tribes. Therefore, every time the Persians tried to control them they withdrew their boats to islands near the coast and stayed there until circumstances allowed them to return. More importantly, these tribes, as we shall see, were bound by many alliances with Arabs of Oman or Al-Qawasim against the Persian ruler, particularly when Karim Khan tried to put an end to independent rule on the east coast of the Arabian Gulf[248].

Despite all of that, Persian authority along the east coast of the Arabian Gulf was not clear during the eighteenth century. Even Nadir Shah did not succeed in his many attempts to dominate the tribes in the region. In his last days, as Kelili says, he decided to force the residents on the eastern coast to emigrate to the coast of the Caspian Sea and to replace them with tribes from that region, but this plan did not see the light of the day because of Nadir Shah's death[249].

Karim Khan tried from 1179 AH /1765 AD until his death in 1193 AH /1779 AD to put an end to the independence of the Arabian states on the eastern coast of the Arabian Gulf. And despite his ability to dominate some areas, including Bandar Abbas and Bushehr for some time, his success did not last long, because he lacked a strong maritime fleet to support his efforts. At the time of his death in 1193 AH /1779 AD the Arab tribes living on the eastern coast rebelled against the rule of Shiraz and kept their independence for the next 20 years, refusing to acknowledge the authority of any ruler except their own tribal sheikhs[250].

It is worth mentioning that some areas on the eastern coast were independent of Persian authority until the end of nineteenth century. For example the Arab tribe which ruled Bushehr kept their independence until 1267 AH /1850 AD; and Al-Qawasim tribe ruled Lingeh until 1305 AH /1887 AD, when an order was made by Persia to put all harbours on the eastern coast of the Gulf, including Lingeh, under Persian authority, and so Al-Qawasim reign in the region was ended[251].

However, this is only one aspect of Karim Khan's policies towards the eastern coast of the Arabian Gulf. Another was his maritime policy. It was known that Karim Khan did not have land marine forces in the Arabian Gulf as was in the case of Nadir Shah. Therefore, Karim Khan tried to benefit from the maritime experience of the population along the eastern coast of the Arabian Gulf as well as their maritime fleets. But these people tried to emphasize their independence in the Gulf rather than support Karim Khan[252].

When Karim Khan did not succeed in gaining what he wanted, he asked the help of representatives of the English East India Company to provide him with one or two military war ships in order to maintain security in the Arabian Gulf. In return he granted the Company commercial privileges in Persia, and he opened commercial offices in Bushehr. This step was aimed at imposing maritime domination throughout the Arabian Gulf, to be followed by another to enforce Persian authority upon Arab tribes resident in the eastern coast of the Arabian Gulf, in order to put them directly under Persian administration[253]. After that he concentrated his efforts on an attempt to invade and occupy Oman.

Karim Khan's Policy Towards Oman

Persia was an internally divided state after the death of Nadir Shah in 1160 AH /1747 AD. This situation pre-occupied his successors and especially Karim Khan. However, once Karim Khan strengthened his authority, he renewed his policy towards the Arabian states in the Gulf in general and Oman in particular. He tried to gain benefit from the military war ships of the English East India Company and others, because they were the only means to wage war on Oman, the strongest maritime power at the time. Nevertheless, Karim Khan did not do anything against Oman until 1183 AH /1769 AD. Perhaps the reputation of Imam Ahmed's navy and the magnitude of his resources more than anything else deterred Karim Khan from attacking Oman after Imam Ahmed bin Said took power[254]. The follower of Karim Khan's policy will find that Karim Khan directed his efforts many times towards dominating and invading Oman, from 1183 AH /1769 AD until his death in 1193 AH /1779 AD, in order to bring it under his control. In 1183 AH/1769 AD he demanded that Imam Ahmed return a large ship that the Imam had bought from Hormuz's ruler, claiming that this ship belonged to the Persians, but Imam Ahmed refused to do so[255]. This event led to tension in the relations between the two countries.

In fact, the main reason for this tense relationship was that Karim Khan demanded an annual taxation, and Imam Ahmed, the liberator of Oman from the Persian invasion, was not prepared to respond to such a demand. This attitude was reflected in his letter to Karim Khan in which he contended that the ship mentioned had indeed been bought entirely legally from Sheikh Abdullah, Hormuz's ruler, and the rest of the claim concerning the Omani payment of an annual tax to Persia was decidedly illegal. He stated that if Karim Khan insisted on his demands, then the only answer would be artillery shells and guns[256].

From that date, relations between Persia and Oman were tense. Many maritime battles were waged between the two parties and Persia was involved in other aggressive incidents against Omani maritime ships and even against Oman itself. In one of these events, the Persian forces, around 7000 soldiers, crossed to Lingeh island intending to attack Oman. Imam Ahmed immediately launched a siege on the island, forcing the Persians to withdraw back to their own country[257]. Meanwhile, the Persians captured two ships loaded with coffee and other goods which were on their way to Basra, prompting Imam Ahmed to carry out an attack in 1184 AH /1770 AD, against Bushehr harbour and to demand full compensation in return for the Persian capture of the two Omani ships. The maritime fleet then return to Muscat[258].

At the end of 1187 AH /1773 AD, the Persian maritime fleet, including a stolen English ship *Tiger*, assembled to fight against the Imam, but many men of the Arabian tribes, whom Karim Khan had called to join, declined to collaborate in the action, thus ensuring the failure of the Persian maritime expedition[259].

It seems that the tense Omani-Persian relationship was not only due to factors mentioned above, but also because Oman had succeeded in dominating many regions and islands in the Arabian Gulf and on its eastern coasts, such as Shamil, Menat, Qeshm and Hormuz. This is apart from the signing of alliances with the Arabian powers in the west and east of the Arabian Gulf, especially when danger threatened. Indeed, these alliances weakened Karim's Khan resolve to dominate the Arabian regions and/or to invade Oman[260].

In the year 1187 AH /1773 AD, a treaty was signed between Imam Ahmed bin Said and the Al-Qawasim Sheikh, in order to confront Karim Khan's threats against the western coast of the Arabian Gulf. In this regard, a treaty was signed between Sheikh Rashid, the ruler of Ras Al-Khaimah, and Sheikh Khalfan, the governor of Muscat harbour. Both attacked Bandar Abbas harbour destroyed two ships there, as well as destroying a military ammunition store which the Persians had built in Lingeh harbour[261].

The Al-Busaid rulers of Oman also tried to strengthen their relations with the Arab tribes, in particular with the Arabian Ka'b tribes, on the western coast of the Arabian Gulf, in order to confront and defeat Karim Khan's threats. It is certain that the tribes reached their peak during Sheikh Salman bin Sultan's rule (1150-1181 AH /1737-1767 AD). The establishment and the progress of this Ka'bi state coincided with the escalating struggle between the Persians and the Omanis to control the region, and in order for this state not to be subject to either of the two conflicting authorities, better relations were sought with the strong Arabian countries in Oman during Ahmed bin Said's era. Oman's technical assistance was requested to build its maritime fleet and to strengthen its military forces, in order to preserve its independence and to face foreign aggression[262]. The Ka'bi's request received a quick response from the Omani Imam who was endeavouring to establish alliances with Arab powers on the eastern and western coasts of the Arabian Gulf, in order to withstand foreign aggression. Thus, the Ka'b tribe obtained Omani technical experience in strengthening and enforcing the Ka'b maritime fleet, and it therefore became one of the most important maritime fleets in the Arabian Gulf at that time[263].

The Ka'bis did not forget Oman's good deed towards them. In this regard, Lorimer reminds us that when Karim Khan tried to attack Muscat in 1187-1188 AH /1773-1774 AD, he asked for assistance from the Ka'bi Sheikh, but the Sheikh: 'pierced a few of his ships and they were shown in this state to the vice-deputies as evidence of his inability to obey his commands'[264]. It is very clear that the Ka'bi Sheikh wanted to give an excuse not to fulfil Karim Khan's demands since his aggression was directed against Oman with which the Ka'bi were linked by great ties. However, friendly relations between Oman and the eastern coastal states of the Arabian Gulf and in particular with the Ka'bi tribe, roused the ire of Karim Khan. Thus he struck an alliance between these powers, even before he started his siege around Basra (in 1189 AH /1775 AD)[265].

Because Karim Khan was occupied with the internal conflicts inside Persia, he left Sheikh Nasir Al-Makhtur, the ruler of Bushehr, to manage naval affairs and gave him the authority to continue the war or to make a peace treaty with Oman. The Imam of Oman showed his desire for peace and for ending the conflict, with the condition that the negotiations be based upon friendly and amicable principles, and not subject to any conditions that would erode the sovereignty and independence of his country. But Sheikh Nasir, Karim Khan's representative, put forward old conditions which the Imam considered to be humiliating and so he refused them out of hand[266]. Therefore, the negotiations failed, and with this failure, Omani-Persian relations returned to their previous state. As a result, India sent delegations and contacted both Oman and Persia in order to end the escalating war between these two sides, especially as it affected trade movement in the Arabian Gulf and among other countries including India. One of these delegations arrived in 1188 AH /1774 AD, after huge preparations made by Karim Khan to invade Oman[267].

The Persian Invasion of Basra and the Omani Rescue

Persian Invasion of Basra and the Siege

While it not possible to enumerate and examine all of the reasons for the Persian invasion of Basra, it is beneficial to study briefly some direct reasons for this invasion in general and concerning Oman and Basra in particular, since this study will throw some light on the nature of Arab -Persian relations during the invasion of Basra and its siege.

It is known that the success which Basra had achieved during the second half of the eighteenth century led to the commercial ruination of Persia's ports. This success was one of the reasons why Karim Khan declared war on Basra city. However, this was not the only reason because the flourishing trade which Basra had enjoyed had declined, and even its traces were wiped out as a result of the horrible frightening plague this city had to face in 1187 AH/1773 AD. The representative of the English East India Company who described the city after his return to it at the end of that year said: 'There was in the city only a small garrison, empty buildings, a commercial recession and a few weak people left untouched by the disease' [268]. The situation was far more complex than that, since Karim Khan armed himself with other reasons to attack and occupy Basra, as the events which followed underline.

The Persian attack on Basra was neither surprising nor unexpected. The threat of attack against the city remained for a year before it actually happened. It seems that the Turkish rulers in Iraq were expecting that, as a reaction to the victories they had won against Karim Khan in northern Iraq, Karim Khan would avenge himself upon either Baghdad or Basra, and Basra was a more likely target than Baghdad. However, the Persians started to attack northern Iraq. This attack was only a part of Persia's distracting and misleading tactics, because at the same time huge preparations were underway in Persia to invade Basra[269].

The reasons, which Karim Khan used to excuse his action were ill-treatment and taxes imposed on Persian visitors when they were passing through Baghdad on their way to sacred sites in Najaf and Karbala. It seems he forwarded to the ruling authority in Iraq demands for payment which could not be accepted. Olivie mentioned that Karim Khan: 'demanded from Al-Bab Ali, the head of Omar Basha [deputy of Baghdad] and he threatened to send an army to the

Tigris and Iraq if they did not fulfil his demands. Also, if they did not cancel the tax which was imposed by Al-Bab on every pilgrim'[270]. Obviously, as Olivie says : 'It is difficult for Al-Bab Ali to sacrifice one of the important officials in the Ottoman government in Iraq, just because of Persian accusations; thus he did not accept the accusations. This was the reason why relations were severed'[271].

The collaboration between Basra and Oman was another reason for severing relations between Karim Khan and the deputies of Baghdad and Basra. Reputable sources point out that the Persian Shah demanded naval assistance from the governor of Basra[272] and the representatives of the English East India Company early in 1188 AH/1774 AD, to attack Oman, or he would send a force to destroy Basra, but both the governor of Basra and the representatives of the English East India Company apologized for not fulfilling the Shah's command. The refusal of the governor and the representatives made Karim Khan seize a few officials of the Company in Shiraz. Therefore, the governor of Basra undertook some precautionary preparations in light of the Persian threat[273].

In fact, collaboration between Basra and Oman was based on profound national feeling. Not only did the governor of Basra not want to provide help to the Persian Shah against the Imam of Oman, he was also more than satisfied and content to increase the power of the Omani Imam as a bulwark against external powers. In addition, the existence of a strong Omani maritime fleet in the Arabian Gulf would not only be a barrier to foreign challenges, but also secure the trade affairs of the two countries, the profits being shared by both parties[274].

The reports of the English East India Company go further than that. It is mentioned that Karim Khan made an attempt to attack Muscat in 1188 AH/1774 AD, but that the maritime fleet of Basra obstructed and dispersed it[275]. This clearly shows the depth of the relationship between Basra and Oman. Those aforementioned reports also point out that Persian sources accused Suleiman Agha, the governor of Basra and the deputy of Baghdad, of providing unlimited aid to the Omanis during this period, and that they considered it the main reason for Karim Khan's hatred of Basra[276].

It was natural in this situation for Karim Khan to decide to invade Basra. He thus prepared a large army, estimated to be 30,000 combatants, under the command of his brother Sadiq Khan, which arrived at the city early in 1189 AH/1775 AD. In Basra, Suleiman Agha and the people of Basra stood firm against the Persian invading army for more than a year. Suleiman Agha had great ability: since he had become aware of Karim Khan's preparations to invade Basra he had started quickly to gather supplies and ammunition. He armed anyone who could be armed from the army and the people, and tried to increase the capabilities of the maritime fleet in Basra. He was hoping that these preparations would help him break the siege or at least hold out until the deputy of Baghdad, Omar Basha, could send him aid[277].

But these preparations only enabled Suleiman Agha and the people of Basra to resist for over a year. They withstood, throughout the year, the advancing army who surrounded the city from every side and then started to shell it with all the cannons it possessed. Supplies continued to come through the Shatt Al-Arab on Karim Khan's ships[278]. Despite the Persian aggression and the magnitude of the artillery which they used to shell the city, the people of Basra sacrificed themselves with great devotion to defend it. They also retaliated as much as possible. This situation continued until their means ran out. It was expected after this long siege that the deputies of Baghdad would send military supplies to save the city. However, a letter sent by the new deputy of Baghdad, Mustafa Basha, to Basra's governor professed his inability to supply Basra with any forces[279]. The representatives of the English East India Company in Baghdad were also of little help. They had promised to protect the city from the river, and when the siege strengthened they suddenly withdrew[280]. This unsupportable action taken by the Turkish deputies and the English emphasizes the obvious fact that no one will defend the land but its children, i.e. the Arab youths. These circumstances forced the people of Basra to request relief from their Omani brothers.

Circumstances Surrounding the Omani Relief of Basra

The circumstances surrounding Omani aid to Basra in the 1870s were not so much connected with the events of the Persian invasion of this city in 1189 AH/1775 AD, as they were related to many other factors. First of all, Imam Ahmed bin Said fully comprehended the expansionist dimensions of Karim Khan's policies, whether in relation to Basra or his own territory, since the occupation of either region would lead to the utmost damage to the other. Therefore, Imam Ahmed rushed to respond to the plea for help[281].

The older and more modern sources differ as to the direction from which help was requested from the Omani Imam. Some of these sources mention the deputy of Baghdad[282], others the deputy of Basra[283], the rest the people of Basra, and specifically the Muntafeq tribes [284]. However, if one probes carefully and deeply into these narrations, one will find that the later sources are more accurate and verifiable. For example, the author of *History of Oman* who was close to the event, referred specifically to this issue when he said :'the people of Basra sent to our lord the Imam, requesting victory from him, then he supplied them with people and boats'[285]. And he mentioned in another place, when Omani aid arrived, Thamer bin Abdullah Al-Sa'adun, the Sheikh of Muntafeq tribes, received it and said:'Oh, my brother [i.e. the Omani commander], we are sick and you are our doctors for our disease and the healer is Allah'[286]. Again, this narration proves that the relationship had strengthened between the people and the figureheads of Basra on the one hand and the Omanis on the other. Whatever the issue, Imam Ahmed bin Said completed the preparations of the Omani maritime fleet in the middle of August 1189 AH/1775 AD. One of these preparations was the joining of

The Omani relief expedition to Basra 1775-1776 AD.

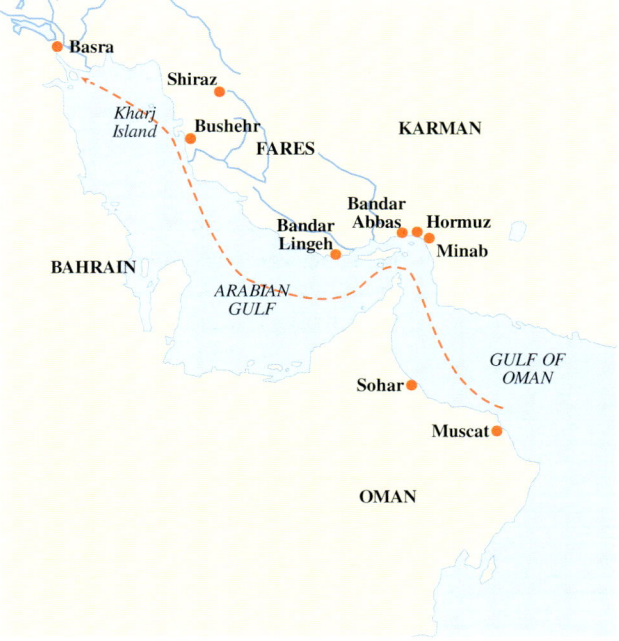

his maritime fleet with the two armed ships of the Baghdad deputy. These two armed ships (*Dejla and Furat*) were brought by the representative of the English East India Company to Muscat, where they were handed over to the Imam immediately at the request of the Baghdad deputy. Then the Imam hoisted the Omani flag to be ready for action[287].

Besides this, the Imam got ready a large number of Omani ships which were described to us by the English traveller Parsons, when he visited Muscat and saw those preparations himself. He said: 'And it was the striking force in the maritime fleet not less than 34 ships, four of them were built in Bombay and carrying 44 cannons, five ships of the frigate type armed with [18-24] cannons and the rest were small ships armed with between [8-14] cannons which were built in Muscat ports and elsewhere in other harbours'[288].

Omani sources estimated the number of ships in the fleet to be 80, including the flag ship of the Imam (*Rahmani*) which was carrying a force consisting of 10,000 men, as Ibn Ruzaiq has recorded[289]. Hilal bin Imam Ahmed commanded the fleet and he was accompanied by his brother[290]. On the eleventh day of September, this maritime fleet passed by Bushehr on its way to Basra, and a few days later docked at the river mouth of the Shatt Al-Arab. When the Omani maritime fleet arrived at Shatt Al-Arab, it found an iron chain across the river, attached by the Persians to the two river banks in order to prevent the passing of any aid to the besieged city. They had also placed a large garrison armed with cannons in the same place for the same purpose. The Omani maritime fleet had to wait in **a** secure position until the end of the month, and did not attempt to cut the chain. However, if they had tried then the opportunity for victory against Karim Khan would have been much greater, especially since his arrival was not immediately expected. The delay enabled the Persians to prepare for battle[291].

According to Ibn Ruzaiq, the Omani maritime fleet was able to break the iron chain at the entrance of the Shatt Al-Arab by ramming it with the flag ship *Rahmani*[292]. Despite heavy artillery shelling from the Persian side, the Omani maritime fleet entered the Shatt Al-Arab in the middle of Rajab 1189 AH, on the fourteenth day of October 1775 AD to the unbounding joy of the people of Basra who were behind city walls. Sadiq Khan's forces were not able to prevent the supplies and men from reaching the people of Basra and being used to launch an attack against the siege the very next day. In a fierce battle between the two sides, the Persian commander promised a reward to his soldiers in order to increase their zeal in facing the Arab attackers. The reward, designed to obstruct the off-loading operations of the Omani soldiers, consisted of three tumanats for the killing of any person and five for every prisoner of war. However, this method did not succeed, because the Omanis and Basrans fought in close combat with the enemy, and were able to wipe out many of their opponents. The great courage displayed by the Arab fighters who repulsed the Persian attacks on the 19 October has been admired and respected by researchers into these events[293].

Despite all of that, the battle was not decisive, the proof being that clashes between the two sides continued for the next few months, quite apart from the continuation of Omani aid to Basra. This aid had played a major role in easing the military pressure around the people of Basra and lifting their morale, particularly once the Omani fleet had established a strong position in the northern region of the Gulf and Basra. Control of the Shatt Al-Arab by the Omani fleet since it had arrived there in the middle of 1189 AH/1775 AD enabled supplies to be delivered to the besieged city. However, as time passed, Omani provisions started to decline. Neither was there any aid forthcoming from the Ottoman Sultan nor from the deputy of Baghdad whereas provisions and men continued to arrive to the Persians from Shiraz[294]. The commander of the Omani fleet decided to withdraw at the beginning of 1190 AH/1776 AD, because he was afraid that the shortage of provisions would affect his soldiers. He also feared that Karim Khan would take advantage of the opportunity presented to him by the absence of the Omani fleet and attack Oman[295].

Despite all the circumstances we have mentioned which did not permit the Omanis to stay in Basra for long, their sincere assistance in defending the city had a lasting effect on the people of Basra and its rulers. Therefore, they decided to reward Oman with an annual payment from the bank of Basra. This reward continued from the time of Imam Ahmed bin Said until the time of Sultan Said bin Sultan[296].

The natural inclination of the Imam in the circumstances outlined above had been to stand beside Basra during its trouble. This led to strengthening of the relationship between Oman and Basra, and once the Persian occupation had been lifted from Basra, immediately trade relations between the two countries were renewed and the annual Omani coffee fleet began to come to the city as it had done before[297].

Whatever interpretation can be put on this collaboration, Landen obviously regarded it as a self-standing alliance between the Ottomans and the Omanis, when he pointed out that: 'Ahmed bin Said concluded an alliance with the Ottomans which filled his coffers with a huge sum of money every year, in return for Omani protection in the south wing of Iraq'[298]. In fact, there was not an alliance in its traditional definition, between the two sides as much as their understanding of the value of the maritime collaboration between themselves. This is what made the people of Basra ready to offer an annual monetary aid from their own state bank, in honour of the efforts paid by the Omanis in defending their city during its siege by Karim Khan. Perhaps this reason amongst others encouraged Karim Khan to wait for the opportunity to dominate Oman. As Lorimer pointed out: 'It was Karim Khan, since the occupation of Basra in 1190 AH/1776 AD, who demanded that his commanders prepare reports on the possibility of moving by land from Basra to Oman'[299]. As a result, Imam Ahmed was forced to keep his maritime fleet in the Arabian Gulf, as a precautionary move. However, the danger passed with the death of Karim Khan in 1193 AH/1779 AD, and the Persians had to withdraw back to their own country in the same year.

Imam Ahmed bin Said, for his part, achieved Omani unity, prevented the Persian danger and confronted them when they attacked Basra. As Sheikh Nur Al-Din Al-Salimi said, 'he has great potential, honourable ambition, courage and daring'[300]. Imam Ahmed bin Said is regarded as the founder of the Al-Busaidi government, the builder of its pillars, the erector of its outstanding characteristics and the bulwark of its throne. He died 1188 AH/1778 AD having achieved his great ambitions[301].

Barka Fort.

The Leadership of Said bin Ahmed bin Said[302]

The death of Imam Ahmed bin Said was a great loss to Oman and its people. It is not clear from the history books whether his son Said bin Ahmed who took over after his death inherited the leadership, or was instated by collective agreement of the *ulema*[303].

Since Imam Said was not interested in administrative affairs, his son Hamad took care of these matters and established Muscat as the headquarters of the government, while his father Said stayed in Rustaq. With the passing of time, the power and the authority of Hamad increased until the effective authority became his entirely[304].

Some of his achievements are mentioned in the history books. He built a tower beside the sea at the entrance to Muscat harbour and armed it with big cannons, in order to fortify the city. He built the fort of Bait Al-Fulaij in Ruwi and another in Barka, and armed it with huge cannons to defend the city against a foreign attack, and he also ordered the building of a ship in Zanzibar named *Rahmani* which became very famous during the Al-Busaidi era, because of its huge size and skilful manufacture[305]. In addition, Hamed bin Said prayed regularly in congregation, doing the compulsory and Sunnah (Extra) prayers, and he used to study the Qur'an. His piety increased the people's love for him, and he became very famous and well respected. Unfortunately, he fell ill and died from his sickness on the eighth day of Rajab 1206 AH/ March 1792 AD[306].

Sayyid Sultan bin Ahmed bin Said

After the death of Hamad bin Said administrative matters, which Hamad had taken care of while Said resided in Rustaq, were put under the control of Sayyid Sultan bin Ahmed bin Said. Sayyid Sultan assumed control of the country's affairs soon after the death of his brother Said bin Ahmed. Following in the footsteps of his father, Imam Ahmed bin Said, he was even more generous with his wealth, and was reluctant to refuse any request asked of him. As a result he retained nothing that could be given away. Thus, the people loved him, regarded him highly and respected him[307].

Sayyid Sultan bin Imam Ahmed bin Said was the first of the Imam's children to be called by the name Sayyid. He faced some internal problems and tribal wars but he overcame them with skilful politics and military prowess. He immediately turned to building internal structures, fortifying Muscat by building a huge castle on Al-Rawiya land, and he built a tower opposite to it and the south-eastern tower in three months. With that the city was fortified completely[308]. Then he built inside the city a huge palace call Bait Alalam which he constructed on the land of the existing Alalam palace, and made it his personal residence[309]. And he built Al-Fulaij fort in an oasis, also known by the same name as Al-Fulaij Oasis. Situated between Barka and Muscat, he made it his family residence away from the storms, wars and the political turmoil. He housed some of his family there and he used to visit them very often, away from politics and administrative problems[310]. After that, Sayyid Sultan bin Ahmed directed his attention outside of Oman, attempting to take back its possessions which had been lost over time. He carried out many military expeditions to recover Qeshm island, Hormuz and Bahrain[311] as a precaution against external threats, including the danger of Persian and European inter-ference, and also against the Wahabi danger which threatened Oman during that period. Concerning this issue, Sheikh Salim bin Hamoud Al-Siyabi said the Wahabis invaded Oman in those days[312], and they made an alliance with the people of Bahrain, therefore it was necessary for Sayyid Sultan to impose his authority on these islands, so he conquered Bahrain and appointed deputies. Then almost immediately he established domination over important ports on Makran coast and he captured Shahbar and Juwadar harbours. This led to the strengthening of relations between Oman and Baluchistan and the emigration of

Al-Alam palace in Muscat.

Baluchis to Oman increased in huge numbers, due to this new relationship. He also ensured the safety of his country by capturing Bandar Abbas harbour with the help of the powerful Omani navy. Sources mention that the Omani maritime fleet at this time had increased in number by more than 500 ships, with a displacement of between 250 to 1000 tons, apart from 100 ships which were owned by the people of Sur. It seems these ships traded and fought as required, because the sources pointed out that large ships assigned solely for combat were not more than three[313].

Because of Omani naval and military power, which amounted to not less than 12,000 fighters, Sayyid Sultan bin Ahmed was able to stop the Wahabi invasion and regain his authority in Bahrain. This followed an incident involving the Sheikhs of Bahrain who spirited Sayyid Sultan's deputy out of the city with the help of the Wahabis; they then concluded an alliance with them and entered under their authority[314].

As regards the international struggle between the French and the British in the Indian Ocean and Gulf waters which was escalating during that period, Sayyid Sultan decided to use this conflict for the benefit of his people, since each side wished to strengthen its relations with Oman to the detriment of the other side. This matter was ended by an agreement between Sayyid Sultan and the English in Jumada Al'Ula 1213 AH/ October 1798 AD ceasing his friendship with the French for many reasons. Among the reasons were first of all, Omani dependence on British-dominated India for the provision of rice, the staple food of most the people on the Arabian peninsula. Secondly, frequent attacks by French pirates against Omani ships. Lastly, the anxiety of princes and rulers, including the rulers of Oman, over the expansionist policies of the French, particularly after the French occupation of Egypt in 1213 AH/1798 AD[315].

Despite all of that, many of the articles of the agreement were not fully executed, because Sayyid Sultan bin Ahmed did not in fact cease trade relations with the French on Mauritius island, and it was not in his power to force the owners of the Omani ship to do so. Also, ending trade relations was harmful to his people's affairs. The significance of this agreement was the acceptance of an English political representative in the capital Oman for the first time in 1215 AH/1800 AD[316]. `

In this manner, Sayyid Sultan bin Ahmed balanced his external policy between British and French ambitions in the Gulf region. He also boosted his own authority in the region, in order to ensure the security and the safety of the Gulf, since Oman depended on maritime commerce. At the end of this continual striving, Sayyid Sultan bin Ahmed was killed on 13 Sha'aban 1219 AH/ 30 November 1804 AD by some pirates during a sea voyage between Basra and Oman[317]. He was succeeded by his famous son Sayyid Said bin Sultan.

Before we discuss the period of Sayyid Said bin Sultan, it is important to ponder some details of the development of relations between Oman and the French. These relations were active between the two sides, from the middle of the seventeenth until the end of the end of the eighteenth century (AD). Since they have only been alluded to very briefly in the discussion on Imam Ahmed and his sons Sayyid Sultan, it is necessary to go into the subject in more detail.

Omani-French Relations During the Second Half of the Eighteenth Century

After Imam Ahmed had proved his ability to unify the Omani tribes and to direct their potential towards naval and commercial activity, Oman became once again a centre for economic activity in the Gulf of Oman and the Arabian Gulf.

At this time, English-French competitiveness was getting tougher in India and the eastern seas. This competition was in fact an extension of the struggle between the two powers for supremacy in Europe. In these circumstances, Oman was prepared, because of its significant strategic position, to try and attract both French and English attention, hoping one or other of them would become an important ally. Imam Ahmed, with his profound vision, realized that he had to be strictly neutral with these two powers, and he persistently refused to allow the establishment of a European centre in Oman: as was mentioned before. France was very interested in Muscat since early times. In 1078 AH/ 1667 AD, the French ambassdor to Persia, de Lalain, suggested to his government that it would be necessary to dominate Muscat and to keep it as an important maritime base[318]. More explicitly, a number of representatives in Persia composed memoranda and treaty proposals - one of them was Peter Paul - in order to conclude alliances. The treaties contained provisions for the occupation and domination of Muscat. These documents even specified the French share of the benefits which might be gained from occupying Muscat with its two castles, Mirani and Jalali[319] . However, nothing was achieved from these proposals, and France was able to gain a more practical objective by capturing Mauritius island in Ramadan 1127 AH/ September 1715 AD and calling it Ile de France[320].

The establishment of Ile de France as a French naval base had to lead, sooner or later, to the definite involvement of Muscat in the English-French struggle, because one of the main aims of the base was to attack English trade from all sides[321], especially along the Cape route which passed to the south of Port Louis. The other important focal point for attack was the north route from Bombay to Muscat passing by the Gulf or the Red Sea[322]. The French made Muscat port a market for their spoils of ships and goods[323]. Therefore, neutrality, the offering of protection and water, amongst other things, arose naturally. Despite Omani efforts to keep aloof from this struggle and to avoid interference with any side, they realized that neither commercial affairs, friendship, traditions, nor international customs were able to protect them from becoming involved with the fighting in Europe, simply because it is difficult to live in peace in the middle of a battle field[324].

Soon enough, Oman witnessed many fights between the French and the English. The first incident happened in 1173 AH/ 1759 AD, when three French privateers[325], without any regard to Omani neutrality, obstructed the way of a British trade ship and forced it to move out of Muscat harbour. The deputy, Khalfan bin Mohammed, was annoyed by this aggressive action and he fired at them from two castles (Mirani and Jalali) forcing them to withdraw[326]. The French made another similar attempt in 1175 AH/ 1761 AD, when two French privateers coming from Ile de France (Mauritius) arrived in Muscat and tried to attack an English ship which was docking there, ignoring all the neutrality laws. Again the deputy Khalfan bin Mohammed immediately tried to protect the English ship and to avenge the humiliation to the Omani flag, so he fired at the two French ships[327]. Another similar incident happened in 1192 AH/1778 AD, but it failed due to the action of the same deputy, which cost the French the death of five people[328].

This stand taken by the deputy of Muscat, in defending the English ship which was seeking protection in the harbour, must not be regarded as proof that Oman favoured one side against the other. The basis of this action is contained in the inherited Arabic tradition of protecting the intruder or the refugee, even with armed force, no matter the nationality or religion of the person. The entrance of the British ship into Muscat port as it tried to escape from French danger, amounted to a seeking of refuge and the natural reaction was to follow traditional customs concerning protection. Naturally the British did not pay any fee in return for this vital assistance[329].

Despite these incidents, there was no animosity between Oman and France. Usually the French sought the Imam's forgiveness for what they had done inside his territory, presenting their reasons and compensation[330] on the one hand, and on the other maintaining good commercial relations between Oman and Ile de France (Mauritius), during the second half of the eighteenth century. So the island exported sugar and other cargo to Muscat, and in return imported food products, such as corn, salt, fish, dates and coffee[331]. Omani trade with the French also benefited considerably because the French frequently used Arab ships to transport supplies and provisions to their colonies[332].

Omani-French relations had been under severe strain in 1195 AH/ 1781 AD, when a small detachment of the French maritime fleet, consisting of three ships, under the command of Captain de Cheny, captured a frigate called *Saleh* armed with 50 cannon, near Sohar. This ship was loaded with English cargo and was travelling from India to Basra[333]. The three French ships had already captured the British ship *Beglerbeg,* and entered Muscat harbour, where they tried again to capture another English ship that was docking there, but they failed to achieve their aim because the deputy of Muscat defended it. Due to this clash, they withdrew, moving towards the Gulf mouth where they met the Omani ship and captured it[334]. Immediately, Oman prepared to defend its dignity and enforce its independence. Two months after the capture of *Saleh*, a French ship, *La Philippine*, came for supplies, whereupon the Imam instantly ordered two of his ships to attack it. After a fight lasting for two hours, the French ship was forced to surrender[335].

However, there was no desire in Muscat to continue the struggle with the French, particularly among those whose interests lay with Ile de France (Mauritius). Therefore, the Imam and his officials came up with a diplomatic compromise ordering *La Philippine* and its crew to Port Louis with a strong objection to its governor Vicomte de Souillac for the violation of Omani neutrality. The Imam also wrote a letter to King Louis XVI revealing his wish to maintain friendly relations between Oman and France[336]. The Imam received a strong endorsement from the governor of Ile de France, thus the French authorities in Paris decided to deal with the matter wisely. They apologized and sent their ship *Courier de I France* as compensation to the Imam for the loss of his ship *Saleh*. Despite the capture of French ship by a British ship on its way to Muscat, good relations were restored between the two sides[337].

As proof of the improvement in relationships in Dhu Al-Qa'adah 1199 AH/ September 1785 AD, a small detachment of the French maritime fleet, under the command of Captain Count de Roselie, consisting of the frigate *Venus* armed with 44 cannon, and two ships (*Prevoyance and Amphitrite*), arrived in Muscat. The Count met officially with the ruler of Muscat, Hamad bin Said. According to some sources, Hamad gave permission, which had been sought for a long time, to establish a French centre in Muscat[338]. But other sources deny this and mention that the Count requested permission to establish a centre and that the request received the same refusal as before[339] . However, if the first version is true, the French did not establish that centre, for two reasons, first, two years after that event, William Franklin realized during his stoppage in Muscat in 1202 AH/ 1787 AD that the restriction was still on; even the English East India Company had a local mediator in the harbour[340]: the British received this privilege in return for the flexibility which was shown by Bengal regarding the salt monopoly, whereby they allowed Omani ships to import limited quantities from Calcutta[341] .The second proof concerning the good state of Omani-French relations was the provision of another ship to compensate for the *Saleh* . This did not take place until 1205 AH/ 1790 AD, when France sent the *Escurial* later renamed *Saleh*, to Muscat accompanied by the frigate *La Thetis* and presented it in an official ceremony to the Omani authorities[342].

Despite French slowness in compensating the Omanis with the new ship, and as Hamad bin Said said, it was very small, less than one quarter of the size of the old one, their action nevertheless left a deep impression in strengthening the good feeling towards the French, so the governor of Muscat not only offered to appoint a French consul, he also offered to provide him with an official residential house without any return[343]. Therefore, Omani-French relations progressed, and one year before the start of the French revolution, the French government decided that it was necessary to have a consulate in Muscat, because of the utmost importance of the harbour. Roselie persisted with his request and pointed out the strong relations between Oman and the local organizations in India, and the fact that he regarded the consular establishment in Muscat as a basic part of the French naval system in the Indian seas[344]. The French government's aim was to achieve two goals at the same time: making Muscat a monitoring point for British activities in India, and as a source of provisions for Ile de France, which were to be transported by Arab sailors in case of a renewal of hostilities with the British[345]. However, the French revolution erupted in 1204 AH/ 1789 AD and obstructed the execution of this decision which was in effect ignored. It seems that the French did not grasp hold of the opportunity offered by the handing-over of the ship *Saleh* to Muscat, and the offer made by its governor to appoint a consul in Muscat[346].

When general war broke out in 1208 AH/ 1793 AD, the French realized the necessity of strengthening their influence in Oman, therefore they argued for the establishment of a consul in Muscat. This project was discussed for more than ten years. Then a resolution passed in Shaban 1209 AH/ March 1795 by the General Security Council called for the establishment of a consulate and appointed M. Beauchamp, a scholar and a traveller, to occupy the position[347].

The instructions passed to him in the middle of 1210 AH/ beginning of 1796 contained the information that the consulate in Muscat was established to spy on English movements in India by studying the internal situations in those countries, and also to study the routes that could be possibly used by the French to invade the east[348]. Nevertheless, M. Beauchamp did not take up office, because when he arrived in Egypt, at the beginning of 1214 AH/1799 AD[349], N. Bonaparte sent him to Constantinople (Istanbul), where he was arrested and put into prison[350]. In fact, no French consul arrived in Muscat until 1312 AH/ 1894 AD, when Monsieur Ottavi came to take over the consular duties[351].

British doubts were stimulated in 1211 AH/1796 AD when the Omani government lifted its neutrality, according to reports which pointed out that Omani commercial ships carried information about British ship movements to Ile de France, and that the French were passing through Muscat very frequently on their way to Persia and the Near East. Those doubts and their effects were supported by the information which was gleaned from the Portuguese that Omani merchants gained huge profits from the sale of merchandise and British ships which were captured for the French. Also, the British siege around Ile de France and Bourbon in 1209 AH/1794 AD[352] had weakened trade activity between Muscat and Port Louis[353]. The lack of a permanent British Company presence on the coast proved to be a dangerous weakness on the British side in the escalating struggle with France, and it meant that the British could not do anything to prevent Muscat being used as a base for destructive attacks by French privateers against British navigation in the Indian Ocean, except by using force or by obtaining control of that harbour. However, the British authorities in India were entirely preoccupied with their own problems there, and could not even consider taking on something which would embroil Britain in dangerous policies on the Arabian peninsula. Therefore, they were satisfied to maintain friendly relations with the Omani government as much as possible, since these relations would ease passage on the usual trade routes to the west and the north. Despite this, Oman kept its neutrality and continued active commercial relations with the French between the French islands and Muscat[354]. The government in Bombay did not raise the subject again, until the appearance of N. Bonaparte in Egypt in 1213 AH/ 1798 AD. His appearance on the scene brought a new dimension to the the stance of the Omani Sultan. Immediately the Omani government started to take serious steps to try and prevent French domination, not only in Oman, but also in other places in the Arabian Gulf [355]. This was at the time when Oman was approaching a new phase in its history after its ruler Sayyid Said bin Sultan took over.

The Sultan Said bin Sultan

The grandson of the founder of the Al-Busaid family, his reign coincided with the most flourishing period that Oman experienced during the nineteenth century, despite the many difficulties he faced in order to advance his country. Historians consider Sayyid Said bin Sultan, without any doubt, to be the most notable member of the Al-Busaid family who played a role in the history of Oman, the Gulf and East Africa. It would not be an overstatement to say that we consider him to be one of the most important statesmen in contemporary and modern Arab history[356].

From the time he took over in Oman in 1219 AH/1804 AD, he was faced with various difficulties: internally, there were disputes with a few tribes who were endeavouring to reject his domination and wanted to enjoy their independence, as was the case with all tribes in the Middle East; another problem was the competition from the Qawasim, from Ras Al-Khaimah, over navigation in the Arabian Gulf. He was also faced with some external difficulties, primarily the Wahabi invasion of the Dhahira region and their capture of the Buraimi oasis. But he also had to contend with a Persian attempt to take back Bandar Abbas port, which is situated on the east coast of the Arabian Gulf, from Omani authority.

The historians regard Sayyid Said bin Sultan's rule to be truly a golden period in modern Omani history for many important reasons:

- The wide expansion of Omani domination in a way that had not been seen before; all the regions between Bandar Abbas, on the east coast of the Arabian Gulf, to Zanzibar on the east coast of Africa, were under Omani authority. In addition to many islands at the entrance and parallel to the east coast of the Arabian Gulf, and the islands in the Arabian Sea and Indian Ocean. In addition, the Comoros islands were under Omani authority.
- The high status which Sultan Said bin Sultan occupied internationally; he was highly respected by the rulers of Europe, Asia, Africa and the United States of America at that time over and above his wide popularity among the people of his own country.
- The stability of Omani rule, despite foreign aggressive desires and conspiracies; at a time, when intra-Arab conflicts were continuing on the Arabian Gulf coasts, and when the Arabian peninsula witnessed constant wars between Mohammed Ali Basha and the Salafi movement. In addition, Oman was subjected to the aggressive desires of the British, the French and the Persians, Sayyid Said worked hard to preserve his country's independence using skilful diplomacy rather than force to reach his aims. The outcome of his intricate balancing act led to the signing of commercial agreements with France, the United States, Holland and Portugal. Sayyid Said's policies were based on realistic principles and diplomatic adroitness, which established Oman as the most influential and greatest of the Arab countries at large, during his reign.
- The strength of the Omani economy which was based on maritime trade was dependent to a large degree on a huge commercial maritime fleet supported by a remarkable maritime force. In addition to extensive Omani trade with China, south-east Asia, India, Ceylon, and Iran, Sayyid Said bin Sultan improved his possessions in East Africa to a point that, in the second half of his rule, most of the Omani government's income was coming from Africa. Omani ships transported coffee from Yemen and East Africa, cloves from Zanzibar, hemp and its yarns from the Ethiopian coast. At the same time, they were used to export these products to Middle East countries and Europe. They also transported from India and the East Indian islands' woods, spices and silk to the Arabian Gulf countries, Iran, Basra and Yemen. In order to

Sultan Said bin Sultan.

advance commercial and economic interests, it was necessary for Oman to have a huge merchant fleet and a naval fleet to protect the ports and the coasts of Oman. Sayyid Said established this maritime fleet, and thus Oman possessed a strong naval fleet and a merchant fleet which included many Omani ships.

The Omani Maritime Fleet

The first half of the nineteenth century witnessed a great focus on building both the merchant and navy fleet, during Sayyid Said bin Sultan's rule. Omani ports, such as Matrah, Muscat, Sur and Shinas, had the most important ship-building yards, where ships were constructed using imported wood from India and Java. Omani wood was also used, as well as palm trees to build small boats. Sayyid Said bin Sultan gave the order to build many commercial and military ships in Indian ports and especially in Bombay. The most distinguished ships in the history of the Omani navy, were ships called *Taj Bux, Caroline, Shah Allum, Liverpool, Sultanah and Taje.* Sayyid Said gave the ship *Liverpool* as a present to the British King William IV in 1240 AH/1824 AD. The King called it *The Imam* in honour of its presenter Sayyid Said bin Sultan. The military ship *Sultanah* was indeed one of the most important ships of the Omani maritime fleet, and it was sent to New York, carrying gifts to the American president. As a result of Sayyid Said bin Sultan's efforts in building the Omani maritime fleet, including its merchant and military wing, during the first half of the nineteenth century it was the biggest maritime fleet at large and the second after the British fleet. This huge maritime fleet had its main bases on the east coast of the Arabian Gulf in Bandar Abbas, Jask, Shaml, Saiab, Lingeh, Qeshm island, Hormuz, Larg and bases on the Omani coast, Matrah and Masirah island. On the African coast, Oman had maritime bases in Mombasa, Lamu, Merca, Madagascar and Zanzibar.

Sayyid Said bin Sultan, the Sultan of Oman who ruled more than half a century, had a vast state in the Arabian Gulf and Indian ocean. He used to travel between his territories in Oman and the African coast and spent a long time on board ship checking on the towns of this vast state. In the last few years of his reign, he used to prefer to spend the longest possible time in Zanzibar, to keep a watch on Omani possessions on the African coast. He had extensive relations with the leaders of the African tribes and kings of the states and islands, such as Madagascar, by which he was able to dominate them.

Despite the maritime force he controlled, he was described as very cautious, so he limited his domination to the coasts rather than take on risky ventures in territorial expansion, either on the coast of the Arabian Gulf or on the African coast. Omani merchants undertook the responsibility to penetrate inside Africa and they arrived at what is known nowadays as Kenya and the African lakes. They traded with the people, spread Islam, and were the first cultural bridge which linked the Arab with middle Africa. A clear picture of the strength of the Omani maritime fleet is given by an American merchant when he visited Zanzibar in the early part of the nineteenth century. He mentioned that Sayyid Said had arrived in the country commanding a force consisting of a ship armed with 64 cannons, three frigates, each of them armed with 36 cannon, two vessels each armed with 14 cannons, and 100 boats loaded with 6000 fighters. Even though the Omani possessions were at a distance from Oman of more than 5000 miles, the Omani maritime fleet was strong enough to guard these wide possessions, spread between Bandar Abbas and Zanzibar. Also, it was able to guard dozens of harbours along the Arab and African coasts and numerous islands throughout the Arabian Gulf and Indian Ocean.

In addition to the establishment of this vast state and the construction of a strong commercial and military maritime fleet, which had been used to maintain this state, Sayyid Said bin Sultan was able to establish a strong international relationship with Egypt and some European countries and the United States of America. Regarding the relationship of Sayyid Said bin Sultan with Egypt and its ruler Mohammed Ali, the relations between these two men were described as mutually respectful. Even though both men were in conflict with Wahabi activity on the Arabian peninsula, letters exchanged between Sayyid Said and Mohammed Ali were few. They do express Sayyid Said's amazement at the modernized government system which Mohammed Ali had established in Egypt and they also contain Sayyid Said's wish to build strong relations with the Basha of Egypt[357].

To enhance the warm relations between these two men and because Mohammed Ali appreciated the role which Sayyid Said bin Sultan carried out in resisting Wahabi activity in Oman during 1221-1234 -AH/1806-1818 AD, Mohammad Ali and the Sherif of Mecca, Yahya bin Sroor, gave a warm reception to Sayyid Said when he came to perform the pilgrimage in 1240 AH/1824 AD. Mohammed Ali sent a group of his high ranking army officers to receive and salute Sayyid Said bin Sultan, and the guns in Jeddah harbour discharged a salute to him while the Omani ship *Liverpool* was approaching, and when he returned back to Muscat he was carrying with him many gifts from Mohammed Ali and the Sherif of Mecca.

The relations between the two men continued to be good despite the British adversarial stand against Egyptian activity in the peninsula and the Arabian Gulf in particular. This stand was one which Sayyid Said could not ignore because of the special relationship which tied him to the British who helped him against his enemies. Despite that, Sayyid Said did not take any adversarial action against Mohammed Ali; the Egyptian documents even point out that Sayyid Said sent a letter to Mohammed Ali in 1255 AH/ 1840 AD requesting him to send quickly one artillery division of soldiers[358].

Sayyid Said bin Sultan's good relationships with foreign countries is obvious from his welcome of the conclusion of a commercial agreement with the United States of America in 1249 AH/1833 AD, in his welcome of the American consul to the Sultanate of Oman, and by the conclusion of an agreement between the Sultanate of Oman and Britain in Rabi Al-Awal 1255 AH/May

1839 AD. Most articles of this agreement deal with the organization of trade and navigation between the two countries, and with an offer of the necessary facilities to the British ships in Omani harbours. Another part of this agreement gave the British consul the right to judge any dispute which might occur between the British people resident in the Sultanate of Oman, and to regard his opinion in the cases which might emerge between British and Arab people.

Another aspect of the Omani Sultanate's external relations can be gleaned from a trade agreement with France in 1260 AH/1844 AD. According to this agreement, France obtained similar commercial and judicial privileges to those stated in the agreement with the British in 1255 AH/1839 AD.

During his reign, Sayyid Said did not refuse any proposal presented to him by any country which wanted to conclude trade agreements or treaties. He favoured trade over everything else. When the European countries and specially Britain requested him to ban the slave trade throughout his territories, and to collaborate with them to fight this type of trade throughout the Arabian Gulf and the Indian Ocean, he accepted this suggestion and forbade the slave trade which had given huge financial profits. He vigorously fought the activities of the pirates of different European nationalities who were involved in this trade. Worldwide public opinion responded positively to this stance at the time. The British national papers and the British House of Commons spoke highly of Sayyid Said and and praised his efforts in fighting the slave trade and his protection of human rights.

Despite the status of Sayyid Said bin Sultan's relations with the above mentioned countries, his relations with the United States of America were deeper and wider. As a result of these relations, Oman was the first Arab country in the Arabian Gulf and Arabian peninsula at that time to generate such relations with that vast country. Therefore, it is worthwhile to include a more detailed analysis of Omani-American relations.

Omani-American Relations During Sayyid Said bin Sultan's Reign

The United States and its relations with the Arab countries

The United States of America only declared its independence in 1190 AH/1776 AD. Therefore concern about its relationship with Arab countries and the Arabian peninsula in particular came later than that of European countries, such as Portugal, Holland, France and Britain. In fact when America gained its independence it was influenced by the policy of its first founder George Washington who encouraged isolationism, a policy which the United States followed for more than a century[359].

As a result, relations with the Middle East came slowly in parallel with the means of this new government, and its wish to be free to build a new country on American soil without the interference of others, and its desire not to be involved in the problems of others, as was mentioned by President James Monroe in his famous declaration in 1239 AH/1823 AD.

The Arab countries were largely unknown to the Americans, except for whatever they had read about them in literature such as Arabian Nights and the

Pharonic History of the Nile valley. The Arab countries, for their part, did not know anything about the the United States of America, since its independence came late in the eighteenth century. However, America expressed its wish to conclude friendly commercial treaties with European countries, and to open the trade gates before the American merchants to Europe, and the Arab countries of North Africa. It indeed succeeded in achieving these goals, whether in the Arab countries in North Africa or in the Arabian east.

The Alawi government of what is now Morocco was the first country to recognize the independence of the United States, since the relations between the two countries remained strong and friendly. We see for instance that the American Congress proposed to the government in 1201 AH/1786 AD that the United States conclude a friendly commercial treaty with Morocco and also requested the mediation of Al-Mou'la Mohammed bin Abdullah, the Moroccan ruler, with the representatives of Tunisia, and West Tripoli to stop their ships from attacking American ships which were trading in the Mediterranean Sea.

When George Washington was elected as President of the United States of America in 1204 AH/1789 AD, he praised the friendship between the two countries since the dawn of American independence, in a letter he sent to the Moroccan government. In fact, the correspondence of Al-Mou'la Mohammed bin Abdullah with the American Congress since independence was regarded as the first international recognition of the government of the United States of America. The United States will never forget Morocco's actions in this regard, and there will always be an American consul in the Moroccan city of Tangiers. This was the first foreign consulate established in Morocco in 1236 AH/1820 AD[360].

If Morocco was the first Arab country to establish friendly trade relations with the United States of America, then the Omani Sultanate was the second such country to establish these relations, and the first country in the Arabian Gulf and Arabian peninsula. Perhaps we can find some similarity between Morocco and Oman, from the viewpoint of the United States at that time. This is because the United States had recently gained independence from the British and their counterpart the French, both with a colonial history. Also it was striving to achieve economic goals and it did not have any clear colonial intentions. In addition, at least the Arabs did not have any painful colonial experience which would make them reluctant or afraid to establish relations with America. Therefore, Morocco worked to establish strong relations with the United States, in order to face any European colonial conspiracy against itself. The Omani Sultanate similarly established strong relations with the United States, in order to achieve a balance with the other foreign powers who were eagerly seeking to extend their domination throughout the Gulf, Indian Ocean and North Africa.

Economic interests were the central point in American policy towards the Arab world. The missionaries - more precisely the Christianizers - supported and facilitated the way by their activities. The American Christian missionaries commenced their activities in the Arab countries at the beginning of the nineteenth century, when they started to build hospitals, schools and churches in Egypt, Syria and the Arabian Gulf region from 1235 AH/1819 AD. Therefore, the conclusion of the agreement between Oman and the United

States of America in 1294 AH/1833 AD came in parallel with United States policy in the Arab region. In other words, the signing of this agreement by Oman cannot be viewed as an individual action by Oman separate from other Arab countries; rather Oman was quicker than other Arab states in concluding an official agreement with the government of the United States of America, or what was then called the New World.

The Trade Agreement Between Oman and the United States in 1833 AD

As regards American economic activity, Oman attracted the attention of Americans from the beginning of the nineteenth century, because of its strategic location along the route to India and the Far East and its position at the entrance to the Arabian Gulf, as well as the fact that it was the focal point of relations with the rest of the Arab countries, Iran, and Africa[361].

In East Africa in particular, Oman was the dominant figure with an influence and power unmatched by any other country. This is because the Omani Sultanate, during Sayyid Said bin Sultan's reign, extended as far as East Africa where Zanzibar was linked to the mainland of Oman. Zanzibar had been under Omani rule from the middle of the seventh century, but not enough attention was given to its development until the arrival of Sayyid Said bin Sultan in the second decade of the nineteenth century, when he introduced clove cultivation in Zanzibar and treated it as a commercial product. He established many plantations and encouraged Omani merchants to penetrate deep into the African continent to trade with the Africans. He was also of immense help to the European explorers who went on numerous expeditions into Africa during the first half of the nineteenth century.

The progress of Oman's African component during Sayyid Said bin Sultan's reign, particularly the trading centre in Zanzibar, was an added attraction for foreign powers to strengthen their relations with the Omani Sultanate. The United States of America was the first foreign power to try and open Zanzibar's markets for American merchants to sell American products and buy African products from other countries. The primary step in trade relations between Oman and the United States of America took place when the American merchant, Captain Edmond Roberts from Newhampshire, visited Zanzibar in 1243 AH/1827 AD seeking to make a substantial profit there, but he could not avail of the same facilities as the British who were very friendly with Sayyid Said bin Sultan. Therefore, he returned to the United States with the idea of concluding a treaty with the Omani government in order to promote American trade in its possessions[362].

The American President Andrew Jackson, agreeing with the idea of concluding a treaty between the United States and Oman, granted permission to Edmond Roberts to start the necessary negotiations. The arrival of the American ship *Be Quick* carrying Roberts's envoy to Muscat was not only proof of American interest in Asia and Africa, but an indication also of the singular importance of Oman to the United States of America. Therefore, the signing of the trade agreement between Oman and the United States was completed in Jummada Al'Ula 1249 AH/ 21 September 1833 AD, and it was the first agreement signed by Sayyid Said bin Sultan and a large state. This agreement became the guide line which Oman followed in its agreements with

Britain in 1255 AH/1839 AD and France in 1260 AH/1844 AD. The American-Omani agreement was in effect until 1378 AH/1958 AD when it was replaced by a new treaty of friendly relations, economic and consular rights between both sides.

According to the 1833 agreement, Americans had economic and judicial privileges within the Arab and African possessions of the Sultan. Thus the Americans were able to trade inside the vast Omani territories; they were permitted to dock in its harbours, paying only 5 per cent fees for the cargo they were bringing into these Omani harbours, and they were relieved of any other taxes on export or import products. They were also relieved of annual pilot fees in Omani ports. The American consul had the right to deal with disputes between his countrymen, and also included was the right of the Omani consul to handle disputes between Omanis in the United States[363].

In our evaluation of the Omani-American commercial agreement, we note that it underlined the importance of Sayyid Said bin Sultan and showed his ability to negotiate an agreement with a large country. This encouraged him to lean towards strengthening of his relations with the Americans and to offer them special commercial privileges in East Africa, on the condition that they stand beside him and support him with arms to place Mombasa under his domination. In addition, the conclusion of an agreement with such an important country gave Sayyid Said bin Sultan considerable leverage with other big powers, especially England and France, in his bid to gain international status for Oman. Thus his country would have international recognition which the new emerging countries in Africa, Asia and even Latin America were seeking at that time.

On the American side, the American president Andrew Jackson received the Sultan's letter in a dignified manner. This letter and the text of the agreement were carried to him by Edmond Roberts upon his return to the United States. The letter conveyed Sayyid Sultan's good wishes to the American President, and expressed his thanks for the letter delivered to him by Roberts which included the goodwill of and respect from the American president to Sayyid Said. Included in the letter of Sayyid Said to President Jackson was the following: 'And we did respond to all of the desires of His Excellency your Ambassador Roberts by concluding the friendly and commercial treaty between our two beloved countries. This treaty which we will be bound to with sincerity, I, and who ever will succeed me, and Your Excellency can be assured that all American ships, which dock in the harbours belonging to me, will meet the same generous treatment which ours are receiving in the harbours of your countries. And I wish from all my heart that Your Excellency will regard me always as your sincere friend, and my friendship to Your Excellency will not vanish with time, but it will continue to strengthen'[364].

The letter and the text of the agreement emphasized the strengthening of relations with the United States. As a result, the reaction in the United States to this agreement was favourable and ratification was completed without any delay. Understandably so however, since the agreement did not place any oblig- ations on the United States towards Oman, and furthermore the United States was binding itself to a friendship with an African-Asian power which was justly proud of owning a maritime fleet larger than the American maritime fleet itself:

the Omani fleet consisted of about 75 ships of different sizes, each armed with a number of cannon between four and 56. Furthermore, Omani commercial ships, as it was noted by the American envoy Roberts, were sailing east to India, Ceylon and Java, besides visiting East African ports.

We may add that, even though this agreement contained a provision which gave the American consul in Oman the right to deal with disputes between his people and the reciprocal right to the Omani consul - if one existed in the United States - to deal with disputes which might arise between Omani people there, this article was more advantageous to the United States than to the Omani government, since it was unlikely that Omanis would reside and trade in the United States. However, this provision did benefit Sayyid Said, in so much as it relieved him of the duty of dealing with disputes which might occur between foreign residents in Oman, thereby avoiding a lot of trouble for him .

The British reaction to the Omani-American agreement was proof of British policy towards the Arabian Gulf, East Africa and the Indian Ocean in general. This policy was centred on domination and elimination of competition, whether from an external big power or even an internal one. For this reason, by the end of the 1820s Britain had bound the Sheikhs of the Omani coastal states with a set of agreements after it destroyed the power of Al-Qawasim in Ras Al-Khaimah. These agreements gave the British unchallengeable authority and they forbade those states from concluding any agreement, even if it were a commercial one, without the approval of the British government.

Because of the friendship between Sayyid Said and the British, Sayyid Said received a warning to be aware of the United States' desires on Omani possessions. Sayyid Said appreciated the British point of view, and concluded a treaty with the British similar in its content to that of the treaty with the Americans in 1255 AH/1839 AD.

The Omani-American commercial agreement resulted in a burgeoning of American trade throughout the African states of Oman, much more so than at Muscat. The number of American ships which were docking in Zanzibar increased rapidly, because these ships were importing an American strong cotton fabric which quickly became very popular in East Africa, the Arabian Gulf and the Arabian peninsula. Other valued trade goods were kitchenware, rifles, gunpowder, watches and shoes. In return the Americans exported Zanzibar cloves, ivory, gum copal which was used in manufacturing paints, copra and spices[365].

Due to the increase in American commercial activity throughout the Omani possessions in East Africa, in 1252 AH/ 1836 AD the American government chose one of its people by the name of Mr Richard Waters to be the first American consul in Muscat in 1254 AH/1838 AD.

However, American commercial activity with Zanzibar was clearly greater than such activity in Muscat. For example, only three American ships visited Muscat during 1254-1255 AH/1838-1839 AD, with the value of their cargoes which were delivered to Muscat harbour at around $1100 only, and dates were the main cargo in Omani-American trade until World War I.

Relations between Oman and United States of America remained friendly until the middle of the nineteenth century, i.e. for a period of nearly 20 years after the trade agreement was concluded between the two sides in 1249

AH/1833 AD. However, these relations were disrupted by a number of factors. Some of these factors are:

- Firstly, Sayyid Said's wish to modify the second article of the 1833 treaty which stated that American merchants had the right to enter all ports which are under the authority of the Sultan. Sultan Said insisted that this second article indicated - in his opinion - that the right was limited to one main port, Zanzibar port. The American government did not wish to respond to the Sultan's wish or to deprive its merchants from trading legally at the rest of Oman's African and Asian ports, and it was afraid these ports would be opened up to the merchants of other countries.
- Secondly, the controversy between Sayyid Said and the Americans concerning the limits of American consular authority over American people in Oman. This controversy arose because of the killing of an Arab by an American navigator, and was also due to the conflicts which often happened between the Americans in Omani territories and the Indian merchants known as Al-Banian - Hindus were not of the 'People of The Book' - and they were under British protection[366].

The American consul in Zanzibar, Charles Ward, who assumed his duties in the African port of the Omani empire in Muharram 1262 AH/ 24 January 1846 AD, played a role in the deterioration of relations between Sayyid Said and the United States resulting in the severing of the link between the two countries in Ramadan 1266 AH/July 1850 AD. Ward believed that the British consul in Zanzibar was behind the worsening of relations between the United States and Oman, and he expected the breakdown of the government after the death of Sayyid Said. This issue became widely known and that angered Sayyid Said to a great extent.

Even though Sayyid Said was prudent enough to permit the continuation of relations with the United States, he was forced to freeze this relationship after he had exhausted the means available in order to solve the problems which had risen between the two sides. Sayyid Said sent a letter to the American government in Ramadan 1263 AH/ September 1847 AD, but he did not receive an answer to it. This compelled him to stick to his interpretation of the second article of the treaty concluded between the two sides. The letter requested specific American guarantees concerning the precise limitation of American trade to parts of the East African coast which belonged to the Omani government, and it also demanded a detailed description of the judicial duties of the American consul in Oman, and the cessation of any interference by the American consul in the internal affairs of Oman.

The United States did not want to lose the friendship with the Sultan, so the American President (Millard Fillmore) sent a goodwill letter to Sayyid Said borne by his envoy Commodore Olic whilst Ward left Oman for the United States. When Olic arrived at Zanzibar on 1 Safar 1268 AH/1 December 1851 AD, he met with the American merchants before presenting the letter to Sayyid Said. He learned at first hand the extent of Sayyid Said's friendship with them, that they had more privileges in Oman than any other foreign merchants, and that Sayyid Said had not offended the American flag as Ward had claimed.

When the American envoy departed from Zanzibar, he left a good impression with its people and its rulers. From 1269 AH/1852 AD, American consuls worked hard at improving the relations between the Omani Sultanate and the United States of America. In fact, the reports of those consuls were filled with admiration for the goodwill which Sayyid Said had shown towards the Americans, and the commercial relations between the two countries were firm and stable[367].

It is worth mentioning that because of the interest of the United States in the African side of the Omani state, the appointment of American consuls to Zanzibar took precedence over the appointment of their colleagues in Muscat. The American consulate in Muscat was actually left vacant for some time and it was even put under the authority of the American consul in Zanzibar. The first consul to arrive in Zanzibar in 1252 AH/1836 AD was Richard Waters, who has been mentioned above, and the last United States consul left Zanzibar in 1309 AH/1891 AD, after the country came under British control. Whereas Mr Henry Marshall took up his job as a consul for the United States in Muscat in 1254 AH/1838 AD, the American consulate was left vacant during the period 1261-1297 AH/1845-1880 AD when Mr Magbour was appointed as a consul for the United States of America in Muscat, even though he was a British merchant. Subsequently in the year 1298 AH/1881 AD, France also recognized him as its consul in Oman.

The voyages of m.v. Sultanah to New York and London and the m.v. Caroline to Marseilles.

Even though relations between Oman and United Sates were good from the signing of the trade treaty (in 1249 AH/1833 AD) and lasting almost for the next 100 years, they were not of huge importance in the view of either side. However, the mere existence of the treaty was an indication of a new era in the domain of international relations, and in the friendly policy which linked Oman and the United States.

The Visit of Sayyid Said 's Ship *Sultanah* to New York

To further enhance the friendly relationship between the Omani empire and the United States which started with the treaty concluded in 1249 AH/1833 AD, Sayyid Said sent his ship *Sultanah* on a voyage to the American port of New York in 1256 AH/1840 AD. As well as strengthening relations with the United States, and general trading he wished to buy weaponry which he needed during his struggle with the Portuguese in Mozambique. The ship was navigated by a British captain, William Soloman, and Sayyid Said chose his private secretary Haj Ahmed bin Nu'man, to be his envoy to the United States. More significantly, he was the first Omani envoy to the United States.

Haj Ahmed bin Nu'man carried with him Sayyid Said's gifts to the American president. These consisted of two Arabian horses, some jewellery and a gold-mounted sword, along with some perfumes. The American president presented Sayyid Said with a large ship furnished with luxurious furniture, and four repeating revolvers and similar rifles.

Ahmed bin Nu'man, the first Omani envoy to the United States of America.

Furthermore the *Sultanah* carried more than 1000 bags of Omani dates, around 20 bales of Iranian carpets, 100 bags of coffee (mocca), 108 ivory tusks, around 80 bags of gum copal, 135 bags of cloves and 1000 of dried animal skins. All this cargo was sold on behalf of Sayyid Said in New York[368]. On the return voyage, the ship was loaded with various goods from New York. They consisted of 125 loads of grey sheets (*mercani* or American), 24 dresses of kermes coloured fabric, 13 bags of red, white and blue beads, 20 dozen of printed fabric, 300 muskets, gunpowder, China plates and few personal things for Sayyid Said[369].

When the *Sultanah* arrived at New York harbour, its passengers were vexed by the behaviour of some of the American public; the Arabic appearance of the Omanis with their distinct clothing attracted the attention of the people in the New York streets, so the public followed them. However their annoyance quickly disappeared when they were honoured and welcomed by the mayor of Brooklyn and the president of the naval club in New York. Then the American President Van Buren and the Secretary for the Navy granted permission for the *Sultanah* to enter into the harbour reserved for the American naval fleet so that it could be readied for sailing at the expense of the American government, and be loaded with the American products which we have mentioned above for the return voyage to Sayyid Said.

The duration of the *Sultanah* 's voyage, from the time it had left Zanzibar until it returned there, was around ten months. On its way back it was navigated by an American captain who was able to safely cross the the turbulent waves of the Atlantic. It returned carrying the envoy of Sayyid Said, Haj Ahmed bin Nu'man after he had completed his mission in far-off lands as ambassador on behalf of his country in a most successful manner.

If the voyage of the *Sultanah* proved anything, it was the wish of Oman and the United States of America, during Sayyid Said reign, to strengthen and to continue friendly relations between the two sides, especially in economic matters which were the chief concern of American merchants. At that time the United States of America was not interested in interfering in political problems due to the isolationist policy which it had followed since it had declared its independence from England. These of course indicate the importance of the economic relations which were built between the Omani Sultanate and the United States during the reign of Sayyid Said bin Sultan.

The Importance of the Contacts Between Oman and the United States of America at the Regional and International Level

Relations between Oman and the United States had an important effect on the stance of both countries. The United States benefited by its trade which flourished for more than half a century. The years 1249-1268 AH/1833-1851 AD witnessed a continuous progress in profits from American trade; thus in the year 1249 AH/1833 AD, the total number of American ships which arrived at Zanzibar was nine, whereas the number of English ships was only four; the number of American ships which arrived at Zanzibar in 1273 AH/1856 AD - this is the year in which Sayyid Said died - had increased to 26, whereas the number of English ships did not exceed two. This means that Sayyid Said did ensure that the United States experienced great progress in its interests in the region.

On the other hand, Oman benefited from its relations with the United States because of the existence of strong American trade in the empire. The fact that this made the sovereignty and the independence of these countries, even after the death of Sayyid Said, a settled issue does not need any discussion, and even after the country was divided between the two sons of Sayyid Said, Majed in Zanzibar and Thuwaini in Muscat, the Omani Sultanate in Muscat was spared colonial conflict, because its sovereignty was guaranteed by international agreements, whereas Zanzibar fell prey to the two colonists, England and Germany.

A report from 1365 AH/1946 AD outlined American foreign policy towards the states in the Arabian Gulf in general and Oman in particular[370]: 'At the time the United States recognized the special status of Great Britain in Kuwait, Qatar emirates and the coast of Oman, which we are in agreement with, and it is our policy -i.e. the policy of the American government - towards this region which takes into account the special status of the British in the emirates, that this will not result in harm to American interests or the interests of the local residents and the existing governments. And our policy towards Oman is based on one of our oldest treaties which is still in effect. This is the treaty on trade and friendly relations signed between the two sides entered into in Jumada Al'Ula 1249 AH/ 21 September 1833 AD' .

The report points out, in order to stress the importance of the relationship between the United States and Oman, that the hundredth anniversary of the signing of the agreement which was celebrated in middle of Dhu Al-Qa'adah 1352 AH/March 1934 AD featured a visit of a special American diplomatic envoy to Muscat. The report also indicates that in 1356 AH/1937 AD the American president, Franklin Roosevelt received in Washington Sultan Said bin Taimur, the Sultan of Oman, as his personal guest.

The report ended with comparisons between the treaties which the Arabian Gulf emirates signed with Great Britain, from the beginning of the nineteenth century, and the Omani-British treaties. The Arabian Gulf emirates promised to collaborate with Britain from 1236 AH/1820 AD in stamping out piracy in the Arabian Gulf, and to put a limit to the weaponry and slaves entering their countries. Also through a series of treaties, the emirates' rulers gave the British the right to use their territories in return for British protection. During the years 1331-1342 AH/1913-1923 AD the rulers of the Arabian Gulf emirates bound themselves even more, when they promised not to give exploration privileges for petroleum to any country without the agreement and the approval of the British.

Yet the Sultan of Oman agreed in 1342 AH/1923 AD only to consult the British political representative in the Gulf and the British Indian government before the exploration for petroleum commenced in the Omani Sultanate. This indicates how far Omani independence had prospered during that period and since Sayyid Said bin Sultan's reign. This was not as a result of the strong international relations which were concluded by the Sultan with America and others of those countries which we have mentioned.

If the interest of the United States, in particular, was directed to a great degree, as we saw, towards Omani possessions on the East African coast, then this focus should lead us to designate a particular chapter to examine these possessions, in order that we can understand how important they were and to see how strongly they were linked with Oman, the mother land, ever since the reign of Imam Ahmed bin Said.

The Foreign Economic and Political Relations of Sultan Said bin Sultan

After he expelled the Persians from Oman and successfully established the Al-Busaidi state, Imam Ahmed bin Said focused his attention on the eastern coast of Africa with which Oman had deeply rooted historical connections. We mentioned earlier that the Sultan exercised considerable power in certain parts of this coastline; in fact he went on to expand his supremacy over other regions as well. Nonetheless, he was only able to appoint governors for Kilwa, Zanzibar and Mombasa since his influence in these other regions was not strong enough to allow him to forge close political and economic relations[371].

The Al-Busaidi state, during the reign of Ahmed Said, had adopted a clear-cut political policy in Africa. That policy was particularly obvious during the entire reign of Sultan Said bin Sultan (1804-1856). In this historical epoch, Oman became a naval power with territory extending from Oman to Pemba Island and Zanzibar on the East African coast towards the hinterlands of the African Sahara, surrounding Mombasa and Dar es Salaam. The area also extended from north of Mozambique to Somalia[372]. Although Sayyid Said had considerable influence over most parts of eastern Africa, islands and coasts alike, the strong Mazrui tribes in Mombasa declined to pay their dues to the Sultan. In 1826, the Sultan issued an ultimatum to the Mazrui tribes. However, it took until 1837 and several expeditions led by the Sultan himself against Mombasa before the power of this tribe was smashed[373].

At the same time as he was endeavouring to seize Mombasa, the Sultan decided to take Zanzibar as a milestone for his African projects[374]. Indeed, Zanzibar occupied an important economic position because of its intermediate location between East African Islamic ports, and its large navigable port made it safer than other coastal sites[375]. Moreover, the island had a moderate climate, fertile soil and the purest drinking water in all of East Africa, as Said himself believed[376]. Zanzibar turned out to be not only the best of the Sultan's projects in Africa, but the most favoured of all his properties, even those in Muscat, delighting the Sultan with its charming nature and moderate climate[377]. In addition, Zanzibar contributed greatly to boosting trade exchange and transit trade all over East Africa[378]. The Sultan's move to Zanzibar was understandable: in the few years preceding his movement to the island, the Sultan had experienced severe internal problems some of which were family-related. Furthermore, Wahabis and Qawasim had frequently attacked the Arabian regions of the Sultanate[379].

Generally speaking, the decision taken by Sayyid Said to reside in Zanzibar as the second capital of the large sultanate was a critical one. The distance between the two capitals was in the range of 2500 miles; and to travel from Oman to Zanzibar was a process mostly governed by seasonal wind direction and speed[380]. Perhaps it was almost impossible for the Omani government to actually control its properties in the remote areas of East Africa. None the less, Sayyid Said opted for a policy to strengthen his power and control over the newly possessed lands. That policy would certainly constitute the most significant reason beyond his decision to transfer his office far from the Arab land to Zanzibar in 1832. There he stayed for the remainder of his life[381]. Although the Sultan preferred to administer Oman's affairs from Zanzibar, he had to travel frequently from Zanzibar to confront and solve problems in Oman[382]. However, he stayed for long periods in Zanzibar and the African island officially remained a part of Oman.

Prior to the reign of Sayyid Said, most of Zanzibar's inhabitants were of Swahili origin. But in the new state, a large Arab population came to reside on the island. In fact, the Sultan had encouraged Arabs to immigrate to Pemba and Zanzibar[383]. All in all, economic factors probably outweighed all other considerations in the Sultan's choice of Zanzibar[384] as his permanent residence over Mombasa, Kilwa, Pemba and other important cities in East Africa[385]. No other site was more suitable for Sayyid Said to implement his ambitious economic policies. That seems to be why he finally resided on the island rather than at Mombasa, Kilwa or other important cities in East Africa. Said confirmed that economic development was his main concern, as well as the stability and security of the island. More than likely, he was the first to introduce clove production in Zanzibar and Pemba. By the end of the nineteenth century, the two islands produced collectively 90 per cent of the world's cloves[386].

The Sultan's interest in clove production was accompanied by a similar attention paid to commercial activities. Accordingly, Arab caravans travelled to various parts of the African continent[387], reaching as far as the Congo.

Sayyid Said did not rely entirely on commercial enterprises as a sole source of revenue. (It should be borne in mind that there was no strict difference between the state's treasury and that of the Sultan). In fact, the nation benefited greatly from customs dues and trade monopoly. With respect to customs, the Sultan imposed a tax of 5 per cent on imports. This was met with sigh of relief on the part of Europeans who believed that such an action would rule out the imposition of any further high taxes by an independent ruler along the coastline. Exports, on the other hand, were exempted from customs. The Sultan also monopolized trade in ivory and gum. As these commodities were mainly exported from the southern seaports of the state, the area extending from Kilwa to Benjani was closed to foreign navigation. Consequently, the two commodities were under the monopolistic control of the Sultan who sold them to foreign tradesmen in Zanzibar. Undoubtedly, trade along the coastal areas had boosted commercial activity in the interior. Caravans, carrying gum and ivory, were on the increase[388]. Sayyid Said bin Sultan was convinced that entrance to the interior of the African continent would certainly enrich the coastal areas. Based on this conviction, he encouraged Arab adventurers that had come with him from Oman to travel along old trade routes[389]. Though Arabs had explored the continent sometime earlier, it was only during the reign of Sayyid Said (particularly since 1840) that periodical caravan tours were organized. Such tours penetrated deeply into the lakes. David Livingstone, the Scottish missionary explorer, saw Arab boats on certain islands in central African lakes such as Victoria, Tanganyika and Nyasa. Arab stations were established in some islands amid Lakes Ujiji and Kazanji[390]. Moreover, Arab centres were established along the trade routes where caravans would usually require provisions. For this reason special warehouses were built, protected by armed guards[391].

The most important route in use at that time was the one beginning at Bejmoyo, opposite to Zanzibar Island, moving straight ahead to the south, then bending in a north-eastern direction to avoid encountering the high mountains ahead. Along this route, with its destination at Lake Tanganyika, the most important Arab centres were located starting at a distance of 600 miles from the coast[392]. Arab traders had frequently visited the capital of the Ugandan kingdom and had been quite near to other Arab tradesmen travelling to these areas from the Sudan. In reality, there should have been some contact between the two groups unless the king of Uganda prevented Arabs of the coastal areas from passing by his kingdom. But, the subsequent establishment of Arab centres along the caravan routes made it possible for traders to penetrate deeper into the continent. In 1870, European travellers saw these caravans journeying far to the west of Tanganyika, and 100 miles to the eastern part of the Congo basin. However, this penetration certainly commenced in the last days of Sayyid Said[393].

The very existence of Arab centres that were completely surrounded by African lands encouraged these centres to be vehemently loyal to the sultan of Zanzibar. After all, it was a loyalty that had not entailed any major financial burden other than the taking of small gifts by the chiefs of these tribes to the sultan in the capital[394]. The general pattern was that the big Arab traders travelled the routes to and fro, whereas others with relatively limited enterprises would reside in the African metropolises. As a consequence, the Sultanate of Oman dominated almost every corner in eastern and central Africa[395], its fame extending from the Indian Ocean to the Congo. A notable saying at that time went that 'if a flautist plays his flute in Zanzibar, people dance to the sound on the Lakes'[396].

Therefore, a positive phase of Afro-Arab relations was ushered in. It was more than a mere relationship, it was an intimacy between Arabs and Africans, between Muscat and Zanzibar within the framework of one sultanate whose dominance had extended over all eastern and central parts of Africa; a sultanate under one ruler who established his residence in Zanzibar. But the colonialist powers, for their part, chose to disturb this close relationship between Arabs and Africans.

The second phase of this study commences with the partition of the Afro-Arab Sultanate as a prelude to the final fragmentation of the state. Undoubtedly, the main objective of this intervention was to halt the Afro-Arab cooperation in East Africa, which had reached its climax during the reign of Sayyid Said. In the last years of his rule, the Al-Busaidi state was outstandingly vast. It included Oman and certain eastern lands along the Arabian Gulf[397] such as Bandar Abbas - which the Al-Busaidi state had rented from Persia for 20 years effective from 1855[398]. The African territory of the state, on the other hand, covered the eastern coast of the continent, from Cape Guardafui north to Cape Delgado in the southern part. In addition, there were several areas under the protection of the Sultanate, such as Mogadishu, Lamu and Patta[399]. The hinterlands, frequently visited by Arab traders, were also included insofar as their peoples expressed loyalty of a certain degree to the Sultan. By and large, the territory under the control of the Sultanate were not only confined to the above mentioned land, since Oman had not enforced its actual control over many other areas such as Bahrain, Zeila, Aden and others[400].

Al-Busaidi State from the Mid-Nineteenth Century to the Beginning of the Early Renaissance

The death of Sultan Said on 19 October 1856 brought to a conclusion the reign of a prominent Arab leader. It was undoubtedly the most prosperous phase within the framework of the traditional civilization of the region and its older dynamic system. But, British supremacy and the accompanying modernization process greatly influenced the overall political landscape. In other words, almost all of Said's sons were bereft of the required efficiency and adequate political acceptance to rule the Afro-Arab Sultanate and maintain its unity. Said had appointed two of his sons to rule in his absence, one for the African part and the other for the Asian part of the Sultanate. Since 1833, however, Thuwaini had been in charge of Muscat; whereas the second son, Majed, had acted as deputy to his father in Zanzibar since 1854. Ever since, each had entertained immense authority in his respective region, but without the ability to annex the other region to his rule. Furthermore, Said had not selected one of his sons to assume office after his death[401]. Consequently, the struggle between his sons remained as one of the outstanding features of the history of Oman during the remaining years of the nineteenth century. They could have maintained the state, both its Arab and African parts, if they were able to properly utilize the economic and political resources within their reach.

As a result of the political disturbances sweeping Oman after the death of Sultan Said, however, a civil war was staged between the heirs of the late Sultan with the result that the state was threatened by devastation and ruin. Apparently, the foreign powers had exploited the situation and had greatly escalated the dispute between the two brothers, Majed and Thuwaini.

Britain and France, in particular, played varied roles in using this dispute to their own advantage. Politicians, officials and armed forces of the two countries mobilized their resources to promote the interests of their respective nations. Great effort was exerted, and an apparent movement between Muscat and Zanzibar undertaken with the intention of providing protection and guardianship. In fact, the two powers were actually encouraging the struggle between the two brothers while feigning to mediate.

Conflict was also at a height between France and Britain as to which of the brothers would win the feud. Both countries mobilized forces and fleets along the Omani and African coasts, expressing sympathy with this or that party to the conflict. However, the interests of the two big powers in East Africa were self-evident. They had recurrently tried to find a footing along the Afro-Arab coast and to this end disseminated rumors and fabricated accounts in a bid to prevent any agreement between the two brothers. They even alleged that the late Sultan had left documents which attested to his wish to partition the Sultanate and distribute it between his sons: supposedly Majed was to get Zanzibar as a region, independent and separate from the Omani motherland. In fact, there is abundant evidence to rebut the allegation that the late Sultan had signed any such documents. Furthermore, the two brothers were on good terms till foreign intervention created a lack of confidence and suspicion among them.

England, for its part, was eager for the partition of the Sultanate and opposed the idea of merging the properties of the two brothers. That is why it backed Majed, giving the justification that any war between the brothers would threaten its interests along the maritime route to India[402]. Thuwaini tried hard to re-unify the state. He started to prepare for the 1859 campaign to Zanzibar. But, the British authorities in India rapidly sent Colonel Russell, one of the officer of the Indian navy, to stop the progress of the campaign. As a result, Thuwaini was compelled to return back to Muscat as the British fleet blocked his way[403].

British reports blamed France for the crisis, claiming that France was desperately trying to get a concession from either Sayyid Thuwaini or Sayyid Barghash for some areas in East Africa such as Mombasa or Brawa and were therefore supporting Thuwaini against Majed. In addition, it was claimed that France intended to revive the slave trade due to its growing demand for African workers in its newly annexed colonies[404]. In reality, France was more concerned with Zanzibar because of the growing trade it maintained with the eastern coasts of Africa during the 1860s. In view of this, Majed obtained Britain's support and began preparing himself for a final fight back[405]. England,

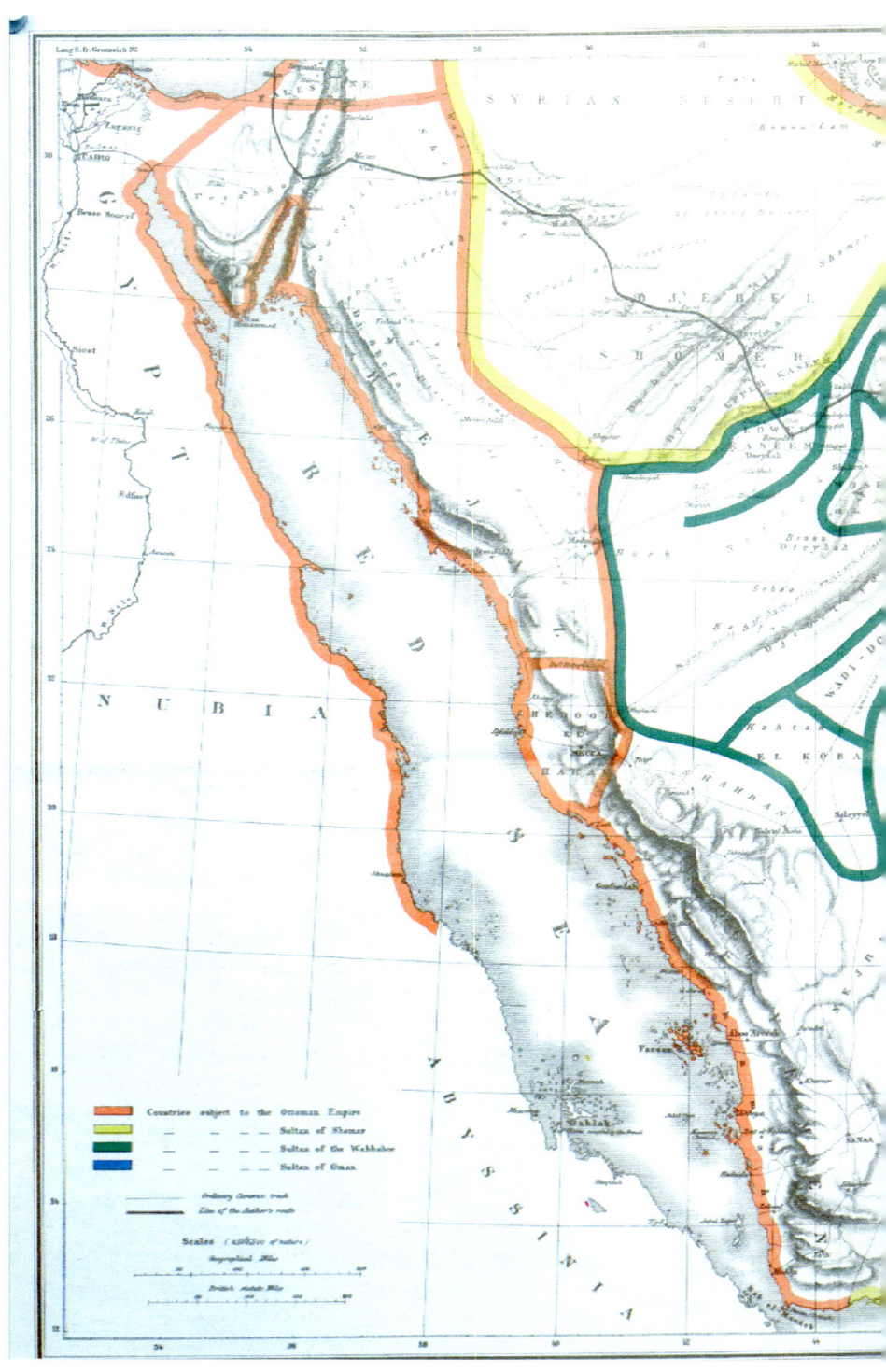

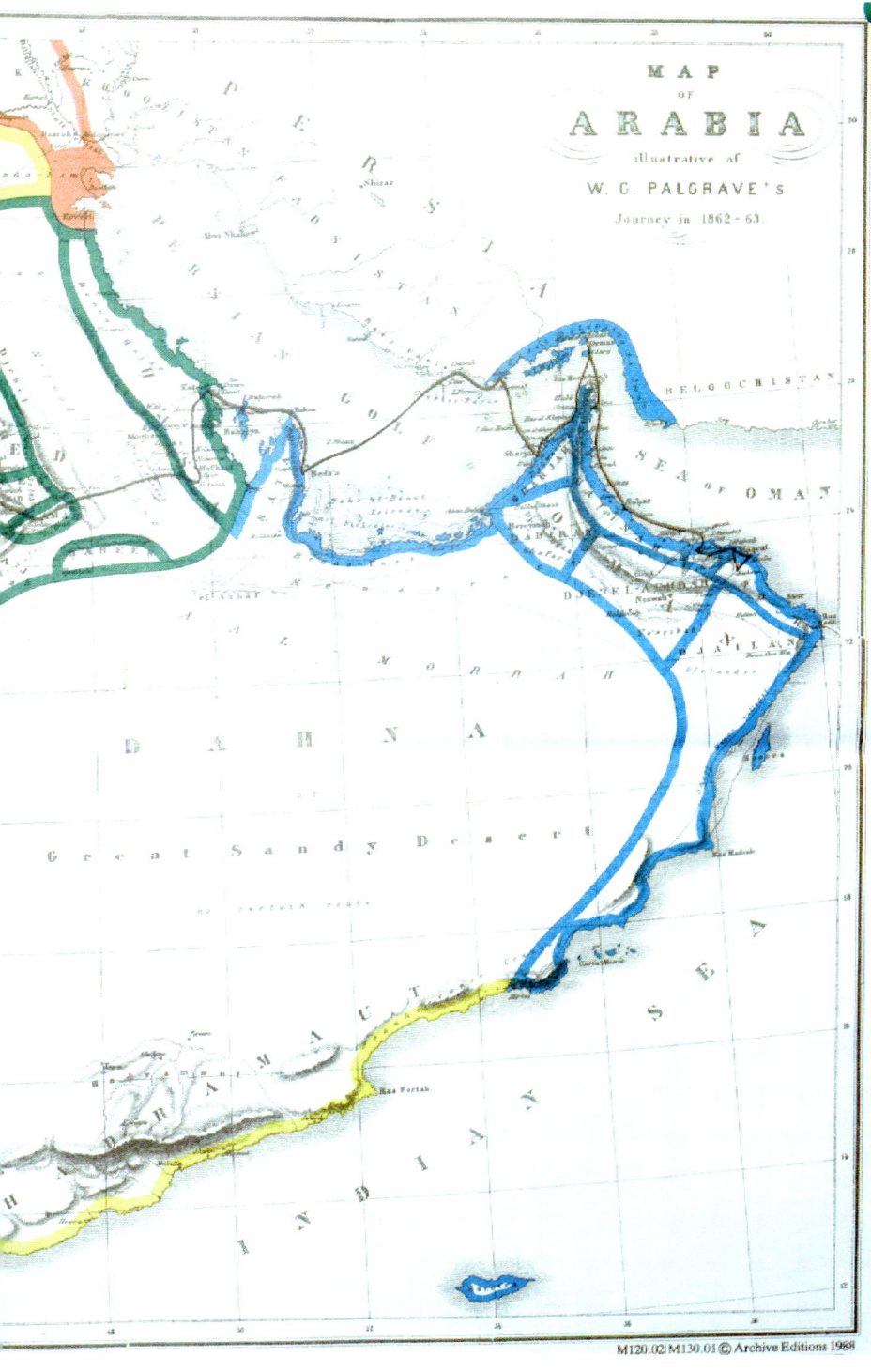

however, did not confine itself to the provision of assistance, but tried to find a solution acceptable to both sides, being prepared to impose one on them if deemed necessary. Therefore, it actively intervened in the dispute between Muscat and Zanzibar - in any way it thought appropriate - in order to restore peace and tranquillity. Otherwise, British interests would certainly be jeopardized, especially along the access route to its empire in India. Owing to this, the British government sent a mission to Muscat and Zanzibar in 1860 in order to investigate the reasons beyond the existing dispute. The mission was headed by Colonel Coughlan, the resident political officer in Aden[406].

Perhaps that was the main objective of the mission, but the tacit goal was to restore normal relations between the two countries so that French intervention in the critical areas along the sea route to India could be averted accordingly. Coughlan, before the commencement of the mission, toured the Red Sea from Aden on 16 January 1860 accompanied by G. P. Badger. The tour included Brim, Masawa, Kharayib Adolis and Zula in Anssili Bay. Coghlan found that the Turks were suspicious of the French moves. He further remarked that such moves should be paid due attention to by the British government insofar as they might create barriers to transport between Britain and India[407]. Anyhow the mission arrived at Muscat in June 1860 to ascertain Thuwaini's requirements. It then sailed to Zanzibar in September of the same year. The mission, in studies it conducted, mentioned that members of Al-Busaidi dynasty were elected to power. And that, after the death of Sayyid Said, the population of Zanzibar had elected Majed as a legitimate ruler[408].Therefore, Thuwaini's claim to Zanzibar was unfounded and each of them should confine his authority to the designated portion of the Sultanate.

The mission submitted its report to Lord Canning, the general administrator of India. On the basis of this report, Lord Canning formulated the reputable arbitration resolution of 1861. Under that decision, Majed was declared governor of Zanzibar and the African properties of the Sultanate; that is, to assume the position of his late father[409]. Moreover, he should pay an annual amount of 40,000 rials to the ruler of Muscat as well as the dues outstanding for the last two years, calculated on this basis[410]. The decision also stated that neither the rulers of Muscat nor the tribes of Oman should interfere in Zanzibar's affairs.

Canning was clear on the point that the amount paid by Zanzibar's ruler to the ruler of Muscat should indicate no subordination on the part of the former. Rather, it was intended to achieve a kind of inheritance equity among the two brothers insofar as Zanzibar's lands were much richer than Muscat's[411].

Lord Canning wrote to both Thuwaini and Majed explaining his conviction that these provisions were just[412]. On 15 May 1861 Thuwaini, for his part, sent a letter to Lord Canning expressing his appreciation and acknowledgment of the resolutions reached[413]. Finally, and mainly due to the results of this arbitration process, the relationship between Zanzibar and Muscat became a mere financial one — that is, Zanzibar was to pay an annual subsidy to Muscat. Otherwise, the relationship between the two parts of the Sultanate was extremely fragile.

It should be noted, however, that Zanzibar during the reign of Majed had assumed a greater African character owing to severed relations with the mother nation. In fact, Majed adopted certain procedures which had ultimately

Land routes of Omani trade in East Africa in the nineteenth century.

weakened relations between Zanzibar and Muscat. In 1864, for instance, he prohibited Muscat's ships from navigating in Zanzibar's regional waters unless documents showed that they were trading in legitimate goods. He also wrote to sheikhs of the Arabian Gulf to ask them to withhold sending their ships to Zanzibar. To even further frustrate relations, he ordered Zanzibar's citizens not to rent houses to Arab traders coming from the Arabian peninsula. Finally, he banned the custom whereby Zanzibar's rulers used to present gifts to Omani tribes. This course of action certainly indicated that Majed was not enthusiastic about the idea of a unified sultanate as in the reign of his late father[414].

Undoubtedly, Muscat was in urgent need of that specific annual amount from Zanzibar in order to afford paying Persia the rent of Bandar Abbas. Indeed this was the other side of the matter. Though Bandar Abbas seemed to be removed from the Muscat-Zanzibar dispute, nonetheless it was relevant[415] because Persia had entered into contractual arrangements with Oman whereby Bandar Abbas would be rented for a term of 20 years[416] commencing in 1855, at an annual rate of 16,000 rials. But the agreement dictated that the Shah of Persia could terminate the contract if the government in Muscat was forcibly seized. And so it was claimed that Sayyid Salim, the son of Sayyid Thuwaini who had originally concluded the contract with Persia, had illegitimately seized power after committing patricide. The point at stake in this respect was that Muscat used to pay the annual rent from the subsidy received from Zanzibar. Thus, once Zanzibar declined to pay the subsidy, Muscat was no longer able to meet its commitment to Persia[417]. The Bandar Abbas issue was directly based on the relationship between Muscat and Zanzibar. Sayyid Salim himself said that, 'since I do not receive the due amount of subsidy from Zanzibar, which was guaranteed to my father by the British government, I cannot afford to pay the due rent of Bandar Abbas to Persia'[418]. Therefore, it was apparent that this subsidy was central for Muscat to maintain holding Bandar Abbas.

Sayyid Salim went further and quarreled with Persia over its trade in the Gulf. And the latter had had no choice but to resort to Britain, a great power who supported Salim[419] to solve the dilemma and prevent the potential damage to the Persian interests. In conclusion, and since Salim refused to pay the rent, Persia was in no position but to request termination of the concession arrangement. From the viewpoint of Britain, Persia seemed to be over-eager to gain control of the Gulf littoral area. But was this consistent with the British strategy? If it wasn't what could it do to prevent Persia from implementing these detrimental policies? The Indian government, in particular, considered it to be highly significant for British interests whether or not Bandar Abbas was in the hands of Muscat. 'During the reign of Sayyid Said we had more confidence in him than in the Shah of Persia who was by then whimsical and unreliable, only concerned with collecting money by any means. But the present government is more stable than that in the reign of Shah Fat'h Ali. In addition, the designated minister in Tehran will be able to convince the Persian government that any Persian governor for Bandar Abbas can deal with us as Muscat's representatives used to'[420].

The partition of the Omani empire was at the root of all these problems. Persia was compelled to hold back Bandar Abbas and engage in an immense maritime activity in the Gulf. In consequence, British presence and influence in the region were strengthened. Yet the relations between Britain on one hand and Muscat, Zanzibar and all sheikhs and emirs along the coast of the Arabian Gulf, on the other, had been regulated by a set of agreements and commitments. These legal instruments were signed by British officers, on behalf of the British government but in their capacities as governors of India and Bombay. At this particular point, however, the conflict between Zanzibar and Muscat had overshadowed the administrative aspect of these areas. The question posed was whether such areas would remain a part of India or be under the direct responsibility of the British Ministry of Foreign Affairs.

As stated previously, Canning's arbitration resolution had obliged Sayyid Majed to pay his brother Thuwaini an annual subsidy, and the Indian government had guaranteed payment. But, would the government of the King accept this measure and implement it, and pay from the Royal Treasury if necessary? On the other hand, would the Indian government pay the amount of subsidy without participating in the negotiations and procedures meant to correct the situation from its own point of view at least? The Indian government elucidated its viewpoint on the fact that its existing relations with the southern Arabian peninsula and the Gulf had great significance for India; and that such relations were consistent with Indian attempts to prevent piracy in Indian territorial waters: 'We have found a cooperative ally in this respect, that is Sayyid Said who was the ruler of Oman for more than 40 years. He was both a trader as well as a statesman. He had ships with commercial engagements with Calcutta and ports of west India. And those who have complaints pertaining to these commercial operations should voice their opinions to the Minister of Foreign Affairs in order for them to be duly assessed. Due to the present conventions concluded with India, it is deemed necessary that our relations with it would be regulated by officers appointed by India and having a direct contact with it'.

By the end of 1869, a special conference was held at the British Foreign Office to discuss the eastern slave trade. The conference was attended by John Kee, representing India, and representatives of the Ministry of Colonies, Admiralty and Treasury. On 24 January, the conference forwarded its report to the Earl of Clarendon, Minister of Foreign Affairs at that time. In its eightieth section, the report stated: 'We now believe that it is important to declare that, in addition to his other charges, the consul in Zanzibar is entirely responsible for termination of the slave trade in the region. Therefore, the appropriate arrangements must be set to share the costs of the consulate in Zanzibar and its subsidiaries between the Royal

Sultan Al-Sayyid Majed bin Said bin Sultan.

and the Indian Treasuries'[421].That is all there is about British policy with respect to the administration of these areas. On the other hand, we have seen how Britain, in order to maintain the status quo in relations between Muscat and Zanzibar, arranged for annual payment of the subsidy through its resident political secretary in Muscat. However, Britain would ultimately be reimbursed by Zanzibar. Therefore, in effect Zanzibar continued paying the subsidy until 1868[422] when the throne of Muscat was taken by Imam Azzan bin Qais, a member of a branch of the Al-Busaidi family other than that to which Sayyid Said belonged. Majed took this for a justification to decline paying the annual amount to Muscat, which was previously paid through the British resident political secretary.

But Azzan bin Qais did not hold on to Muscat for long. Sayyid Turki bin Said took his place in 1871. The reign of Turki bin Said coincided with the rule of his brother Barghash in Zanzibar. In either 1871 or 1872, Turki wrote to Barghash requesting resumption of the subsidy to be paid by Zanzibar; he even threatened to invade Zanzibar. This emerging conflict was solved upon approval by Turki of the slave accord. According to an agreement, Turki would be repaid the amount of subsidy in arrears, which were estimated at 40,000 rials, together with the outstanding amounts for the last six months (that is, in the range 20,000 rials), to be paid within three months from the date of the agreement.

The British resident political secretary in the Gulf, Ross, was authorized to pay the subsidy to Turki on a regular basis provided that he maintained his commitments and respected his friendship with Britain. In fact, this subsidy was

Sultan Al-Sayyid Turki bin Said bin Sultan.

Sultan Al-Sayyid Bargash bin Said bin Sultan

paid in 1873, equally shared between India and Britain. Its amount was in the range of 86,400 rupees, which was then equivalent to 40,000 rials. Indeed, the subsidy continued to be paid without suspension. In most cases, it was paid prior to its due date, so that the Muscat government could meet its immediate requirements. Upon the request of the Sultan, the subsidy, which was previously paid bi-annually, was paid from 1876 on a three-month basis; then it became a monthly payment from 1879.

From September 1883, the British government decided to totally disengage itself from Zanzibar's affairs, including the financial aspects. As a result, India was compelled to pay the subsidy from then on. It should be noted that Turki and Barghash had been on good terms with each other ever since the British government guaranteed payment of the subsidy from Zanzibar. This cordial relationship made it possible for Turki to abdicate the rule of Oman to his brother Barghash. The Indian government was greatly surprised at this news. It immediately contacted Ross, the British resident secretary in the Gulf, to inquire into the matter. Ross replied that certain contacts and negotiations had been underway between Barghash and Turki, and, after all, the issue was quite public. But India instantly authorized its political agent in the Gulf to interfere if unity between Oman and Zanzibar was attempted. This would certainly explain the extent to which Britain was frustrated by the slightest notion of a unified Omani state.

It seemed, therefore, that Britain had put pressure on Turki to abstain from abdication of the throne; for it knew quite well that he might do so.

The two brothers remained on good terms after the failure of their efforts towards unity and they continued to exchange gifts. In 1884, for instance, Barghash gave his brother 22,000 rupees to tackle the internal turbulence in Oman. In 1886, once again, he presented him with the steamer *Sultani* and the yacht *Dar es-Salaam*. In March 1888, Barghash visited Oman, staying for a week in Bushar's hot springs in an attempt to cure a disease with which he was afflicted. Turki extended every respect and cordiality to his brother. Later, upon his return to Zanzibar, Barghash sent a gift of 50,000 rupees to his brother. Both died within three months after their latest meeting.

The latter period of Turki's rule, until his death in 1888, was peaceful. He left a well-regulated and stable kingdom for his heir, Sayyid Faisal. Evidently, Faisal assumed power at a time when the Arab world was beset by a rising wave of European colonialist influence, particularly that of Britain and France who occupied several parts of the Arab world. Only a few Arab countries were able to escape this fierce colonialist attack. Among these was Oman; for Faisal bin Turki had skilfully established his rule amidst an overall climate of turbulence. He also paid great attention to the internal situation in a bid to strengthen the national front. Thus he set up a powerful army, vesting its leadership in his brother Fahad who had firmly established security throughout Oman.

Faisal's policy was to establish a balanced relationship with England and France. In 1894, he approved the setting-up of a French consulate in Muscat; he also granted the French permission to install a coal warehouse at Al-Jassa in 1898[423]. Upon receiving this news, Britain dispatched Lord Landsdowne, the Crown Deputy in India, and Lord Salisbury, the Foreign Secretary, in 1890. Their discussion with Faisal concluded that Oman had the right to forge foreign relations with any nation; and that it was ready to draw-up trade and friendship conventions with Britain. Faisal's reign continued until October 1913, the date of his death, when he was replaced by his elder son, Taimur.

Sultan Taimur assumed power at a critical time on both the internal and external fronts. Oman was beset by severe internal conflicts. On the foreign arena, the shadow of the First World War (1914-18) was on the horizon; whereas economic crisis was almost strangling the entire globe. Taimur tried his best to avert difficulties and crises. In particular, he attempted to create political stability in order to induce an improvement in the economic situation. Thus in 1920 he signed the Seeb Agreement.

In the aftermath of the First World War, Omani trade started to flourish once again. But it soon encountered the suffocating climate of the global economic depression of the early 1930s. Nevertheless, Taimur went on to adopt economic reform with the help of three Egyptian experts who were recruited to develop a system for customs in Muscat. Furthermore, he formed a Council of Ministers which was the first of its kind in Omani history. The Council was chaired by Nadir bin Faisal; later on, in 1929, Taimur appointed his son Said to this position.

Taimur's reign witnessed certain important events such as the 1925 agreement between Oman and D. Arky Co.[424] concerning oil exploration in the Sultanate. But, no oil was discovered whilst he was in power. Taimur relinquished control for health reasons in 1932 and his son,

Sultan Al-Sayyid Faisal bin Turki bin Said.

Sultan Al-Sayyid Taimur bin Faisal.

Sultan Al-Sayyid Said bin Taimur

H.M. Sultan Qaboos bin Said meets the people.

Sayyid Said took over soon afterwards.

Sultan Said bin Taimur was immediately aware that the world was experiencing a severe economic crisis. Therefore, he had to adopt a financial policy that would relieve the nation of the burden of foreign debts, for such debts are the deeply rooted reason behind the malfunctioning of the economy and they could certainly constitute the basis for foreign powers to interfere in internal affairs. The decision taken accordingly was to spend within the limits of the nation's resources together with a commitment to repay outstanding debts. He had also taken specific measures to strengthen the foreign relations his country maintained. In 1937 he visited the U. S. and Japan. In the U. S., for example, he met its president Franklin Roosevelt (1933-1945) with whom he exchanged gifts. Said was the first Arab ruler to visit the U. S. From there he left for Britain, where he was warmly met by King George V, then to France, Italy and India[425]. In 1944, he once again visited Egypt, where he met King Farouq; from there he went to Jerusalem, the capital of Palestine.

Two major events should be borne in mind concerning the reign of Said. The first was the settlement of outstanding disputes with Saudi Arabia over the Buraimi oasis. Of course, Said had a fundamental belief in the integrity of Omani territory. The second was the granting of a concession for oil exploration to the Petroleum Development of Oman Company. Subsequently, oil was discovered and its exportation started in August 1968.

The first event brought internal peace and stability; whereas the second provided the financial support necessary to unleash an overall economic development. Perhaps, this development had actually begun during the reign of his son Sultan Qaboos bin Said in what would later come to be known as the modern Omani renaissance.

Having discussed the political changes in Oman from the late nineteenth century to the early renaissance, it is equally significant to shed light on the African part of the state — i.e., Zanzibar. In Zanzibar, though, things took a completely reverse course of action, especially after Britain declared Zanzibar a protectorate in 1891.

Political Developments and the Omani Presence in Zanzibar

After Britain declared Zanzibar to be a protectorate in 1891, the political reality dictated that the Sultan would become a mere honorary symbol. Policy-making was entirely vested in the British consul or resident secretary, who would often seek the assistance of the senior British experts and officials.

In the first phase of this newly emerging relationship, executive and legislative councils were formed to function as advisory bodies. To state the obvious, however, most of the members of such councils were appointed by the British administration. The seats of the legislature were distributed among Arab, Sherazi, African and Asian (particularly Indian and Pakistani) tribes and sects. As a consequence of British measures to strengthen and expand its influence in Zanzibar, racist movements had emerged to protect and promote their respective interests[426]. The Arab Zanzibar Society, for instance, denounced these British policies which were formulated mainly on the notorious principle of 'divide and rule'. The Society went further to request abolition of the election system which was based on ethnic and sectarian grounds and called instead for a unified list for all candidates on the basis of a general election; it also asked for adoption of a ministerial regulation to prepare for the elections[427].

Early in 1955, the first Arab party was established in Zanzibar. In cooperation with the Arab Zanzibar Society, the National Zanzibar Party, headed by Alī bin Muhsin, called for general elections on a popular rather than ethnic basis. It also requested Britain to withdraw from the island.

Meanwhile, the British administration encouraged other elements to establish their own parties and political gatherings[428]. In reality, the British call focussed primarily on the Afro-Sherazi bloc which was able to establish the Afro-Sherazi Party, chaired by Obeid Amin Karomi, who was renowned for his hatred of Arabs.

In the 1957 elections, the Afro-Sherazi Party[429]won all seats except a single one taken by a Pakistani candidate. Nevertheless, NZP continued its calls for the people's right to representation. In the final outcome, Britain endorsed a general franchise for all adults, male and female alike. And the council's seats were increased from 12 to 22. After the 1961 elections, a coalition of NZP and the Peoples Party, a recently formed group seceded from the Sherazi gathering, set up the first national government in the history of Zanzibar. This government seemed to be an expression of the popular will[430].

In 1963, once again, a coalition of the two parties won the election, defeating Afro-Sherazi and the Ummat Party, which had been recently broken up from the NZP. The second cabinet was formed under the rule of the Sultan Jamshid bin Abdullah Al-Busaidi, one of the sons of Sultan Said. He emphatically requested Britain to decide on a date for independence[431].

On 10 December 1963, Zanzibar achieved independence. It has subsequently become a member of the United Nations. In January 1964, Jamal Nasir was accredited as the first Zanzibar ambassador to Egypt. In fact, that was the first and the last diplomatic accreditation of Zanzibar as an independent Arab state with UN membership[432]. After independence, the Arab regime in Zanzibar did not continue for long. On 2 January 1964, John Okello spearheaded a bloody revolt against the Arab sultanate. The aim of the revolt was to establish a presidential regime headed by Obeid Karomi, the chairman of the Afro-Sherazi party[433]. In the savage massacres resulting from the aborted revolution, 15,000 to 20,000 Arabs were killed in an obvious attempt to totally eradicate the Arab ethnic group on the island[434]. The Afro-Sherazi party, to impose its ideology calling for an uprooting of the Arabs from Zanzibar, officially declared union with Tanganyika on 26 April 1964. The offspring of the marriage was the United Republic of Tanzania, which took Dar es Salaam as its capital. The newly adopted constitution stated that a president of the republic should be from Tanganyika. Accordingly, Julius Nyerere, then the head of Tanganyika Republic, became president of the new nation; the first vice-president [435], who had to be selected from Zanzibar, was Obeid Karomi. He was assassinated in 1972 in the aftermath of a coup led by an opposing group. And finally, therefore, the Arab state in Zanzibar was a part of history.

Omani Civilization in East Africa During Al-Busaidi Rule

Without doubt, the golden age of the Omani presence in East Africa was under Al-Busaidi rule. The reign of Sayyid Said bin Sultan (1804-1856), in particular, represents the peak of Islamic and Arab civilization in the region. It was an intensely human and cultural civilization which promoted and enriched various facets of social, economic and political life. This fact directly refutes certain African and European studies conducted by authors with a Western colonialist orientation. The aim of those biased studies was to distort the history of Arabs in Africa by the accumulation of suspect evidence in order to create an ever widening gap between Arabs and Africans[436].

Postage stamp issued on the occasion of the 200th anniversary of Al-Busaidi rule in Zanzibar.

The Omani presence in East Africa during the Al-Busaidi era led to the establishment of a modernized state with all its political, economic and social dimensions. Several factors were at play to accentuate the impact of Omani civilization in the region. These factors include, among others:

- The active participation of Omani people in all aspects of the emerging civilization, including domestic and international trade, underpinned by their vast experience in transversing the world's seas. The Omani effort to extend trade to areas in East Africa was remarkable and Omani merchants and sailors certainly played an essential role in this regard.
- The Omanis, as shown by their commercial and social conduct, were compliant and friendly. This greatly strengthened the healthy cultural environment to which the good reputation Oman enjoyed could be attributed. Africans were accordingly willing to embrace this cultural experience and to become an integral part of its political and social texture.
- Oman's rulers greatly encouraged traders and commercial activity in general. As a result, Omani merchant fleets toured the remotest coasts of the Indian Ocean and the eastern coastline of Africa. The rulers of Al-Busaidi dynasty were concerned to provide Omani trade with the means by which it could flourish. Thus, custom tariffs were reduced to less than 5 per cent in an initial step to give traders attractive incentives. In addition to this, the rulers enforced protection of Omani sailors and traders. A set of governmental measures was adopted to reinforce efforts exerted by the public in order to boost trade. However, governmental encouragement was not only confined to Omani citizens, during the reign of Sayyid Said bin Sultan, in particular, it covered foreign traders such as Americans, French, British, Germans and Indians as well[437].

- Oman's location and ports contributed greatly to its civilizing influence. Omanis had sailed across seas and oceans, armed with a vast experience that enabled them to mingle in a friendly manner with all nations in Africa as well as in Asia.

Indeed, as we have already mentioned, the golden age for the impact of Omani civilization on East Africa was that of the reign of Sayyid Said. Political stability, which was due mainly to the strength and diplomacy exhibited by the country's leaders, had greatly contributed to the success of the great state in various ways. The imprint of Omani culture on Zanzibar's history was of immeasurable magnitude. This culture had extended to cover all African coastal areas. Omani influence was so great in East Africa as to encompass several aspects, all of which we will deal with under the following headings.

Political and Administrative Structures

The political and administrative structures in Zanzibar and its peripheral emirates, which were formulated by Al-Busaidi rulers, were primarily influenced by the Arab and Islamic traditions prevailing in Oman. Sayyid Said was largely responsible for firmly establishing Islamic and Arab administrative systems. Local and foreign sources described him as the most efficient ruler as far as administration was concerned. He was undoubtedly one of the most prominent politicians in the history of Asia and Africa during the nineteenth century[438]. His political and administrative genius was evident insofar as he selected Zanzibar in 1832 as the capital of East Africa. He successfully developed the island from a small centre to a metropolis of political and economic enlightenment for all of eastern and central Africa. Omanis, under his reasoned leadership, were able to reinforce their regime in Africa, extending it from Mogadishu in the north to Cape Delgado on the southern coast of the eastern coastline. In the north-western direction, however, Omani influence went even deeper to reach the Ugandan Kingdom and the hinterlands of Congo (Zaire) to the west[439].

The influence of the Al-Busaidi dynasty on eastern and central Africa was so enormous that its echo has been heard worldwide. This is particularly so with respect to the foreign politics and diplomatic vigour experienced by the region for the first time in its history. It would be appropriate to quote Said Hamid Heraiz, an expert in sociology who has given us an accurate account on the role of this Afro-Arab state. He states[440], 'the region became part of a diplomatic movement extending as far as England, Germany, France and the United States. The area had known European consulates and political and economic openness since the second half of the last century, at a time when the majority of Arab, Asian and European nations were far removed from this pattern of diplomatic relations. The journey undertaken by the ship *Sultanah* to the United States in 1840 was the earliest attempt at an Arab-American discourse'.

Cultural Features of the Omani Regime in East Africa
The Al-Busaidi regime in East Africa was characterized by a distinctive set of features, the most important of which was the recruitment of a large number of advisors and scientists in various fields of expertise. These advisors and experts were charged with the day-to-day duties of administration. Most of them were *walis,* judges and senior army or navy commanders. Local and foreign sources indicated that advisors and scientists had undertaken outstanding roles. The dominant features of the age were tolerance and a lack of fanaticism with respect to ethnic or sectarian factors. Sayyid Said treated citizens and leaders alike with leniency, respect and cordiality. Equality for the whole population, irrespective of ethnic origins, was the most fundamental feature of Said's rule[441].

Historic house in Zanzibar.

Cultural values also prevailed in this African community. Many scientists and knowledgeable Muslims had immigrated to the island and established good relations with Al-Busaidi rulers. In turn, these rulers gained legitimacy; for these scientists had a great influence on African society. Moreover, Al-Busaidi rulers paid great attention to the implementation of the Islamic Shari'a and equality among Arabs and Africans. This was obvious from the pamphlets issued by Al-Busaidi rulers to their *walis* and *qadhis* throughout the state. Some Omani references provide us with a good insight into such pamphlets. A circular issued by Sayyid Majed bin Said, for instance, was rightly considered as a constitution that would reflect the extent to which equality and justice prevailed in the African part of the Omani empire. This particular document emphatically emphasized principles of equality in litigation; the pressing need to safeguard peoples' lives and properties; and the necessity to ensure that such concerns were within the scope of the state's duties so that it could maintain stability[442].

Majed, to the satisfaction of his father as well as his people, adhered to the method of governance followed by his father. This became clear when he emphasized that justice, precision in decision-making and good conduct were to be given the utmost priority[443]. Such efforts made it possible to firmly establish the Arab-Omani presence in East Africa. Omanis were therefore considered the messengers of civilization and cultural progress due to the outstanding development of East Africa. Many European nations began to keep a close eye on the newly emerging nation with the tacit intent of dividing it up amongst themselves.

Ministers, Judges and Advisors

Al-Busaidi rulers sought the administrative assistance of talented persons and from their ranks were chosen ministers, judges and other experts. This tradition had been adhered to since the reign of Imam Ahmed bin Said, the founder of the Al-Busaidi state. In the course of time, however, the tradition had become even more firmly established. During the reign of Sayyid Said bin Sultan, for

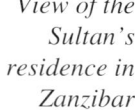

View of the Sultan's residence in Zanzibar

Bait Al-Aja'ib (the House of Marvels), Zanzibar.

instance, it became an essential component of the state's administrative framework. One of the foremost of these advisors was Sayyid Suleiman bin Hamad bin Said Al-Busaidi (1782-1873), who was from a prominent family in Zanzibar. Upon his arrival on the island, the Sultan appointed Said as prime minister and he continued to occupy this position until his death in 1873. Said therefore worked with Sayyid Barghash; he was a powerful and courteous person. Sultan Said bin Sultan used to delegate sufficient authority to his advisors to allow them to govern in his absence. However, as the Sultan's sons matured, they took over when their father was away[444].

Al-Busaidi rulers administered the state's affairs with justice, selecting the most qualified persons, irrespective of their ethnic origins or background, to carry out executive duties. Nonetheless, Ibadhism remained the official sect of the state[445]. Consequently, an athmosphere of cordiality and friendship amongst all social circles prevailed. This was paricularly obvious among scientists and Islamic teachers from Ibadhi and Sunni sects. Accordingly, some of the judges, appointed by Sayyid Said bin Sultan in Zanzibar, were Sunnis whereas others were Ibadhis.

Sunni judges had the utmost freedom to hold trials at their own homes, or in mosques, at whatever time they chose. However, major lawsuits of public interest would be tried at the official headquarters of the government[446]. Sheikh Mehudin Al-Qahtani Al-Wai'ili (1790-1869) was an eminent Sunni judge who was later designated a judge of the Shaffi sect in Zanzibar in 1837. During the rule of Majed bin Said, Al-Wai'ili assumed the position of the island's *mufti* (expounder of Islamic law). Informed sources indicated that Al-Wai'ili was one of the notable advisors to Sayyid Said and his son Majed. Sayyid Said often relied on him, particularly in facing difficulties such as the disputes that raged in Sewa in 1845-1846. Al-Wai'ili's efforts proved successful as he was able to conclude a peace accord in favor of Sayyid Said. Foreign and local sources unanimously agreed that Al-Wai'ili earned the respect of all peoples in all parts of East Africa[447].

Arab Tribes in East Africa During the Rule of the Al-Busaidi Dynasty

Al-Busaidi rulers were very successful in forging unity amongst Arab tribes in East Africa. In the framework of this policy, Sayyid Said was particularly concerned with setting up good relations with tribal chiefs. Sheikh Nasir bin Ja'id Al-Kharousi, one of these tribal leaders, was a famous Ibadhi scholar and the Sultan used to consult with him on state affairs especially with respect to Oman and the problems encountered by Sayyid Thuwaini, the then deputy of his father in Muscat.

Al-Kharousi frequently travelled to Oman to render assistance to Thuwaini. Available references confirm that he was honoured by Sayyid Said and, consequently, allowed to reside in the personal palace of the Sultan till his death in 1847[448].

Arabs from Hadramaut, in southern Yemen, were an influential group in Zanzibar and East Africa, having populated the island and rendered their service to the state.

Omar Al-Qaddi Al-Shatri Al-Alawi, one of their famous leaders, was very powerful and a confidant of Sayyid Said. In fact, the Shatri tribe, to which Al-Alawi belonged, was among the first Arab groups to reside in Zanzibar. They subsequently inter-married with the former Zanzibar rulers (Moeni Macho)[449]. Sultan Said conferred great respect and appreciation on this family and never intervened in their affairs. As a result they wholeheartedly supported Al-Busaidis.

Shura, or the Islamic equivalent of democracy, was adhered to during Al-Busaidi rule in East Africa, as was manifest in the so-called Sultani councils (or royal councils) convened by the rulers to keep abreast of the peoples' problems and to engage in consultation on matters of state. Everybody had the right to attend such meetings which were held in the Sultan's office on Fridays and Mondays in two sessions, the first from nine in the morning to two o'clock in the afternoon; the second from the afternoon onwards. Those attending were granted freedom of speech: when the session ended the ruler would stand up to indicate that the meeting was over, allowing everybody, apart from those with particular concerns, to depart. The ruler would then meet separately with each one of them[450].

Sayyid Said bin Sultan's rule was a model of justice, *Shura* and forbearance, traits usually found in good rulers. Said, himself, was pious, gracious and courteous, never haughty or domineering. Furthermore, he never hesitated to visit one of his servants to offer his congratulations on a happy occasion or to express condolences on a sad event[451].

Thus all efforts were made to spread Omani civilization in East Africa. As a result, the coastal African cities embraced aspects of Islamic and Arab civilization; these were particularly obvious in the mosques and schools which constituted a spring-board from which the Arabic language spread among Africans along the coastal areas of East Africa as well as in certain parts of the interior reached by Omani traders. The Arab-Omani heritage, as manifested in several architectural and archaeological sites[452], is still obvious in East Africa.

The Army and the Fleet

The expansion of the Omani empire during Al-Busaidi rule brought numerous challenges. Provision of security, stability and protection for the remote areas of the empire were the most significant difficulties encountered. A strong army was envisaged as a pressing need to fight the land and sea wars waged against the state.

Frequently, Sayyid Said bin Sultan himself led the army in an attempt to persuade rebellious emirates and mutinous movements to become obedient to the state. A case in point was the subjection of Mombasa and its surroundings[453]. Although command of the army was the exclusive responsibility of the Sultan, due to the vastness of the state and its numerous strongholds and fortresses, an emir was appointed to command the army in each emirate[454].

Sheikh Mohammed bin Juma'a Al-Barwani was one of the outstanding military leaders on whom Sultan Said relied in East Africa. He was a fierce fighter who had led the army to the coast of Lake Tanganyika and brought all the ports there under his control, after expelling the people of Malagasy[455].

As far as the naval fleet was concerned, all Sultan Said's ships, mercantile and military, were equipped with sail. At that particular time, however, steam boats had not been introduced on a wide scale. The most famous military sailing boat was *Liverpool*, built in Bombay in 1826. With a crew of 150 officers and sailors, the boat was equipped with 74 cannons. *Liverpool* was later presented to the King of England as a gift from Sayyid Said, to be subsequently renamed *Imam* in acknowledgment of the Sultan. The King of England, for his part, gave the Sultan a boat - *The Crown Prince* - as a gift[456].

During Al-Busaidi rule, the navy command was held by famous officers such as Hamad bin Suleiman Al-Busaidi, Sheikh Hassan Al-Farsi and Ahmed bin Nu'man Al-Ka'bi. The latter led the journey on board *Sultanah* to New York in 1840. He also sailed to France and had a good command of both English and French, with a fair knowledge of the oceanography relevant to the Indian Ocean and the Atlantic. Al-Busaidi state relied heavily on such greatly experienced people.

Sheikh Al-Ka'bi, for example, was appointed Minister of Foreign Affairs and also Finance in the aftermath of the death of Hassan Al-Farsi. Al-Ka'bi died during the rule of Sayyid Majed in 1867[457].

The naval fleet had two major duties: to sustain any war and to undertake trade. Oman had put considerable effort into the building of sailing boats which could sail the Indian Ocean and the Arabian Sea. With their large boats, Omanis were able to link Omani shores with the various coasts of Africa even during periods of severe seasonal winds. It would be insufficient to elaborate on the political and administrative structures of Al-Busaidi state without a careful perusal of opinions expressed by orientalists and foreign historians who studied the character of Sultan Said bin Sultan. Apparently, he had gained respect from enemies and friends alike. Richard Burton, the famous traveller, who had dealt with Sayyid Said, spoke about the leadership qualities of the Sultan, saying that, 'one felt that one was before a majestic personality, religious but not intolerant, kind and noble'[458].

Commercial Activity and the African Caravan Trade

Trade activity in East Africa is the most significant feature of the Omani presence requiring thorough study. The urgency of an objective analysis stems partly from the fact that certain European sources, in the context of overwhelming crusading campaigns, focussed primarily on the slave trade. The reader might be forgiven for thinking that it was the only trade in East Africa[459]. In fact, more comprehensive economic objectives were conceived during the Al-Busaidi rule there, particularly in the reign of Sayyid Said bin Sultan who had taken Zanzibar for his headquarters in the region. When departing Oman, Said was careful to take with him those Indian traders who were pivotal to trade activity in Muscat.

Indian traders seemingly achieved momentous economic growth during the reign of Sayyid Said bin Sultan. The Sultan had in fact employed the most qualified among them to undertake administrative duties in economic matters and Indian traders expanded their commercial activities to remote areas like Mozambique, Madagascar and Comoros[460]. But it seems that much of this activity was detrimental to the East African economy. The number of Indian traders increased alarmingly and they started to accumulate possessions through mortgage and direct purchase. During the reign of Sayyid Said, the number of Indians rose to 4000[461]. Consequently, the Sultan ordered hundreds of traders in Oman to come and reside on the island. But the newcomers did not settle only along the coast as anticipated, they advanced into the interior of the continent. The ultimate result was that Zanzibar played a vital cultural role with a far-reaching effect which touched areas beyond the tropical lakes: there were day-to-day commercial and cultural links between Zanzibar and central Africa.

Al-Busaidi efforts in the economic field were quite substantial, especially during the rule of Said bin Sultan. Said's success in this respect had an immense impact on his ability to establish a powerful state. Of great significance was the viable system for customs which he had formulated and which was applied in Muscat as well: customs on imports were no more than 5 per cent; and exports were exempted. This policy was, of course, intended to invigorate trade. Sayyid Said was well aware of the importance of trade incentives, accordingly, he set up a simple monetary system to regulate trade and substitute the dominant currencies on the island - namely, the German, Austrian and Spanish currencies. The new system, whereby a local currency was issued, replaced these currencies[462].

In 1882, Sayyid Barghash coined the new currency in which his name was engraved. This currency was first circulated in 1883; and in 1887, the Sultan once again introduced a new currency carrying the name of Zanzibar, which was actually used after his death and during the reign of Sayyid Khalifa bin Said (1888-1890). Some referred to this currency as Khalifa's baizat (copper coins). In 1936, however, British silver coins were introduced. Yet Khalifa's baizat remained informally in circulation. In tribute to Sayyid Khalifa as a great ruler, citizens requested the government to permit use of baizat. In response to this request, baizat continued to circulate beside the British silver coins.

Sayyid Said was widely known for his eagerness to engage in trade. He thus utilized the nation's naval fleet for the transport of goods far and wide. Ports in

Britain and France commonly received large volumes of African trade. In view of this, foreign political circles considered the Sultan to be a great man who turned his country into a large free trade zone, with unquestionable attraction for foreign nations. Instead of a small port, Zanzibar was now the biggest port in the western part of the Indian Ocean and a main warehouse of African and Asian trade in general. Hamerton, the British consul in Zanzibar, reported that the population of the island had almost doubled during the reign of Sayyid Said. In a twenty-year duration in office, the Sultan had successfully turned the island into one of three or four largest ports along the western waters of the Indian Ocean and increased the economic revenues of the island by nearly ten-fold.

The Sultan tried his best to provide the necessary facilities to stimulate foreign trade. Particular emphasis was given to the Arab caravan trade moving towards the interior parts of the African continent and as a result these caravans were enabled to travel across all trade routes in Africa and old roads were revived. In 1843, the first Arab caravan reached Buganda Kingdom, on the shores of Lake Victoria[463]. Towards the last years of the rule of Sayyid Said (and in 1852 in particular), a new trade route was opened to link the eastern African coast with the western shores through Lake Tanganyika. In the same year, a caravan from Zanzibar arrived to Benguuela along the western coast of Africa[464].

This trade expansion had resulted in the emergence of three major routes for Arab trade caravans:

- The central route extending from Mombasa and Malindi to the Lakes' plateau or the eastern parts of the present Uganda. This road was quite risky due to the raids staged by the warring Masai tribes.
- The intermediate route, which started from the African ports *vis-a-vis* Zanzibar, such as Tanga, Pangani and Bagamoyo, leading toward the centre of Lake Tanganyika. From Tanganyika, the road forked into two, north to the tropical Lakes' plateau, and south to Ujiji area and the Congo river basin. The significance of this route had increased in the nineteenth century owing to a sharp rise in the price of ivory worldwide. Arabs and Swahili people had formed relations with the Nyamezi tribes inhabiting the area and this route was generally considered to be the most important in terms of its lucrative trade revenues.
- The southern route, extending from Kilwa through southern Tanganyika and northern Mozambique to Lake Nyasa. Arabs had been able to forge an alliance with the Yaw tribe, famous for providing ivory and other African goods[465].

Ivory was one of the most significant goods carried by the Arab caravans. In fact, ivory had great importance in Europe and Asia at that time. During the rule of Al-Busaidi dynasty, however, ivory exports increased remarkably. For ivory was now a raw material used in several new industries such as ornaments, musical instruments and sculptures. Numerous commercial centres in, say, Germany, Netherlands and Britain, were built to exclusively trade in ivory[466].

Omani sources confirmed that before the arrival of the Europeans to Africa, Omani travellers had penetrated deeply into the continent. Said bin Mohammed Al-Aisari, Habib bin Salim Al-Afifi, Nasir bin Saif Al-Mamari, Issa bin Abdullah Al-Kharousi and Obeidalla bin Salim Al-Khadouri were the first travellers to reach Africa's hinterlands[467].

To facilitate travel for Omani caravans, permanent centres were established in Tabora, in central Tanganyika and Ujiji. Arab caravans consequently availed of ammunition and food supplies which were stored in these locations. Such centres later became Islamic emirates under the jurisdiction of the Sultan of Zanzibar[468]. H. M. Stanley, the famous European explorer, said that the town of Tabora, located some 1000 kilometres west of the eastern African shores was the most important commercial centre in central Africa for Muscat's and Zanzibar's trade[469].

Humaid bin Mohammed Al-Mirjabi, and his deputy Mohammed bin Khalfan Al-Barwani, were among the renowned Omani travellers who played a vital role in the ivory trade, establishing a vast Arab Islamic emirate in the upper Congo. It was an emirate that had a massive commercial and political influence in the period preceding European domination of the continent. Together with other Arab traders, they also contributed in the establishment of towns such as Kasongo and Nianojui, in a manner typical of Arab architecture and planning, as had previously been adopted in Zanzibar and the eastern coasts of Africa[470].

Commercial transactions relied entirely on barter. Travellers estimated that $2000 worth of ivory in the interior would be sold at $7000 in the coast. In 1859, the British consul in Zanzibar estimated his country's imports of Zanzibar's ivory at 448,600 labels, to the value of some £146,666[471]. Caravan trade proved greatly lucrative to the Africans themselves. Although Arabs deserved the credit for focussing the attention of the Africans on the importance of ivory, the Buganda kings subsequently monopolized trade in ivory in the surrounding areas of their kingdom; and Arabs were ultimately deprived of the right to roam in areas dominated by those kings[472].

Though Zanzibar was now an important source for arms and other vital commodities, particularly cotton textiles for the Buganda kings, their relations with the Al-Busaidi sultans had unexpectedly been severed. Nonetheless, Zanzibar's traders achieved an eminent status in the Buganda and Panyoro kingdoms.

Some of these traders had even been promoted to the position of advisors and consultants in the service of the African kings. Certainly, the increase in economic activity experienced by these kingdoms had stimulated an increase in their political power and, indeed, paved the way for the introduction of Omani cultural values into all the African societies in the region[473]. In reality, the concern shown by Europeans with East Africa was not confined to trade; rather, another activity had suddenly come into focus. This was the crusading fervour which was intimately linked with European exploratory expeditions. European missionaries had thus penetrated into the eastern provinces of Africa since the mid-nineteenth century and were successful in setting up several missionary centres that had paramount significance in the religious and social life of the Africans.

Social Life

Despite the great diversity in ethnic origin and linguistic background of the peoples of Zanzibar and East Africa in the nineteenth century, the newly emerging society evolved in the Arab-Islamic mould. This process was largely attributable to the religious and cultural similarities prevailing throughout the region during the rule of the Al-Busaidi dynasty. However, it is worth mentioning that the Al-Busaidi rulers had shown considerable tolerance and respect for all ethnic aspects and local traditions. Therefore, Africans responded, both spontaneously and positively, to Islam especially among the societies which came into direct contact with Omanis.

In regard to this, Al-Mughairi states that, 'an example of the decency of Zanzibar's sultans was their non-zealous approach to race and religion. All non-Arab races in Zanzibar were treated by the Sultan with due respect to equality in all governmental affairs. Any thorough reading of the history of Zanzibar would reveal no segregation between Arabs and other races'[474]. More than a hundred years ago, an English observer referred to this remarkable phenomenon in African societies by saying: 'Whatever they are, and wherever they go, Muslim missionaries showed kindness and respect to local traditions and tribalism. This factor has been, undoubtedly, behind their success'[475].

The major population groups in Zanzibar were composed of Africans, Arabs and Indians. In addition, there were other minority groups from Comoros, Somalia, the Nubia and other areas[476]. Based on the results of the last official census conducted in 1948 for Zanzibar and Pemba islands, the population amounted to 264,000 persons distributed as follows[477]:

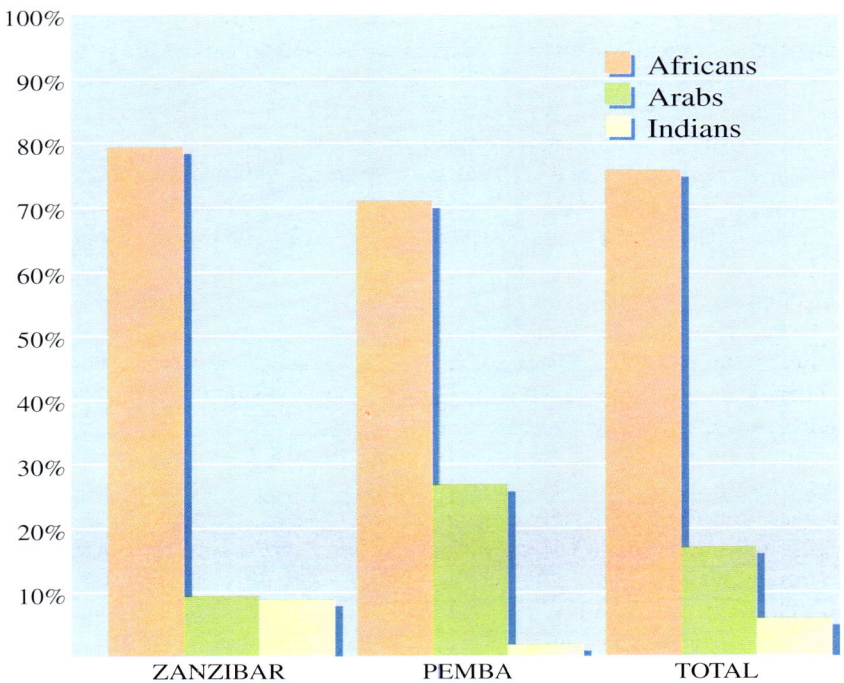

Most of the Arabs in Zanzibar had migrated during the reign of Sayyid Said bin Sultan. These were mainly from the Hurth tribe, who were described by Al-Mughairi as the major contributors to the improvement of social life on the island. Al-Mughairi elaborated on the main branches of this tribes, stating 'that they include Barwana, Khanajira, Gheyoth, Muharima, Samirat, sons of Nadi, Mutawiqa, people of Sinaw and A'asira. Yet other tribes, too, had inhabited this island. But all of them were the followers of the Ibadhi sect'[478].

Foreign and local sources indicated that there were numerous immigrations of Omanis into these areas from earlier times, in addition to a new group of immigrants represented by those accompanying Sayyid Said to Zanzibar in 1832[479]. On the other hand, the Sherazi group was the most significant African community in Zanzibar. Sherazi was in turn divided into two subsections: Makhadimu and Tumbatu. This mother group was generally seen as the aboriginal inhabitants of the island[480]. From the social point of view, however, Sherazi was the closest ethnic community to Arabs as far as traditions are concerned. The intimacy between the two communities was primarily due to their advocacy of Islam. Moreover, intermarriage between the two groups provided further evidence of a close relationship[481].

There were also other African groups from the continent's interior. These were best represented by the Nyamwezi, Sokomo, Zaramu, Haya, Yao, Angoni, Malonde and Gogo. They immigrated into Zanzibar and Pemba in great numbers to work on the clove farms which were expanded in the nineteenth century. Others were connected with transportation of goods during the period of caravan trade mentioned previously. But agriculture was the major reason for the settling of these tribes in Zanzibar and Pemba[482].

The ruling dynasty of sultans, advisors, ministers and *walis* were at the top of the social hierarchy in Zanzibar and East Africa. Then came, in terms of relative significance, big traders and the well-educated population who constituted the intellectual elite, leaders in religious and cultural aspects. These worked in the judiciary, education and other consultative posts in the sultan's office[483].

One of the most far-reaching impacts of Oman, in the regions under the jurisdiction of Al-Busaidi state in eastern and central Africa, was the role it played in combating the primitive habit of nakedness. Nakedness was previously quite common in many parts of the African interior. African communities not only accepted Arabic culture and Islamic religion, but they imitated Arab dress, too. Thus, Africans were no longer naked; they now dressed exactly like Arabs, putting on white loose garments and covering their heads with the so-called *umama*.

Arab impact and Islamic influence were clear in both male and female dress. For men, Kanzu dress was the distinctive wear for Swahili communities as well as African groups in the hinterland. This was an Arab-Islamic white garment, covering the body to the feet and arms - the same garment now widely known in Oman as *dishdasha*[484]. Closely linked to Islam in Africa, it would usually be completed by wearing the head-cover, commonly known as *koufi'yah*[485]. The wearing of this dress granted Muslims and Africans respect and esteem. Swahili families descending from Arab-Omani origins also wore a sword and half-circled knife in addition to the Arab common dress. Generally speaking, men's dress was quite similar to that worn by Omanis. Swahili people dressed in this manner up to the early twentieth century[486].

Likewise, women's dress reflected the impact of Arab, Omani and the Islamic essence. The most important wear in this respect was the black gown, or what was termed in Kiswahili as *buibui*. This clothing consisted of two pieces, the major one to be wrapped around the body, covering it to the feet; whereas the second piece was a band-like silky cloth to cover the head. The overall dress was similar to the women's gown presently used in Oman and other Gulf nations[487].

In a pilot study a European researcher has analyzed the major patterns and social characteristics of the Omani immigrations to central Africa since the last century. The study concludes that these immigrations had stimulated the development of urbanized communities inhabited by people of Arab ethnic origin[488]. These Omani communities could be found in Rwanda and Burundi, in addition to the eastern parts of Zaire (Kivu and Shaba regions in particular)[489]. The urbanization of these communities was largely due to the economic activity exercised by a considerable number of Omanis. Many Omani travellers were engaged in business, living in large capitals such as Kigali and Bujumbura[490].

A remarkable social phenomenon was that Omanis in Africa were characterized by a tendency to readily mix with other groups. This was directly related to their activity as merchants, in addition to their persistent search for ways to make a living. For instance, Meizon said that Omani men frequently married African women in the villages or towns through which they travelled on business. They might sometimes marry daughters of tribal chiefs in a bid to strengthen their social and economic influence in the respective regions. Meizon, in fact, attended marriages between three Omani brothers and three African women[491].

This social tolerance and co-existence during the rule of Al-Busaidi dynasty had great implications in the context of Afro-Arab relations. The Omani pioneers, those who had promoted Arab Islamic culture in the dark of the African continent, were a magnificent example of positive intermingling with the original populations. They adopted an Islamic way of life which did not countenance segregation on racial grounds. Consequently, a large portion of the African groups in East Africa mixed with Arab blood. And numerous Africans were proud of their Arab origin as well as of their Islamic identity[492].

Religious and Cultural Life

Expansion of Islam in Africa

Indeed the cultural role played by Omani Arabs in the last century was primarily focussed on Islamic missionary work. The era of Al-Busaidi rulers was a significant period along the line of Islamic *call* in East Africa. For the first time, Islam was advocated in Uganda, the upper Congo river, Rwanda and Burundi, in addition to the interior of Lake Tanganyika. Zanzibar was a source of Islamic radiation since it had become the capital for Sayyid Said bin Sultan in 1832, as already mentioned.

On this issue, one of the contemporary propagandists, who visited Zanzibar in 1973, confirmed that, 'the old rule had gone, both its delights and agonies. All advocated Islam. Islam is the prevailing religion in all of the island which is characterized by two distinguishing phenomena: first, the salient Islamic features; and, secondly, the Arab pattern of urbanization as manifest in buildings and roads. This is largely attributable to the authenticity of Islam which was embraced early on by the various inhabitants. In short, Zanzibar and Pemba, though small islands, include some 375 mosques - a mosque for each hundred persons (women excluded). Until quite recently, Zanzibar was a veritable East African forum; the teachings delivered in mosques had given birth to an intellectual elite who had attained the highest levels of religious knowledge'[493].

Islam was spread during the reign of the Al-Busaidi dynasty by the Omani caravan trade which travelled from Zanzibar and other coastal cities. These merchants, commonly named in foreign and local references as Zanzibaris, traded extensively in the mid-nineteenth century. By and large, it was an Islamic call based entirely on peaceful propaganda and conviction practised by numerous propagandists who had no resources other than their firm beliefs.

Among the most important early propagandists was Sheikh Ahmed bin Ibrahim Al-Amri, who had a great influence on the spread of Islam in Uganda. His arrival at the King Sunna court in the Buganda kingdom was a turning point in the history of the kingdom, marking as it did the early introduction of Islam to Uganda. Informed sources indicated that Al-Amri was the first Muslim trader to reach the kingdom ever. In his memoirs, Emin Pasha, an Egyptian historian, said that Al-Amri's first visit to Uganda was in 1843[494].

European and local sources agreed that the commercial excursions conducted by Arab traders were usually accompanied by an exchange of views and ideas. This paved the way for Islam to spread far and wide in these remote areas in eastern and central Africa. Furthermore, during this period, Al-Amri showed unprecedented courage in opposing certain barbaric practices in the court, such as the manslaughter of innocent people in response to the superstitious requirements of the Lubaare heretical belief. Lubaare was advocated by a considerable number of Bugandan people, primarily the *Kabaka* (or the king) who represented both the secular and spiritual authority in that societal system. The Kabaka, at one time, ordered a massacre in accordance with the traditional barbarous rites. To the surprise of all attending, Al-Amri stood up to oppose the Kabaka. Loudly expressing denunciation of the deed, he said to the King, 'those subjects to be unjustly killed, are but creatures of Almighty Allah, who has created you and lavished the kingdom upon you'[495].

The King maintained his composure to reply that his gods had conferred the kingdom upon him. Still, Al-Amri bravely continued to reiterate his denunciation of the action, repeatedly reminding the King that Allah was great, until the King started to ask who was Allah. Al-Amri elaborated, explaining his ideas very clearly. Gradually, the King began to respond, requesting Al-Amri to teach him even more about the one God. The literature indicated that Al-Amri was finally able to teach the Kabaka four parts of the Holy Qur'an before he died in 1856. In this way, a wide opening was made for the spread of Islam in Uganda and its surroundings[496].

This was a typical example of the work undertaken by Muslim propagandists in Africa. Al-Amri was in fact a magnificent example of a Muslim propagandist. A strong, brave charismatic personality, with clear-cut morals, he would never compromise as regards God's cause. And though he combined trade with propaganda, he would sometimes devote his time to the latter. This was the firm basis laid down by Al-Amri and the subsequent Muslim propagandists during the time of King Motisa I (1856-1884) of the Buganda kingdom. The King showed unprecedented enthusiasm toward Islam; he exerted all efforts to spread Islam not only among his people in Buganda, but in the surrounding kingdoms as well. He wrote to Kabarega, the King of Bunyoro, calling him to embrace Islam.

During his rule Omani traders were respected and taken on as advisors. He also exchanged gifts with Zanzibar's sultans, especially Majed and Barghash. Moreover, he vested some Swahili people with the authority necessary to administer the local affairs of their respective areas. For the first time in Bugandan history, he introduced the Hegira calendar in all parts of the kingdom; and he also requested commitment to Islamic morality and conduct in all day-to-day and social transactions.

The role of Omanis in the diffusion of Islam in eastern and central Africa during Al-Busaidi rule is in need of more extensive research and study, particularly from an Islamic and Arab point of view. References written by Muslims are relatively scarce. There were, for instance, several unknown propagandists about which only scanty information was found scattered in European sources such as the official documents and reports prepared by missionaries. Among these, were Sheikh Khamis bin Jum'a, who had stimulated King Motisa to embrace Islam and Sheikh Abdul Rahman bin Obeid Ibn Hamoud, the personal envoy of Sayyid Barghash at the court of King Kabarija of Bonyoro. The latter had undertaken substantial efforts in the Islamic call by constructing mosques and leading the Islamic community of Zanzibar's merchants and national figures[497].

It would be advisable to mention in this respect the pioneer role undertaken by the most famous Omani merchant: Sheikh Humaid bin Mohammed Al-Marjabi - as well as his assistant Sheikh Mohammed bin Khalfan Al-Barwani[498]. These two notable figures had established an Islamic Arab emirate in the upper Congo; administratively, the emirate was loyal to Zanzibar[499]. Al-Mughairi summed up this activity in the following lines: 'Omani Arabs, the subjects of Sayyid Said, had undoubtedly established trade centres in the hinterlands of Africa. They also excelled in knowledge of its roads and built Arab colonies as well to ultimately become centres for Islamic teaching and the promotion of the Sultanate of Zanzibar'[500].

Contemporary references on Arab activity in central Africa and the role of Omani Arabs are numerous. As already mentioned, Omani Arabs were instrumental in the dissemination of Islam and their work was helped substantially by their role as traders in the Congo region. One of the contemporary references mentioned that the Arabs had never put any political pressure on the nationals of the region; they did not impose their civilization and religion by force, but they went beyond the simple act of trading by encouraging the nationals to embrace Islam in a peaceful and voluntary manner. The reasons for their success in this respect could be numerous: the most important of all was that Arabs were socially esteemed by Africans; and they were also free from intolerance. The same reference confirmed that Africans had promptly embraced Islam to avoid enslavement, for a Muslim should not be taken as a slave[501].

In the same manner, Omanis evidently contributed to the introduction of Islam in Burundi and Rwanda. We have previously mentioned the study conducted by a French sociologist in these countries. This researcher has come up with the social features of the Islamic community which was formed as a consequence of waves of immigrations of the Omani Hurth tribes. Islam was also introduced to these areas in central Africa by the peaceful means that usually accompanied trade and intermingling with the recipient societies. Through time, urbanized communities were created; for the majority of the Omani immigrants had lived in large cities. The French sociologist stated that about 30 per cent of Rwanda's Muslims were in Kigali, whereas 70 per cent of Muslims in Burundi inhabited Bujumbura, the capital of the nation[502].

Muslim Scholars in Zanzibar and East Africa

Al-Busaidi rulers had tremendous respect for scholars and knowledgeable Muslims. This was one of the most outstanding features of the Al-Busaidi State advocated by Sayyid Said bin Sultan, its founder who lavished great respect and care on scholars from all sects; and it seems religious tolerance was one of the basic features of his state policy. As a result, close relations prevailed between scholars of the Ibadhi sect - which was the official doctrine of the state - and the Shaffii sect of Islam advocated by a majority of Sunnis in East Africa[503]. This trend had first appeared among scholars and judges from both sides in the meetings presided over by the Sultan and, afterwards, when some of them were appointed to executive posts, or as advisors to the sultan or, later on, to his sons[504].

Knowledgeable Muslims and scholars were the real force in Zanzibar in several ways. They had numerous duties including implementation of Shari'a on the island and its surroundings. They were also charged with the responsibility of supervising education, and consequently were able to spread Islamic values among the community in Zanzibar and East Africa[505]. They accordingly devoted a large portion of their time to reading and understanding Islamic jurisprudence; and they also participated in the compilation of numerous books on Islamic subjects. They had, accordingly, organized visits for the purpose of research to the original sources of knowledge, the large distinguished Islamic centres in the Holy Lands, Oman and Hadramaut. As time passed, they gained a high status for themselves in society; and were granted the same esteem as scholars from the traditional Islamic centres[506].

This group of scholars had actively participated in the dissemination of Islamic culture, by teaching, writing and partaking in the social momentum. A large number of inhabitants of Zanzibar and the East African hinterlands had benefited from efforts exerted by these fervent scholars. This study will later illuminate the role of a selected group of such distinguished scholars from the last century who had written many books, few of which are presently published in Arabic or Kiswahili. It is clear, however, that they discuss diverse aspects pertaining to Islamic heritage in East Africa which is to date not well appreciated.

Only relatively few names are to be found in European references and scarce Arabic ones. Of significance among these names are Sheikh Muhyi Addin Al-Qahtani (1790-1869)[507]; Sheikh Ali bin Khamis Al-Barwani (1852-1886) who was taught by the elite of the Ibadhi sect during the reign of Sultan Barghash (such as Al-Manthiri and Al-Khusaibi)[508]; Sheikh Monsib bin Ali (1863-1927), Sheikh Ali bin Abdullah Al-Mazrui (1825-1894)[509], Sheikh Abdul Aziz Alamawi (1832-1896)[510]; Sheikh Abdullah bin Mohammed Bakithir Al-Kindi (1864-1925)[511], Sheikh Ahmed bin Sumait (1861-1925), and Sheikh Al-Amin bin Ali Al-Mazrui (1891-1947)[512].

Education

The early nucleus of education was to be found in the Qur'anic (elementary) schools and the lessons taught in mosques and the houses of *ulema*. Both constituted the basic foundation of education in Zanzibar and the other Islamic centres in East Africa such as Pemba, Lamu, Mombasa, Malindi and Kilwa[513]. Muslim scholars played a vital role in the education process and these educational institutions were the mould in which Swahili culture was formed. The early stages of education in Swahili societies were therefore closely linked to Islam. In consequence, education followed obvious Islamic guidelines in both its methods and essence. This was the case in all the Islamic centres where male and female students were taught Qur'an, Islamic jurisprudence and Arabic language. The teaching was designed to instill Islamic values and proper conduct into the students[514].

This massive effort is best illustrated by the activities of Sheikh Al-Amin bin Ali Mazrui (1891-1947), who was a good example of the Muslim scholars and their role in education. In an introductory note to one of the rare pieces of literature that gave detailed accounts on the history of East Africa, the following comments were made on the pivotal role played by Mazrui: 'Devoting himself to the righteous call and public guidance, he taught frequently in Mombasa and all other places he visited. He opened two schools, one in Mombasa and the other in Goi village nearby. He spent his own money on them as well as that collected from the donations of a few good people. He also wrote about 30 books in Swahili, the African language commonly used in East Africa and in the Latin alphabet'.

Indeed, of all his books, *Hidayat Alatfal* - that is, guidance for children-which was taught in all East African mosques and schools, stands out as a masterpiece worthy of appreciation. He also had written books on Hadith - the Prophet's teachings - and other aspects of Islamic jurisprudence[515].

Thus we note that during the Islamic Sultanate of Zanzibar, Omanis and other Arabs from Hadramaut were at the forefront of efforts to disseminate education in East Africa. By the nineteenth century, Zanzibar was a forum for students from all over the coastal cities and the hinterlands of East Africa, attracting huge numbers of scholars, teachers and students who came from remote areas such as Djawa, eastern Indian islands, Oman and Hardramaut.

Shortly thereafter, educational methods developed so that studies encompassed Quranic science, interpretation, Islamic jurisprudence and language, including Arabic language studies, rhetoric and poetry. In fact, teaching methods were quite similar to those followed in Oman, Hadramaut, and the

Holy Areas in Hijaz. The most reputable centre then was the institute set up within Maskiti Gofu mosque in Zanzibar. This institute was established by one of the members of the Al-Jamal Allayl family, famous for its knowledge and massive efforts in the Islamic call in East Africa[516].

Indeed, many Africans underwent instruction as a result of educational developments during Al-Busaidi rule. This process continued and the Islamic influences on education remained overwhelming in the coastal region in general. It should be reiterated that the pioneers of education were Omani Arabs and that the Arab and Islamic culture was passed on to the Africans by the Arab teachers. Finally, illiteracy was abolished and the African communities were ultimately linked to the Islamic and Arab world. Thus, African Muslims openly expressed their Islamic orientation and loyalty as well as their close intimacy to the Arab elements in several ways[517].

Printing and Emergence of the Press in Zanzibar

The establishment of the Sultanate's printing press in Zanzibar during the reign of Sultan Barghash (1870-1888) was one of the major factors in further boosting a scientific renaissance in East Africa. The printers published numerous Omani books, particularly religious ones[518]. An Omani source described the role of this printing shop, at the same time commending the efforts of Sultan Barghash in this respect: 'An Arabic printing press was established to undertake printing of religious and literary works as well as other diverse topics. The most distinguished books it published included *Hayman Azzad*, an Islamic Shari'a dictionary, *Mukhtasar Al-Khissal*, Bisawi collection, *Manzoomat Madarij Al-Kamal*[519].This remarkable achievement made it possible to promote public awareness and disseminate Islamic and Arab culture in the region.

The printed press was therefore established for the first time in the history of Zanzibar and that of East Africa as well. Omanis founded newspapers such as *Falaq*, *Nahda* and *Islah*, to mention but a few. Great people like Sheikh Ahmed bin Hamdoun Al-Harithi, Sheikh Hashil Al-Maskari. Sheikh Abdullah bin Hamoud Al-Harithi and Al-Amin bin Ali Al-Mazrui were among the outstanding figures to take over the duties of editors-in-chief of the fledgling papers. Numerous Omani literary figures, whether residents of Zanzibar or the homeland, participated by writing for the press[520]. The new newspapers were instrumental in fostering literary and religious awareness among Muslims in East Africa so that Muslim communities were armed with the means to encounter threats to their way of life; similarly, they became quite vigilant of the principles and values that should be observed to maintain the coherence of their Islamic and Arab identity[521].

Expansion of Arabic Language and Swahili Culture

The Arabic language spread amongst the various sectors of the population in East Africa. Indeed, it became the language of the intellectual elite as well as merchants and statesmen. However, the vast majority of ordinary Muslim Africans mastered a relatively limited knowledge of the language which barely allowed them to exercise the Islamic rituals and recite Qur'an.

Notably, though, the spread of Arabic went hand in hand with the diffusion of Islam. European travellers were astonished that Kings Motisa and Kabarija, and other African chiefs, spoke Arabic fluently as well as Kiswahili[522]. Nonetheless, Kiswahili remained the day-to-day medium of communication between ordinary people, especially in the interior of East Africa. But Kiswahili was imbued with Arabic terms that express Islamic concepts. Obviously, the empire had opted early on for Kiswahili as the official language of the state. Yet Arabic maintained its position as the medium commonly in use at the Sultan's office and governmental offices. For the governors of the Arab African areas were Omani Arabs, advocating Islam and speaking Arabic as their mother tongue. Therefore, it is reasonable to find that Zanzibar, the capital of the empire, adopted Arabic, as well as the Islamic culture. Zanzibar, as a result, turned into a source of cultural radiation. Ultimately, Kiswahili and Arabic were maintained hand in hand with the Omani influence in all areas accessed by Omanis in East Africa[523].

Swahili culture, in its typical form, which can still be observed on East Africa's islands and coastal areas together with the central African cities, was a reflection of the Islamic creed. It also governed the very names of people, their traditions, costumes, architecture, arts, proverbs and medium of daily communi-cation. It was above all an African-Arab-Islamic culture[524]. Accordingly, 'Swahili', as a term, was much used to describe the peoples of the eastern coast of Africa who were closely linked with the Arab World by bonds of culture and trade. Most of this population had advocated Islam and adopted Arab and Islamic life-styles.

During the rule of the Al-Busaidi dynasty, the development of trade and the movement of caravans deep into Africa, all contributed to strengthen the position of Kiswahili as a language of people with mutual interests. In fact, the caravan trade, was largely instrumental in introducing this language to central Africa[525]. Generally speaking, however, this Omani role had far-reaching effects on contemporary aspects of culture and politics. Kiswahili is presently the most significant *lingua franca* in Africa, followed by Arabic in terms of the geographic distribution and number of speakers. Kiswahili is the national language of Tanzania and the official one in Kenya. It is also widely used in southern Somalia and Uganda together with a large number of metropolises in Burundi, Rwanda, eastern Zaire, northern Mozambique and Comoros. The total number of Swahili speakers is estimated at 40 million. It is also taught in linguistics colleges in Africa, Europe, America and Asia. The United Nations Educational, Scientific and Cultural Organization (UNESCO) has recently adopted Kiswahili as one of the languages of its bulletins.

Navigation and Trade in the First Century of Al-Busaidi Rule

The first hundred years of Al-Busaidi rule was unequivocally successful. Omanis had achieved great progress in navigation and trade. Thus, if the preceding Al-Ya'ruba nation could be labelled as a 'maritime military state', then the Al-Busaidi nation could best be seen as a 'mercantile marine state', if not an empire.

Numerous internal and external factors were set in play to permit Omanis to undertake a distinctive role in navigation and trade during the first century of the Al-Busaidi regime. Such factors included the development of expertise in navigation and commercial skills. Omanis had in fact gained this vast experience through a long pathway of historic events coupled with a strategic geographical location. The other factor was the relative stability of Oman in general and its seaports in particular at a time when all other ports in the region were in disarray. Omani ports, the most important of which was Muscat, were the subject of strong governmental control that provided security and protection for all those involved in trade. Indeed Omani trade, immense and successful as it was, would have had its own commercial ships as well as military warships to protect shipping and the coastal cities as well.

All these factors could be considered as internal, intrinsic ones, which had contributed to the prosperity of Omani trade at that time. The other factor, outside the scope of these internal ones, was that pertaining to international and regional trade. This was closely related to trade into the Asian ports, already underway in the Asian ports to the east and west of the Indian subcontinent. Considerable in volume and types of commodities, a large portion of this trade was under the control of Omani traders, which constituted the main commercial relationship between the Indian subcontinent, on the one hand, and the Arabian Gulf, Red Sea and East African region on the other. Omani domination of this area was primarily due to the withdrawal of the Europeans, and particularly the British, who were previously engaged in this trade. The Europeans ventured further to the east mainly toward China. This change had its effect on trade relations existing to the west and Asian traders were ready to fill the gap. Omanis were at the forefront of those prepared to take the lead.

The volume of trade managed by Omanis and transported by their ships was incredible. By now, Muscat was the major entrepôt for the transshipment of goods to the western Indian Ocean. The wealth thus accumulated by Omanis during this era was enormous. Some would say that the Omanis' trade in sugar and coffee alone was enough to describe them as wealthy. Coffee imported from Yemen's ports of Mukhha and Al-Hudaydah, almost half of the annual production of Yemen, satisfied the demand for it in Iran, Arabia, Iraq, Armenia and Anatolia as well as part of the demand in Syria, the European part of the Ottoman Empire, Germany, Poland, Russia and North Europe. Sugar from Batavia, on the other hand, was imported in sufficient quantity as to meet the demand in Iran, Iraq, Armenia, Arabia and Anatolia.

Trade of this volume required Al-Busaidi rulers to adopt specific policies in order to maintain the distinguished commercial status of the nation. Policies so undertaken could be summarized as follows:

- A focus on maintaining supremacy overseas; including efforts to meet external threats and a commitment to protect Omani coastal areas and ports. This would ultimately lead to full security for all shipping in the area.
- An attempt at controlling areas of strategic and commercial significance, with particular emphasis on the Arabian Gulf and East Africa. Omani rulers considered these areas as significant for the strengthening and expansion of their commercial state.
- Adoption of special trade policies designed to coordinate existing commercial relations between the Indian coasts, Arabian Gulf, the Red Sea and East Africa. These relations were organized in a manner that ensured Oman's supremacy and excellence in the field of navigation and trade.

In this chapter we will discuss the extent to which the Al-Busaidi regime had successfully implemented these policies. However, it will be necessary to first elaborate on the developments in the field of trade and navigation in Oman and the Indian Ocean.

Early Developments in Respect to Trade and Navigation in the Al-Busaidi State

Ahmed bin Said Al-Busaidi, the governor of Sohar, expelled the Persians from the region, and was consequently elected Imam in 1157 AH/1744 AD, remaining in office until his death in 1197 AH/1783 AD. During his reign, Oman was powerful, stable and secure. In several aspects, however, Al-Busaidi rule was a continuation of the preceding Ya'ruba regime from 1034 AH/1624 to 1153 AH/1740 AD. Yet each had certain distinguishing features.

Generally speaking, the Ya'ruba state could have been aptly described as a marine military state[526]. The Ya'ruba fleet was the strongest local fleet in the Arabian Gulf and the Red Sea, and even in the Indian Ocean. In 1695, the fleet consisted of five large ships, each of which could carry up to 1500 men[527]. In 1715, however, and according to Hamilton's account, the fleet included a large ship that carried 74 cannons, two boats with 60 cannons each, a boat with 50 cannons and 18 other small boats each equipped with 4-8 cannons[528]. Armed with this naval power, Al-Ya'ruba was able to achieve much success in the fields of politics and war.

The struggle against the Portuguese was a distinctive feature of the Ya'ruba era. Indeed, the fight Oman waged against the Portuguese in the Arabian Gulf was unprecedented in the history of the nation. Omanis were not only able to

MEDITERRANEAN SEA

Bushihr
Bandar Abbas
Hormuz
Jawadar
Karachi

CHINA

Basra
Sohar
Muscat
Sur
ARABIAN PENINSULA
Suakin
Massawa
Mukha
Shihr
Salalah
Berbera

Surat
Calcutta
INDIA
Goa
Madras
Ceylon

Canton
Luqin

Mogadishu
Lamu
Mombasa
Zanzibar
Kilwa

INDIAN OCEAN

Malqa

INDONESIA

Surabaya

Mozambique

Mauritius

Safala

MADAGASCAR

Territory of Oman
Oman's Sea Trade Routes
Oman's Land Trade Routes
Oman's Trade Centres

The Omani State and its trading practices in the eighteenth and nineteenth centuries.

expel the Portuguese from their homeland, but they were successful in pursuing them in the other Arabian Gulf areas and as far away as India and East Africa[529].

In fact, there was more than one local[530] dominant naval power competing with Omanis in the Indian Ocean and the surrounding waters.

It should be noted that the Persian coasts were continuously threatened by the Omani naval fleet and crucial parts of the Arab coasts and islands of the Arabian Gulf fell under the supremacy of the Omani state. Cogent evidence of the strength and power of the Omanis could be seen in the extent of the fear shown by Britain and the Netherlands toward the Omani naval force. The two great nations had even requested their agencies in the region to avoid committing any act that might arouse or provoke Oman[531].

In the second half of the eighteenth century and the first few decades of the nineteenth, the Omani naval and commercial role was expanded. But, before going on to discuss the trade and naval activities of Oman during that particular epoch, it would seem appropriate to have a look at the overall situation and the emerging conditions which might have had great impact on Omani naval and trade activity. Some of these factors were intimately related to the presence of European and local powers on the Indian subcontinent and the Arabian Gulf. The Portuguese and Dutch were no longer in the Gulf; whereas France was unable to secure considerable political, military or commercial influence on the Indian subcontinent and in the Arabian Gulf alike; this was despite persistent French attempts to find a footing in the region. On the other hand, the British, represented by the East India Company, were able to impose domination over the Bengal region towards the second half of the eighteenth century. This relative success was only possible after they emerged victorious from the battle of Plassey in 1757. Shortly afterwards, the East India Company expanded its domination to other regions as well. It was then prepared to pay unprecedented attention to the Arabian Gulf region.

Apart from the situation pertaining to the European powers, some local powers in the region, represented by influential tribes, were on the rise. In the southern section of the Arabian Gulf the Qawasim tribe emerged[532] to exhibit a growing influence having captured Nadir Shah's fleet, following the death of the Shah and the final collapse of the central government of Persia. The Qawasim quickly used this fleet to achieve their particular interests and ambitions[533]. At the further end of the Gulf, were the sheikhs of Bushehr who were also able to snatch another part of the Shah's fleet. Nearby, also were the rulers of the small Bandar Rig and the neighbouring Kharj island.

To the far north, Utoob Bedouins had strengthened their hold on certain parts of the northern Gulf, particularly Kuwait and Bahrain, in the last decades of the eighteenth century. They channeled almost all their efforts into trade and navigation, in which they were apparently successful[534].To the farthest north of the Gulf, was the Ka'b tribe, garrisoned at Shatt Al-Arab and spreading around the basin of Karoon river[535]. Most importantly for Omanis in this period was the emergence of the Wahabi movement in Nejd, Arabia. The Wahabi sect was on the increase at this time, with more and more adherents threatening Oman. The Wahhabis later allied with the Qawasim to further challenge Oman. While Wahhabis continued to impose pressure on land, the Qawasim threatened the state along the Omani coastline and ports.

The picture would not be complete unless the role of the Ottoman Empire, which was in control of Iraq, is briefly discussed. Paradoxically, though, the intervention of the Ottoman and Persian empires in Gulf affairs was relatively limited. This was due to numerous factors, the most significant of which was the weakness of the two empires in the field of naval power[536].

Although there were many competing powers as already said, Oman did not loose its vigour and integrity; it proved to be particularly successful in its efforts to adapt to the new emerging situations, as well as maintain its identity and interests. Furthermore, Oman, especially during Al-Busaidi rule, mobilized efforts to boost trade. As a result, it was able to realize phenomenal achievements in this regard. This is therefore the subject matter of this study.

Numerous factors helped Oman achieve success and excellence in trade and navigation during the first century of the state. The most significant of these factors was the skill and expertise exhibited by Omanis in the field of trade and navigation. They gained such vast experience from endless historical events together with a strategic geographical location and an eternal heritage[537]. The other important factor in this context, however, was the relative stability experienced by Oman in general and its ports in particular. In contrast most of the other Gulf ports were in disarray. Bandar Abbas, on the one hand, was gradually starting to lose its strategic importance in the region. Previously, the port, being on the inlet of the Arabian Gulf, was a major centre of political, commercial and navigational activity for more than a half century. By the mid-eighteenth century, however, it was on the decline. This was mainly due to the chaos prevailing in Persia in the aftermath of the death of Nadir Shah in

1747[538]. The central authority was no longer able to influence the course of events in this port. Likewise, local governors engaged in a fierce competition to dominate the city. Most important of all was that a large part of the Shah's naval fleet, for which Bandar Abbas was the major base, had fallen under control of the Arab tribes residing nearby. War was waged between these tribes, to add to an already deteriorating situation. This was coupled with the greediness and rigidity of the Persian rulers, which had been increasingly detrimental to trade and navigational activity in the port. The Dutch East India Company could do nothing but withdraw from Bandar Abbas in 1752; the British Company soon followed suit in 1763. The remaining merchants were scattered here and there to other ports but Muscat was probably a destination for a good number of them. The English East India Company finally relocated its operation from Bandar Abbas to Basra, a new major centre from then on.

In this particular period in the history of the region, stability was gradually maintained in certain parts of the Persian coastline. Karim Khan Zand expanded his territory to capture the waters surrounding Bushehr port to the northern end of the Gulf. By the time the English agency was shifted from Bandar Abbas to Basra, on April 1763, exactly, the company's Bushehr agent, O. I. Price, visited Sheikh Sa'adoon, the port's designated emir, and forged an agreement with him, whereby the company had had to open its headquarters there. Karim Khan endorsed the agreement; and the office was actually established[539]. But very soon, the situation had once again deteriorated because of the war between Persians and Mir Mihana in the neighborhood of Bushehr. The Dutch and British were utterly entangled in its snares. Thus, trade activity was halted in the port to a large extent. Moreover, a sudden dispute erupted between the Persians and the British, who were only recently allied against Mir Mihana. Finally, the British withdrew from the port in 1769, satisfied with their main centre in Basra[540].

Unfortunately, the situation in Basra was on the decline, too. In fact, the city was riddled with crises and difficulties; the power of Mir Mihana, the governor of Kharj Island and the port of Bandar Rig, coupled with his violent war against the Dutch, British and Persians, had further hindered trade in much of the northern Arabian Gulf. Most important, too, was the dispute between the strong Ka'b tribe and the Ottomans. The former had intercepted navigation in the Shatt al-Arab; and even had from time to time laid siege to Basra. In 1767, a blustering war was raged between the Ka'b tribe, on one hand, and the British and Ottomans on the other. This war was likely to entirely block any commercial activity for years to come[541]. Crises came in quick succession for Basra. In 1773, the plague hit the city, followed very shortly by the severe siege staged by the Persians and their subsequent occupation in 1776. This occupation had a detrimental impact on trade. Basra was by now completely cut-off from the other parts of Iraq. Caravans previously travelling to Aleppo and other destinations were no longer in operation.

Following the Persian occupation of Basra, the situation required years of indefatigable effort to restore the former commercial status of the port. Due to all these unfortunate events, trade activity had moved to other ports along the Gulf, such as Kuwait, Bahrain, Bushehr and, most importantly, Muscat.

During the last two or three decades of the eighteenth century, Muscat was the most favoured port in the region. In addition to factors favouring trade, the port was under an authority strong enough to enforce security, order, justice and protection. Perhaps that was the fundamental reason why traders, bankers, ship owners and speculators from all races rushed to reside in Muscat. Of Arab, Indian and Persian origin, and from all spectrums of belief, there were also Armenians, Jews and Europeans of all nationalities[542]. And there were boundless instances of the tolerance exercised by the Omani authority as well of the tremendous security prevailing. For example, Ibrahim Burenster, who visited Muscat in 1775, remarked that traders would often leave their commodities stacked on the street during the night; since the government exercised vigilance and enforced security in the region[543]. In their report submitted to the English East India Company and the British government, S. Monesty and H. Jones described the Arab authorities in the Gulf in general and Muscat in particular as follows:

It is commonly recognized that Arab governments entertain a considerable share of respect. This especially applies to Muscat. Though it is quite rigid in pursuing justice, yet the very justice it serves will alleviate the burden of such rigidity. The Imam, the ruler of the state, resides in Rustaq, far from Muscat; but he has his representative in this port. The present representative is Skeikh Khalfan who bestows protection on traders, foreigners, residents and frequent visitors alike. He is easily accessible. Khalfan is specially concerned with the demands and complaints of traders; he is quite careful to serve justice. Therefore, all believe that their properties are entirely secured, and that their lives are free from threat[544].

Taxes would undoubtedly constitute a factor of paramount significance for failure or success, recession or growth of trade in any port. With respect to this factor, Omani policy was fairly advantageous, just and consistent. Muscat's authorities imposed 6.5 per cent taxes on any commodity whatsoever. No exemption was ever conferred on any particular group of traders[545]. In light of this, traders were able to perform their jobs, without any fear of injustice, uncertainty or rigidity. The situation can be better understood by comparison with other ports which were under the jurisdiction of the Ottoman Empire or that of Persia. In the Ottoman ports, traders had not only complained of burdensome taxes, but of arbitrariness in the levying processes and blackmailing accompanying the same. Taxes were even liable to fluctuate up or down, depending on the temperament and greed of the officials in charge. In Basra, for instance, which was under control of the Ottomans, taxes were seen as burdensome at best[546]. Such taxes had motivated most traders, towards the end of the eighteenth century, to transport their goods, originally destined to Aleppo, from the Kuwaiti port direct through the desert to Aleppo without passing by Basra.

Thus some traders were able to reach Shatt Al-Arab by one way or another. Though this pattern of commercial conduct had resulted in lucrative profits, it was quite detrimental to honest traders who were opposed to such illegal practices[547]. In addition, there was no equality in levying taxes. Whereas taxes of no less than 7.5 per cent were imposed on most local traders and all Asians, they did not exceed 3 per cent on most European tradesmen[548]. This encompassed the previous advantages conferred by the Ottoman Sultan on Europeans. Indeed, this variation had conferred a relative advantage on European traders when others in the same situation would incur severe damages.

Despite the economic recession dominating the Gulf region and its surroundings for a period towards the end of the eighteenth century, trade remained as rich and voluminous as ever. For trade in this part of the region was never dependent on limited local demand; rather, it supplied vast and remote areas, through the Arabian Gulf and the Red Sea. Both waterways were among the oldest international trade routes. Asian goods would move through these water passages to reach their destinations as far as Iraq, Arabia, Persia, Asia Minor and Syria. From these destinations, though, goods would be carried further to the coasts of the Mediterranean Sea and the Black Sea. Similarly, ports along the Arabian Gulf and the Red Sea were transshipping Asian goods to East Africa and the coasts of the Indian subcontinent.

Therefore, a trade of this size could hardly feel the effects of recession, no matter the extent of the troubles and crises it encountered. So since Omanis were in control of a considerable portion of this trade, Muscat had turned into the largest and most significant commercial centre throughout the Indian Ocean. It was even highly significant on the international scale of things as well.

The documents of the British East India Company and reports written by some European travellers would certainly provide us with indispensable information about Omani merchant ships and the naval fleet. In a letter sent from the Company to the British government, a clear-cut elaboration on the existing conditions in the Arabian Gulf in the late 1760s was given. The Company reminded us of the relative significance of Oman and its fleet of six battleships, each with 14-20 cannons; and that the Imam of Oman had a great number of small ships with proper weaponry[549]. By 1765, the Omani fleet consisted of 50 ships, ranging from small to large. The fleet was now able to undertake yearly expeditions to the various ports to the east of Basra and up to Malaga in the west[550].

Among the expeditions which gave the Omani trade fleet its resounding fame was the so-called 'Coffee Fleet' journey. This journey would start from Yemen to Basra, where coffee was distributed to all corners of the Near East. Christian Niebuhr, who visited the region in 1765, described Omanis as, 'the most skilful among Arabs in aspect of navigation. they will annually send 50 ships (*turanki*[551]) loaded with coffee to Basra'[552].

By the turn of the eighteenth century, however, a major development was in effect with respect to the number of Omani merchant ships. Perhaps the giant leap made by the European ship industry, beginning early in the sixteenth century, had greatly benefited the Asian fleets. By the end of the eighteenth century, though, Oman had made huge strides in availing of the current advancement in the European nations in general and in Portuguese ship-building technology in particular. This advancement focussed on the squaring of the ship's hull and the use of nails instead of threads. Thus, a ship had a much greater flexibility then ever before.

O. H. Morland believed that Omani Arabs had begun building their ships on the Portuguese model in 1507[553]. Many European travellers were indeed amazed at the change. Most Omani ships, built mainly in Muscat, Sohar and

Sur, were quite similar to the European ones. They were very large, and owing to this emerging industry, Oman started to import large quantities of wood from India, in addition to buying ships from Europeans.

According to the account related by a traveller visiting Oman in 1775 who saw the nation's fleet prepared to sail to Basra in order to lift the Persian siege, there were about 34 ships, 'four of which were built in Bombay with as much as 18-24 cannons in each; whereas the remainder of the fleet was of the so-called *ketches and galiots*, each of which was carrying 8-14 cannons'[554].

Perhaps, the reign of Sayyid Sultan bin Ahmed (1792-1804) is a better indication of the extent to which the Omani ships had been developed in terms of quality, technology, number, forces and capabilities. By then, the Omani merchant fleet, on the one hand, was in the range of 15 large ships, each of which would carry 400-700 tons in addition to hundreds of vessels of various sizes[555]. The naval fleet, on the other hand, was extremely strong and efficient. For instance, the lead vessel of the fleet, known as *Janjana*, had a loading capacity of 1000 tons, with 32 cannons. In addition to a hundred smaller, armoured ships, the fleet consisted of a further three ships, each carrying 20 cannons and built in the European style[556].

The reign of Sayyid Said bin Sultan (1804-1856) was by far the most outstanding period for the growth of the Omani fleet, both commercial and military. As indicated in the following table, the fleet force had undergone a remarkable expansion which was seen to be proportional to the expansion of the state's Asian and African boundaries[557]:

Year	Name of Ship	Description	Number of Cannon	Load
1802	Taj Box	passenger boat	-	737
1814	Caroline	frigate	36	575
1819	Shah Allam	181 ft frigate	56	1111
1822	Nousari	-	-	164
1826	Liverpool	180 ft third class	74	1715
1832	Sultanah	passenger boat	12	312
1834	Taja	-	12	205
1835	Nousari	-	-	179

In reality, the first half of the nineteenth century was the richest in the history of Oman. The naval fleet had witnessed remarkable progress, for Sayyid Said bin Sultan was largely concerned with the building of ships in the Omani ports such as Matrah, Muscat and Sur. He also ordered the construction of numerous commercial and navy ships in the shipyards of India and Bombay in particular. Among the superb battleships of the day were *Taj Baksar, Caroline, Shah Allam, Liverpool, Sultanah and Taja*. In 1824, he presented the frigate *Liverpool* to William IV of England as a gift. The latter renamed it *Imam* in gratitude to the Sultan. The navy battleship, *Sultanah*, on the other hand, was sent to New York in an expedition carrying gifts to the American president.

The Omani fleet in the first half of the nineteenth century was of great power and significance. It was ranked second, immediately behind England's, in terms of strength and influence. To give a good idea of the extent to which the fleet was developed, one must refer to the accounts of American traders who visited Oman in the early 1830s. They said that Sayyid Said arrived at the homeland in a convoy consisting of a ship equipped with 64 cannons, three frigates each of which was equipped with 36 cannons, two boats each with 14 cannons and 100 passenger boats carrying 6000 fighters. Though the Omani properties in Africa were some 2000 miles from Muscat, the fleet was strong enough to effectively control a vast area extending from Bandar Abbas to Zanzibar together with numerous ports located along the Arabian and African coasts, scattered and remote islands in the Arabian Gulf and the Indian Ocean.

With respect to trade, fortunately there is enough reliable information to give an idea about the volume of trade and expansion of operations in the Indian Ocean in general and the Arabian Gulf and the Red Sea in particular. Such information and estimates were basically contained in official reports[558] and the books written by travellers and those concerned with trade. H. Malcolm wrote a report submitted to the British East India Company in which he estimated the volume of trade in the Gulf at 16 million rupees. Trade between India and the Gulf constituted the largest share of this volume[559].

Perhaps the report written by S. Monesty and H. Jones was the most important insofar as it contained detailed accounts of the trade between India and the Gulf. It also spoke about the significance of Muscat and the paramount role played by Omanis in trade and navigation. The report confirmed that Oman, a naturally barren land with poor soil, had been turned by trade into a rich prosperous nation. The wealth of Omanis was enormous. The nation was at that time importing coffee from Al-Hudaydah and Mukha and sugar from Batavia. It was rightly said that Oman's trade in sugar and coffee alone was enough to turn it into a rich country[560]. As already mentioned, imports of coffee would meet demand in Iran, Arabia, Iraq, Armenia and Anatolia as well as part of the demand in Syria, the European part of the Ottoman Empire, Germany, Poland, Russia and North Europe. Whereas sugar imported from Batavia, on the other hand, was in a sufficient quantity as to meet demands in Iran, Kurdistan, Iraq, Armenia, Arabia and Anatolia[561].

Other trade of considerable importance to Omanis included pearls, salt, sulphur, copper, arsenic, saffron, incense, dried fruits and various sorts of herbs. They used to take these goods and return back with cotton textiles, cotton, wool, wood, and several other spices and commodities[562]. A trade of this volume would undoubtedly require Omanis to formulate certain policies geared to maintain the nation's excellence at sea and to protect their valuable economic gains. These policies can be outlined in brief as follows:

- Focus on maintaining supremacy at sea; efforts to meet external threats and a commitment to protect Omani coastal areas and ports.
- An attempt at controlling areas of strategic and commercial significance, with particular emphasis on the Arabian Gulf and East Africa.
- Adoption of special trade policies to improve coordination in existing

commercial relations between the Indian coasts, Arabian Gulf, the Red Sea and East Africa. We have seen in the previous pages how these policies had greatly succeeded. It was a success which had been manifested in a trade boom that was at its peak during the first half of the nineteenth century - the reign of Sayyid Said bin Sultan (1804-1856). In this particular period, however, trade progress in the state was quite remarkable. This progress could be attributed to the following factors:

- Efficient Omani leadership represented by Sayyid Said whose reign was characterized by stability and sound diplomatic relations with other nations. Oman entertained good diplomatic and consular relations with about 20 nations including Britain, the United States, Netherlands, France, Portugal, Spain and Germany. Despite the great expansion of the naval force during Said's rule, the wars engaged in were relatively few compared to the long duration of the period in question. The fleet was, therefore, basically used to safeguard trade routes and to protect the various commodities transported. Sayyid Said was also willing to give money to the Arab tribes in the Empty Quarter who could potentially threaten the Omani coastline. This measure was not indicative of weakness on the part of the Sultan; rather, what he offered was relatively meagre compared to the huge benefits realized as a result of stable trade.
- A well- developed Omani fleet that could reach as far as the China Sea, Bengal Gulf, Indian Ocean, the African coasts, the Red Sea, the European coasts and America.
- The diplomatic success of the Sultan; it was a diplomacy that largely benefited from ongoing regional and international conflicts. Thus, Oman was able to control ports on the eastern coast of the Arabian Gulf such as Bandar Abbas, Lingeh, Qeshm and Hormuz. Oman had benefited in particular from the perpetual conflicts between the Ottoman empire and Mohammed Ali of Egypt with whom the Sultan had had good relations. Because of this, Oman was granted massive privileges in the Red Sea. Likewise, the Sultan entertained good relations with the rulers of India, Ceylon, Maldives and Madagascar. Moreover, he never rejected any proposal for regional or international trade agreements, since he favoured trade over any other activity. Thus, when the European nations, and especially England, requested him to abolish the slave trade within the framework of his state, he accepted the deal. Soon afterwards, he prohibited the slave trade even though it was fairly lucrative for a number of Omani traders. He also went on fighting piracy from all sides, particularly when Europeans were involved in the slave trade. The measure was widely applauded by international public opinion. In England, for instance, the newspapers commended the action as did the House of Commons.
- The intensive agricultural development that was experienced by Oman and its lands in Africa. This development focussed primarily on farming cloves, cotton, hemp and the management of the huge wealth engendered. Sayyid Said appointed representatives to levy taxes on the various parts of the African eastern coast.
- The improved relations with numerous countries. On 16 June 1809, for

instance, the Sultan concluded an agreement with General Duncan, the governor of the French Comoros islands on 16 June 1807. The agreement endorsed the utter impartiality of Oman as regards the ongoing dispute between France and England. France had also pledged to abstain from intercepting Omani ships in exchange for approval of a French representative in Muscat.

In 1817, once again, the Sultan signed an accord with the ruler of De Bourbon (Reunion) island, whereby each country granted the other preferential trade advantages. On 10 September 1826, the Sultan and the English governor of Mauritius concluded a joint communiqué aimed at encouraging trade between Oman and England. In the same year, furthermore, another accord was concluded with the Portuguese governor of Mozambique. This accord confirmed the mutual friendship between Oman and Portugal and the readiness of the two nations to facilitate trade. The taxes to be imposed on trade between the two countries was also defined at 10 per cent.

In 1827, a commercial agreement was signed with the Portuguese concerning taxes on trade. With the United States, on the other hand, an accord was signed to limit sales of American weapons to the Sultan's government in Zanzibar. The U. S. had also pledged to pay 5 per cent in taxes on the American goods exported to Oman and its possessions.

On 31 March 1839, the first general trade agreement was drawn up between Oman and England. It was signed by Sayyid Said himself whereas the British consul in Muscat represented the British government. This accord included diverse commercial issues besides the issue of cooperation between the two parties with respect to consular matters and attempts to abolish the slave trade. To further indicate its fervent efforts to combat the slave trade, England convinced the Sultan to exert his efforts to persuade the Sheikhs of the Arabian Gulf emirates of the necessity to abolish this trade. The Sultan went even further and prohibited other parties from using Omani ports along East Africa's coasts for this purpose.

On 20 November 1843, Said concluded an agreement with the Portuguese government regarding the regulation of visits by Omani ships to Portuguese ports. The agreement included arrangements concerning the documents to be carried by these ships. However, a year later, in 1844 to be exact, Said also concluded a friendship agreement with France. The French side was represented at this time by Roman Defois, the governor of Madagascar and Bourbon. The French agreement was quite similar to the friendship accords signed with Britain and the U.S., except for the fact that Said had promised to permit France to build warehouses in Zanzibar.

Whereas Sultan Said had voluntarily accepted the call to abolish the slave trade, the British government paid £200,000 to the King of Spain to merely endorse the principle of prohibition. Said had further approved the British parliament's decision No. 28 for 1845 on prohibition of the slave trade. In reality, he was the only ruler throughout the Indian Ocean to totally advocate laws and international regulations on the issue. The Portuguese and Spanish, on the other hand, vehemently opposed the implementation of such regulations.

As the Omani fleet increased its trade activities and augmented its capacity, trade in the Arabian Gulf, and especially in the coastal cities under the jurisdiction of Sultan Said, had grown remarkably. Under an agreement between Sultan Said and Persia's Shah, concluded in April 1856, Oman had delegated authority to Omani governors for Bandar Abbas, Qeshm, Hormuz, Larg and Lingeh ports for a duration of 20 years. In return, the Shah would get an annual rent of 16,000 toman against his pledge not to accept any foreign representatives in these ports.

International trade in which Oman was a partner had gathered momentum. The growth of commercial activity was accompanied by an increase in production of pearls from the pearl fisheries of Bahrain, Qatar, Kuwait and Abu Dhabi. Indeed, the Gulf in the first half of the nineteenth century was the site of the major international pearl market. Local merchants, together with British, Indians and Persians, entered into a bitter competition in acquiring Gulf pearls, insofar as they were considered to be the best of their kind worldwide. Historical literature indicated that Sultan Said himself was holding a considerable number of rare pearls. The Sultan's wives were said to have marvelous pearls as ornaments.

Thus, the Sultanate of Oman exercised its influence over a vast area of lands extending from Asia to Africa. This influence was even more expansive in so much as it covered all parts of the Arabian Gulf, the African east coast and the Red Sea.

Suddenly, however, the state fell victim to the negative impact of the death of one of its most illustrious sons, Sultan Said bin Sultan, aboard the ship *Victoria* near Seychelles in 1856. Soon afterwards, the nation started a bloody internal conflict which split the Al-Busaidi family. The dispute did not end until 1862, when an agreement to divide the country into two parts was concluded between the two brothers: Thuwaini and Majed. Under the new arrangement, the former was declared ruler of Oman and its surroundings in the Arabian Gulf; the latter ruler of Zanzibar and the Omani lands in East Africa. The agreement was concluded with the assistance of Lord Canning, England's Foreign Minister at the time, who acted as intermediary. The superpowers of the time, especially France, Britain and Portugal, had found a great opportunity to partition the Omani lands.

In the period from 1856 to 1862, when the fierce dispute between the two brothers was at its height, the commercial and naval fleet fell apart. The brothers competed with each other to sell parts of the fleet to the European nations which had rapidly dominated most of the islands located within the archipelago of Zanzibar and Comoros. Persia's rulers, despite their relative weakness, had also moved swiftly to extend their influence over the eastern coast of the Arabian Gulf. Though Oman remained active in international trade, it lacked efficient leadership and the collapse of the fleet apparently contributed to the subsequent setback that had a detrimental impact on the image of the nation in the second half of the nineteenth century.

In conclusion, the unmatched leadership of Sultan Said had made it possible for Oman to turn into a powerful nation in the Arabian Gulf and the Indian Ocean. During his reign, Oman had concluded several conventions and agreements to usher in viable diplomatic and commercial cooperation, and was duly acknowledged for these achievements. In 1837, for instance, the Sultan was elected by the Asian Royal Society in London as an honorary member owing to his contribution to the advancement of oceanography and ship-building as well as his role in developing trade, and the prevalence of peace and stability along the coasts of the Arabian Gulf and the Indian Ocean. Therefore, one can rightly say that Sultan Said was the most famous Arab ruler of the first half of the nineteenth century. Under his rule, Oman's fleet became one of the strongest marine powers in the Indian Ocean. Trade, too, reached a peak.

The Administrative Organization of the Al-Busaidi State

This chapter describes the administrative organization of the state of Oman during the reign of the Al-Busaidi family from 1744 to 1970, one of Oman's renaissance periods. Historical analysis indicates that there is a mutual relationship between a state's administrative system and the effectiveness of its institutions and agencies. This is confirmed by our study of Oman's historical heritage, both past and present.

Despite the fact that the historical period of particular interest to this chapter lasted for almost two and a half centuries we shall in fact deal with it in brief.

Imam Ahmed bin Said Al-Busaidi

First we start with the reign of Imam Ahmed bin Said Al-Busaidi, the founder of the Al-Busaidi state. This era was characterized by numerous distinguishing features which contributed to the prosperity of the Omani state in the administrative and organizational fields[563]. Imam Ahmed bin Said had many leadership qualities, high administrative efficiency and great foresight, all of which contributed to his selection by Imam Saif bin Sultan Al-Ya'rubi as governor of Sohar. Moreover, he was an active merchant with great financial and commercial astuteness and a thorough knowledge of both internal and external affairs. Imam Ahmed bin Said was upright, just, brave and generous, as well as an efficient administrator, personality attributes which greatly helped him to achieve national unity in Oman, including reunification of all the tribes.

Appointment of Governors and Administrative Leaders
Imam Ahmed bin Said paid considerable attention to the appointment of *Walis* (governors) in all parts of the Omani state. He was eager to select governors with good administrative capabilities, sufficiently experienced to run the affairs of state. Meanwhile, Imam Ahmed bin Said concentrated on training his sons in administrative as well as political and organizational affairs so that they could acquire leadership skills. Consequently, a number of his sons were appointed as governors. However, one of the most significant governors and administrative leaders during Ahmed bin Said's rule was Khalfan bin Mohammed bin Abdullah Al-Busaidi, who was appointed governor of Muscat and charged with the responsibility of levying money, land taxes (*khiraj*) and customs duties in Omani ports. Likewise, a number of governors were carefully selected for eastern Africa. Those who were able to restore security included

governor Mohammed bin Ja'id Al-Busaidi.

Justice, Judiciary and Security

Imam Ahmed bin Said was actively involved in maintaining law and order in the country and uniting the tribes. He appointed Khamis bin Salim Al-Busaidi in Muscat and Matrah to firmly establish justice and equality among the population during his reign. Imam Said also selected those judges who were renowned for their ability, including the notable judge Sheikh Mohammed bin Amir bin Ariq Al-Adwani.

The Army and the Naval Fleet

One of the most outstanding achievements of Imam Ahmed bin Said was the formation of a large, well-equipped, well-organized army and navy. In forming the army, he was particuary dependent on Omani nationals. In addition to the regular forces, the army and navy also consisted of reserves. As a result of their high level of organization, Omani forces were able to expel the Persians who held certain parts of Oman in 1737. Furthermore, the strength of the naval fleet assisted in crushing several piracy movements in the Gulf and the Indian Ocean, thereby providing traders with the security they needed. The formation of a disciplined army also helped Imam Ahmed bin Said to annex the north-western part of Oman. The army also responded to an appeal from the Ottoman Empire to guard Basra and southern Iraq against a potential Persian threat. Ultimately, the army was able to defeat the Persians in the Shatt Al-Arab[564].

Commerce and Economy

The effects of these administrative and organizational changes were felt within the commercial sector. With the establishment of the commercial maritime fleet, Imam Ahmed bin Said was able to turn the Gulf and the Omani coastline into a free trade zone. He selected the most efficient administrative leaders to handle accounting and financial affairs such as customs and land taxes. For instance, he appointed Ruzaiq bin Najib bin Said bin Ghassan to organize financial affairs in Omani ports. As a result, customs regulations for shipping, exports and imports were effectively reorganized.

International Relations

It is difficult to fully appreciate the administrative organization of the commercial sector, the naval fleet or maritime trade without focussing on Oman's international relations. Imam Ahmed bin Said was single-minded in his determination to forge fair and equitable international relations covering all aspects of commerce and the economy, similar to the links established with India, Britain and the Ottoman Empire. Furthermore, he paid great attention to the security of trade, counteracting the Persian threat from Basra with a strong army and formidable naval fleet. Several commercial agreements were concluded, comparable to present day trade representation arrangements, with the aim of invigorating economic and commercial relations. In order to secure Omani territory, Imam Ahmed bin Said was particularly concerned with maintaining friendly and balanced international relations with Britain and France.

Whilst the above summary covers the most important features of the administrative organization in Oman during the reign of Imam Ahmed bin Said, it is not really possible to fully comprehend the extent of the organizational infra-structure without a more thorough analysis of all aspects involved in the process. The nature of economic and commercial progress is central to this analysis. In short, the reign of Imam Ahmed bin Said was one of the most significant historical periods and a turning point in terms of administrative competence. Many different factors contributed to the administrative and organizational edifice of the state[565].

Imam Sultan bin Ahmed

The Military Aspect.
Imam Sultan established a naval fleet of several large ships in addition to medium- and small-sized sailing boats. The fleet enabled Oman to maintain security, stability and sovereignty over the Gulf, the Indian Ocean and as far as the eastern coast of Africa. The Omani commercial fleet consisted of 16 medium-sized ships, 5 sailing boats and 55 small boats. Imam Sultan took additional steps to pursue commercial benefits in the interest of the country. He proceeded to rent Bandar Abbas seaport from the Shah of Iran in 1794. The annual rental amount agreed upon would certainly confirm the effectiveness of the Omani naval fleet. This focus upon defensive capability was a major factor in maintaining the security of the Omani coastline in the Gulf.

The Commercial Aspect.
Apart from the organization of the naval fleet, the state was able to achieve an overwhelming trade prosperity in all its ports, particular Muscat seaport. Almost all of the commercial activities were in the hands of Omani tradesmen. Generally, annual trade volume of the state was estimated at over £2.5 million with Oman earning more than half of this amount. Moreover, Imam Sultan increased customs tariff on imports to 6.5 per cent. This greatly contributed to the growth of the state's financial resources. Likewise, taxes were levied on farm products, whereas land taxes were imposed in East Africa.

Several historians[566] justifiably believe that the obvious commercial devel-opment of this period is evidence of an effective administrative organization and a revival of Muscat's role as a trade centre. Financial resources were readily available owing to the procedures and systems instituted, especially in the last two decades of the eighteenth century. Omani trade was not merely limited to countries such as Britain and France; several factories in the Netherlands, for instance, entered into close relations with Omani businessmen.

International Relations
Pursuing policies to expand trade relations with Britain, France, Netherlands and several other neighbouring nations, Imam Sultan established a firm basis for friendly foreign relations. Unfortunately, this period was also one of insta-bility in the relationship between the Wahabi and Qawasim tribes[567]. Nonetheless, Imam Sultan, much like his predecessors[568], was able to organize viable international relations in order to both ensure stability in the area and contribute to trade promotion.

By and large, Imam Sultan brought about friendly relations with foreign nations such as the Ottoman Empire, Britain and France, particularly subsequent to the arrival of Napoleon in Egypt.

Sultan Sayyid Said bin Sultan

Thanks to his efforts in organizational and administrative matters, Sayyid Said bin Sultan initiated significant steps towards the creation of a modernized state. In view of the significance of this particular period in Oman's history, it is worth reviewing the nature of administration during the reign of Sayyid Sultan, i.e. from 1804 to 1856.

Military Organization

In fact, Sayyid Said bin Sultan's concerns over administrative affairs were unequivocal in terms of the proper organization of the army. He evenly distributed his time between Muscat and other Omani territory in East Africa. Moreover, he trained his sons in administration and leadership skills. Thus, during his absence, he would designate one of his sons to be temporarily in charge.

A large portion of the state's resources were mobilized in order to establish a military and commercial fleet. At times of peace, however, the entire fleet would be put into commercial service. Manpower recruited to work in the fleet numbered 20,000 combatants[569].

Justice and the Judiciary

Sayyid Said bin Sultan paid considerable attention to the creation of a distinct judiciary system. He was eager to obtain the best governors, in Oman, the Green Isle and Zanzibar. For instance, eight governors were appointed in the Green Isle. Judges included outstanding persons like Said bin Hamad bin Khalfan Al-Habsi, Saif Al-Ma'wali and Said bin Abdullah bin Abdul Salam. In Zanzibar governors included Suleiman bin Hamad Al-Busaidi, who later participated in the negotiations between Sayyid Bargash and Great Britain. This particular governor was a remarkable politician as far as organization and administrative matters are concerned. Other governors in Zanzibar included Nasir bin Hamad bin Said Al-Busaidi and Hamad bin Saif bin Badr Al-Busaidi[570].

Trade and Economic Factors

Sayyid Said distributed and reorganized the commercial centres in the Sultanate. Muscat was no longer the sole trade centre in the state, albeit it retained its major commercial significance in the Gulf region. From 1820, the Sultan took major steps to turn Zanzibar into the centre of his rule over the African part of the Sultanate. Zanzibar benefited from this so that new agricultural crops were developed, including, among others, clove and coconut. Zanzibar's seaport became an open international trade centre which was considerably attractive to tradesmen from India, Britain and America. On the other hand, the economic growth of Zanzibar greatly contributed to the financial resources of the Omani Empire producing almost twice what was previously available from the Asian parts of Oman.

The broad boundaries of Oman provided a valuable source of income over and above that which was directly related to its trading activities. In 1840, for example, the revenues of Oman were estimated at some £120,000. The increased national income was the result of additional funding sources coming on line, such as taxes, customs, rentals, commercial profits and others. Significantly, sales of the clove crops, produced by the Sultan's property in Zanzibar, were around £40,000, amounting to almost one-third of the total revenues of the state[571].

International Relations

The Omani state withstood several internal and external disturbances during the reign of Sayyid Said bin Sultan. Despite this, the regime was generally characterized by modernization and progress. Consequently, the Sultan was able to maintain the properties of the state owing to his diplomacy and sound financial judgement. Meanwhile, he was inclined to maintain a peaceful cooperation with Britain, and especially to combat the slave trade[572].

During the reign of Sayyid Said bin Sultan, numerous international treaties were concluded including ones with India, the U. S. (in 1833), Britain (in 1839) and France[573] (in 1844). The true significance of these agreements was largely founded upon their emphasis on trade and friendly relations between Oman and the respective nations. It is clear from them that Oman as a nation was overwhelmingly preoccupied with efforts to improve its economic and commercial resources as well as boosting economic activity in its seaports.

Trade arrangements at the time of Sultan Said bin Sultan.

In addition to the serious concern paid by the Al-Busaidi rulers to develop the administrative and organizational structure of the state, certain factors played their part in the second half of the nineteenth century to usher in

outstanding rates of growth and prosperity in the economic, commercial and military fields. The following are the most significant catalytic factors:

- Firstly, the organization of the military and commercial fleets of the state. This was coupled with vigorous maritime activity, helping to maintain security along the trade routes extending from the Indian Ocean as far as the Indonesian coast to the east and the East African coast to the west.
- Secondly, the positive contribution of Omani businessmen and their organization of the economic and commercial activity in the state. Economic recession in the Iranian ports, as well as in other Gulf areas, were in Oman's favour: Muscat became the most important commercial port in the Gulf region.
- Thirdly, an increase in the financial revenues effected by Al-Busaidi rulers together with their far ranging efforts to boost economic and commercial resources[574].

Significant Changes 1870-1920

Despite the division of the Omani Empire after the death of Sayyid Said into two parts, one African and the other Asian, the main interests of the Al-Busaidi rulers were maintained. The family's rule and influence remained strong and effective as far as the social and economic life is concerned. This is particularly apparent in the reign of Sayyid Majed (1856-1870) and Sayyid Bargash (1870-1888).

From the early 1870s right up to the early 1920s, Oman experienced many significant changes. These changes provided a vital basis upon which the present shape of the administrative structure of the state is founded. Particular emphasis, in this regard, should be given to the reign of Sultan Turki, and his son Sultan Faisal. Sultan Turki created many valuable administrative and financial systems which helped to support the development of government institutions. The Sultan was eager to combine traditional ruling procedures with modern administrative methods. Two particular factors were pivotal. First, Sultan Turki attempted to improve the state's administrative structure in order to achieve internal

Currency minted in Muscat in the time of Al Sayyid Faisal bin Turki, 1315 AH/1897 AD.

stability. Secondly, he did his best to strengthen the power and sovereignty of the state *vis-a-vis* the European powers which were then engaged in a severe dispute between each other over control of the Gulf area.

The most significant features of the administrative organization of the state during this periodwere as follows[575].

The Charismatic Personality of the Sultan

Sultan Turki was highly efficient and had unyielding enthusiasm. Because of these traits, he was able to fully control the state. He involved members of the ruling family in the state's administration and sought assistance from notable tribal leaders and Muscat's businessmen. In addition he made good use of foreign expertise in aspects of modern development, having several foreign advisors at his disposal.

The Ministers

Ministerial positions were among the most important administrative and political posts in the state. A minister was considered as the Sultan's first aide. The positions were mostly occupied by members of the ruling Al-Busaidi family, and especially those members who had exhibited personal strengths such as Sayyid Abdul Aziz bin Said.

Consultants and Special Aides

These positions were occupied by governors and army leaders. The holders of these posts were in the good graces of the Sultan due to their organizational and administrative competence; as was the case with Suleiman bin Suweilim who was designated governor of Sur and Dhofar.

Governors

Sultan Turki's administration was characterized by an innovative centralized system of governance organized into several regional units. In the coastal areas, governors were appointed personally by the Sultan. They enjoyed great authority to the extent of enabling them to carry out all the Sultan's decisions and decrees in various aspects of administration, military and finance. The centres to which they reported were designated according to their specific geographic locations. Among the most important administrative centres were Muscat, Matrah, Sohar, Dhofar and Sama'il.

Administration of Sohar was at all times the most difficult insofar as it entailed supervision of assistant governors in smaller areas such as Sham, Liwa and Shinas. Generally speaking, a governor would supervise officials in the strategic areas and internal, mountainous terrain. But, in the rural plain areas governorship was designated in accordance with the relative importance of the area in question. By and large, the Sultan almost always selected governors who possessed the best administrative qualifications in order to properly supervise public agencies. The most significant administrative institutions, which were the representative of the organizational structure of the state, are listed below.

Judges and the Judiciary

This administration was undertaken by judges appointed by the Sultan. For major lawsuits and criminal offences, the Sultan himself would assume control. But, in minor offences the governors, through the designated judges, would make appropriate judgments. In reality, there were neither court panels nor written laws. The Holy Qur'an or the tenets of the Islamic Shari'a constituted the main frame of reference. As previously mentioned, the Sultan would preside over major cases and tribal disputes of considerable repercussions.

Financial Affairs Management

To properly manage this department, the Sultan sought assistance from governors, officials, businessmen and tradesmen. Customs made up the most important financial revenues; annual customs income from Muscat and Matrah seaports amounted to some 110,000 Austrian schillings. This income continued throughout the reign of Sultan Turki. Customs revenues from Gwadar seaport reached an annual amount of 20,000-30,000 Austrian schillings. However, the Sultan was committed to establish further customs facilities in Sur seaport.

Furthermore, financial management included levying *zakat* on exports of agricultural crops. The treasury also included rental income from governmental buildings and lands. Financial aid from Zanzibar further augmented the state's revenues.

Management of the Army and Security Affairs

Sultan Turki supervised army organization and military operations. He sought assistance from his senior aides and governors. But, there was no clear-cut distinction between civil and military institutions. The regular army mainly comprised over 1000 soldiers covering all posts. Relevant tribes would usually undertake protection of internal posts.

In reality, the Sultan did not make serious efforts to renew the Omani naval fleet which had been considerably affected by the division in the Omani Empire. However, he provided certain members of the ruling family in Zanzibar with a number of yachts and ships in an attempt to enable them to bolster the Omani naval force there.

Sultan Taimur bin Faisal

Documentary evidence from this period confirms that Sultan Taimur bin Faisal inherited a number of financial and economic problems in addition to uneasy relations with Britain and a troubled internal front. These all had a bearing upon the political, social and economic structure of the maritime regions of the Omani state. The Sultan took a number of steps aimed at improving administrative structures so that the various public agencies could cope better with successive crises.

During the period 1913-1920, the internal situation was quite unstable, resulting in inevitable distractions for Sultan Taimur whose best efforts were needed to handle the situation. Financial and economic tensions, fuelled by fluctuating international currency exchanges and the First World War, combined to create a worsening picture. But the Sultan did his best to stabilize internal conditions. Thus, in 1920, the Seeb Accord was signed between Sheikh Isa bin Saleh, the representative of the Imam, and Sayyid Taimur bin Faisal[576].

In the early 1920s, Sultan Taimur attempted to strengthen the financial status of Muscat, to develop the governmental agencies by boosting their efficiency and, at the same time, retain the best of the existing administrative structures. He appointed qualified administrative experts from Europe, Egypt and India to work alongside his Omani assistants. British influence was clearly on the increase, as was evidenced by the prominence of British advisors assisting with administrative matters and advising on a wide range of policy issues.

The following is a brief account of the outstanding administrative and organizational features of the reign of Sultan Taimur in the early 1920s[577]

Executive and Administrative Aspects

In an attempt at developing the administrative organization of the state, Sultan Taimur established a council of senior Omani executive administrators. In 1921, the Sultan formed a four-member Ministerial Council chaired by his brother Sayyid Nadir bin Faisal. The Sultan attended all sessions of the Ministerial Council and was keen to facilitate important executive, political and administrative decisions. The council's main task was to focus on ways to improve Oman's financial, economic and external security situation.

In 1929, Sayyid Said bin Taimur was appointed prime minister. This enabled him to play a more active role in government and focus on the actual administration of the nation's affairs. Since the early 1930s, his father, Sultan Taimur, had been keen to transfer such responsibilities to him.

The Financial and Economic Field.

In the early 1920s, Sultan Taimur prepared a sound budget that remained deficit-free to 1923. In fact, the Sultan adopted austerity measures to avoid the financial and economic crises during this significant period in Oman's history. Shortly afterwards, he appointed three Egyptians to manage the customs system in Muscat. Thus the Sultan aimed to reorganize customs administration so that revenues made from the seaport could ultimately be boosted. This objective was further emphasized by the appointment of an Irish expert, Ronald Malcolm, as a minister of finance. In reality, the financial conditions of the state were greatly affected by a host of unfavourable external circumstances. But, in the aftermath of the First World War, an economic recovery was beginning to take effect. Due to efforts exerted by Sultan Taimur, the state was able to make remarkable progress in its bid to solve the financial crises. The respite however was all too brief for the nation suffered a series of financial set-backs resulting from the Great Depression of the 1930s. Thus, whereas Oman's trade was estimated at £575,603 in the fiscal year 1919-20, this figure increased to £637,817 in 1925-26 then dropped significantly to £474,202 in the subsequent year. In 1933-34, the figure decreased even further to a low of £364,905. However, after the end of the world economic crises of the 1930s, trade once more recovered to register a record high of £400,00[578].

Reunification of the Omani lands after the failure of Imamate in 1955 was one of the important events during the reign of Sultan Said bin Taimur. The economic conditions prevailing in Oman since the early 1930s, coupled with scarcity of resources and recurrent monetary crises, greatly hampered Oman's attempts at imposing its supremacy over the Gulf region. Internal instability was also a factor. The immediate result was that the country was unable to afford a much needed modernization of its naval forces to bring them in line with technological advances of the age, including the emergence of steam boats.

Inevitably, all these factors combined to push the administrative and organizational systems of the state into gradual recession resulting in an inability to confront the internal as well as external challenges. It was even too weak to handle the financial and routine administrative affairs within its borders. In consequence many financial and economic resources were lost.

We briefly review below the administrative system during the reign of Said bin Taimur, taking into account the prevailing economic and social circumstances[579].

Sultan Sayyid Said bin Taimur

The Executive and Administrative System

The government structure remained as it had been since the early 1920s with the addition of some foreign advisors who assisted in the administration of local affairs. Internal affairs were placed under the direction of Sayyid Ahmed bin Ibrahim. In fact, this government ministry was the only such ministry existing in Oman prior to 1970. Ahmed bin Ibrahim sought assistance from available administrative and professional elite. For long periods, Sultan Said remained in Salalah, whereas Sayyid Ahmed, responsible for internal affairs, undertook supervision of all governmental matters. In this he received the support and assistance of the relevant governors.

Administrative control in the interior areas was, however, left to tribal chiefs and local dignatories who were, in turn, supervised by the Sultan through his respective governors.

Management of Economic and Commercial Affairs

The country experienced severe economic conditions due mainly to the economic crises inherited from the previous century. Oil exploration began in the early 1930s and oil was first discovered in commercial quantities in 1963 when the Oman Petroleum Development Company was established. The export of oil finally began in 1967. But, until the early 1960s, Omani trade remained relatively meagre. For instance, annual total imports were confined to £3.7 million with no more than a miniscule £700,000 of exports.

Certain regulations were adopted to further thwart trade between coastal and interior areas in the Sultanate. And customs were raised to reach 300 per cent on some goods and commodities. These restrictions seriously impaired trade and commerce.

Management of Development

A directorate to manage development was established in 1959. This directorate was given the task of supervising the three sectors of health, agriculture and public works beside social welfare. With respect to health, some clinics and hospitals were constructed. The best equipped of these was the Hospital of the American Mission in Matrah. In the agricultural field, on the other hand, two experimental farms were established in Nizwa and Sohar. But neither farm met with success, partly as a consequence of inadequate financial resources.

Coin from the time of Al- Sayyid Said bin Taimur.

By 1970, the number of schools was about three. In fact, Oman's first school was established in 1914 whilst the second opened in 1940, under the name of Al-Busaidi School. In 1955, another school, also called Al-Busaidi School, was established. Later, administrative buildings and a number of small projects for electricity and potable water were realized.

The Military Aspect

Sultan Said bin Taimur aimed to develop the administrative and organizational structures of the army; a need that had become very apparent in the late 1960s when Oman's internal situation was his major concern. Under this focus the army was provided with experts and advisors to help in both training and upgrading of military efficiency. Certain units were established which later formed the nucleus of Omani land forces and Sultan Armed Forces.

International Relations

There was an improvement of international relations during the latter period of the reign of Sultan Said bin Taimur. Good relations were forged with Britain and India, together with other nations such as France and Germany. Moreover, a friendship accord was concluded between Oman and the United States in 1958. This accord came into force in 1960, succeeding its predecessor which was signed as long ago as 1833. Unfortunately, there were no trade relations with other Arab countries. Oman only joined the Arab League in 1971 and the country's representation in the United Nations was effected in October of the same year. These positive changes were due to efforts exerted by the administration of Sultan Qaboos bin Said who introduced the nation to an entirely new era.

By and large, the main characteristics of organization and infrastructure in the reign of Sultan Said bin Taimur were reflected by the social, economic and commercial conditions. This period, extending from 1931-1970, was a real transitional period from an historical point of view.

Notes for Part Five

[1]   Mohammed Mustafa Ziada, *Egypt and the Crusaders' Wars.*
[2]   Mohammed Ali Al-Dawood, 'The History of Omani Domination in the Indian Ocean'. *College of Arts Magazine*, No. 5, April 1962, p 260.
[3]   Mohammed Rashid Abbas, 'Political Developments in Oman and its Historical Relations'. M.A.Thesis, Baghdad 1988, p 14.
[4]   Salih Mohammed Ala'abid, *The Role of Al-Qawasim in the Arabian Gulf 1747-183,* Baghdad, 1976, p 21-23.
[5]   Abdul Amir Mohammed Amin, *The Naval Forces in the Arabian Gulf.* Baghdad, 1966, p 5.
[6]   Said Nawfal, *The Political Situation of the Emirates of the Arabian Gulf and the Southern Peninsula.* second edition, The Higher Institute of Arabic Studies, Cairo, 1961, p 42.
[7]   *Ibid.*
[8]   Abdullah Salih Al-Mutawa'a, 'The Collars of Pearls in the Days of the Saudi Family in Oman'. Written transcript, p 17-18.
[9]   Mohammed Abdullah Al-Salimi, *Oman- History Speaks*, Damascus, 1963, p 191.
[10] Dr Salih Mohammed Ala'abid, *The British Attitude towards French Activities in the Arabian Gulf 1798-1810.* Baghdad, 1979, p 7-8.
[11] Dr Mohammed Ali Al-Dawood, *op.cit.,* p 260.
[12] Dr Salih Mohammed Ala'abid, *The Role of Al -Qawasim.* Page 24-26.
[13] *Ibid.,* p 27.
[14] Amin Abdul Amir Mohammed, *ibid.,* p 5.
[15] Salih Mohammed Ala'abid, *The Role of Al -Qawasim.* p 28.
[16] *Encyclopaedia Britannica*, London, 1987. vol. 15, p 98.
[17] Abdul Amir Amin, *British Interests in the 'Persian Gulf'*. London, 1967, p 14.
[18] Humaid bin Mohammed bin Ruzaiq, *Al-Fet'h Al-Mubeen fi Sirat As-Sadah Al-Busaidiyeen,* edited by Abdul Moni'm Amir and and Dr Mohammed Mursi Abdullah, p 250.
[19] *Ibid.*
[20] Sarhan bin Said Al-Azkawi, *The History of Oman*, adapted from the book *Kashef Al Gumah* the collection of national news, edited by Abdul Majed Al-Qaisi, published by the Ministry of National Heritage and Culture, Sultanate of Oman, 1980, p 75-76.
[21] Minab is an important area situated on the Iranian shore at the entrance of the Gulf. Lorimer, *Gazetteer of the Gulf*, geography section, vol. 4, p 1526.

22   Sarhan bin Said Al-Azkawi, *op. cit., supra,* p 98-99, Aisha Al-Sayyar, *The State of Al Ya'ruba,* p 46, Dar Alquds, Lebanon.
23   Humaid bin Mohammed bin Ruzaiq, *op. cit., supra,* p 263, Al-Azkawi: *op. cit.,* p 99.
24   1034 AH /1624 AD.
25   Humaid bin Mohammed bin Ruzaiq, *op. cit., supra* p 246; Jamal Zakariya Qasim, *op. cit., supra,* p 129, Aisha Al-Sayyar. *op. cit., supra,* p 49.
26   Nur Al-Din Al-Salimi, *op. cit.* . vol. 2, p 5, Al-Azkawi, p 98-99.
27   Nur Al-Din Al-Salimi, *op. cit., supra,* vol. 2, p 5.
28   R. G. Landen, *Oman Path and Fate*, Arabic translation by Abdullah Mohammed Amin, p 19.
29   Nur Al-Din Al-Salimi, *op. cit., supra,* p 5-6.
30   *Ibid.,* p 6-7; Al-Azkawi, op. cit., p 100. Aisha Al-Sayyar, p21.
31   *Ibid.,* Al-Azkawi, *op. cit.,* p 101.
32   Nur Al-Din Al-Salimi, *op. cit.,* p 101.
33   Al-Azkawi, *ibid.,* p 102-103. *Oman Across History.* vol. 3, p 201.
34   Lorimer, *Gazetteer of the Gulf,* As-Seyabi's history section, vol. 2, p 633
35   S.B.Miles, *Countries and Tribes of the Persian Gulf.* vol. 2, p 196-197.
36   Humaid bin Mohammed bin Ruzaiq, *op. cit., supra,* p 275. Al-Azkawi, p 106. Al-Salimi, vol.2, p 12-13.
37   The Portuguese had succeeded in signing a treaty with the English in 1634. The treaty opened an exchange of relations between the colonies of the two countries
38   Dr Salah Al-A'aqad, *The Political Trends in the Arabian Gulf,* Cairo, 1983, p 45.
39   Al-Azkawi, *op. cit.,* p 105-106. Al-Siyabi, *op. cit.,* vol. 3, p 207.
40   J. Kelly, *Britain and the Persian Gulf.* London, 1968, p 15.
41   Miles *op. cit.,* p 218.
42   Mustafa A'aqeel, *International Competition in the Arabian Gulf 1622-1763,* p 109.
43   Dr Jamal Zakariya Qasim, *The Arabian Gulf, op. cit.,* p 112.
44   *Ibid.*
45   Lorimer, *op. cit.,* vol.2, p 640.
46   A. Wilson, *The Persian Gulf,* p 194.
47   Falih Handhal, *Details of the Arab Emirates' History*, p 103.
48   The most prominent document said he died in 1059 AH/23 April 1649.
49   Humaid bin Mohammed bin Ruzaiq, *Al-Fet'h Al-Mubeen fi Sirat As Sadah Al-Busaidiyeen,* edited by Al bu Munaem A'amir Mursi, p 275.
50   Lorimer, *op. cit.,* history section, vol. 2p 635-636.
51   Dr Jamal Zakariya Qasim, *The Arabian Gulf at the time of the First European Expansion,* p 106; C. R. Boxer, *Some Aspects of the Struggle between the Omanis and the Portuguese 1650-1730,* p27.
52   Dr Tariq Nafi Al-Hamdani, 'The Role of Omani Arabs in the Expulsion of the Portuguese from the Arabian Gulf during the first half of the Seventeenth Century.' *The Magazine of the Institute of Arabic Research and Studies,* vol. 13, p 277.
53   Abdullah bin Khalfan bin Qaysar, *The Biography of Imam Nasir bin Murshid,* edited by Abdul Majed Al-Qaisi, p 46, Al-Azkawi, p 104.
54   Dr Tariq Nafi Al-Hamdani, *op.cit.* ,p 279.
55   Ibn Ruzaiq, *ibid.,* p 284.
56   For more information about this attack, read the interesting story which is mentioned in most of the Omani folklore books, eg. Ibn Ruzaiq, *op. cit.,* p 286; Nur Al-Din Al-Salimi, *op. cit.,* vol. 2, p 65.
57   Lorimer, *op. cit.,* history section, vol. 2, p 636.
58   Ibn Ruzaiq, *op. cit.,* p 290.
59   Dr Tariq Nafi Al-Hamdani, *The Role of Omani Arabs in the Expulsion of the Portuguese from the Arabian Gulf during the First Half of the Seventeenth Century,* p 281.
60   Mustafa A'aqeel, 'The Political Trends in the Arabian Gulf 1622-1763', p 24.
61   Lorimer, *op. cit.,* vol. 2, p 67.
62   Mustafa A'aqeel, *op. cit.,* p 125.
63   Salih Mohammed Ala'abid, *The Role of Al -Qawasim,* p 40.
64   Dr Mohammed Ali Al-Dawood, *op. cit.,* p 261. Haifae Abdul Aziz Karim, *The Dutch Invasion of the Arabian Gulf and Arab Resistance.* An M.A Thesis, 1988, p 116.
65   Dr Mohammed Ali Al-Dawood, *op. cit.,,* p 261.
66   Salih Mohammed Ala'abid, *The Role of Al -Qawasim,* p 42
67   Haifae Abdul Aziz Karim, *ibid.,* p 114.
68   Aisha Al-Sayyar, *op. cit.,* p 122.
69   Salih Mohammed Ala'abid, *The Role of Al-Qasim,* p 42.
70   Haifae Abdul Aziz Karim, *op. cit.,*p 116.
71   Jamal Zakariya Qasim, *The Arabian Gulf, op. cit.,* p 117.

72 Said bin Ali Al-Mughairi, *Jahinat Al Akhbar fi Tarikh Zanzibar,* vol 2, 1986, p 195.
73 Al-Sayyar , *op. cit.,* p 76.
74 *Ibid.,*p 78.
75 Jamal Zakariya Qasim, *ibid.,* p 168.
76 Documents on the following Imams, Bal'arab bin Sultan, Saif bin Sultan, Sultan bin Saif the Second, are summarized from the historical sources by Salim bin Mohammed Al-Abri.
77 He may mean the city of Al-Rustaq and Al-Batinah in the north.
78 Al-Salimi, *Tohfat Al -'Ayian bi Sirat Ahl Oman,* vol. 2, p 115. Ibn Ruzaiq, *op. cit.,* p 301.
79 Sheikh Nur Al-Din Al-Salimi, *op. cit.,* vol. 2, p 115.
80 In Arabic 'Amam' means 'in front of you' while 'Imam', i.e.what the crowd heard, means 'your caliph'.
81 Nur Al-Din' Al-Salimi, *op. cit.,* vol. 2, p 117.
82 Humaid bin Mohammed bin Ruzaiq, *op. cit.,* p 303.
83 Salim Al-Siyabi, *Oman Across History,* vol. 4, p 102-104.
84 *Ibid.,* p 104-105.
85 Mohammed Hassan Qudos, *Nadir Nama,* Tehran, 1339 AH, p 122
86 Mustafa A'aqeel, *International Competition in the Arabian Gulf* 1622-1763, p 277.
87 Nur Al-Din Al-Salimi, *Tohfat Al 'Ayian,* vol. 2, p 98.
88 Jamal Zakariya Qasim, The Al-Busaid State, p 4.
89 Laurence Lockhart, *Nadir Shah: A Critical Study Based Upon Contemporary Sources,* London, 1938, p 184.
90 Nur Al-Din Al-Salimi, *Tohfat Al ' Ayian.* vol .2, p 154.
91 Wendell Philips, *Oman: a history,* p 77.
92 Al-Azkawi, *op. cit.,* p 149.
93 *Ibid.,*p 151
94 For this subject refer to *Al-Fet'h Al-Mubeen*, p 344. Wendell Philips, *Oman: a history,* p 78; Al-Azkawi, p 152.
95 Humaid bin Mohammed bin Ruzaiq, *Al-Fet'h Al-Mubeen fi Sirat As Sadah Al-Busaidiyeen,* 351.
96 A.H. Al-Tazi, *Historical Relations between Morocco and Oman,* The Proceedings of the Seminar of Council of Omani Studies, ch. 3, p 131.
    Dr J. Z. Qasim, *The Arabian Gulf in the Age of the First European Expansion,* p 96.
97 Samuel Miles, *Countries and Tribes of the Persian Gulf,* p 161.
98 B. J. Silut, *The Arabs of the Gulf,* 1602–1784 AD, translated by Ayidah Khouri, United Arab Emirates Publications, p146.
99 *Ibid.,* p174-5.
100 Miles, *op. cit.,* p 221.
101 Silut, *op. cit.,* p178.
102 *Ibid.*
103 Dr Salah Al-A'aqad, Dr. J. Z. Qasim, *Zanzibar, op. cit.,*p31.
104 Miles, *op. cit.,* p224.
105 Silut, *op.cit.,* pp197 and 199.
106 Silut, p196-7.
107 It is said that his death occurred in 1679 while some sources mention that it was in 1680.
108 Silut, *op. cit.,* p 216.
109 Humaid bin Mohammed bin Ruzaiq, *Al-Fet'h Al-Mubeen fi Sirat As Sadah Al-Busaidiyeen,* pp 293-4.
110 Dr. A. Al-Sayyar, *op. cit.,* pp68-69.
111 Agent for the British East India Company in Iran.
112 Lorimer, *Gazetteer of the Gulf:* historical section, vol. 1, p132.
113 B. J. Silut, *op. cit.,* p217.
114 *Ibid.,* p126.
115 Lorimer, *op. cit.,* vol. 1, pp116-7.
116 B. J. Silut, *op. cit.,* p226.
117 Guillain, Tome I p 320.
118 Dr. J. Z. Qasim , *op. cit.,* p111.
119 Abd al-Fattah Ibrahim, *On the Road to India,* Baghdad, 1935, p30.
120 James Morrier, *A Journey Through Persia, Armenia and Asia Minor to Constantinople,* 1809, p375.
121 Guillain, *op. cit.,* Tome 11, p528.
122 Dr. J. Z. Qasim, , *op. cit.,* p114.
123 *Ibid.,* p 114-5.
124 Dr Jamal Zakariya Qasim, Dr Saleh Al-A'aqad, *Zanzibar* p 31.
125 S.B. Miles, *On the Border of the Great Desert: A Journey in Oman*, p 161.

[126] Dr. J. Z. Qasim , *op. cit.,* p115.

[127] Qasim, pp116-7, and Miles, vol 11, London, 1919, p 150.

[128] Qasim, p118.

[129] Silut, *op. cit.,* p234.

[130] Dr. J. Z. Qasim, *op. cit.,* p118.

[131] Silut, *op. cit.,* p237.

[132] Alexander Hamilton, *A New Account of East India,* vol. 1, p57.

[133] Ian Skeet, *Muscat and Oman, The End of an Era,* London, 1974, p 65.

[134] Firouz Kajare, *Le Sultan de Oman,* pp165-7.

[135] Ian Skeet, *Muscat and Oman, The End of an Era,* London, 1974, p 65.

[136] Lorimer, *op. cit.,* p111.

[137] Aisha Al-Sayyar, *The Al-Ya'ruba Dynasty in Oman and East Africa 1624-71,* p170.

[138] Falih Handhal, *The History of the Arabic Emirates,* vol. 1, p98.
Qasim, *op. cit.,* p111.

[139] Dr. Z. J. Qasim, *op. cit.,* p111.

[140] *Ibid.*.

[141] C. Boxer, *New Light on the Relationship of Oman and the Portugese 1650-1730,* pps.29-30.

[142] Dr. J. Z. Qasim, *op. cit.,* p113.

[143] Lorimer, *op. cit.,* vol. 1, p111.

[45] Lorimer, *op. cit.,* vol. 1, p27.

[144] Lorimer, *op. cit.,* vol.1, p.67.

[145] *Ibid.,* p27.

[146] Dr Aisha Al-Sayyar, *op. cit.,* p176.

[147] Lorimer, *op. cit.,* vol.1, p67.

[148] *Ibid.,* p67.

[149] *Ibid.,* p68 from *The Portuguese Asia,* vol. 3, p382, translation by Stevenson of F. Soma's book.

[150] Sadanaha, *State Papers, op. cit.,* p524. Miles, *op. cit.,* p212.

[151] Dr. J. Z. Qasim, *op. cit.,* p115.

[152] Qasim, p116-7.

[153] Samuel Miles, *op. cit.,* p150.

[154] Miles, p118.

[155] The commercial and strategic importance of Muscat increased day by day, however it was not the capital of Oman.

[156] Dr. Jamal Hamdan, *The Character of Egypt,* vol. 2, Cairo, 1981, pp690-691.

[157] H. Ingrams, *Arabia and the Isles,* London, 1960, pp3-4.

[158] Dr J. Z. Qasim, *Historical Roots for the Afro -Arab Relationships,* Cairo, 1975, p61.

[159] *Ibid.,* p63.

[160] Al-Mas'udi, *Murooj Al-Thahab,* vol 2 pp29-33.

[161] Basil Davidson, *Africa Beneath New Lights,* trans.(Arabic) Jamal Hamad, Beirut, 1965, pp 264-5.

[162] Some sources indicate that he acceeded to the Imamate in 1649, others that it was in 1650.

[163] Lewis Krapf, *Travels, Research and Missionary Labours during an Eighteen Years Residence in Eastern Africa,* London, 1860, p522

[164] Dr A. Al-Sayyar, *op. cit.,* p95.

[165] Qasim, *op. cit.,* p109.

[166] M. F. Hofer, *L'Univers, Histoire et Description de tous les peuples Afrique Orientale et Centrale,* Paris, 1848, pp163-166.

[167] Dr A. Al-Sayyar, op.cit., p97.

[168] Dr J. Z. Qasim, *op. cit.,* p110.

[169] 'Abd Al-Rahman Badawi, 'African and Arabic Culture', no.48, magazine *Nahda Ifriqiyya,* year 4, October, 1961.

[170] Dr J. Z. Qasim, *Historical Roots for Afro-Arab Relationships,* p112.

[171] Reginald Coupland, *East Africa and its Invaders from the Earliest Times to the death of Sayyid Said in 1856,* pp17-22.

[172] Basil Davidson, *op.cit.,* p265.

[173] L. Lockhart, *Nadir Shah, A Critical Study Based Upon Contemporary Sources,* p 182, London, 1938.

[174] Dr Jamal Zakariya Qasim, *The Arabian Gulf During the First Period of European Expansion,* p 42.

[175] B. J. Silut, *Arabs of the Gulf,* p 291.

[176] Dr Jamal Zakariya Qasim, *op. cit.,* p139.

[177] B. J. Silut, *Arabs of the Gulf,* p 192.

[178] Silut, *op. cit.,* p 293.

[179] Dr Jamal Zakariya Qasim, *The Arabian Gulf During the First Period of European Expansion,*

p 140. Falih Handhal, *op. cit., supra*, p 176.

[180] Humaid bin Mohammed Ruzaiq, *Al-Fet'h Al-Mubeen fi Sirat Al-Sadah Al-Busaidiyeen,* p 348.

[181] B. J. Silut, *op. cit., supra*, p 295.

[182] It is said by Ibn Ruzaiq that the trick which Saif bin Sultan had plotted had nearly succeeded, but Ahmed bin Said received a warning from Ibn Ruzaiq and discovered the plot, and was forever indebted to Ibn Ruzaiq and his descendants.

[183] Salim bin Hamoud Al-Siyabi, vol. 2, p 48.

[184] Dr Jamal Zakariya Qasim, *op. cit supra*, p143.

[185] Falih Handhal, *The History of the Arab Emirates*, vol. 1, p 178-179.

[186] Al-Salimi, *Tohfat Al-'Ayian fi Sirat Ahl Oman*, vol. 2, p 148-149.

[187] B. J. Silut, *op. cit.,* p 222.

[188] Sarhan bin Said Al-Azkawi, *History of Oman,* Adapted from the book *Kashef Al-Ghumah Aljama'a Li'Akhbar Al-Ummah*, research by Abd Al-Majed Al-Qaisi, p 155.

[189] Dr Mohammed Ali Al-Dawood, 'The Omani Issue', Lectures in The Political Developement of Oman, Cairo 1964, p 21-23.

[190] Ibn Ruzaiq, *Al -Fet'h Al-Mubeen fi Sirat Al-Sadah Al-Busaidiyeen,* p 330.

[191] Donald Hawley, *Oman and its Modern Development*, translated by Fu'ad Haddad and Adel Salahi, no date, p 44.

[192] Dr A'la Aldeen Nawras, *Iranian Politics in The Arabian Gulf during Karim Khan's reign 1757 - 1979,* Baghdad, 1982, p 56.

[193] B. J. Silut, *op. cit., supra*, p 324.

[194] *Ibid*

[195] John Kelly, *Britain and The Gulf,* 1795 -1870 A.D., vol. 1, p 21-22.

[196] Maine Records, vol. 891, August 15, p 178.

[197] Dr Jamal Zakariya Qasim, *op. cit., supra*, p 208.

[198] Wendell Phillips, *Oman: a history,* translated into Arabic, Muscat, The Ministry of National Heritage and Culture 1989, p 79.

[199] *Ibid*, see also Dr Jamal Zakariya Qasim, Al-Busaid Government in Oman and East Africa 1741-1871, Cairo, The Modern Egyptian Library, 1967.

[200] Sadiq Abduwani, 'The Omani Government, Its Development and Flourishing', *Proceedings of the Conference for Omani Studies*, Muscat 1980 p 69.

[201] Wendell Phillips, *op. cit., supra* p 80.

[202] Mohammed Mursi Abdullah, *Emirates of the Coast, Oman and the First Saudi government (1793-1818),* vol. 1, Cairo, The Modern Egyptian Library, 1978, p 87.

[203] Persia tried particularly during Nadir Shah's time to establish a distinct maritime fleet, see L. Lockhart, 'The Navy of Nadir Shah'. *Proceedings of the Iranian Society*, vol. 1, London, 1936.

[204] Dr Jamal Zakariya Qasim, *op. cit.*, p 118.

[205] *Ibid.*

[206] Qasim, *op. cit.* p 119.

[207] Mustafa Aqeel Al-Khateeb, *International Competition in the Arabian Gulf (1622-1763),* Beirut, Egyptian Library, 1981, p 271. Also, George Curzon, *Persia and the Persian Question*, vol. 1, London Longmans, Green and Co. 1892, p 375.

[208] Sadiq Abduwani, *op. cit., supra* p 66.

[209] Robert Landen, *op. cit., supra*, p 71.

[210] S. B. Miles, *Countries and Tribes of the Persian Gulf,* 2nd ed. London, Frank Cass & Co. Ltd., 1966, Arabic translation published in Muscat, The Ministry of National Heritage and Culture 1986, p 227. See also, Mustafa Abdulqader Al-Najar, *The Political History of the Eastern Border of the Arab Country in the Shatt Al-Arab*, a documentary study, Basra, publication of Jama' it Aldifa'an'n Urobet Alkhaleeg, 1974, p 57-58.

[211] Salim bin Hamoud Al-Siyabi, *Oman Across History,* Muscat, The Ministry of National Heriage and Culture 1986, p 154.

[212] Miles, *op. cit., supra*, p 71.

[213] In addition to the trade relations which linked Oman with Maurititius island, there was also good relations with the rulers and very often gifts were exchanged between them.

[214] Miles, *op. cit., supra*, p 226.

[215] It should be mentioned here that Omani-French relations had been gone through some bad patches, especially during 1195 AH/1781 AD, when French pirates captured the 50 cannon ship *Saleh* which was on a trade voyage from India to Basra. The Imam protested against the action and demanded from the French compensation of 1,00,200 rupees. At the request of the French consul in Baghdad, France sent a ship *(La Thetiq)* to Muscat where it was presented as compensation to the Imam for the *Saleh* and he also sent an apology from the French government, see Sadiq Abduwani, *op. cit., supra*, p 71.

[216] Dr Jamal Zakariya Qasim, *op. cit.,* p 181. What is interesting here is that, the Imam Ahmed refused a similar request which England had presented to establish a trade office in Muscat, in

the same year. This explain how strong Omani-French relations were during that period.

[217] The French official Rozilly wrote about this point saying : 'The people of Muscat, as it seems to me, like the French and hate the British because of their domineering and proud ways'. See, Dr Jamal Zakariya Qasim, *op. cit., supra*, p 181.

[218] Salah Al-A'qa'ad, *op. cit., supra*, p 61.

[219] *Ibid.*

[220] Olivie, *The Olivie Voyage to Iraq, (1794-1796)*, translated by Dr Yousef Hibbi, Press of the Iraq Scientific Council 1988, p 100.

[221] Olivie, *op. cit., supra*, p 95-96.

[222] Dr Mustafa Abu Hekmah, *The Modern History of Kuwait* (1750-1965), That Alsalsel Press, Kuwait 3rd ed., 1984, p 43-44.

[223] Olivie, *op. cit., supra* p 106. also see John B. Kelly, *Britain and the Gulf,* Oxford, Clarendon Press 1968, Arabic translation by Mohammed Amin Abdullah,1979, vol 1, p 65. Dr Abd Alamir Mohammed Amin, *The Maritime Forces in the Arabian Gulf During the Eighteenth Century,* Asa'ad Press, Baghdad 1966, p 11-12.

[224] Amin, *op. cit., supra*, p 10.

[225] J. G. Lorimer, *Gazetteer of the Gulf,* historical section, Calcutta 1908-15, and Press of Ali bin Ali Aldouha, Qatar, vol. 1, p 236.

[226] Lorimer, *op. cit., supra* vol. 2, p 656. See also, S.B. Miles, *Countries and Tribes of the Persian Gulf,* translated into Arabic by Mohammed Amin Abdullah, Amoun Liltajlied and Altiba'ah 3rd ed., 1986, p 223.

[227] Abraham Parsons, *Travels in Asia and Africa*, London 1808, p 209.

[228] Dr Jamal Zakariya Qasim, The Arabian Gulf, a *Study of the History of Arab Emirates during the Period of European expansion 1507-1840*, Dar Alfikr Al-Arabi, Cairo, 1985, p 149-150.

[229] Humaid bin Mohammed bin Ruzaiq, *Al-Fet'h Al-Mubeen fi Sirat Al-Sadah Al-Bu saidiyeen,*, study by Abdul Mon'im Amir and Dr Mohammed Mursi Abdullah, Cairo, 2nd ed., 1983, p 365.

[230] Fenzinzo, known as Sheikh Mansour History of Sayyid Said, translated by Dr Mahmoud Fadhil, The Arabic Encyclopedia, Beirut, 1980, p 84.

[231] Lorimer, *op. cit.,* vol. 2, p 656.

[232] Fenzinzo, *op. cit.,* p 84-85.

[233] Lorimer, *op. cit.,* vol. 1, p 2250.

[234] Parsons, *op. cit.,* p 206.

[235] For developments in Omani ship manufacturing see, Robert Geran Landen, *Oman since 1856*. Princeton, 1967, translated by Mohammed Amin Abdullah, 1970, p 57; Sultanate of Oman, Ministry of Information & Culture *Oman A Seafaring Nation, England, 1979* p 74; Parsons, *op. cit.*, p 207.

[236] Miles, *op. cit., supra*, vol. 2, p 223. See also, John Townsend, *Oman the Making of the Modern State*, Croom Helm London, 1977, p 39.

[237] Dr Abdulamir Mohammed Amin, 'British Interests in the Arabian Gulf 1747-1778', translated by Hashem Kat'a Lazem, *Publications of the Arabian Gulf Studies in Basra University*, Alerrshad Press, Baghdad, 1977,p 232.

[238] Parsons, *op. cit.* p 207. See also Kelly, *op. cit., supra*, p 28.

[239] Parsons, *op. cit.* p 208.

[240] *History of Sayyid Said, Sultan of Oman,* p 79.

[241] For further details about this subject see John R. Perry, *Karim Khan Zand, A History of Iran 1747-1779* , University of Chicago Press, 1979, p 13-149.

[242] Lorimer, *op. cit., supra*, vol. 5, p 2597.

[243] Perry, *op. cit.*, p 279.

[244] Rasul Al-Karkukli, *A Beautiful Baghdad Event*, translated from Turkish language Musa Kathem Nours, Dar Al-Kitab Al-Arabi, Beirut, p 149-150; Amin, *The Maritime Forces,* p 64.

[245] Olivie, *op. cit., supra*, p 106.

[246] *Ibid.*

[247] Dr Jamal Zakariya Qasim, 'False Iranian Claims in the Arabian Gulf', *The Egyptian History magazine*, vol 20 (1973), p 175.

[248] Kelly, *op. cit.,* vol. 1, p 69-70.

[249] Kelly, *op. cit.,* vol. 1, p 69.

[250] Kelly, *op. cit.,* vol. 1, p 35, pp 69-70.

[251] Lorimer, *op. cit.,* vol. 5, pp 2969-2970.

[252] Landen, *op. cit., supra*, vol. 1 p 28.

[253] Dr Abdulaziz AbduAlghani Ibrahim, *The Relationsip of the Omani Coast with Britain* , A documentary study (Riyadh 1982) p 114.

[254] Lorimer, *op. cit., supra*, vol. 2, p 694.

[255] Miles, *op. cit., supra*, p 226.

[256] Francis Warden, 'Historical Sketch of the Rise and Progress of the Government of Muscat 1694- 1891' in *Selections from the Records of Bombay (B.G.S.R.)*, Oleander Press, England, 1982 p 170. See also Lorimer, *op. cit., supra*, vol 2, p 650. and Dr Jamal Zakariya Qasim, *The Arabian Gulf, during the Period of European Expansion*, p 150.

[257] Unknown author, Book of Omani History, published in chapter eight of the book *Kashef Al-Ghumah Al -Jami' Li'Akhbar Al Ummah* written by Sarhan bin Said Al-Azkawi, study by Abd Al-Majed Haseeb Al-Qaisi, Sejel Al-Arab Press, 1980, p 158.

[258] Warden, B.G.S.R. *op. cit.* p 170. also see Lorimer, *op. cit.*, vol. 2, p 650.

[259] Lorimer, *op. cit.*, vol. 1, p 235, vol. 2, p 650., vol. 5, p 2419.

[260] Qasim, *The Arabian Gulf*, p 146. See, also Fadel Mohammed Abdul Husain Jaber, *Oman during Ahmed bin Said period* (1749- 1783), an unpublished M.A. thesis. College of Education, Baghdad University (1988), p 130.

[261] B.G.S.R, *op. cit.*, 'Historical Sketch of Joaseem Arab Tribes of Oman', vol. XXIV, p 301. Also see Ibrahim: *op. cit., supra*, p114.

[262] Jaber, *op. cit., supra*. See also, Mustafa Abdulqader Al-Najar, *The Political History of Arabistan Emirate* (1897-1925), Dar Alma'aref, Egypt, 1971, p 45.

[263] Al-Najar, *op. cit.* p 45.

[264] *Gazetteer of the Gulf*, historical section, vol. 5, p 2419-2420.

[265] Qasim, *The Arabian Gulf*, p 151.

[266] B.G.S.R, *op. cit.*, *Historical sketch of Muscat*, vol. XXIV, p 170. See also see Lorimer, *op. cit.*. vol. 5, p 2640-2641, vol. 2, p 651.

[267] Perry, *op. cit,.* p 271. See also Lorimer, *op. cit., supra*, vol. 1, p 253. Jaber, *op. cit., supra*, p 99-100.

[268] Steven Hemsley Longrigg, *Four Centuries of Modern Iraq*, Oxford, Clarendon Press, 1925, translated into Arabic by Ja'afer Khai'at , Dar Al-Kash'af, Beirut, 1949, p 177.

[269] Perry, *op. cit.*, p 192.

[270] The Olivie voyage to Iraq, p 104.

[271] *Ibid.*

[272] Lorimer, *op. cit., supra*, vol. 4, p 1845, vol. 5, p 2639; Amin, *The Maritime Forces* from *Letters from Bussora, Gombroon*, etc., vol. 17, May I, 1774.

[273] Lorimer, *op. cit., supra*, vol. 4, p 1845. In additon to what was mentioned, according to Persian sources, the Basha (the Baghdad deputy) also refused to allow the Zand's army to cross his territory in order to pass to the Arabian coasts and enforce Zaki Khan's expedition against Oman. However, such an expedition was not expected. As Perry said, Karim Khan wanted to move against Basra, Perry, op. cit, p 172.

[274] Amin, *The Maritime Forces*, p 63. Perry, *op. cit.*, p 172.

[275] Perry, *op. cit.*, p 159.

[276] *Ibid.*

[277] Concerning the preparations by the deputy of Basra, see Al-Karkukli, *op. cit., supra*, p 152. Olivie, *op. cit., supra*, p 106.

[278] Olivie, *op. cit., supra*, p 106.

[279] Concerning a letter from Baghdad's Governor to the Deputy of Basra, see Othman bin Sanad, *Albasrri*, Matali Alsau'ad Betaaib Akhbar Alwali Baghdad, summary by Sheikh Amin bin Mohammed Alhilwani Almadani, *Fifty-five years of Iraqi History 1188-1242*, Al Salafaih Press, Cairo, 1377, p 10.

[280] Amin, *The Maritime Forces,* p 70.

[281] Longrigg, *op. cit.. supra* p 179. Miles, *op. cit., supra*, p 227.

[282] Miles, *op. cit., supra*, Sultanate of Oman, Ministry of Information and Culture, *Oman's Maritime History*, p 7, Saleh Mohammed Al-A'bed, 'Basra During the Trouble' 1775-1779, *Almawred*, vol. 14, No. 3,1985, p 45.

[283] Falih Handhal, *The History of the United Arab Emirates*, Dar Alfikr Litiba'ah and Nashir, Abu Dhabi,vol. 1, p 229. Dr Abdaziz Sulaiman Nawar, *Daoud Basha*, Dar Alkitab Alabrabi Litiba'ah and Nashir 1967, p 223.

[284] Author Unknown, *History of Oman*, p 158; G. P .Badger, Jaber *op. cit., supra*, p 130.

[285] Author unknown. op. cit *supra*, p 158.

[286] Author unknown. *op. cit., supra* p 159.

[287] Parsons, *op. cit.,* p 206.

[288] *Ibid.*

[289] *Al-Fet'h Al-Mubeen*, p 370.

[290] The source indicates, without any research, that Imam Ahmed bin Said led the Omani fleet by himself. The authentic Omani sources emphasize that the leadership of this fleet was in the hands of Majed bin Said and not Imam Ahmed. Author Unknown , *op. cit.*, p 159.

[291] Amin, *The Maritime Forces*, footnote 35, p 85. Perry, *op cit.,* p 180.

[292] Ibn Ruzaiq *op. cit.*, p 370.

[293] For more detail on this subject see Perry, *op. cit*, p 181.

[294] Badger, *op. cit,* p 170. See also Author unknown, *op. cit.,* p 159.

[295] Amin, *The Maritime Forces,* p 73; Handhal, *op. cit.,* vol. 1, p 231.

[296] Fenzinzo, *op. cit..* p 67, Ibn Ruzaiq, *op. cit.,* p 370, 438.

[297] Lorimer, *op. cit.* vol. 2, p 652.

[298] *Oman since 1856* , p 54.

[299] *Gazetteer of the Gulf,* vol. 2, p 652.

[300] Nur Al-Din Al-Salimi, *Tohfat Al-'Ayian,* vol. 2, p 172.

[301] Salim Al-Siyabi, *Oman Across History,* vol. 2, p 14.

[302] Commentaries on the leadership of Said bin Ahmed and Sayyid Sultan bin Ahmed, prepared by Dr. Rajab Mohammed Abduhalim

[303] *Op cit., supra,* vol. 4, pp 221-223.

[304] *Ibid.,* pp 225-235.

[305] *Ibid.,* p 241.

[306] *Ibid.,* pp 242-252.

[307] *Ibid., ,* pp 257-267.

[308] *Ibid.,* p 279.

[309] *Ibid.,* p 291.

[310] *Ibid.,* p 291.

[311] *Ibid.,* 268.

[312] *Ibid.,* p 268.

[313] Salah Al-A'qa'ad, 'The Role of Sultan bin Ahmed Al-Bu said in Modern Omani History', from *Fa'aliat wa Mansahit Almuntada AlAdabi* for the year 1989/90, Muscat, p 378-379.

[314] Salim bin Hamoud Al-Siyabi, *op. cit.,* vol. , p 294, pp 302-303.

[315] Salah Al-A'qa'ad, *op. cit.,* pp 380-382.

[316] *Ibid.,* p 380-383.

[317] Salim bin Hamoud Al-Siyabi, *op. cit.,* vol. 4, p 268-269.

[318] Ian Skeet, *Muscat and Oman,* London, 1974, p 40.

[319] *Ibid,* p 40-41.

[320] The credit for establishing this dangerous base 1111-1167 AH/1699-1753 AD belongs to La Bourdonais who was appointed as its governor (in 1735 AD). He succeeded during his reign (ten years) in creating a flourishing strategically important colony out of it. He developed the island's excellent natural port, established ship-building and concentrated his efforts on making it stronger, as well as establishing a new capital, Port Louis. Bourdonais was able to carry out fierce attacks against the British in India, during the Austrian war 1153-1161 AH/1740-1748 AD. For further details see G.A. Ballard, *Rulers of the Indian Ocean* , London, 1927, pp 248-259. This island was very important in the view of France and they regarded it as the key to the Indian Ocean . See Herbert Richmond, *The Navy in India, 1963-1783,* London 1931, p 122.

[321] Other aims: Observing the developments in India, inciting Indian princes against British existence, and taking it as a base for assembling the forces and weaponry to invade India, at suitable circumstances.

[322] S.P. Sen, *The French in India,* 1763-1810, New Delhi, 2nd ed., 1971, p 533; G.S. Graham, *Tides of Empire,* Montreal 1972, p 59.

[323] Coupland, *East Africa and its Invaders,* Oxford, 1961, p 84.

[324] Zeki Saleh, *Mesopotamia 1600-1914* , Baghdad 1957, p 51.

[325] Privateers: a ship 'licensed' by the government to capture and plunder enemy ships in the manner of pirates. The French indulged in this practice during their struggle in the Indian Ocean against Britain for naval supremacy, at a great loss to the British. During this period (1773-1797 AD), the Franch captured 2266 British ships of various sizes. See G.B. Malleson, *Final French Struggle in India and on the Indian seas* , London 1878, p 813.

[326] In the following three years they captured another 1200 ships. C.C. Lloyd, *Armed Forces and the Naval Art of War* , the *New Cambridge Modern History,* Cambridge 1965, vol. IX, p 76. The reaction of the British government was to pass legislation in 1798, whereby weaponry had to be installed on every ship, and they sent a maritime fleet to police the danger zones, resulting in an increase in the maritime force, and subsequently the number of sailors also increased from 24,000 in 1783 AD to 120,000 1797. *Ibid* p 78-84; G.B. Malleson, *The Final French Struggle in India and on the Indian Seas,* London 1878, p 79-157. Coupland, p 85, Saleh, p 52. Miles and Skeet are wrong in specifying the date of this incident as 1749; S.B. Miles, *Countries and Tribes of the Gulf,* London 2nd ed., imp., 1966, p 268.

[327] Miles, p 269-270; Saleh, p 51.

[328] Miles, p 274-275.

[329] Saleh, p 52.

[330] Saleh, pp 52-3.

[331] Miles, p 270; Coupland, p 84.

[332] Salah Al-A'qa'ad, *The Political Streams in the Arabian Gulf*, Cairo (no date), p 44.

[333] Skeet, p 41.

[334] Miles, p 277; Coupland, p 85, Saleh, p 53.

[335] Miles, p 277-278; Coupland, p 85.

[336] Coupland, p 85.

[337] Miles, p 278; Saleh, *op. cit.*, p 53.

[338] L. H. Prentout, *Ile de France sous de Caen,* 1803-1810, Paris 1901, p 332; Coupland, p 86.

[339] Miles, p 282.

[340] William Feankline, *Observations made on a Tour from Bengal to Persia in the Years 1786-1787*, London 1790, p 37.

[341] J. Kelly, *Britain and The Gulf 1795-1880*, Oxford 1968, p 65.

[342] Miles, p 278; Coupland, p 86.

[343] Prentout, p 325.

[344] Prentout p 332; Coupland, p 87.

[345] Salah Al-A'qa'ad, *The Political Streams in the Arabian Gulf*, p 64.

[346] Skeet, p 41.

[347] Coupland, p 87-88.

[348] Salah Al-A'qa'ad, *The Political Streams in the Arabian Gulf,* p 66.

[349] The reason given by Dr Al-A'qa'ad for Beauchamp's delay was that his instructions were to visit the Black Sea first, then Syria, Lebanon, Palestine, Jordan and Egypt, and also to study the routes which lead to India. Beauchamp then found a good reason to excuse himself from carrying out his mission in Muscat. This reason was the ill-feeling against France, which had spread throughout the Islamic world because of the French expedition on Egypt, *op. cit., supra*, p 66.

[350] Coupland, p 89.

[351] Skeet, p 42.

[352] For further details see, *The British Reaction to French Activity*, p 283-284.

[353] Kelly, p 65; Coupland, p 90.

[354] *Ibid*, from Broker at Muscat to Duncan, Dec. 27, 1797.

[355] Dr. Saleh Mohammed Al A'bed, *The British Reaction to French Activity in the Arabian Gulf (1798-1810)* Baghdad 1979, pp 79-136.

[356] Dr. Salah Al-A'qa'ad, *The Political Streams in the Arabian Gulf*, p 116.

[357] A'qa'ad, *op. cit.. supra*, p 139.

[358] Dar Al-Mahfouthat Altareekhiah, Mahafez Al-Hijaz no. 269, document 38, date 11 Du Alqa'ada 1255 AH.

[359] Dr Sama'an Putrus, *International Political Relations in the Twentieth Century*, vol. 1, p 276.

[360] Dr Jalal Yahya, *The Great East, Modern Times*, p 74.

[361] Lorimer, *op. cit., supra* vol. 2, p 728.

[362] Dr Richard Stevens, 'Review of the Beginning s of American Trade -consular Relation s with the Sultanate of Oman and Muscat (1833-1856)', *The Gulf and Arabian Peninsula Studies*, p 122.

[363] Stevens, p 125.

[364] Stevens, p 126.

[365] Donald Hawley, *Oman and its Modern Development*, p 187.

[366] Stevens, *op. cit., supra* p 130.

[367] Stevens, *op. cit., supra*, p 133.

[368] Donald Hawley, *op. cit., supra*, p 188.

[369] Hawley, *op. cit., supra*, p 189.

[370] Memorandum Prepared in the Department of State (secret) Washington, March 15, 1946, no. 790 0014 - 946 'Current U.S. Policy towards the Arab Principalities of the Persian Gulf and the Gulf of Oman'.

[371] Robert G. Landen, *Oman Since 1856*; translated by Mohammed Amin Abdullah, Beirut, 1970, p 54.

[372] Rudolph Said-Reute, *Sultanate of Oman During the Reign of Sayyid Said bin Sultan* (1791-1856); translated by Abdul Majed H. Al-Qaisi, The Arabian Gulf Studies Center, Basrah University, 1983, pp 43-44.

[373] Holingsworth, *op. cit.,* p 5.

[374] Zoe Marsh and G. W. Kingsourth, *An Introduction to the History of East Africa*, Cambridge, The University Press, 1965, p 25.

[375] Al-A'qa'ad and Qasim, *Zanzibar*, p 60.

[376] Zoe Marsh and G. W. Kingsourth, *op. cit.,* p 25.

[377] Qasim, *Al-Busaid State in Oman and East Africa* (1741-1861), p 208.

[378] R. Coupland, *East Africa and Its Invaders (From the Earliest Times to the Death of Sayyid in*

1856), p 295.

[379] Qasim, *op. cit.,* p 208.

[380] Zoe Marsh and G. W. Kingsourth, *op. cit.,* p 6.

[381] R. Coupland, *op. cit., p 6.*

[382] Qasim, *op. cit.,* p 24.

[383] F. B. Pearce, *Zanzibar,* p 125.

[384] Coupland, *op. cit.,* p 297.

[385] F. B. Pearce, *Zanzibar*, p 215.

[386] Zoe Marsh and G. W. Kingsourth, *op. cit.,* p 26.

[387] Salah Al-A'qa'ad, and Zakariya Qasim, *Zanzibar, op. cit.,* p24.

[388] *Ibid.,* pp76-77.

[389] Holingsworth, *op. cit.,* p 6.

[390] Salah Al-A'qa'ad and Zakariya, Qasim, *op. cit.,* p 77.

[391] Said Rajab Heraiz, *Britain and East Africa from Colonialism to Independence,* Arab Institute of Research and Studies, 1971, p 22.

[392] Salah Al-A'qa'ad, and Zakariya Qasim, , *op. cit.,* pp 77-78.

[393] R. Burton, *Zanzibar, City, Island and Coast*, vol. 2, p 151.

[394] Salah Al-A'qa'ad, and Zakariya Qasim, *op. cit.,* p120.

[395] Said Rajab Heraiz, *op. cit.,* p 22.

[396] Holingsworth, *op. cit.,* p 7. See also: Salah Al-A'qa'ad, and Zakariya Qasim, *op. cit.,* p 79; and Said Rajab Heraiz, , *op. cit.,* p 22.

[397] Qasim, *op. cit.* p 254.

[398] I. O. L. political and Secret Dept., B. 2. Confidential, Zanzibar, Muscat and Persia, a memo by the political secretary, J. W. Kate. 1st July 1968, p 3.

[399] Qasim, *op. cit. pp.* 254-255.

[400] O. Burton, *Zanzibar, City and Coast*, vol. 1, pp. 307-308.

[401] Robert Nunez Lyne, *Zanzibar in Contemporary Times*, London, 1950, pp. 44-50.

[402] Holingsworth, *op. cit.,* p 12.

[403] Salah Al-A'qa'ad and Zakariya Qasim, *op. cit.,* p 121.

[404] E. B. Russel Charles, *General Rigby, Zanzibar and the Slave Trade,* pp. 159-160.

[405] Zakariya Qasim, *op. cit.,* pp. 264-265.

[406] I. O. L. Political and Secret Dept. B. 8. Memo on the Turkish Claim to Sovereignity over the Eastern Shores of the Red Sea and the Whole of Arabia, and on the Egyptian Claim to the Whole of the Western Shores of the Red Sea, including the African Coast from Suez to Cape Guardafui; printed for the use of the F. O. Hertzlet, 10 March 1874.

[407] I. O. L. Political and Secret Dept. B. 2. Confidential. Memorandum by Eastwick, 15 July 1968, p 1.

[408] Aitchison, *op. cit.,* vol. XI, p 225.

[409] I. O. L. B. 2, Memo on Muscat and Zanzibar Affairs. H. P. Freyer, 20 July 1868, p 1.

[410] Aitchison, *op. cit.,* vol. XI, p 225.

[411] I. O. L. B. 2, Memorandum by Captain W. M. S. Eastwick, 15 July 1968, p 6.

[412] Aitchison, op. cit., vol. XI, p 75.

[413] Salah Al-A'qa'ad, and Zakariya Qasim, *op. cit.,* p 130.

[414] I. O. L. Political and Secret Dept. B. 2. Confidential memo. Zanzibar, Arabia and the Persian Gulf, T. Princep, I. O., 15 July 1868, p 4.

[415] Lyne, *op. cit.,* p 45.

[416] I. O. L. Political and Secret Dept. B. 2. Confidential. Zanzibar, Muscat and Persia, Memo by the political secretary J. W. Kaye. 1st July 1868, p 4.

[417] I.O.L. Political & Secretarary Dept. B.2, Confidential Memo, Zanzibar, Arabia and the Persian Gulf, H.T. Princep, 1868 p 45.

[418] I. O. L. Political and Persia. Memo by the political secretary, J. W. Kaye. 1st July 1868, p 3.

[419] I. O. L. Political and Secretary Dept. B. 2. Confidential memo. Zanzibar, Arabia and the Persian Gulf, H. T. Princep, 15 July 1868, pp 4-5.

[420] I. O. L. Political and Secret Dept. B. 2. Confidential memo: Zanzibar, Arabia and the Persian Gulf. H. I. Princep, I. O., 15 July 1868, pp 1-2.

[421] I. O. L. Political and Secret Dept. B. 14, memorandum, M. O. L., Zanzibar Agency and Consulate Expenses, A. W. M., 17 August 1867.

[422] Salah Al-A'qa'ad and Zakariya Qasim, *op. cit.,* p 161.

[423] *Ibid.,* pp 332-334.

[424] D. Arky Exploration Company.

[425] J. E. Peterson, *Oman in the Twentieth Century*, Croom Helm, Kent, 1984, p 53.

[426] Sana Mohammed Abdul Jabbar Al-Tay, *Omanis in East Africa*, Arabian Gulf States Information Documentation Centre, Baghdad, 1988, p 120.

[427] Dr Jad Muhammad Taha, *Afro-Arab Relations*, the Institute of Arab Research and Studies,

Cairo, 1977, p 137.

[428] These societies and political parties include:

a) The Arab Society, established in 1925 to represent Arab interests;

b) Sheraz Society, established in 1930 to represent Swahilis who commonly call themselves the Sherazis;

c) the African Association, established in 1931, to advocate the interests of Africans in the eastern coasline of Africa. These are mostly Christians and pagans;

d) the Comoros Society with members from Comoro Island;

e) the National Indian Society, established in 1924 to include the Indian population in the island; and

f) Zanzibar Liberation Front.

For further details see *Zanzibar in History* (undated), pp 13-15.

[429] *Ibid.,* p 22.

[430] *Ibid.,* p 24.

[431] *A History of Africa 1918-1967,* Moscow, 1968, p 371.

[432] *Zanzibar Liberation Front, op. cit.,* pp 30-31.

[433] *A History of Africa, op. cit.*

[434] *Zanzibar Liberation Front, op. cit.,* pp 33-34.

[435] Abdul Mulik Oudda, 'The One-Party System and Application of Socialism in Tanzania', *International Politics,* issue III, Cairo, 1967.

[436] J. Zakariya Qasim, *The History of Arabs in Africa,* a title in the series on Arabs in Africa, Historical Roots and Contemporary Reality, Cairo, 1987, pp. 24-25.

[437] R. Coupland, *The Exploitation of East Africa* 1856-1890, London, 1939, p. 4.

[438] Said bin Ali Al-Mughairi, *Jahinat Al-Akhbar fi Tarikh Zanzibar,* edited by Abdulmoneim Amir, 1979, pp. 139-165. See also Abdullah bin Saleh Al-Farsi, *Al Busaidis the Rulers of Zanzibar*; translated by M. Amin Abdullah, pp. 164-165.

[439] F. B. Pearce, *Zanzibar: the Island Metropolis of Eastern Africa,* London, 1920, pp. 119-120. See also Ibrahim Al-Zain Sughairoon, *The Omani and South Arabian Muslim Factor in East Africa,* Riyadh, 1984, pp. 23-25.

[440] Said bin Hamid Heraiz, *Arab Elements in the Swahili Culture,* Beirut, 1988, pp. 21-22.

[441] Al-Mughairi, *op. cit.,*pp. 145, 150, 180, and 184,Al-Farsi, *ibid.,* pp. 56-59.

[442] Al-Mughairi, *op. cit.,*pp. 211-212.

[443] Al-Farsi, *op. cit.,*p. 63.

[444] Al-Mughairi, *op. cit.,*pp. 174-180.

[445] Al-Farsi, *op. cit.,*p. 73.

[446] *Ibid.*

[447] Al-Mughairi, *op. cit.,*p. 174; and Al-Farsi, *op. cit.,*p. 75.

[448] B. G. Martin, 'Notes on Some Members of the Learned Classes of Zanzibar and East Africa in the Nineteenth Century', *The International Journal of African Historical Studies,* vol. 4, part 3, 1971, pp. 525-545.

[449] J. M. Gray, 'The Hadimu and Tumbatu of Zanzibar', *Tanzanian Records,* Nos. 18 and 82, 1977, pp. 135, 137 and 139.

[450] Al-Farsi, *op. cit.,*pp. 56-61.

[451] Sayyida Salima bint Said bin Sultan, *Memoirs of an Arab Princess,* translated by Abdul Majed Al-Qubaisi, Oman, 1983, p. 60.

[452] Qasim, *op. cit.,*p. 211.

[453] Al-Farsi, *op. cit.,*pp. 114 and 125.

[454] Al-Mughairi, *op. cit.,*p. 159.

[455] Al-Farsi, *op. cit.,*p. 80.

[456] Al-Mughairi, *op. cit.,*p. 155.

[457] Al-Qasimi, *op. cit.,*p. 59.

[458] R. F. Burton, *The Lake Regions of Central Africa,* London, 1860, vol. 2, pp. 194-195.

[459] R. Coupland, *East Africa and Its Invaders,* Oxford, 1938.

[460] R. Coupland, *ibid.,* pp. 302-303.

[461] Qasim, *op. cit.,*pp. 1741-1861.

[462] R. Coupland, *East Africa and Its Invaders,* p. 304.

[463] Qasim, *op. cit.,*p. 215.

[464] Said Hammid Heraiz, *op. cit.,*p. 20.

[465] M. Mohammed Mosailihi, *Commercial Activity in East Africa in the Nineteenth Century to the Early period of the European Colonialism* (in Arabic), pp. 179-182.

[466] R. W. Beachey, 'East African Ivory Trade in the Nineteenth Century', *Journal of African History,* volumes 8 and 2, 1967.

[467] Al-Mughairi, *op. cit.,*pp. 217-220.

[468] *Ibid.,* pp. 159-160.

469 H. M. Stanley, *Through the Dark Continent*, London, 1878, vol. 2, p. 362.

470 Al-Mughairi, *op. cit.,*p. 223.

471 Mosailihi, *op. cit.,*p. 204.

472 Mosailihi, *op. cit.,* pp. 197-198.

473 Sughairoon, *The Omani and South Arabian Muslim Factor in East Africa*, pp 133-153

474 Al-Mughairi, *op. cit.,*p. 63.

475 Modathir Abdul Rahim, *Islam and Social Uniformity in Africa,* The Islamic African Centre, Khartoum, 1985, issue I, p. 16

476 Ibrahim Al-Zain Sughairoon, *The Sudanese Muslim Factor in Uganda*, University of Khartoum Press, 1981.

477 Heraiz, *op. cit.,*p. 27.

478 Al-Mughairi, *op. cit.,*p. 19.

479 B. G. Martin, *op. cit.,*p. 572.

480 J. M. Gray, *op. cit.,*pp. 136-137.

481 Al-Farsi, *op. cit.,*pp. 56-58. Also see Al-Mughairi, *op. cit.*, p. 167; and Heraiz, *op. cit.*, p. 37.

482 Heraiz, *op. cit.,*p. 29.

483 Al-Farsi, *op. cit.,* pp. 62-99. See also B. G. Martin, *op. cit.*, pp 525-545.

484 M. Hassan Al-Iyadarous, 'Sultan Said and the Afro-Arab Relations', *The Arab Historian* (journal), issue 37, 1988, p. 26.

485 I. Al-Zain Sughairoon, *The Omani and South Arabian Muslim Factor in East Africa*, pp. 145, 147, 190 and 191.

486 Heraiz, *op. cit.,*p. 52.

487 Salima bint Said, *op. cit.,*pp. 132 -137 and 232.

488 Collette Meizon, *Hurth Immigrations to Central Africa*, Ministry of National Heritage and Culture, issue 61, November 1984, p. 6.

489 *Ibid.,* pp. 6-7.

490 *Ibid.,* p. 7.

491 Meizon, *op. cit.* p.11.

492 Abdul Rahim, *op. cit.,*pp. 18-19.

493 Mohammed Al-Haddad, *Facts about Arabs and Islam in East Africa,* 1973, pp. 123-124

494 John Gray, 'Amin Diaries, Ext. 1'., *Uganda Journal*, vol. 25, No. 1, 1961, entry for 11 August 1867, p. 10.

495 Apolo Kagwa, 'How Religion Came to Buganda,' *Mengo Notes*, vol. 3, No. 5, May 1902.

496 Al-Zain Sughairoon, *Historical Glimpse of the Spread of Islam in Uganda,* p. 22.

497 *Ibid.,* p.23.

498 F. O. 403/108 Emin Pasha to Colonel Euan Smith, Wadelai, 20 August 1887.

499 F. O. 403/97 Acting Consul, General Holwood to the Marquis of Salisbury, Zanzibar, 8 January 1887; see also F. O. 403/127 Report by Mr. H. H. Johnston, Her Majesty's Consul on the Nyasa-Tanganyika Expedition 1889-90, Note with reference to the Arabs in Central Africa, pp. 34-39.

500 Al-Mughairi, *op. cit.,*p. 159.

501 Marquis, *op. cit.,*p. 228.

502 Meizon, *op. cit.,*p. 8.

503 Al-Mughairi, *op. cit.,*pp. 166 and 174; see also Al-Farsi, *op. cit.,*p. 73.

504 Al-Farsi, *op. cit.,*pp. 73-80.

505 B. G. Martin, *op. cit.,*pp. 526-527.

506 *The Swahili-Speaking Peoples of Kenya's Coast, 1895-1965*, Nairobi, 1973, pp. 159-168.

507 Al-Farsi, *op. cit.,*pp. 75-76; and see also Al-Mughairi, *op. cit.,*pp. 125-26 and 130-31.

508 B. G. Martin, *op. cit.,*p. 535.

509 Al-Farsi, *op. cit.,*pp. 73-74; and Sughairoon, *op. cit.,*pp. 17-18.

510 Al-Farsi, *op. cit.,*pp. 77-79.

511 B. G. Martin, *op. cit.,*pp. 538-39.

512 Al-Farsi, *op. cit.,*pp. 73-80.

513 Sughairoon, *op. cit.,*pp. 16-24.

514 Heraiz, *op. cit.,*pp. 57-58.

515 Sughairoon, 'Islamic Heritage in East Africa', a preliminary study in a foreword for a book on the history of Mazrui's tribe in East Africa written by Al-Amin bin Ali Mazrui, the Book World Journal, vol. 6, issue II, Riyadh, 1985, pp. 190-218, and page 5 of the manuscript.

516 Al-Mughairi, *op. cit.,*pp. 305-307; see also Al-Farsi, *op. cit.,*pp. 97-98.

517 Heraiz, *op. cit.,*p. 85.

518 B. G. Martin, *op. cit.,*p. 535.

519 Al-Mughairi, *op. cit.,*p. 233.

520 Ahmed Al-Falahi, Publication in Oman, Books World Journal, vol. 3, issue 4, Riyadh, 1983.

521 Ahmed Eeda Salim, *The Swahili-Speaking Peoples of Kenya's Coast 1895-1965*, pp. 159-168.

[522] Several European works included references to this phenomenon. Among these, see Col. C. Chaille, *Central Africa,* London, 1876, p. 106; J. M. Gray, 'The Diaries of Emin Pasha', extract II, *Uganda Journal,* vol. 25, No. 2, 1960-1961, p. 159.

[523] Heraiz, *op. cit.,*pp. 88-89.

[524] Heraiz, 'A Study on Swahili Culture, Its Origins, Elements and Developments', in *The Relation between Arab and African Cultures,* Tunis, 1985, p. 152.

[525] Heraiz, *Arab Influences in Swahili Culture,* p. 44.

[526] For detailed accounts of the history of Oman during the Al-Ya'ruba period, see: Humaid bin Mohammed Ruzaiq, *Al-Fet'h Al-Mubeen fi Sirat As Sadah al Busaidiyeen,* edited by Abdul Mon'im Amir and Mohammed Mursi Abdullah, 1857; Nur Al-Din Al-Salimi, *Tohfat Al-'Ayian bi Sirat Ahl Oman,* Cairo, 1931; Abdullah Khalfan Qaissar, *Sirat Imam Nasir bin Murshid,* edited by Abdul Majed Haseeb Al-Qaisi, 1983, Salim bin Hamoud bin Shamis, *Oman Across History,* vol. 4 1982. Among foreign references one is advised particularly to see: B. Miles, *The Countries and the Tribes of the Persian Gulf,* 2 volumes, 1919; and J. G. Lorimer, *Gazetteer of the Persian Gulf,* 2 volumes, India, 1908.

[527] Lorimer, *op. cit.,* vol. 1, p 403.

[528] A. Hamilton, *A New Account of the East Indies, 1688-1723,* 2 volumes, 1727, vol. 1, pp. 43-45.

[529] Miles, *op. cit.,* vol. 1, p 220.

[530] Local power is used here to mean any non-European power.

[531] Lorimer, *op. cit.,* p 402.

[532] S. Mohammed Al-Aa'abid, *The Role of Al-Qawasim in the Arabian Gulf,* Baghdad, 1976.

[533] Abdel Amir Amin, *The Naval Powers in the Arabian Gulf in the Eighteenth Century,* Baghdad, 1966.

[534] Meymona Khaliffa Sabah, 'The Establishment of Kuwait and Its Development in the Eighteenth Century', *The Gulf and Arabia* (journal), No. 46, Year 12.

[535] M. Abdul Qadir Al-Najar, *The Political History of Arabistan Emirate,* Dar Al-Ma'arif Publications, Egypt, 1971

[536] Amin, *op. cit.*

[537] *Oman A Seafaring Nation,* a publication by the Ministry of Information and Culture, Oman, 1979.

[538] Abdul Amir Amin, *British Interests in the Arabian Gulf (1747- 1778)* Baghdad, 1977, pp. 46-50.

[539] *Ibid.,* pp. 119-121.

[540] *Ibid.,* pp. 170-172.

[541] Amin, *The Naval Powers in the Arabian Gulf,* pp. 40-45.

[542] A. Parsons, *Travel in Asia and Africa,* London, 1808, p 220.

[543] *Ibid.*

[544] Marine Records, vol. 891, 15 August 1790, Reports on Trade of Arabia and Persia by Samuel Monesty and Hartford Jones.

[545] *Ibid.*

[546] *Ibid.*

[547] *Ibid.*

[548] *Ibid.*

[549] India Office: Factory Records, Letters from Bussors Gambroon, letter from Basra, 21 September 1769.

[550] Lorimer, *op. cit.,* p 416.

[551] *Turkani* was a category of sailing boat common in the first half of the eighteenth century.

[552] Lorimer, *op. cit.,* p 416.

[553] R. Boxer, *Portuguese Conquest and Commerce in Southern Asia,* London, 1933, p 428.

[554] Parsons, *Travel in Asia and Africa,* London, 1808, p 220.

[555] Lorimer, *op. cit.,* p 435.

[556] *Ibid.*

[557] *Oman A Seafaring Nation,* p 77.

[558] To get an idea about this aspect of the Omani history, see the following reference: F. R. Letters, etc. 21, 1800 Report on the State of Trade between Persia and India and suggestion as to the means of improving it, by Captain J. Malcolm; Marine Record, vol. 891, 15 August 1790, Report on the Commerce of Arabia and Persia by Samuel Monesty and Hartford Jones; Early preliminary papers related to India collection No. 2, December 1791; and Third Report of the selected Committee appointed to take into consideration the export trade from Great Britain to the East Indies.

[559] Factory Records, Letters etc., vol. 21, 1800.

[560] Marine Records, vol. 891, 15 August 1790.

[561] *Ibid.*

[562] *Ibid.*

[563] For further details refer to the following titles:

Salim bin Hamoud bin Shamis Al-Siyabi, *Oman Across History* , vol. 4, Ministry of National Heritage and Culture, Muscat, Oriental Press, 1982, pp. 113-115.

Robert G. Landen, *Oman Since 856;* translated into Arabic by Mohammed Amin Abdullah, Ministry of National Heritage and Culture, Matrah, Oriental Press, 1981, pp 53-54.

Wendell Philips, *Oman: a history;* translated into Arabic by Mohammed Amin Abdullah, Ministry of National Heritage and Culture, the International Press (3rd ed. 1989), chapter II.

Abdul Majed Al-Qaisi, in a foreword to the book, *Diary of an Arab Princess'* by Salima bint Sayyid Said bin Sultan, Sultan of Muscat and Zanzibar, 5th ed., Ministry of National Heritage and Culture, Amon press, 1985, p15.

Humaid bin Ruzaiq, *Al-Fet'h Al-Mubeen fi Sirat Al-Sadah Al-Busaidiyeen,* edited by Abdul Mon'im Amir and Mohammed Mursi, Ministry of National Heritage and Culture, Sijil Al-Arab Printing Press, 1977, pp 35-87.

Sheikh Nur Al-Din Abdullah Al-Salimi, *Tohfat Al-'Ayan bi Sirat Ahl Oman,* Istiqama Bookstore (undated), pp150-168. Ahmed bin Hamoud Al Ma'meri, *Oman and East Africa,* translated into Arabic by Mohammed Amin Abdullah, Ministry of National Heritage and Culture, Sijil al Arab Printing Press, 1980, p 70.

[564] Sadiq Hassan Abdowani, *Omani State, Its Establishment, Development and Progress,* Proceedings of a symposium on Omani studies, vol. 2, November 1980, Ministry of National Heritage and Culture, Sijil Al-Arab Printing Press, 1981, pp 5-129; see also Robert G. Landen, *op. cit.*

[565] For further details see, Abdowani, *Omani State,* pp 76-87; see also Al-Siyabi, *Oman Across History* vol. 4, p 70; and Al-Qaisi, in his foreword to the book, *Diary of an Arab Princess.*

[566] For further details on the volume of trade and customs revenue during that period, see P. Risso, *Oman & Muscat: Early History,* London, Croom Helm, 1986, pp 100-102 and 107.

[567] Abdowani, *op. cit.*, pp 80-83. More details can be found in: Zuhdi Abdul Majed Samur, *Oman, Political History in the Second Half of the 19th Century*, vol. 2 , Kuwait, Dar al-Sallasil Publications, 1985, chapter IV.

[568] See also Risso, *op. cit.*, chapters 8 and 9.

[569] Dr Sultan bin Mohammed Al-Qasimi, *The Division of the Omani Empire* (1856-1862), Dubai, Al-Bayan Press, 1989, first chapter.

[570] For detailed accounts on this point see Said bin Ali Al-Mughairi, *Jahinat Al-Akhbar fi Tarikh Zanzibar,* edited by Mohammed Ali Al-Saleibi, Ministry of National Heritage and Culture, 1986, pp 245-250.

[571] Landen, *op. cit.*, pp 58-60.

[572] Jamal Zakariya Qasim, 'The Historic Roots of the Omani Issue', *Arab Journal of Historical Studies*, Issue 12, Cairo, 1964-1965.

[573] Abdowani, *op. cit.*, pp. 113-118; Phillips, *op. cit.*, pp 124-138; Al Ma'meri, *op. cit.* p 28; and Al-Qasmi, *op. cit.*, pp 23-68.

[574] Landen, *op. cit.*, p 55.

[575] See Landen, *op. cit.*, pp 304-349.

[576] For further details on Seeb Accord see Al-Ma'meri, *op. cit.*, pp 121-122; Phillips, *op. cit.*, p 189; Qasim, *op. cit.*, pp 180-181 and Landen, *op. cit.*, p358.

[577] Phillips, *op. cit.*, p 178-181.

[578] Landen, *op. cit.*, pp 355-361.

[579] In its analysis of this period, this paper has relied extensively on the following titles:

Al-Ma'meri, *op. cit.*, pp 117-127; Phillips, *op. cit.*, pp 179-183; Landen, *op. cit.*, pp 367-376.

For more details see Jamal Zakariya Qasim, *The Arabian Gulf: The Contemporary History 1945-1977*, Arab League Educational, Cultural and Scientific Organization, 1974, chapter VII.

APPENDIX

Researchers who presented studies for the conference on *Oman in History*, held during the period September 24 -27, 1994.

Dr Sughairoon, Ibrahim Al-Zain, Professor of History, Sultan Qaboos University, Sultanate of Oman.

Dr Shalabi, Ahmed, Senior Professor, Dar Al-Uloom College, Cairo University, Arab Egyptian Rep.

Dr Khalil, Amal Mohammed, Professor of History, College for Girls, Ayn Shams Univ., Arab Egyptian Rep.

Dr Al-Ziani, Amal. Consultant at the Ministry of Foreign Affairs, State of Bahrain.

Dr Taha, Jad Mohammed, Dean of College of Arts, Sultan Qaboos Univ., Sultanate of Oman.

Dr Zarins, Juris, Consultant Archaeologist, Southwest Missouri State Univ. , U.S.A.

Dr Al-Azzi, Member of Arab Historians Union, Rep. of Iraq.

Dr Hassan, Khalil Shakir, Prof. of History, Al-Mustansiryah Univ., Member of Arab Historians Union, Rep. of Iraq.

Dr Al-Sheikh, Ra'fat Ghunaimi, Head of Dept. of History, College of Arts, Al-Zaqaziq Univ., Arab Egyptian Rep.

Dr Al-Hashimi, Ridha Jawad, Prof. of History, Baghdad Univ., Rep. Of Iraq.

Dr Al-Atraqchi, Ramzia Mohammed, Prof., Institute of Science Heritage, Baghdad Univ., Member of Arab Historians Union., Rep. of Iraq.

Dr Ata, Zubaida, Head of Hist. Dept., College of Arts, Al-Minia Univ., Arab Egyptian Rep.

Dr Abdul Aziz, Sahar Assayyid, Assist. Prof., College of Arts, Alexandria Univ., Arab Egyptian Rep.

Dr Al-Humaidi, Sa'ad bin Said, Prof., College of Language and Social Sciences, Abha Univ., Kingdom of Saudi Arabia.

Al-Saqlawi, Said bin Mohammed, (Engineer), Sultanate of Oman.

Dr Taha, Samir Mohammed, Prof. of Hist., College of Arts, Suhaj Univ., Arab Egyptian Rep.

Dr Al-Taei, Sana Mohammed, Memb. of The Arab Historians' Union., Rep. of Iraq.

Dr Salim, Al-Sayyid Abdul Aziz, Prof. of Hist., College of Arts, Alexandria Univ., Arab Egyptian Univ.

Dr. Al-Kashif, Saida Ismail, Prof. of Hist., College for Girls, Ayn Shams Univ., Arab Egyptian Univ.

Dr Abdul Munaem, Shakir Mahmoud, Prof. of Hist., Almustansiryah Univ., Rep. of Iraq.

Dr Al-Aa'abid, Salih Mohammed, Prof. of Hist., Univ. of Baghdad, Rep. of Iraq.

Dr Al-Sheikhli, Sabah Ibrahim, Prof. of Hist., Univ. of Baghdad, Rep. of Iraq.

Dr Al-Hamdani, Tariq Nafi', Prof. of Hist., Univ. of Baghdad, Rep. of Iraq.

Dr Amin, Abdul Amir Mohammed, Prof. of Hist., Univ. of Al-Yarmouk, Jordan.

Dr Al-Mawafi, Abdul Hamid, Oman News Agency, Sultanate of Oman.

Mr Al-Harithi, Abdullah bin Nasir, Sultan Qaboos Univ., Sultanate of Oman.

Dr Abdul Rahman, Abdullah Mohammed, Assistant Prof. Social Studies Dept., College of Arts, Alexandria Univ., Arab Egyptian Rep.

Dr Al-Rumaihi, Abdul Latif, General Director, Office of His Excellency Al Sheikh, the Prime Minister. State of Bahrain.

Prof. Abu A'alia, Abdul Fattah Hasan, Prof. College of Islamic Sciences, Univ. of Imam Mohammed bin Saud, Kingdom of Saudi Arabia.

Dr Al-Qahtani, Abdul Qadir Hammood, Dept. of Hist., College of Humanities and Social Science, Qatar Univ., State of Qatar.

Dr Sultan, Abdul Munaem Abdul Hamid, Prof. of Hist. College of Arts, Univ. of Sohaj, Arab Egyptian Rep.

Dr Hassanain, Abdul Na'eem Mohammed, Prof. of Hist., College of Arts, Ayn Shams Univ., Arab Egyptian Rep.

Prof. Nasir, Ali Mansour, Prof. of Hist., Univ. of Bahrain, State of Bahrain.

Dr Mohammed, Ghazi Rajab, Member of Arab Historians Union, Rep. of Iraq.

Dr Al-Ja'beeri, Farhat Ali, Prof. of Hist., Univ. of Al-Qairawan, Tunisia.

Dr Shihab, Fouad, Prof. of Hist., Univ. of Bahrain, State of Bahrain.

Dr Rashid, Fawzi, Member of Arab Historians Union, Rep. of Iraq.

Dr Faraj, Lutfi Ja'far, Prof. of Hist., Univ. of Al-Mustansiryah, Rep. of Iraq.

Dr Al Hussaini, Mohammed Baqir, Member of Arab Historians' Union, Rep. of Iraq.

Dr Ferzat, Mohammed Harb, Prof. of Hist., College of Humanities and Social Sciences, Univ. of Qatar, State of Qatar.

Dr Ramzi, Mohammed, Prof. of Hist., Univ. of Damascus, Syrian Arab Rep.

Dr Shukri, Mohammed Said, Prof. of Hist., Univ. of Aden, Rep. of Yemen

Dr Arab, Mohammed Sabir, Prof. of Hist., Univ. of Al-Azhar, Arab Egyptian Rep.

Dr. Al-Suroji, Mohammed Mahmoud, Senior Prof., College of Arts, Alexandria Univ., Arab Egyptian Rep.

Prof. Al-Dawood, Mohammed Ali, Member of Arab Historians' Union, Rep. of Iraq.

Prof. Al-Shak'a, Mustafa, Senior Prof., College of Arts, Univ. of Ayn Shams, Arab Egyptian Rep.

Dr. Al-Najjar, Mustafa Abdul Qadir, Member of Arab Historians' Union, Rep.of Iraq.

Dr. Aqeel, Mustafa, Prof. of Hist., Univ. of Qatar, State of Qatar.

Dr. Taha, Muneer Yosuf, The Museum of Iraq, The Centre for Archaeology and Heritage, Rep. of Iraq.

Dr. Daftar, Nahidh Abdul Razaq, Assistant Prof., Dept. of Archaeology, College of Arts, Univ. of Baghdad, Rep. of Iraq.

Mr. Al-Sharooni, Yosuf, Arab Egyptian Rep.

Prof. Ghowanma, Yosuf Hassan, Dean of College of Arts, Univ. of Jordan, Kingdom of Jordan.

Prof. Na'aisa, Yosuf, Prof. of Hist., Univ. of Damascus, Syrian Arab Rep.

Contributors to the Conference 'Oman in History', Held during the period September 24 -27, 1994.

Mr Tadmuri, Ahmed Jalal, Director of Archives and Researches, The Royal Diwan, Ras Al-Khaimah, United Arab Emirates.

Prof Mustafa, Ahmed Abdul Rahim, Ayn Shams Univ., College of Arts, Dept. of Hist., Arab Egyptian Rep.

Prof. Abdul Razzaq, Ahmed, Head of Dept. of Hist., College of Arts, Ayn Shams Univ., Arab Egyptian Rep.

Prof. Al-Naqshabandi, Osama Nasir, Head of the Centre of Arab Historians, Member of Arab Historians' Union, Rep. of Iraq.

Prof. Abdul Halim, Ismael Al-Haj, Prof. of Islamic Hist., The National Univ. of Kuala Lumpur, Malaysia.

Ms Al-Hamdani, Amna Rashid, Head of Research., Centre for Folklore Heritage, State of Qatar.

Prof. Sayyid, Ayman Fouad, Prof. Higher Studies Hist., Univ. of Cairo, Arab Egyptian Rep.

Dr. Boreeqa, Al-Tijani bin Hummadi, Dept. of Literature, Prof. of Higher Education, Univ. of Al Zaitona, Rep. of Tunisia.

Dr. Al-Khalifa, Khalid, Univ. of Bahrain, State of Bahrain.

Dr. Saiqali, Samir, Prof. Dept. of Hist., American Univ., Rep. of Lebanon.

Dr Al-Nasiri, Sayyid Ahmed Ali, Head of Dept. of Hist., College of Arts, Univ. of Cairo, Arab Egyptian Rep.

Dr Hasanain, Shireen Abdul Munaem, Prof. College of Arts, Univ. of Ayn Shams, Arab Egyptian Rep.

Prof Basarrah, Salih Ali, Head of Dept. of Hist., College of Education, Univ. of Aden, Rep. of Yemen.

Prof. Al-Shamlan, Abdul Rahman Rashid, Prof. of Hist., Univ. of King Saud, Member of Saudi Historical Society, Kingdom of Saudi Arabia.

Prof. Abdul Rahim, Abdul Rahim Abdul Rahman, Head of Dept. of Hist., Univ. of Al-Ain, United Arab Emirates.

Dr. Al-Hulabi, Abdul Aziz bin Salih, Prof. of Hist., College of Arts, Univ. of King Saud, Kingdom of Saudi Arabia.

Prof. Karim, Abdul Karim, Head of the Morocco Historians Society, Univ. of Mohammed Al-Khamis, Kingdom of Morocco.

Prof. Ahmed, Labeed Ibrahim, Director of Al-Hikma Institute, Univ. of Baghdad, Rep. of Iraq.

Prof. Rabee', Mohammed Hasanain, Dean of College of Arts, Univ. of Cairo, Arab Egyptian Rep.

Prof. Al-Mash Hadani, Mohammed Jasim Hammadi, Assistant General Secretary of the Arab Historians Union, Baghdad, Rep. of Iraq.

Prof. Omaira, Mohammed, Dean of Institue of Hist., Univ. of Algeria, Rep. of Algeria.

Prof bin Ahmado, Mohammed Al-Mukhtar, General Secretary of Mauritanian Historians, Mauritania.

Dr. Abdullah, Mohammed Mursi, Director of Archives and Researches Centre, Abu Dhabi, United Arab Emirates.

Prof. Al-A'abid, Mufeed, Head of Dept. of Hist., Univ. of Damascus, Syrian Arab Rep.

Prof. Al-A'awlaqi, Nasr, Vice President, Univ. of Sana'a, Rep. of Yemen.

Prof. Zeyada, Niqcla, Prof. Dept. of Hist., American Univ., Rep. of Lebanon.

Prof. Hassan, Yosuf Fadhl, Prof. of Hist. Khartoum Univ., Rep. of Sudan.

Prof. Abdullah, Yosuf Mohammed, Vice President of Heritage and Libraries Committee, Sana'a, Rep. of Yemen.

Prof. Rizq, Younan Labeeb, Head of Dept. of Hist., College for Girls, Ayn Shams Univ., Arab Egyptian Rep.

Prof. Abdul Haleem, Rajab, Prof. And Head of Dept. of Hist., Institute for African Studies, Univ. of Cairo, Arab Egyptian Rep.

The Chief Supervisory Committee for the Preparation of the Book, 'Oman in History'.

His Excellency, Al-Rawwas, Abdul Aziz bin Mohammed, Chairman of the Committee.

His Excellency, Al- Rashidi, Hamad bin Mohammed, Vice Chairman.

His Excellency, Al-Nabhani, Sheikh Yahya bin Abdullah, Member of the Committee.

Al-Siyabi, Sheikh Ahmed bin Saud, Member of the Committee.

Al-Battashi, Sheikh Saif bin Saud, Member of the Committee.

Al-Hinaei, Sheikh Mahmoud bin Zahir, Member of the Committee.

His Excellency, Al-Ka'bi, Sheikh Ahmed bin Obeid, Member of the Committee.

Al-Wuhaibi, Mohammed bin Said, Member of the Committee.

Al-Maskari, Saif bin Hamad, Member of the Committee.

Tabash, Khaleel bin Hamad, Member of the Committee.

Al-Kharousi, Sheikh Muhanna bin Khalfan, Member of the Committee.

His Excellency, Al-Abri, Sheikh Salim bin Mohammed, General Secretary of the Committee.

Al-Rahbi, Abdullah bin Nasir, Assistant General Secretary of the Committee.

INDEX